Sport and Physical Activity

Other Titles From E & FN Spon

Biomechanics and Medicine in Swimming
T. Reilly, A. Lees, M. Hughes, D. MacLaren

Drugs in Sport
D.R. Mottram

Exercise
Benefits, limits and adaptations
T. Reilly, C. Williams, D. McLeod, R. Maughan and M. Nimmo

Exercise Physiology for Health Professionals
S. Bird

Foods, Nutrition and Sports Performance
J.T. Devlin and C. Williams

Intermittent High Intensity Exercise
D. McLeod

Leisure and Recreation Management, Third edition
George Torkildsen

Physiology of Sports
T. Reilly, N. Secher, P. Snell and C. Williams

Sport and Recreation
An economic analysis
C. Gratton and P. Taylor

Writing Successfully in Science
M. O'Connor

For more information about these and other titles published by us please contact:
The Promotion Department, E & FN Spon, 2–6 Boundary Row, London SE1 8HN

Sport and Physical Activity

Moving towards excellence

Edited by

T. Williams
Loughborough University

L. Almond
Loughborough University

A. Sparkes
Exeter University

In association with
A. Byrne
G. Doll-Tepper
P. Gardonyi
and S. Glyptis

The Proceedings of the AIESEP World Convention
July 20–25, 1990
Loughborough University
UK

E & FN SPON
An Imprint of Chapman & Hall

London · New York · Tokyo · Melbourne · Madras

Published by E & FN Spon, an imprint of Chapman & Hall, 2–6 Boundary Row, London SE1 8HN

Chapman & Hall, 2–6 Boundary Row, London SE1 8HN, UK

Chapman & Hall, 29 West 35th Street, New York NY10001, USA

Chapman & Hall Japan, Thomson Publishing Japan, Hirakawacho Nemoto Building, 6F, 1–7–11 Hirakawa-cho, Chiyoda-ku, Tokyo 102, Japan

Chapman & Hall Australia, Thomas Nelson Australia, 102 Dodds Street, South Melbourne, Victoria 3205, Australia

Chapman & Hall India, R. Seshadri, 32 Second Main Road, CIT East, Madras 600 035, India

First edition 1992

© 1992 E & FN Spon

Printed in Great Britain by St Edmundsbury Press Ltd, Bury St Edmunds, Suffolk

ISBN 0 419 17080 4

A catalogue record for this book is available from the British Library

Library of Congress Cataloging-in-Publication data available

CONTENTS

Part Two

Special Populations

Part Four

Coach Education

Part Five

Sport and Leisure

FOREWORD

This was the first occasion that the AIESEP World Congress had been held in the United Kingdom and Loughborough University was delighted to have had the opportunity to host the event with the support of the British Council of Physical Education. The University is committed to the notion of excellence and building on the tradition of quality developed within the AIESEP movement the theme of the 1990 World Congress was designated 'Moving Towards Excellence'. It is this concept of excellence in research which drew together a variety of perspectives and traditions that included the following:

New Directions in Sports Coaching
Sport Pedagogy
The Teaching of Health Related Exercise
Sport and Exercise for Special Populations
Rethinking Sport Sciences
A National Physical Education Curriculum
Sport and Leisure

The contents of these proceedings reflect the multidisciplinary interests expressed throughout the Congress. The task of organizing and selecting from the large and varied number of contributions that were submitted was a difficult task given the quality that characterized the programme. However, choices have had to be made and we have attempted to group these resulting papers within the framework outlined below.

Sport Pedagogy
Special Populations
Health Related Exercise
Coach Education
Sport and Leisure

The opening section concentrates on the domain of Sport Pedagogy. The emerging focus on a variety of research forms is evident in the contributions to this section. This range of interest along with the sense of excitement and the tensions they bring to the research agenda is signalled by the keynote addresses of Linda Bain, Richard Tinning and John Evans. In the second section the emphasis is placed on Special Populations. The keynote papers by Karen dePauw and Bob Steadward address aspects of the close relationship between research and practice that currently dominate the field of adapted physical activity. The teaching of health-related exercise in schools has become a major change of focus in the past few years. The papers in the third section, Health Related Exercise, highlight the diversity of views emerging in this area and they provide a critical perspective that will enhance future developments in the field. The fourth section represents a major international interest in the developing area of Coach Education. The keynote speaker, Sue Campbell, looks towards the future as sport and coaching come closer together. The final section places sport in the broader contexts of leisure and lifestyles. The keynote paper by Sue Glyptis identifies 'winners' and 'losers' in the world of leisure opportunity and the ensuing papers examine aspects of leisure in relation to social, political and economic change.

There was a total of 280 full-time participants plus invited guests and speakers together with 130 day delegates from 35 countries attending the conference. The highlight of the Opening Ceremony was the presence of H.R.H. The Princess Royal, a distinguished sport performer who presented the Juan Samaranch Prize for Sport Pedagogy to Prof. Dr. Udo Hanke, delivered the Opening Address and formally opened the Congress.

We would like to extend our thanks to the British Council of Physical Education, the members of the Scientific Committee and the Organizing Committee for the success of the Congress . We would like to pay special tribute to the tireless efforts of those who staffed the Congress Office with such grace and humour, and finally to Jayne Simonetti for her endurance and patience in typing and bringing together these proceedings.

Editors
Trevor Williams
Len Almond
Andrew Sparkes

PART ONE

SPORT PEDAGOGY

RESEARCH IN SPORT PEDAGOGY: PAST, PRESENT AND FUTURE

LINDA L. BAIN
California State University, Northridge, USA

Abstract
The paper provides an analysis of sport pedagogy research in the USA. The emergence of sport pedagogy as a scientific area of study is traced by reviewing the work of key scholars. The impact of current research on practice is examined within each of three paradigms: behaviourist, socialization, and critical theory research. The implications for future research of the post-structural challenge to positivism are discussed.
Keywords: Paradigms, Behaviourist, Socialization, Critical Theory, Post-structuralism.

1 Introduction

The title of this paper implies a rather ambitious project, an analysis of the past, present and future of sport pedagogy. My goals are considerably more modest than the title. First, my discussion will be primarily limited to an examination of North American research because of my greater familiarity with that literature and my inability to read literature published in languages other than English. Second, the historical analysis will focus on the last 25 years and will provide not a complete description but a backdrop for a discussion of current research. Third, the paper will identify issues rather than attempt to summarize results of the research. (For reviews and summaries of the research, see Bain, 1990a; Locke, 1984; Siedentop, 1983b; Steinhardt, in press; Templin & Schempp, 1989; as well as a number of topical reviews published in the Journal of Teaching in Physical Education.)

I recognize that an analysis of research in North America is not directly applicable to scholarly work in other countries. My hope is that an examination of North American research will serve as a case study that may provide insight into issues that confront all sport pedagogy researchers.

Crum (1986) identified three research tasks which sport pedagogy researchers need to address:

(a)   The hermeneutic research task - dealing with the ideological clarification of the relationships between fundamental conceptions, sports education objectives, and criteria for the quality of sport pedagogy;
(b)   The descriptive-explanatory research task - dealing with the description and explanation of the empirical relationships between actual presage, process, product and context variables of sport pedagogy;
(c)   The constructive research task - dealing with design, controlled implementation, and evaluation of sport pedagogical improvements.

This list of research tasks provides a scheme for classifying the research done within sport pedagogy. Crum (1986) conducted an analysis of pedagogical journals in which he identified two major subcultures within sport pedagogy as West Germany and North America. He concluded that they have emphasized different research tasks. His view is that the West German scholars neglect descriptive-explanatory research while North American pedagogical science is 'characterized by almost a denial of the hermeneutic research task' (p.216).

I would add to Crum's list a fourth task, that of deconstruction. A more complete discussion of post-structualism and deconstruction will be postponed until the final section of the paper, but I want to briefly introduce the concept of deconstruction at this point. Sarup (1989, p.59) explains, 'In the move from hermeneutics and semiotics to deconstruction there is a shift of focus from identities to differences, unities to fragmentations, ontology to philosophy of language, epistemology to rhetoric, presence to absence'.

To some extent this paper will be an attempt to deconstruct research on sport pedagogy in the USA. For that reason, the analysis will not attempt to create a linear explanation of the history of sport pedagogy but will employ an approach called genealogical analysis. Genealogy is a form of critique which attempts 'to establish and preserve the singularity of events' and 'to reveal the multiplicity of factors behind an event' (Sarup, 1989, p.64). The paper will examine differences within sport pedagogy and the continuing struggle over meaning within the field.

2 The Recent Past

In the Introduction to the Terminology of Sport Pedagogy recently published by AIESEP, the authors acknowledge that one of their most difficult tasks was to define sport pedagogy itself (Piéron, Cheffers & Barrette, 1990). They suggest that disagreement regarding the term is based on philosophic and cultural differences and propose the following as a workable definition: 'Disciplined inquiry from different perspectives into teaching and coaching in a variety of contexts in order to inform and improve practice' (p.24). To some extent, the difficulty in definition is seen as based on the relative youth of sport pedagogy as a field of study. This perspective is exemplified by a statement made by Metzler in a recent review article, 'However one might define it, and whether one might want to include or exclude certain parts of it, there is little doubt that a serious contributing science of sport pedagogy has been around for only a few years' (Metzler, 1989, p.87). This portrayal of sport pedagogy as a new area of study is disputed by Dewar (1990, p.70) who notes, 'It is the standards for judging what constitutes a science of sport pedagogy that are relatively new, not the existence of pedagogy in physical education'. Dewar's point is well taken. There is a large body of pedagogical literature published before the recent surge of pedagogical scientific work.

The original focus of the field of physical education was the preparation of teachers, and pedagogical concerns were central in college and university programmes and in the literature from 1860 to 1960 (Spears & Swanson, 1978; Ziegler, 1975). Using the categories described by Crum, most of this early pedagogical literature could be classified as hermeneutic or constructive; that is, it dealt with the goals of physical education and how programmes could be designed to meet those goals. With the advent of the disciplinary movement in the 1960's, the focus of the field of physical education shifted from the preparation of teachers to the scientific study of human movement (Lawson, 1984).

In response to this change, a few pedagogy scholars associated with major research universities in the USA began a struggle to establish sport pedagogy as a scientific area of study. Their efforts were marked by an emphasis on descriptive-explanatory research that has come to characterize North American sport pedagogy (Crum, 1986). Identifying sport pedagogy as a new area of study was a rhetorical device for distancing recent research from earlier pedagogical work and establishing the credentials of pedagogy scholars in the scientific community. The literature tends to give the impression that all North American sport pedagogy scholars undertook a similar programme of research on teaching. However, a closer examination of the past 25 years reveals differences and contradictions within the field that may help us understand the current paradigmatic debates.

My analysis will focus on a handful of key pedagogy scholars. Focusing on individuals rather than trends directs our attention to the singularity of events. The individuals selected were chosen because of their influence on the development of sport pedagogy in North America. That influence derived in part from their writings but also from their roles as leaders of major doctoral programmes in sport pedagogy. Of necessity, my discussion must omit many other scholars who also made significant contributions to the development of the field.

William Anderson was one of the first USA scholars to begin a programme of research involving systematic observation of teaching in physical education within the doctoral programme at Teachers College, Columbia University. His 1971 article in Quest and his co-edited monograph, What's Going on in Gym (Anderson & Barrette, 1978), introduced descriptive-analytic research on teaching to the physical education profession. However, an interesting transition has occurred in the Teachers College programme which Anderson described at the 1982 AIESEP convention in Boston. Anderson (1982, p.209) indicates that he 'got a little tired of studying teaching--particularly of coding teacher/student behaviour' and 'decided that maybe instead of just studying what was happening in physical education, we ought to try to change it'. The result was a shift to programme development research in which doctoral students from Teachers' College work with physical education teachers to improve programmes and simultaneously conduct case studies of the programme development process (Anderson, 1989).

Another of the scholars who helped to establish a scientific tradition within sport pedagogy in the USA is Larry Locke. Locke served as co-author of the chapter on physical education research in the influential Second Handbook of Research on Teaching (Nixon & Locke, 1973) and as author of a monograph summarizing research on teacher education (Locke, 1984). Both of these reviews are written within the process-product framework that characterizes positivist research on teaching. In addition to serving as a spokesperson for pedagogical research, Locke established a doctoral programme at the University of Massachusetts that focuses on physical education teacher education. Locke's work also shows a shift of emphasis from the 1970's to the 1980's and, to some extent, contradictory perspectives. While Locke's review articles were based on the positivist process-product paradigm, most of the recent doctoral work at the University of Massachusetts has used qualitative research methods based on the interpretive paradigm. Locke's (1989) tutorial on qualitative research methods in the Research Quarterly for Exercise and Sport has been an important contribution to the legitimation of such methods within the field. The University of Massachusetts programme under the leadership of Locke and his colleagues (Patt Dodds, Pat Griffin and Judy Placek) has emerged as perhaps the leading doctoral programme in the USA for training qualitative researchers in sport pedagogy.

Another of the doctoral programmes in the USA that initiated a systematic programme of research on teaching in the early 1970's was the Ohio State University programme under the leadership of Daryl Siedentop. The Ohio State programme is based on behaviour analysis and modification and the research has focused on procedures for training teachers (Siedentop, 1972; 1981, 1983a, 1983b, 1986). Siedentop's work has been influential in North America because of his extensive publications and because of the large number of pedagogy specialists trained in the Ohio State programme. As universities began to increase their emphasis on research and publication, the scientific skills of Siedentop's students made them successful candidates for faculty positions across the USA. In contrast to the shifts that have occurred in the programmes at Teachers College and Massachusetts, the Ohio State programme has maintained its emphasis on behaviour analysis. Although in the 1980's an increasing number of Ohio State doctoral dissertations have employed qualitative methods, this does not reflect a shift in the philosophic basis of the programme. Instead, these studies have been viewed as exploratory research that could identify variables and hypotheses to be examined in subsequent experimental research (Siedentop, 1989).

While Siedentop's research on teaching has maintained a consistent emphasis on behavioural research, it should be noted that his other major scholarly contribution has been the explication of a curriculum model that he labels the sports education model (Siedentop, 1980; Siedentop, Mand & Taggart, 1986). This work, which has been both hermeneutic and constructive, tends to be viewed as separate from and unrelated to Siedentop's sport pedagogy research. This separation reflects a tendency in North America to differentiate curriculum work from research on teaching and to view the latter not the former as legitimate sport pedagogy research.

This distinction between curriculum and instruction has had a significant effect on the way the work of Ann Jewett has been received in the USA. Jewett is a curriculum scholar whose primary professional contributions have been the authoring of textbooks (Nixon & Jewett, 1980) and the development of the Purpose Process Curriculum Framework (Jewett, Jones, Luneke & Robinson, 1971; Jewett & Mullan, 1977). Although Jewett's doctoral students at the University of Wisconsin and the University of Georgia have conducted a number of empirical studies to validate the curriculum framework (Jewett & Bain, 1987), the primary emphasis of her work has been hermeneutic.

Jewett's other major contribution to hermeneutic scholarship in the USA has been to organize a biennial curriculum theory conference starting in 1979. (The seventh such conference is scheduled in March, 1991 at the University of Georgia and proceedings from previous conferences are available from that institution.) Jewett has also recently initiated a curriculum research and development centre affiliated with the National Association for Sport and Physical Education. The centre organizes research on programme development at various sites throughout the USA. Jewett's work exemplifies hermeneutic and constructive work within sport pedagogy. However, because of the hermeneutic emphasis of Jewett's work, she tends to be viewed as a theorist not a researcher by the scientific sport pedagogy community.

The four people I have just described have probably been the most influential in sport pedagogy in the USA in the past 25 years. However, I also want to talk about two other people whose influence has been more recent. I will not attempt to recognize all those scholars who have made important contributions to the knowledge about teaching, but will limit my attention to two individuals who have influenced the paradigmatic debate within the field.

Hal Lawson (1983b, 1986, 1988) has emerged in the 1980's as the major spokesperson for the socialization perspective in research on teaching and teacher education. Lawson (1983a) was also one of the first North American scholars to discuss alternative paradigms for sport pedagogy research. One of Lawson's important contributions has been to provide a theoretical foundation for the growing number of qualitative research studies within the field.

Another individual whose role in the sport pedagogy paradigmatic debate is worth noting is Don Hellison. Hellison (1978, 1985), who has been somewhat of a maverick, has spent 15 years developing and field testing a curriculum model he calls the social development model. Only recently have he (1983, 1988) and others (Bain & Jewett, 1987) begun to describe his work as research. In effect, Hellison was conducting case studies that attempted to empower participants before the critical theory perspective justifying such an approach as research appeared in the sport pedagogy literature. Despite recent efforts to locate his work within the critical theory paradigm, some scholars grounded in the positivist paradigm continue to dismiss his work as anecdotal.

It should be noted that while Lawson and Hellison have had influence through their publications and presentations, neither has been in an institution with a doctoral programme so they have not played a role in training the next generation of pedagogy scholars. Nevertheless, they have helped to frame the paradigmatic debates.

What does this brief examination of pedagogy scholars reveal? Despite generalizations about the scientific orthodoxy within North American sport pedagogy, diversity has existed among the leaders. Although there has been a focus on descriptive-explanatory research, there have been strong elements of hermeneutic and constructive work. To some extent, this contradicts Crum's conclusion that North American scholarship has ignored the hermeneutic task. However, the hermeneutic and constructive work has frequently not been legitimized as research and this may have contributed to his conclusion.

There has also been considerable variation in the types of descriptive-explanatory research conducted. The empirical research has included not only process-product research but qualitative research based on interpretive or critical perspectives.

In addition to the diversity among leaders, individual scholars have had shifting and sometimes contradictory approaches to pedagogical work. Some have shifted over time from a positivist position to constructivist research. Some have seemed to embrace interpretive work while clinging to some of the tenets of positivism. This observation is not intended as a criticism but as a recognition that individuals as well as social groups are characterized by complexity and ambiguity. In a recent article in Quest I have acknowledged the shifting and contradictory elements of my own work (Bain, 1990b).

I should note that gender appears to have had an influence on the development of sport pedagogy in the USA. Although 56% of physical education teacher education faculty are female, men are more likely to have a doctoral degree and to publish (Metzler & Freedman, 1985). Many early women leaders had an interest in pedagogy, but most of those who led the effort to transform sport pedagogy into a scientific area of study were men. However, the curriculum component of the field has been dominated by women, primarily Jewett and her students. This gender pattern may have reinforced the dominance of the empirical study of teaching and the lesser status of the hermeneutic examination of curriculum.

While a narrow definition of positivist empiricism has been the dominant philosophy propounded by those seeking academic credibility for sport pedagogy, threads of hermeneutic and constructive work as well as alternative paradigms for empirical research existed. Sport pedagogy has, not a singular past, but a multiplicity of histories. Recognizing this may help us to situate and understand the complexity of the field in the present.

3 The Present

As noted in the definition of sport pedagogy cited earlier, the fundamental purpose of pedagogical research is to guide and improve educational practice. For that reason, it seems appropriate to organize a review of the present status of sport pedagogy research around the question of how well this purpose has been achieved.

Any discussion of the impact and implications of research must begin with a recognition that research is a socially-constructed enterprise and that part of the construction is a view of the relationship between research and practice. When we ask, 'Has research had an impact on practice?', the meaning of the question and the basis for the answer derive from our paradigmatic assumptions. The question as posed implies a cause-effect relationship between two distinct entities, a view derived from a 'research and development' perspective. Our examination of pedagogical research in physical education will reveal that the traditional R & D model is based on positivist assumptions and is less compatible with other research paradigms.

There are three distinct research traditions within North American physical education pedagogy, and each defines research and its relationship to practice differently. The dominant research paradigms are behaviourist research and socialization research. There is also an emerging area of research based on critical theory. We will explore the view of research and practice embedded within each tradition and examine the impact of research based on each paradigm's definitions and standards.

3.1 *Behaviourist Paradigm*

The behaviourist or natural science paradigm of research on teaching and teacher education is based on positivist assumptions that view the purpose of research as the discovery of generalizable laws of human behaviour. The initial focus of the work is on the description of effective teaching, usually through process-product research that identifies teaching variables which relate to student learning outcomes. Much of this research, including that in physical education, has lead to the delineation of models of 'direct teaching' and 'active teaching' seen as effective in producing student learning (Siedentop, 1983). Some have criticized the research for focusing on basic skills rather than higher order learning and on generic management behaviours rather than content related teaching behaviours. However, advocates of the behaviourist paradigm argue that a substantial body of information about teaching has been identified and that future research can extend the work to more complex teaching and learning situations.

The second phase of behaviourist research is to develop training procedures that enable teachers to acquire the teaching behaviours identified as effective in process-product research. It is at this point that the behaviourist becomes concerned with impact on practice. Daryl Siedentop (1986), the primary spokesperson for the behaviourist perspective in physical education pedagogy, identifies the following as necessary characteristics of teacher education research based on a natural science of behaviour:

> First, the studies would have to focus on teacher behaviour as a natural phenomenon studied for its own value rather than as an epiphenomenon studied only to infer something about other less accessible variables....Second, the training intervention would have to be defined with sufficient specificity to allow for replication. And finally, the research design would have to allow for some internally valid means for attributing changes to the presence and absence of the training strategy. (p.5)

The goal of such research is to identify procedures for developing effective training programmes for teachers.

A substantial body of research has applied behavioural analysis principles to the training of pre-service and inservice teachers in physical education. Selected behaviours are targeted for change, and an intervention consisting of goals, explanatory materials, regular observation, and feedback is provided. Such interventions have been successful in producing changes in targeted behaviours, and evidence indicates that university supervisors, co-operating teachers, school principals, peers or teachers themselves can be trained to act as change agents (Borys, 1986; Cusimano, 1987; Mancini, Clark & Wuest, 1987; Ratliffe, 1986; Siedentop, 1981, 1986).

One could argue that there is a strong case for the impact of behaviourist research on teaching and teacher education in physical education. However, there are two issues that must be examined before reaching that conclusion. The first is whether skills attained through behavioural training are sustained after the completion of the programme. The second deals with the extent to which the behavioural training model has been or will be adopted by pre-service and inservice teacher educators.

The issues of transfer of teaching skills from training to practice and retention of those skills over time are complex problems. Locke (1984) identifies factors that seem to influence transfer and retention as including a degree of initial mastery, context, and trainee acceptance or rejection of skills. Siedentop (1986) notes that behavioural and developmental theories make different assumptions regarding the problem. The developmental or socialization perspective assumes that what needs to be modified is some 'inner essence which, once changed, is permanent' and that is reflected in behaviour (pp.12-13). The behavioural perspective assumes that generalization from training programme to work place requires bringing the behaviour under the control of contingencies that will continue to be present in the work place and that support the desired behaviour. For example, teachers need to be trained to respond to indicators of student learning as reinforcers rather than to student enjoyment as their primary satisfaction.

While Siedentop's explanation provides a theoretically consistent view of the problem, it is unclear whether behavioural training can actually accomplish transfer and retention of teaching skills in the diverse and often constraining circumstances in which physical educators teach. Will there be indicators of student learning to which teachers can respond in overcrowded, underequipped classes? Will the reinforcing power of teaching physical education outweigh the pressures and contingencies associated with coaching? Research seems to indicate that teachers, even distinctive teachers, find student enjoyment a more powerful reward than student achievement (Earls, 1981; Placek, 1983) and that when learning does occur teachers may think it is due to factors outside their control (Veal, 1988). Research also indicates that coaching is often of greater importance than teaching to physical educators, especially males (Bain & Wendt, 1983; Chu, 1978; Sage, 1989; Segrave, 1980), and this may weaken the strength of reinforcers in the physical education setting. The extent to which behavioural training can address these contextual constraints has not been answered.

The second major issue related to impact or influence of behaviourist pedagogical research is that despite a growing body of research based on the paradigm, the behavioural training approach to physical education teacher education programmes has not been widely implemented. Several reasons have been suggested including cost, inability of faculty to conduct such a programme, and incompatibility of such a training programme with the norms and values of the university (Siedentop, 1985). While some public school systems in the USA have installed teacher supervision systems based on process-product research (most notably the Madeline Hunter model), physical education behavioural research seems to have had relatively little influence on teacher education or public schools.

It is difficult to explain this lack of influence of behaviourist research from within the tradition itself. Examining decisions about teacher education programme design raises questions about the beliefs and values of the decision-makers and the politics of universities and school systems. However, behaviourists do not study beliefs and politics. To understand their dissemination problem, behaviourists may have to turn to the second research tradition, socialization research.

3.2 *Socialization Research*

The second major theoretical paradigm for pedagogical research in physical education has been socialization research or what Lawson (1983a) has called research on teachers rather than research on teaching. Occupational socialization 'includes all of the kinds of socialization that initially influence persons to enter the field of physical education and that later are responsible for their perceptions and actions as teacher educators and teachers' (Lawson, 1986, p.107). Research based on this perspective studies not just teachers' behaviours but their characteristics, perceptions and beliefs.

Most of the socialization research in physical education can be classified as post-positivist. Phillips (1989) defines post-positivism as the search for 'warranted assertions' rather than truth. The goal of science remains the development of generalizable theory but all theory is seen as tentative and temporary. Assertions are warranted when they survive criticism from multiple perspectives, but those warrants are based on probability not certainty. Objectivity is viewed not as an attainable reality but as a 'regulative ideal' in which one's work withstands critiques by peers. While some early socialization research has been based on a deterministic perspective characteristic of positivism, more recent work has suggested that socialization is 'problematic, not automatic' and that 'while institutions try to typecast individual acts and actions, people also try to transform institutions' (Lawson, 1983b, p.4).

Researchers within the socialization paradigm see their research as providing insight and understanding that can serve to guide but not prescribe teaching decisions and policy decisions. Major themes in socialization research relate to teachers' perceptions of their work and how these perceptions influence their actions. Studies of recruitment improve our understanding of the characteristics and beliefs of those who choose a career in physical education (Dewar & Lawson, 1984; Templin, Woodford & Mulling, 1982). Studies of students' experiences in professional training programmes provide insight into how students interpret and negotiate in such programmes (Graber, 1989; Tousignant & Brunelle, 1987; Steen, 1986). Studies of induction into the work place shed light on the effects of bureaucratic socialization.

An area of socialization research of particular relevance to our topic today is the examination of teachers' utilization of information sources. The evidence seems to indicate that teachers rely on peers rather than research as a primary source of information (Campbell, 1988; Earls, 1981; Vertinsky, 1989). One explanation might relate to the contrast that Lawson (1985) has drawn between the knowledge systems of researchers and practitioners. He suggests that practitioners prefer not scholarly, scientific knowledge but working knowledge that blends selectively perceived, scientific knowledge with professional ideology and experiential knowledge. Such an interpretation views practitioners not merely as consumers of information but also as active participants in the generation and reinvention of knowledge.

What this suggests is that research can potentially provide a guide to thinking but not a guide to action. Reid (1978) defines educational decisions as uncertain practical problems in which action must be taken within a specific, unique set of circumstances and the consequences of alternatives not chosen can never be known. He sees theory and research as providing, 'Not statements of lawful relationships which might tend to devalue the role of responsible judgment, but data that help us to identify and define problems for decision and that increase our capacity for generating alternative solutions and for improving the quality of our deliberations about which of these should be adopted' (p.27).

Thus, from within the socialization perspective, the question is not 'Does research affect practice?' but instead becomes, 'How well has pedagogical research served as a guide to thinking about practical problems in physical education?' The answer to that question is difficult to determine. Within higher education, it may have changed the language we use to discuss teaching and teacher education programmes. However, there is little evidence that research has changed the ways in which physical education teachers view teaching. What has been called 'knowledge creep' may have permitted some research findings to find their way into work organizations (Weiss, 1980), but such indirect influence has had limited effect on practitioners' discourse and actions.

Some would argue that this limitation can be overcome only if the separation between research and practice is removed. This position has been endorsed by those within the third perspective, that of critical theory.

3.3 *Critical Theory*

Although most North American pedagogical research in physical education is based on the behaviourist or the socialization perspectives, a few scholars are examining teaching and teacher education from a critical theory perspective (Bain, 1989, 1990; Bain & Jewett, 1987). G.L. Anderson (1989) provides the following summary of critical research:

> Critical ethnographers seek research accounts sensitive to the dialectical relationship between the social structural constraints on human actors and the relative autonomy of human agency. Unlike other interpretivisit research, the over-riding goal of critical ethnography is to free individuals from sources of domination and repression. (p.249)

The critical theorist declares that all research is value-based not value-free and inescapably tied to issues of power and legitimacy. A goal of much of the research is to empower those being researched, that is, to provide them with the insight necessary to demystify and critique their own social circumstances and to choose actions to improve their lives (Lather, 1985). Most critical research is grounded in feminism or neo-Marxism and focuses on issues of gender, race or class. These value-based research programmes are committed to research that challenges the status quo and contributes to a more egalitarian order.

Pedagogical research based on the critical theory perspective treats practitioners as participants in the research process rather than subjects to be studied. Participants help to frame questions, to interpret data, and to examine how insights might serve as a basis for action. Lather (1986) suggests that the validity of critical research depends not only on the trustworthiness and credibility of the interpretation, but also on what she labels catalytic validity, that is, the effectiveness of the process in empowering the participants. It should be noted that some critical research studies the oppressor rather than the oppressed, and therefore aims at extending our understanding of power relations but not empowering those studied. Nevertheless, such research shares the emancipatory goal of critical research.

For the critical researcher, impact on practice is an issue to be addressed throughout the research rather than after the study is completed. Therefore, for the critical theory paradigm, the question is not 'Does research affect practice?' but 'Has this research project empowered participants to act more effectively on their own behalf?' The primary focus is on impact in the specific setting in which the research was conducted. However, critical theorists do choose to publish their work with the intention that it have a broader impact. The hope is not that the results can be directly applied in other settings but that reading the study will inspire others to critically examine their own circumstances. The research dissemination process seeks to provide 'consciousness-raising' experiences for the reader.

Relatively little critical research has been conducted in physical education pedagogy in the USA. Some researchers have begun to conduct feminist critical research (Bain, 1985; Bain, Wilson & Chaikind, 1989; Dewar, 1987; Griffin, 1989b) and Hellison (1978, 1983, 1985) has established a research programme with 'at-risk' students that may fit within the empowerment tradition.

It is difficult to assess the impact of critical research on practice in physical education. Many of the research reports provide relatively little information about the 'catalytic validity' of the study; that is, how effective the project was in enabling participants to understand their own behaviours and make choices based on that understanding. In addition, the consciousness-raising effects of the research reports depend on their accessibility to teachers as well as other researchers. Hellison's work seems to have had relatively broad impact based on several factors: a programme of work conducted over more than 15 years, publications and presentations that are accessible to teachers, and a personal style that enhances credibility with practitioners. However, Hellison's work seems to have focused on human agency and personal growth but has given little attention to social structural issues. It is too early to judge the impact of the more recent feminist critical research, but one might conjecture that its radical feminist roots will be perceived as threatening by many in the mainstream of physical education, especially given the conservatism of physical educators (Hendry & Whiting, 1972; Kenyon, 1965; Locke, 1962; Sage, 1980).

3.4 *Summary of Current Research*

What conclusions can we draw and what are the implications? The first conclusion is that the question about the relationship of research and practice must be asked differently for each of the research paradigms. For the behaviourist paradigm, the traditional R&D question, 'Does research affect practice?', is appropriate. For socialization research, the question becomes, 'Does research influence the ways in which we think about practical problems?' For the critical researcher, the question is, 'Does this research empower participants to change their lives?'

Within each of the three paradigms, there is reason for optimism as well as discouragement. The behaviourists have developed a body of technical knowledge about teaching, some of which is indirectly affecting teachers and teacher educators through a process of 'knowledge creep'. The socialization researchers have established a solid base of qualitative research that provides greater insight into the daily lives of physical education teachers. Critical researchers have begun to establish a foothold and to create a critical discourse within the field. Each of the research traditions has matured to a point where it has a cadre of well-trained researchers ready to move beyond descriptions of existing programmes to seek an impact on practice. However, the problems of school physical education are enormous and the progress made in addressing those issues has been slight (Dodds & Locke, 1984).

As indicated earlier, this review has focused on research and practice within the USA. Despite the tendency for North American scholars to be isolated from other cultures, they have had some contact with the work of sport pedagogy scholars from other countries. This awareness tends to be limited to publications in English and to presentations at international meetings such as AIESEP. Behaviourists are familiar with the work of Maurice Piéron (1986) from Belgium. Those interested in curriculum have read Herbert Haag (1978) of West Germany, Len Almond (1986) of England, and Peter Arnold (1979, 1988) of Scotland. Scholars with an interest in interpretive and critical research know the work of John Evans (1986, 1988) and Andrew Sparkes (1986, 1988) of England and of David Kirk (1988) (Kirk & Tinning, 1990), Richard Tinning (1987, 1988) and Jennifer Gore (1990) of Australia.

These international contacts seem to have been particularly helpful in nurturing alternatives to the dominant positivistic, behaviourist paradigm. As Crum (1986) noted, hermeneutic work has thrived in Europe. Interpretive and critical research have also had a stronger if not dominant presence in England and Australia. The emergence of alternatives to positivism seems likely to be the most salient characteristic of the immediate future of sport pedagogy research.

4 The Immediate Future

Our examination of the future of sport pedagogy research must be situated in an understanding of the status of social theory and research. The most notable development in the past thirty years has been the growing rejection of the assumptions of positivism and objectivism. Objectivism is the 'basic conviction that there is or must be some permanent, ahistorical matrix or framework to which we can ultimately appeal in determining the nature of rationality, knowledge, truth, goodness, or rightness' (Bernstein, 1985, p.8). The assumption is that there is a reality 'out there' that we can discover through rigorous scientific study. At the heart of this new era is a questioning of the basic assumptions of positivist science: neutrality, objectivity, and observable facts. Lather (1989) summarizes the critique:

> Facts are not given but constructed by the questions we ask of events. All researchers construct their object of inquiry out of the materials their culture provides and values play a central role in this linguistically, ideologically, and historically embedded project that we call science. (p.5)

Bernstein (1985, p.8) concludes that the concepts of truth, reality, and so forth 'must be understood as relative to a particular conceptual scheme, theoretical framework, paradigm, form of life, society, or culture'.

What has emerged from this rejection of positivist science has been a collection of views labelled post-structuralism or postmodernism. One element of post-structuralism focuses on the role of language in creating rather than mirroring reality. Any text has multiple and shifting meanings that are created by the reader as well as the producer of the text. Post-structuralists employ the method of deconstruction created by Derrida to examine texts in order to reveal inconsistent and paradoxical use of concepts (Sarup, 1989). Rejection of the objectivist perspective has also changed our understanding of human cognition (Lakoff, 1987; Lakoff & Johnson, 1980; Johnson, 1987). The process by which humans categorize and interpret their experience is not a mirror of reality but reflects both experience and imagination. Human beings create metaphors based on preconceptual bodily experience and social experience; these metaphors create as well as describe reality.

Because there are multiple interpretations rather than a single reality, post-structuralists are also interested in the ways in which power relates to the creation of knowledge. Power is reflected in what Foucalt (1980) calls regimes of truth, in which status and power determine who is 'charged with saying what counts as true' (p.131). Power is envisioned not merely as conscious repression, constraint or prohibition, but as the creation of ways of viewing the world which legitimize certain knowledge and practices. Power permeates all social relations and an understanding of power and knowledge is central to our understanding of the social world.

The result of the post-structural analysis is a rejection of what Lyotard (1984) calls 'metanarratives' which attempt to provide overarching explanations of history and first-order principles for the discovery of truth. Instead, legitimation of knowledge and action becomes plural and local. Fraser and Nicholson (1990) summarize:

> Instead of hovering above, legitimation descends to the level of practice and becomes immanent in it. There are no special tribunals set apart from the sites where inquiry is practiced. Rather, practitioners assume responsibility for legitimizing their own practice. (p.23)

In this nonfoundational view of science, knowledge is no longer seen as absolute but as plural and context specific. The result is a recognition that the world is 'spoken from many sites' (Lather, 1989).

The unresolved and troubling issue is how to reconcile the post-structuralist view with the political commitment to social justice. Fraser and Nicholson (1990) state the dilemma for feminists as follows:

> How can we combine a postmodernist incredulity toward metanarratives with social-critical power of feminism? How can we conceive a version of criticism without philosophy which is robust enough to handle the tough job of analyzing sexism in all its endless variety and monotonous similarity? (p.34)

Post-structuralism has been criticized by some as being apolitical and perhaps neoconservative (Sarup, 1989). Hartstock (1990) notes that just as those who have been silenced begin to form theories about the world and to talk about changes, 'ideas of progress and the possibility of systematically and rationally organizing human society become dubious and suspect' (p.164). While no assumption is made of a conspiracy, the issue remains of how to ground one's political beliefs and actions without resorting to metanarratives.

Several answers have been proposed. Lather (1989) proposes that inquiry in the post-structural world involves not a quest for certainty but a celebration of ambiguity and competing discourses. Cherryholmes (1988) suggests that we consciously create a dialectic of construction-deconstruction in order to avoid despair:

> Constructors must realize that what is built is temporal, fallible, limited, compromised, negotiated, and incomplete or contradictory. Each construction will eventually be replaced. And deconstructive arguments must be shaped so that construction will be encouraged and follow. (p.143)

Flax (1990) discusses the implications for feminism, saying:

> Feminist theories, like other forms of postmodernism, should encourage us to tolerate and interpret ambivalence, ambiguity, and multiplicity as well as to expose the roots of our needs for imposing order and structure no matter how arbitrary and oppressive these needs may be. If we do our work well, reality will appear even more unstable, complex, and disorderly than it does now. (p.56)

In this disorderly world, political action must be local, diffused and strategic (Sarup, 1989).

What are the implications of the decline of positivism and the emergence of post-structural thought for sport pedagogy research? The first is that there will continue to be multiple paradigms for pedagogical research and that an increase in interpretive and critical research seems likely. However, the struggle for acceptance of alternative paradigm research will be slow. It will be made more difficult by the conservatism of physical educators, the dominance of positivist research in exercise and sport science, and the marginal status of sport pedagogy within the broader field of kinesiology. As indicated by the post-structural view, the struggle will occur at local sites (e.g. tenure decisions within specific academic departments and manuscript reviews by editorial boards of particular journals). The outcome of the struggle will not be a consensus about the right way to teach or to train teachers or to do research, but an ongoing dialogue about these issues.

The second implication is that as sport pedagogy scholars become more familiar with post-structural thought, we will begin to recognize the shifting and contradictory nature of our discourse and practices. This recognition will result in scholarly activities that fall within the broad category of deconstruction. Some examples have begun to appear such as Jennifer Gore's (1990) analysis of pedagogy as text with multiple meanings, Andrew Sparkes (in press) examination of the rhetoric of research reports, and Richard Tinning's (1990) keynote address at this meeting. Although we may expect that relatively few will undertake such analyses and that deconstruction will remain at the fringes of sport pedagogy, the publication of such work will change the perspectives of most sport pedagogy scholars and increase the sense of uncertainty and ambiguity within the field.

Because of our commitment to the improvement of practice, this uncertainty will be especially difficult for sport pedagogy scholars. Our tendency is to search for the right answer, the best way to teach. Our task will be to accept the ambiguity and uncertainty of the post-structural era without retreating from a commitment to action. The benefit of ambiguity may be to enable us to build what Young (1990) has called a politics of difference:

> A politics of difference lays down institutional and ideological means for recognizing and affirming differently identifying groups in two basic senses: giving political representation to group interests and celebrating the distinctive cultures and characteristics of different groups. (p.319)

However, such affirmation of difference is not a necessary outcome of the post-structural era or perhaps even a likely one.

In developing the conclusion for this paper, I have had to resist historicism or the notion that there is an overall pattern in history. The temptation has been to embrace the metanarrative that progress is inevitable and that the uncertainty of the age will lead to a better future. Instead, I must conclude that the future is also uncertain and that we must live with the joys and the frustrations of the here and now.

5 References

Almond, L. (1986) Research-based teaching in games. In J. Evans (ed), **Physical Education, Sport and Schooling**. London: Falmer Press.

Anderson, G.L. (1989) Critical ethnography in education: Origins, current status, and new directions. **Review of Educational Research**, 59 (3), 249-270.

Anderson, W.G. (1971) Descriptive-analytic research on teaching. **Quest**, 15, 1-8.

Anderson, W.G. (1982) Working with inservice teachers: Suggestions for teacher educators. **Journal of Teaching in Physical Education**, 1(3), 15-21.

Anderson, W.G. (1989) Curriculum and program research in physical education: Selected approaches. **Journal of Teaching in Physical Education**, 8 (2), 113-122.

Anderson, W.G. and Barrette, G.T. (1978) What's going on in Gym. Monograph 1, **Motor Skills: Theory into Practice**.

Arnold, P.J. (1979) **Meaning in movement, sport and physical education**. London: Heinemann.

Arnold, P.J. (1988) **Education, Movement and the Curriculum**. London: Falmer Press.

Bain, L.L. (1985) A naturalistic study of students' responses to an exercise class. **Journal of Teaching in Physical Education**, 5, 2-12.

Bain, L.L. (1989) Interpretive and critical research in sport and physical education. **Research Quarterly for Exercise and Sport**, 60 (1), 21-24.

Bain, L.L. (1990a) Physical education teacher education. In W.R. Houston (ed), **Handbook of Research on Teacher Education**. New York: MacMillan.

Bain, L.L. (1990b) Visions and Voices. **Quest**, 42(1), 1-12.

Bain, L.L., and Jewett, A.E. (1987) Future research and theory-building. **Journal of Teaching in Physical Education**, 6(3), 346-364.

Bain, L.L., and Wendt, J.C. (1983) Undergraduate physical education majors' perceptions of the roles of teacher and coach. **Research Quarterly for Exercise and Sport**, 54(2), 112-118.

Bain, L.L., Wilson, T. and Chaikind, E. (1989) Participant perceptions of exercise programs for overweight women. **Research Quarterly for Exercise and Sport**, 60(2), 134-143.

Bernstein, R. (1985) **Beyond objectivism and relativism**. Philadelphia: University of Pennsylvania Press.

Borys, A.H. (1986) Development of a training procedure to increase pupil motor engagement time (MET). In M. Piéron and G. Graham (eds), **Sport pedagogy**, (pp. 19-26). Champaign, IL: Human Kinetics.

Campbell, S. (1988) From research to practice: Functioning processes of knowledge dissemination in physical education. **Dissertation Abstracts International**, 48, 2276A.

Cherryholmes, C.H. (1988) **Power and criticism: Poststructural investigations in education**. New York: Teachers College, Columbia University.

Chu, D. (1978) A foundational study of the occupational induction of physical education teacher/coaches as it is affected by the organizational requirements of the training institution and its environment. **Dissertation Abstracts International**, 39, 3860A.

Crum, B. (1986) Concerning the quality of the development of knowledge in sport pedagogy. **Journal of Teaching in Physical Education**, 5 (4), 209-210.

Cusimano, B.E. (1987) Effects of self-assessment and goal setting on verbal behaviour of elementary physical education teachers. **Journal of Teaching in Physical Education**, 6(2), 166-173.

Dewar, A.M. (1987) The social construction of gender in physical education. **Women's Studies International Forum**, 10(4), 453-466.

Dewar, A.M. (1990) Oppression and privilege in physical education: Struggles in the negotiation of gender in a university programme. In D. Kirk and R. Tinning (eds), **Physical Education, Curriculum and Culture: Critical Issues in the Contemporary Crisis**. London: Falmer Press.

Dewar, A.M. and Lawson, H.A. (1984) The subjective warrant and recruitment into physical education. **Quest**, 36(1), 15-25.

Dodds, P. and Locke, L.F. (1984) Is physical education in American schools worth saving? Evidence, alternatives, judgment. In N. Struna (ed), **Proceedings, National Association for Physical Education in Higher Education**, Vol. 5, (pp. 76-90). Champaign, IL: Human Kinetics.

Earls, N. (1981) Distinctive teachers' personal qualities, perceptions of teacher education, and realities of teaching. **Journal of Teaching in Physical Education**, 1(1), 59-70.

Evans, J. (Ed.) (1986) **Physical Education, sport and schooling**. London: Falmer Press.

Evans, J. (Ed.) (1988) **Teachers, teaching and control in physical education**. London: Falmer Press.

Flax, J. (1990) Postmodernism and gender relations in feminist theory. In L.J. Nicholson (ed), **Feminism/Postmodernism**. London: Routledge, Chapman & Hall.

Foucalt, M. (1980) **Power/Knowledge**. New York: Pantheon.

Fraser, N. and Nicholson, L.J. (1990) Social criticism without philosophy: An encounter between feminism and postmodernism. In L.J. Nicholson (ed), **Feminism/Postmodernism**. London: Routledge, Chapman & Hall.

Friere, P. (1973) **Pedagogy of the oppressed**. New York: Seabury Press.

Gore, J.M. (1990) Pedagogy as text in physical education teacher education: Beyond the preferred reading. In D. Kirk & R. Tinning (eds), **Physical Education, Curriculum and Culture: Critical Issues in the Contemporary crisis**. London: Falmer Press.

Graber, K.C. (1989) Teaching tomorrow's teachers: Professional preparation as an agent of socialization. In T.J. Templin & P.G. Schempp (eds), **Socialization into physical education: Learning to teach** (pp. 59-80). Indianapolis, In: Benchmark Press.

Griffin, P.S. (1989b April) **Using participatory research to empower gay and lesbian educators**. Paper presented at the annual meeting of the American Educational Research Association, San Francisco.

Haag, H. (1978) **Sport Pedagogy Content and Methodology**. Baltimore: University Park Press.

Hartsock, N. (1990) Foucault on power: A theory for women? In L.J. Nicholson (ed), **Feminism/Postmodernism**. London: Routledge, Chapman & Hall.

Hellison, D. (1978) **Beyond balls and bats**. Washington, DC: American Alliance for Health, Physical Education, Recreation and Dance.

Hellison, D. (1983) It only takes one case to prove a possibility...and beyond. In T.J. Templin and J.K. Olson (eds), **Teaching in physical education**. Champaign, IL: Human Kinetics.

Hellison, D. (1985) **Goals and strategies for teaching physical education**. Champaign, IL: Human Kinetics.

Hellison, D. (1988) Our constructed reality: Some contributions of an alternative perspective to physical education pedagogy. **Quest**, 40(1), 84-90.

Hendry, L.B. & Whiting, H.T.A. (1972) General course and specialist physical education student characteristics. **Educational Research**, 14(2), 152-156.

Jewett, A.E. and Bain, L.L. (eds), (1987) The Purpose Process Curriculum Framework: A personal meaning model for physical education. **Journal of Teaching in Physical Education**, 6(3).

Jewett, A.E., Jones, L.S., Luneke, S.M. and Robinson, S.M. (1971) Educational change through a taxonomy for writing physical education objectives. **Quest**, 15, 32-38.

Jewett, A.E. and Mullan, M.R. (1977) **Curriculum design: Purposes and processes in physical education teaching-learning**. Washington, D.C.: AAHPER.

Johnson, M. (1987) **The Body in the Mind**. Chicago: University of Chicago Press.

Kenyon, G.S. (1965) Certain psychosocial and cultural characteristics unique to prospective teachers of physical education. **Research Quarterly**, 36 (1), 105-142.

Kirk, D. (1988) **Physical Education and Curriculum Study**. London: Croon Helm.

Kirk, D. and Tinning, R. (eds), (1990) **Physical Education, Curriculum and Culture: Critical Issues in the Contemporary Crisis**. London: Falmer Press.

Lakoff, G. (1987) **Women, Fire and Dangerous Things**. Chicago: University of Chicago Press.

Lakoff, G. and Johnson, M. (1980) **Metaphors We Live By**. Chicago: University of Chicago Press.

Lather, P. (1985) **Empowering research methodologies**. Paper presented at the annual meeting of the American Educational Research Association, Chicago, IL.

Lather, P. (1986) Issues of validity in openly ideological research: Between a rock and a soft place. **Interchange**, 17(4), 63-84.

Lather, P. (1989) **Reinscribing otherwise: The play of values in the practices of the human sciences**. Paper presented at the Phi Delta Kappa Alternative Paradigms Conference, San Francisco.

Lawson, H.A. (1983a) Paradigms for research on teaching and teachers. In **Teaching in physical education** (eds.T.J. Templin and J.K. Olson), 339-358. Champaign, IL: Human Kinetics.

Lawson, H.A. (1983b) Toward a model of teacher socialization in physical education: The subjective warrant, recruitment teacher education (Part 1). **Journal of Teaching in Physical Education**, 2(3), 3-16.

Lawson, H.A. (1984) Problem-setting for physical education and sport. **Quest**, 36 (1), 48-60.

Lawson, H.A. (1985) Knowledge for work in the physical education profession. **Sociology of Sport Journal**, 2(1), 9-24.

Lawson, H.A. (1986) Occupational socialization and the design of teacher education programs. **Journal of Teaching in Physical Education**, 5 (2), 107-116.

Lawson, H.A. (1988) Occupational socialization, cultural studies, and the physical education curriculum. **Journal of Teaching in Physical Education**, 7 (4), 265-288.

Lawson, H.A. (in press) Sport pedagogy research: From information-gathering to useful knowledge. **Journal of Teaching in Physical Education.**

Locke, L.F. (1962) Performance of administration oriented male physical educators on selected psychological tests. **Research Quarterly**, 33(1), 418-429.

Locke, L.F. (1984) Research on teaching teachers: Where are we now? **Journal of Teaching in Physical Education Monograph 2.**

Locke, L.F. (1989) Qualitative research as a form of scientific inquiry in sport and physical education. **Research Quarterly for Exercise and Sport**, 60(1), 1-20.

Lakoff, G. and Johnson, M. (1980) **Metaphors We Live By.** Chicago: University of Chicago Press.

Lyotard, J.F. (1984) **The Postmodern Condition: A Report on Knowledge.** (translated G. Bennington & B. Massumi). Minneapolis: University of Minnesota Press.

Mancini, V. II., Clark, E.K., & Wuest, D.A. (1987) Short and long-term effects of supervisory feedback on the interaction patterns of an intercollegiate field hockey coach. **Journal of Teaching in Physical Education**, 6(4), 404-410.

Metzler, M. (1989) A review of research on time in sport pedagogy. **Journal of Teaching in Physical Education**, 8(2), 87-103.

Metzler, M.W. and Freedman, M.S. (1985) Here's looking at you, Pete: A profile of physical education teacher education faculty. **Journal of Teaching in Physical Education**, 4(2), 123-133.

Nixon, J.E. and Jewett, A.E. (1980) **Introduction to physical education.** Philadelphia: W.B. Saunders.

Nixon, J.E. and Locke, L.F. (1973) Research on teaching physical education. In R.M. Travers (ed), **Second Handbook of Research on Teaching.** Chicago: Rand McNally.

O'Sullivan, M. (1989) Failing gym is like failing lunch or recess: Two beginning teachers' struggle for legitimacy. **Journal of Teaching in Physical Education**, 8(3), 227-242.

Piéron, M. (1986) Analysis of the research based on observation of the teaching of physical education. In M. Pieron and G. Graham (eds), **Sport Pedagogy** (pp. 193-202). Champaign, IL.: Human Kinetics.

Piéron, M., Cheffers, J. and Barrette, G. (1990) **An Introduction to the Terminology of Sport Pedagogy.** Liege, Belgium: AIESEP.

Phillips, D.C. (1989) **Post-positivistic science: Myths and realities.** Paper presented at the Phi Delta Kappa Alternative Paradigms Conference, San Francisco, CA.

Placek, J. II. (1983) Conceptions of success in teaching: Busy, happy and good? In T.J. Templin and J.K. Olson (eds), **Teaching in physical education** (pp. 46-56). Champaign, IL: Human Kinetics.

Ratliffe, T. (1986) The influence of school principals on management time and student activity time for two elementary physical education teachers. **Journal of Teaching in Physical Education**, 5(2), 117-125.

Reid, W.A. (1978) **Thinking About the Curriculum.** London: Routledge & Kegan Paul.

Sage, G.H. (1980) Sociology of physical educator/coaches: Personal attributes controversy. **Research Quarterly for Exercise and Sport**, 51(1), 110-121.

Sage, G.H. (1989) Becoming a high school coach: From playing sports to coaching. **Research Quarterly for Exercise and Sport**, 60(1), 81-92.

Sarup, M. (1989) **An Introductory Guide to Post-Structuralism and Postmodernism.** Athens, GA: University of Georgia Press.

Segrave, J.O. (1980) Role preferences among prospective physical education teacher/coaches. In V. Crafts (ed), **Proceedings, National Association for Physical Education in Higher Education** (Vol. 11, pp. 53-61). Champaign: Human Kinetics.

Siedentop, D. (1972) Behaviour analysis and teacher training. **Quest**, 18, 26-32.

Siedentop, D. (1980) **Physical Education Introductory Analysis.** Dubuque, IA: Wm. C. Brown.

Siedentop, D. (1981) The Ohio State University supervision research program summary report. **Journal of Teaching in Physical Education** (Introductory issue), 30-38.

Siedentop, D. (1983a) **Developing teaching skills in physical education.** Palo Alto, CA: Mayfield.

Siedentop, D. (1983b) Research on teaching in physical education. In T.J. Templin and J.K. Olson (eds), **Teaching in physical education** (pp. 3015). Champaign, IL: Human Kinetics.

Siedentop, D. (1985) The great teacher education legend. In H.A. Hoffman and J.E. Rink (eds), **Physical education professional preparation: Insights and foresights** (pp. 48-57). Reston, VA: American Alliance for Health, Physical Education, Recreation and Dance.

Siedentop, D. (1986) The modification of teacher behaviour. In M. Piéron and G. Graham (eds), **Sport pedagogy** (pp. 3-18). Champaign, IL: Human Kinetics.

Siedentop, D. (1989) Do the lockers really smell? **Research Quarterly for Exercise and Sport**, 60(1), 36-41.

Siedentop, D., Mand, C. and Taggart, A. (1986) **Physical Education: Teaching and curriculum strategies for grades 5 to 12.** Palo Alto, CA: Mayfield.

Sparkes, A.C. (1986) Strangers and structures in the process of innovation. In J. Evans (ed), **Physical Education, Sport and Schooling.** London: Falmer Press.

Sparkes, A.C. (1988) The micropolitics of innovation in the physical education curriculum. In J. Evans (ed), **Teachers, Teaching and Control in Physical Education.** London: Falmer Press.

Sparkes, A.C. (in press) Towards understanding, dialogue and polyvocality in the research community: Extending the boundaries in the paradigms debate. **Journal of Teaching in Physical Education.**

Spears, B. and Swanson, R.A. (1978) **History of sport and physical activity in the United States.** Dubuque, IA: William C. Brown.

Steen, T.B. (1986) A case study of teacher socialization in physical education during early training experiences: A qualitative analysis. **Dissertation Abstracts International**, 46, 2668A.

Steinhardt, M.A. (in press) Physical Education. In P. Jackson (ed) **Handbook of Research on Curriculum.** New York: MacMillan.

Templin, T.J. and Schempp, P.G. (eds) (1989) **Socialization into physical education: Learning to teach.** Indianapolis: Benchmark Press.

Templin, T.J., Woodford, R. and Mulling, C. (1982) On becoming a physical educator: Occupational choice and the anticipatory socialization process. **Quest**, 34(2), 119-133.

Tinning, R.I. (1987) Beyond the development of a utilitarian teaching perspective: An Australian case study of action research in teacher preparation. In G.T. Barrette, R.S. Feingold, C.R. Rees and M. Piéron (eds), **Myths, models, & methods in sport pedagogy** (pp. 113-122). Champaign, IL: Human Kinetics.

Tinning, R.I. (1990) **Pedagogy in teacher education: Dominant discourses and the process of problem-setting.** Paper presented at the world convention of the Association Internationale Des Écoles Supérieures d'Éducation Physique, Loughborough, England.

Tinning, R.I. (1988) Student teaching and the pedagogy of necessity. **Journal of Teaching in Physical Education**, 7(2), 82-89.

Tousignant, M. and Brunelle, J. (1987) Personalized instruction: A relief for some and a pain for others. In G.T. Barrette, R.S. Feingold, C.R. Rees and M. Piéron (eds), **Myths, models & methods in sport pedagogy** (pp. 215-224). Champaign, IL: Human Kinetics.

Veal, M.L. (1988) Pupil assessment perceptions and practices of secondary teachers. **Journal of Teaching in Physical Education**, 7(4), 327-342.

Vertinsky, P. (1989) Information source utilization and teachers' attributes in physical education: A preliminary test of a rational paradigm. **Research Quarterly for Exercise and Sport**, 60(3), 268-279.

Weiss, C.H. (1980) Knowledge creep and decision accretion. **Knowledge: Creation, Diffusion, Utilization**, 1(3), 381-404.

Young, I.M. (1990) The ideal of community and the politics of difference. In L.J. Nicholson (ed), **Feminism/Postmodernism**. London: Routledge, Chapman & Hall.

Ziegler, E.F. (1975) A history of undergraduate professional preparation for physical education in the United States, 1861-1961. In E.F. Ziegler (ed), **A history of physical education and sport in the United States and Canada**. Champaign, IL.: Stipes.

TEACHER EDUCATION PEDAGOGY: DOMINANT DISCOURSES AND THE PROCESS OF PROBLEM-SETTING

RICHARD TINNING
School of Education, Deakin University, Australia

Abstract

Pedagogy is a major concern of teacher education. Within this paper three pedagogies are discussed: performance pedagogy, critical pedagogy, and postmodern pedagogy. The case is made that in order to understand which particular pedagogies are privileged within physical education teacher education it is useful to analyse the discourses on which they are based and the process of problem-setting which acts to define or set certain problems which require certain solutions. The problems which dominate the physical education profession tend to be those which address technical or instrumental issues which in turn privilege performance pedagogy as the appropriate solution. The political processes involved in such problem-setting are discussed with reference to dominant discourses and the nature of contemporary professional practice. It is argued that privileging performance pedagogy in teacher education is limited in vision and continues to produce physical education teachers who conceive of teaching as essentially a technical matter with little sense of the social, moral and political aspects of their work.

Keywords: Pedagogy, Teacher Education, Physical Education, Discourse, Text, Problem-Setting. Ideology.

1   Introduction

Hariman, 1989: 226, 'Pedagogy should be construed less as an interesting application of theory and more as a means of reconstructing the arena for intellectual debate.'

In this paper I wish to address the notion of pedagogy in teacher education. I want to discuss how pedagogy has been **defined as a problem** in teacher education and some of the solutions which have been articulated for solving the problem. At the outset I wish to point out that this paper is an analysis of **discourse** within physical education teacher education. By discourse I mean a regular, recurrent pattern of language which both shapes and reflects the user's basic intellectual commitments (Sparkes, 1990). As such this paper will not be an analysis of teacher education as it is practiced, but more of the way in which it is conceived, thought about, and theorized. Some of the discourses I shall discuss have, as yet, little or no practical referent within physical education, but does so within teacher education more generally. But I also want to make it clear that I am not presenting a theory/practice dichotomy, rather my discussion is predicated on the understanding that the ideas we use and the ways in which we think about pedagogy are necessarily interrelated to our practice as teachers or teacher educators. Moreover, like Sneja Gunew (1982) I take the view that 'those who control language control all, even our most secret thoughts. For the **way** we think is entirely produced by the **language** in which we think' (p1. original emphasis). Thus, the way we think about and practice physical education is controlled by the language we use to describe it, and those who control the language control the practice. Since language is the medium through which most discourse is expressed, an analysis of discourse is, therefore, of vital significance in a consideration of pedagogy in teacher education.

The term pedagogy is significant in the official discourse of PETE and moreover it is a word of considerable currency within teacher education in general. But pedagogy means different things to different people and a discussion of these multiple meanings is an essential feature of this paper. As an example of discourse in pedagogy within teacher education I would like to consider the following scenario which could have taken place in almost any physical education teacher education programme around the world. It is an example to which I will return throughout the paper.

A student teacher named Kim was responsible for teaching a lesson on throwing and catching to a class of grade 6 pupils (ages about 11 or 12 years) in a local primary school. Observing her teach the lesson was the class teacher (Ms Bianca) and Mr Pasteur, the supervisor who teaches the 'methods' course back at university. This was an 'assessable' lesson so the student teacher was attempting to put on the best performance possible. The lesson consisted of the usual warm up activities, some skill development and a culminating segment on the application of the skills in a game situation. At the conclusion of the lesson Kim, Ms Bianca and Mr Pasteur sat down and discussed the lesson. Mr Pasteur had a lesson evaluation format which had been prepared over many years by the staff responsible for the methods courses. It was a very focussed format which required judgements to be made about such things as: was the lesson planned using the correct college format (a modified Glaser model); were the objectives for the lesson stated in behavioural terms; did the chosen activities provide sufficient variety to maintain the interest of the class; was the class managed with sufficient control; were teacher instructions kept to a minimum; were the instructions given with clarity; was the teacher enthusiastic; was the class kept active and on-task for most of the time; were the lesson objectives met?

Rather than use a specific evaluation format, Ms Bianca gave her feedback in the form of general comments. She simply observed the lesson and wrote comments on such things as use of voice, movement around the class, ways to arrange for the more efficient distribution of equipment and so on. She always wanted to encourage student teachers so never wrote anything which might be read as negative or critical.

In the post-lesson discussion Kim listened to the reports of both evaluators and essentially said very little. She realized that the evaluators were there to make a judgement on her teaching and she knew that to disagree would not enhance her grading. It was best just to 'bite your tongue' and appear grateful for the 'constructive' criticism. As it happened, Kim managed to keep most of the class busy, behaving appropriately, and it seemed that she had indeed met her lesson objectives. She received a good report for the lesson.

For the purposes of the argument of this paper I would like to consider Kim's lesson and its evaluation to be a 'text' of pedagogy (after Gore, 1990) which is made up of numerous discourses[1] . Importantly, as Sparkes tells us, '...all discourses are socially constructed and contain rules that guide their use...the rules, both tacit and explicit govern what is said and what remains unsaid when we speak or write..."(p.9). 'Text' refers to a particular concrete manifestation of practices organized within particular discourses. Examples of text include written passages, oral communications, non-verbal communications and visual forms of communication such as photographs, paintings and sculpture. Thus the lesson, like such things as curriculum materials, textbooks, newspapers, visual media etc., can be viewed as a text embodying discourses which articulate ideas, beliefs, values and practices. The concept of 'text' as it is used in discourse analysis is not a single version or account of reality but, rather, will have many meanings depending on who is doing the 'reading'. The case of Kim's lesson, therefore, considered from the perspective of pedagogy as text will have different meanings (readings) depending on the history (in particular the values and ideological dispositions) of the reader. However, I will contend that there is a dominant set of discourses within the text of pedagogy as it is represented in this example and they are also the dominant discourses of physical education teacher education.

I shall also distinguish between what I will call 'performance pedagogy', 'critical pedagogy', and 'postmodern pedagogy' and will claim that each of these pedagogies are defined by different discourses which are, in turn, responses to problems which can be understood by analysing the process of problem-setting (Lawson, 1984).

At the outset I wish to put my position with respect to pedagogy clearly up front. I take the view that pedagogy as a term is misused and has been co-opted by the dominant discourse. I agree with John Smyth's (1987) claim that 'the notion of pedagogy...has come to be misconstrued as the science of teaching or instruction, and to that extent it represents a narrowly scientistic view that deserves to be severely discredited'(p.1). Accordingly I will contend, like Stuart Hall, that 'There is no general pedagogy, only pedagogies. Like horses for courses' (Hall, 1983, p.6). A major question for this paper is that given multiple pedagogies why is there a hierarchy of pedagogies and why is the 'scientific' the dominant pedagogical

---

[1]   I think it is useful to think of a text using the metaphor of a rug with a particular design. A rug (text) is made up of numerous threads (discourses) each of which is necessary for the integrity of the rug. But some threads, because of their colour or texture, are foregrounded to represent the pattern on the rug. So a text will be made up of numerous discourses but some will be foregrounded and represent the dominant discourses of the text.

discourse in PETE? But before discussing specific pedagogies I shall consider the process by which certain pedagogies become defined as problems.

2   Pedagogy as a Problem

In pursuing the question of why particular discourses have become dominant within the pedagogies of physical education teacher education, it is useful to consider how the profession defines or sets its problems. A beginning assumption of this analysis is that if a major problem for teacher education is what form of pedagogy is most appropriate, then 'performance', 'critical' and 'postmodern' pedagogies are particular **responses** to that problem. Some teacher educators define or set the key problems of pedagogy as 'How can we train student teachers to become effective teachers?'

'How can we best develop the teaching skills of student teachers? (such are the questions of the major reviews of teacher education in the U.S.A. at least). Others define them as 'How can we produce teachers who have a critical social perspective who will work to build a just society?' 'How can we train teachers to be reflective of their work in ways which see a teacher's role as more than technician?'

The sorts of pedagogies we advocate or support for teacher education will be specific responses to what we consider to be the central problems of teacher education. How we define or set the central problem will be a reflection of what we consider to be the purposes of schooling. Should schooling merely reproduce the culture or should it have a transformative role as well? My position on this issue is clear. As I have argued elsewhere (Tinning, 1987), much of what stands for physical education in our schools is miseducative and makes little or no contribution to a better social world. As John Evans has told us, physical education makes both friends and enemies of children in schools. My sense is that it often makes friends of some kids (and adults) by reinforcing certain socially questionable values; for example that one can only succeed in a competitive environment if there is a loser; that girls are inferior to boys in the domain of the physical; that the slim mesomorph body is the preferred body shape to which we should all aspire, and so on. For me our physical education programmes should be challenging such values and consciously working to transform those aspects of the practice of sport and physical activity which are unjust, immoral, divisive, insensitive and limiting. To this end, a teacher education programme should educate teachers to consider their role as transforming school physical education not merely reproducing it.

3   Problem-Setting as a Framework for Analysing Pedagogy

What is meant by problem-setting? How we go about defining or setting the central problems of physical education teacher education is of central concern in an attempt to understand pedagogy. According to Hal Lawson (1984, p.49) 'problems are not just 'out there' like objects of nature; they are socially constructed...'. They are socially constructed in the process of what he calls problem-setting. Problem-setting involves a form of social editing where some possible problems are eliminated from consideration and other possibilities are foregrounded and become the focus of attention. Problem-setting is a political act which is intimately linked with power, control and what counts as legitimate knowledge in the culture or profession. It is significant not only in what it defines as a problem but also in what it chooses not to define as a problem.

Thus, for Lawson, 'Problem-setting begins with... a fundamental, ideological disturbance and proceeds as people frame selectively and then name as problems either part, or the entirety, of the aforementioned trends and conditions'. Then 'once problems have been selectively framed and named, attention may be directed toward their solutions' (Lawson, 1984, p.49). The process of problem-setting proceeds through the complementary process of framing then naming. **Frames** provide a perspective for defining a problem as a problem. They are 'editing mechanisms that function to transform the unfamiliar into familiar categories and situations' (p.52). Professionals bring to a particular situation a number of frames or perspectives which they use in order to interpret and locate a particular 'problem'. Importantly, they 'frequently are unable to identify the composition and consequences of their frames because they are tacit' (p.52). In this sense, frames are ideological and the ideological work done by such frames masks the interests which are being served by a particular practice. Also, given that 'The names professionals affix to problems... demonstrate their preference for a solution. Names thus provide a backdoor entry to understanding frames and the larger process of problem-setting' (p.56).

I would argue that when Lawson is referring to frames and names, he is essentially talking about discourse. Given that discourse is the medium through which professional practice is constituted, then the process of framing and naming is the process of contesting discourses. The discourses in which problems of the profession are expressed can thus be analysed through the process of framing and naming.

The process through which problems become defined. Lawson contends that there are usually two ways in which problems become defined in a profession. One is that the profession recognizes certain social trends or conditions which are considered ripe for exploitation and accordingly the profession changes its 'mission' statement (of aims, objectives) to accommodate responses to these trends. I would call this process 'opportunism'. It's rather like the profession recognizing that its cause can be advanced by attachment to a new social concern. He cites the changing cultural role prescriptions for women and the heightened interest in fitness and lifestyle as two examples which the physical education profession have been able to capitalize on by increasing what it has to offer.

The other way in which problems become defined is where a trend in society or cultural practice is considered to be controversial, troublesome or potentially dangerous (to the profession) in that they threaten the ideals of the profession. I would call this a response to 'threat'. In this context, rather than accept a change in ideals, the profession attempts to change the trend.

What Lawson is referring to are the dominant problems of the profession. Or, said another way, the problems considered central by those whose preferred discourses dominate the profession. Of course there will be other problems considered as central by those members of the profession who reject the dominant discourse, and often the solutions to these 'non-mainstream' problems take the form of resistance to the mainstream or dominant problems and their solutions. As we will see shortly, both critical and postmodern pedagogies are cases in point.

A useful way of thinking about mainstream (or dominant) and other problems and their solutions is to locate them within a typology which Paulston (1976) has devised. In essence Paulston argues that there are different ways of conceiving research problems in the social sciences; there are those studies which start with the assumption that essentially society is 'on track' and that all we need to do is a better job of working (through consensus) within the current social frameworks (the structuralist and functionalist studies represent this view); and there are studies which assume as their starting point that there are fundamental problems with the structure of society and that the way to improve the situation is via conflict and contestation with those who defend the status quo (Radical feminist, Marxist and neo-Marxist studies represent examples of this view). Thus problems of pedagogy conceived within a consensus model will foreground different discourses to those conceived within the conflict model. They will be framed and named differently.

Herein rests a concern I have for the way in which Lawson has described the process of problem-setting. Although the foregrounded discourse of Lawson's framework can be located in the critical tradition because of its emphasis on the importance of questions of power, values, control and conflict, his examples of the ways problems are defined in a profession through 'opportunism' and 'threat' are both conceived within the consensus model which foreground the discourses related to efficiency, accountability, measurement, validity and science. Moreover, 'opportunism' and 'threat' both represent essentially non-radical scenarios and they do not cover the range of processes or reasons for problem-setting. I would argue that solutions to the problems considered central to the profession do not have to be designed to 'put the profession back on track' in response to a particular ideological disturbance. Rather, for some members of the profession who operate within a conflict model of society in which discourses related to power, values and contestation are foregrounded, the solution may be intended to chart a different course or track for the profession. Perhaps a track that is in opposition to the current direction of the profession. The work of the critical and postmodern pedagogues finds its expression within this conflict paradigm. I find my work located within this paradigm. The work of the performance pedagogue however finds its expression within the consensus paradigm.

I will return to the issue of dominant discourses later but first I want to address the question of **what are the different frames and names which operate in problem-setting for pedagogy within teacher education?** In addressing this question I will be essentially describing the discourses which make up teacher education and the foregrounding of some discourses at the expense of others within particular pedagogies.

4   Framing and Naming Performance Pedagogy

I think there is little doubt that within PETE the dominant form of pedagogy is what I will call 'performance pedagogy'. This pedagogy is based on structured discourses which foreground utility and which are concerned with the problem of 'how' to teach physical education. It is perhaps best characterized by Daryl Siedentop's (1983) book **Improving Teaching Skills in Physical Education**. It is also no coincidence that for his authorship of this book Siedentop was awarded the Samaranch prize for the 'greatest scholarly contribution to the field of sport and physical education research'. It is a book which spoke (and in large part shaped) the dominant discourses in physical education teacher education for the 1980s.

Siedentop, like many others who champion performance pedagogy, believes in the pursuit of a technology of teaching and 'that it is to our advantage to pursue such a technology goes without saying' (1983 p.49). The fundamental beliefs which underpin performance pedagogy are that teaching is (or at least should be) a science. The main structuring questions in this discourse centre around techniques and strategies which are concerned with the most efficient ways to achieve essentially non-problematic ends.`

The framing of performance pedagogy had its roots in the perceived shortcomings of what David Kirk (1986) called 'traditional' discourse in teacher education. According to this discourse, teacher education is primarily a process of professional socialization and induction. On the job (that is in school) 'reality' is most highly valued and skills, knowledge and attitudes are passed on to prospective teachers by way of word of mouth. The dominant pedagogical knowledge in what might be called 'craft pedagogy' (after Tom, 1984) is cast in such 'rules of thumb' as 'start off firm then you can relax later', 'be consistent in your treatment of students' etc. Theory about teaching is little valued and the main focus of 'methods' courses is on tips for how to teach. Teacher education programmes which champion this discourse favour long periods of practicum with student teachers taking the role of apprentices.

During the 1960s and 70s there were two parallel research movements which in part created the conditions for performance pedagogy as an alternative to the craft pedagogy. The first was research into the student teaching process (see Tinning, 1984) which overwhelmingly revealed that the time spent by student teachers in schools was often a form of modelling which reproduced existing inadequacies in teaching and provided students with little capacity to analyse teaching. This research provided a contextual background for the claims made by the other research movement - namely the scientific analysis of teaching. Writing in the mid 1980s David Berliner (1986) put the position for a performance pedagogy as follows 'there now exists a body of knowledge and a fresh set of conceptions about teaching on which to base teacher education. Recent and numerous advances in pedagogical knowledge can now, for the first time, be used to provide teacher education with a scientific foundation' (p.7).

The discourses which are foregrounded in performance pedagogy are those of 'science' in which there is an acceptance of the primacy of rational thought and in particular scientific logic. By the application of reductionist logic, teaching could be distilled to a discrete series of skills which could be isolated, practiced, and applied in a systematic manner. There was a search for, and a belief in, a set of universal principles of teaching, a generalizable grand theory. Moreover, practice was 'naturally' separated from theory in that researchers 'discovered' or generated theory and the role of the teacher was to implement the findings. It represented classic 'modernist' thought (see Giroux, 1990). These discourses of performance have underwritten most of the research in pedagogy which is reported in physical education journals such as the **Journal of Teaching in Physical Education**.

In the case of performance pedagogy the language which constitutes the discourse is avowedly one of technocratic rationality. As I have described elsewhere this is a language of efficiency in which terms like effectiveness, fidelity (of treatment), facts, and objectivity are frequently used. The moralistic naming associated with performance pedagogy is reflected in terms like 'good' teaching, efficiency, rationality, objectivity, and science as 'truth'. The value positions represented by such terms are not considered to be problematic. According to its critics, technocratic rationality leads to 'radical deafness' toward any non-approved questions. Questions of efficiency are of major concern, and as such educational issues are defined as technical issues to be solved in the most efficient manner. Moreover technocratic rationality presupposes that means and ends are logically distinct. Issues of concern become what is the most efficient means to achieve a particular end. The desirability of the end is not contested and ceases to be an issue.

One interpretation of the ideology of technocratic rationality in physical education was outlined by Charles (1971) almost 20 years ago and it is strikingly similar to the contemporary analyses of scholars like Whitson & Macintosh (1990) and Kirk (1990). Although Charles's analysis suffers from an over-zealous application of reproduction theory (that is accepting the premise that individuals are essentially at the mercy of powerful dominant social forces) it is worth noting. Charles claims that physical education is characterized by what he calls technocentric curriculum and pedagogy. The cornerstones of this perspective are mechanisticity, reproducibility, componentiality, and measurability. 'Technological advances in society at large are reflected in physical education by the view-point of man as machine. In technocentric physical education, productivity and efficiency are measured in terms of physical performance in which case the human body may assume paramount importance' (p.277).

Within this pedagogy there is a heavy emphasis on management and class control skills because, in sympathy with the Fuller & Bown (1972) developmental model for student teachers 'that's where student teachers are at'. B.O. Smith in his famous 'Model for a School of Pedagogy' reveals very clearly what he considers to be the principle concern of teacher education: 'The pre-service student should not be exposed to theories and practices derived from ideologies and philosophies about the way schools should be. The rule should be to teach thoroughly, the knowledge and skills that equip beginning teachers to work successfully in today's classrooms' (1980, p.23). Of course this begs the question of what knowledge and skills are necessary in today's classrooms and this is a key point in the advocacy of both critical and postmodern pedagogies as we will see shortly. Also, as Beyer (1984) has claimed 'Just because teachers appear to develop in a particular way under present circumstances does not imply that this is the way we ought to help teachers grow' (p.23).

Consideration of Kim's lesson and its evaluation reveals that the discourses which are dominant are those of performance pedagogy which are embedded in the values and assumptions articulated by Mr Pasteur. Ms Bianca's discourse is that of craft pedagogy but it is backgrounded and has little influence in the text compared with the scientific discourse of Mr Pasteur. If we consider Kim's lesson as a text which provides some clues to the solutions the profession deems appropriate for the problem of teacher education we can readily identify a vocabulary of technical efficiency which Lawson has suggested is one of two common vocabularies located in the process of problem-setting. The lesson evaluation format 'talks' of control, management, time efficiency, clarity of instructions, and the statement and achievement of behavioural objectives. Morality, the other vocabulary suggested by Lawson, is rather more obscure but perhaps there is a sort of moral imperative implicit in the emphasis on time management - wasting time is associated with indolence, lack of dedication to task, and generally repugnant to the Protestant work ethic. The ideological frames which are foregrounded in the discourses of the evaluation format and the whole evaluation episode for Kim are, I would argue, consistent with the dominant discourses of the profession which are articulated in performance pedagogy.

5   Framing and Naming Critical Pedagogy

'Critical pedagogy', a relative newcomer to pedagogy in physical education, rejects the discourses of science as the most appropriate for teacher education and instead uses a social justice discourse in which the key concepts are emancipation, dialogue, critique and student voice. Critical pedagogy foregrounds questions of power, vested interests, struggle and contestation and so shares some of the concerns of feminist theory, Marxism and neo-Marxism. In a critical pedagogy, a teacher education institution would be considered a site of cultural politics and that any consideration of appropriate pedagogy not only should take accout of how to teach questions but also questions of 'how we come to know'. According to David Lusted (1986) 'How one teaches is therefore of central interest but, through the prism of (critical) pedagogy, it becomes inseparable from what is being taught and, crucially, how one learns' (p.3). A critical pedagogy will ask questions related to ethical, moral and political issues. It is concerned with rendering the means and ends of teacher education problematic and hence an explicit part of the teacher education curriculum. The writings of David Kirk (1986, 1988) represent the best articulation of this position within the physical education literature.

Advocates of critical pedagogy do not consider that the central problem of teacher education is how to create the conditions in which student teachers can learn and practice the supposed fundamental/basic skills of teaching. Critical pedagogy is a solution to a conception of a **different central problem** of teacher education. Advocates of critical pedagogy argue that all discourse in teacher education is ideological. Indeed, there is no such thing as a value free education. To this end a teacher education programme should have as its central problem the relationship of school to society, the way in which knowledge is created, disseminated and legitimated, and the nature of teaching itself. Schools and teacher education programmes are considered as sites of cultural production and reproduction and a key problematic is the power relations which mediate these processes.

As Kirk (1986) has claimed, 'the notion of inquiry oriented teacher education, and the critical pedagogy it entails, marks a radical departure from other approaches to teacher education by its emphasis on the political dimension of schooling' (p.231). Indeed, at the very time that the advocates of performance pedagogy were finding 'truth' in the findings from the research on teaching to which Berliner referred, the advocates of the critical perspective were attacking many of the assumptions upon which the research on teaching were based and, equally importantly, the appropriateness of using such research as the cornerstone for programmes of teacher education.

Critical pedagogy locates itself in opposition to positivistic conceptions of teaching. Opposition takes place on a number of issues in the context of teacher education. First, a teacher education based on performance pedagogies produces teachers, it is claimed, who are unable to step back from their daily practice to reflect on the social, moral and political nature of their work. Second, the preoccupation with efficiency ignores the problematic of the goals of education and gives.teachers no sense of what they **ought** to teach. Third, the critical pedagogue refuses to countenance that theory and practice are separate. They argue that all practice involves theories-of-action and also that notions of theory versus practice create an artificial hierarchy in which those who practice are considered of lower status to those who theorize. Performance pedagogy which conceives of the teacher as the implementer of the ideas (theories) created by the researcher implicitly endorses a theory/practice distinction. According to Adler & Goodman (1986)

> Critical theory contains a number of implications for teacher education generally and for the teaching of methods courses more specifically. Traditionally, methods courses have emphasised the development of specific skills such as planning lessons, managing basal programmes, and disciplining children, which represents competent and effective teaching. A critical perspective, **on the other hand**, fosters a questioning attitude towards teaching, learning, knowledge, the curriculum, and toward the role of schools in society (p.4). (my emphasis)

The phrase 'on the other hand' is particularly worrying within this quotation for it presents critical pedagogy and the development of teaching skills as necessarily incompatible. It's as if, by adopting a critical pedagogy it is not possible to also develop teaching skills. Critical pedagogy, as I just mentioned, is itself in part a response to the conception theory and practice as dichotomous. Moreover, as a response, it will necessarily appropriate and incorporate some of the 'old' ideas within new contexts. Recognition of such a contradiction apparently eluded Adler & Goodman and many other critical pedagogues as well. The tendency of educators (including critical pedagogues) to present concepts as binary opposites or dichotomous is one of the criticisms to which postmodern pedagogy is a response.

If Kim's lesson had been evaluated by someone who valued the discourses foregrounded in a critical pedagogy, the dominant concern would not have been on management, control, efficiency and technical competence. It's not that such aspects of Kim's teaching would be considered unimportant, but rather that other considerations would also feature strongly in making a judgement of the quality of the lesson. For example, the evaluator would consider the extent to which Kim's lesson reinforced sexism by differentially favouring boys in the choice of activity and in the nature and extent of her interactions with boys and girls. Also, judgements would be made about the extent to which Kim catered for all pupils in the class and not just those who were physically more capable. Similar judgements would be made with respect to racism. Also, given that a critical pedagogy would openly work toward a non-hierarchial relationship between teacher, supervisor and student teacher, it is most likely that all judgements made would be discussed with the expectation that Kim's opinion is valid and important. A critical pedagogy evaluation would also recognize the context specific nature of teaching and judgements would be based on a recognition of the specific context in which the lesson took place.

6   Framing and Naming Postmodern Pedagogy[2]

'Postmodern pedagogy' is **the** new kid on the block in terms of pedagogical discourses in teacher education. To my knowledge, with the exception of some work by scholars like Linda Bain, Jenny Gore and Andy Sparkes, postmodernism hasn't even been considered in the discourse of physical education to this date. But it is also probably the most illusive to pin down to a definition. It is difficult to define in terms other than as a response to the perceived shortcomings of critical pedagogy and I will simply suggest that a postmodern pedagogy is an attempt to match pedagogy with what has been called the 'postmodern condition'. Stanley Aronowitz (1987/88) says that 'we are living in a transitional era in which emerging social conditions call into question the ability of old orthodoxies to name and understand the changes that are ushering us into the 21st century' (in Giroux, 1990, p.16). A postmodern pedagogy, like critical pedagogy, has as its basis a questioning of the assumptions of positivist science. However, unlike critical pedagogy, it rejects the modernist notion of a grand narrative (in this case a dominant discourse) and the notion that truth is to be found through the application of rational thought processes or 'enlightenment'. It also recognizes multiple readings or interpretations of a text and values eclecticism rather than one method.

Personally, for me it is easier (given my particular biography) to understand the linear rational argument of performance pedagogy. It's just that while I understand it

---

2   When I first heard the term 'postmodernism' I immediately thought 'how can I understand this when I don't even know what modernism is and I didn't know I missed it'. In this sense I think poststructuralism is a better term because it doesn't have the same temporal confusions. However it is possible to define the characteristics of what has become know as 'modernism' about which postmodernism takes issue. Modernism is characterized by an emphasis on the Enlightenment ideals of critical thought and individuals exercising social responsibility. There is a faith in rationality and science and technology, in indivudals as self-motivating subjects, and in the grand narrative of human progress.

I don't believe it as an adequate explanation of current practice nor as a focus for a teacher education which can contribute to a better social world. On the other hand critical pedagogy is, for me, more difficult to understand but, paradoxically perhaps, it is more believable as a pedagogy for teacher education which is better able to prepare teachers for the social problems of the 1990s. Postmodernist discourse further challenges - its language is obtuse, heavy (and probably elitist) but it's driven by many of the best minds in the contemporary fields of social and cultural theory. While we should be sensitive to avoid jumping on the bandwagon of every new movement or theory, we should take notice of what they are saying and attempt to learn from them. I am not saying that I understand postmodernism or what a postmodern pedagogy would look like - rather I am flagging it as a discourse which we should be considering.

Postmodernism, according to Henry Giroux (1990) is both an intellectual position, a form of cultural criticism, and a response to an emerging set of social, cultural and economic conditions that characterize an age of global capitalism and individualism. Patti Lather (in press B, p.5) contends that, 'In essence, the postmodern argument is that the dualisms which continue to dominate Western thought are inadequate for understanding a world of multiple causes and effects interacting in complex and non-linear ways, all of which are rooted in a limitless array of historical and cultural specificities'. Within this context Lindsay Fitzclarence (1985) tells us that teacher educators have

> 'a long history of dealing with key concepts and ideas in curriculum by seeing them as binary oppositions or dichotomous. For example we have presented the world of teaching...as theoretical/practical, process/product, academic/functional, physical/mental, child centred/teacher directed, high status/low status knowledge'. (p.3)

We certainly know where physical education has been positioned with respect to such binaries and that it is not to our advantage to have our field of endeavour represented in such a way. We can also easily identify the way in which such binaries operate **within** our profession to the advantage of some and the disadvantage of others. Analysis of the dominant discourses in physical education teacher education reveal the use of such dichotomies and continue to reinforce a black or white conception of reality. It is worth recalling the claim I made at the start of this paper that those who control the dominant discourses control the way we think about our professional practice.

A postmodern pedagogy is a pedagogy which is intended to recognize the nature of the postmodern condition and it is a response to the considered failure of critical pedagogy to live up to its own claims. Elizabeth Ellsworth (1989) argues that critical pedagogy fails in the fulfillment of its emancipatory ideals and argues that although 'the literature states implicitly or explicitly that critical pedagogy is political, there has been no sustained research attempts to explore whether or how the practices it prescribes actually alter specific power relations outside or inside schools' (p.301). Jenny Gore (1990) asserts that pedagogies which claim to be radical, such as critical or feminist pedagogies, mostly do not address pedagogy at all except in abstract ways. She argues, correctly I think, that most writers of critical pedagogy ignore the process of knowledge production in either their own arguments or the classrooms to which they refer. In essence much of what stands for critical pedagogy fails to acknowledge the **pedagogy of the theorizing** itself. Gore also claims that critical pedagogy lacks reflexivity in that it lacks a sense of history and as such decontextualizes its focus. It focusses out on others (for example it is teachers who are 'given' the responsibility for changing the social world) and ignores the pedagogy of its own theorizing. David Lusted is of similar mind and he tells us that most critical pedagogy is based on two unquestioned assumptions: First that merely to transmit ideas is enough, and second that the pedagogy of any address follows its production rather than being integral to it, 'as if there is no pedagogy in the fact of theorising or teaching itself' (Lusted, 1986 p.5) he further claims that 'to be sensitive to the pedagogy of teaching and of theory...is to undermine the conventional transmission model wherein knowledge is produced, conveyed and received' (p.4).

Postmodern scholars are actually discourse theorists and employ a process called deconstruction to examine the meanings created of cultural practices. 'Deconstruction reveals that meanings are shifting and diffuse rather than firmly grounded in observation' (Bain, 1990 p.4). Thus we need to hear many voices, what Sparkes calls 'polyvocality', in any portrayal of meaning. But postmodern scholars are faced with a contradiction in that the intellectual tools they use for the deconstruction of cultural practice are the very ones which they consider as part of the contemporary crisis. Arguing against what they call 'a crisis of Enlightenment rationality' (Lather, in press B, p.7) they seem forced to use rational thought processes.

Examples of postmodern pedagogy are even more difficult to find in the literature than examples of critical pedagogy. Henry Giroux (1990), however, provides an account of what might constitute a postmodern pedagogy in what he calls 'Border pedagogy'. According to Giroux

> the notion of border pedagogy presupposes not merely an acknowledgement of the shifting borders that both undermine and reterritorialise different configurations of power and knowledge; it also links the notion of pedagogy to a more substantive struggle for a democratic society. It is a pedagogy that attempts to link an emancipatory notion of modernism with a postmodernism of resistance (p.33).

It is important to note that it is not a simple rejection of modernism but a 'different modulation of its themes and categories'. Notice how postmodern pedagogy contains many of the same discourses which we heard characterize critical pedagogy. Concern is still with issues of power and knowledge and a better social world, but the processes of rational thought and enlightenment are not considered to be the *sine qua non* for change.

To 'read' Kim's lesson evaluation from the perspective of postmodernism we can see that the 'truth' about the nature of good teaching is portrayed as one reality - a technical efficiency reality. Moreover the 'truth' of good teaching is to be pursued through the application of rational thought processes and scientific logic. The episode also reaffirms dominant power relations which position the knowledge and the reality of the student teacher at the bottom of the hierarchy. At this point, however, while there are numerous postmodern critiques of the practice of critical pedagogy (e.g. Ellsworth, 1989, Lather, in press) it is not possible for me to describe what a postmodern pedagogy would be like in practice let alone the limitations of such practice. Accordingly, at this time a postmodern analysis of Kim's teaching is, for me, not possible.

7   The Politics of Problem-Setting for Pedagogies: Issues of Power and Knowledge

Why is there a dominant pedagogy? Don Hellison (1988) has suggested that 'Some alternative breezes are blowing across the study of physical education, calling for more attention to the subjectivity of experience, social problems, reflection and empowerment of teachers and students, and alternatives to the empirical-analytical research paradigm' (p.88). These alternative breezes as Hellison calls them are, I would argue, mere zephyrs against the dominant prevailing trade wind in teacher education. That prevailing wind is the discourse of technocratic rationality.

Within teacher education there are different groups of scholars arguing for and against particular pedagogies on the basis of certain ideological and political stances. These stances contain certain positions of power or responses to power. All teachers/scholars/researchers are positioned within power networks and the questions they consider to be worth asking (and those which they do not ask) are influenced by such positions. Linda Bain (1990, p.4) has remarked that 'The question is not **what** knowledge but **whose** knowledge counts' (my emphasis). Accordingly, any analysis of pedagogies within teacher education will require a consideration of power relations. According to Canadians Whitson & Macintosh (1990, p.46)

> 'Different interest groups and proponents of different paradigms vie to define the profession's 'mission'. They combine to reproduce, in physical education, what Aronowitz & Giroux (1985) refer to as the technicist tendency in North American undergraduate and professional education. This involves an emphasis on technical and management 'skills', and a corresponding de-emphasis on...analysis and questioning of the social relations within which professional skills are applied.'

Whitson & Macintosh provide a vivid analysis of what they call the 'scientization of physical education' in Canada. They claim that the dominant discourse of the profession is now the **discourse of performance** specifically related to elite sport. Also the sports scientists and 'performance technocrats' who promote a positivist, technically oriented knowledge structure that seeks to map the way to increased levels of achievement in high performance sport, are in opposition to a shifting coalition of philosophers, sociologists and educators who promote a self-critical scholarship that aims to question the social and ethical nature of high performance sport. Importantly, those who question the discourse of performance are becoming marginalized and losing ground as sports science takes further footholds in the academy of physical education. A similar argument is put by Kirk (1990) in his paper on 'Knowledge, science and the rise and rise of human movement studies'.

While oppositional forms of pedagogical discourse are gaining considerable attention within mainstream teacher education they are still in their infancy in physical education teacher education. Indeed, despite Bain's (1990) claim that 'within physical education pedagogy...critical research is beginning to emerge' (p.8), I am unconvinced that it will offer a substantial challenge to the dominance of performance pedagogy. But it is, and will continue to be, an important 'other' voice which must be heard.

8   The Nature of Professional Practice and the Failure of Performance Pedagogy

Throughout the world professionals of all kinds are being confronted with situations in which the tasks they are being asked to perform no longer bear any relationship to tasks for which they have been trained. The work of Donald Schon (1984) has been useful in shedding light on this process across many professions including teaching. Schon's argument is, according to Smyth (1989), 'a neat counter to the simplistic criticism and outcries for a return to 'excellence in teaching' by merely tidying up on the technicalities of teaching' (p.4). I believe that we need to recognize some of the consequences of pursuing performance pedagogy with its technocratic discourse in the context of the nature of contemporary professional practice.

Firstly, we should recognize that we are not alone in our reverence of technocratic rationality. Schon (1984) provides ample evidence that it is the underpinning epistemology of all professions. Indeed the very notion of contemporary professional knowledge rests on the capacity to apply standardized knowledge in the form of general principles to concrete problems. A performance pedagogy attempts to define just such knowledge and principles. However, as Schon points out, technocratic rationality is failing to deal with contemporary professional practice that is increasingly unpredictable, complex, situation specific and value laden.

Why then if Schon is correct, and I believe he is, do we have performance pedagogy as the dominant discourse in PETE and in the **Journal of Teaching in Physical Education**? Lawson (1984) asserts that 'Critics have assailed all professions for their inherent conservatism and self-serving tendencies and their approaches to problem-setting are, in large part responsible' (p.56). I think that Foucault's (1980) notion of **'regimes of truth'** is useful in seeking to answer this question. The frames in which problems are defined by the profession are themselves embedded within power relations. For Foucault power is attributed to 'truth' and 'Truth' is linked in a circular relation with systems of power which produce and sustain it, and to the effects of power which it induces and which extend it' (p.133). This is what is meant by a 'regime of truth'. Although Gore (1990) argues that **all** pedagogies operate as regimes of truth, I believe that the regime of truth which is represented by the discourse of technocratic rationality is **the most powerful** in shaping our professional consciousness and practice in physical education. It is the dominant consciousness within our profession. It constitutes the rules and language against which other discourses find they must defend themselves. The recent debate in the **Journal of Teaching in Physical Education** on the methodological paradigmatic contests within physical education is a case in point.

One of the consequences for the operation of technocratic rationality as **the** regime of truth is that pedagogical problems are defined as essentially individual problems. The irony here is that professions define their valued knowledge in generalistic or nomothetic terms and such knowledge is contradictory to the very discourse of technocratic rationality which underpins their conception of professional practice. It is little wonder that Schon tells us that such generalistic knowledge has been impotent in solving individual problems of practice. Technocratic rationality locates the causes of contemporary social problems within individuals and, as Lawson (1984) has told us, problems which are framed and named in a person-centered way preserve and reproduce existing political institutions and their operations.

9   In Conclusion

Yes, both Hellison (1988) and Bain (1990) are right to claim that discourses other than technocratic rationality are now part of the 'official' discourses in pedagogy as represented by conference papers and journal articles. However, I believe that the regime of truth which shapes our professional consciousness and practice remains essentially unmoved. Although Foucault (1980) states 'The problem is not changing people's consciousness - or what's in their heads - but the political, economic, institutional regime of the production of truth' (p.133), at least recognizing that the way in which we define or set the central problems with respect to teacher education is itself constituted **within** that regime of truth is, nevertheless, a small step towards creating a teacher education which has the potential to contribute to a more humane social life. And it is one worth taking.

If, as I have claimed, the case of Kim is representative of the typical experience for student teachers, then the chances of teacher education contributing to more informed and committed educational practice is limited. It is limited because teaching is conceived mainly as a technical matter. The discourses of performance pedagogy value efficiency and technical competence but do not address, or even consider, issues related to the social world experienced within the lesson itself and the form of social world the lesson represents. The discourses of critical pedagogy have helped us begin to ask questions relating to power, knowledge and social mission but has given us few practical referents to consider in creating such a pedagogy. The discourses of postmodern pedagogy have raised questions about the nature of truth and the existence of regimes of truth in which most contemporary thought is conceived. There are, as yet, no practical referents for this pedagogy, instead, '...something is emerging, something embryonic, liminal, not yet in place' (Lather, 1989, p.14).

In our pursuit for pedagogical practices (including discourse) which are more appropriate for teacher education in the 1990s, we should begin with some of the emancipatory concerns which both critical and postmodern pedagogies address. Pedagogy should become 'a site not for working through more effective transmission strategies but for helping us to learn to analyze the discourses available to us, which ones we are invested in, how we are inscribed by the dominant, how we are outside of, other than the dominant, consciously/unconsciously, always partially, contradictorily' (Lather, in press A, p.178).

As our social world changes so we will need new discourses and new pedagogies in order to both understand and improve what stands for teacher education in our colleges. By accepting the discourses of performance pedagogy as the foundation of our teacher education we will be in danger of continuing to prepare teachers who remain ignorant of the ways in which physical education itself is implicated in producing and reproducing many of the unjust social practices which characterize much contemporary educational experience. But to consider any of the pedagogical discourses outlined in this paper to be **the answer** is to fall victim to the persuasion of the discourse itself. 'True believers' of any one answer seem too ready to stop listening, to stop challenging, and to stop questioning.

10 References

Alder, S. and Goodman, J. (1986) Critical theory as a foundation for methods courses. **Journal of Teacher education**, 2-7.

Aronowitz, S. (1987/1988) Postmodernism and politics. **Social Text**, 11 (3), 99-115.

Bain, L. (1990) Visions and voices. **QUEST**, 42 (1), 2012.

Barrette, G., Feingold, R., Rees, C. and Picron, M, (1987) **Myths, models, and methods in sport pedagogy** (eds), Human Kinetics, Champaign, Illinois.

Berliner, D. (1986) Reform in teacher education: The case for pedagogy. Unpublished report, University of Arizona.

Beyer, L. (1984) Field experience, ideology, and the development of critical reflectivity. **Journal of Teacher Education**, 25 (3), 36-41.

Charles, J. (1979) Technocentric ideology in physical education. **QUEST**, 31:2, 277-284.

Ellsworth, E. (1989) Why doesn't this feel empowering? Working through the repressive myths of critical pedagogy. **Harvard Educational Review**, 59 (3), 297-324.

Evans, J. (1986) **Physical Education, Sport and Schooling: Studies in the Sociology of Physical Education** (ed), London, Lewes: Falmer.

Fitzclarence, L. (1985) Beyond dichotomy. Paper prepared for the School of Education Directions Day 1985, Deakin University, Geelong.

Foucault, M. (1980) Truth and power, in **Power/knowledge: Selected interviews and other writings 1972-1977**, (ed C. Gordon), Pantheon Books, New York.

Fuller, F. and Bown, O. (1975) On becoming a teacher. In **Teacher Education** (ed K Ryan), The 74th Yearbook of N.S.S.E. Chicago: University of Chicago press.

Giroux, H. (1990) **Curriculum Discourse as Postmodernist Critical Practice**, Deakin University Press, Geelong, Australia.

Gore, J. (1990) Pedagogy as text in physical education teacher education: Beyond the preferred reading. In **Physical Education, Curriculum and Culture: Critical Issues in the Contemporary Crisis.** (eds D. Kirk and R. Tinning), The Falmer Press, London.

Gore, J. (1989) The struggle for pedagogies: Critical and feminist discourses as 'regimes of truth'. Unpublished paper, University of Wisconsin-Madison.

Gunew, S. (1982) Discourses of otherness, in **Displacements: migrant story-tellers**, Deakin University, Victoria, Australia.

Hall, S. (1983) Education in crisis. In **Is There Anyone Here From Education?** (eds J. Donald & A. Wolpe), Pluto, London.

Hariman, R. (1989) **Getting Smart! Empowering Approaches to Research and Pedagogy**, Quoted in P. Lather (in press), Routledge, London.

Harrington, W. (1987) An ethnographic study of one teacher and two classes. In **Myths, models, and methods in sport pedagogy** (eds Gary Barrette et al.), Human Kinetics, Champaign, Illinois.

Hellison, D. (1988) Our constructed reality: Some contributions of an alternative perspective to physical education pedagogy. **QUEST**, 40, 80-90.

Kirk, D. (1986) Beyond the limits of theoretical discourse in teacher education: Towards a critical pedagogy. **Teaching & Teacher Education**, 2 (2), 155-167.

Kirk, D. (1986) A critical pedagogy for teacher education: Toward an inquiry-oriented approach. **Journal of Teaching in Physical Education**, 5, 230-246.

Kirk, D. (1988) **Physical Education and Curriculum Study: A Critical Introduction**, Croom Helm, London.

Kirk, D. (1990) Knowledge, science and the rise and rise of human movement studies. **ACHPER National Journal**, 127, 8-12.

Lather, P. Staying dumb? Student resistance to liberatory curriculum. In **Getting Smart! Empowering Approaches to Research and Pedagogy** (in press a), Routledge, London.

Lather, P. (1989) Postmodernism and the politics of enlightenment. **Educational Foundations**, 3 (3), 7-28.

Lather, P. Postmodernism and the discourses of emancipation: Precedents, parallels and interruptions. In **Getting Smart! Empowering Approaches to Research and Pedagogy** (in press b), Routledge, London.

Lawson, H. (1984) Problem-setting for physical education, **QUEST**, 36, 48-60.

Lusted, D. (1986) Why pedagogy? **Screen**, 27 (5), 2-14.

Paulston, R. (1976) **Conflicting theories of social and educational change: A typological review**. University Centre for International Studies, University of Pittsburg.

Rothing, P. (1987) Reflections on researching sport pedagogy. In **Myths, models and methods in sport pedagogy** (eds Gary Barrette et al.), Human Kinetics, Champaign, Illinois.

Schon, D. (1984) **The Reflective Practitioner: How professionals Think in Action**. Basic books, New York.

Siedentop, D. (1983) **Developing Teaching Skills in Physical Education**. 2nd edition, Mayfield Publishing Co, California.

Smith, B. (1980) A Design for a School of Pedagogy. Department of Education, Washington, D.C. ERIC Document No ED 193 215.

Smyth, J. (1987) **A Rationale for Teachers' Critical Pedagogy: A Handbook**. Deakin University, Geelong.

Smyth, J. (1989) A critical pedagogy of classroom practice. **Journal of Curriculum Studies**, 21 (6), 483-502.

Smyth, J. (1987) Introduction: Educating teachers; changing the nature of pedagogical knowledge. In **Educating Teachers: Changing The Nature of Pedagogical Knowledge** (ed J. Smyth), The Falmer Press, London.

Sparkes, A. Towards understanding, dialogue and polyvocality in the research community: Extending the boundaries of the paradigm debate. **Journal of Teaching in Physical Education** (in press).

Sparkes, A. (1987) Strategic rhetoric: A constraint in changing the practice of teachers. **British Journal of Sociology of Education**, 8, 37-54.

Tinning, R. (1984) The student teaching experience: All that glitters is not gold. **The Australian Journal of Teaching Practice**, 4 (2), 53-63.

Tinning, R. (1987) **Improving Teaching in Physical Education**, Geelong, Deakin University Press.

Tinning, R. (1987) Beyond the development of a utilitarian teaching perspective: An Australian case study of action research in teacher preparation. In **Myths, models, and methods in sport pedagogy** (eds Gary Barrette et al.), Human Kinetics, Champaign, Illinois.

Tom, A. (1984) **Teaching as a Moral Craft**. Longman, New York.

Whitson, D. and Macintosh, D. (1990) The scientization of physical education: Discourse of performance. **Quest**, 42 (1), 40-51.

RESEARCHING PEDAGOGY AND REFLECTIVE TEACHING

JOHN EVANS
University of Southampton, Southampton, England

Richard Tinning's paper is challenging and properly provocative and I want to endorse much of what he has to say. I also want to set his views within the United Kingdom educational scene to search out their applicability to Teacher Education and research on pedagogy in this country. My claim will be that in the UK we are going to need all the friends we can get in the next few years if we are to sustain, better still develop, the position of PE as an **educational** rather than a **training** enterprise within the educational system. To this end we are also going to have to adopt a pretty healthy and progressive attitude towards the curriculum and pedagogy of Teacher Education if we are to produce teachers able and willing to engage in critical reflection upon what they do and if research on pedagogy is to survive and thrive within the current conditions of educational work. By progressive I mean an attitude of mind which is as capable of embracing the perspectives or discourses outlined in Richard's paper as it is of taking a critically reflective stance toward's each of them. This won't be easy given that, as Richard has pointed out, embedded in each are personal and professional interests and value systems and also domain assumptions not only about the nature of knowledge but also about what the individual and society is and ought to be. Neither of the 'discourses' outlined by Richard can yet lay claim to having discovered how or what research on teaching or pedagogy ought to be, though at times each seems close to doing so. Each has enormous strengths and some substantial limitations. None of them come close, in my view, to exhausting the agenda of what the study of pedagogy in Teacher Education should look like or what research on pedagogy should embrace, given the problems facing educational practitioners in the UK, and elsewhere.

Richard's paper lays great stress on the analyses of the discourses which feature in Teacher Education and of the texts in which they are embedded. This form of analyses is undoubtedly extremely important and should occupy our serious attention. Discourse analyses is a means of unveiling the nature and the distribution of power in our work places, and the mechanisms of cultural production and social control. There are, however, substantial problems in viewing **all** social phenomena as texts along with the producers of discourse and language as the absolute captors of our minds, innermost secrets and imaginations. As others have argued, if textual authority were as efficacious as some literary critics would have us believe then, 'writers would be kings' (Sangren, 1988, p.411). I think Richard is right to hint that there may be a certain elitism in this view, in the writings of post modernism. Sangren makes the point that:

> by making textual authority stand for cultural authority in general, the literary critic, as fabricator and deconstructor of that authority, places himself or herself in a position of transcendent power - if not that of a king, at least that of a high priest. Although this appropriation of power may be socially effective in academic institutions such authority does not seriously threaten other ways of constituting and reproducing authority in society as a whole. (Ibid, p.411).

In my view Sangren isn't far off the mark when he contests the merits of equating the logic of the production of texts with the logic of social and cultural reproduction as a whole. He argues:

> culture and society encompass texts and empirically the latter are constrained within the former; nonetheless texts are in some important senses 'free' of the material conditions (productions, life and death, reproduction, competition with other societies) that constrain forms of social reproduction. So too is the actor's point of view in some respects 'free' to misunderstand both the nature of social reproduction and its own encompassment within social reproduction. (p.414).

Others too have argued that the 'multilevel operations of power within social practices cannot be understood exclusively with reference to language and discourse' (Stephanson, 1988, p.273 quoted in Giroux, 1988). Giroux's (1988) critique of the postmodern (over) emphasis on language and textuality seems particularly pertinent to Physical Educationists for whom expression and understanding through the body and movement is as (if not more) important than linguistic/literary or oral communication. He claims:

> Language is not the sole source of meaning; it cannot capture through the totalizing belief in textuality, the range of habits, practices, and social relations that constitute what can be called the 'thick' side of human life. Those aspects of social practice in which power operates to maim and torture as well as to forge collective struggles whose strength are rooted in lived experiences, felt empathy, and concrete solidarity exceeds the insights offered by way of linguistic models. (p.23).

These are dangerous times for the discipline of Physical Education, and uncomfortable ones for PE teachers and teacher educators. The present Conservative administration has shown itself more willing than any of its predecessors to intervene directly (for example through the Council for the Accreditation of Teacher Education) to control not only the curriculum of schooling, but also the nature of Teacher Education in both the public sector and in Universities. This may not be all bad news, but other Teacher Educators have pointed out (Barton and Whitty, 1988) the attempt to control Teacher Education is not just an attempt at control for its own sake. It has its roots in a vision of a desirable social order. In recent years those working in the field of Teacher Education will have felt the sharp thrust of policy interventions which have squeezed educational studies components of teacher education courses, privileged practice **rather than** theory, and which seem bent on producing a teaching force characterized by specific forms of subjectivity which it is hoped have little place for critical or reflective theory. Changing the ways in which teachers and pupils think about the world has, as Barton and Whitty (1988) argue, become an open and acknowledged task of the present government. Its educational policy initiatives have been informed by a narrow, instrumental, technocratic view of schooling, increasingly concerned with evaluating the quality and effectiveness of teachers and schools, in terms of their, the Government's or industries' pre-specified needs and visions of what education ought to be. The latest expression of paranoia about the putative poor quality of Teacher Education is found in a recent White Paper, which claims amongst other things that B.Ed. courses are distinguished by an absence of rigour.

> Time which could be spent giving future teachers a grounding in core National Curriculum subjects such as English or Mathematics is dissipated on such non-academic pursuits as dance or movement. There is, it is claimed, a continuing and questionable emphasis on 'special needs', 'multicultural' education and 'gender'. The curriculum, that is to say, still reflects many of the sociological obsessions of the 1970's. (*The Times*, 11.5.90).

Now all this does not sound like reference to a form of Teacher Education in which a scientific discourse is dominant. Though the last thing we should do is assume that the claims of these authors are based on evidence from systematic research or that they constitute accurate representation of what takes place in teacher education. In recent years the New Right in Britain has been expert at creating the impression that there is a crisis in education when in reality either none or little more than a minor problem is to be found (Evans and Davies, 1990). Even more disturbing is the absence in this and other policy documents of any suggestion that social critique might be an important part of the teachers role and thus of a course in teacher education and this at a time when teachers are having to deal with great uncertainty, with more and more often contradictory demands; and when young people will need to face increasing social divisions, discriminations, tensions and challenges within their local communities and wider societies. Yet the whole notion of criticism, an essential pre-condition of positive social change, is itself being challenged (Barton and Whitty, p.18). The point to be stressed here, however, is that the New Right discourse of critique (which isn't undifferentiated or without contradiction by any means) which has been directed at teacher education and teachers in schools in the last 10 years, not only speaks **past** educationists to address the 'public at large', it also simultaneously addresses particular discourses **within** the profession. In this way it privileges certain factions of the education community and the social relations, power and status positions they enjoy along with the discourse which has helped support and sustain them. In Physical Education the 'privileged' may be the discourse and purveyors of what Richard refers to as a Performance Pedagogy.

The point is well made in Richard's paper that there are hierarchies of knowledge in the discursive field of Physical Education. Discursive fields according to Michael Foucault consist of competing ways of giving meaning to the world and of organizing social institutions and processes. They offer individuals (teachers, in this case) a range of subjectivity. Within a discursive field not all discourses carry equal status, weight or power. Some will account for and justify the appropriateness of the *status quo*. Others will challenge existing practices from within or will contest the very basis of current organization and the selective interests which it represents. Such discourses are likely to be on the margin or periphery of existing practices perhaps dismissed by the hegemonic system of meanings and practices as irrelevant or bad (Weedon, 1987,). Richard is right to point out that in PE, the discourse of scientific or performance pedagogy, is privileged above all others (and this doesn't make science inherently a bad thing) though its position has not gone uncontested. If it were we wouldn't have had the fuss about the putative demise of competition, or sport and the relentless advance of egalitarianism that we've had in recent years. Such privilege is not arbitrary, it reflects long established interests and positions of power and reaches out to a wider social system and cultural climate which values and affords high status to certain forms of knowledge. Others have made this point better than I can. Margaret Talbot (1989) has implored us to consider why PE students in America and in the UK. undervalue the human studies in relation to the physical sciences and even question their relevance to their professional training. She asks:

> are our students required as part of their higher education to confront the ethical and social issues which form the context for and influence their profession? Can they afford not to at a time when the rapidly changing social world in which we live makes it essential that future professionals possess the conceptual and reasoning tools to make rational and ethical decisions' (p.22).

The pursuit of technical ability and expertise (predominantly, but not solely the quest of performance pedagogy) without any grasp of the moral, ethical, social or political issues (predominantly, but not solely, the interests of Critical Theory and Post Modernism) is as Margaret goes on to say, 'likely to lead to inconsistent and partial decisions, which together become the root cause of accusations of incompetence and unprofessional behaviour'. With Richard, and others (Beyer, 1988), I'd argue for a form of Teacher Education, which encourages and helps develop a critical consciousness, which is committed equally to reflection and committed action and which aims at developing a more just, humane and satisfying environment. Like Beyer, I'd claim that 'Reflectivity is not just on analytica] tool based on some abstract ideal'. It is a process that should lead to intervention strategies that work towards changing the experience of teachers and children; and indeed it may well be the case that in the process reflection and action, 'thought and action, theory and practice, and continuity and change become unified' (p.196). Of course the achievement of this is easier said than done, but it's unlikely to be accomlished unless the interests of critical theorists, post modernists and performance pedagogues, can co-exist or better still, co-mingle in the curriculum of teacher education. Arguably such will have to be the case if we want our students to be curriculum **decision makers,** confident re-creators of the variety of policies and discourses which will frame their work, and not just curriculum **delivery service workers** (Ginsberg, 1988), purveyors of the Government's or other people's latest policy whim.

So in this cultural and political climate, building blocks between the interest groups or factions which co-exist within the PE profession at this period is just what we can't afford to do. Like Richard, I would stress that we certainly need to be sorting out our stall in Teacher Education so as to produce teachers capable not only of reflecting critically on the range of discourses and policies which will bear upon their practices as teachers, but also of then acting constructively towards them. This is a matter to which I will return below. For the moment, however, I simply want to put us on our guard and stress that given that educational research or more specifically the study of pedagogy is social science applying its wares alongside a little history and philosophy in Teacher Education we would do well to recognize, as Brian Davies (1988) has neatly stated, that 'this is the Age of Control of the Means of Ennunciation (ACME). Our Government and their academic spokepersons will think nothing of turning the screws on certain forms of knowledge and action in schools and teacher education. There are, as Brian says, 'bullies but no innocents left in social science'. This leaves me, with him, in strong support of Patricia Broadfoot's (1988) view (expressed in her Presidential Address to the British Educational Research Association) that there has never been a period more in need of educational researchers whacking in the evidence to check and purify the purposes of ideologically driven, untested educational policy. In England and Wales, we are faced with teacher testing, National Curriculum, Local Financial Management of schools, and opting out, and new and different ways of producing a future supply of teachers. All of this as far as their implications for PE and sport are concerned, is currently badly, sadly under researched. This brings me again to Richard's paper. Given the political and cultural climate in which we work we simply cannot afford either the reductionism which is inherent in sports performance pedagogy, or in my view, the solipsistic tendencies of post modern methodology. The focus of the former (perhaps unavoidably), on the what and how rather than on the why of teaching does leave important research questions and interests largely untouched and also ethical, moral and political issues explicitly un-addressed. Thinking of performance pedagogy reminds me of that scene in the big screen version of Joseph Heller's **Catch 22.** Captain Yossarian and his co-pilot are lying amidst the mangled debris in the fuselage of their crashed B52 bomber. Yossarian is uninjured but Snowden, his radio-gunner bombadier propped up against the mangled wreckage, is not so lucky. His leg, evidently, is badly gashed and Yossarian, focusing his attention on this very obvious problem desperately searches for something to curb the gushing flow of blood. He comforts Snowden, gives him a cigarette and re-assures him that once he's applied a tourniquet to his leg to stem the flow of blood all will be well. Unable or unwilling to find anything about his own person capable of serving this purpose, he looks to the bombadier's white but blood stained, silky shirt. He grabs hold of this and tears away a sizeable strip. From the gaping aperture slumps the innards, the intestines of his now obviously fatally wounded friend. The look of horror and incomprehension on Yossarian's face brilliantly announce his feelings for the predicament he's in. He has misunderstood his friends problem and mis-directed his own attentions. His friend will die. He seems to wearily ask himself, not what should I do next, but why on earth am I here?

Richard is right to point out the shortcomings of performance pedagogy discourse, it does reduce the study of pedagogy to the study of **instruction.** It's probably fair to say that in much of the social psychological and psychological (systematic observation) research on teaching the quest is a relentless documentation of an assumed relationship between teacher behaviours (stimulus) and student learning outcomes (response). The complexities of the teaching process and the cultural, material and organizational contexts in which it is located seem often to be of little concern. Teaching is described in psychological terms based on the analysis of a single individual. The focus **is** on the **how**, rather than the **why** of teaching. But in postmodern pedagogy (as far as I can currently tell) the teacher is also superordinate in the research focus though strangely and ironically in decentreing the 'self' the person often seems to disappear. The subject is not only subordinate to the text (constituted in and through it) or radically decentred, it sometimes ceases to exist entirely. In Giroux's (1988, p.23) view:

> The subject bears no responsibility for agency since he or she is merely a heap of fragments bereft of any self-consciousness regarding the contradictory nature of her own experience .... There is little sense of the ways in which different historical, social and gendered representations of learning and desire are actually mediated and taken up subjectively by real, concrete individuals

or (I would add) of how consciousness is 'shaped' by the structured realities of peoples' everyday lives. The construction and deconstruction of our own and others' pedagogies as texts would be at the centre of a post-modern pedagogy in teacher education. This focus and form of analyses is extremely important, but what we don't yet clearly see is how a particular pedagogy as text, along with its embedded discourses, are situated in social practices, how the text is related to an exterior material and social world, or how individuals both frame and are framed by the recursive conditions of their everyday lives. We need also beware of the pluralism of some post-modern discourse in which various groups, discourses or texts appear to be ascribed an equal status or equal voice. Giroux (1988) identifies the weaknesses in this position, arguing that there is a failure within this type of analyses to develop forms of social analysis, critique, or understanding of how particular voices and social formations are formed in oppositional struggle, rather than in dialogue (p.19). Marginal voices, texts or discourses are privileged but the important issue of what social conditions need to exist before such voices can actually exercise forms of self and social empowerment is not engaged. There are then substantial dangers to a post-modern discourse if it reduces pedagogy to 'a lifeless methodological imperative of teaching conflicting interpretations of what counts as knowledge' (Graff, 1987) rather than 'a pedagogy informed by a political project that links the creation of citizens to the development of critical democracy' (Giroux, 1988, p.27).

The issue here is not how or whether we replace a scientific discourse or performance pedagogy with critical theory or post-modernist methodology. That's neither possible nor desirable. Our starting point might be to ask, with Beyer (1988, p.l87) what kind of Teacher Education in form and content, is most appropriate and justifiable given the nature and demands of modernity? What kind of curriculum and pedagogy do we have to construct within Teacher Education to create possibilities for teachers to treat teaching as a moral, political and social act? How are we to prepare teachers to routinely reflect upon the kind of world they are helping to build by the environment they construct in their classrooms and also about the kind of moral principles and action guides that they should use in making educational choices (Ibid, p.l87). Answers to these questions take us way beyond the brief of this conference, but re-thinking how we conceptualize science and pedagogy, is as good a place as any to begin.

It may well be the case that in Britain, perhaps unlike in the USA and Australia, the problem is not that a scientific discourse has dominated the study of pedagogy, but rather that such activity, the study of pedagogy, has hardly featured at all in the curriculum of Teacher Education. Maybe this is no bad thing given the conservative tendencies, the lack of reflection and self criticism which apparently is evident in such practice (Dewar, 1990, p.67) where it occurs. In the UK it's possible to argue that either the study of pedagogy in PE has arrived and nobody has noticed it or it simply failed to get started in the first place; both propositions are partly true. Neither in PE nor in other curriculum areas in Teacher Education has the study of pedagogy featured high amongst the interests of teacher educators. Some years ago Brian Simon (1985) offered an explanation for this in a chapter entitled 'Why no Pedagogy in Britain'? He pointed to the powerful and ubiquitous influence of the public school system and within it the attitude of mind which posits that all one needs for entry to the teaching profession is the correct cultural habitus and an appropriate set of technical (subject specific) skills; an attitude which the New Right in Britain are all too ready to cultivate both in the wider public mind and the discourse and practice of teacher education. In this view approaches to teaching are handed down from generation to generation. 'The (historical) denigration of the value of professional training by the public schools implies a disdain for the concept of pedagogy, or a science of teaching, since the function of professional training is, in theory, to lay the basis in science of the practices **of the art of teaching**' (p.338). Like Brian Simon I, too, would argue for a 'science of pedagogy' if pedagogy is re-conceptualized to embrace teaching (the processes or modes of transmission), curriculum and the producers (teachers) of both and if science (following Giddens, 1990) is thought of and engaged in as reflexive practice. As Giddens says:

> reflexivity is a defining characteristic of all human action but with the advent of modernity, reflexivity takes on a different character. It is introduced into the very basis of system reproduction, such that thought and action are constantly refracted back upon one another. (p.38). [1]

---

[1] The reflexivity of modern social life consists in the fact that social practices are constantly examined and re-formed in the light of incoming information about those very practices, thus constitutively altering their character (Giddens, 1990, p.38).

'Modernity is constituted in and through reflexively applied knowledge, but the equation of knowledge with certainty has turned out to be misconceived'. Such a claim is not new. As Giddens goes on to point out:

> Even philosophers who most staunchly defend the claims of science to certitude, such as Karl Popper, acknowledge that, as he expresses it, 'all science rests upon shifting sand'. In science **nothing** is certain, and nothing can be proved, even if scientific endeavour provides us with the most dependable information about the world to which we can aspire. In the heart of the world of hard science, modernity floats free' (p.39). [2]

Adopting this view has implications both for how we think about the study of pedagogy in Teacher Education and how we go about doing research on teaching. It certainly blurs the boundaries between doing science and practicing the 'art of teaching' in a way which brings us close to the prescriptions for reflective teaching which are found in a variety of recent Teacher Education literature. Schon (1983), for example, proposes a fundamental re-organization of the ways in which we think about teacher education and the relationship of theory to practice. He re-constructs the position of **practice**, removing it from its' inferior status in relation to theory, and contests the 'model of Technical Rationality' which has shaped thinking about research, education and practice in Teacher Education. A model in which professional activity consists in instrumental problem solving made vigorous by the application of scientific theory and technique (p.21). By contrast, Schon argues for 'the production of 'reflective practitioners' - characterized by an ability to recognize and explore puzzling events that occur during the activities of practice. 'Where Technical Rationality separate means from ends, research from practice, and knowing from doing, reflection-in-action unites these categories: practice is a kind of research, means and ends are framed interdependently ..., enquiry is a transaction with the situation in which knowing and doing are inseparable' (1987, p.165).

All this can sound like good news, but others have pointed out while Schon's work goes some distance towards describing what the reflective teacher is like it provides very little in the way of how we might (in either schools or teacher education) achieve such a laudable position/condition (Munby and Russell, 1989). Gore (1990), and Smyth (1989) currently may be our best examples of what reflective teaching, as a form of practice or praxis might look like, and Richard's claims for a wider adoption of critical and post-modernist discourse and pedagogy in teacher education might go some way towards enhancing the supply of teachers endowed with the ability and attitude to engage in activity of this kind.

The discussion so far, however, has concentrated attention on what should be the nature, place and purpose of pedagogy and the study of pedagogy in teacher education. This should not exhaust our concern or interests in what research on

---

[2]   It should also be noted that Giddens goes on to make the point, and it is one that I would share, that we should 'dismiss as unworthy of serious intellectual consideration the ideas that no systematic knowledge of human action or trends of social development is possible. Were anyone to hold such a view (and if indeed it is not incohate in the first place), they could scarcely write a book about it. The only possibility would be to repudiate intellectual activity altogether' (p.47).

teaching these days should be, given the conditions of practice which young teachers will encounter. Neither the treatment of pedagogy as text, critical theorizing as a reflective practitioner's, nor the systematic observation of classroom events, are the be all and end all of research on pedagogy. While it is hard to think of either pedagogy or teaching without thinking of teachers, students or classrooms, research on both need neither always begin nor end with a focus on these phenomena only. Like Brian Davies (1990) I would argue that while it is probably inevitable and important that we should continue to carry on with the measurement of the easily accessible (usually the remit of the systematic observers within sports pedagogy research), a task taken on with increasing technical efficiency and refinement in the UK by the school effectiveness movement[3], at the moment it is even more important that we should also look for patient and fundamental enquiry at the level of detail in the daily work world of students and teachers, and at the way in which educational policies and discourse help construct and frame the environment of learning. This, as Davies goes on to point out, doesn't mean more of the indulgent circularity of the ethnographic (or case-study) teacher and pupil strategies literature which over provides 'accounts of classrooms as low technology, poorly understood workplaces where everything is likely to happen and does, apart from adequate teaching and learning' (Ibid, p.l). Neither this nor the critical analyses of 'radical theorists' have much to offer if it remains more concerned with deconstructing teaching than with how it is to be put back together again. There are signs that this is now happening in radical critical theory[4].

David Halpin (1990) recently makes a similar point as he usefully outlines what for me is an important agenda for research on teaching in PE. He stresses that for far too long the discipline of sociology has avoided direct engagement with curricular policy advocacy preferring to 'hover around the margins of such work showing little awareness of initiatives that lack a specific sociological bent. Given this tendency it is hardly surprising that the discourse of scientific pedagogy with its promise of utility, amelioration and democratic teaching and a developing field of curriculum studies have captured the interests and imaginations of teachers and teacher educators, at the expense of the development of sociological research on teaching, or critical or post-modern pedagogy in Teacher Education. Halpin is just about right when he argues that what is needed now are forms of research and analyses which will assist progressive local authorities, schools and teachers to integrate their everyday priorities and practices with the requirements of recent educational legislation. This will require more than ideas about **means** about how to teach

---

3   One should read Davies (1990) for a challenging critique of research on effective teaching. He comments, "The sort of people that 'good teachers' are sums up the concern in educational discourse which has ensured the neglect of pedagogy in appropriate organisational and policy frameworks that would enable us to refloat 'educability' work, capable of going somewhere. The search for the individual (and, I would add, the institutional or organisational) correlates of effectiveness is an inevitably doomed activity, very largely in the interests of the status quo" (p.13).

4   Early radical theory, claim Giroux and Friere (1987), failed to address the experience of those educators, parents and others whose works in and with school had very little to say about advocating the discourse of democracy in either a formal or substantive sense, which in turn made it difficult for this position to be related to the historical experiences, legacies and aspirations of those groups who still believed in such a discourse.

effectively. The choices are as Halpin states both moral and political. The prescriptions which he goes on to offer, neatly embrace the discourses and the concomitant research interests and methodologies which Richard has outlined. His vision is of action and policy orientated research. Amongst other things this would mean consolidating and extending current efforts to research and thereby illuminate the ways in which educational policy (for example Health Education initiatives, or the Education Reform Act) make their impact on teachers, teaching and learning.

In this view, and it is one that I would share, there is a key role for policy orientated ethnography (Finch, 1988). It would also mean work by student teachers, teacher educators and professional researchers on the construction and deconstruction of education policy documents. Within Teacher Education this would mean assisting teachers to 'read' the significance of educational policy texts. Critical analysis of policy texts surrounding new legislation (The Education Reform Act, ERA) or new initiative (for example in Games teaching, or Health Related Exercise) should or would become part of the curriculum of student teachers both at initial and inservice levels. As Halpin properly notes, 'to be able to relate one's own work as a teacher to the requirements of ERA or any other educational policy statement, entails not simply knowing what it says but also being able to interpret its ideological effect in relation to other competing perspectives on schooling' (p.31). Finally, he claims that we need studies of how policy develops inside and outside schools, of who plays the key roles and of who are benefitted and disbenefitted when innovations take place.

More than ever then, we need to create opportunities within Teacher Education, both in the organizational form of our practices and the content of our curriculum, for students, and indeed serving teachers and Teacher Educators, to engage in reflection and research on pedagogy. This will require a critical analysis of social and knowledge hierarchies; it will also mean the adoption of the interests and methodologies of critical theorists and post-modernists. We might then begin to help our students make those essential links between theory and experience, between biography and history, between their private troubles (as teachers) and public issues, that lie at the heart of the sociological imagination (Barton and Whitty, 1988).

References

Barton, L. and Whitty, G. (1988) Exercising The Sociological Imagination in Adversity: Sociologists and Teachers Under Thatcherism. Paper presented to the International Sociology of Education Conference, Faro, Portugal, April 1988.

Beyer, L. (1988) **Knowing and Acting: inquiry and educational studies,** Basingstoke, The Falmer Press.

Broadfoot, P. (1988) Educational Research: two cultures and three estates. **British Journal of Educational Research,** 14 (1), 3-15.

Davies, B. (1988) Research in a Department Without ITT. Text of talk given to the Education Department, University College, Cardiff, April, 1988.

Davies, B. (1990) Social Class, School Effectiveness and Cultural Diversity. Paper presented to AERA Conference, 1990.

Dewar, A. (1990) Oppression and Privilege in Physical Education: Struggles in the Negotiation of Gender in a University Programme. In Kirk, D. and Tinning, R. (eds) **Physical Education, Curriculum and Culture,** The Falmer Press, pp.67-101.

Evans, J. and Davies, B. (1990) Power to the People? The Great Education Reform Act and Tomorrows Schools. In Lauder, H. and Wylie, C. (eds) **Towards Successful Schooling,** The Falmer Press, pp.53-73.

Finch, J. (1988) Ethnography and Public policy. In Pollard, A., Purvis, J. and Walford, G. (eds) **Education, Training and the New Vocationalism.** The Open University Press, pp.185-201.

Foucault, M. (1979) **Discipline and Punish.** Hammersmith: Penguin

Foucault, M. (1981) **The History of Sexuality,** Volume one, An Introduction. Hammersmith: Viking.

Foucault, M. (1986) **The History of Sexuality,** Volume Two, The Use of Pleasure. Hammondworth: Viking.

Giddens, A. (1990) **The Consequences of Modernity.** Polity Press.

Ginsburg, M. (1988) **Contradictions in Teacher Education and Society: a critical analysis.** Basingstoke, The Falmer Press.

Giroux, H.A. and Friere, P. (1987) 'Serious Introduction', in Livingstoke, D.W. and Contributors, (eds) **Critical Pedagogy and Cultural Power,** London, Macmillan Education Ltd., pp.XI-XVI.

Giroux, H.A. (1988) Postmodernism and The Discourse of Education Criticism, in **Journal of Education,** Vol.170, No.3, 1988, pp.5-30.

Gore, J.M. (1990) Pedagogy as Text in Physical Education Teacher Education: Beyond the Preferred Reading. In Kirk, D. and Tinning, R. (eds) 1990, pp.101-139.

Graff, G. (1987) **Professing literature: An institutional history.** Chicago: University of Chicago Press.

Halpin, D. (1990) The Sociology of Education and the National Curriculum. In **British Journal of Sociology of Education,** Vol.11, No.1, 1990, pp.21-37.

Munby, H. and Russell, T. (1989) Educating the reflective teacher: an essay review of two books by Donald Schon, in **Journal of Curriculum Studies 1989,** Vol.21, No.1, pp.71-80.

Sangren, P. (1988) Rhetoric and the Authority of Ethnography, in **Current Anthropology, Vol.29,** No.3, June 1988, pp.405-423.

Schon, D. (1983) **The Reflective Practitioner.** Basic Books, New York.

Schon, D. (1987) **Educating the Reflective Practitioner: Toward a New Design for Teaching and Learning in the Profession.** Jossey-Bass, San Francisco.

Simon, B. (1985) **Does Education Matter?** Lawrence and Wishart.

Smyth, J. (1989) A Critical Pedagogy of classroom practice. In **Journal of Curriculum Studies,** Vol.21, No.6, pp.483-502.

Talbot, M. (1989) Equality, Education and Physical Education. Paper presented at the Faculty of Educational Studies, University of Southampton, 1989.

The Times (1990) Misteaching Teachers. **The Times,** 11th June, 1990.

Weedon, C. (1987) **Feminist Practice & Poststructuralist Theory.** Basil Blackwell.

HOW CAN SPORT PEDAGOGY MOVE TOWARDS EXCELLENCE?

ROLAND NAUL
Sportpedagogy, University of Essen, Germany

Abstract
The paper points out two different meanings of the title: how can sport pedagogy as a discipline move towards excellence and how can sport pedagogy approach the topic of sporting excellence? The development from theory of PE to modern sport pedagogy in the FRG is reviewed methodologically. A hermeneutic paradigm based on qualitative methods has to be re-established. The lack of knowledge about sporting excellence in sport pedagogy is criticized. Qualitative life cycle research of elite athletes should be a field in sport pedagogy. Both meanings of the title have to be combined to increase the quality of sport pedagogy.
Keywords: Theory of PE, Sport Pedagogy, Qualitative Methods, Excellence, Competitive Sports, Elite Athlete, Life Cycle Research, FRG.

1   Introduction

The title, according to the linguistic feeling of an anglophile German, supports two different interpretations:

(a)   How can the qualitative level of sport pedagogy as a discipline in the sports sciences be increased?
(b)   How can sport pedagogy as a discipline approach the topic of excellence in sports?

A qualitative improvement of our discipline is possible and feasible without including competitive sports in the concept. However, the question remains whether sport pedagogy should exclude this field of sports reality and whether this would be an advantage for its own further development and structure. The field of competitive sports seems to pose some interesting questions and worthwhile problems from a pedagogical point of view, which also arise in other fields of sports but have not been looked into yet and thus can be regarded as a neglected subject of research in sport pedagogy.

Before these questions can be answered we have to find out which aspects of sport pedagogy today seem relevant in order to achieve a qualitative improvement of the discipline (2) and what sport pedagogy can contribute in the field of competitive sports (3). At least some conclusions (4) will point out what sport pedagogy has to consider in any way when moving towards excellence.

2 How can the quality of sport pedagogy be improved?

Although this question is answered from a national point of view with a short analysis of the development in the FRG so far, some of the tendencies refered to may as well be relevant to the perspective of a comparative sport pedagogy in other countries. Here a comparative analysis cannot be given (see Krotee/Jaeger, 1986).

In the eighties the term 'sport pedagogy' has more and more become the internationally accepted term for our discipline. The term has increasingly found acceptance even in the USA (see Piéron/Graham, 1986; Barette et al., 1987; Siedentop, 1987), where it was little known before and therefore could not be adequately integrated into the structure of the sport sciences.

In the FRG the term was introduced at the end of the sixties and the beginning of the seventies as a new programme, so to say, for PE in schools (see Grupe, 1969; Hecker/Trebels, 1970; Haag, 1978). Sport pedagogy implied a break with tradition, with the norms and values, content and methods of an earlier PE at schools because its theoretical foundation and legitimacy had started to disintegrate since the reality of PE at schools displayed contours different from those the theory anticipated or presupposed.

Four characteristics typical of the central differences to the previous PE represent the new sport pedagogy as a discipline at the beginning of the 70's:

(a) Educational aims such as a willingness to compete, comradeship etc. are no longer regarded as a transfer achievement of PE. Realistic values and goals derived from sports itself such as health and purposeful leisure activities supplant an old catalogue of virtues.

(b) The old canon of the classical school sports like gymnastics, track and field, and swimming has been enlarged by a multitude of new kinds of sports that have become very popular with students outside the school system, e.g. games.

(c) In view of new findings in psychological research the strict differentiation of developmental phases for age groups and the development of motor abilities are given up.

(d) New methods of instruction and presentation are introduced to PE The teacher's role no longer is defined as a model of instruction, who does not mark the class only according to his own motor performance. The teacher himself rather became one variable in a complex instruction process that increasingly is influenced by the student's response and his individual interests as well as by the multitude of different orientations in sports and the structural characteristics of the new kinds of school sports (see Kurz 1977, 29ff).

Summing up, we can say that in the early 70's sport pedagogy dismissed a new philosophical-ethical foundation as well as a sociological analysis of the theoretical outlines and tradition of the former PE movement. Pragmatically the new paradigm of sport pedagogy took the here and now, the objective and recognizable new facts of the modern sports and of the children's and adolescent's actual individual interests (e.g. motivation) and needs of sports (e.g. socialization) as its point of orientation (see ADL, 1971, 1974).

The relation to societal reality, objectively as well as subjectively, was made the benchmark to clarify sport pedagoggy as a new discipline in the canon of sport sciences (see Haag, 1976; Meusel, 1976; 18ff; Schmitz, 1979, 17ff). The empirical and analytical concept of science and research was established in sport pedagogy in order to objectify this relation (see Willimczik, 1968, 65ff; Joch, 1975, 18; Grössing, 1976, 15; Meinberg, 1979, 183ff; Meinberg, 1981, 68ff). The appearance of West German sport pedagogy with regard to the empirical-analytical science paradigm may seem to have achieved little (see Kurz, 1987; Erdmann, 1987). However, the perceived lack of achievement, especially from a comparative point of view (see Piéron/Cheffers, 1988), does not call into question the importance of the implicitly empirical-analytical research paradigm for studies in the fields of sport pedagogy in the FRG during the 70's and early 80's (see e.g. the volumes of 'Sportunterricht,' 1974-82).

Today, almost 20 years after the change in theory from PE to sport pedagogy, this discipline itself confronts a crisis of identity because the fixation on the factual here and now was not able to bring into focus the desired and in part necessary changes in the reality of sports in the FRG. The inheritance of the old theory of PE previously ignored has already returned (see Meinberg, 1986, 1987). In different and modern concepts it is formulated by sport philosophers, sport sociologists, and sport historians as well as by some younger sport pedagogues, who criticize:

(a)   a lack of ethical and moral values such as e.g. fairness or fair play in the behavioural patterns of sports dominant at present; they demand a new prescriptive and normative behavioural regulation in terms of an educational and anthropological theory (see Scherler, 1990);

(b)   the 'structure of sports'; for instance, they regard the regard of dominant goal-benefit relation based on the principle of optimization of all sportive behavioural structures and their over-organization as too one-sided. In order to counteract and overcome these limitations they go back to historical sources (see Digel, 1982; Cachay, 1988; Naul, 1990) and to old exercises which can be found in the excercise canon of the theory of PE (for gymnastics see Trebels, 1983; for swimming see John/Johnen, 1986; for games see Dietrich, 1985b; Jonischeit, 1989);

(c)   the empirical-analytical research paradigm for allowing the verification or falsification of perceived needs in school sports while not being able to identify real needs and actual behavioural patterns in physical leisure time activities and school sports. Therefore qualitative methods are needed in order to achieve what sport pedagogy has long held as its goal, to study the reality of sports and the assessment and orientation of sports in and outside the schools (see Brettschneider, 1984; Miethling, 1986).

Today, some 20 years after modern sport pedagogy supplanted the theory of PE, this kind of criticism indicates that the present fixation of sport pedagogy on the possible and factual in general theory and in the gym has been an obstructive self-restriction. Now we can perceive and must understand that any orientation by a temporal reality of PE and sports will change and that any reality is historically changeable in principle. Several studies of the development in youth sports have been emphasizing this point in the course of the last years (see Brettschneider et al., 1989; Sack, 1985). The rediscovery of the historicity of sport pedagogy today restores to the discipline the forgotten inheritance of the theory of PE (see Beckers, 1987; Naul, 1986). The philosophical idea and intention of the old theory of PE, but of course not its conceptual structure, is being restored to sport pedagogy after having been excluded by the self-imposed restriction to an empirical-analytical paradigm. In this case we can help sport pedagogy move towards excellence if we accept the following:

(a) Ethical and moral norms and values are supposed to function as regulative benchmarks for behaviour in sport without having to prove their legitimacy by having their factual success empirically measured, as it was 20 years ago. The potential falsification of values and norms, possible in principle in the context of an empirical-analytical science paradigm, does not necessarily preclude the use of such regulative measures in general.

(b) Qualitative approaches and methods of data analysis and interpretation of behavioural processes in sport are essential in order to explore inter-subjective meaning norms and values and to find and objectify their subjective context of interpretation. The finding of research questions cannot and must not exclude this, and in the same way the explanations based on data records at least presuppose understanding.

(c) Socio-historical reconstructions of any available data are necessary in order to recognize such data and the results of their analysis within the context of their own genesis of data collection. The genesis and effects structure must be pointed out in order to open them to modern research of sport pedagogy in an interpretable and reliable way.

3   How can sport pedagogy as a discipline approach the topic of excellence in sports?

Even if we understand sport pedagogy as determined by its genesis, its structure of effects, and its social differentiation during the last two decades, it can no longer neglect certain elements of the reality of sports. Its traditional limitation to the fields of school sports, interaction processes in the gym, and PE teacher training was a self-imposed restriction not even implied by the theory of PE at the beginning of the 70's, but rather results from the supposed congruence of the educative processes in the schools and the sport clubs. Moreover, training and competition were not excluded from an anthropological orientated theory of PE. The view of the assumed congruence of physical education inside and outside the school system presupposed by the theory of PE was corrected by sport pedagogy. There was, however, a conscious differentiation between the two fields, since exercises of sports practiced in the club environment and its goal of optimizing behaviour and performance was regarded critically from a pedagogical point of view. Many West German sports pedagogues today still regard this type of sport consisting of regular training and competition schedules as not responsible from an educational point of view (see e.g. Dietrich, 1985a; Funke, 1984).

At first some psychologists and sociologists see the development of competitive youth sports and its pedagogical side effects as a challenge for scientific inquiry (see Bette, 1984; Kaminski et al., 1984; Sack, 1980).

The subject of competitive sports as a pedagogical challenge was not accepted in sport pedagogy as a systematic factor of differentiation within the discipline. However, some sport pedagogues perceived social problems in competetive youth sports (see Howald/Hahn, 1982) and some others also carried out research projects on the socialization process into elite sports and the drop out dilemma (see Holz, 1981,1988; Kröger, 1987). However, from a theoretical perspective only a few sport pedagogues accept the field of competitive sports as a challenge to sport pedagogy and its structure so far (see Kurz, 1988; Naul, 1989a; Naul/Quanz, 1990). The majority of scholars in the area of sport pedagogy of course focus on the actual forms of sports and clearly distinguish between school sports and club sports as well. Most of them actually refuse to take competitive sports into account, either for teaching or for councelling or for research purposes, because they disagree with this type of sport from a educational point of view.

Today, 20 years after sport pedagogy was established, there are some critics of this limitation, which some sport pedagogues see as precipitate and as no longer conducive to a systematic sport pedagogy. If the subject of sport pedagogy is the different forms of sports in society, then, so to say, each of these forms must be regarded as a subject of the discipline. This is true for the sports of the disabled or that of the elderly as well as for competitive sports and any other form of sports practised by people in a certain age bracket who associate distinct behavioural motives with their sport.

This does not mean that the same problems and questions as well as the same framework of methods and approaches may be used within the several fields of sport pedagogy. There are of course some fundamental differences between the fields of competitive sports and the classical field of research in school sports. The task of a sport pedagogy confronting the subject of competitive sports might be described as follows:

The field of interest is the biography and the course of career of an athlete within the social system of competitive sports and in his private social context (e.g. school, job etc). The role and career of the athlete in its several person-environment relations can be differentiated socio-ecologically (see Baur 1989).

The micro-system is the club or performance centre where the athlete does his training. His coach and his athlete colleagues thus are his most immediate persons of reference, comparable to a family. The meso-system characterizes the correlation between the athlete and other persons, such as his doctor, his teacher or vocational instructor. The exo-system represents the competitive cadre, his team mates and competitors in sport as well as in his profession. The macro-system encompasses all systems and organizations, such as the sports association, functionaries and other persons, and the norms and values that they define for him or for the practice of his sport, e.g. qualification norms, membership in differentiated performance cadres, bonuses etc. (see Naul/Quanz, 1990).

Increasingly there is a conflict of interests in the biography of athletes today when their careers as competitive athletes is to be harmonized with their school education and their vocational training. This is not only true for West German society because there are very similar problems in the USA and Canada as well as in some socialist countries (see Murphy et al., 1989; Pawlak, 1984). This conflict potential is reinforced by two antagonistic development processes in the athlete's biography:

(a) The typical development processes in the sports career become shorter because the basic and the competitive training are increasingly advanced to a younger age. Thus the athletes at the peak of their careers tend to be younger and they are likely to finish their sports career earlier than athletes 20 or 30 years ago did.

(b) The typical development processes in education and vocational training, on the other hand, increase in length. Training and job security today take longer to achieve, often until the end of the third decade of life.

The dynamics of both career patterns run antagonistically, causing a conflict potential in the athlete's biography and leading either to early retirement before reaching the top of excellence in the sports career or will fail to lead to a job placement after retirement as an elite athlete.

The challenge to sport pedagogy in its attempt to achieve excellence in sports is to establish a socio-ecological career research that analyses the different person-environment relations and anticipates the arising conflicts between the different career patterns. Information and counselling are necessary in order to prevent an early end of the sports career and prevent problems in later job placement by a variable educational structure attuned to the athletes' time schedule (see Naul, 1989b).

Such a sport pedagogy in the field of elite sports functions in a preventive way. I describe it as a preventive sport pedagogy because it wants to secure a successful education and vocational training for the athlete by preventing difficulties and problems as social effects caused by a competitive sports career without having to advise the athlete to break off his sports career.

4   Conclusion

There are scientific standards and criteria that are valid for some scientific fields in the sports sciences. With regard to the importance of this kind of empirical-analytical sport pedagogy in some other European countries and in the U.S. there may be a need to catch up in Germany (see Piéron/Cheffers, 1988; Crum, 1988).

Nonetheless a qualitative improvement of the discipline of sport pedagogy is only feasible with the acceptance and implementation of other research paradigms, as the recent discussion in the USA indicated in an impressive way, especially the articles by Locke (1989) and Bain (1989).

Furthermore, accepting the challenge to sport pedagogy to approach competitive sports means dropping the exclusiveness of a paradigm that is only focused on the generalizable and objective and in addition to that initiating qualitative research as biographical research. Only in this way can the athletes' problems and needs in their sports and professional careers be understood subjectively, recorded and made available to research. Counselling athletes demands first of all judgements for the individual case with only subjective relevance in order to help and to give support individually.

By following a complex biographical research pattern in competitive sports, sport pedagogy will generally be able to provide results valid for an encompassing biographical research in sports from a methodological point of view. Thus there could be a better understanding for the behaviour of PE teachers in the gym and their socialization into this role as well as for the different kinds of participation in sports by the students in schools and outside the school systems, if we can take into account their individual social life patterns and their developmental processes.

Coming back to my original question, I would like to conclude that a qualitative improvement of sport pedagogy and moving towards excellence in general will only be possible:

(a)   if the exclusion from sport pedagogy of certain fields of sports in society is avoided in future;

(b)   if old ethical and moral values in PE theory are redefined and rethought as regulative factors for today and, above all, are accepted for new research in sport pedagogy to find their modern equivalents;

(c)   if new inter-subjective senses of norms and values in sports which already exists in different age groups are laid open, and accepted individually for all age brackets and will be related to more detailed research work;

(d)   and finally, if socio-historical reconstruction of sports and its related social settings are accepted as the source of pedagogical subjects, questions, and processes in sport pedagogy in any way and in any time.

5   References

ADL, ed. (1971) **Motivation im Sport**. Schorndorf.

ADL, ed. (1974) **Sozialization im Sport**. Schorndorf.

Bain, L. L. (1989) Interpretive and Critical Research in Sport and Physical Education. **Research Quarterly,** 60, 21-24.

Barette, G. T. et al., eds. (1987) **Myths, Models, and Methods in Sport Pedagogy.** Champaign, Ill.

Baur, J. (1989) **Körper- und Bewegungskarrieren.** Schorndorf.

Beckers, E. (1987) Durch Rückkehr zur Zukunft? Anmerkungen zur Entwicklung der Sportpädagogik. **Sportwissenschaft,** 17, 241-257.

Bette, K. H. (1984) **Strukturelle Aspekte des Hochleistungssports in der Bundesrepublik.** St. Augustin.

Brettschneider, W. D., ed. (1984) **Alltagsbewußtsein und Handlungsorientierungen von Sportlehrern.** Schorndorf.

Brettschneider, W. D. et al., eds. (1989) **Sport im Alltag von Jugendlichen.** Schorndorf.

Cachay, K. (1988) **Sport und Gesellschaft.** Schorndorf.

Crum, B. (1988) Zur Entwicklung sportpädagogischer Forschung-Ein Vergleich zweier maßgebender Subkulturen. **Sportwissenschaft,** 18, 176-184.

Dietrich, K. (1985a) Leistungssport für Kinder?-Kinder für den Leistungssport! **Sportunterricht,** 34, 169-176.

Dietrich, K., ed. (1985b) **Sportspiele.** Reinbek.

Digel, H. **(1982) Sport verstehen und gestalten,** Reinbek.

Erdmann, R. (1987) Zum empirisch-analytischen Forschungsansatz in der Sportpädagogik - vom Erbsenzahlen zur Minestrone, in **Forschungskonzepte in der Sportpadagogik** (eds Brehm, W.and Kurz, D.), ClausthalZellerfeld, pp. 57-73.

Funke, J. (1984) Kinder im Hochleistungssport, in **Schüler im Sport - Sport für Schüler** (eds ADL) Schorndorf, pp. 141 bis 148.

Grössing, St. (1976) Überlegungen zum Wissenschaftscharakter der Sportpädagogik, in **Forschen, Lehren, Handeln** (eds Andrecs, H.and Redl, S.) Wien, pp. 13-22.

Grupe, O. (1969) **Grundlagen der Sportpädagogik.** München.

Haag, H. (1978) **Sport Pedagogy. Content and Methodology.** Baltimore.

Haag, H. (1976) Zur inhaltlichen Konzipierung der Sportpädagogik als Aspekt der Sportwissenschaft, in **Forschen, Lehren, Handeln** (eds Andrecs, H.and Redl, S.) Wien, pp 23-33.

Hecker, G.and Trebels, A. (1970) **Sportdidaktik,** Wuppertal.

Holz, P. (1981) Nachwuchsathleten im Spannungsfeld sozialer Wirklichkeit. **Leistungssport,** 11, 5-19.

Holz, P. (1988) Probleme des Ausstiegs von Jugendlichen aus dem Leistungssport. **Leistungssport,** 18, 5-10.

Howald, H.and Hahn, E., eds. (1982) **Kinder im Leistungssport.** Basel.

Joch, W. (1975) Probleme und Position der Sportpädagogik innerhalb der Sportwissenschaft(en). **International Journal of Physical Education,** 12, 1, 13-21.

John, H. G.and Johnen. (1986) **Alternatives Schwimmen.** Aachen.

Jonischeit, L. (1989) Historische Turnspiele. **betrifft: sport,** 6.

Kaminski, G. et al. (1984) **Kinder und Jugendliche im Hochleistungssport,** Schorndorf.

Kröger, C. (1987) **Zur Drop-out Problematik im Jugendleistungssport,** Frankfurt.

Krotee, M.and Jaeger, E., eds. (1986) **Comparative Physical Education and Sport,** vol. 3. Champaign/Ill.

Kurz, D. (1977) **Elemente des Schulsports.** Schorndorf.

Kurz, D. et al. (1988) **Pädagogische Grundlagen des Trainings.** Schorndorf (Studienbrief 4).

Kurz, D. (1987) Zur Situation sportpädagogischer Forschung in der Bundesrepublik Deutschland wissenschaftspolitische Provokationen, in **Forschungskonzepte in der Sportpädagogik** (eds Brehm, W.and Kurz, D.) Clausthal-Zellerfeld, pp. 7-18.

Locke, L. F. (1989) Qualitative Research as a Form of Scientific Inquiry in Sport and Physical Education. **Research Quarterly,** 60, 1-21.

Meinberg, E. (1986) Die Körperkonjunktur und ihre Wurzeln. **Sportwissenschaft,** 16, 129-147.

Meinberg, E. (1987) Warum Theorien sportlichen Handelns Anthropologie benötigen! **Sportwissenschaft,** 17, 20-36.

Meinberg, E. (1979) **Erziehungswissenschaft und Sportpädagogik.** St. Augustin.

Meinberg, E. (1981) **Sportpädagogik,** Stuttgart.

Meusel, H. (1976) **Einführung in die Sportpädagogik.** Munchen.

Miethling, W. D. (1986) **Belastungssituationen im Selbstverständnis junger Sportlehrer.** Schorndorf.

Murphy, S. M. et al. (1989) Athletes in Transition: Helping Athletes with the Career Development Process, in **First IOC World Congress on Sport Sciences** (ed USOC). Colorado Springs, pp. 406-413.

Naul, R. (1989a) Olympic Headquarters: A New Challenge to Sport Pedagogy in the Federal Republic of Germany, in **Comparative Physical Education and Sport,** vol. 6 (eds Fu, F. et al.) Hong Kong, pp. 199-204.

Naul, R. (1986) Schulsportgeschichte-Sportgeschichte im Schulsport. **Sportunterricht,** 35, 445-447.

Naul, R. (1990) The Renaissance of the History of School Sports-Back to the Future? **Journal of Sport History,** 17, H. 1.

Naul, R. (1989b) **Berufsanalyse für Spitzensportler und Netzplanung für flexible Qualifikationswege in der beruflichen Laufbahn der Athleten.** Essen (unpubl. Ms).

Naul, R.and Quanz, R. Präventive Sportpädagogik-Was kommt nach der sportlichen Karriere? in **Kongressbericht lo. Hochschultag** (ed Dvs). Schorndorf (in press).

Pawlak, A. (1984) The Status and Style of Life of Polish Olympians after Completion of their Sports Career. **Rev. for Soc. of Sport,** 19, 169-183.

Piéron, M.and Cheffers, J. (1988) **Research in Sport Pedagogy.** Schorndorf.

Piéron, M.and Graham, G., eds. (1986) **Sport Pedagogy.** Champaign, Ill.

Sack, H. G,. (1980) **Zur Psychologie des jugendlichen Leistungssportlers.** Schorndorf.

Sack, H. G. (1985) **Soziale Funktionen des Sportvereins im Jugendalter,** Bd. 1/2. Frankfurt.

Scherler, K. H., ed. (1990) **Normative Sportpädagogik.** Clausthal-Zellerfeld.

Siedentop, D. (1987) Sport Pedagogy Research: Methods and Assumptions, in **The Physical Education Teacher and Coach Today,** vol. 1 (eds Rieder, H.and Hanke, U.) Cologne, pp. 295-310.

Schmitz, J. (1979) Entwicklung und Stand der Sportpädagogik in der Bundesrepublik Deutschland. **International Journal of Physical Education,** 16, 1, 15-22.

Trebels, A. (1983) **Turnen an Geräten.** Reinbek.

Willimczik, K. (1968) **Wissenschaftstheoretische Aspekte der Sportwissenschaft.** Frankfurt.

PROFESSIONAL DEVELOPMENT OF CO-OPERATING TEACHERS

M. O'SULLIVAN
The Ohio State University, Columbus, Ohio, USA

Abstract

The purpose of this paper is to describe the professional development of three co-operating teachers during their first experience mentoring a student teacher. The co-operating teachers completed a 30 hour workshop on instructional supervision in physical education where a number of supervisory perspectives were discussed. The research questions were: (a) What do these teachers see as the role of the co-operating teacher and university supervisor during the student teaching experience? (b) What events during the student teaching experience are viewed as successful and problematic by the co-operating teachers? (c) What impact do the co-operating teachers perceive they will have on the student teachers and they on them? Interviews, critical incidents, and weekly review sheets of the supervisory experiences were the major sources of data. The findings indicate these co-operating teachers see themselves as facilitators helping student teachers improve their teaching behaviours and providing opportunities for student teachers to reflect and self manage their teaching. The university supervisor was seen to play a significant role as resource and quality control person and liaison for the co-operating teacher to the outside professional world. Despite training these teachers received, they still had concerns about their abilities to provide quality supervision specifically as it related to getting students to be reflective about teaching.

Keywords: Co-operating teachers, Supervision of physical education.

1 Introduction

Student teaching is considered by many as the most critical component in the professional preparation of the pre-service teacher (Lanier and Little, 1986; Richardson-Koehler, 1988) and the co-operating teacher as the most critical person in the life of a student teacher during this experience. Concern, however, has been expressed about the nature of this co-operating teacher (CT) influence (Dodds, 1989; Zimpher, de Voss and Nott, 1980; Yee, 1969). For example, Chandler (in Glickman & Bey, 1990) found co-operating teachers dominated over 60 % of the talk in post teaching conferences.

Tannehill and Zakrajsek (1988) suggested that due to lack of supervisory training, co-operating teachers provide minimal supervision of student teachers in physical education. Tinning and Siedentop, (1985) reported co-operating teachers (CTs) relied on informal accountability systems and partially explicit tasks to supervise student teachers. Although supervisory training for co-operating teachers as well as university personnel has been shown to effect the quality of early field experiences and student teaching (Appelgate and Lasley, 1984; Killian and McIntyre, 1986), little attention has been given to determining the nature of the supervisory skills and knowledges necessary to provide quality student teacher experiences (Barnes and Edwards, 1984; Guyton and McIntyre, 1990; Nagel et al, 1988; Richardson-Koehler, 1988). In the recent **Handbook of Research on Teacher Education**, Gyton and McIntyre (1990) claimed 'supervision processes are what make up the event called student teaching... to learn about student teaching, one needs to know what occurs in student teaching, and the most significant occurrences centre around supervision processes' (p. 527).

2   Purpose of the Study

The purpose of this study was to describe the professional development of three co-operating teachers during their first experience supervising a student teacher. This article is based on a larger database gathered to study this issue. The following research questions are the focus of this paper:

(a)   What do these teachers see as the role of the co-operating teacher and university supervisor during the student teaching experience?

(b)   What events during the student teaching experience are viewed as successful and problematic by the co-operating teachers?

(c)   What impact do the co-operating teachers perceive they will have on the student teachers and they on them?

3   Subjects and Procedures

3.1 *Subjects*

Participants in the study were 3 experienced teachers. Each had completed a 30 contact hour workshop on supervision of physical education during the summer and received their first student teacher in the fall. Debbie was a senior high school teacher with 18 years of experience and Mark and Megen[1] were elementary physical education specialists with 4 years teaching experience. One university supervisor was assigned to all three co-operating teachers.

---

[1]   Megen reviewed the text of this manuscript to confirm the validity of the authors findings and conclusions. In her reaction she stated 'this paper describes extremely well the experience of being a first time CT. You definitely hit the real issues involved in being a CT.'

3.2 *Data Collection*

A series of data collection strategies were used to provide information on the research questions:

(a) The co-operating teachers were interviewed three times, once before, during, and upon completion of the 10 week student teaching period. Each of the interviews was transcribed and an inductive analysis of the data completed.

(b) Each of the co-operating teachers kept a weekly log of significant incidents (Flanagan, 1954) that occurred during the student teaching period. This log prompted the teachers to address relationships with their student teacher and university supervisor, the development of their supervisory skills, impact of the students teacher on them, and critical incidents of significance in the development of their roles as co-operating teachers.

(c) The co-operating teacher provided a copy of the conference planning guide used with the student teacher in post teaching conferences. It summarized the goals they would work on during subsequent lessons. ALT-PE data collected by the co-operating was also available.

(d) The university supervisor (US) kept a weekly log of her interactions with each of the 3 co-operating teachers and the concerns and questions addressed to her in the role of US. Little of that data is used in this paper.

4   Results

Data for the three research questions are drawn from several sources and are compiled and presented by research question. Findings will be discussed later in the paper.

4.1 *Role of the co-operating teacher and university supervisor*

Interviews with the co-operating teachers before, during and after the student teaching experience were the main sources of information for this research question. The co-operating teachers saw their role as a facilitator helping the student teachers improve and self manage their teaching. In an interview before student teaching began, Megen said:

> My role is to be a facilitator for better teaching and that would be done having the ST develop his skills, helping him feel comfortable in his role as a teacher, that he understands it is OK that things don't always work out as planned. That is going to happen and should be expected and it is OK to work through those problems.

In a second interview midway throught the experience, Megen spoke about facilitating reflection of the ST on their teaching performance, saying:

> Some days I am really conscious of the fact that I have to question him... what was the most important part of your lesson and did you accomplish your goals. I am really tuned in to asking them questions.

Mark, the second elementary specialist described the role in similar terms acting:

> mostly as a facilitator trying to work with the [university] programme so the ST will experience some success... Involving the CT more would help to point out the background of the situation. The ST will be able to go through all the phases from purchasing equipment to teaching a group and he will have an opportunity to do it his way and to explore his ways... I have gone out of my way to make sure the schedule has a cross section of elementary PE. I have not eliminated any problems which I could easily have done... [as] I am not convinced that is the right way to do it. This is what it will be like and that is part of the educational process.

Debbie, the secondary school CT, saw her role as an extension of the university in helping to fulfill the objectives of the teacher preparation programme using practical knowledge of an experienced teacher with specific supervisory skills to

(a)   take data that gives information to her [ST]
(b)   help her interpret the data as to how she wants it best to fit into her scheme of things as far as her personality goes
(c)   help her develop a teaching style that has characteristics of that specified by the university and the things she thinks are important.

In a second interview she explained how important it is for the ST to observe and critique her teaching and would encourage the ST 'to ask questions about what I did and why I did them'.

The CTs described the qualities of an effective co-operating teacher first as a series of traits: a good listener, someone who wants to spend time with a ST to help them solve their problems. In essence someone to help the student teachers be problem solvers as well a sproblem setters. The CT is flexible and patient, and confident in their own teaching. Megen's comments reflected the view of the others when she said:

> You definitely have to be flexible and patient... you have to be comfortable with your setting, your position, yourself.

Secondly, they described a series of competencies of an effective CT; that they observe and collect information on the teaching performance of the ST, demonstrate conferencing skills that allows ST to reflect and critique the appropriateness of their teaching decisions in that educational situation. Mark said that since taking the supervisory course:

> I am a better observer (of physical education lessons) and I think I am more critical. I know what to look for and how to look for it... You can (also) pick up a lot more information if you can listen to them (ST) and really find out what they are trying to say.

Megan suggested:

> They would have to know something about the research in their profession... the importance of activity time and transition time... they would have to know what is expected of them as a supervisor (and) willing to give of their own time to learn these things for the good of the profession.

The university supervisor (US) was described by the CT's as a resource for both the CT and the ST and a liaison between the school and the university. As a first time CT, Debbie wanted the US to give her guidance by helping her delineate what she was doing right and wrong. Megen saw the US as:

> a sounding board and... a helper. I don't have all the answers so he (ST) needs to feel he can go to her (US) and I feel I should be able to go to her when I am not clear on something or there is a problem between the ST and me.

Mark saw the US as an organizer and somebody who would ensure 'all the requirements will be met and that I am doing my job and that we are co-ordinated together.' During the experience, the CT's always spoke and wrote positively about their interaction with the US. Megen's comment was representative of all three CTs:.

> It definitely made for a more enjoyable experience. She (US) usually tried to make time to talk to me, to the ST, to the three of us together. I enjoyed one on one with her. She would ask me things about my teaching that she could apply to the ST.

Megan perceived this as 'lending credibility' to her discussions with the ST. Again and again, the CT teachers saw this as an important link with the outside professional community. All three teachers related how important it was for them to be with other physical educators and be associated with the university and looked forward to the bi-weekly visits of the university supervisor. Half way through the experience Debbie said:

> I really like working with people from the university. It is positive for me. It is positive for the kids here. They like seeing the university people working with their teacher... They understand that there are true purposes to teaching and they are evaluating her (student teacher).

4.2 *Successes and concerns of the co-operating teacher*

Critical incidents written by the co-operating teachers, nine interviews with the researcher before, during and after student teachig, and weekly review sheets describing the co-operating teachers' greatest improvements and biggest concerns were the data sources for this research question. An inductive analysis of these data sources was completed.

Success for the CT's related to student teachers successful efforts at learning to teach, the collegiality associated with having a student teacher, and maintaining accountability for the student teacher.

Learning to teach. Intially the co-operating teachers were most pleased when they saw improvements in the student teachers' teaching performance. A variety of teacher and student behaviours were the foci of post teaching conferences and together the CT and ST set explicit goals for subsequent lessons. Several strategies to achieve the goals were discussed by the CT and the ST. Use of names in teacher interactions with students, use of appropriate demonstrations for skills and drills, providing specific feedback to students during practice, and active supervisions in the gymnasium are characteristic of CT-ST targeted behaviours. Topics of these post teaching conferences included discussion on what Ocansey (1989) called substantive tasks on the appropriateness of specific drills and activities and who benefits from these activities (see Evans, 1989). These discussions relate what Sparkes (1988) described as the micropolitics of physical education. Mark said:

> We don't have to agree on everything which is nice. We have some arguments that get your blood going. I look to argue about PE and to talk about what should be done. I had (Bill) attend the teacher conference day in PE... A lot came out of that I was very upset about. I was curious about which ones upset him. We were able to talk about the political aspects of some of the things that were said -- to distinguish between what was true physical education and what was politics.

A second source of satisfaction for the CTs related to the quality of student teacher reflections during post teaching conferences and other informal discussions. The CTs liked to see the STs engaging in a dialogue with them on the success or failure of their teaching performance objectives and explore what might be learned from such situations. In these instances, the student teacher examined what happened not wanting the co-operating teacher to provide him/her with a list of prescriptions to improve the next lesson. All three co-operating teachers shared incidents where they felt they were effective as co-operating teachers because the student teacher showed independent professional judgement and a willingness to present their own ideas about improving student learning in physical education settings. This was not always a daily or weekly event so the co-operating teachers reported them as highlights of the day or the week when they occurred.

The co-operating teachers also learned about their own teaching from these interactions. Megen in her final interview following the experience said:

> I really enjoyed it. I learned a lot about my teaching... by telling him to try this and try that. He told me once that he was surprised I knew so much about teaching being as young as I am. You know you don't know how much you know until you turn and tell it to somebody else. I knew it but it never came out in any vocal sense... It really made me think about my own teaching. It made me conscious about the amount of management time, my feedback or my negative

desists etc. from the fact that I had to do it for him. Even if I didn't write it down it was clicking in my head what I was doing.

Collegiality. The co-operating teachers reported they enjoyed the opportunity to talk to 'someone who cared about physical education schools'. Mark saw it as a chance to 'have a conversation about professional issues in teaching physical education' with other professionals. Megen noted 'that has been the most exciting thing. Being able to talk to someone who understands, has the same language or who even gives a hoot you know'. These conversations, in some cases lasting several hours a week, provided an opportunity for the CTs to share their knowledge and beliefs about teaching in general and the physical education profession in particular. It was also an opportunity for the CT to hear new perspectives and participate in philosophical analyses of their beliefs and orientations to a profession they felt all too often goes unquestioned and not cared for by their colleagues and administration. Such opportunities were particularly important to the elementary specialists who were the only physical education teachers in their schools. Megen said

'It is nice to have someone around who understands physical education. We really had nice conversations about professionalism and methodology and things like that. Being the specialist here, there isn't anyone else who could understand'.

The three CTs were guest participants in the student teachers' senior seminar on campus and shared their perspectives on teaching. It was a positive experience for all and Megen reflected the others views when she wrote:

I thoroughly enjoyed the seminar. I also learned quite a lot from Mark and Debbie about their programmes. This was very positive as (I) don't get to brag about my programme to people who care very often.

Debbie commented:

The individuals (Mark and Megen) have made a tremendous impact on me and where I can reach out for help. The invitation to take a day and come to my school and watch me teach from Mark was wonderful. Watching the contrast of the two personalities has been very positive and valuable for me.

Having a student teacher and using the observation and conference skills she developed through the co-operating teacher workshop brought Megen prestige among her colleagues. Megen wrote:

When they knew what I was doing with the daily sheets (systematically monitoring their lessons) they were really impressed with that. I took the time to sit down and explain it to them. This was how much time a kid was involved in waiting. They really were impressed with that (quality of analysis).

Accountability. Holding the ST accountable was a difficult task for all three CTs so when they did hold the ST accountable or when the ST held him/herself accountable for lesson plans, unit plans, or some aspect of their teaching, they felt very positive about their role in that incident. These incidents revolved mostly around the ability of the student teacher to carry out something they had difficulty accomplishing. A series of critical incidents written by Megen show how she failed to hold him accountable for planning and she believed the ST's lessons began to show the effects. Finally, she decided 'to break the unit plan into steps and make him responsible for one step per day. This has worked well... I was struggling with the situation and he was not making any headway on his own unit plan. Now he feels progress and growth, as I do'.

The three main areas of CTs concerns during this experience were issues related to workload, holding student teachers accountable, and supervisory skills. While Megen estimated she spent 10 hours extra a week above and beyond class time with the ST, none of the CTs felt they had enough time for 'going over his lessons and units and just talking... what happened that day... about what he was going to do the next day, asking what was going on in his planning... thinking to say things I thought about the night before that I didn't get to say the day before'. It was as Mark stated the 'energy you exert rather than the actual time spent... Now I get to eat lunch and have some time to relax'. Mark wondered if in fact it is a good idea to have a ST when he was in season as a coach. Even lunch time was work as he introduced the ST to other staff, discussed morning lessons, or previewed the next day's lessons. He felt he could not relax from when he arrived in the morning until he left for home in the afternoon.

Another major concern of the CTs was holding the STs accountable for their work. For all three, this was something from the outset of the experience they thought they would have little difficulty with as they were used to holding students accountable for learning and behaviour. However, each of them had difficulty when it came to holding another adult accountable for their teaching performance. Upon reflection Debbie felt she put her ST at a disadvantage, 'I didn't have enough time after school. I didn't make time for her to talk. I left her to schedule a time and things could grow and grow and things were put aside'.

None of them liked the idea of giving up their students to anybody including a student teacher. Mark said:

> These are my children... I care very much about them... I am very protective of them. The work I have started here is extremely important to me. I don't want to see that (lost)... It is easy to have fun and not learn anything new but it is much more difficult to have fun and be trying to transfer a child to a higher skill level.

All three teachers indicated it was difficult to balance their concern for pupil learning with the student teachers's need to experiment and try his/her own approach to teaching physical education.

The final concern related to the CTs questioning of their supervisory skills throughout the experience. They felt they were not doing their job if the student teachers did not show consistent improvement in a teaching behaviour they had been working on for a period of days. They attributed lack of student teacher's success to their inability to 'motivate the student teacher' or to provide the 'right answer'. Prior to the experience the two female teachers, Debbie and Megen, talked about their nervousness. Would they be able to provide the kind of information to the student that would ensure a quality experience. While not stating he was nervous, Mark questioned if he would be able to let go of his students and allow the ST the freedom to explore teaching for himself. From the beginning of the experience, the CTs reflected a concern for self analysis by the ST. In the second weekly review sheet Megen wrote 'Am I giving him too much information and not letting him do enough self analysis'. Megen's goal for week 4 of her supervisions related to this again and she worked on not being 'quick to answer his (STs) questions, (rather) help him to figure out answers'. Early in the experience, Debbie wrote 'I move too fast and take over too much... I need to find ways to relinquish my power'. Mark perceived his own major weakness was in 'figuring out ways to get the ST to go into longer statements about what he was doing and I think I filled in the blanks on it for him even though I know I should not do that'.

4.3 *Co-operating teachers and student teachers: Impact?*

In the first interview each of the CTs was asked to describe the kind of impact they hoped to have on their student teacher? The consensus was to stress with these neophyte professionals the importance and value of teaching physical education. Mark said, 'It makes up such a small amount of time (in schools)... and even though that is the reality, things can be taught in that amount of time... (that ST can have) a tremendous impact on children'. Debbie summarized her feelings to the question saying, 'My biggest thing is that she understands and loves all the different kinds of kids... that they have value... If she really loves physical education, she will get that across. It is very hard to like the kids if you don't like your subject matter'. Megen said, 'I hope my enthusiasm will have an effect on him, my enthusiasm for the kids, for the school, to search for better ways... I am always looking for ways to make things better'. When asked midway through the experience to reflect on what they felt they had accomplished with the student teacher to this point, the co-operating teachers provided specific examples of student teacher behaviour change. For Mark it was the student teacher's ability to differentiate between student activity and student learning: 'active and learning are not the same. I collect the number of trials by practice sessions across drills and modified (3 by 5 minute observations). Kids can be active in a game but not necessarily learning anything... He (ST) really understood that and has made some improvements in that'. Megan was pleased with specific improvement in student names, and the quality of feedback and 'we really have good conversations about the value of our profession... we are both open to each others views'. For Debbie, the student teacher was 'developing well from a student teacher to a student of teaching. I believe even though she may not be a teacher, she is becoming a student of teaching... she is thinking where do I want that student to be at the end of the unit and what is she offering that student... that is the great emergence I have seen'. In the final interviews, the CTs noted their greatest impact was in helping the student teachers to use the knowledge base from their theory courses in planning, instructing, and evaluating what it was their students were learning. When asked what impact the student teacher might have on them, all three hoped they would get some ideas from new teaching methods to new content ideas. After the experience had ended they responded to that question with the same thoughts. Their experience working and talking with a student teacher and university supervisor caused each of them to take a finer look at their own teaching and their own perspectives on teaching physical education.. It made them bring to the fore the tacit knowledge about teaching that they didn't even realize they knew. It was, they felt, the best contribution the ST could make to their professional development.

5   Discussion

Co-operating teachers in this study completed a supervision workshop prior to this experience. The workshop included a description of the student teacher's professional preparation programme. The co-operating teachers developed systematic observation skills, conferencing skills, received an overview of the knowledge base on teaching and engaged in discussion on alternative perspectives on the purposes of supervision and teacher education (cf. Zeichner, 1983; Tinning, 1988). Many topics from the workshop were reiterated by the three participants in various ways throughout the study.

Three themes emerged from the findings. First, the co-operating teachers struggled with what Feiman-Nemser (1983) described as the 'cross purposes pitfall' of learning to teach in the naturalistic environment. Although the CTs wanted the student teacher to have freedom to experiment with teaching styles while learning to teach they felt obligated to ensure their pupils received a safe quality instruction. It was hard for them to sit on the side lines and watch their students, knowing that if they could only tell them to try a task a particular way they could be successful. Midway through the experience, Mark began 'coaching' the student teacher from the side of the gym even though in later conversations he admitted that while the student teacher liked this process, he should have left the student teacher to deal with the students.

Second, having someone take over their programme and work with their students was more anxiety provoking than they had anticipated. Their programmes were going public for the first time and each was unsure how the 'audience' (ST and US) would react. It was the first time anybody would take a close up view of what they were doing in their programmes. While they felt confident about their programmes, they worried 'lest the students would let them down' or the student teachers or university supervisor would find more to criticize than to praise of their efforts.

Third, and most importantly, the co-operating teachers struggled to provide a balance in their supervision to develop technical competence in discrete teaching skills with interaction patterns that allowed critical reflection and self analysis by the student teachers. The major goal for these co-operating teachers was to ensure STs had opportunities to practice and improve planning, instruction,and managerial skills with different groups of pupils. At the same time, they wanted to establish a positive and supportive environment where student teachers would learn to self manage their teaching by setting goals for subsequent lessons, deciding on strategies to reach those goals, and using the co-operating teacher and university supervisor as resources to discuss the implications of their decisions.

These co-operating teachers shared what Sharon Feiman-Nemser (1990) described as a technological orientation to their supervision. The co-operating teachers collected data and helped develop explicit task statements and strategies to accomplish these tasks in subsequent lessons. This was influenced in part by the orientation of the teacher preparation programme and the supervision workshop they completed. Their supervision training and the teacher preparation programme was theoretically driven by a behavioural orientation and empirically based. Such programmes have come under increasing criticism recently by advocates of a critical theory perspective describing them as 'technocratic physical education' having a limited contribution to make to prospective physical education teachers learning to teach. McKay, Gore & Kirk (1990) described technocratic physical education as a one dimensional view of teaching physical education with the 'near absence of critical or reflective approaches' (p.56). The authors dichotomized teachers, and by implication supervisors, as either technicians or reflective intellectuals. It should be noted however that the notion of teachers as intellectuals or what Giroux and McLaren (1986) describe as 'transformative intellectuals' may be an example of Hegelian idealism (Lynch, 1989). In a recent critique of neo-Marxists in education Lynch reminds us how much theorizing by critical theorists such as Apple, Giroux and others suffers from 'an indifference to empirical research - be that research historical ethnographic or statistical... This is something neo-Marxists rarely do'.(p.10). Lynch argues ' to be transformative in education we need to confront reality as it is (and that means fully recognizing the interests, forces and structures established to maintain the status quo) not as we would like it to be. What seems to be happening is that... critical theorists have emphasized the power of human agency despite empirical evidence to the contrary, at least in certain societies' (p.16). No support for a dichotomy of teachers as intellectuals or teachers as technicians was found in this study. On the contrary, these co-operating teachers struggled to balance the development of technical expertise of student teachers with critical self analysis by the STs on the nature and implications of their planning and teaching decisions.

Mark held an academic orientation to teaching and supervision in conjunction with a technological orientation (Feiman-Nemser, 1990). He wanted the student teacher to be concerned 'with helping students learn worthwhile things they could not pick up on their own'. Mark saw the teacher's responsibility to use his/her time to improve students' proficiency and joy for physical activities. While his discussions with the ST revolved around those issues, he constantly reflected on his own supervision style to ensure that Bill (ST) had the opportunity to critique that position and formulate his own perspective on teaching physical education. Debbie demonstrated a technological and personal orientation to supervision. She worked on having the ST be independent and encouraged the ST to seek alternative strategies to modelling the CT's behaviour. She tried to provide what she considered a safe environment for risk taking and experimentation by the student teacher. In reality, she found herself playing a much more directive role in monitoring and directing the student teacher's behaviour at the outset because of what Debbie perceived as weak managerial skills of the student teacher and safety issues associated with the first unit (archery). The CT found herself trying to help the ST develop these competencies while providing opportunities for self directed reflection by the ST on the nature of the experience and what students were learning from her teaching. The struggle between directive and non-directive supervision between attention to technical and critical issues lasted throughout the experience.

These co-operating teachers looked to the US and ST as professional links to the outside world from the isolation of the gymnasium. It was a chance to talk about professional issues nobody else on staff either cared about or understood. At the same time the experience provided an opportunity for a renewal and review of their own teaching. It was as Tannehill (1989) suggested 'a time to converse with a colleague about professional matters relevant to their classroom that ultimately confirmed, challenged, reinforced, or supported what they were doing for children' (p.253). It was in many ways one of the more beneficial forms of professional development for these experienced teachers. If we believe teachers ought to be collaborators in the professional education of prospective teachers then we need to pay attention to what it is they are telling us about how we can help them attend to this task productively.

6   References

Applegate, J. and Lasley, T. (1984) What co-operating teachers expect from preservice field experience students. **Teacher Education**, 24, pp.70-82.
Barnes, S and Edwards, S. (1984) Effective student teaching experience: A qualitative-quantitative study (Report No. 9060). Austin, TX: Research and Development Center for Teacher Education, The University of Texas at Austin.
Dodds, P. (1989) Trainees, field experiences, and socialization into teaching. In T. Templin and P. Schempp (eds) **Socialization into physical education: Learning to teach** (pp.81-104) Indianapolis, IN: Benchmark.
Evans, J. (1989) **Teachers, teaching and control in physical education curriculum: Studies in the sociology of physical education**. Lewes: Falmer Press.
Feiman-Nemser, S. (1990) Teacher preparation: Structural and conceptual alternatives. In W. Houston (ed) **Handbook of research on teacher education** (pp.212-233) New York: Macmillan.
Flanagan, J. (1954) The critical incident technique. **Psychological Bulletin**, 4, 327-358.
Glickman, C. and Bey, T. (1990) Supervision. In R. Houston (ed) **Handbook of research on teacher education** (pp.549-566), New York: Macmillan.
Giroux, H. and McLaren, P. (1986) Teacher education and the politics of engagement: The case for democratic schooling. **Harvard Educational Review**, 56(3), 213-238.
Guyton, E. and McIntyre, J. (1990) Student teaching and school experiences. In R. Houston (ed) **Handbook of research on teacher education** (pp.514-534), New York: Macmillan.
Kagan, D. (1988) Research on the supervision of counsellors and teachers in training: Linking two bodies of literature. **Review of Educational Research**, 58(1), 1-24.
Killian, J. and McIntyre, D. (1986) Quality in the early field experiences: A product of grade level and co-operating teachers' training. **Teaching and Teacher Education**, 2(4), 367-376.
Lanier, J. and Little, J. (1986) Research on teacher education. In M.C. Wittrock, (ed) **Handbook of research on teaching**. New York: Macmillan.
Lynch, K. (1989) **The hidden curriculum: Reproduction in education, an appraisal**. London, Falmer Press.

McKay, J., Gore, J. and Kirk, D. (1990) Beyond the limits of technocratic physical education **Quest**, 44, 52-76.

Nagel, A, Berg, M., Malian, I. and Murphy, D. (1988) Changing supervisory performance through training intervention. Paper presentation at the American Educational Research Association annual meeting, New Orleans.

Ocansey, R. (1989) The effects of behavioral model of supervision on the supervisory behavior of cooperating teachers. **Journal of Teaching in Physical Education**, 8(1), 46-63.

Richardson-Koehler, V. (1988) Barriers to effective supervision of student teaching: A field study. **Journal of Teacher Education**, 39(2), 28-34.

Sparkes, A. (1988) The micropolitics of innovation in the physical education curriculum. In Evans, J. (ed), **Teachers, teaching and control in the physical education curriculum: Studies in the sociology of physical education**. London: Falmer Press.

Tannehill, D. (1989) Student teaching: A view from the other side. **Journal of Teaching in Physical Education**, 8(3), 243-253.

Tannehill, D. and Zakrajsek, D. (1988) What's happeining in supervision of student teachers in secondary physical education? **Journal of Teaching in Physical Education**, 8(1), 1-12.

Tinning, R. (1988) Student teaching and the pedagogy of necessity. **Journal of teaching in physical education**, 7(2), 82-89.

Tinning, R. and Siedentop, D. (1985) The characteristics of tasks and accountability in student teaching. **Journal of Teaching in Physical Education**, 4(4), 286-299.

Yee, A. (1969) Do cooperating teachers influence the attitudes of student teachers? **Journal of Educational Psychology**, 60(4), 327-332.

Zeichner, K. (1983) Alternative paradigms for teacher education. **Journal of Teacher Education**, 34(3), 3-9.

Zimpher, N., de Voss, G. and Nott, D. (1980) A closer look at university student teacher supervision, **Journal of Teacher Education**, 31(4), 11-15.

WHAT PRICE VICTORY? MYTHS, RITUALS, ATHLETICS AND THE DILEMMA OF SCHOOLING [1]

C. ROGER REES
Department of Physical Education, Adelphi University, Garden City, New York, USA

Abstract

This paper draws on the work of Basil Bernstein to show how high school sports and physical education provide consensual rituals which help bind the school together as a unit, and differentiating rituals which mark off the students into different sub-groups. These rituals have made real the myth that 'sport builds character' and supported the expressive function of the school as an agent of moral development for children. Changes in the rituals of sport and physical education under conditions in which the instrumental function of the school gains importance over the expressive function are described, and the implications of these changes for the physical education curriculum are discussed.

Keywords: Invented tradition, Consensual rituals, Differentiating rituals, High school, Cliques, Sport, Physical education, Curriculum.

1   Introduction

This paper is concerned with what sociologists of education have called the dilemma of schooling. For Hurn (1985, pp. 281-282) this dilemma is found in the problem of how schools minimize control and coercion without impairing the motivation of the students to learn, for Lesko (1980) it is the issue of balancing the goals of individual success and public welfare, the battle of contest and community. Behind both examples is the broader issue of how schools adjust to changes in the structure and process of cultural transmission.

   Since this question has been one of the preoccupations of sociologist Basil Bernstein, I will use his early work on ritual in education to describe the process of cultural transmission at the micro level of the school. I am particularly interested in the role of physical education and sport in implementing this transmission, and will concentrate on how these elements of the school curriculum provide what Bernstein

---

[1]   I appreciate the help of Professors Alan Sadovnik and Devin Thornburg, School of Education, Adelphi University, in the preparation of this paper.

(1975)[2] has called consensual rituals which sustain a sense of school community, and differentiating rituals which mark off different groups within the school. Understanding the ritual functions of physical education is important because they effect the possibilities of moral and physical development through sport and physical activity.

2   Theoretical assumptions

Recent reviews of the work of Basil Bernstein (Atkinson, 1985; Sadovnik, in press) have characterized it within a structuralist tradition stemming from but not constrained by the theories of Emile Durkheim. Specifically, Atkinson (1985, pp. 24-25) notes that while he used Durkheim's model of social differentiation characterized by mechanical and organic solidarity as a starting point, Bernstein constructed several such principles or codes which he feels regulate the selection and combination of cultural elements. These codes (for example, the now infamous elaborated and restricted code of language) allow for different modes of understanding and meaning (Atkinson, 1985, p.132), not between societies as Durkheim had invisaged, but among members of the same society. The concept of codes is used as a device for understanding the process of transformation in social roles, language, and knowledge which occurs through the shift from mechanical to organic solidarity, and how this process effects the structure and content of education. One consequence of this shift is the blurring of the 'sacred' and the 'profane' which causes knowledge and morality to be less universally accepted, and makes ambiguous the value system of the school (Atkinson, 1985, p. 12, also p. 173).

If the issue of the sacredness of institutional control is central to a structuralist analysis of schools then sport provides a particularly apt focus. According to historian Eric Hobsbawm (1983b) sport was one of the many 'invented traditions' developed during the latter half of the nineteenth century and the beginning of the twentieth century:

> The term 'invented tradition' is taken to mean a set of practices, normally governed by overtly or tacitly accepted rules and of a ritual or symbolic nature, which work to incalcate certain values and norms of behaviour by repetition, which automatically implies continuity with the past. (Hobsbawm, 1983a, p. 1)

These inventions were a response to the unprecedented historical change involving the growth of democracy and mass politics, the development of the concept of 'nations' and the change from social relations based on 'Gemeinschaft' to social relations based on 'Gessellschaft'. Since old traditions had broken down, new ones had to be invented, or old ones updated.

The last three decades of the nineteenth century marked the institutionalization of sport on a national and international scale. One element of this institutionalization

---

2   This paper was originally published with H. Elwin and R.S. Peters in *Phil. Transactions of the Royal Society*, series B, 251, 1966. The present reference is to *Class, Codes and Control*, 3, pp. 67-75, henceforward abbreviated to CCC with the appropriate volume number.

was the assimilation of previously upper class recreational activities by the middle class and the attempt to segregate these activities from the working class via the concept of amateurism. This is the era of 'muscular christianity' and the cult of compulsory games so prevalent in the curricula of British private schools. The myth made legitimate by the ritual of compulsory games was that 'sport builds character', which meant that through playing team sports middle class boys could learn the moral values of manliness and leadership. It is perhaps more than coincidental that the first application to school sports of Bernstein's theory of ritual was made in the context of British private schools (Mangan, 1981, Chaper 7). At the macro level of society the invented tradition of sport was used to legitimize middle class values of morality, while the development of international sporting festivals such as the Olympic Games helped to promote a sense of nationalism while simultaneously reinforcing the idea of character development through amateurism (Rees, 1989).

Hobsbawm makes specific reference to the importance of invented tradition in America because of the problem of how to assimilate a heterogeneous mass of immigrants[3]. He notes (1983b, p. 279) that the education system was transformed into a machine for political socialization. In this context however the myth made real through sport was altered slightly to reduce the elitist overtones of amateurism. In America not just participating in sport but winning in sport built character, because through winning moral superiority was demonstrated (Mrozek, 1983).

3   Bernstein's theory of ritual in education

Atkinson (1985, p. 22) notes that one characteristic of Bernstein's early work was his concern with changes in the moral order of schools as transmitters of systems of meanings and values. These changes are discussed in three papers written in the 1960's and reprinted in *Class, Codes and Control, volume 3*. In 'Open schools - open society?' (CCC, 3, pp. 67-75) Bernstein discussed the effect of mechanical and organic solidarity upon the organization of the school. Under the 'old' order ability is seen as a fixed, genetic attribute and is used as the basis of streaming. Pupils are classified on what are perceived as ascribed roles. There are strong symbolic bounderies separating domains of knowledge which make up the curriculum. Under the 'new' organization the value system of the school becomes more ambiguous, ability is seen as changeable, and roles are achieved.

In *Ritual in education* (CCC, 3, pp. 54-66) Bernstein contrasts two models of schools, 'stratified' and 'differentiated' in relation to two types of ritual. He defines rituals as (p. 54) 'relatively rigid patterns of acts, specific to a situation, which construct a framework of meaning over and beyond the specific situational meanings.'

Bernstein posits two types of rituals, consensual and differentiating, responsible for transmitting the expressive order and the instrumental order. Consensual rituals function to bind together all members of the school, staff and pupils as a moral community, giving the school an identity and helping with the inculcation of a coherent set of shared values which reflect those of wider society. These rituals also

---

3   Bernstein makes a similar point at the level of the school (1975, CCC, p. 66).

serve to prevent the questioning of these values and the social order which transmits them. Differentiating rituals separate and mark off groups within the school (for example, those based on ability, gender or age), foster loyalty within these groups and help establish social distance between them.

Bernstein makes several predictions based upon this classification. For example, the more the school resembles a total institution the greater the ritualization of the expressive order. This has led educational anthropologists such as Kepferer (1981) to suggest that there are more expressive rituals in private schools than in state schools. Bernstein also anticipates a crisis in the expressive functions of schools characterized by the weakening of consensual rituals as schools try to adjust to social and economic diversity. In this paper sporting activities are mentioned as forms of differentiating rituals demonstrating gender differences in coeducational schools although, in a footnote, he also refers to them as consensual rituals.

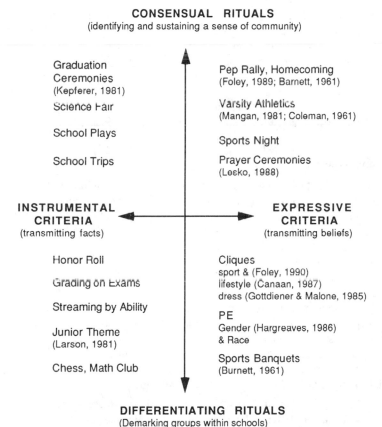

CONSENSUAL RITUALS
(identifying and sustaining a sense of community)

Graduation
Ceremonies
(Kepferer, 1981)

Science Fair

School Plays

School Trips

Pep Rally, Homecoming
(Foley, 1989; Barnett, 1961)

Varsity Athletics
(Mangan, 1981; Coleman, 1961)

Sports Night

Prayer Ceremonies
(Leeko, 1988)

**INSTRUMENTAL
CRITERIA**
(transmitting facts)

**EXPRESSIVE
CRITERIA**
(transmitting beliefs)

Honor Roll

Grading on Exams

Streaming by Ability

Junior Theme
(Larson, 1981)

Chess, Math Club

Cliques
sport & (Foley, 1990)
lifestyle (Canaan, 1987)
dress (Gottdiener & Malone, 1985)

PE
Gender (Hargreaves, 1986)
& Race

Sports Banquets
(Burnett, 1961)

DIFFERENTIATING RITUALS
(Demarking groups within schools)

Figure 1 *Rituals in Education*

Finally, in *Sources of consensus and disaffection in education* (CCC, 3, pp. 37-53) Bernstein addresses how school culture is transmitted. He anticipates tension between the expressive order and the instrumental order of the school, particularly when the instrumental order is greatly stressed.

It is interesting to note the similarity of Bernstein's theory of ritual in education to Hobsbawm's idea of 'invented tradition' discussed above. In both cases the source is the structuralist concern with the sacred and the profane discussed at different analytic levels. Sport is an important element of ritual at both levels.

Bernstein's theory of ritual in education is explored in Figure 1. Here the examples of ritual are located along two dimensions denoting type of ritual, consensual/differentiating, and type of function, instrumental/expressive.

As with all Bernstein's codes, these do not signify separate categories, but rather differences by degree (Atkinson, 1985, p. 31). For example, the ritual of graduation ceremonies may well reinforce the idea of the school as a community, but at the same time, differentiation based on ability is present. Students receive awards for instrumental criteria such as educational attainment and effort. On the other hand, consensual rituals surrounding sporting events or religious ceremonies in which the whole school takes part are more clearly based on the expressive criteria of shared beliefs. Hence the location of graduation and prayer ceremonies in different segments of the figure. Furthermore, although sporting rituals dominate the expressive/consensual quadrant, particularly in non-religious school, sport and physical education also play a part in differentiating rituals since sport is an important criterion of status in clique formation. The tension between these ritual functions has important implications for curriculum theory and practice in physical education.

4   Sport and consensual rituals

Given the previous comments about the importance of the expressive order to American education it is surprising that sociologists have not attached more importance to rituals in school life or to the value of sport in providing such rituals (an exception is Burnett, 1969). In her description of the culture of a Catholic high school for girls Nancy Lesko (1988, p. 117) notes that rituals are typically undervalued in America and seen as 'empty social routines'. She provides an excellent analysis of how students deal with the tensions between individualism and community through the rituals of friendship groups, and school rituals such as spirit assembly and all-school mass, but references to sport are noticeably absent. The importance of sport as ritual is also missing from Cookson and Persell's (1985) account of the 'prep' students' rite of passage through the elite private schools of America. They agree (p. 78) that athletics is the most important extracurricular activity at most of the private schools they studied but also note (p. 139) that 'in place of rituals, schools are apt to substitute collective games.'

Coleman, in his classic study of state schools in the 1950's, placed sport at the centre of school life, and characterized it as a method by which educational institutions solve the problem of generating enthusiasm for and identifying with the school and drawing the energy of adolescents into the school culture. However, he felt that schools pay a high price for this involvement since students no longer have education as a central concern (Coleman, 1961b). In other words expressive rituals took presidence over instrumental rituals in the schools Coleman studied.

Burnett (1961) was one of the few sociologists who has recognized the importance of sport in contributing the ritual of school life. Her description of pep rallies and homecoming rituals, which she characterized as rites of passage and intensification, are examples of consensual rituals. Typical was the description of the pep rally which took place every Friday during football season:

> During football season, the order of events of the day ran its familiar course until a special bell rang ten minutes earlier than the usual dismissal bell. At this signal, the entire high school population, including teachers, assembled in the old gymnasium. When all were assembled, the school principal called the group to order and made a few announcements. Then the cheerleaders, as a group, trotted before the audience, and in well-practiced formation initiated cheers to the students and led them in highly synchronized cheers, first for the team, then for the coaches. They retired and one or two of the varsity players (always either seniors or juniors in class standing) stood before the group and gave a pep talk on the coming game. The talks always endend on a note of determination to strive to win. The player was greeted with a cheer; his talk was sometimes interrupted with cheers and always closed with a cheer from the students. Next, the head coach or assistant coach gave a pep talk always concerned with the reputation of this week's opponent and the good features and improvements in the home team. The coach's talk always closed with a statement of his confidence in the players and their determination to play hard and to play to win. Finally, he usually alluded to the helpfulness toward victory of the spirit and support of the rest of the students. Then, the cheerleaders led the entire student body in more cheers and, as the dismissal bell rang, the students filed out, cheering as they went.' (Burnett, 1969, pp. 4,6).

This description captures some of the principle characteristics of consensual rituals. All elements of the school are united behind a common goal, the achievement of which is dependent upon the successful realization of the values of hard work, and dedication, the values espoused by the school. The goal is to win,and, through victory, to prove your moral worth. The slogans of athletics which adorn the locker room walls: 'winners never quit, quitters never win', 'it's not the size of the dog in the fight, it's the size of the fight in the dog', 'winning isn't everything, it's the only thing' exort the student body to encorporate these beliefs, symbolized on the sports field, into their own system of values. In case Burnett's description, taken from the late 1960's, be thought of as out-dated it closely resembles the one given by Foley (1990) in his recent ethnographic study of football in a South Texas rural community. With some regional variations 'character' is still being built by high school sports.

5   Sport and differentiating rituals

Coleman (1961a) in his study of American high schools in the late 1950's found athletic ability to be the key to high status in peer groups. He showed that male students preferred to be remembered at school first as an 'athletic star', second as a 'brilliant student', and third as 'most popular'. Subsequent studies using Coleman's methodology have tended to confirm these results, although athletic ability is less highly valued for female than for male popularity by both boys and girls (Thirer and Wright, 1985). A more detailed analysis of high school cliques confirms this general finding within a more complicated context. A status hierarchy of high school cliques and the descriptive characteristics of each is presented in Figure 2. It is based upon research by Gottdiener and Malone (1985), Canaan, (1987), and my own work with over 250 students in the New York metropolitan area[4].

Canaan (1987) has argued that high school students de-emphasize the cliques as important in their social life, and instead emphasize flexibility and tolerance. Yet all are aware of their existence and are able to describe them. Although ascribed criteria

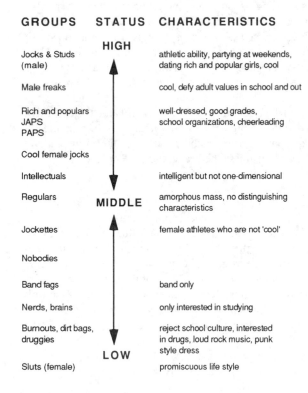

GROUPS	STATUS	CHARACTERISTICS
	HIGH	
Jocks & Studs (male)		athletic ability, partying at weekends, dating rich and popular girls, cool
Male freaks		cool, defy adult values in school and out
Rich and populars JAPS PAPS		well-dressed, good grades, school organizations, cheerleading
Cool female jocks		
Intellectuals		intelligent but not one-dimensional
Regulars	**MIDDLE**	amorphous mass, no distinguishing characteristics
Jockettes		female athletes who are not 'cool'
Nobodies		
Band fags		band only
Nerds, brains		only interested in studying
Burnouts, dirt bags, druggies		reject school culture, interested in drugs, loud rock music, punk style dress
	LOW	
Sluts (female)		promiscuous life style

Figure 2   *Cliques in high school*

---

[4]   Over the last three years all students in my 'Social Issues in Sport and Physical Education' class have constructed a 'sociometric' map of the various cliques in their own high school indicating the characteristics and status of each.

such as gender, race and social class are evident as status criteria (nice clothes and an affluent lifestyle are prerequisites for membership in the 'rich and popular' group), achieved criteria are also important. The key to high status is showing that you are 'cool' or self-confident through behaviour in extra-curricular activities, principally athletics and 'partying'. Part of this self-confidence is being able to 'handle' what are perceived as 'adult' activities such as drinking alcohol, taking drugs, and experimenting with sex. Canaan suggested that the main difference between the jocks and the male freaks lay in the fact that, whereas the freaks partied all the time, the jocks only partied on weekends. During the week the jocks complied with the culture of the school.

Although it was cool to party a total rejection of the culture of the school was not cool. The burnouts or dirt bags (referred to by one interviewee as 'the waste products of society') were accorded low status. There is strong consensus on this point even though sampling bias may be a factor (burn-outs do not typically seek higher education and often do not graduate from high school). Intellectual ability is a high status attribute provided it is accompanied by some other characteristic such as athletic ability. As one male interviewee said, 'Everyone in the school respects the athletes, especially the athletes who do well academically.' In general, cliques comprising students interested in only one thing (eg brains, band fags) are low status. The exception to this may be the male jock group, although this varies from school to school and among sport within school. Some interviewees agreed that 'dumb jocks' were high status provided they won.

6   Tensions between types of ritual

The above analysis confirms the importance of sport as a major achieved characteristic in the development of differentiating rituals in schools, albeit with some limitations. Since sport provides many expressive/consensual rituals it becomes identified as part of the school culture. Thus the burnouts are likely to reject athletics because it is perceived as replicating school values. Bernstein (CCC, 3, p. 67-75) anticipated this situation when he suggested that pupils only weakly involved in the instrumental order could be less receptive to consensual rituals supporting the morality of the school. Foley commented on the burnouts' behaviour at pep rallies:

> In sharp contrast, (to the more prominent students) knots and clusters of the more socially marginal students, the 'druggers', and the 'punks and greasers,' usually claimed the seats nearest the exits, thus signaling their indifference to all the rah-rah speeches they had to endure.' Foley (1990, p. 113)

Within the instrumental/differentiating quadrant of Figure 1 are contained rituals which mark off the student body into subgroups based on criteria such as intellectual ability. Such rituals as streaming by ability, or the process of grading and the examination system perform these functions in schools. Sometimes such traditions as a 'senior project' or 'junior theme' (Larson, 1988) are invented by schools as a rite of passage. These present an intellectual challenge to students and require the capacity to think and work on their own. Although I have placed the ritual of clique formation in the differentiating/expressive quadrant (see Figure 1) there is some ambiguity. Membership in the physics or math club would usually qualify students for nerd status (unless they had some other redeeming social characteristic). Despite the earlier point about the high status of the dumb jock it is possible for sport and physical education to provide instrumental/differentiating rituals through which students are classified in a negative manner.

Originally thought of as the moral leaders of the school, 'student athletes' still retain some of this status. However, there are signs that, as 'partying' and experimenting with adult activities becomes more important to adolescents, this behaviour becomes important in the 'jock' clique. Foley (1990) identified a strong 'macho' element in the jock culture he studied. Part of this was to drink, break curfew rules, and 'screw around'. 'Real' men would not let such extracurricular activities impair their ability to play football. While the community, with a strong tradition of (winning) football, accepted and even encouraged this behaviour as part of growing up (high school football as a rite of passage) the dumb jock image of sport has been questioned. In Texas, for example, the no pass/no play laws now make participation in extracurricular activities such as varsity athletics dependent upon a 'C' average.

Besides undermining the expressive dimension of differentiating rituals, the intrusion of intellectual ability into the domain of sport compromises it's effectiveness as an expressive ritual representing the whole school. That students of different racial and ethnic background participate on high school sports teams has symbolized, for many members of the community (particularly the elite groups), an open system free of discrimination. Under the new no pass/ no play laws black and Hispanic students, one third of whom do not maintain a 2.0 grade point average, are hardest hit (Lewis, 1989). Hargreaves (1986, Chapter 8) has suggested that school sports in Britain reproduce ethnic stereotypes by helping to perpetuate the subordinate position of blacks, and has characterized physical education as the most sex-specialized subject on the school curriculum. In spite of Title IX this continues to be true in America. The gender gap is reinforced in clique development based on athletics. Apart from some female college athletes, interviewees invariably attached more status to jocks than to jockettes although Canaan (1987) did assign high status to 'cool female jocks'.

7   Summary

The value system of the school becomes ambiguous as organic solidarity increases. Under these conditions traditions such as high school athletics are invented which bind the school together and link it to the community. In many communities the high school football team may be the only aspect of the school which receives attention in the local community, especially if the team is winning. Athletes become the moral heroes and athletic success forms the basis of clique development. However in situations where instrumental criteria are greatly stressed there is a weakening of the expressive order and tension over what values should be transmitted and how this transmission should take place. To paraphrase Bernstein, the sacredness of sport becomes profane as the morality of the school is contested.

This situation has a number of important implications for the future of physical education. The description of the consensual and differentiating rituals which constitute high school sports are in stark contrast to the ideals of achievement and clean living espoused by many educators. Sport may build character, or a least this myth may be real for many Americans (Rees, Howell and Miracle, 1990). However, character in high school cliques is operationalized as being 'cool', which, for male adolescents at least, means sex, drugs, booze and football. Lawson (1988) and others have noted the 'occupational' socialization of prospective physical education teachers before they come to college, and the difficulty of changing this outlook in four years. In light of what counts for status in adolescent cliques, the idea of teaching moral values, through sport appears problematic, to say nothing of using athletes to persuade adolescents to 'say no to drugs'.

If the sacredness of the moral order of the school is in doubt, then so too is one of the bases of athletics in schools, it's use as a mechanism of socialization and social control. Should we abandon sham of character development and move to the entertainment model of professional and quasi professional (college) athletics (Sage, 1990)? Or should we concentrate on fitness and try to develop a more inclusive model of interscholastic athletics?

Since this paper has dealt with the issue of social control the primary concern is with the principles of collective and individualized values within the school, but Bernstein's recent work is with the organization and transmission of knowledge, in particular what constitutes curriculum content and how this knowledge is transmitted and assessed (Atkinson, 1985, Chapters 7 and 8; Sadovnik, in press). He is particularly interested in 'the rules regulating the production, reproduction, inter-relation and change of what counts as legitimate pedagogic texts' (Bernstein quoted in Atkinson, 1985, p. 171). The theme of movement from the sacred to the profane is maintained, this time in the context of the curriculum. Applying this work to physical education may help us decide what rules govern the inclusion of one type of knowledge in the curriculum rather than another, what myths should be developed to establish this knowledge as an important part of the larger curriculum of the school, and what traditions need to be invented to make this knowledge sacred for groups that control what is taught in schools.

8   References

Atkinson, P. (1985) **Language, Structure and Reproduction: An Introduction to the Sociology of Basil Bernstein**. Metheun, London.

Burnett, J.H. (1969) Ceremony, rites, and economy in the student system of an American high school. **Human Organization**, 28 (1), 1-10.

Bernstein, B. (1975) **Class, Codes and Control, Volume 3. Towards a Theory of Educational Transmissions**. Routledge and Kegan Paul, London.

Caanan, J. (1987) A comparative analysis of American suburban middle class, middle school, and high school teenage cliques, in **Interpretive Ethnography and Education** (eds G. Spindler and L. Spindler), Erlbaum Press, Hillsdale, NJ, pp. 385-406.

Coleman, J. (1961a) **The Adolescent Society**. Free Press, NY.

Coleman, J. (1961b) Athletics in high school. **Annls. American Acad. of Polit. and Soc. Sc.**, 338, 33-43.

Cookson, P.W. and Persell, C.H. (1985) **Preparing for Power: America's Elite Boarding Schools**. Basic Books, NY.

Foley, D.F. (1990) The great American football ritual: reproducing race, class, and gender inequality. **Soc. Sport J.**, 7(2), 111-135.

Gottdiener, M. and Malone, D. (1985) Group differentiation in a metropolitan high school: the influence of race, class, gender and culture. **Qualitative Soc.**, 8(1), 29-41.

Hargreaves, J. (1986) **Sport, Power and Culture**. St. Martin's Press, NY.

Hobsbawm, E. (1983a) Introduction: invented traditions, in **The Invention of Tradition** (eds E. Hobsbawm and T. Ranger), University of Cambridge Press, Cambridge, pp. 1-14.

Hobsbawm, E. (1983b) Mass-producing traditions: Europe, 1870-1914, in **The Invention of Tradition** (eds E. Hobsbawm and T. Ranger), University of Cambridge Press, Cambridge, pp. 263-307.

Hurn, C. (1985) **The Limits and Possibilities of Schooling**. Allyn and Bacon, Boston.

Kepferer, J.L. (1981) Socialization and the symbolic order of the school. **Anthro. and Educ. Qua.**, 12(4), 258-274.

Larson, R. (1988) The high school 'junior theme' as an adolescent rite of passage. **J. Youth and Adol.**, 17(4), 267-283.

Lawson, H.A. (1988) Occupational socialization, cultural studies, and the physical education curriculum. **J. Teaching in PE.**, 7, 265-288.

Lesko, N. (1988) **Symbolizing Society: Stories, Rites and Structure in a Catholic High School**. Falmer Press, NY.

Lewis, A. (1989) The not so extra curriculum. **Phi Delta Kappan**, 70(9), 1-8.

Mangan, J.A. (1981) **Athleticism in the Victorian and Edwardian Public School**. Cambridge University Press, Cambridge.

Mrozek, D.J. (1983) **Sport and the American Mentality,** 1880-1910. University of Tennessee Press, Knoxville.

Rees, C.R. (1989) Pax olympics and the myth of peace and international understanding through sport. Paper presented at the ICHPER Congress, Frostburg State University, Frostburg, Md., July 20.

Rees, C.R., Howell, F.M. and Miracle, A.W. (1990) Do high school sports build character? A quasi-experiment on a national sample. **Soc. Sci. J.**, 27(3), 303-315.

Sadovnik, A.R. (in press) Basil Bernstein's theory of pedagogic practice: a structuralist approach to curriculum and pedagogy. **Soc. of Ed.**

Sage, G.H. (1990) High school and college sports in the United States. **JOPERD**, Feb., 59,61,63.

Thirer, J. and Wright, S.D. (1985) Sport and social status for adolescent males and females. **Soc. Sport J.**, 2(2), 164-171.

COMPETING ORIENTATIONS FOR PE CURRICULUM DEVELOPMENT: THE TREND TOWARDS A CONSENSUS IN THE NETHERLANDS AND AN INTERNATIONAL COMPARISON

BART CRUM
Amsterdam, Netherlands

Abstract
This paper is based on a report written in pursuance of a study assignment by the Dutch Foundation for Curriculum Development. The task was to chart, to compare and to evaluate the curriculum orientations that are dominant in the process of curriculum development in nine selected countries. Assuming that every PE curriculum is characterized by its explicit and/or tacit assumptions concerning corporeality, movement, movement culture and schooling, five ideal-typical PE curriculum ideologies are distinguished. This classification forms the frame for the comparative evaluation. The five conceptions are outlined. The working groups that are engaged in the development of a new Dutch PE curriculum for the secondary school have come to a consensus in favour of the so called 'critical-constructive movement socialization conception'. The rationale for this choice is briefly elucidated. Finally the results of the comparative evaluation of the official curriculum documents of nine states are schematically summarized.
Keywords: PE curriculum ideologies, Classification model, International comparison.

1   Introduction

In the Netherlands a radical innovation of the curricula for the first three grades of secondary education (age 12-15) was initiated in the second half of the eighties. The development of an obligatory PE curriculum is included in this process. Until today such a curriculum did not exist for PE, because it is a non-examination subject It is evident that the Dutch PE profession views the curriculum development enterprise as rather drastic and challenging at the same time.

The Dutch Foundation for Curriculum Development is responsible for the co-ordination of the curriculum innovation in general. At the end of 1988 this agency asked me to carry out a comparative study concerning trends in PE curriculum innovation which can be identified in other countries (states). The report should be useful as background support for the ongoing developmental process in the Netherlands. Since only a short time was available, I had to restrict myself to an analysis of the official national curriculum documents which were present either in the library of the Foundation or in my private collection. Thus besides the Netherlands eight foreign states have been included: Baden-Wurttemberg and Nordrhein-Westfalen (both belonging to the Federal Republic of Germany), Sweden, France, Scotland, California, New York State, and Quebec.

The final report contains more than 80 pages. Since time is short here, I can only share with you some selected elements. Consequently I will, briefly, pay attention to (1) the frame of reference that has been used for the comparative identification of curricular trends, (2) the considerations that form the rationale for the consensus which has been slowly accomplished between and within the official discussion platforms in the Netherlands, and (3) the summary of the outcomes of the international comparative study.

2   The classification frame

Eisner and Vallance (1974) are pioneers in the field of curriculum classification. They distinguish five competing conceptions of curriculum:

(a)   Development of Cognitive Processes;
(b)   Academic Rationalism;
(c)   Personal Relevance;
(d)   Social Adaptation and Social Reconstruction;
(e)   Curriculum as Technology.

The model of Eisner/Vallance was developed with regard to the so called 'academic' subjects and it is not really appropriate for a classification of curriculum orientations in the field of PE In their book 'The Curriculum Process in Physical Education', Jewett and Bain (1985) present a classification of curriculum orientations 'in terms of major emphasis, focus and implications for practice, as well as value positions' (p.24). Their classification is closely allied to that of Eisner and Vallancen. Jewett and Bain distinguish:

(a)   Learning Process (cp.: Development of Cognitive Processes);
(b)   Disciplinary Mastery (cp.: Academic Rationalism);
(c)   Self Actualization (cp.: Personal Relevance);
(d)   Social Reconstruction (cp.: Social Adaptation/Reconstruction);
(e)   Ecological Validity.

However, Jewett and Bain recognize that this classification is not adequate for a description of the curricular shifts in the field of PE . They point out that these shifts were often not caused by changes in value orientation, but rather proceeded from changes in the definition of the subject matter. For that reason Jewett and Bain conclude that the following questions are decisive for the identification of PE curricula:

> '(1) What is the value perspective toward personal or individual development, toward social-cultural goals, and toward subject matter content ? (2) To what extent is any of these three elements valued above the other two ?' (p.33).

When Jewett and Bain subsequently develop their PE specific classification, they omit a consistent back coupling with these indeed very relevant questions. Consequently they present a rather opportunistic catalogue of PE curriculum orientations, mainly reflecting the orientations that emerge in the USA PE reality. The following seven orientations are distinguished:

(a) Developmental Education (based on the idea that traditional gymnastic, play, sport, and dance activities have a special potential for general individual development);

(b) Humanistic Physical Education (central assumptions: every student is unique and movement is an excellent medium for the development of personal identity');

(c) Fitness (two variants can be distinguished within this orientation: (a) the traditional 'education-of-the-physical' idea, and (b) the variant in which training of anatomical and physiological parameters is combined with teaching of fitness related knowledge);

(d) Movement Education (interpreted according to the typical Anglo-Saxon use of the term; the main idea here is not moving to learn or to develop, but learning to move; moreover, it is important that a very special system for the analysis and description of human movement forms the starting point);

(e) Kinesiological Studies (based on the idea that students, who know the principles derived from the human movement sciences, are more capable of solving the problems which they meet when participating in sport);

(f) Play Education (based on the assumption that play and sport have an intrinsic value and that the objectives of PE should not be formulated in subject transcending, pie in the sky, terms, but in terms of competencies that are needed in order to participate in everyday play and sport);

(g) Personal Meaning (main assumptions: 1. an experience can only have pedagogical value if it is meaningful for the child concerned; 2. movement experiences can be intrinsically as well as extrinsically meaningful).

In my opinion, due to its opportunistic character the Jewett/Bain catalogue is not suitable for an adequate comparative description of the basic ideologies of both European and North American PE curricula. Thus I felt obliged to develop a new classification model.

To that end I started from the assumption that general curricular decisions, namely decisions on objectives and contents of education, are dependent on value-bound views concerning (a) children and their potential and desirable development, (b) the expected and the desired changes in the social-cultural context, (c) the role of schooling, and finally (d) considerations concerning the connection between (a), (b) and (c). A specification of this assumption for PE leads to the thesis that PE curriculum ideologies are characterized by their implicit and/or explicit assumptions concerning (a) corporeality and movement, (b) movement culture, and (c) physical education as a school subject. My starting point is schematically represented in Figure 1.

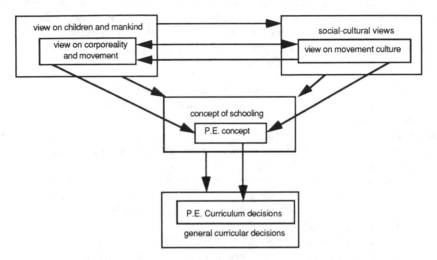

Figure 1   *The relationship between fundamental views and curricular decisions*

Against the background of this scheme I put the following two questions (which are in fact quite similar to the decisive questions of Jewett and Bain):

(a)   What is the view on (i) corporeality and movement, (ii) movement culture, and (iii) PE as a school subject on which a curriculum document is based ?

(b)   To what extent is the perspective through the upper left box or the perspective through the upper right box dominating ? In other words: is 'personal development' valued above 'social-cultural goals' or is it the other way around ?

In reply to the second question I distinguish three curriculum orientations that are mainly based on assumptions concerning the upper left box, one orientation which is mainly based on assumptions concerning the upper right box, and finally one orientation with a kind of balance between the perspectives of the upper right and the upper left box.

I label these five PE curriculum orientations as follows:

(a)   the biologistic training-of-the-physical concept;
(b)   the pedagogistic education-through-movement concept;
(c)   the personalistic movement education concept;
(d)   the conformistic sport socialization concept;
(e)   the critical-constructive movement socialization concept.

Within this brief paper an outline of each of these orientations can only be given by short, catchword-like, sentences.

2.1 *The biologistic training-of-the-physical concept*

This orientation has its origins in the system of the Swedish gymnastics (Ling). Under influence of the increase of coronary diseases and the new healthism in PE there is now a revival of this concept. A basic assumption is that the human body is a machine, an instrument that should be kept in good shape. There are no explicit considerations concerning movement culture (movement as a social-cultural domain). The objectives are formulated in terms of training of anatomical and physiological variables: flexibility, cardiovascular endurance, muscular power and endurance. Content description is in terms of exercises for improvement of flexibility, cardiovascular endurance and muscle power and endurance (exercises classified according to body-parts). The main methodological principles are: keep them busy with a high level of exertion and frequent repetitions of simple exercises. Product evaluation is by means of standardized fitness tests. The main theoretical frames of reference are the biological and medical sciences.

2.2 *The pedagogistic education-through-movement concept*

The origins lay in Philantropinism, GutsMuths' ideas on 'Leibesübungen' and later the so called 'Austrian School of PE'. The basic assumption is that movement is an outstanding medium for exploration, general personal development and communication. Main motto is not 'learning to move' but 'moving to learn'. There are no explicit considerations concerning movement culture. Objectives are formulated in abstract terms of general personal development, character building (will-power, perseverance, discipline), social and aesthetic education. Content description is in terms of the traditional catalogue of gymnastic, play, sport and dance activities. The main methodological principle is: organize these activities orderly and in good atmosphere. Process evaluation (order, atmosphere, child-orientation) is emphasized and there are no substantial directions for product evaluation. The main theoretical frames of reference are phenomenology, hermeneutic pedagogy and humanistic psychology.

2.3 *The personalistic movement development concept*

The basic ideas are that corporeality has subject-character (the body-subject) and that movement action is a mode of being with an intrinsic value for development and human existence. The main motto: 'learning to move'. There are no explicit considerations concerning movement culture. The objectives are formulated in terms of realization of a personal movement identity. The content description depends on the chosen movement concept (the Anglo-Saxon 'movement education' tradition with its physical movement concept versus European options with a relational movement-as-action concept). Main methodological principles are: orientation towards the individuality of the student and guided discovery. Process evaluation is dominant. The theoretical frames of reference are phenomenology, hermeneutic pedagogy, humanistic psychology, general educational (teaching) theory.

2.4 *The conformistic sport socialization concept*

The basic ideas are: the school is pre-eminently an agency for transference of cultural techniques; organized sport is a relevant and important social-cultural domain; the learning individual is a role-taker; dominance of competitive sport in movement culture and its selective character are taken for granted; orientation towards sportive status quo. In this orientation there are no explicit considerations concerning individuality and personal development. The objectives are formulated in terms of physical fitness and technical and tactical capabilities needed for participation in sport. The content description is based on techniques and tactics of the most popular forms of sport. The main methodological principles are teacher orientation, efficiency and control. Product evaluation is by means of testing of well-defined sports skills, tactical control and knowledge of official rules. The theoretical frames of reference are functional sociology, kinesiology, behavioural analysis and general teaching theory.

2.5 *The critical-constructive movement socialization concept*

The basic ideas are: the school is not only an agency for cultural adaptation, but also for cultural innovation; participation in movement culture according to personal possibilities and needs is an important factor for the quality of daily life; competitive sport is only one mode of movement culture and the dominance of this mode should be criticized because of its selective and excluding traits; uniqueness of the individual and relevance of personal development are acknowledged: the learning individual is not only a role-taker but also a role-maker; learning orientation towards a range of meaning perspectives in movement culture. The objectives are formulated in terms of motor-instrumental, socio-motor and reflective competencies needed for a personal and social satisfying, life-long participation in movement culture (also with regard of individual responsibility for physical fitness and health). The content is thematically organized. The main methodological principles are thematic and methodological openness. Process as well as product evaluation is seen as important and the latter is done according to individual standards. The theoretical frames of reference are interactive sociology, critical theory, humanistic psychology, cognitive psychology and general teaching theory.

3   The rationale for the growing consensus in the Netherlands

In the Netherlands a consensus in favour of the critical-constructive movement socialization concept gradually emerges. That is to say, by now this concept is generally acknowledged by the official platforms that take part in the discussion about the development of a new and obligatory curriculum for the first three grades of the secondary school. However the impact of this concept is still relatively weak in the daily reality of PE classes.

The rationale for the mentioned consensus is formed by a composition of factors. Briefly they include:

(a)   The evidence that the claims of the biologistic concept (physical fitness can be improved in 2 or 3 PE classes a week given under the conditions of the school) can not be substantiated.

(b)   The evidence that the pie-in-the-sky claims concerning general personal development and character building of the pedagogistic concept can neither be substantiated and that the vagueness of the practical directions that can be derived from this concept carries the risk of an uncommitted PE practice.

(c)   The recognition that it is pre-eminently the task of the school to enhance the development of personal potentials of the students in the light of a critical-constructive transference of culture regarding future participation as a member of society.

(d)   The insight that PE will be judged as a school subject like all other subjects and that it will fail to keep its place in the core curriculum if it can not make plausible (i) that its product-claims can be substantiated, (ii) that its product-claims can not sufficiently be realized by other agencies (e.g. sportclubs), and (iii) that its product-claims are emancipating in the sense that they are valuable for social-cultural participation and that they contribute to the quality of daily life.

4   Summary of the international comparison

The most recent official PE curriculum documents were reviewed for the international comparison. There is, however, one exception. Since I am unable to read Swedish, I had to content myself with reviewing the official English summary published by the Swedish Board of Education.

The inspection of each document was directed to two levels. Firstly the level of the legitimation of PE as a school subject and the formulation of objectives and secondly the level of curriculum content (activities to be done). On both levels I searched for explicit or tacit indications of the underlying ideologies (see Table 1)

Table 1.   *Summary of a comparative evaluation of official PE curriculum documents*

		Biol. Concept	Pedagog. Concept	Person. Concept	Conform. Concept	Cr-const. Concept
Baden-Wb	f.l.	X	X	-	-	-
	c.l.	+	+/-	-	X	-
NRW	f.l.	+/-	-	-	-	X
	c.l.	+/-	-	-	X	-
Sweden	f.l.	+/-	-	+	-	X
	c.l.	+/-	-	+/-	+	+/-
France	f.l.	X	X	+	-	-
	c.l.	+	+/-	-	+	-
Scotland	f.l.	-	-	+	+	+
	c.l.	-	-	-	X	+
Calif.	f.l.	+	X	+	+/-	-
	c.l.	-	-	+	X	-
New Y.S.	f.l.	-	X	+	-	-
	c.l.	-	+/-	+/-	X	-
Quebec	f.l.	-	-	X	-	X
	c.l.	-	-	X	X	+/-
Netherl.	d.l.	-	-	-	-	X
	p.l.	+	X	+	X	+

f.l. : fundamental level   c.l. : content level   d.l. : discussion level
p.l. : practical level   X : dominant emphasis   + : clear influence
+/- : influence unclear   - : no substantial influence

Finally a few comments:

(a) From my point of view it should be welcomed that the critical constructive movement socialization concept advances in a number of countries (besides the Netherlands also Quebec, Sweden, Nordrhein-Westfalen and Scotland).

(b) The general discrepancy between the curriculum ideology (fundamental level) and the concrete elaborations at the content level are striking and problematic.

(c) Using 'ideological orientation' and 'internal consistency' of the documents as evaluation criteria, I recommended the Scottish and the Quebecois documents to the Dutch Foundation for Curriculum Development.

5 References

Advies over de voorlopige eindtermen basisvorming in het voortgezet onderwijs - lichamelijke oefening (1989). DOP, Den Haag.

California State Department of Education (1986) **Handbook for Physical Education.** Sacramento.

Commissie Sport en Lichamelijke Opvoeding (1986) Naar een **geïntegreerd beleid voor lichamelijke opvoeding en sport.** DOP, Den Haag.

Crum, B.J. (1980) Deelschoolwerkplan - Vakconcept - Maatschappelijke Verantwoording. De **Lichamelijke Opvoeding,** 68, 16, 466-469.

Crum, B.J. (1987) Physical Education in Tomorrows Schools; its Legitimation and Recommendations for Curriculum Planning. **International Journal of Physical Education,** 3, 8-12.

Eisner, E.W. and Vallance E. (eds) (1974) **Conflicting conceptions of curriculum.** McCutchan, Berkely, CA.

Jewett, A.E. and Bain, L. (1985) **The curriculum process in physical education.** Wm. C. Brown, Dubuque, IA.

Kultusminister des Landes Nordrhein-Westfalen (1981) **Richtlinien Sport, Band I, II, III.**

Ministerium für Kultus und Sport Baden-Württemberg (1984) **Bildungsplan für die Hauptschule/die Realschule/das Gymnasium.** Neckar Verlag, Villingen-Schwenningen.

Ministère de l'Education Nationale (Frankrijk) (1987a,b,c,) **Programmes et Compléments Classe de Sixième, Classe de Cinquième, Classe de Quatrième et de Troisième.**

Ministère de l'Education du Quebec (1984) **Secondary School Curriculum Physical Education.**

Ministère de l'Education du Québec (1984) **Secondary School Curriculum Guide, Physical Education Cycle One and Cycle Two.**

New York State Education Department, Bureau of Curriculum Development (1986) **Physical Education Syllabus Grades K-12.**

New York State Education Department (1988) **Physical Education Guide Grades K-12.**

Scottish Examination Board (1988) **Standard Grade Arrangements in Physical Education.**

Scottish Examination Board (1988) **Standard Grade Physical Education - Specimen Question Papers.**

Swedish National Board of Education (1988) **Physical Education in Swedish Schools - a health oriented subject.**

Swedish National Board of Education (1988) **Lgr. 80.**

THE PHYSICAL EDUCATOR AS A CURRICULUM LEADER

H. DAVID TURKINGTON
University of Victoria, Victoria, British Columbia, Canada

Abstract
Canadian physical educators have many reasons to be proud of the leadership role they have played in developing excellent curriculum materials and quality programmes. Examples of their work can be found throughout the world. Unfortunately, due to various pressures within the education system, physical education finds itself once again 'fighting' for its existence as a required subject for all students. There are many reasons which can be brought forward to account for this trend but it is the author's contention that physical educators must renew their commitment to becoming curriculum leaders in order for physical education to survive these latest attacks.
Keywords: Physical Education, Curriculum Leaders.

1 Introduction

The place of physical education in the school curriculum is being challenged throughout the world. In some jurisdictions, the quality of our physical education programmes has come under fire while in others it is simply a matter that the education system is being asked to add to the curriculum more and more subjects such as; consumer education, computer education, AIDS education, second language education, multicultural education, equity education and so on. This has created a situation whereby the school day must be increased and/or the amount of time spent on courses which have traditionally been part of the school curriculum must be reduced or simply eliminated. Unfortunately, when discussion takes place on this subject one of the first courses under scrutiny is physical education. It is my contention that not only must the quality of our teaching and curriculum continue to improve, but that we must make a concerted effort to improve our public image if physical education is to remain a viable subject within the school curriculum. Hence the need for physical educators to assume the role of curriculum leader has never been greater. Although this paper will focus on Canadian physical education, it is my belief that it has implications for school programs throughout the world.

Once again the political and societal climate in Canada is favourable for embarking on new initiatives. However, on the negative side, time is limited. Physical educators must make their presence felt in the immediate future or it may be too late to save the day. In Canada we have many reasons to be proud of our quality physical education programmes and curriculum materials. Unfortunately, for the most part, we have not taken the time to publicize our accomplishments and hence many adults only remember the militaristic programmes they were subjected to during their youth. If we want to maintain or improve our present position in schools, we must:

(a) let the public know why physical education and physical activity are important for children, youth and adults;

(b) show and/or tell the public what we are doing. They will be impressed. For example, many local school districts such as Calgary, Coquitlam, Burnaby, Saskatoon, Vancouver, Scarborough, Waterloo and provincial Ministries of Education in British Columbia, Alberta, Quebec, Manitoba and New Brunswick have developed exemplary curriculum guides. There is no lack of quality curriculum materials in Canada. Unfortunately, we have not left time in our busy schedule to do the necessary public relations work.

(c) evaluate the effectiveness of our current programmes and make the necessary changes. Questions that must be addressed include:
  - Do the programmes meet the needs and interests of today's students?
  - Is physical education a pleasant experience for all students? If not, why not?
  - Do the students learn anything or is it a glorified recess?
  - Do the students choose physical education when given the option?
  - Will the programme assist students in developing a physically active lifestyle both now and in the future?

(d) re-evaluate our professional commitment and ensure that we place curriculum leadership at the top of our priorities.

2   The Canadian Context

Luckily many positive initiatives are taking place across Canada. We need to be aware of these initiatives and to use the information to further our cause. For example:

(a) Otto Jelinek (1987), while Minister for Fitness and Amateur Sport in Canada emphatically pointed out the value of quality, daily physical education when he stated, 'Statistics provide us with the evidence that we need to demand change, yes, and I say demand change'. He went on to say, 'The biggest problem that I think we are faced with ... relates to Canada's number one resource. We keep talking about how wealthy we are in this country to have the natural resources we have and that's true, but our number one natural resource is the youth of the nation. It pains me terribly that this number one resource, the youth of this nation, is not receiving the daily physical education activities that are so fundamental to the well being and future of this country.' In closing, he stated, 'It can be done, it can be done. We can't continue to sit back and say, well it can't be done, it should be done, it can be done and it must be done'.

(b)   The fitness boom is still evident across Canada. Adults are exercising like never before. One just has to stroll around any Canadian city to see the number of active Canadians. This new attitude is carrying over to their children. Young adults are flocking to fitness centres in great numbers in an attempt to improve their fitness and to look good.

(c)   Participaction continues to keep the value of physical activity in front of Canadian TV viewers with timely, interesting messages.

(d)   The emergence of CAHPER's Quality Daily Physical Education Project. This programme has as its major goals; to raise public awareness, to recognize quality school programmes, to assist with the implementation of provincial workshops, and to develop resource materials. The federal government is now contributing over $200,000 per year to assist CAHPER with the funding of this project. I am happy to report that this national project is meeting with significant success in communities across Canada.

These initiatives and others are all very positive indicators that we have considerable support for physical education. However, everything is not rosy--we are losing ground in many parts of Canada. For example:

(a)   in British Columbia - physical education is now elective in grade 11 and recent proposals lead one to believe that a further curtailment could take place in the near future;

(b)   in Saskatchewan - there has been a decrease in the number of schools with daily physical education;

(c)   in Manitoba - there has been a decrease in daily physical education in order to provide time for the introduction of French for all students;

(d)   in Ontario - only one course credit is required after grade 8;

(e)   and finally, - district physical education consultants are becoming a memory in many parts of Canada.

To thwart this trend it is necessary for physical educators to renew their efforts to become curriculum leaders. We must be able to overcome these factors and deal with emerging problem areas such as:

(a)   The back to basics movement - This movement is usually directed towards reading, writing and arithmetic at the expense of other subject areas. Although these basics are important skills to learn, it is my belief that there is nothing as basic as a healthy body. Without a healthy body, it is difficult to reach one's potential academically. Physical activity may not make you any smarter but it will allow most people to live an invigorating lifestyle with the potential to relieve stress, to develop endurance and to be well enough to learn efficiently. In addition, physical education provides the opportunity to develop several intellectual skills such as thinking, creativity and problem solving.

(b)   There is a widening of the affluence-poverty continuum among Canadians. There are more opportunities for the well-to-do but less for the poor. As the costs for out-of-school programmes go up, the need for quality physical education in schools increases. Unfortunately, without a renewed effort to develop quality programmes, the difference in skill levels will get wider between the advantaged and disadvantaged students. It is extremely important that everyone develop the skills and attitudes necessary to live a healthy, active lifestyle.

(c) Concern has been expressed in the area of equity. Do our programmes meet the needs of all students - male, female, handicapped, highly skilled and the less skilled? Are physical educators concerned with equity issues? To address these issues takes the knowledge, understanding, time and dedication to make it happen.

(d) Can our programmes stand up to scrutiny or will physical education requirements continue to be eroded? If the programmes are not educationally sound can they remain in the school curriculum?

(e) Many physical educators are torn between teaching and coaching. This is perhaps the most important issue facing physical educators in Canada and I suspect in many parts of the world. There is no doubt that coaching has become a major roadblock to the implementation of quality physical education programmes and physical educators becoming curriculum leaders. I do want to make it very clear that I personally believe interscholastic sports at the secondary school level can be a valuable experience for students. In fact I would go further to state that all schools should have interscholastic sports. There is nothing inherently wrong with these programmes, but, unfortunately, some people who become coaches or who direct athletic programmes, create situations where problems occur, but that is another issue. Here, I am going to address those factors which drive teachers to mediocrity in the teaching of their physical education classes.

3   Avoiding Mediocrity

First, a brief look at the role of the teacher. A teacher is expected to teach and all that entails; to plan lessons, units of instructions and yearly programmes; to supervise activities; to administer their programme; to sit on school committees; to belong to professional organizations; to attend workshops and conferences; to meet with parents and often, to counsel students. These tasks along with many other day-to-day items lead one to say - 'Does the physical educator have time for anything else?' If a physical educator is involved in coaching or administrating interscholastic programmes, something must go and, in most cases, it is quality teaching. Unfortunately, evidence is available to suggest that far too often, physical educators do put less into their teaching than they should in order to put more into their coaching.

Siedentop, Mand and Taggart (1986) in their excellent textbook on teaching and curriculum strategies outline several factors which lead to role conflict and strain. They include:

(a)   Most students who are preparing to become certified as physical education teachers have coaching as their main interest. Unfortunately, even those who enter with a desire to becoming a good teacher soon learn about the unequal set of rewards for the two roles.

(b)   Administrators prefer to hire teachers who can coach.

(c)   Teachers are traditionally evaluated once or twice a year by the principal and if the students behave and are kept busy, the teacher is evaluated highly. However, the coach is evaluated by parents, peers and the general public by their 'won/loss' record.

(d)   When a teacher/coach is observed in a coaching role the practices are highly organized, intense, clearly focused on skill development and strongly accountable and performance oriented. However, in class sessions, the teacher is more neutral, less well managed, only marginally focused on performance and skill development, less concerned with individuals and less accountable-conscious.

(e)   Non-monetary rewards are extremely unequal. It is rare for a teacher to be praised for doing a good job in teaching their physical education class. Coaches on the other hand receive constant feedback in the newspaper, from parents, from school administrators and from the public.

Is it any wonder that most individuals in this situation place most of their effort on coaching at the expense of their teaching?

As stated earlier, physical education is at a crossroad. We have the opportunity to gain from the public's emerging attitude towards physical activity or, if we continue to offer less than quality programmes, to see physical education disappear from the school curriculum. To overcome the role conflict issue, it is suggested that:

(a)   the principal evaluate teachers and, if warranted, reward them for their teaching excellence;

(b)   teachers reduce their commitment to coaching so that it is maintained at a reasonable level, e.g.
- coach one team per year
- limit the number of games
- limit the length of practices and
- limit the length of season.

(c)   teachers develop a renewed commitment to teaching.

(d)   coaches, teachers, administrators and parents discuss the purpose of school athletic programmes. Perhaps the whole question of elite athletics needs to be addressed. Whose responsibility is it to develop elite athletes? It appears to me that in Canadian secondary schools, coaches are getting away from the intended purpose of interscholastic sports, and although most are not paid to coach, they are becoming over-committed to athletics at the expense of their teaching.

If physical educators become curriculum leaders they will develop good programmes and **good programmes do make a difference.** The process of developing curricula should be an ongoing responsibility of physical educators.

When physical education leaders take the time to develop a philosophy, to determine a scope and sequence of content, to select various instructional strategies and to implement evaluation techniques, programme improvement is a definite possibility.

In determining the philosophy, goals and learning outcomes of the physical education programme, consideration must be given to developing a statement of beliefs relative to the students, the school and physical education. The role of equity, co-education, competition, activity selection by students and accountability, needs to be discussed and addressed as we develop our programme philosophy. Once this has been developed, the selection of content and instructional strategies become more meaningful.

The scope and sequencing of content is closely tied to our overall philosophy. What is really important for children and youth to learn? Should all children learn the same things? Should children/youth have the opportunity to select activities that interest them? Should children progress in an individualized manner based on their readiness and interest, or should students progress on a class or grade level basis? Personally, it is my belief that there are no magic activities to which all students must be subjected. What is important is that they learn; to move effectively, to enjoy physical activity and to develop an attitude which will lead them to become active, healthy individuals throughout their lifetime.

Regardless of the teaching strategies used, be it a direct (command), a task/station, a reciprocal, an individualized, a personalized, an inclusive, or an exploratory approach, it is important to ensure that those factors which have been identified as contributing to effective learning are in place. These include; maximum time-on-task, minimum management time, maximum time in which to practice correctly, a matching of tasks to student ability, realistic expectations and holding students accountable.

It should be stressed that student evaluation is part of the learning process. When students are given content specific feedback, they have a much better opportunity to learn than if left to their own devices. When summative evaluation is used for grading purposes, it is important for students to believe that the methods used are fair. When students understand that grading is related to how well they have achieved the goals and learning outcomes of the course, they are better able to cope with the results.

4   Conclusion

Good programmes do make a difference. In fact, if the quality of our programmes does not improve dramatically over the next few years, and we continue to forget to inform the public, we may find the profession in disarray as physical education disappears from our schools.

We have the opportunity like never before to go forward. I have confidence that physical educators in Canada and around the world will meet the challenge and that physical education will flourish. To ensure that this happens it is imperative that all physical educators redefine their 'reason for being' and become the curriculum leaders of the 1990's.

5   References

Jelinek, Otto (1987) Press conference. CAHPER/ICHPER Conference. Vancouver, British Columbia, Canada.

Siedentop, D., Mand, C. and Taggart, A (1986) **Physical Education: Teaching and curriculum strategies for grades 5-12**. Palo Alto: Mayfield.

MOVEMENT EXPERIENCES AND ACADEMIC ENHANCEMENT

EMMI MYOTIN[1]
Universidade Federal de Viçosa, Viçosa, Minas Gerais, Brazil

Abstract

Recent studies have demonstrated that movement experiences can have a beneficial influence on the integral development of children and enhance academic achievement when there is integration of movement activities with academic concept development. Such integration presupposes the need for interaction among disciplines and teachers and the appropriate training of PE teachers otherwise accustomed to working in isolation. Accordingly, this project set itself the following objectives: (1) to develop a programme of physical activities which can foster academic learning and integral development; (2) to assess the viability of an interdisciplinary approach to pre-school and primary teaching; and (3) to equip teachers with the experience and knowledge to participate in this kind of programme. The project was developed in the state school 'Effie Rolfs' in Viçosa, Brazil, in three classes of children between the ages of 5 and 14. Classes were conducted by two qualified PE teachers specially trained to work in the project. Results suggested a clear improvement in PE teachers in conducting classes, class control and teaching content, pupil perceptual-motor development and readiness to assimilate academic concepts and that benefits are to be derived from an interdisciplinary approach to teaching at the pre-school and primary levels.

Keywords: Movement Experiences, Academic Enhancement, Preschool Children, Teacher Training.

1   Introduction

The value of Physical Education and the importance of the active participation of children in physical activities at the pre-school (age group: 5-6) and primary levels (age group: 7-10) is generally acknowledged and much-discussed in the major population centres of Brazil. In contrast, in regions whose populations live far from the relative affluence of these centres, such as the Mata region of Viçosa, Physical Education is marginalized and relegated to a position of secondary importance.

[1]   The author wishes to acknowledge the full collaboration of Catia Mary Volp in the elaboration and implementation of this research project.

The Mata region of Viçosa lacks sufficiently qualified professionals, appropriate premises and installations and special materials; there is also insufficient public awareness of the merits of Physical Education and programmes are ill-suited to the specific needs of the local population. In addition, some educationalists have drawn attention to the difficulties children encounter when they start school and have discovered that they suffer from many deficiencies related to neuro-psychological functions considered fundamental to the development of literacy (MEC, 1975) and which can predetermine poor achievement and inhibit achievement at school. These deficiencies come in static and dynamic balance, visual motor ability, eye-hand coordination, form perception, space-time relationships, etc.

With a view to redressing the diverse and complex shortcomings in the education system of the Mata region of Viçosa the Department of Physical Education (DES) of the Federal University of Viçosa (UFV), with the financial assistance of the National Research Council of Brazil (CNPq) elaborated the following research project. The project ran for three years from 1985 until 1987 and its remit was necessarily restricted by the funding available. In essence, it sought (a) to define a programme of physical activities which can foster academic learning and integral development; (b) to assess the viability of an interdisciplinary approach to pre-school and primary teaching; (c) to equip teachers with the experience and knowledge to participate in this kind of programme.

To begin with, personal contacts were established with the Regional Education Authority of Ponte Nova, Minas Gerais (Delegacia Regional de Ensino de Ponte Nova) and the Local Education Inspectorate (Inspetoria de Ensino) in Viçosa, that is, the two official bodies with responsibility for the administration of education in the region. These contacts aimed to promote their awareness of the role and importance of Physical Education in the pre- and primary school syllabus and, most importantly, to apply for the fullest possible assistance in the implementation of the project.

Once the administrative and financial assistance had been received it was necessary to undertake the central task of enhancing the awareness among all administrative and teaching staff of the value and role of Physical Education at the afore-mentioned levels. This involved the organization of conferences addressing state-of-the-art approaches to Physical Education for the pre-school and primary age groups, the presentation of various retraining courses for Physical Education teachers at these levels, special courses for pre- and primary school teachers not qualified in Physical Education and advice on setting-up teacher training programmes at the pre-school level on Physical Education matters. In total, about 400 teachers attended these events.

However, the most important component of all was the elaboration of a core-project in the state school named 'Effie Rolfs' in Viçosa. The following relates to this in detail.

2   Experiences in the 'Effie Rolfs' state school

2.1   *Theoretical framework of the project*

Results obtained from research into the relation between perceptual-motor abilities and academic achievement have demonstrated that movement experiences can enhance academic learning. Accordingly, movement experience programmes structured to develop such abilities were employed in the project in order to improve academic learning principally for pupils with learning difficulties. These programmes were also used as a preparation at the pre-school level for the prevention of learning difficulties at the primary level, in particular in the first year of literacy acquisition. They were also designed to integrate movement activities with academic concepts taught in the classroom. Some authors have illustrated practical examples of the specific forms of activities which can effectively facilitate the acquisition of academic concepts in an enjoyable way by adopting an approach which, unlike the traditional classroom approach, appeals to the active participation of the child in the learning process.

The current project used activities suggested by Cratty (1971), Gallahue, Werner and Luedke (1975) and Gallahue (1982), adapted where necessary. The academic concepts developed included those related to mathematics and language, e.g. in order to assist the child in the development of the concept of mathematical sets various experiences in the classification of objects and people were used. Here, children were asked to name all objects in the shape of a square and to bounce only blue balls. Children were also assisted in learning about geometric shapes by means of body pose or forming ropes into different geometric shapes. The same procedure was repeated in number concepts where children were asked to make body numbers. To develop reading and writing skills children played with square blocks of wood with letters painted on their sides. This activity helped them to recognize letters of the alphabet and later, to construct words. Other concepts such as quantity, size, relative body position, space, sense of distance and weight were also developed. We also devised our own movement activities in, for example, materials and music better suited to the cultural identities of the pupils in the participating school.

The implementation of active movement experiences command a central position in the project since we wished to avoid the mere transposition of the learning environment from the classroom to the sportsfield. In addition, it was extremely important to seek to provide pleasure and enjoyment in order to foster interest and active participation in the exploration of movement whilst ensuring that the discipline fundamental to any learning environment was maintained. The basic point of departure of the project thus remained faithful to the objective of Physical Education at this level: 'learning through movement'.

2.2   *Project scope and methodology*

The core-project implemented in this school involved intensive work in the four-month semester with two groups of pre-school children and one first-year primary group, close liaison with the class teachers and the two teachers trained in Physical Education. The supervision and direction remained the responsibility of the two lecturers from the Department of Physical Education at the Federal University of Viçosa who co-ordinated the project.

After securing approval and assistance in the implementation of the project the co-ordinators visited the school to assess the facilities available and to establish first contact with those children who would participate and with their class teachers with whom the project content was discussed. In the following meeting the Physical Education teachers selected to conduct Physical Education classes were introduced to the class teachers and a discussion followed relating to both the academic concepts which were being studied in the classroom and the general academic performance of the children. This enabled their learning difficulties to be raised in advance of the attention focussed on them in the Physical Education lesson itself.

In this preparatory stage and during the implementation of the project itself both co-ordinator and Physical Education teachers maintained periodic contact with the children in the classroom so as to observe them and to enable informal appraisal of the state of their perceptual-motor development and school progress and foster closer relations with them. This approach facilitated an appreciation of the learning difficulties which were to be surmounted by means of movement experience and which movement abilities were to be improved.

These observations formed the basis upon which teaching units were planned. These would run for eight weeks with two sessions per week on alternate days. Each unit contained: the specific objectives to be attained by the children; concepts and abilities to be taught; the appropriate sequence; specific movement activities to be used in the development of these concepts and abilities; the requisite equipment and material; and appraisal methods to be employed in assessing goal attainment. Moreover, these unit plans foresaw teaching methods and techniques appropriate to each different class and activity. This provided an outline of those activities and concepts in which classes would be involved throughout the project. Attention was also paid to the possible influences of climatic change on the choice of either indoor or outdoor activities . The teaching unit plan for each class was developed into daily lesson plans and each lesson consisted of fifty minutes spent in leaving the classroom, physical activities, hygiene and returning to the classroom. These lesson plans encompassed the objectives to be reached in one day, the activities chosen to enhance concepts and movement abilities and selection of relevant material and equipment. In implementing these daily lessons the Physical Education teachers were aware of the need to take safety precautions, to promote total class participation and ensure the progress of each pupil toward the accomplishment of the aims of the lesson. Finally, in order to maximize effectiveness the teachers adopted a variety of teaching approaches coupled with their own creativity, interest and enthusiasm.

3   Results and conclusion

The final evaluation of the project demonstrated a clear improvement in Physical Education teachers in conducting classes, mastering control technique, forms of discipline and teaching content, in addition to an increased readiness to work in conjunction with the classroom teacher. By the same token, the pupils showed not only an improvement in their perceptual-motor abilities and readiness to assimilate academic concepts but also a clear interest and enthusiasm for Physical Education classes. In conclusion, it may be suggested from these findings that benefits are to be derived from the adoption of an interdisciplinary approach to Physical Education teaching at the pre-school and primary levels.

4 References

Cratty, B.J. (1971) **Active learning: games to enhance academic abilities.** Prentice Hall Inc., Naglewood Cliffs, New Jersey.

Gallahue, D.L., Werner, P.H. and Luedke, G.C. (1975) **A conceptual approach to moving and learning.** John Wiley and Sons Inc., New York, N.Y.

Gallahue, D.L. (1982) **Developmental movement experiences for children.** John Wiley and Sons Inc., New York, N.Y.

MEC. Departamento de Ensino Fundamental (1975) **Diagnóstico preliminar de educação pré-escolar no Brasil.** Brasilia.

GETTING STUDENTS TO TAKE RESPONSIBILITY FOR THEIR LEARNING: A CONCERN OF PRIMARY IMPORTANCE FOR DANCE TEACHERS

M. TOUSIGNANT, J. BRUNELLE, M. LAFORGE, AND D. TURCOTTE
Laval University, Department of Physical Education, and L'Ecole de danse de Québec, Québec City, Canada

Abstract

The purpose of this presentation is to characterize the teaching-learning process in terms of the goals dance teachers set for their students, and to elaborate on an aspect identified as an area in need of improvement, i.e. getting students to take responsibility for their learning. Five dance instructors were observed regularly by researchers who used ethnographic techniques. The results were presented to the teachers in order to check the data credibility and to obtain a tacit theory regarding their practice. The results indicate that dance teachers primarily used a Direct Instruction approach to help their students 'learn to do' and 'learn to feel' a variety of movements. However, they did not limit their teaching strategies to asking students to imitate their demonstrations. They strongly believed that students must shoulder the responsibility of their learning. The method most frequently used to nurture this ability consisted in teachers urging dancers to assume responsibility. The teachers' reflection on their action led them to realize that the strategies used in motivating the students to become more responsible for their learning needed improvement.
Keywords: Teaching Practice, Dance Technique Classes, Qualitative Study.

1 Introduction

The main goal of this research project was to shed some light on what dance teachers want students to learn, what they do to help them achieve their goals, and why they believe it is important to act as they do.

Relatively little is known about the daily practice of dance teachers. The literature on teaching dance resembles that which exists for teaching in general and for physical education. Thus, the research aimed at identifying the best methods of teaching dance was plagued with research design weaknesses identical to those of studies conducted in academic settings, and no significant conclusions emerged from this body of literature. Several researchers conducted descriptive studies involving systematic observation with predetermined categories of teacher behaviour and, occasionally, of student behaviour (e.g.: Brunelle and De Carufel, 1982; Fortin, 1986; Gray, 1983; Lord, 1981-82; Lord and Petiot, 1986; O' Sullivan, 1985; Piéron and Géoris, 1983; Piéron and Delmelle, 1983). In her review of the research literature on teaching dance, Lord (1986) discusses what was learned from these studies. Thus, she states:

> Results show that, like most physical activity teachers, dance teachers rely on three main behaviours during technique classes. In order of quantitative importance, they are: to support or guide students' motor activities, to prepare for motor activities and to provide feedback. Dance teacher skills mainly differ from those of physical education teachers in the substantially greater amount of non-verbal communication, as well as in the wider variety of strategies involved. (p. 18)

In her conclusions, Lord (1986) expressed a need for more qualitative descriptive studies of the way dance is taught.

Numerous authors have pointed out the limitations of the traditional approaches to produce knowledge about practitioners' actions in the natural context of their practice (Argyris and Schön, 1974; Argyris, 1980; Schön, 1983, 1987). The usefulness of an epistemology of practice is more widely recognized. A close examination of what goes on in 'the complex, unstable, uncertain and conflictual world of practice' is likely to yield a better understanding of the practice. The study of the routine application of procedures as well as 'professional artistry, that is, the competence by which practioners actually handle the indeterminate zones of practice' (Schön, 1983, p. 13) plays a central role in the description of professional practice and in the process of reflecting on the action needed to seek ways to improve practice.

Quite obviously, the traditional teaching model is the one most used in the teaching of dance. Indeed, if this type of teaching process has produced outstanding dance performers, why should it be challenged? Apparently, dance teachers are not generally inclined to question the limitations of the usual model for teaching dance when their students do not produce the expected results. They realize that the dominant model encourages students' obedience; nonetheless, they hope that dancers will act on their own initiative. Thus, it was hypothesized that a research process aimed at increasing teachers' awareness of their teaching and their attitudes concerning their role as educator could lead them to acknowledge what Schön calls 'indeterminate zones', areas in which both students and teachers feel dissatisfied when they experience difficulties in reaching some of their goals (for example, goals related to mastering artistic qualities), and to engage in a process of searching for innovative teaching methods.

2   The purposes of the study

One purpose of this project was to characterize the teaching-learning process
naturally taking place in the context of technique dance classes in terms of the goals
pursued and the teaching strategies used. An accompanying purpose of this
collaborative endeavour between a group of dance teachers and three researchers was
to describe the outcome of a process aimed at raising the teachers' awareness of their
teaching strategies. Thus, the teachers were informed of the preliminary results of
this qualitative study, were asked to reflect on the tacit theories underlying their
teaching strategies, and were invited to identify specific areas in need of
improvement.

3   Procedures

3.1 *Participants and setting*

This investigation of the teaching-learning process in dance classes took place in a
private dance school specializing in classical and modern dance. The school's
programme has both a professional training and a recreational component.

The research team consisted of two senior researchers and a dance teacher who
had recently completed her Ph. D. pedagogy. To gain access to the school, the
research team met first with the person directing the school and then with all the
teaching staff to explain the purposes of the project. Several dance instructors
indicated their willingness to get involved in the process of becoming more aware of
their teaching strategies and improving selected aspects. Five were included in the
study; their role basically consisted in being observed and in reflecting on their action
by reacting to the preliminary results presented by the researchers.

All five participants were women with training in dance teaching. One had over
20 years of teaching experience, one had only one year's experience, and the other
three had taught dance for 8 to 12 years. The lessons observed were technique
classes: three groups of classical and two of modern dance.

A programme guideline was provided by the school, and each teacher was
responsible for designing the content of the lessons. A typical lesson consisted of 10
to 12 technical exercises including various basic steps. These exercises were
repeated two to four times during a lesson and remained part of the lesson for two or
three weeks. A session lasted 11 to 14 weeks, with two or three 90-minute lessons a
week, depending on the group level. The lessons took place in the school's studios,
which were equipped with the usual barres, mirrors, spring floor, and a musician or
a cassette player. The classes were scheduled from 4:00 to 10:00 p.m. The average
number of participants in the groups was 12; however, this number varied between 4
and 20. Participants included young girls, adolescents, young adults hoping to
become professional, and adults participating in the recreational programme.

3.2 *Data collection and data analysis*

A series of methodological techniques were used for collecting data.

Observation Five groups were chosen to be observed once a week (one group for each teacher participating in the study), throughout the autumn session. A total of 45 lessons were observed by the three researchers trained to use ethnographic techniques to describe what occurred during the classes (Bogdan and Biklen, 1982). The researchers focused their attention on the teachers' and dancers' behaviour while learning tasks were carried out. The Pedagogical Moves model (structuring, soliciting, responding and reacting) developed by Bellack, Kliebard, Hyman and Smith (1966) served as the theoretical framework on which the data collection procedures were focused. The specific questions used in the collection of data for this qualitative research were as follows:

(a) What strategies were used by teachers to introduce the learning activities, i.e., how did they structure the tasks?

(b) What did the teachers do to get the learners to carry out the learning tasks, i.e., how did they **solicit** students' responses?

(c) What did the students do when given opportunities to respond, i.e., how did students **respond** and how did they perceive the learning conditions being offered to them?

(d) What did the teachers do when the students carried out the learning activities, i.e., how did they **react** to the students' responses?

The notes taken during the lesson were subsequently expanded and transcribed as soon as possible. Peer debriefing sessions among the three observers took place every week to ensure that they had a similar understanding of the research questions. As they were sharing their observation data, they began to carry out a constant comparative analysis of the data (Glaser and Strauss, 1967), and to develop a taxonomy of teacher and student behaviour (Spradley, 1976). The emerging themes, sub-themes and categories were recorded and circulated among the researchers. Week after week, they coded their data using the identified themes and collected new themes. In the meantime, they gathered examples to illustrate the themes, sub-themes and categories of behaviours.

Critical incidents Each of the 60 students participating in the observed classes was asked several times to write short stories relating specific events associated with positive and less positive feelings about the learning conditions offered to them. The content of the dancers' subjective appraisal of the learning conditions obtained by means of the critical incident questionnaires was sorted according to the themes that emerged from the analysis of the observation, and added to the taxonomy under a specific heading called 'students' perceptions'.

Interviews Two interviews were conducted with each teacher. Four weeks after the beginning of the study, the teachers were first individually presented with the preliminary results of the observation of their classes and the data from their students' critical incidents. The purpose of these meetings was to check the credibility of the data analysis process, and to gather data on the teachers' tacit theory on their teaching methods. The interviews were recorded and transcribed for further analysis. The teachers' perceptions were added to the developing taxonomy.

Second, at the end of the session, the composite profile of the teaching strategies that had emerged from the analysis of all the data was presented to the group of teachers (a) to make them more aware of the variety of ways in which dance is taught, (b) to obtain their reactions to the profile, and (c) to identify areas in need of improvement.

4   Results and discussion

Three major goals characterized the teaching-learning processes taking place in the various dance classes:

(a) **Learning to do** refers to improvement in the students' ability to perform the movements appropriately.
(b) **Learning to feel** is associated with the learners' ability to sense from an inner perspective the movements that they are executing, to live in or inhabit them.
(c) **Learning to take responsibility for one's learning** is related to the development of the student's autonomy and sense of initiative.

4.1   *Learning to do*

An inductive analysis of the descriptive data on the teaching-learning process taking place in the technique dance classes revealed that the most frequently observed patterns in the methods by which students were helped to learn the movements consisted of the following phases:

(a) The teachers presented the learning tasks by demonstrating and explaining the basic features of the technical exercises, and by insisting on a few specific aspects of the techniques to be performed (Ex.: 'Today, we are doing ..., you will pay particular attention to the position of your shoulders while turning, see... not too far back').
(b) The students promptly followed the directions and executed the exercises with a high degree of concentration and, generally, a high success rate.
(c) While the students were carrying out the tasks, teachers observed, provided guidance, and gave concomitant feedback of various forms, either to the group or to individuals.
(d) Each repetition of a technical exercise was followed by information on the quality of the responses, and by additional instruction on what should be improved. Such information was given either to an individual, to small groups or to the whole group, depending on the teachers' perception of their students' needs.

The interview data emphasized that the dance teachers were committed to providing the dancers with numerous opportunities to practice tasks well adapted to their skill level. They also believed that feedback is an essential component of the learning process. The students' perceptions revealed their appreciation for receiving teachers' corrections.

This most frequently used pattern contains the main features of what is generally called Direct Instruction (Rosenshine, 1979). It is highly structured and teacher-directed, and the main task of the student is to imitate the teachers' demonstrations.

4.2 *Learning to feel*

Our data revealed that dance teachers did not limit their teaching strategy to asking the students to imitate demonstrations. Interview data indicated that the teachers strongly believed that 'students must feel what they are doing'. For example, the teachers used sentences like: 'If the student only imitates what he sees, he is too mechanical', 'They must be able to combine technical skills and feelings', 'Not only must they learn the vocabulary and the grammar, they must also contact their feelings'. Observational data showed that, as learning activities were being carried out, teachers asked the dancers to feel what they were doing, to concentrate on what they perceived from an inner perspective, and to avoid merely focusing on the projected impression. For example, they told the students: 'Make sure that you feel that your weight is on the balls of your feet...'. Also, they used imagery to help the learners concentrate on their feelings, for example, 'Your hands must feel as if they were carrying a precious object'.

It should be emphasized that 'learning to feel', that is, the particular aspect of the teaching-learning process aimed at helping the dancers 'learn to live in, to inhabit their movements' also pertains to the Direct Instruction model. Indeed, most of the time the teachers provided specific information on what sensation the students should be looking for or created images that could help the students feel the movement. This is also part of the traditional teaching model.

However, this appears to be an example of what Schön (1987) called an 'indeterminate zone'. Much remains to be understood about the tacit theory underlying this particular aspect of the artistry of teaching dance, since teachers seemed to follow rules that have not yet been made explicit.

4.3 *Taking responsibility for their learning*

The data also revealed that occasionally the dance teachers seemed to have run out of tools to help the students learn. Several incidents indicated that when the teachers had exhausted the resources of the Direct Instruction model, they felt helpless and somewhat frustrated. For example, after a rather long session of providing specific feedback and observing students' responses which did not seem to show much improvement, a teacher threw her arms down and said: 'I can only tell you what needs to be worked on, I can't do it for you. You need to concentrate on the problem', then she went on with a lecture on the necessity of dancers disciplining themselves and shouldering the responsibility of learning.

Several events relating to teachers' impressions of helplessness were connected with the memorization of sequences: 'I took the time to explain it, I expected that you had learned it', 'Make more effort to memorize quickly so that we can concentrate on the quality of your movement', or 'You do not memorize fast enough, it is your responsibility, ...I have the feeling you are relying on me too much!'

The interview data also indicated feelings of helplessness: 'There are times when I don't know what to do to help them!', 'I feel that I keep repeating the same things over and over'. All five teachers mentioned at some point that they strongly believed that learning to dance is not something that they can do for their students. For example, Louise, referring to the students said: 'Becoming a dancer must be their goal, they cannot rely only on what I can do for them'. Rachel mentioned: 'It is difficult. I have the feeling I must do everything, I must be everything, a psychologist, a mother, as well as a teacher. It is especially hard with the ones who lack self-discipline'. Denise added: 'They must not expect everything from the teacher!'. Some teachers had the tendency to blame the students' attitudes: 'They are not dedicated enough', 'They are too detached', 'Learning to dance must become an obsession'.

A systematic analysis of the specific data on what was actually done to get students to take responsibility for their learning indicated that on several occasions (a) the teachers talked about the need for students to take a more active part in the teaching-learning process, (b) the teachers allowed students to take some initiative to help their learning, and (c) a number of 'implicit goals' existed.

Teachers urged dancers to assume responsibility   The teachers gave lectures on the need for students to shoulder the responsibility for their learning. Also, they encouraged them to have confidence in their learning ability by saying things like: 'Do not get angry at yourself, give yourself time and try again'. Moreover, they gave individualized instruction: 'Diane, just do this..., concentrate on the turn', or 'Keep working on this while the others are doing the whole sequence'. Very occasionally, they asked students to evaluate their own performance, or to watch each other.

Teachers allowed students to take some initiative   When a student repeated an exercise while the teacher was busy helping someone else and the teacher saw that student, she was likely to give some positive feedback. Students were also encouraged to pay attention to corrections given to someone else. Teachers allowed some students to spontaneously help each other, providing that it was not disturbing the class activity. Consequently, a few dancers asked each other for information or commented on their performances from time to time.

Dance teachers expected their students to develop the basic attitudes and usual manners required of a dancer   Students were supposed to arrive on time, to dress appropriately, and to assume and maintain the starting and finishing positions as long as needed. They were also expected to pay constant attention to what the teacher was saying, to keep going whenever they made an error, to be able to count and follow the music, and to find out when it was time for them to take their turn. They were responsible for learning the vocabulary, practicing individually and identifying the ways of performing a movement that could lead to injuries.

On the other hand, the learning activities were not directly related to these 'implicit goals'. These goals were subtly communicated to students through occasional feedback (for example: 'I am glad to see that all of you arrived on time today!') or comments (for example: 'You must get into the habit of listening to the music yourself, I am not going to count for you all the time'). During her interview, a teacher mentioned that she regularly observed without saying anything: 'They must learn to manage by themselves'.

It should be emphasized that with regard to the second purpose of this study, after practitioners reflected on their teaching strategies, they came to acknowledge the limitations of the traditional teaching model with regard to **getting the students to take responsibility for their learning.**

This concern, which emerged from the reflection on the practice of dance teachers, can also be found in a variety of points of view expressed in educational literature (for example, some of the of teaching models identified by Joyce and Weil, 1972 or by Bilbrough and Jones, 1970, or the humanistic individualized instruction presented by Heitmann and Kneer, 1976). The need to pay attention to the roles played by students in the learning process was also recognized in the literature about teaching effectiveness (for example, see Doyle, 1986).

5   Conclusions

This article, in addition to characterizing the teaching learning process in dance classes according to the teachers' explicit and implicit goals, illustrates how dance teachers, when presented with the results of a qualitative description of their teaching strategies, came to realize that (a) they were using rather effectively a large repertoire of skills associated with the Direct Instruction model, but that (b) from time to time they experienced some frustration as they faced the limitations of that dominant model. Using Direct Instruction as the principal method of helping students learn to do and feel the basic movements appears appropriate. Moreover, this method has produced outstanding dancers time after time . Consequently, whenever dancers experience some difficulties in learning, teachers are tempted to blame it on the students' attitudes and motivation, and to resort to urging, hoping that it will make them become more responsible.

The findings of the observation contrasted somewhat with the teachers' desire (which was evident in their interviews) to involve participants in their learning. Their strong commitment to helping their students become more autonomous was not associated with the deliberate use of systematic teaching strategies. It appears very difficult, scary, and even hazardous to switch from a Direct Instruction model, even for short periods of time, to indirect teaching strategies which would require that the students play a more active role in their learning, while respecting the established traditions for teaching dance.

Several questions can be raised regarding the information obtained from studies on teaching which can help in the understanding of what it means to make students more responsible for their own learning and why this is difficult to implement. For example, the literature on 'teacher thinking' suggests that teachers may be uncomfortable with major changes in the decision making process and with sharing their role with learners. Likewise, the findings on 'teacher socialization' indicate that the difficulty in challenging the usual methods of teaching can be based on the traditional model used for training dancers, and on what has been recognized as effective teaching for several centuries. Is the main problem related to choosing methods of conveying the meaning of assuming responsibility in a field where teachers have not been 'socialized' to do so?

Other issues arise from the teaching effectiveness literature: Is the difficulty built into the accountability system? Could it be that dance teachers are perceived as 'masters' who are entirely responsible for making decisions about the quality of the learners' responses and that the students do not feel that they can take an active part in the evaluation process? The literature on teaching effectiveness has also pointed to the overwhelming impact of the learners' background on their achievement. Thus, perhaps the dance teachers believe that autonomy and a sense of responsibility are qualities dancers should possess naturally, or learn by themselves, not something they have to teach. The 'why and how' of making the learners responsible for their learning in the context of dance classes seems to be an example of what Schön (1987) has labelled an indeterminate zone of the artistry of teaching dance. It remains an intriguing question which could serve as prime focus in the search for improvements to the teacher repertoire of strategies to help students become better dancers.

6   References

Argyris, C. (1980) **Inner Contradictions of Rigorous Research,** Academic Press, New York.

Argyris, C and Schön, D.A. (1974) **Theory in practice: Increasing Professional Effectiveness,** Jossey-Bass, San Francisco.

Bellack, A.A., Kliebard, H.M., Hyman, R.T. and Smith, F.L. (1966) **The Language of The Classroom,** Teachers College Press, New York.

Bogdan, C.B. and Biklen, S.K. (1982) **Qualitative Research for Education: An Introduction to Theory and Methods,** Allyn and Bacon, Boston.

Bilbrough, A. and Jones, P. (1970) **Physical Education in the Primary School,** University of London Press, London.

Brunelle, J. and De Carufel, F. (1982) Analyse des feedback émis par des maîtres de l'enseignement de la danse moderne. **La Revue Québécoise de l'Activité Physique,** 2, 1, 3-9.

Doyle, W. (1986) Classroom Organization and Management, in **Handbook of Research on Teaching** (ed M.C. Wittrock), Macmillan Pub., New York, pp. 392-431.

Fortin, S . (1986) **L' efficacité des Feedback de Correction telle que Perçue par des Etudiants et des Professeurs en Classe de Danse Moderne.** Unpublished master's thesis, Universite de Montreal.

Glaser, B.G. and Strauss, A.L. (1967) **The Discovery of Grounded Theory: Strategies for Qualitative Research,** Aldine Pub., Hawthorne, N.Y.

Gray, J. (1983) The science of teaching the act of dance: A description of a computer-aided system for recording and analyzing dance instructional behaviors. **Journal of Education for Teaching,** 9, 3, 264-279.

Heitmann, H.M. and Kneer, M.E. (1976) **Physical Education Instructional Techniques: An Individualized Humanistic Approach,** Prentice-Hall, Englewood Cliffs.

Joyce, B. and Weil, M. (1972) **Models of Teaching,** Prentice-Hall, Englewood Cliffs.

Lord, M. (1981-82) A characterization of dance teacher behavior in choreography and technique classes, **Dance Research Journal,** 14, 1, 15-24.

Lord, M. (1986) What do we know about the teaching of dance. **Proceedings of the VIII Commonwealth and International Conference on Sport, Physical Education, Dance, Recreation and Health,** University Press, Cambridge, pp. 15-24.

Lord, M. and Petiot, B. (1986) Analyse de l' organisation temporelle des comportements d'enseignants en classes de danse, **Revue Canadienne de l'Education.**

O' Sullivan, M. (1985) A descriptive analytical study of student teacher effectiveness and student behaviors in secondary school physical education, in **Teaching Effectiveness Research** (eds. B.L. Howe and J.J. Jackson), University of Victoria, Canada, pp. 22-30.

Piéron, M. and Delmelle, V. (1983) Les réactions à la prestation de l'élève: Etude dans l'enseignement de la danse moderne, **Revue de l'Education Physique,** 23, 4, 35-4 1 .

Piéron, M. and Géoris, M. (1983) Comportements d'enseignants et interactions avec leurs élèves, observation dans l'enseignement de la danse moderne, **Revue de l'Education Physique,** 23, 4, 42-46.

Rosenshine, B. (1979) Content, time and direct instruction, in **Research on Teaching: Concepts, Findings, and Implications** (eds P. Peterson and H. Walberg), McCutchan, Berkeley, Calif.

Schön, D.A. (1983) **The Reflective Practitioner**, Basic Books, New York.

Schön, D.A. (1987) **Educating The Reflective Practitioner**, Jossey-Bass, San Francisco.

Spradley, J. (1976). **Participant Observation**, Holt, Rinehart and Winston, New York.

MOVING TOWARDS EXCELLENCE IN THE TEACHING OF PHYSICAL EDUCATION IN THE SECONDARY SCHOOL

G. L. UNDERWOOD
Christ Church College, Canterbury, England

Abstract
The research involved in-depth case studies in five schools. The schools were selected based on the responses of 1,780 male and female pupils in the 4th year (14 years old) in 14 schools to a Physical Education 'Learner Report' questionnaire. They included the two highest scoring schools (S1 and S2) whose scores were significantly different from the two lowest scoring schools (S4 and S5) and a control school (S3). This gave rise to the main hypothesis that the more effective teaching and learning would take place in S1 and S2. In order to test this hypothesis, the author spent one week observing lessons, interviewing staff and pupils, analysing syllabuses and teaching in each of the five schools. ALT-PE recording of 74 lessons were mainly non-supportive of the hypothesis. Particular consideration is given to ways of increasing 'motor time' and ensuring logical progression in lessons. Qualitative data highlighted the importance of emphasizing the use of principles in teaching. This is considered in relation to the teaching of games and the principles of fitness training. Finally, attention is drawn to the importance of integrating the male and female departments into a single well co-ordinated unit.
Keywords: Participant observation, Motor time, Teaching principles, Integrated Department.

1 Introduction

Most delegates would heartily endorse the central theme of this conference of 'moving towards excellence' in their physical education teaching and it is certainly a goal to which teachers in Great Britain aspire. It is the purpose of this paper firstly, to examine some of the main trends of this movement based on the author's recent research and secondly, to suggest ways in which this movement might be accelerated.

2   The Research

In an extensive study of pupil-teacher interaction in secondary school physical education, Underwood (1988) investigated the teaching behaviour of male and female physical education teachers in secondary schools and its effect on pupils' behaviour in the naturalistic setting of the school environment. The starting point of the research involved videotaping male and female teachers teaching six educational gymnastic and six basketball/netball lessons. The multi-dimensional analyis of this pilot study identified aspects of learning and teaching which could be addressed in greater detail in the main study. Subsequently, in order to broaden the scope, a number of case studies were conducted in physical education departments in schools. Five schools were chosen which were selected on the basis of the responses of 1,780 male and female pupils in the 4th year (aged 14 to 15 years) in fourteen schools to Crum's (1984) Physical Education 'Learner Report' questionnaire. Based on the pupils' assessment of their own learning, two were designated high-scoring schools (S1 and S2) and two low-scoring (S4 and S5), and both pairs were statistically significant from one another. In addition, a control school (S3) which was not significantly different from either pair was also chosen. The main hypothesis was that the physical education departments in S1 and S2 would be more effective than those in S4 and S5. The author spent one week as a participant observer observing the teaching of physical education in each of the five schools.

Seventy-four lessons were observed and each was analysed through ALT-PE (Academic Learning Time - Physical Education) at the Context and Learner Involvement levels. As well as generating quantitative data through this observational method a number of qualitative evaluations were also made. These included judgements about effective communication between the teacher and pupils, the working atmosphere, class organization, related progression and levels of structured interviews were conducted with the staff in every school about their overall curriculum planning and implementation procedures based on the author's previous national survey in 1983. Each school had a written physical education syllabus and these were also analysed. The opinions of pupils and their attitudes to physical education were obtained through informal discussions, during and after lessons as well as through a number of interviews with 20 boys and girls of high and low motor ability. Thus an eclectic research approach was deemed appropriate to investigate such a complex and highly interrelated set of variables as teaching and learning in physical education and each of the research strategies provided insight to the enquiry.

It is not the intention (nor would it be possible) to present all the findings from the investigation in this paper but rather to abstract some of the main findings and consider their implications for the future.

3   Quantitative results

In the conduct of almost all lessons, a certain proportion of time must be allocated to organization and management, and a reasonable expectation would be that the teachers in the more efficient schools would spend less time in the ALT-PE General

Content categories. In this way, non-movement time would be reduced to a minimum and free time which could be devoted to the development of skill and understanding. The input of PE Knowledge would depend on the skills being taught and the stage of development, but in general terms, the application of technique (Strategy) should predominate. With regard to the PE Motor element, because the physical is so central to the learning of skills in physical education, the expectation would be that the motor element would comprise the major proportion of the time allocation. These assumptions are now examined in relation to the 74 lessons observed in the five schools.

3.1 *Academic Learning Time - Physical Education (ALT-PE)*

Firstly, the quantitative data generated from the ALT-PE Context Level analysis is presented and analysed in Table 1. The mean percentage scores for each school showed the distribution of time in each category and the Kruskal-Wallis ANOVA indicated the level of statistical significance.

Table 1.   *ALT-PE context level. Mean scores and Kruskal-Wallis one-way ANOVA by sub-section and category for S1-S5*

	S1	S2	S3	S4	S5	H	p
	N=13	N=13	N=11	N=19	N=18		
General Content							
Transition	12.9	18.5	20.5	10.5	16.7	13.25	<0.05
Management	1.4	0.1	2.3	1.1	0.5	9.26	N.S.
Break	0.2	0	0.5	0.6	0	-	-
Warm-up	3.8	5.2	4.0	3.5	4.4	0.93	N.S.
Providing Eqpt.	6.4	4.2	4.0	3.5	1.1	17.97	<0.01
Sub-section	24.7	28.0	31.3	19.2	22.7	7.74	N.S.
PE Knowledge							
Technique	9.8	12.2	9.5	6.8	4.8	7.18	N.S.
Strategy	7.7	9.8	16.6	13.8	11.1	2.53	N.S.
Rules	0.1	1.2	0.3	0	0.3	-	-
Social behaviour	0.2	0	0.2	0	0	-	-
Background	0	0.2	1.5	2.4	0.2	-	-
Sub-section	17.8	23.4	28.1	23.0	16.4	4.1	N.S.
PE Motor							
Practice	18.9	18.0	17.2	9.8	13.5	6.07	N.S.
Skill/scrimmage	20.6	30.5	21.2	44.8	46.7	13.74	<0.01
Game	17.5	0.4	2.5	1.3	0.7	9.37	N.S.
Fitness	0	0	0	2.1	0	-	-
Sub-section	57.0	48.9	40.9	58.0	60.9	0.35	N.S.

As a result of this analysis, a number of statements can be made in relation to the context within which the pupil behaviour occurred. (Where significance was reached, the schools with the more favourable scores are indicated in brackets).

(a) There were no significant differences in the General Content, PE Knowledge and PE Motor sub-sections.
(b) There were no significant differences in the distribution of time spent in the management, warm up, technique, strategy, practice and game categories.
(c) Significant differences were apparent in the transition (S1 and S4), providing equipment (S2, S3, S4 and S5) and skills application (S4 and S5) categories.

Table 2.   *ALT-PE learner involvement. Mean scores and Kruskal-Wallis one-way ANOVA by sub-section and category for S1-S5*

	S1	S2	S3	S4	S5	H	p
	N=13	N=13	N=11	N=19	N=18		
Not Motor Engaged							
Interim	0.4	0	0.6	0.3	0.6	-	-
Waiting	18.1	22.9	19.1	10.7	14.5	6.93	N.S.
Off-task	0.3	0.1	2.0	0.4	0.2	6.55	N.S.
On-task	19.8	15.9	8.1	13.3	15.6	7.23	N.S.
Cognitive	20.2	28.1	43.0	25.7	21.7	10.80	<0.05
Sub-section	58.8	67.0	72.8	50.4	52.6	5.69	N.S.
Motor Engaged							
Motor appropriate	40.8	32.8	27.2	49.5	47.5	9.47	<0.05
Motor inappropriate	0.2	0	0	0	0.2	-	-
Motor supporting	0.5	0.2	0	0.2	0	-	-
Sub-section	41.5	33.0	27.2	49.7	47.7	0.70	N.S.

Secondly, the ALT-PE Learner Involvement focused on individual pupils and these results are presented and analysed in Table 2.

At the Learner Involvement level, three general statements can be made.

(a) There were no significant differences in the Not Motor Engaged and Motor Engaged sub-sections.
(b) There were no significant differences between schools in the waiting, off-task, and on-task categories.
(c) Significant differences were reached in the cognitive (S1) and motor appropriate (S4) categories.

Clearly, most of the results did not support the main contention that the high-scoring school would provide a different and more favourable teaching context for their physical education lessons. This may suggest that a ranking order based on pupils' assessment of their own learning may not be a valid method of judging the effectiveness of a physical education programme. Also, there was no denying the pupils' perceptions differed even though there were few significant differences in the context within which pupil behaviour occurred.

3.2 *Motor time*

As expected, the PE Motor element did comprise the major proportion of time in the five schools (54.4%) and this was reflected in the Motor Appropriate category of learner involvement (39.6%). However, this percentage was probably an overestimate as the definition of motor appropriate is related to the pupils performing at an 'easy level of difficulty' and the author was often unable to discriminate according to this criterion. This was because of the constraints imposed by live recording and a lack of knowledge about each pupils' ability. Consequently, the true percentage would almost certainly have been lower. Considering that motor involvement is the main process through which children learn physical skills, no complacency can be felt about this percentage and consideration needs to be given to increasing the amount of time teachers make available for the motor aspect of lessons.

Based on subjective evaluations of the lessons, there are a number of ways in which this might have been achieved. Periods of time which were exclusively allocated to physiological warm up could, with minor adaptations, have been skill orientated and thus increased the 'motor time'. Games lessons which began with runs round the field or tag relays could easily be adapted to simple individual or group practices which involved all pupils in purposeful skill activity. Some of the teachers' explanations were rather excessively long and could have been more effective had they been shorter and more sharply focused on relevant teaching points. This would initially involve careful thought and planning in the presentation of instructions and lesson material but would eventually become part of an effective verbal teaching pattern. Allowing groups to show their work to other groups at the end of every lesson was not uncommon and is a doubtful and time consuming practice. There are two main reasons for using this type of group demonstration. The first is to show the rest of the class what the group has achieved, a laudable aim at the end of several weeks work, but not at the end of one lesson when the standard and development of the work is still in its infancy. The second reason is to give pupils ideas how to interpret a theme or task, for example, in gymnastics or games. The flaw here is that once all the groups have shown their work the apparatus is put away and there is little chance that any ideas which might have been gleaned will carry over to the next lesson. Ensuring that pupils are involved in the lesson at all times would be a prime aim of all teachers and it was therefore disturbing to find that, on average, pupils spent 16% of the lesson either waiting to take part or to receive instructions. Teacher behaviour which reduced this waiting time would be seen as beneficial to the learning environment.

All lessons should have clearly defined objectives which are logically developed in pursuit of their achievement. Whilst lesson themes and objectives were apparent in most lessons, there were occasions when the theme became dissipated as the lesson progressed. Gymnastic themes practised on the floor were sometimes not transferred to the apparatus because of the nature of the task set and/or the arrangement of the apparatus. Similarly, the techniques practised in the initial part of the games lessons were not always transferred to the applied skills or games playing part of the lesson.

The implication from the above is that not only can the amount of time in the motor categories be increased but also that it can be used more effectively with intelligent pre-planning in the organization and presentation of the material.

4   Qualitative data

The qualitative data was a little more revealing and highlighted three issues which could improve the teaching and organization of physical education in the secondary school and these are examined in a little more detail.

4.1   *Teaching principles*

With the advent of the National Curriculum and the likely reduction of curriculum time allocated to physical education being reduced to 5%, even less time will be available in the quest to achieve excellence. Many will consider that this will result in a slowing down in the movement towards our eventual goal of achieving excellence and they may well be right. However, this need not necessarily be the case but it is likely that we may have to rethink the methods of achieving some of our aims. For example, games play a dominant role in British education but many of the games appear to be taught as separate components with little emphasis placed on the common elements or principles of games playing. Based on the evidence from the interviews with pupils, it was abundantly clear that the pupils had little or no idea about such principles as creating and moving into space in attack or denying space to the opposition in defence and this was an aspect which was either absent or ineffective in the teaching strategies of most teachers. A greater emphasis on the principles of teaching for transfer could result in more effective teaching.

Similarly, is it necessary for every child to experience playing a large selection of games or would it be sufficient for children to have experience of one or two of invasion (e.g. hockey and basketball), over-the-net (e.g. badminton and volleyball) and striking and fielding games (e.g. cricket and rounders) as three categories identified in the Games for Understanding approach? Thus a coherent programme of work planned along these lines would result in principles being applied to a smaller range of games than is currently being taught in schools. This might prove to be an alternative as well as effective way of coping with a reduction in curriculum time.

4.2   *Principles of fitness*

The development of organic fitness is a common aim for physical education but the sample of lessons observed in this study suggested that the physical is being somewhat neglected in the amount of time devoted to the physical practice as well as to the intensity of the workload. Certainly there was little evidence that pupils were exercising for any length of time in the 'training zone' from which maximum benefit is derived. It could be argued that there is insufficient time allocated to the subject for this to happen and is an unrealistic objective in any case. With a potential reduction of curriculum time in the future it is even less likely that physical education will be able to develop personal fitness levels during lessons. Consequently, it is even more important that children understand the principles of fitness training and have experience of planning and taking responsibility for their own fitness levels. There was some encouraging evidence of this in a few lessons but the vast majority of pupils were unsure and confused about how to develop the different components of fitness. Misconceptions were commonplace and this is an unfortunate reflection on the effectiveness of the teaching in one of the core elements of the physical education curriculum.

Three of the questions on the questionnaire were related to health and fitness. Two of the schools had a coherently planned course in HRF but, surprisingly, had the least positive scores. This suggested that the pupils in these schools had the least positive perceptions about their learning and that more positive results were being obtained in schools where there was no specific course planning in the area. Overall, the evaluation of childrens' learning in this area was disappointing in view of the emphasis on health related fitness in the professional literature and in in-service education over the last few years.

If physical education is to have a life-long effect on the lifestyle of teenagers, a coherent and logical programme must be planned which emphasizes the importance of a healthy life style. More importantly, it must be taught effectively and be based on personal experience. This will obviously be multi-disciplinary in nature and may well link with other subjects such as science and personal and social education. It is important that this core element is practically based but that the related theory is incorporated into the teaching. But above all, it is essential that the principles of achieving and maintaining a healthy lifestyle are learnt by the pupils and incorporated into their normal living. This should become one of the major thrusts of the subject in the future and need not necessarily take up excessive amounts of curriculum time if a 'principles approach' is adopted.

4.3 *Departmental planning*

All the schools had boys' and girls' departments but only in one school were the two departments fully integrated. This was clearly reflected in the integrated and well-planned syllabus which had been devised, discussed and agreed by all the staff. The main components of curriculum planning, viz: aims and objectives, content, method and evaluation were all considered at regular monthly department meetings. This had resulted in a cohesive department with a shared ideology. All the other schools had quite separate and autonomous departments with an administrative head and it was exceptional for the staff to meet to discuss the programme. It is difficult to justify this segregation when the aims and content of the subject are so similar. As a result, the best use was not being made of the available staff resources. With the advent of mixed physical education in secondary schools, there will be greater pressure and even more justification for a 'coming together' of the male and female staff in the planning and implementation of the physical education curriculum in the future. As a result, a more efficient and effective programme could emerge.

5   Summary

From the evidence presented in this research study, it would appear that the standard of teaching and learning was rather mixed. There was some evidence of excellence but the majority of the teaching and learning suggested that the movement towards excellence was not proceeding as fast as it might. The suggestions which have been made in this paper should help to accelerate this movement as well as to cope with the potential reduction of physical education time in the school curriculum.

6   References

Crum, B.J. (1984) The use of learner reports for exploring teacher effectiveness in physical education. Paper presented at the Olympic Scientific Congress, University of Oregon.
Underwood G.L. (1983) **The physical education curriculum in the secondary school: planning and implementation.** Falmer Press.
Underwood G.L. (1988) **Teaching and learning in physical education: a social psychological perspective.** Falmer Press.

A COMMENTED ANALYSIS OF THE QUÉBEC TEACHER INDUCTION SYSTEM: ONE LAW, TWO WAYS OF LIVING IT!

A. HUPÉ[1], C. PARÉ[2] AND A.M. LOISELLE[1]
[1]*Université du Québec à Montréal, Montréal, Canada*
[2]*Université du Québec à Trois-Rivières, Trois-Rivières, Canada*

Abstract
This paper analyses the Québec Teacher Probation System, a two-year programme designed originally to support the integration of new teachers into the profession. Since it got under way in 1969, it has been through more downs than ups. The time frame is divided in three sections: before 1969, 1969 to present day, and what lies ahead for the 90's. The analysis is conducted from two standpoints, the formal intentions and the informal, day to day reality as seen through two cultural biases, two sets of different perspectives. Before 1969 there was no formal teacher induction in Québec. The probation system was tested then implemented between 1969 and 1971. It was conceived as a natural outcome of the professional requirements for teacher certification. However, as early as 1970 the formal induction period was doomed for political and administrative reasons. Some schools found ways of making the system work while others turned it exclusively into a testing period for beginning teachers. As for the future, two distinct options seem to emerge, one is characterized by collaborative efforts between the work place and the universities, and the other consists of eliminating probation altogether while integrating the induction objective into a two-year teacher education programme after a three year non-teaching university degree.
Keywords: Teacher Induction, Certification, Québec, Probation, Integration.

1 Introduction

This paper considers teacher induction as the first two years of professional practice, and as such will analyse the Québec Teacher Probation System from two standpoints: the formal intentions, and the informal, day to day reality as seen through cultural and political biases, through different sets of perspectives. It will also allude to what lies ahead, to what shapes seem to emerge for the teacher induction process from the new multicultural, 'global village', collaborative partnership that is slowly characterizing Québec.

In Canada, Education comes under the jurisdiction of provinces. Thus Québec enacted statutes concerning induction into teaching.

2 What is teacher induction?

The writings consulted on teacher induction used key words like transition, adaptation, assistance, orientation, autonomous full-time involvement, full-load, to qualify the **'most crucial period in a teacher's career'** (Dillon-Peterson, in Varah 1982).

In the teaching profession we have a very particular way of welcoming a neophyte into the ranks. In fact, in many countries including Canada, teaching is the only profession in which a neophyte is placed, immediately upon graduation, in the arena and asked to tame the lions. And to make the challenge even greater, often this new teacher is even given the most difficult students under the worst working conditions. In other professions, the neophyte is not allowed to practice alone for a year or two, as he (she) is overseen continuously by a tutor (a senior professional), and is given simple tasks to perform. Why is it not so in teaching?

We have to think seriously about what **induction** means. Do we want it to be an integral part of the teacher selection process, of the hiring process, because, in that capacity, induction becomes the survival of the fittest in running the gauntlet of professional competition. Or does it include both objectives! It is up to us, as a profession, to decide. Could these be good questions to be addressed by all participants at this symposium on teacher induction!

For the purpose of this paper, **induction** is seen under the form of the Québec Teaching Probation system which entails a two-year full-time teaching period in which a candidate, having satisfied partially the qualifying components or certification, demonstrates the required abilities to obtain a teaching certificate (Legendre, 1988; El Masri, 1971).

Coach will be used to refer to the 'assistance-orientation' aspects of induction, while **evaluate** or **judge** will characterize the summative evaluative concerns found in analysing the Québec Teacher Probation System.

3 Methodology

The data for this paper come firstly from a review of pertinent literature, and secondly from interviews conducted with eight carefully selected individuals which are, or have been, significantly involved directly in the Québec Teacher Probation System. In order to account for the varied points of view on the subject we have solicited opinions respecting a multifaceted matrix (Catholic/Protestant and French/English, for the Québec Ministry of Education, schools, teachers' unions, and universities).

4   The evolution of the Québec teacher induction system: then and now!

Since the Québec Teacher Probation System was introduced in 1969 it has been 'lived' under different contexts and with more downs than ups. These particularities stem from labour/management confrontations and from cultural groundings.

4.1 *Before 1969*

Before 1969 there was no **formal** teacher induction in Québec. Upon graduation from 'Normal Schools' or universities teachers received 'full certification', and were *ipso facto* full-fledged teachers. In this context, the 'better' principals practised some informal, common sense assistance to beginning teachers, and government 'inspectors' were attentive towards new-comers. However, there was an interesting intentional procedural gap on the 'Protestant' side of the coin, as McGill University insisted that each neophyte be involved in a period of in-the-field-full-time successful supervised teaching before recommending to the government the issuance of a teaching certificate (see Fig. 1).

4.2 *As of 1969*

The Parent Report, which in 1965 overhauled the educational system, suggested the institution of a two-year probationary period for all teachers entering the profession. That recommendation was tested then implemented between 1969 and 1971. In 1969, the Normal Schools were abolished as the full mandate to train teachers was given to universities.

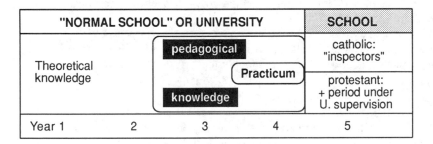

Figure 1.   *Before 1969*

As illustrated in the Figure 2, the Québec Probation System was conceived as a natural outcome of the professional requirements for teacher certification. The Reglement no.4 issued in April of 1966, contains the basic elements that must be met by all Québec teacher training programmes, regardless of level, subject matter, or speciality. Figure 3 presents the seven criteria for teaching certification.

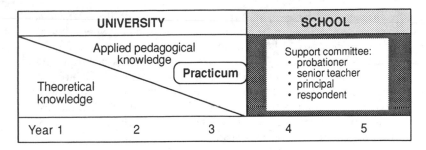

Figure 2. *As of 1969, as conceived by the developers*

Responsibility		Qualifying component	Certification
U	1.	Personality adapted to teaching	
N			
I	2.	Mastery of teaching language (French or	
V		English)	
E	3.	Aptitude for practice teaching	
R	4.	Knowledge in pedagogy	Permit
S	5.	Knowledge of Quebec school system	
I	6.	Knowledge of teaching field (content, level)	
T			
Y			
Minister under recommendation from probation committee	7.	Knowledge, abilities to exercise professional practice (Probation)	'Brevet'

Figure 3. *Teaching Certification Criteria*

4.3 *From 1969 to today*

At the onset, the teacher induction system seemed to flourish. However, as early as 1970 the formal induction period was doomed for three main reasons. Firstly, the large Catholic teachers' union convinced its membership to **coach** the new colleagues but to refuse to **judge** the performance of peers; thus jeopardizing the entire concept. This came about since a tripartite 'encadrement' (professional support) was at the core of the system. In fact, the neophyte, a senior colleague, and the school principal constituted the 'probationary committee'. This committee had to agree unanimously for the teacher-candidate to be certified. However, this requirement has shrunk with the passage of time. From unanimity it went to majority, and finally to only one decision, the administrator's.

Secondly, in reaction to the teachers' refusal, enhanced by a desire to affirm their responsibilities, some principals and government employees took it upon themselves to run the system on their own. Thus, the emphasis slid from 'formative' to 'summative', and then to 'selective' policies. Many administrators saw the hiring of teachers as their responsibility and probation as being 'one' aspect of the hiring process. Furthermore, they invented and cultivated what they called **temporary equivalent full-time** teaching appointments which were held, for example, by some individuals for seven years before occupying a tenure track position. This reinforced the **selective** dimension of probation.

Thirdly, a factor with gruesome results, especially when mixed with the previously mentioned difficulties, came from the oversupply of Catholic teachers. This situation rendered the two-year probation within a five year period impossible for large numbers of candidates since very few teaching appointments were available. Thus the spirit of a full-time two-year massive integration was transformed, for a large segment of the new formula of equivalent full-time teaching. Moreover these part-time opportunities were done in different settings (subject matter, level, ...); factors which did not favour continuity of training.

Ever since that 1970 day, the teacher probation system has been in limbo for lack of **political will** on the government's part, even though there is an **institutional will**.

Probation has been 'lived' basically under two interpretations expressed in Figure 4.

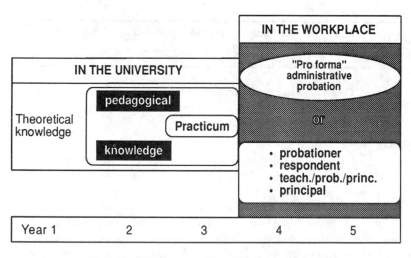

Figure 4.   *How it was transformed and as it stands today*

In 1981, officials from the Québec Ministry of Education proceeded to re-write the procedures in order to make the probation system work. In so doing they indicated minimum and maximum structures. This led basically to two interpretations as expressed in Figure 4. In **situation A** school administrators have taken over the system for what they say is a lack of support from 'the other side' (teachers' unions), and have developed 'pro forma' administrative and normative procedures under a literal interpretation of the 1981 minimal requirements for teacher probation. In **situation B** other principals have interpreted the same policies differently, and proceeded, with the co-operation of senior teachers, to operationalize a larger five-person committee. Since this formula involved more people it tended to be less conflictual, less political, while still maintaining the non-involvement of teachers in the **evaluation** process, yet positively supporting the **coaching** aspects of induction. In this structure the committee involved the probationer, the respondent (a senior teacher chosen by the probationer), the principal, a person chosen by the principal, and another senior teacher chosen jointly by the probationer and the principal.

5   What is emerging in the 90's

As powerful, yet slowly and firmly, rising swells of change are beginning to assert themselves throughout the world, they are too being felt in Québec. These changes have political, cultural, economical, and more specifically educational consequences. Some of these have profound implications for teacher induction as they touch the very definition of schooling. These are, among others: a very powerful shift in paradigm from 'positivism' to 'neo-positivism' to 'post-positivism'; from 'disciplinary' to 'multi-disciplinary' to 'cross disciplinary' to 'trans-disciplinary' development of knowledge; from 'knowing' to 'being' in the definition of objectives; from 'summative' to 'formative evaluation'; from 'individual production' to 'collective/co-operative /collaborative productions' (Van der Maren, 1986). These trends have been mentioned in one form or another by 10 out of the 12 speakers at the 'Active Living' conference organised by Ottawa last March in which 200 'decision makers' from across Canada were gathered, to 'think strategies for change' (Fitness Canada, 1990).

Specifically, concerning teacher induction in Québec we are confronted with two distinct options. One, expressed in Figure 5 as a re-visited version of figure 2 served with a 'sauce' of the 90's and characterized by collaborative efforts between the work place (schools, school boards) and the universities. Or another expressed in Figure 6, a more dramatic and pragmatic solution, which consists of shooting induction into oblivion, or so to speak, going back to square one, back to Figure 1. In this situation the teacher preparation is taken over exclusively by the teacher training institutions. As an old grandfather used to say: 'The more things change the more they stay the same!'.

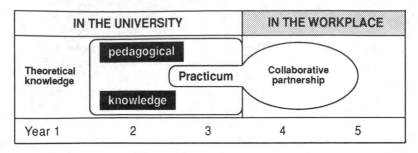

Figure 5.   *Option 1 emerging in the 90's*

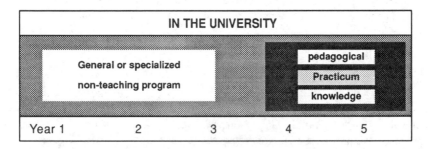

Figure 6.   *Option 2 emerging in the 90's, or variations on the same theme*

Education in Québec is facing difficult challenges. To name a few: the intentional shift from religiously to linguistically defined parameters, the ageing of teaching personnel which leads the school authorities and the teachers' unions to want to be involved in the preparation of the next generation of teachers as 50% of teachers are retiring in 5 years and 75% in 8 years, and lastly the demographic phenomenon of immigration which is tilting the scales; for example in some Montreal schools the student body is 80% allophone, to mean other than French or English speaking.

6   Conclusion

It is hard to foresee exactly from the literature consulted or from the people interviewed which road Québecers will choose concerning teacher induction. However, we can say that just as Québecers have had recently to create the 'Québecois de souche' concept to cope with the ever complex and dynamic reality of our modern society, they will adapt. Even though the two founding communities have strongholds and roots, the multi-ethnic demographic impact has already begun to erode the past structures and mould an open-end future for Québec.

7 References

Daoust, J. (1969) La Certification des Maîtres: Projet de Recherche 4211, **Service de Recherche,** Corporation des Enseignants du Québec, Québec.

El Masri, W. (1971) **Le Système de Probation des Enseignants,** Université du Quèbec à Montréal, Montréal.

Fédération des Cégeps, (ND). Le Règlement No 4 et le Niveau Collégial (la certification des maîtres), proposition du comité de la fédération des Cégeps (Version provisoire), **Fédération des Cégeps,** Montreal.

Fitness Canada (1990) **Active and Healthy Living: a Dialogue on Teacher Preparation,** A Joint Venture of six Governmental, Para Governmental, and Private Agencies or Associations Co-ordinated by Fitness Canada, Ottawa.

Guba, E. and Lincoln, Y. (1989) **Fourth Generation Evaluation,** SAGE Publications, Newburg Park, CA.

Guba, E. and Lincoln, Y. (1985) **Naturalistic Inquiry,** SAGE Publications, Newburg Park, CA.

Legendre, R. (1988) **Dictionnaire Actuel de l'Éducation,** Larousse; Paris-Montréal.

Pagé, L. (1990) La Formation des Maîtres: Enjeux et Défis Actuels, Notes pour l'intervention de Lorraine Pagé, présidente de la **CEQ,** à l'occasion des fêtes du XXe anniversaire de l'Université du Québec à Montréal, **CEQ,** Montréal.

Parent, A.-M. (1965) **Rapport de la Commission Royale d'Enquête sur l'Enseignement dans la Province de Québec,** Gouvernement de la province de Québec, tome II, Québec.

Stewart, D.K. (1986) The Eric Clearinghouse on Teacher Education. **Journal of Teacher Education,** 27, 1, 35-37.

Van Der Maren, J. M. (1986) Revoir la Recherche en Éducation; Cesser de Prédire pour Mieux Comprendre. **Repères,** 6, 100-140.

Varah, L.J. et al., (1976) Beginning Teachers: Sink or Swim? **Journal of Teacher Education,** 27, 1, 30-34.

CRITICAL ISSUES IN ELEMENTARY SCHOOL EDUCATION: INTEGRATION AND THE CURRICULUM

G.J. FISHBURNE[1] AND I.R. HASLAM[2]
[1]*University of Alberta, Edmonton, Canada*
[2]*University of Western Ontario, London, Canada*

Abstract

In Alberta the Government publication 'Program of Studies for Elementary Schools' (1988) lays the foundation for discrete subject area delineation and dictates the minimum percentage of time to be allocated to each area. This is done in order to indicate the 'degree of importance' to be attached to each discrete subject. The wisdom of such an approach has been questioned elsewhere (see Fishburne, 1983a and Boras and Fishburne, 1986). Such legislation produces a typical timetable which is dominated by language arts (Fishburne, 1989) and emphasizes a group of discrete subject areas deemed 'core'. Non-core subject areas receive little emphasis and are usually treated as frills or extras compared to the important 'core' subjects. The major thesis of this paper is that the development of the whole child should be the overriding factor in curriculum design and that discrete subject area delineation, ranked on degree of importance, should be eliminated. Instead, an integrated approach to learning is advocated at the elementary school level, with all subject areas forming equally important criteria for inclusion. Results from two research projects, which support the benefits of an integrated approach to learning, are reviewed and discussed with reference to curriculum planning and teacher education.
<u>Keywords:</u> Integration, Curriculum, Critical Issues, Elementary School.

1   Introduction

Observing children in an elementary school setting is quite an enlightening experience. As children move from classroom to gymnasium, teachers often experience difflculty in controlling the children's eagerness and natural excitement. Given the opportunity, children would run to the gymnasium. Such is not the case when children are confronted with the subject area of mathematics. Usually, children do not 'run' to mathematics; they do not seem to think that mathematics is an exciting subject area, one that needs to be learned as part of the school curriculum. Yet, it is mathematics that is deemed 'basic' to a child's development, and not physical education. In fact, physical education does not even make the list of 'core' subjects in the opinion of many educators. The result is a school subject area that gets little attention, is poorly planned for, is hardly ever evaluated properly, and is used as extrinsic motivator or as punishment to control the behavior of children. It would be difficult to find, or even imagine, another school subject area that is abused to the same degree.

Any time a large area is needed for school activities, the gymnasium is taken over and physical education is cancelled. The school play, Christmas concert, band practice, examinations, etc., are all considered to be valued educational experiences and so it is felt justified to take over the gymnasium. Instead of making alternative arrangements, physical education is often cancelled. If a child misbehaves, the child is often held back from physical education. If a child needs remedial help in one of the 'core' subject areas, they are often provided with the extra tuition during the physical education curriculum time. No other subject area is treated with such disrespect, although music and art fair only slightly better.

The 'non-core' subject areas of physical education, music and art rightfully claim their place in the elementary school curriculum, yet in practice these subject areas are frequently treated as extras or frills. They are not felt to be part of the total process of education, contributing to the development of the whole child; for if they were, they would not be treated as 'non-core', 'non-basic' subjects.

2   Basic Education

The real question is, 'what is basic?' Historically the three R's have come to be known as the basics and clearly these three areas do play a very important role in a child's development. Yet, are these areas more 'basic' and more 'important' than other areas of development? Is physical and motor development not 'basic' to life? Could we get by in life without movement? Could we get by in life without reading or without a knowledge of algebra? Clearly, if a person was unable to move it would be difficult to suggest they would be able to function independently in society and experience much of life. One might argue the same for an illiterate person. However, according to the Southam Literacy Survey (1987) almost one quarter of the Canadian adult population is functionally illiterate, yet these people function in society. Evidence of this is revealed in the Southam Survey; of the 24% functionally illiterate, the Survey revealed that 75% of these people did not feel handicapped and had no intention of seeking remedial help to provide them with the 'basics' they had failed to grasp in school.

3   An Integrated Approach to Learning

It has been suggested that at the elementary school level discrete subject area delineation should be de-emphasized and that a more integrated approach should be utilized. However, is there any evidence to suggest that an integrated approach would be a better way to educate elementary school children? Would there be any benefit, for example, if 'movement' was given greater emphasis in the learning situation? Surveying the educational literature reveals a wealth of evidence to suggest that what is occurring in today's typical elementary school classroom is not necessarily in the best interest of children. For example, Plato wrote in 'The Republic' over two thousand years ago, 'do not, then my friend keep children to their studies by compulsion but by play' (cited in Kline, 1977, p.199). No doubt Plato realized the importance of the sensory modes associated with the natural enjoyment of movement and play, and how it is necessary to capitalize on these sensory experiences when a child is learning any subject area.

Today, teachers rely almost entirely on the child's sensory experiences of vision and hearing as the modes of communication when learning situations are planned. It is not uncommon to see children spend many hours doing sedentary seat work, having to rely on vision and hearing as their major form of sensory input. However, this would seem to be at odds with what we know about brain development. Almost a quarter of a century ago Steinhaus (1966) reported that,

> A larger portion of the nervous system is devoted to receiving and integrating sensory input originating in the muscles and joint structures than is devoted to the eye and ear combined. (p.38)

The brain has evolved to devote so much of its functional area to movement, and yet our schools have evolved to devote so little of its curriculum to movement. Educators have been slow to respond to the research and thoughts surrounding the integrated nature of learning and to the unique link between mind and body. J. Welton, a Professor of Education, wrote over three quarters of a century ago in 1912,

> ...the need of children for bodily activity is being increasingly acknowledged in practice, though slowly and somewhat grudgingly. Despite all the indications of nature, children of five years of age and upwards are still made to sit for long hours at desks, mainly looking and listening. Public opinion is satisfied if a few minutes daily be spent in the playground and if, two or three times a week, the children be put through some form of bodily drill. Even these deliverances from the desks are, however, advocated purely from a physical standpoint. Consequently, as long as bodily growth goes on normally everything is regarded as satisfactory. Modern knowledge enables us to go further and to affirm that the relation between body and mind is so intimate and constant that the intelligence is dwarfed whenever the demand for bodily activity is not met. (p.78)

Welton quoted 'modern knowledge' as the source linking mind and body, and this was almost eighty years ago. Since this time there have been many research citations to support and verify the connection between movement and development. For example, Johnson (1987) recently published a book entitled: 'The Body in the Mind' where he shows how all knowledge originates in bodily experiences. Even with this lengthy history linking movement to learning, little has been done to incorporate movement into the classroom. In fact, the educational thrust over the years would appear to have been to almost eliminate movement, rather than to capitalize on its contribution to learning!

4   Integrated Learning - Research Evidence

The findings from two research studies will be briefly outlined here to provide evidence of the effectiveness of an integrated approach to learning. Brown, Sherrill, and Gench (1981) reported on the effects of an integrated physical education and music programme in changing early childhood perceptual motor performance. They used two approaches to facilitate perceptual-motor development in children. One group of children (experimental group) received an integrated physical education/music programme based upon the concepts forwarded by the prominent music educators Kodaly and Dalcroze. The control group of children experienced a movement programme for an equivalent length of time. Although movement exploration was stressed, there was no music or singing in the control group's programme. At the completion of the two programmes, significant differences were found between the two groups of children. The integrated physical education/music programme was more effective in improving children's motor, auditory, and language aspects of perceptual-motor performance. Brown et al. stated that music should not be taught as a separate unit but instead, integrated with all movement experiences.

The second study to be reviewed is a research project that was undertaken at the University of Alberta by Boras (1988), where an integrated teaching approach with grade one children was employed. Specifically, the study was undertaken to evaluate and compare the difference between an Orff-Schulwerk music programme and the more traditional approach of teaching music education. Motor development, music skill acquisition, and children's attitude toward school and subject area were the variables under consideration. Boras reported that the quality of movement displayed by the Orff-Schulwerk group of children far surpassed the movement of the non-Orff group of children; thus adding credence to Brown et al.'s earlier findings of superior learning when an integrated approach is employed. Boras also noted that while the Orff students did not significantly differ from the more traditionally taught music students on music skill acquisition, it was apparent that their attitude toward music and the development of music skills was more positive than that displayed by the non-Orff group of students. It is not feasible in this paper to discuss the entire findings emanating for the Boras (1988) study. However, one of the main points recorded was the incredible integration available through the Orff-Schulwerk approach. The educational experiences the children underwent naturally crossed the artificial subject area boundaries in a truly integrated manner. The children were bound up in the excitement of an approach that encompassed dance, music, poetry, story, art, movement and drama, in addition to many other areas of the curriculum, as themes naturally flowed across all curricula areas. In addition to the children who enjoyed the Orff-Schulwerk integrated approach, the teachers involved in the Boras study also enjoyed such an integrated programme and viewed the Orff-Schulwerk approach as being:

(a)   An approach which requires the total involvement of the children motorically, cognitively and emotionally;

(b)   An approach which is child-centered. The teacher and student exist in a symbiotic relationship;

(c)   An approach which utilizes activities suited to the child's developmental level and interest level;

(d)   An approach which contributes to skill and conceptual development. All children are involved all of the time thereby refining their skills;

(e)   An approach which can assist children in feelings of self-confidence. Since the children are involved in a 'fun' way, they are more relaxed and less likely to harbor feelings of 'I can't!' - Positive feelings of self-esteem are more likely to emerge.

(Boras, 1988. pp.115-116)

The studies by Brown et al. (1981) and Boras (1988) clearly indicate the link between mind and body in learning and development. Children's movement experiences are intimately connected with their intellectual, emotional, aesthetic, social, physical and motor development. In other words, movement is tied to human development (Fishburne, 1983b). To abuse and play down the importance of movement/physical education in elementary school education is to affect the integrated nature of natural human development.

5   Teacher Education and Curriculum Planning

It was suggested earlier that educational change is a slow process. Indeed, the discrete subject area approach is firmly entrenched in both our school systems and in the teacher education programs which produce, train and educate new elementary school teachers. Changes must occur at all levels if a more meaningful education of young children is to take place. The evidence is available to show the link between mind and body; what is needed now is a firm commitment from all parties who carry a vested interest in the education of children and who currently influence elementary school education. This will require changes in attitude and educational policy all the way from Government agencies and teacher education programmes, to school teachers, Principals and finally parents. They must be educated into knowing what Williams clearly identified in 1983 when he wrote,

Children come to school as integrated people with thoughts and feelings, words and pictures, ideas and fantasies. They are intensely curious about the world. They are scientists, artists, musicians, historians, dancers and runners, tellers of stories, and mathematicians. The challenge we face as teachers is to use the wealth they bring us. (p. 189)

If teachers can provide these 'integrated people' with a truly integrated curriculum, then perhaps children will 'run' to school and not just to 'non-core' discrete subject areas like physical education.

6   References

Boras, C.M. (1988) The Orff-Schulwerk and Traditional Music Education: A Comparison of Approach. Unpublished Masters Thesis, University of Alberta, Alberta, Canada.

Boras, C.M. and Fishburne, G.J. (1986) Music and educational legitimacy: A time for change. **Elements: A Journal for Elementary Education,** 18(1), 4-8.

Brown, J., Sherrill, C. and Gench, B. (1981) Effects of an integrated physical education/music program in changing early childhood perceptual-motor performance. **Perceptual and Motor Skills,** 53, 151- 154.

Fishburne, G.J. (1983a) Is reading more important than physical education? **Elements: A Journal for Elementary Education,** 15(1), 3-5.

Fishburne, G.J. (1983b) Explaining the mystery of movement. **Elements: A Journal for Elementary Education,** 15(1), 18-21.

Fishburne, G.J. (1989) The link between mind and body: Implications for curriculum planning, in **Issues in Teacher Education: Proceedings of the 1989 ATEPE Society Annual Meeting** (eds G.J.Fishburne and D.A.Sande). Faculty of Education Publication, University of Alberta, Edmonton, pp.24-43.

Johnson, M. (1987) **The Body in the Mind: The Bodily Basis of Meaning, Imagination and Reason.** University of Chicago Press, Chicago.

Kline, M. (1977) **Why the Professor Can't Teach: Mathematics and the Dilemma of University Education.** Academic Press, New York.

Program of Studies for Elementary Schools. (1988) Alberta Education (Provincial Government), Edmonton.

Southam Literacy Survey. (1987) Southam News, Ottawa, Ontario.

Steinhaus, A.H. (1966, September) Your muscles see more than your eyes. **Journal of Health, Physical Education, and Recreation,** 38-40.

Welton, J. (1912) **The Psychology of Education.** MacMillan, London.

Williams, L.V. (1983) **Teaching for the Two Sided Mind.** Simon & Schuster, New York.

MODIFIED AUSTRALIAN SPORTS — QUALITY PARTICIPATION FOR ALL CHILDREN — AN EVALUATION UPDATE

KEN HAWKINS[1]
Ballarat University College, Ballarat, Australia

Abstract

This paper overviews a comprehensive national programme developed by the Australian Sports Commission and The Australian Council for Health, Physical Education and Recreation aimed at providing students in the final three years of primary school with a diversified and improved quality of sports participation, and provides an evaluation of its effectiveness in meeting the following aims: (a) help promote existing sporting and physical education programmes; (b) promote modified sports for children, allowing them to play sport which is suited to the physical, intellectual and emotional development of each child; (c) encourage social, personal and skill development rather than the 'win at all costs' attitude; (d) provide incentives for children to begin and continue participating in a variety of sports; (e) encourage parent and community involvement in children's sport whether it be through the school or local sports club; (f) give resource assistance by providing teachers and other interested people with educational materials and suggested teaching activities for over 30 sports; (g) provide information and suggested teaching activities to tackle a number of major sporting issues. For example, drugs in sports, the importance of good behaviour in sport, sports first aid and the historical and social significance of sport in Australia. The major research strategies adopted by the evaluators were: (a) Surveys of participant schools; (b) Interviews with Aussie Sports personnel; (c) Collation of data collected by Aussie Sports co-ordinators; (d) Telephone interviews with non-participant schools.

---

[1] I would acknowledge the work of J. Clough and R. Traill in the preparation of the reports listed in the references upon which this paper has been based. The tables presented in this paper are taken directly from the Clough and Traill reports.

1   Introduction

Concern about junior sport participation has received widespread debate over many years in Australian educational and sporting institutions. On the basis of these discussions and data collected by many researchers able to make observations relating to the role of modified sports in Australian sports participation, a modified junior sports programme called 'Aussie Sports' was developed and promoted for use through school and community sporting organizations. This comprehensive national programme and associated coaching development component was launched in 1986 for all children in their last three years of Primary School with the aims of:

(a)   To improve the quality, quantity and variety of sporting activities available to Australian children.
(b)   To provide all children with the opportunity to participate in appropriate sporting activities.
(c)   To encourage participation and skill development in a variety of sports.
(d)   To reduce the emphasis on 'win at all costs' and promote enjoyment and good competition through participation in sport.
(e)   To promote the principles of good sporting behaviour.
(f)   To improve the quality of sports instruction available to Australian children.

This Aussie Sports programme was a unique development in Australian and educational history in response to concerns expressed by the teaching profession, sports administrators and government ministers that children's sport, in particular, should be diversified and improved. It was also a reflection of the belief that all sectors of the community should pay more attention to attitudes and behaviour in sport participation.

In order to gauge the impact of the programme, annual evaluations in 1986, 1987 and 1988, were carried out. Evidence from these studies indicated that modified sports were producing outcomes such as increased enthusiasm from children aged 7 to 12 years towards sports, improved participation rates among children and particularly girls, and an increase in skill levels in a variety of sports.

In evaluating the Aussie Sports programme, four major research processes were adopted viz.:

(a)   Surveys of participant schools
(b)   Interviews with Aussie Sports personnel
(c)   Collation of data collected by Aussie Sports co-ordinators
(d)   Telephone interviews with non-participant schools

It is worth noting the growth of Aussie Sports programmes adopted by schools. In 1986, 449 schools were involved in the programme, in 1987 this had increased to 919 schools while in 1988, 2,040 schools indicated adoption of the Aussie Sports curriculum. This figure, however, only represents 26% of Australian Primary Schools.

2   Findings

Some of the more interesting findings from the Aussie Sports evaluations are now presented.

2.1 *Participation rates*

Participation rates were found to be evenly distributed across grade 4 to 7 groupings, thus confirming the Australian Sports Commission plans for Aussie Sports to be used by all children in the later years of Primary Schools (Table 1). There is also strong agreement that Aussie Sports continues to result in more Primary School children participating in sports than had previously been achieved and that such participation was leading to increased self-esteem in these children (Table 2). Similarly there is evidence that increased participation rates in sports in schools is transferring to children participating in larger numbers in community sport. This phenomena is to be evaluated further in the next stage.

Table 1.   Participation Rates in Schools

| | No. of Children in School | | | No. of Children participating in Aussie Sports | | |
Class	Boys	Girls	Total	Boys	Girls	Total
K-3	162	151	313	157	133	290
4	1080	992	2072	934	855	1789
5	1097	1073	2170	976	937	1913
6	1077	1033	2110	952	931	1883
7	328	379	707	314	369	683
Totals	3744	3628	7372	3333	3225	6558

Table 2.   *Reasons for Joining Aussie Sports*

Reason	No. of Schools Stating Reason
Increased children's participation in sport	46
Variety of sports	42
Skills development	38
Modified versions of sports	25
Quality of instruction	13
Improved sporting behaviour	12
Positive, healthy lifestyle	8
Non-competitive sport	7
Less emphasis on winning	6
Equal opportunity for girls	6
Awards scheme	3
Attracted by publicity	3

2.2 *The Variety of Sports*

The variety of sports presented in the Aussie Sports programme and reflected in Table 3 continues to be highly valued by teachers. The main sports utilized are Kanga Cricket (modified Cricket), Netball, Minkey (modified Hockey), Tee Ball (modified Baseball/Softball), Basketball and Soccer.

Table 3. *Aussie Sports in Schools (N = 37)*

Sport Category	No. of Schools	Sport Category	No. of Schools
Athletics	9	Rollerskating	1
Mini-athletics	1	Mini-footy	2
Australian Football	3	Mini-rugby	3
Aussie Footy	5	Soccer	11
Badminton	2	Mini-soccer	7
Ball games and skills	1	Football	5
Baseball	2	Softball	10
Tee-ball	19	Junior softball	1
Basketball	8	Squash	1
Mini-basketball	2	Table Tennis	1
Bike riding	1	Tennis	5
Cricket	6	Mini tennis	1
Kanga cricket	22	Touch	9
Dancing/Skipping	3	Mini-touch	1
Gymnastics	3	Trampolining	1
Gym-fun	1	Underwater sports	1
Hockey	8	Volleyball	10
Marching	1	Mini-volleyball	7
Minkey	19	Flippa ball	1
Judo	1	Royal Water Safety	1
Korfball	2	Wrestling	1
Sof-crosse	14	Swimming	8
Netball	14	Newcombe	2
Netta netball	6	Paddle/hand Tennis	2
Orienteering	2	Contin.cricket/Indoor Cricket/Vigaro	2

2.3 *Parental Influence*

There is evidence that there is an improvement in the way children view their parents' participation in and knowledge of the Aussie Sports programme. It may be argued that increased publicity of the programme, particularly through television media, was a factor in increasing the knowledge of parents about Aussie Sports.

3   Modified Sports at Community Level

One of the findings described above indicated the influence of Aussie Sports in Schools upon participation rates by children in community sport. The Australian Sports Commission conducted a national survey to determine the extent to which various sports associations and clubs were modifying their sports at junior level and to determine what links were developing between sporting associations and clubs and schools, particularly in promoting modified sports.

A number of general conclusions were derived from the data and are summarized below.

3.1   *Modifications*

The use of modified versions of sports is a well accepted practice in Australian sport. Of the 34 sports surveyed, 33 reported having made some modification to their respective sports. Some of these modifications are reflected in Table 4. The degree of modifications varies between individual sports, nonetheless 140 of the 166 sporting associations stated that the modifications they had developed had enhanced their particular sport.

3.2   *Aussie Sports and Community Sports Links*

Survey findings indicate that there is a strong link between the 34 sports, their modified programmes and the Aussie Sports programme. 30 of the 34 sports indicated being involved in Aussie Sports, while also indicating coaching personnel taking an active role in teaching of Aussie Sports. In relation to coaching, 133 of the 166 associations stated they had policies relating to coaching development programmes for personnel involved in coaching roles in their sports.

Table 4.   Characteristics of Modified Sports

Modification	Version A		Version B		Version C	
	Yes	No	Yes	No	Yes	No
Scaled down area	107	12	57	8	17	15
Modified equipment	115	8	69	12	24	18
Shorter playing time	103	12	58	12	22	11
Rotation of players	91	15	49	15	16	12
Team selection	42	52	31	25	16	9
Fewer players	54	39	30	26	7	6
Competition	93	14	50	16	19	10

3.3 *Perceived Strengths of Modified Sports Programmes*

Sporting associations surveyed nominated the following strengths of modified sports programmes such as Aussie Sports to be:

(a)   Ability to create wider participation
(b)   Presentation of a variety of sports
(c)   Emphasis on skills development
(d)   Creation of a sense of enjoyment of sport for the participants

Perceived strengths of the Aussie Sports programme are reflected in Table 5.

Table 5.   *Major Strengths of Aussie Sports*

Major Strengths	No. of Schools Supporting View
Variety of sports	40
Increased participation	36
Self confidence of children	20
Quality sports instruction	17
Skills development	15
Improved sporting behaviour	11
Enjoyment of Sport	9
Awards scheme	7
Sequential development in school programme	6
Assists teachers	6
Supplements other sports programmes	5
Equipment	5
Availability of coaches	4

3.4 *Difficulties*

Despite the positive feedback regarding the Aussie Sports programme, sports associations noted the following concerns:

(a)   Lack of knowledge and active participation in the programme from school teachers
(b)   Limited resources
(c)   Lack of publicity for programme

4   Conclusion

In terms of the organization of sport in our school and community settings some of the following points warrant consideration. First we need from school principals, guidance and acceptance that physical education and sport education are integral parts of school curriculums and as such should occur on a regular basis emphasizing both fitness and skills development. A second priority in the school curriculum should be the organization, modification and time allowance for participants to learn and experience a diverse range of sports appropriate to their physical and mental growth and development.

In terms of sport education within our schools and community clubs, the emphasis should be on the teaching and coaching of sports skills and techniques required to develop controlled efficient movement and game strategies rather than concentrating on just outstanding performance and the need to win the game at all costs. Participants should be encouraged to strive for excellence in self-performance at their own level of ability rather than striving to beat one's opponents.

Aussie Sports offers resources and advice for the conduct of sport programmes in order that teachers and coaches can make sport experiences more meaningful, relevant and enjoyable for participants. Life was not meant to be easy however, and the role of the teacher or coach is a complex and busy one. Nevertheless I am convinced that the degree of success of sport education programmes will ultimately be determined by the commitment of the teachers and coaches to modify programmes and the level of expertise they bring in delivering the programmes in the most positive environment that can be generated.

5   References

Australian Sports Commission (1985) **Children in Sport Program - Aussie Sports,** Australian Government Printers, Canberra, A.C.T.

Australian Sports Commission (1990) **Aussie Sports Fun - Resource Manual,** Sport and Recreation - Victoria

Clough, J. and Traill, R (1989) **Report of Australian Sports Commission Study of Modified Sports,** Australian Government Printers, Canberra, A.C.T.

Clough, J. and Traill, R. (1989) **The 1988 Evaluation of Aussie Sports,** Australian Government Printers, Canberra, A.C.T.

Ministry of Education (Schools Division), Victoria (1987) **Sport Education** The Education Shop - Materials Production, Melbourne, Victoria.

ASSESSING PUPILS' GAMES PERFORMANCE IN THE SECONDARY SCHOOL: AN EXPLORATION USING REPERTORY GRID TECHNIQUE

ANDREW J BALSDON AND STEPHEN M CLIFT[1]
Christ Church College, Canterbury, England

Abstract
This paper explores the criteria which physical education teachers use in making judgements about pupil performance in basketball and badminton. Ten physical education teachers were asked to make assessments of a video recording of skills and game performance in basketball and a further eleven teachers were asked to make assessments of a video recording of skills and game performance in badminton. The pupils performing in the video recordings were in their fourth year at secondary school and had completed a ten week course in either basketball or badminton as part of their GCSE programme. Twelve pupils participated in the badminton video and ten pupils participated in the basketball video. Personal constructs were elicited from each teacher. The most common constructs identified by the teachers for each game were used to produce a separate composite grid for basketball and badminton. In both cases the grid was divided into skills performance and game performance. Each performance by a pupil was rated using a ten-point scale. Completed grids were analysed individually and comparisons made within and across the badminton and basketball grids. The results reveal substantial consistency in the teachers' independent ratings of pupils' relative performance in both games. There was some variation, however, in absolute grading of performance with some teachers being consistently 'harder' in grading and others 'easier'. The implications of the results for teaching and learning strategies and assessment of physical education in schools are discussed .
Keywords: Assessment, Games performance, Secondary pupils, Teachers constructs, Repertory grid technique.

1   Thanks are due to the Principal and Governing Body of Christ Church College, Canterbury and to the twenty-one teachers and twenty-two pupils who gave so generously of their time and made this study possible.

I   Introduction

In recent years attention has focused on exploring the relationships between different aspects of the physical education curriculum, such as its aims, objectives, methods of delivery, assessment and evaluation. These components are seen to be part of a dynamic interactive process by curriculum theorists (eg Eraut et al, 1985) and as Jewett and Bain (1985) put it, the curriculum process 'is an ongoing cycle of planning, implementation and evaluation' (p 224). The process of evaluation is of particular importance as it serves to guide further planning and implementation of the curriculum.

Assessment of pupil performance is clearly an important part of evaluation in the context of physical education, but such assessment raises difficult issues concerning the criteria to be employed. Some sports performances can be gauged objectively by reference to established norms as, for example, in swimming and athletics, where distances and times serve to provide a basis for grading performance. Such objective standards are not available, however, for assessing performances in team games, racket games, gymnastics and dance. In these areas, grading depends on the skilled observation and experience of the assessors who assign grades using their own personal criteria, (Balsdon and Clift, 1990). The specific criteria and standards adopted by one assessor may differ from those adopted by another. These two factors are likely to account for most of the disagreements which may arise between independent assessments of the same performance. Making these criteria and standards explicit should serve to clarify the basis of disagreements in assessment and help to resolve them.

In addition, some improvement in the quality of practical performance might be achieved through making these criteria explicit and making them available to pupils. A clearer understanding of the criteria by which performance is assessed could serve to encourage pupil self-assessment and help them focus more effectively on the areas of their performance they could usefully work on. It is hoped that the research reported in this paper will go some way towards meeting these goals.

In the secondary school physical education curriculum, a broad, balanced and relevant programme might include the teaching of games, gymnastics, dance, swimming, athletics and outdoor pursuits (DES 1989). The amount of time a pupil would spend on these activities would depend on staff expertise, the time-table and resources available. Practical assessment is a central issue under debate in physical education circles and is particularly pressing at the secondary level given the introduction of GCSE and implementation of the National Curriculum. Both of these innovations in physical education require teachers to make regular assessments of pupils' practical skills. However, the measurement of skills is only part of the assessment process in physical education. As studies by Cope (1985), Kane (1977) and Underwood (1983) have revealed, consideration must also be given to such issues as 'the development of a good attitude', 'enjoyment', and 'social awareness and responsibility' issues which many physical education teachers regard as important objectives in their work with young people.

The development of attainment targets and standard assessment tasks with the introduction of the National Curriculum, should support learning and make it possible for pupils to discuss with teachers the criteria used to assess their performance in physical education. This should help them to develop a clearer understanding of their level of achievement. It is also important for physical education teachers to evaluate their work but as yet, evaluation procedures have not featured very strongly. As Underwood (1983) found, physical education teachers evaluated less than 5% of the syllabus and most of the evaluation undertaken was focused on curriculum content and teaching methods.

1.1 *Personal construct theory and repertory grid technique*

In the present research, the issue of subjective criteria used in assessing physical performance is approached from the perspective of Kelly's (1955) Personal Construct Theory, and use is made of a specially devised form of repertory grid technique to explore the constructions of badminton and basketball performance held by a group of physical education teachers.

Kelly developed his ideas on the basis of his work as a psychotherapist and educator in clinical psychology and saw the person as a practical scientist concerned to understand, predict and control himself and the environment around him. He regarded the search for meaning as central to human psychology and believed that in the process of making sense of experience each person elaborates a set of personal theories for organizing and predicting events within and around him. For Kelly, our constructions of the world are best understood as hypotheses which serve to guide our expectations for the future. This assumption is formally stated in the fundamental postulate which forms the starting point for his theory: 'A person's processes are psychologically channellized by the ways in which he anticipates events'. This postulate is further elaborated by a series of eleven corollaries which provide an account of how construct systems are organized, how they develop and how they change. Kelly also believed that each person's construct system is unique both in its content and structure (the individuality corollary), but that equally, individuals often hold common constructions of the same events (the commonality corollary) and are capable of looking at the world from another's point of view so construing another person's constructions (the sociality corollary).

Basic to the theory is the notion of a construct which Kelly regarded as a discrimination made within an array of similar events (eg people, situations, objects, ideas). A construct is defined as a way in which at least two of these events is similar and thereby different from a third and is always bi-polar, for example, some people may be seen as 'warm' and others by contrast as 'cold'.

One of the techniques Kelly devised for exploring an individual's construct system is the repertory grid. Since its initial development, this technique has been elaborated in several directions and many different forms of repertory grid technique exist (Fransella and Bannister, 1977). The essential features of this approach remain unchanged however. Individuals producing a grid are asked to identify, or are given, a set of elements to construe. These, typically, are people known to the person, but they can be situations, objects, events etc. The person is then asked to consider the elements and identify ways in which they vary from one another. A common approach to help them do this is the triadic elicitation technique. In this method three elements are selected and the person is asked to identify a way in which two are similar to one another and thereby different from the third. Other approaches to elicitation may be adopted where the triadic technique is not practicable. Alternatively, bipolar constructs can be suggested to the person.

Once a construct is identified it can be applied systematically to all elements in the grid. This can be done in a variety of ways, but commonly the person is asked to rate each of the elements on the construct using a 5, 7, or 10 point scale. Eventually, a matrix of ratings is produced which represents the application of all the constructs identified to the set of elements under consideration. This matrix can then be analysed in various ways to clarify the structures of meaning employed by the individual in making sense of his experience.

1.2 *Assessment in physical education and personal construct theory*

It has already been noted that in certain areas of physical performance norms are available to allow for objective assessment eg the time taken to run 100m. However, there are many areas of physical performance where such clear and objective criteria for assessing performance are not available and the teacher/examiner has to draw on his personal experience in making judgements of quality. Clearly, individuals are able to explain the basis of their judgements and criteria of assessment can be discussed, negotiated and agreed to some extent, but inevitably, there is scope for individual variation in the nature of the criteria employed and the standards of judgement made. It is also the case that an individual's skill in assessment will vary according to experience and the level and quality of their interaction with other assessors.

These points are well illustrated by the results of a recent study, (Balsdon and Clift 1990), in which repertory grid technique was used to explore the constructions of undergraduate students' gymnastic performances held by movement studies specialists all of whom had experience of work in a higher education context. Ten specialists viewed video recordings of ten gymnastic routines performed by students as part of their final examinations. Personal constructs of performance qualities were elicited via free description of the routines and discussion. Ten constructs were identified for each participant which were used together with the provided construct 'excellent-poor' to rate each of the performances in turn. Analysis of the resulting grids produced several interesting findings:

(a) Despite grading performances on eleven distinct criteria, a very high degree of internal consistency in the gradings was apparent for all participants. Anchor analysis (Higginbothom and Bannister, 1983) identified only one component for each of the grids.

(b) Overall judgements of performance quality showed substantial levels of concordance across the ten specialists, indicating high levels of agreement in the relative ranking of performances in terms of quality. The participants who were more experienced in the area of gymnastics appeared to be better judges of the relative performance quality.

(c) Despite the high level of agreement over relative rankings, the participants differed substantially in the gradings given, with some assessors consistently over-marking relative to the group and others consistently under-marking.

(d) Analysis of the personal criteria employed revealed a considerable variety of discriminations.

Thus, looked at from a personal construct perspective, teachers/examiners working in the area of physical education will have developed a system of constructs for discriminating among physical performances and making judgements of quality. The constructs employed can be identified and their relationships explored by means of repertory grid technique. In this way, it is possible to clarify the nature of the constructs employed in making assessments, look at the standards implicit in the application of constructs and compare the constructs and standards of application of two or more assessors in making judgements in the same area of physical movement.

1.3 *The present study*

In the present study twenty-one physical education teachers were asked to produce grids based on video-recordings of badminton and basketball skill and game performances. The recordings were of fourth-year pupils who had completed a ten week course as part of GCSE requirements. The objectives of the study were:

(a) to identify the principal criteria teachers use in assessing performance;
(b) to explore the level of agreement in relative ranking of performances and examine the issue of over- and under-assessments of quality, and
(c) to investigate the level of correspondence in making judgements of skill and game performance.

2   Method

2.1 *Sample*

Twenty-one physical education teachers from five state secondary schools and one independent school in East Kent, were invited to participate in this study. The teachers (10 men, 11 females) had differing levels of expertise in either the game of badminton or basketball but all were qualified and experienced in physical education. Fourteen of the teachers had taught physical education for at least five years and fourteen had taught in only one school. Eleven had been in their current school for less than five years. Of the six schools participating in the study, three were involved in teaching GCSE with a total of nine teachers engaged in examination work.

2.2 *Video material employed*

Two video tapes were produced showing badminton and basketball with fourth-year pupils performing skills routines followed by participation in a game. The complete recording for badminton took 24 minutes to view and the basketball took 20 minutes to view.

2.3 *Procedure for grid production*

Eleven teachers viewed the badminton video and ten the basketball video. Two school visits were required, each lasting approximately one hour. On the first visit each participant was asked to watch the video and describe any positive or negative aspect of the performances by the pupils as they occurred. The descriptive comments were recorded. These descriptions were taken to represent the emergent poles of bipolar constructs and once the viewing was complete each participant was asked to identify the contrast poles for each descriptive word or phrase. For example, if a performer had been described as 'consistent' the teacher would be asked: 'What would the opposite of a consistent performance be?' or 'If a performance were not consistent, how would you describe it?' The process of identifying constructs involved some discussion with each teacher to ensure that the distinctions being drawn were clear and to avoid any obvious repetition of constructs. This approach to construct identification was employed since the nature of the video material used in this study would have made it very difficult and time-consuming to use the standard triadic elicitation technique. Following this procedure each teacher was asked to rank order the constructs identified for the skill and game sequences in terms of their importance in making assessments of performance quality. On the basis of the rank order, five of the most important and commonly occurring constructs relating to the skill and to the game contexts were identified for both badminton and basketball. The ten constructs for each game were then used in the second stage of the procedure.

On the second visit the teachers viewed the video again and rated the pupils' skill and game performances on the ten selected constructs using a ten-point rating scale. (see Tables 1 and 2 for examples of completed grids for badminton and basketball). A rating of 1 indicated that the first pole definitely applied and a rating of 10 that the contrasting pole definitely applied. A 10-point scale has no mid-point and required the teachers to decide whether the pupil was at one pole or at the other in varying degrees. Furthermore, a 10-point scale is the marking band used, for assessing practical activities for the Southern Examining Board's GCSE physical education examination which was adopted by three of the participating schools. After scoring each performance the scores were covered so that they would not influence the next set of scores. The teachers could review performances as necessary to enable them to give the appropriate grade.

2.4 *Methods of analysis*

Having obtained repertory grids from the twenty-one teachers, the following forms of analysis were undertaken:

(a) For each teacher mean ratings of each pupil's performance across constructs were calculated and comparisons made across teachers to assess the degree of consistency in their judgements of performance quality. In other words, to what extent did the teachers agree regarding 'good' and 'poor' performances?

(b) In order to assess the levels of over- and under-marking, teachers' mean ratings over all constructs and performances were compared with the overall mean score for all teachers.

(c)   In order to determine whether higher scores were given for skill or game performances teachers' mean ratings over the skill and game constructs for all performances were compared.

3   Results

3.1   *The constructs*

Tables 1 and 2 report completed examples of the repertory grids used by teachers in grading badminton and basketball performance. In both cases constructs 1-5 relate to the skills routine and constructs 6-10 relate to the game situation.

Table 1.   *Repertory grid rating sheet for assessing practical performance in Badminton completed by Teacher One*

CONSTRUCTS	ELEMENTS											
	1	2	3	4	5	6	7	8	9	10	11	12
Skill												
1 Correct body position vs Incorrect body position	4	5	6	3	4	2	6	4	7	8	8	9
2 Correct skill execution vs Incorrect skill execution	5	5	5	4	4	3	6	4	7	7	7	9
3 Good footwork vs Poor footwork	4	4	6	3	5	2	6	3	7	9	7	9
4 Very mobile vs Lack of mobility	4	4	6	3	5	2	5	3	7	8	7	8
5 Good use of the wrist vs Poor use of the wrist	5	5	6	5	4	3	5	3	8	8	8	9
Game												
6 Able to select shots vs Unable to select shots	5	4	4	2	3	2	4	4	7	8	7	9
7 Aware of court position vs Unaware of court position	4	3	3	3	4	2	4	3	8	8	7	9
8 Able to vary shots vs Unable to vary shots	4	3	3	2	3	2	4	3	7	8	7	9
9 Good spatial awareness vs Poor spatial awareness	5	3	3	2	3	2	3	2	7	7	8	9
10 Communicates with partner vs Poor communication with partner	4	3	3	2	2	2	3	2	8	8	8	9

Rating Scale

1 = Very poor   2, 3, 4, 5 = Average   6, 7, 8, 9, 10 = Exceptional

Table 2.   *Repertory grid rating sheet for assessing practical performance in Basketball completed by Teacher One*

CONSTRUCTS	ELEMENTS									
	1	2	3	4	5	6	7	8	9	10
Skill										
1 Demonstrates good technique vs Demonstrates poor technique	7	7	4	6	5	8	6	6	7	6
2 Good application of skills vs Poor application of skills	7	7	4	6	5	8	6	6	7	5
3 Good use of footwork vs Poor use of footwork	6	8	4	6	6	7	5	6	5	6
4 Consistent performance vs Inconsistent performance	7	8	5	5	5	7	6	6	7	5
5 Confident ball handling vs Lacks confidence in ball handling	6	8	4	6	4	7	6	7	8	5
Game										
6 Good individual & team play vs Poor individual & team play	6	6	6	5	6	6	6	6	7	4
7 Shows all-round skill vs Limited skills	6	6	5	4	7	7	7	6	7	6
8 Good spatial understanding vs Poor spatial understanding	6	6	6	5	6	6	7	6	7	5
9 Good concentration and awareness vs Poor concentration and awareness	6	5	6	6	7	7	7	6	7	5
10 Able to change pace vs Unable to change pace	5	5	4	4	6	7	6	5	6	5

Rating Scale

1 = Very poor   2, 3, 4, 5 = Average   6, 7, 8, 9, 10 = Exceptional

The bi-polar constructs included in the grids are based upon the results obtained from eliciting personal constructs from each participant in the study. The skill constructs focus on the pupils' display of technical ability in a non-pressurized activity, whereas the game constructs relate to their performance in an on-going competitive game situation.

There are clear similarities between the two sets of skill constructs for badminton and basketball, for example, reference to 'good technique', 'skill application', and 'footwork'. However, less similarity emerges for the constructs related to the game situation. In both games, constructs relating to pupils' understanding of spatial concepts emerged but other constructs appear specific to the particular game under consideration.

3.2 *The level of consistency in teachers' ratings of pupils' performance*

Kendall's coefficient of concordance (W) (Siegel, 1956) was used to assess the degree of consistency in teachers' judgements of pupils' performance. For both games, pupils were rank ordered in terms of individual teacher's summed

assessments across all constructs. For badminton, W = 0.772, p<0.00I and for
basketball, W = 0.529, p<0.00I. These results clearly indicate a substantial degree
of agreement among teachers in their independent assessments of overall pupil
performance for each game. It appears, however, that greater agreement in relative
assessments occurred for badminton compared with basketball.

3.3 *The level of under- and over-marking*

To explore the variation in the patterns of assessment among the teachers, the mean
score awarded to each performance was calculated and compared with the overall
mean of means for all teachers. Tables 3 and 4 report the teachers' mean scores, the
overall mean of means score and the deviation score for each teacher from the group
mean.

Table 3.   *Badminton: Under/Over Marking*

Teachers	Teachers Mean Score	Extent of Over-or Under-marking
1	5.0	-0.2
2	3.8	-1.4
3	4.4	0.8
4	6.1	+0.9
5	5.9	+0.7
6	4.5	-0.7
7	4.9	-0.3
8	5.4	+0.2
9	6.2	+1.0
10	6.7	+1.5
11	4.5	-0.7
Overall mean	5.2	

For badminton, the individual means ranged from 3.8 (1.4 points below the group
mean) to 6.7 (1.5 points above the group mean). Relative to the overall mean,
teacher 2 showed the greatest tendency to under-mark and teacher 10 the greatest
tendency to over-mark. In general the teachers' means did not vary greatly from the
overall mean score. For basketball, individual means ranged from 4.1 (1.8 below
the group mean) to 6.9 (0.9 above the group mean). Relative to the overall mean,
teacher 10 showed the greatest tendency to undermark and teacher 7 the greatest
tendency to over-mark. As with the badminton results the teachers' means did not
vary substantially from the overall mean.

Table 4.   *Basketball: Under/Over Marking*

Teachers	Teachers Mean Score	Extent of Over- or Under-Marking
1	6.0	+0.1
2	6.6	+0.7
3	5.8	-0.1
4	5.3	-0.6
5	6.5	+0.6
6	6.4	+0.5
7	6.8	+0.9
8	5.9	0.0
9	5.7	-0.2
10	4.1	-1.8
Overall mean	5.9	

3.4 *The level of scoring for skill and game*

In order to investigate the teachers' scores in more detail, the level of scoring for skill and game performance was examined by calculating the mean ratings across skill and game constructs for all performances for individual teachers. These results indicate whether higher ratings had been given for skill or game performance.

Table 5 reports the results for badminton and shows a clear tendency for skill performance to receive higher marks than game performance (correlated t-test: $t = 4.56$, $p<0.001$, one-tailed). Ten of the eleven teachers gave marks in favour of skill. Only one teacher gave marks in favour of game performance and then by a margin of only 0.1.

Table 5.   *Level of Scoring Skill and Game Performance: Badminton*

Teacher	Skill	Mean Game	Score Difference	Game/Skill
1	5.4	4.6	0.8	Skill
2	4.1	3.4	0.7	Skill
3	4.8	3.8	1.0	Skill
4	6.5	5.7	0.8	Skill
5	5.9	5.8	0.1	Skill
6	5.1	3.9	1.2	Skill
7	5.2	4.5	0.7	Skill
8	5.3	5.4	0.1	Game
9	6.3	6.0	0.3	Skill
10	6.8	6.6	0.2	Skill
11	4.7	4.3	0.4	Skill
Means of means	5.5	5.0	0.6	Skill 10 Game 1

Table 6 reports the basketball results and shows that the majority of teachers gave scores favouring skill performance with only three teacher's scores favouring game performance. The difference observed very nearly achieves statistical significance at the 0.05 level (correlated t-test: t = 1.78, p<0.054, one-tailed). Although three teacher's scores are biased towards game performance the difference in each case is less than 0.3.

Table 6.   *Level of Scoring for Skill and Game Performance: Basketball*

Teacher	Skill	Mean Game	Score Difference	Game/Skill
1	6.0	5.8	0.2	Skill
2	6.5	6.7	0.2	Game
3	6.2	5.3	0.9	Skill
4	5.6	5.0	0.6	Skill
5	6.5	6.4	0.1	Skill
6	6.1	6.5	0.4	Game
7	6.9	5.4	1.5	Skill
8	6.1	5.6	0.5	Skill
9	5.5	5.8	0.3	Game
10	4.3	3.9	0.4	Skill
Means of means	6.0	5.6	0.5	Skill 7 Game 3

4   Discussion

This study has attempted to explore the personal criteria employed by physical education teachers in their assessment of fourth-year pupils' practical performance in badminton and basketball. Twenty-one teachers were asked to complete a repertory grid based on video recordings of a skills routine and a game context for either badminton or basketball. The teachers showed a strong level of agreement about the criteria they employ when grading practical performance. This was reflected in the constructs elicited which were the basis for the grid rating sheets for each game (Balsdon 1990). In the grids, the skill constructs referring to technique were similar for both games, whereas the game constructs were more specific to each game under consideration.

The level of agreement in the relative ranking of the performances was high among the teachers for both games, but a greater agreement in relative assessments occurred for badminton. In addition, the examination of under- and over-marking showed that the teachers' mean ratings did not vary greatly and there was little deviation, in general, from the overall mean score. It is of interest, however, that the teacher who showed the greatest tendency to over-mark in badminton (10) and the teacher who most strongly over-marked in basketball (7) worked at the same school. Similarly, the teacher who most strongly under-marked in badminton (2) and the teacher who showed the highest level of under-marking in basketball (10) also taught in the same school. This points to a high level of internal consistency in the standards of judgement among teachers within these same departments. It is a matter of concern, however, that the levels of marking between the two schools involved was so different, especially when both of them were involved in GCSE work. With this commonality of experience one would expect to find greater consistency given that teachers involved in examination work are likely to have had experience of moderation exercises with teachers from other schools.

The two teachers showing the greatest tendency to over-mark for both games were the class tutors for the pupils that took part in the video material. This result suggests that personal knowledge of the performers over a period of time (not just the information available from the video), prompted them to mark towards the higher end of the rating scale. The teachers endorsed this point during a feedback session to discuss the results which had emerged from the study.

Examination of the scores given for skill and game showed that higher scores were generally given for the skills performances than the performances in the game context. This is not surprising given the greater complexity and difficulty of the game situation and given also that a good standard of skill execution will tend to be a necessary but not sufficient condition for good performances in a games context. Nevertheless the absolute difference in skill and game ratings was not very substantial. There was some evidence, however, that similar scoring patterns emerged from teachers from the same school. Examples of this are provided by the teachers from school B who both showed a tendency to mark higher for skill performance and the teachers from school F who both gave marks favouring game performance.

4.1 *Future research and practical implications*

Future research should explore the extent to which the methodology employed here could be adapted to examine the construing of performance in other games, for example, tennis and soccer. It could also be used to compare the judgements made at different levels of performance, in different areas, by assessors of differing levels of expertise. Whilst centred on the secondary level, the research carried out could equally be applied to the primary level.

On a more practical level, the exercise developed here could be undertaken by physical education professionals working within the same institution to explore the criteria and standards they employ in making judgements of different forms of practical performance. It could be used by a teacher with groups of pupils to help them appreciate the ways in which physical performance can be judged and to understand the criteria to be employed in the assessment of their performance skills. Such a process may help to develop self-assessment skills among pupils and so improve their actual levels of performance.

6 References

Balsdon, A J (1990) **The Criteria used by Physical Education Teachers in Assessing the Practical Performance of Secondary School Pupils: An Application of Repertory Grid Technique.** Unpublished masters dissertation. Christ Church College, Canterbury.

Balsdon,A J and Clift, S M (1990) Assessing Gymnastic Performance: An Exploration using Repertory Grid Technique. **Physical Education Review** Spring 1990 vol 13, no 1, 48-59.

Cope, E (1985) Evaluation in Physical Education. **Journal of Psycho-Social Aspects.** Occasional Papers No 1.

DES (1989) **Physical Education from 5-16** London: HMSO.

Eraut, M, Goad, L and Smith, G (1985) **The Analysis of Curriculum Materials.** University of Sussex Education Area. Occasional Paper No 2.

Fransella, F and Bannister, D (1977) **A Manual for Repertory Grid Technique.** London: Academic Press.

Higginbotham, P G and Bannister, D (1983) **The GAB Computer Program for the Analysis of Repertory Grid Data.** Department of Psychology, University of Leeds, England.

Jewett, A E and Bain, L (1985) **The Curriculum Process in Physical Education.** University of Georgia: W C Brown.

Kane, J E (1977) **Movement Studies and Physical Education.** London: Routledge and Kegan Paul.

Kelly, G (1955) **The Psychology of Personal Constructs Vols 1 and 2.** New York: Norton.

Siegel, S (1956) **Non Paramedic Statistics.** New York: McGraw-Hill.

Underwood G L (1983) **The Physical Education Curriculum in the Secondary School: Planning and Implementation.** Lewes: The Falmer Press.

COVERING AN OPPONENT IN TEAM SPORTS: EVOLUTION OF ACTIONS MANIFESTED BY 3RD, 4TH AND 5TH GRADERS

C. PELCHAT[1], A. HUPÉ[1], C. SARRAZIN[2] AND C. ALAIN[2]
[1] *Université du Québec à Montréal, Montréal, Québec*
[2] *Université de Montréal, Montréal, Québec*

Abstract
This paper deals with the evolution of covering actions manifested by primary school students. Typical covering behaviours ranging from the beginner's behaviours to the higher order solutions behaviours for covering, have served as the guiding framework in this study dealing with the different forms and sequences of progress in this activity, as well as with the internal logic guiding its evolution. One basic question was answered through a tentative model of 14 different covering behaviours elaborated from empirical data grounded in team sports experience, as well as from a Piagetian and neo-Piagetian theoretical viewpoint. This qualitative research, analysing covering behaviours of 156 students (grade 3, 4, 5, boys and girls) playing a modified game, has shown that all the 14 covering behaviours identified have been used by the students learning that ability. Qualitative analyses of frequencies has shown also that from grades 3 to 5, for girls and boys, the highest frequencies move from less to more elaborated behaviours. These 'movements' of frequencies would be due to the subject's procedural adjustments associated to the exploration of new and more efficient surveillance conditions for the opponent.
Keywords: Covering an opponent, Team sports, Defence behaviour, Observation, Sport ethnology, Evolution of actions.

1   Introduction

In a research project financed by the Social Sciences and Humanities Research Council of Canada, we have conducted a study on 'covering' in team sports to elucidate the evolution of this skill from the point of view of the student learning it. This study tried to point out the elements and moments of appropriation of a specific motor ability by a subject. Since this study analysed **covering an opponent** through systematic observation and under the mode of appropriation used by the subject in this defensive ability, it can be classified as a 'process' study (Tousignant, Brunelle and Godbout, 1986).

In team sports, numerous experts and authors (Bayer, 1979; Caron and Pelchat, 1975; Mercier, 1968a, 1968b) consider covering offensive players, eventual relay receivers, as the key element of success in defence. Unfortunately, defence in team sports has never been systematically and scientifically studied. At best, covering is defined descriptively as 'a tactical defensive action where a player defending his goal places himself between the carrier and the eventual receiver in order to stop this player from participating in his team-mate's play and, as the case may be, intercept the pass and recapture the control of the relay '(Mikes, 1987; Pruden, 1987; Errais and Weisz, 1984; Palmer, 1984; Ferrarese and Pousset, 1977; Watt, 1971). Therefore, it stands to reason that teaching covering has been generally conducted under the elements contained in the preceding descriptive definition.

2   The problem

Experience supported by simple yet structured empirical observation show, however, that to recapture the relay as soon as possible or to stop an attacker from receiving a pass from a team-mate gives rise to a gamut of more or less elaborated behaviours expressed by the subject in a learning context. This range of behaviours exceeds what served as the traditional lower end of the spectrum and fills the gap between the two extremes of the 'standard' definition mentioned previously. Formerly there was, on one hand, the defender who operates in the immediate environment of the carrier and who attempts to intercept the pass as soon as it is sent. This subject 'sticks' closely to the carrier: at approximately arm's length. His displacement follows that of the carrier's. If the carrier jumps, he jumps; if the other one pivots laterally, the defender manoeuvres in order to face the carrier in the same direction. If the carrier moves the ball without changing his body position, he follows the movement of the ball and projects his hands toward it, even if it means to stretch on the carrier, and force him to bend backward, to the side, or even to step backward (Fig. 1). This is the most general and typical 'beginner's' behaviour mentioned in many team sports.

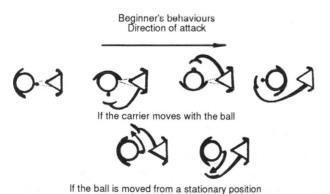

Beginner's behaviours
Direction of attack

If the carrier moves with the ball

If the ball is moved from a stationary position

Figure 1.   *Construction of the carrier and his projections: behaviour E*

There was also, on the other hand, the defender who deliberately and coyly stayed at a safe distance away from the eventual receiver, in order to entice the passer to target this particular team-mate, so that he may intercept the pass. Situated near the attacker which he has identified as the potential receiver, the subject observed moves laterally away from him, one or two arms spans, while the passer seeks a pass receiver. He watches alternately the passer and the receiver. Here, distancing is an intentional move: the subject looks for a placement which leaves the field of vision of the receiver, while at the same time, he adopts an apparent passive stance (arms along side the body) facing the carrier. However, other attitudes (knees flexed, wide feet stance, heels not touching the floor, trunk slightly bent forward, eyes fixed on the passer) indicate that he is ready to move on the ball as soon as it is passed (Fig. 2). This last type of covering constitutes a provoked interception; it is also the most elaborate form of individual covering observable in collective sports.

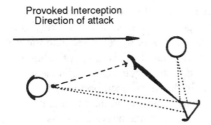

Figure 2.   *Construction of the provoked*
             interception: behaviour N

Our empirical observation of these former 'extreme' covering behaviours has shown the presence of an ability for which the continuum of performance is much larger than that offered by the previous generally accepted definition of this important defensive ability. In fact we have observed four behaviours which we have classified as the construction the defensive field, and which serve as stepping stones to the former lower extreme.

Furthermore, the observation of the intermediate behaviours between the two former extremes mentioned before have generated two general questions which gave birth to this study. Firstly, we wanted to know if in the process of mastering the ability to cover an opponent the intermediate behaviours observed are related to learning this ability, or whether they are random manifestations, without particular significance to covering. Secondly, we wanted to know if these intermediate behaviours corresponded or not to a taking into account by the defender of elements or factors for which the importance of proprieties that they have been attributed, would determine the progressive mastery of this skill. That is to say, the evolution would pass successively from behaviour A to behaviour B, and from this behaviour to behaviour C, and so on until behaviour N (provoked interception) identified as the most elaborate behaviour. However, in the present paper, we will deal only with the first question.

3   The development of the observational grid and its validity

The study of the aforementioned questions necessitated the elaboration of a complete and exhaustive observational grid of multiple covering manifestations. The construction of this observational instrument was realized in many stages; it stemmed from inductive and deductive processes, in the sense that it has been equally induced from observations grounded in a long experience of teaching team sports, as well as deducted from Piagetian theory (Brief, 1986a, 1986b, 1983; Piaget, 1977, 1974a, 1974b). The consideration of these practical and theoretical inputs in the development of the covering observational instrument has allowed, firstly, to structure the behavioural field of this motoric ability, at the **macroscopic level** in five basic components called, for the purpose of this study, **evolution phases.** These are linked, (1) to the construction of the defensive field, (2) to the carrier and his projections, (3) to the ball's trajectory and its falling point, (4) to the ball receiver and, finally, (5) to the provoked interception. Secondly, successive viewings of sequences of a game called 'player-goal' have permitted a schematic illustration of each concrete production of each covering behaviour identified. Thirdly, additional viewings have generated precise illustrations by incorporating displacement forms, players orientation, distances, etc., and the formulation of detailed descriptions of the fundamental characteristics. The latter operations have offered the opportunity to observe, from a **microscopic level,** the specific covering behaviour manifestations and their identification and illustration in fourteen mutually exclusive categories, which constituted our general observational grid.

Table 1 shows how each of these specific covering behaviours are grouped according to the evolution phases. In the grid's final developmental stage the list of fourteen covering behaviours identified, illustrated and described, as well as the five evolution phases, have been submitted to the judgement of eight 'teachers/experts' for a construct validity test. The results show that teachers/experts have judged the evolution phases and their sequential order in conformity with what they themselves have observed in their teaching of team sports; the same pattern can be witnessed for the intermediate behaviours. Their evaluation indicates that the list of phases as well as the list of behaviours are complete and that these two instruments define well the diverse aspects of covering as manifested by a subject learning this defensive skill.

Table 1.   Phases of Evolution in Covering

Phase	Characteristic	Behaviour
I	Construction of the defensive field	A B C D
II	Construction of the carrier and his projections	E
III	Construction of the ball's trajectory	F G H
IV	Construction of the ball receiver	I J K
V	Construction of the provoked interception	L M N

4   The data collection procedures

The subjects involved in this study were the grade 3, 4, and 5 students of the Pierre-de-Coubertin elementary school, in the north region of the Montréal Catholic School Board. This school has two classes per grade level and 27 students per class. Third graders are between 8-9 years old, fourth graders between 9-10, and fifth graders range between 10-11 years of age. The students involved in this study included six classes, totalling 156 students. The girls and boys represented respectively 29.5% and 70.5% of the subjects in this study.

The 'player-goal' game has been used in its global form as the context for observing the covering productions displayed by students. This game is a collective/cooperative physical activity stripped of technical or regulational constraints inherent to codified sports activities. It is used for pedagogical reasons in teaching the fundamental and common elements of codified team sports. In its general pedagogical and didactic elements, this activity recalls the 'hot potato' (Caron and Pelchat, 1975) from which it has been derived for a large part by the PE teachers of the Pierre-de-Coubertin school as they wished to adapt its characteristics to elementary school children. The data collection was done by videotaping intra and inter class intramural 'playergoal' competitions, held during the PE class periods. Using the coding procedure suggested by Paré, Lirette and Laurencelle (1986), it has been decided that the behaviour classification would be coded simultaneously (jointly yet independently) by two coders operating by consensus. On more than 4000 classifications, 36 were persistent disagreements which were arbitrated. This represents less than 1% of the total classifications by coders.

5   Intra-inter fidelity of coders

Before proceeding with the observational phase, the coders were trained until their intra and inter coders reliability ratings were acceptable. The reliability test was conducted under the procedures and formula of agreement used by Bellack, Kliebard, Hyman and Smith (1986) which are 'standards' in the field. The consistency of coder 1 and 2 in their personal classifications of covering behaviours were 90.2% and 89.3%. The inter coders mean percentages of agreement was 86.2%. These intra-inter agreement levels between coders are comparable to those of numerous similar studies.

6   Presentation and analysis of results

6.1   *Existence of intermediate covering behaviours*

Demonstrating the existence of intermediate behaviours was a crucial element of this study. In as much as it was possible to observe on one hand, that the grade 3, 4, and 5 students manifested concretely every one of these different behaviours and that teachers/experts, not related to the study, declared on the other hand, having seen students learning covering skills adopt one or the other of the 14 covering behaviours, it was possible to address the first question of this study related to the existence in reality of each of the intermediate behaviours in the learning process of covering. The data showed the spread of the observations by school level, behavioural type, and sex. We have observed that all the intermediate behaviours identified are manifested by the students at one time or another during the learning of this skill. These findings confirmed the construct validity results of the intermediate behaviours by teachers/experts. In fact, the data from students' covering manifestations and from teachers/experts validations reinforce empirical inductions and theoretical deductions by which the observational grid was elaborated. So, this observational grid of covering may constitute a didactical instrument potentially reliable enough for diagnostic and pedagogical purposes. However, some further studies will be conducted to ascertain its full value.

6.2 *Evolution of covering during the learning process*

The second operation concerned the observable evolution of the mastery of these behaviours. We needed to know, in general terms, if there is an evolution pattern in this process, that is to say, if the subject proceeds from a lesser to a more important level of elaboration.

Before this study, common sense logic and our theoretical framework led us to think that the evolution of covering productions would be perceivable on the one hand, by progressively decreasing frequencies of occurrences from the first phase to the fifth phase for the grade 3 students, girls or boys; on the other hand, the frequencies of occurrences totals would rise progressively from phase 1 to phase 5 for grade 5 students, for girls as well as boys. This evolution would be perceivable also by the fact that manifestations of less elaborate behaviours would be more frequent in grade 3 and progressively diminishing in grades 4 and 5. Inversely, the manifestations of more elaborated behaviours should be more frequent in grade 5 and progressively become less frequent in grade 4, than in grade 3, where the manifestation of these behaviours could even be non-existent. In this regard, the analysis of the histograms of frequencies of occurrences specific to each behaviour type have revealed, not only the evolution of covering as a specific learning phenomenon, but also the direction of that evolution.

In order to answer the second part of our first question we have proceeded with a 'macroscopic' verification of the frequencies of appearance of the behaviours in relation to the five evolution phases previously alluded to; these are related to the five realities that a subject would construct while learning that skill. In order to do this, the frequencies of occurrences found for each behaviour associated with each of these realities have been grouped to constitute five blocks of data (Table 2) for which the total respective occurrences frequencies were compared, one to the other.

As for the evolution of covering behaviours from a learning point of view, figure 3 represents the distributions of frequencies of occurrences of covering behaviours grouped in relation to the five phases of evolution in covering, by sex and level of schooling on one hand, and on the other hand for students of the same sex but in relation to different grade levels.

Table 2.   Frequencies of behaviours (%) grouped according to each of the five evolution phases

Phases		I	II	III	IV	V
Behaviours		A B C D	E	F G H	J K	L M N
	G	65.4	27.5	7.0	-	-
3rd	B	26.3	44.6	28.3	0.6	-
	T	43.8	37.0	19.7	0.3	-
	G	43.5	29.6	26.7	-	0.2
4th	B	24.4	38.7	36.6	0.1	0.1
	T	30.3	35.8	33.4	0.06	0.1
	G	32.7	36.6	25.8	4.8	-
5th	B	21.1	31.2	38.5	7.7	1.6
	T	24.5	32.9	34.4	6.7	1.1
Grand	G	49.7	30.8	18.0	1.3	0.06
	B	23.8	37.9	34.8	3.0	0.6
Total	T	33.7	35.2	28.7	2.4	0.4

The first hard fact that emerges from Figure 3 concerns a form of hierarchy of behaviours in waves, one behaviour in relation to the others. We understand by 'hierarchy in waves' of intermediate covering behaviours, a process by which a subject uses fully a behaviour for a certain period of time, then replaces it by another usually more complex behaviour and which becomes momentarily omnipresent. This goes on until the subject judges that his mastery level is sufficient to meet his needs (from his point of view). It is in a way a kind of horizontal hierarchy in which the subject undertakes covering by adopting one after the other certain 'typical' covering behaviours linked just as much to structural components of this skill (the playing surface, the carrier, the receiver, etc.) as to modes of operating related to the means deployed.

According to our theoretical framework, (Inhelder, 1986; Brief, 1983; Inhelder and Piaget, 1979) the subject's action is in fact in the centre, in the heart of his knowledge acquisition process. In order for him to know an object he must exercise on this object an objectification operation, that is to say, exercise on that object different actions, which have for effect, by the different perceptions that it generates from that object, to reveal more and more the particularities (proprieties) and thus the reality of this object. In a complementary manner, when the subject repeats every one of these diverse actions on many different objects, the imperative action adaptation to the diversity of these objects (their particular proprieties) lead the subject to trials and errors which are in fact objectification operations of concrete procedures allowing the subject to establish an operational relationship between the aim (to succeed in the task) and the means (the efficient action). The stabilization of this procedural knowledge linked to action permits in this way the subject to progressively structure (objectify) the objects on which his actions were exercised; this procedural knowledge allows him, in short, to know better and better the object upon which he acts.

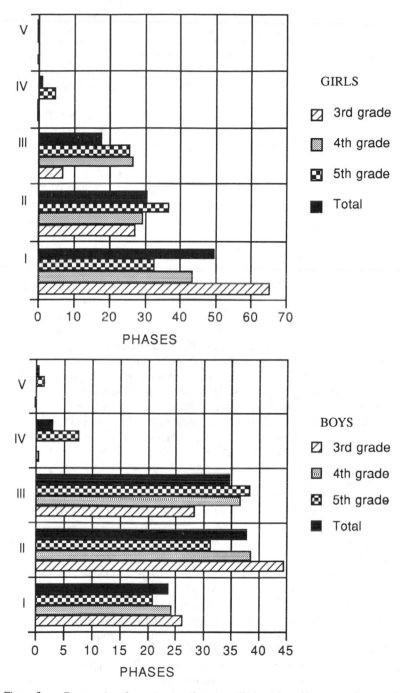

Figure 3. *Frequencies of covering manifestations (%) by girls and boys according to school level and each evolution phase of covering*

7   Conclusion

The general objective of this study was strictly 'exploratory'. We had chosen to observe how children solve problems in an activity for which we benefitted from little scientifically derived information. Just as this study allowed us to formulate the observations mentioned previously, it also permitted us to consider certain new avenues for research.

The first avenue of research concerns directly the fourteen covering behaviours grid. The pedagogical consequences of this research are evident, because, if these behaviours are indeed the behaviours manifested by subjects learning to cover an opponent in team sports and if subjects manifest these behaviours in a definite order when they are attempting to master them, then it is possible to develop, for pedagological purposes, an observational grid of **covering.** Such a grid could be used, just as well, for diagnostic reasons, that is to periodically read the student's level of development in this activity, as for didactical reasons, meaning to help the teacher/coach plan better and organize significant learning situations concerned with covering an opponent (Hupé, Pelchat, Brief and Loiselle, 1989b).

Without dismissing the very important question of validity for pedagological reasons, when one wants to know the **logic of the activity,** as well as the **logic of the subject's acquisition** of this skill (Hupé, Pelchat, Brief and Dostie, 1989a), it is important to reconsider these different behaviours in the enlarged context in which that behaviour was produced. This is so, because it seems reasonable to say that a subject's decision to manifest a specific behaviour is directly related to the elements present in the situation at the time of the decision. Consequently, the observation of covering behaviours must be opened to include this context in order to identify the elements which provoked the production of a given behaviour and find out which of these influence the choice of behaviour.

Even though the present report does not mention it explicitly, the analysis of data showed that some students exhibited a rather large sequence of covering actions. Sometimes these were similar; other times they were different. It seems therefore important, as a second avenue of research, to verify this situation in context, in a game situation. We do not think that the production of these behavioural sequences is done randomly. On the contrary, their presence supposes that the situation contains elements which bring about in the subject the repetition of certain behaviours while the presence of others produce different covering behaviours. The importance of directing this study on covering towards the identification of the factors contributing to the choice by the subject of one covering procedure over another, draws its meaning from the learning process and constitute the third avenue of research. In fact, these elements, whose identification becomes here so important, can be seen as **practical problems,** from a pedagogical viewpoint. These problems act as epistemological obstacles provoking in the subject not only transformations in covering operations for which behaviours are the observable parts, but also in its conceptualizations which, in return, play an important role in the production of a response. The choice of these elements or of certain of their proprieties becomes thus pedagogically important in the production of the desired covering transformations. Lastly, we have noticed differences in covering behaviours between boys and girls and these differences were interpreted on the basis of differences in previous motor experiences. This interpretation opens yet another avenue for research concerning the role played by previous motor acquisitions in the development of a new skill. According to our conceptual framework, the subject's interpretation of a given situation and the responses that he/she subsequently exhibits, are elaborated by the subject from previous knowledge or the knowledge of the means at his disposal. The idea that the diversity, the quantity and the quality of this knowledge could greatly influence the interpretation and the responses thus generated appear to us very promising pedagogically and didactically. Further studies on covering should seriously consider this last but foremost question.

8   References

Bayer, C. (1979) **L'Enseignement des Jeux Sportifs Collectifs**. Éditions Vigot, Paris.

Bellack, A.A., Kliebard, H.M., Hyman, R.T. and Smith, F.L. (1986) **The Language of the Classroom**. Teachers College Press, Columbia University, New York.

Brief, J.C. (1986a) **Problématique des Notions Fondamentales en Éducation**, Cours EDU 7270, Programme de maîtrise en Éducation, Département des sciences de l'éducation, Université du Québec à Montréal, Montréal.

Brief, J.C. (1986b) A Sound Mind in a Healthy Body, or Rather, Minding your Own Body. Conférence d'ouverture, Symposium International **Persons, Mind and Bodies**, Université d'Ottawa, Ottawa.

Brief, J.C. (1983) **Beyond Piaget: A Philosophical Psychology**. Teachers College Press, Columbia University, New York.

Caron, J. and Pelchat, C. (1975) **Apprentissage des Sports Collectifs: Hockey-Basket**. Les Presses de l'Université du Québec, Montréal.

Dunkin, M. and Biddle, B. (1974) **The Study of Teaching**. Holt, Rinehart and Winston, New York.

Errais, M. and Weisz, A. (1984) **Basket-Ball Moderne**. Amphora, Paris. Evertson, C. and Green, J.L. (1986). Observation as Inquiry and Method, in Wittrock, Merlin, Am. Ed. Res., **Handbook of Research on Teaching**, pp.162-213.

Ferrarese, J.F. and Pousset, P. (1977) **Le Handball**, Éditions de Vecchi, Paris.

Hupé, A., Pelchat, C., Brief, J.C. and Dostie, N. (1989a) Les Préceptes Psycho- Génétiques: Guide de Lecture du Développement, in A.I.P.E.L.F., **Les Modèles en Éducation**. Éditions Noir sur Blanc, Montréal, pp.355-366.

Hupé, A., Pelchat, C., Brief, J.C. and Loiselle, A.M. (1989b) L'Évolution de la Chaîne d'Actions Courir et Sauter Propre au Contexte du Franchissement d'Obstacles en Course chez les Enfants de 8 à 12 ans: Représentation et Comportements des Sujets. **Colloque Interdisciplinaire Corporéité, Représentation et Action**. CIRADE, Montréal.

Inhelder, B. (1986) Des Structures aux Procédures, in Piaget, J. Mounoud, P. and Bronkart, J.P., (eds), **Psychologie**. Encyclopédie de la Pléiade, Paris.

Inhelder, B. and Piaget, J. (1979) Procédures et Structures. **Archives de Psychologie**, 47, 165-176.

Mercier, J. (1968a) Attaquer, se Démarquer: Jouer avec et sans Ballon. **E.P.S.**, 94, 85-88.

Mercier, J. (1968b) Attaquer, se Démarquer: Jouer avec et sans Ballon. **E.P.S.**, 95, 73-76.

Mikes, J. (1987) **Basketball Fundamental**. Leisure Press, Champaign.

Palmer, G. (1984) **The Hockey Drill Book**. Leisure Press, New-York.

Paré, C., Lirette, M. and Laurencelle, L. (1986) Rapport Méthodologique sur la Recherche en Enseignement de l'Activité Physique, in Paré, C., Lirette, M. and Piéron, M., (eds), **Méthodologie de la Recherche en Enseignement de l'Activité Physique et**

Sportive, Département des Sciences de l'Activité Physique, Université du Québec à Trois-Rivières, Trois-Rivières.

Piaget, J. (1977) **La Naissance de l'Intelligence chez l'Enfant.** Delachaux and Niestlé, 9e édition, Paris.

Piaget, J. (1974a) **Réussir et Comprendre.** P.U.F., Paris.

Piaget, J. (1974b) **La Prise de Conscience.** P.U.F., Paris.

Pruden, V. (1987) **A Conceptual Approach to Basketball.** Leisure Press, Champaign, Illinois.

Tousignant, M., Brunelle, J. and Godbout, P. (1986) Les Grandes Orientations de Recherche en Intervention au Département d'Éducation Physique de l'Université Laval, in Paré, C., Lirette, M. and Piéron, M., (eds), **Méthodologie de la Recherche en Enseignement de l'Activité Physique et Sportive.** Séminaire international, Département des Sciences de l'Activité Physique, Université du Québec à Trois-Rivières, Trois-Rivières.

Watt, T. (1971) **How to Play Hockey.** Double Day Canada Ltd., Toronto.

9   Appendix A: Symbols

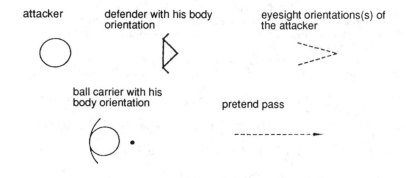

attacker

defender with his body orientation

eyesight orientations(s) of the attacker

ball carrier with his body orientation

pretend pass

TEACHING EFFECTIVENESS: COMPARISON OF MORE AND LESS EFFECTIVE TEACHERS IN AN EXPERIMENTAL TEACHING UNIT

F. CARREIRO DA COSTA AND M. PIÉRON
Technical University, Lisbon, Portugal, and University of Liège, Belgium

Abstract
Two teachers were selected amongst the 18 teachers taking part in an experimental teaching aimed at learning the Fosbury flop. These teachers were located at the extreme ends of the continuum of effectiveness in terms of the qualitative assessment of the criterion task. The ETU involved 10 teaching sessions including student evaluation, 18 teachers, 18 classes and 458 students aged 10 to 16. Classes were of 5th grade (n = 10) and 6th grade (n = 8) levels. Due to drop out the final number of students participating in the total ETU were 393 students (223 males and 170 females). Pre-test and post-test items included: a test of vertical jump, a qualitative analysis of the jumping performance of the Fosbury flop and interviews. All pre-test and post-test were videotaped. During the teaching period, 5 sessions were observed 'live' and 3 were videotaped. The videotape procedures focused, (1) on teacher behaviour, and (2) on student behaviour. The most effective and the least effective teachers differed in most of the process variables. The following variables were higher in the most effective teacher: (1) In class time management: functional time, allocated time for practice, and duration of instruction; (2) In teacher instructional and feedback behavior in the specificity and appropriateness components; (3) In student motor engagement: specificity. Students attending the class led by the least effective teacher were more frequently inactive or involved in deviant or off-task behaviours.
Keywords: Teaching effectiveness, Experimental teaching unit, Teacher behaviour, Pupil behaviour.

1 Introduction

The research on teaching effectiveness attempts to identify the relationships between variables observable during the process of teaching and student achievement (product). In a similar approach researchers are seeking an answer to the question 'What does make a difference between more and less effective teachers?' In that approach behaviours of teacher and pupils are compared in classes where the pupils' learning gain is the highest or the lowest (De Knop, 1983, 1986; Phillips and Carlisle, 1983; Piéron and Piron, 1981).

Data from literature show some convergency towards two types of variables discriminating between classes distributed according to pupils' learnings gains: variables dealing with the time spent on task and variables dealing with the information, especially feedback provided to the learner.

These results arise from experimental teaching units completed in simplified settings (Piéron and Piron; 1981), or in natural settings (Graham, Soares and Harrington, 1983; Neto and Piéron, 1990; Piéron, 1983; Phillips and Carlisle, 1983). They need to be confirmed in natural settings and in using complex motor tasks as learning objectives.

Our purpose was to compare the highest and lowest limits of a continuum of classes ranked according to the qualitative learning gains completed by pupils.

2   Method

The Experimental Teaching Unit design was used involving a learning objective set forth to teachers and pupils, pre- and post-tests of pupils' performance, and the systematic observation of teachers' and pupils' behaviours.

2.1 *Subjects and teaching conditions*

Eighteen teachers, twelve males and six females took part in the study. They were involved in a 10-session-teaching unit in a natural setting. Their teaching experience ranged from two to twenty years. Classes were 5-grade and 6-grade levels with a total of 458 students. Average number of students per class was 25, ranging from 19 to 30. Students' age averaged 12.02 years, ranging from 10 to 16.

At the end of the teaching unit, 393 students (223 boys and 170 girls) were qualified for all the measures necessary for the study.

The experimental teaching unit lasted for an 8 week-period (50 minute-2 weekly sessions). Each class practised the activity during 10 lessons, the first and the last of which were devoted to student evaluation. Two weeks before starting the teaching period, teachers received written and verbal information on the general goal of the teaching unit, the general objectives of the study and more accurate information on the teaching objectives, the organization and development of the unit and the teacher's role in the evaluation sessions.

2.2 *Evaluation*

Students were pre-tested in the first session of the unit in:

(a) a test of vertical jumping ability;
(b) the performance in the high jump (Fosbury flop). The jump was videotaped and analysed for quality (approach, impulsion, trajectory and landing). Two cameras were used to videotape students' performance.
(c) a semi-structured interview was carried on to appraise the participant level of satisfaction.

2.3 *Observation*

Observation was completed as follows:

(a)   3rd, 5th and 8th lessons were videotaped. Videotaping was centered on teacher behaviour and on student behaviour;

(b)   2nd, 4th, 6th, 7th and 9th lessons were directly observed 'live'.

Three main observation systems were used to analyse teaching variables.

(a)   Time management with categories of:
  - functional time
  - instructional time
  - organizational time
  - time allocated to practising physical education activities

(b)   Teacher behaviour (Prof/ULg - Piéron, 1982) including
  - categories of:
  - instruction
  - feedback
  - organization
  - affectivity
  - listening to the student verbal interaction
  - silent observation

Moreover, instruction and feedback were described using a specific multidimensional analysis schedule . A specific observation schedule was developed to appraise the quality of instruction (task presentation) in terms of correctness from a technical point of view. Feedback was observed through the FEED/ULg system (Piéron, 1982) adapted to take into account the feedback value on an appropriate-inappropriate basis (Table 1). The appropriateness of the feedback was largely dependent on the adjustment of diagnostic and prescription to student performance.

Table 1.   *Multidimensional analysis of feedback (adapted from FEED/ULg, Piéron, 1982)*

CONTENT	INTENT
Specific (whole)	Approbatory evaluation
Specific (analytic)	Disapprobatory evaluation
Non Specific	Description (simple)
	Description (specific)
VALUE	Prescription (simple)
Correct	Prescription (justified)
Incorrect	Interrogation
FORM	DIRECTION
Verbal	Individual
Visual	Group
Kinesthetic	Class
Verbal & Visual	
Verbal & Kinesthetic	

(c)   Student behaviour (OBEL/ULg - Piéron, 1982) categories:
- motor engagement in terms of specific or non specific engagement
- organization
- cognitive engagement
- waiting
- off-task behaviours

Student learning gains were appraised under several aspects:

(a)   Quantitative raw progress, measured by substracting the initial height from the final height performed in the jump.
(b)   Qualitative raw progress, based on reduction of errors present in performance, i.e. number of errors observed in the pre-test performance minus number of errors observed in the post-test performance.
(c)   Qualitative relative progress gain score or achievement score adjusted for entry skill level.

2.4   *Analysis of data*

ANOVA, ANCOVA and cluster analysis were used to analyze the data. Teachers were ranked along a continuum based on qualitative learning gains achieved by pupils. The class with the highest learning gain C (+) was compared to the class with the lowest learning gains C (-). Corresponding teachers will be labeled T (+) and T (-) in the text.

3   Results and Discussion

The following topics will be successively analysed: management of class time, pupils' behaviours, teacher's behaviours profile and characterization of teachers and classes.

3.1   *Management of class time (Figure 1)*

A relatively large difference in the amount of functional time was observed between teachers. C (-) class spent 75% of C (+) class in the gym. Although both classes were allocated the same amount of teaching time. Other ratios are also lower in class C instruction time and allocated time to practice.

These observations are consistent with data from classroom research. Rosenshine (1978) reported a significant relationship between student learning gains and time devoted to content. This first level of effectiveness implies that teachers save as much time as possible to spend in the gym. Time spent in dressing room and time used for administrative routine must be kept at a minimum. Usually the functional time variable does not appear as significant in experimental teaching units as it was observed in this study .

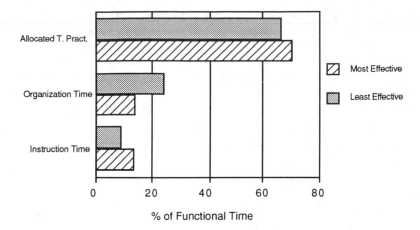

Figure 1   *Comparison of time management between the most effective and the least effective class.*

3.2 *Pupils behaviour*

The profile of pupils' behaviours showed striking differences between the two classes led by the most and the least effective teachers (Figure 2). Although the amount of motor engagement time was slightly in favour of C(-), the specific motor engagement was dramatically higher in C(+): 8.2% vs 2% of the functional time (time spent in the gym). Considering this difference, it is easy to understand that learning gains were higher in C(+) than in C(-).

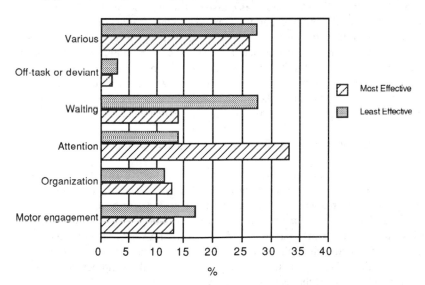

Figure 2   *Comparison of pupils' behaviours between the most effective and the least effective class.*

In C(+), pupils spent a larger part of their time listening to the teacher. On the contrary, their waiting time was approximately half than in C(-). A difference was also observed in the attention devoted by pupils to watching their classmates' performance. It is suggested that businesslike behaviours do not only relate to the motor engagement but also in the general involvement in the whole teaching - learning process.

The behaviour profile of pupils in the most effective class was similar to:

(a)   classes lead by expert teachers (Piéron, 1982)
(b)   classes wherein students achieved higher learning gains (Phillips and Carlisle, 1983; Pieron and Piron, 1981).

In both classes, students spent only a short span of time in deviant or off-task behaviours despite the large amount of waiting time in the least effective class. However, in this class, time spent in deviant behaviours was higher than the mean for the 18 classes observed in the study.

3.3   *Teachers' interventions*

There was a clear predominance of two functions emphasizing the content of teaching in the most effective teacher. Instruction and feedback took a larger part in the teaching profile of T (+) than in T (-). On the other hand T (-) spent more time in silently observing the pupils.

We found in T (+) the same characteristics as those identified in experts or master teachers (Piéron, 1982). In presenting the task the total length of instruction intervention was approximately double in T (+) than in T (-).

A small difference exists in the proportion of specific feedback: 92.2% in T (+) versus 88.3% in P (-). This difference is consistent with data found in the literature. However it is too small for any generalization. We found a more contrasted picture when dealing with the correctness of the feedback. Amongst its specific feedback, T (+) emitted 99% of correct feedback and T (-) 81.4% corresponding roughly to 1 out of 5 incorrect feedback. Let us remind ourselves that correctness is referred to as the usual technique of the Fosbury flop. This fact emphasizes the importance of a knowledge as good as possible of the subject matter taught. The second component of the quality of feedback was its appropriateness, i.e. its match with the learner's performance.

Certainly, being able to provide feedback is within the domain of pedagogical skills.

It will be unwise to limit this ability to its unique quantitative aspect. Its quality seems to be a key issue for its effectiveness. It relies heavily on the teacher's knowledge of subject matter, on his/her ability to identify performance error (diagnosis) and to emit an immediate message (prescription). A specific preparation to observe the learner's performance, based on a profound knowledge of the laws of human movement and their application to sports is a necessary basis to develop this pedagogical skill. Adjusting the reaction to pupil understanding and performance abilities is another facet of the feedback effectiveness.

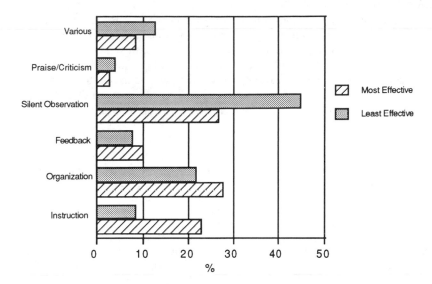

Figure 3   *Comparison of teachers' behaviours between the most effective and the least effective class.*

3.4 *Characteristics of teachers and classes*

Although the teacher identified as the most effective was a man and the least effective was a woman, gender cannot be presumed responsible for the differences observed in the teaching process. When the most and least effective groups were considered, it was observed that the proportions of men and women were the same as in the whole population: 4 men and 2 women.

The least effective teacher had a longer teaching experience (13 years) and was tenured. The most effective teacher had only four years of experience and was not tenured. Experience does not necessarily mean expertise.

The number of pupils in each class was similar: 22 in C(-) and 24 in C(+). A larger proportion of boys (17-7) in C(+) than girls (12-10) in C(-) could explain the emphasis placed on the criterion task in the most effective class.

4   Conclusions

Highest learning gains in a physical education class seemed to be the result of convergent factors:

(a)   The management of class time. From the first instants of a class, effectiveness was characterized by higher amounts of time spent in the gym, of instruction time, and allocated time to practice physical activities.

(b) Pupils' behaviours. Pupils achieving higher learning gains had a higher specific motor engagement time. They were paying more attention to the teacher's interventions and to the activity of their classmates.

(c) Teachers' interventions. Presentation of content, specificity, correctness and appropriateness of feedback were characteristics of the most effective teacher. A sound knowledge of the subject matter taught is a warrant of these interventions when completed by adequate communication skills.

5   References

De Knop, P. (1983). Effectiveness of tennis teaching. In, R. Telama, V. Varstala, J. Tiainen, L. Laakso, and T. Haajanen (eds), **Research in school physical education. Jyväskylä: The foundation for promotion of physical culture and health**, pp.228-234.

De Knop, P. (1986). Relationship of specified instructional teacher behaviors to student gain on tennis. **Journal of Teaching in Physical Education**, 5, 2, 71-78.

Graham, G., Soares, P., and Harrington, W. (1983). Experienced teachers' effectiveness with intact classes: An ETU study. **Journal of Teaching in Physical Education**, 2, 2, 3-14.

Neto,C. and Piéron, M. (1990). Behaviours of 5 to 6 year-old children in teaching situations aiming at acquiring specific motor skills. Paper presented at the Loughborough - AIESEP 1990 International Convention.

Phillips, D., and Carlisle, C. (1983). A comparison of physical education teachers categorized as most and least effective. **Journal of Teaching in Physical Education**, 2, 3, 55-67.

Piéron, M. (1982). Effectiveness of teaching a psycho-motor task. Study in a micro-teaching setting. In, M. Piéron, and J. Cheffers (eds), Studying the teaching in physical education. Liege: AIESEP, pp.79-89.

Piéron, M. (1983). Effectiveness of teaching a psychomotor task (Gymnastic routine). Study in a class setting. In, R. Telama, V. Varstala, J. Tiainen, L. Laakso, and T. Haajanen (eds), **Research in school physical education. Jyväskylä: The foundation for promotion of physical culture and health**, pp.222-227.

Piéron, M., and Piron, J. (1981). Recherche de critères d'efficacité de l'enseignement d'habiletés motrices. **Sport**, 24, 144-161.

Rosenshine, B. (1978). Academic engaged time, content covered, and direct instruction. **Journal of Education (Boston)**, 160, 3, 38-66.

THE EFFECT REFINING AND APPLYING INSTRUCTIONAL TASKS HAVE ON STUDENT ACHIEVEMENT IN AN OPEN MOTOR SKILL

LINDA S. MASSER
Alcona Community Schools, Lincoln, Michigan, U.S.A.

Abstract

This paper combines the results of three studies done to investigate the effect refining and applying instructional tasks have on student achievement in an open motor skill. Some students had previous experience with the skill others did not. All studies took place in a public school rural setting using intact 5 and 6 grade classes. Three groups were involved: a control group, a group receiving mainly refining tasks, and a group receiving mainly applying tasks. All subjects were pre-tested, post-tested immediately following treatment, and post-tested after several months. The pre- and post-test scores were analysed using a one-factor experiment with repeated measures and an analysis of covariance. Results indicated both applying and refining tasks brought about significant improvement in those students working on a new skill but if students had past experience with the skill and long term effects were desired then refining tasks were necessary to bring about significant improvement.

Keywords: Instructional Tasks, Student Achievement, Open Motor Skill.

1 Introduction

There are many skills a teacher must have command of in order to be effective. Among these are content knowledge (McCormick, 1979; Shulman, 1987), classroom management (Doyle, 1985; Graham, Soares, and Harrington, 1983), ability to motivate students (Siedentop, 1983), clarity of instruction (Cruickshank, 1985; Werner and Rink, 1989), keeping students accountable (Gusthart and Sprigings, 1989; Werner and Rink, 1989), and setting a classroom environment conducive to learning (Werner, 1985; Harrison, 1987). Given these skills as factors contributing to effective teaching, researchers must begin to investigate the instructional tasks the teacher gives to the students in an effort to bring about student skill performance improvement. Rink (1985) has written 'at the heart of the instructional process in physical education is the movement task. Movement tasks are motor activities assigned to the student that are related to the content of the lesson'

(Rink, 1985, p. 10). Rink has identified four types of instructional tasks: informing, refining, extending, and applying.

Informing tasks are basic tasks used to introduce the content of the lesson to the students. Refining tasks help students work on the quality involved in the skill being learned. Extending tasks ask students to extend the skill into other dimensions and applying tasks have students use the skill outside the movement itself.

This researcher asked the question - Will each of the types of tasks Rink has identified affect student achievement equally or will a particular type of task have more effect on student achievement than another? An earlier study done by the author (Masser, 1985) investigated informing and refining tasks. Results immediately following treatment found significant ($p<0.05$) improvement in the standing broad jump performance of students in grades K, 1, 2, 3, 4, and 6 when students received mainly refining tasks. Students receiving mainly informing tasks had significant improvement in grades K, 1, and 5. Conclusions drawn from the study indicated the importance of refining tasks if student achievement was the objective.

The next step for this researcher was to compare the effect of refining and applying tasks on student achievement. A series of three studies were done investigating refining and applying tasks with students having no previous experience in a particular open motor skill and students having some previous experience with the skill. This paper compiles the findings of those three studies (Masser, 1988; Masser, 1989).

2 Method

2.1 *Setting*

All three studies took place in the same northern rural elementary school system. Each study was carried out in the regularly scheduled physical education classes. The classes met twice a week with each class period lasting 30 minutes.

A novel piece of equipment - a peteka - was used in the studies to eliminate any practice the students might obtain outside the studies. The peteka has a sponge rubber base with three large feathers extending from the base. It is hit with the bare hand to send it over a net.

2.2 *Subjects*

The subjects were all fifth and sixth grade students (except four excused for medical reasons) during the 1986-87 (N = 97), 1987-88 (N = 144), and 1988-89 (N = 146) school years. Fifth graders had received no previous contact with the peteka. Many of the sixth graders had received instruction and practice involving the peteka as fifth graders.

The teacher/researcher for each study was the regular physical education teacher who had taught in the system for the past 21 years. Since the instructor was also the researcher great care was taken to avoid different types of biases that could enter the studies. Precautions taken included:

(a) students pre-tested before random assignment of intact classes;
(b) dependent variable was chosen because it could be objectively measured; and
(c) all verbal teacher behaviors were coded to determine treatment fidelity.

2.3 *Procedures*

Prior to each study administration approval was obtained and parents were informed. Parent approval was deemed unnecessary since treatment was similar to the regular physical education programme given the students.

Treatment, pre-testing, and immediate post-testing for the students lasted three weeks involving five physical education classes for each of the studies: class one - students pre-tested; classes two, three, and four - students received treatment; class five - students post-tested. All lessons were audio and video taped during treatment. Students were accustomed to being video taped since video taping had occurred on a daily basis in all indoor physical education classes since the 1985 school year. Audio taping was also commonly done.

2.4 *Treatment*

A 'nonequivalent control-group design' as described by Borg and Gall (1983) was used in the 1987 and 1988 studies. The 1986 study was similar but it did not have a control group. The studies were quasi-experiments since groups rather than subjects were randomly assigned to receive the different treatments. Three groups were involved in each study: a C group, and A group, and a R group. The 1986 study had no C (control) group. Instead it had a second R group in which independent variables were manipulated in different ways. This second R group has no bearing on this study and therefore the findings for the group will not be discussed in this paper. The C control group in the 1987 and 1988 studies received no instruction nor practice in the peteka except that which occurred during the pre-test and post-test. They received instruction in indoor field hockey. The A group in all three studies received mainly applying tasks with some informing, refining, and extending tasks along with practise time in using the peteka. The R group in all three studies received mainly refining with some informing, extending, and applying tasks along with practice time in the use of the peteka. Table 1 gives instructional tasks given the A and R groups during treatment.

2.5 *Instrument for coding teacher behavior*

Rink's (1979) Observation System for Content Development - Physical Education (OSCD-PE) was used to code all verbal teacher behaviors in the lessons taught to the experimental A and R groups during each study. Informing, refining, extending, and applying are constructs in the observational system. Rink developed the OSCD-PE in order to have both validity with other instruments similar in nature and reliability determined from different individual's inter and intra coding agreements. Twelve lessons were involved in each study (3 lessons per group). Intra-judge agreement was found to be 93~. Three lessons, two from the A group and one from the R group were randomly selected from the 1986 study and sent to Rink for inter-judge agreement which was 86 per cent. Both inter- and intra-judge agreement was determined using simple percentage of agreement.

Table 1.   *Examples of instructional tasks given R and A groups during treatment*

Some of the Tasks Given A Group

Informing	Use the palm of your hand to strike the peteka above your forehead and see if you can send the peteka straight up above your head. (Teacher demonstrate)
Applying	Count how many continuous overhand strikes you can make.
Extending	Keep using the overhand strike and see if you can send the peteka to your partner in an arching pathway so the peteka will come down directly above your partners forehead. (Teacher demonstrate)
Applying	Count the number of continuous times you and your partner can send the peteka back and forth to each other.
Applying	One person stand on one side of the volleyball net and the other stand on the other side and count how many times you and your partner can send the peteka back and forth to each other.
Applying	Decide whether you want to play cooperatively or competitively. Those working cooperatively see if you can beat the school record of 33 consecutive hits. Those working competitively set up rules for the game you can both agree on and see who is winning in four minutes.

Some of the Tasks Given R Group

Informing	Use the palm of your hand to strike the peteka above your forehead and see if you can send the peteka straight up above your head. (Teacher demonstrate)
Refining	Keep your hand flat and your wrist firm.
Refining	Use a short striking action.
Extending	Be ready to move your feet quickly keeping yourself under the peteka so you can keep striking it upward.
Refining	Keep your knees slightly bent and your weight forward on the balls of your feet.
Extending	Keep using the overhand strike and see if you can send the peteka to your partner in an arching pathway so the peteka will come down directly above your partners forehead. (Teacher demonstrate)
Refining	Make sure you are directing your striking hand upward and toward your partner.
Extending	Try getting a higher arch to the pathway in which you are sending the peteka so your partner has more time to get under it.
Applying	Count how many times you and your partner can send the peteka back and forth to each other.

2.6 Independent variables

Six independent variables were investigated. Two of these involved in the instructional process were manipulated; refining and applying. The other four were analysed to determine if they could have been a factor in affecting student achievement. These four were; informing, extending, allocated learning time and engaged learning time. A significant level of $p < 0.01$ was used on all data involving independent variables which were manipulated in the study. A significant level (p<0.05) was used on data for independent variables not manipulated but calculated to determine if the data could have been a factor in affecting the study in any way.

2.7 Dependent variable

The dependent variable for the studies was the ability of the student to return an aerial object - peteka - to a given area. Students were pre-tested, post-tested immediately following treatment, and post-tested again after a time span of four months for the 1986, five months for the 1987 and 1988 studies. The testing procedure involved a sender (the researcher) sending a peteka in an arching pathway to a subject who then had to return it to a given area. A total of five petekas were sent to the subject in this way. A five foot high volleyball net separated the sender from the subject. Before sending the first peteka, the subject was asked to designate the area he or she intended to return the peteka to. Two areas were marked on the floor across the net from the subject on each side of the sender, one area to the diagonal right of the subject, the other area to the diagonal left. Each area consisted of five concentric circles with the smallest circle having a diameter of two feet and the largest ten feet. Scores for the targeted area were 10, 8, 6, 4, and 2 with 10 points for the smallest circle. If the peteka landed on a line the higher score was given. If the subject sent the peteka over the net but it did not land in the chosen area only one point was given. If the peteka failed to cross the net 0 points were given. The subject's score was the total points achieved from the five attempts.

3   Results

3.1   *Independent variables*

The independent variables manipulated during the three studies were refining and applying instructional tasks. The OSCD-PE was used to calculate the percentage of times these instructional tasks were used during the lessons. A t-test for independent samples was used on each behavior to determine if there was a significant difference given each of the A and R groups. A one-tailed test with a significance level of p<0.01 was used since the variables were manipulated. Results found the R group received significantly more refining tasks than did the A group and the A group received significantly more applying tasks than did the R group. This data may be seen in Table 2.

The independent variables not manipulated during the studies but calculated using the OSCD-PE found no significant differences in the percentage of informing tasks or extending tasks given the A and R groups. This data may also be seen in Table 2.

Allocated learning time was calculated using the video tapes by timing in seconds the total amount of practise time the teacher gave the majority of the students to practise during each lesson. Allocated learning time (class mean average for three lessons) was found to be significant in only the 1987 study between the sixth grade A and R groups (6Ax = 1408.33 sec., 6Rx = 1221.00 sec., t = 4.28, p<0.05).

Table 2.   *Results from each study of the independent t-test comparing the A and R group means for informing, refining, extending, and applying tasks*

Year	Grade	Group	Informing	Refining	Extending	Applying
1986	6	R	8.00	34.33*	2.33	7.00
	6	A	9.67	1.67	1.33	28.33*
	5	R	10.00	37.33*	3.00	7.00
	5	A	9.33	8.67	.33	29.33*
1987	6	R	8.33	47.67*	1.67	5.67
	6	A	6.33	1.00	3.00	36.67*
	5	R	7.67	45.33*	2.00	2.00
	5	A	8.33	3.67	1.00	35.67*
1988	6	R	7.33	37.33*	.67	17.33
	6	A	6.67	.33	.33	44.67*
	5	R	9.67	33.33*	.67	16.67
	5	A	8.67	2.00	.33	40.33*

* $p < 0.01$

The video tapes were also used to determine student engaged time for each of the studies. The researcher counted the number of times each student in the A and R groups struck the peteka during each lesson. Student **engaged time was found to be significantly different $p < 0.05$** between the two fifth grade groups in the 1987 study (5Ax = 453.10, 5Rx = 357.60, t = 4.15) and the two fifth grade groups in the 1988 study (5Ax = 603.86, 5Rx = 511.12, t = 2.49).

3.2 *Dependent variable*

A t-test for independent samples was used on the pre-test peteka scores to determine if there were significant differences ($p < 0.05$) between the sexes. Significant differences were found in all three studies. This data is given in Table 3. Since there were significant differences between the sexes, equal cells were used in the statistical procedures when comparing groups.

An analysis of covariance was done with each grade to determine if there were any significant differences between groups. The independent variable was method and the covariate was the pre-test scores in the peteka. Where significant differences were found a Newman-Keuls test for multiple comparisons was done on the adjusted group means to determine the level of difference. A level of p=0.05 was accepted on this data since the A and R groups were being compared with each other and both groups had received treatment and practice. Significant differences were found each year with the fifth grade groups. In the 1986 study significant differences occurred in long term effects between the adjusted group means of the A and R groups (Rx = 22.88, Ax = 16.11).

Table 3.   *Results from independent t-test comparing dependent variable pre-test group means of boys and girls for each study*

Year	Grade	Boys Group Means	Girls Group Means	df	t
1986	6	22.29	11.92	51	4.79*
	5	9.22	6.90	41	1.11
1987	6	16.56	14.84	69	1.01
	5	9.24	6.11	71	2.37*
1988	6	19.00	14.80	70	2.00*
	5	11.68	7.03	72	2.85*

* $p<.05$

Significant differences were found between the adjusted group means of the 1987 R and C groups immediately following treatment (Rx = 16.36, Cx = 10.76). Significant differences in the 1988 study occurred immediately following treatment between the R and A groups and between the R and C groups (Rx = 19.49, Ax = 14.59, Cx = 13.04). No significant differences were found between the sixth grade groups in any of the studies. This data may be seen in Table 4.

Table 4.   *Analysis of covariance adjusted group means for the R, A, and C groups from immediate and long term post-test scores*

Grade	Year	Post-test	N for Each Group	R Adjusted Mean	A Adjusted Mean	C Adjusted Mean	df	F
5	1986	Immediate	22	22.55	18.43		1/41	3.42
		Long Term	22	22.88* from A	16.11		1/41	14.37
5	1987	Immediate	24	16.36* from C	14.87	10.76	2/68	3.90
		Long Term	24	17.49	15.44	14.13	2/68	1.07
5	1988	Immediate	22	19.49*from A&C	14.59	13.04	2/62	4.78
		Long Term	22	16.04	16.03	11.47	2/62	2.88
6	1986	Immediate	24	28.37	30.27		1/45	.99
		Long Term	24	25.36	22.32		1/45	1.69
6	1987	Immediate	22	20.97	21.27	19.18	2/62	.40
		Long Term	22	21.50	17.06	17.16	2/62	1.71
6	1988	Immediate	22	17.27	21.89	18.31	2/62	2.30
		Long Term	22	22.31	22.26	18.43	2/62	1.75

* $p<.05$ results from Newman-Keuls for multiple comparisons done on adjusted post-test group means

A one factor experiment with repeated measures was used to determine within group differences between pre-test and post-test scores for the C, A, and R groups in each of the studies. A significance level of p<0.01 was used on this data since students in the A and R groups were given treatment and practice with the intention of improving the skill performance of the students. Where F ratios were found to be significant a Newman-Keuls test for multiple comparisons was used on group means to determine column effects. Significant differences were found with the fifth grade A and R groups between pre-test and long term post-test group means. For the sixth grade, significant differences were found between the pre-test and immediately following treatment post-test group means in the 1986 A and R groups and in the 1987 R group. Significant differences were found between the pre-test and long term post-test group means in the 1986, 1987, and 1988 R groups. This data may be seen in Table 5.

Table 5.   *One factor experiment with repeated measures for R, A, and C groups giving pre-test, immediate post-test and long term post-test group means*

Grade	Group	Year	Pre-test	Immediate Post-test	Long Term Post-test	df	F
5	R	1986	7.29	22.19* from P	22.71*from P	40	59.06
		1987	6.96	15.83* from P	17.00*from P	44	17.00
		1988	8.00	18.55* from P	15.36*from P	42	15.53
5	A	1986	8.40	19.20* from P	16.32* from P	38	14.78
		1987	8.33	15.00* from P	15.58* from P	46	10.80
		1988	10.06	15.17* from P	16.44* from P	42	8.08
5	C	1987	8.58	10.98	14.38* from P	46	8.28
		1988	9.77	13.41	11.73	42	4.61
6	R	1986	17.71	28.81* from P	25.52* from P	40	15.10
		1987	14.23	20.55* from P	21.45* from P	42	8.07
		1988	18.34	17.64	22.72* from P	42	5.94
6	A	1986	17.38	30.33* from P&LT	22.33	46	19.69
		1987	15.00	21.14	17.05	42	8.07
		1988	16.32	21.36	21.68	42	4.07
6	C	1987	16.82	19.73	17.23	42	.90
		1988	17.84	18.47	18.60	42	.10

* p<0.01 - results from Newman-Keuls for multiple comparisons done on column means P - pre-test, IP - immediate post-test, LT - long term post-test

4 Discussion

Results of this study found applying tasks to be important if the students were learning a new skill. The old cliche 'practise makes perfect' seems to be true if a new skill is involved. Very little instruction was given the fifth graders (students with no previous experience with the peteka) yet these students had significant gains (p<0.01) when pre-test scores were compared to both immediate and long term post-test scores. Refining tasks also brought about significant gains with the fifth grade students. On the other hand, if students had previous contact with the skill and if long term effects were the desired outcome then refining tasks were necessary in the teaching process. All fifth and sixth grade groups receiving mainly refining tasks achieved significant (p<0.01) improvement between their pre-test group mean scores and their long term post-test group mean scores. Data from the analysis of covariance found the R group receiving mainly refining tasks to have higher adjusted long term group means when compared to the A groups receiving mainly applying tasks and the C control groups. Although this data was usually not at a significant (p<0.05) level it was consistent across both the fifth and sixth grades and across all three studies. Informing, refining, extending, and applying are types of tasks used in the instructional process. These studies seem to indicate refining tasks to be particularly important if student achievement in long term effects are the desired outcome. Future research studies need to examine the accuracy of the refining tasks given. Is the information given in the refining task technically correct in helping students improve their motor performance and does it include a critical cue for students to focus upon as they practice?

5   References

Borg, W.R. and Gall, M.D. (1983) **Educational Research an Introduction** (4th ed.). Longman, NY.

Cruickshank, D.R. (1985) Applying research on teacher clarity. **J. of Teacher Education, 36,** 44-88.

Doyle, W. (1985) Recent research on classroom management: Implications for teacher preparation. **J of Teacher Education, 36,** 31-35.

Graham, G. Soares, P. and Harrington, W. (1983) Experienced teachers' effectiveness with intact classes: An ETU study. **J of Teaching in Physical Education,** 2, 3-14.

Gusthart, J.L. and Sprigings, E.J. (1989) Student learning as a measure of teacher effectiveness in physical education. **J of Teaching in Physical Education,** 8, 298-311.

Harrison, J.M. (1987) A Review of the research on teacher effectiveness and its implications for current practice. **Quest,** 39, 36-55.

Masser, L. (1985) An experimental study investigating the effect of the teaching behavior of refinement on student achievement in a fundamental motor skill. (Doctoral dissertation, Bowling Green State University, Ohio).

Masser, L. (1988) An experimental study investigating the effect instructional tasks have on sixth grade student achievement in an open motor skill. Paper presented at the 1988 Olympic Scientific Congress. Seoul, Korea.

Masser, L. (1989) An experimental study investigating the effect instructional tasks have on student achievement in an open motor skill. Paper presented at the 1989 AIESEP World Convention. Jyvaskyla, Finland.

McCormick, W.J. (1979) Teachers can learn to teach more effectively. **Educational Leadership,** 37, 59-60.

Rink, J.E. (1979) The development of an observation system for content development in physical education (Doctoral dissertation, The Ohio State University). **Dissertation Abstracts International,** 40, 4476A.

Rink, J.E. (1985) **Teaching Physical Education for Learning.** Times Mirror/Mosby, St. Lotlis, MO.

Shulman, L.S. (1987) Knowledge and teaching: Foundations of the new reform. **Harvard Educational Review,** 57, 1-22.

Siedentop, D. (1983) **Developing Teaching Skills in Physical Education** (2nd ed.). Mayfield, Palo Alto, CA.

Werner, P. (1985) The learning environment, in **Teaching Physical Education for Learning** (ed J.E. Rink), Times Mirror/Mosby, St. Louis, MO, pp. 48-79.

Werner, P. and Rink, J. (1989) Case studies of teacher effectiveness in second grade physical education. **J of Teaching in Physical Education**, 8, 280-297.

MEASURING RELIABILITY WITH DYADS IN PHYSICAL EDUCATION

RICHARD J. NASTASI[1] AND JOHN CHEFFERS[2]
[1]*Ballarat University College, Ballarat, Australia*
[2]*Boston University, Boston, United States*

Abstract

This study described the dyadic interactions of one experienced physical education teacher in a lab classroom setting. The researcher used the Individual Reaction Gestalt (IRG III) as a primary method for observing teacher–student behaviour. A heart rate monitor was also employed to provide data in the psychophysiological dimension. Previous studies explored crowd behaviour using IRG-III (Goodman, 1989; Nastasi, 1989). Prior investigation has also been done in dyadic behaviour in the classroom using Cheffers Adaptation of Flanders Interaction Analysis System (CAFIAS). This study combined the dyadic implications of IRG-III with the classroom setting for the first time. The design established one male physical education teacher (age 27) working with inner city fourth graders in a natural setting. The instrument's primary task was to measure emotionality and involvement. Using the Kendall Tau, an inter-rater reliability coefficient of 0.923 (corrected for ties) was obtained. Since the sample was slightly over ten (n=12), a Spearman Rho was also computed. A coefficient of 0.964 (corrected for ties) was obtained. The results of the study were: 1) IRG-III is a valid instrument for measuring student-teacher dyadic behaviour in a physical education setting. 2) Unlike the engrossed behaviours of the singular spectators, dyads exhibit spasmodic involvement due to various pastoral behaviours initially expected and confirmed by the study. It was concluded that this type of spasmodic behaviour was desirable for the majority of crowd situations. It is also to be expected in classroom settings and while this type of behaviour can initiate learning opportunities, the problem of spasmodic distraction is inherent in this type of behaviour.

Keywords: Individual Reaction Gestalt, Dyad, Social Learning Theory, Expressive Relationship, Spasmodic Involvement, Inter-rater Reliability.

1   Introduction

Emile Durkheim spoke of the education experience as 'the actual process of exerting influence on children.' Researchers interested in the intimacies derived from such influence need only examine the teacher-student dyad.

The concept of dyadic behaviour in the classroom/gymnasium has not been given a great deal of attention. Martinek and Johnson (1979) broke ground with significant data relating to the effects of teachers' expectations on specific student-teacher behaviours. The authors developed the Dyadic Adaptation of CAFIAS (DAC) for the study, expressing a hope that researchers would continue to use DAC as well as other instruments to measure dyadic behaviour in the school physical education setting.

The use of the Individual Reaction Gestalt (IRG) has been a popular measurement for the degree of involvement of an individual or a group in a diversity of activities and settings. While this measure has been used in school settings (Crowley-Sullivan, 1990), the use of IRG-III in the exploration of dyadic behaviour between teacher and student has not occurred.

This study was interested in the verbal and nonverbal attention rates given by teachers to individual students as opposed to a group of students (either part of or the whole class). Of primary concern was the validation of IRG as a tool to measure dyadic behaviour in the physical education classroom setting. Since dyadic observation involving teacher and student requires unique observation techniques, the concept of inter-rater reliability is critical. Cheffers et al. (1978) notes that Flanders (1960) suggested that reliability among or between observers is dependent on group training, knowledge or common ground rules, an understanding of each observer's own unique biases and regular meetings after training sessions to discuss unusual categorization problems. As student-teacher dyadic behaviour differs from previous IRG-III applications, the question of appropriateness (by inter-rater reliability) was tested. Having established inter-rater reliability, a secondary concern was to ascertain the quality of time spent when the teacher and a student were having a dyadic interaction.

The study of teacher-student dyadic behaviour is a critical issue in education:

> By studying the interactions of teacher-student dyads, the teacher becomes more sensitive to and aware of students characteristic behaviours and individuality, as well as the manner in which they interact with other students (Martinek, 1978)

Social Learning Theory gives additional credence to these investigations as the prospect of modelling in the physical education classroom can be significant. Students tend to perceive teachers in a positive modelling construct. Greedorfer and Lewko (1978) call this interaction 'expressive relationship behaviour'. This creates a rich modelling situation where student attention is 'discriminate' in nature. This behaviour is one of the requisite conditions for observational learning. Recent work in expressive relationship dyads (Nastasi, 1989) in sporting crowds yielded significant correlations between the level of the relationship and the modelling which took place.

2 Methodology

The investigator observed an experienced (six years teaching) primary school level physical education teacher (with three undergraduate assistants), on three separate teaching occasions (a total of six hours). During the observation, the teacher worked with the same Boston inner city fourth grade class (n=15), teaching a three lesson unit on skills development. During these sessions, two trained coders measured the dyadic relationship between the teacher and students. Prior to the experiment, training of the coders consisted of twenty practice hours of paired coding, achieving a 0.75 inter-rater reliability rating using the Spearman Rank Order Coefficient. After the coding had been completed, inter-rater coefficients (Spearman Rho and Kendall Tau) were derived to establish the reliability of IRG-III in this setting. The IRG-III data was analysed to determine the ratios of time spent within each of the four basic IRG-III categories. The teacher also wore a heart rate monitor to supply a psychophysiological component to the inquiry.

3 Results

The primary concern of this investigation was to prove the reliability of IRG-III in describing dyadic behaviour in the physical education classroom. The coders established an inter-rater reliability of 0.964 (corrected for ties) using the Spearman Rank Order Coefficient and a 0.923 (corrected for ties) using the Kendall Tau. These results led the researchers to affirm the measurement used as reliable in the natural setting which we described.

Table 1.   *Individual Reaction Gestalt III (IRG-III)*

Verbal	Non-verbal	Category	Description	Concepts
1	11	No Apparent Involvement	Wandering around the learning area doing something not on task	Low Involvement
2	12	Distracted Involvement	Present, but not giving the lesson concentration. Talking to someone	Low Involvement
3	13	Spasmodic Involvement	No permanent focus. Fluctuates on and off task	Spasmodic Involvement
4	14	Engrossed Involvement	Permanent focus. No apparent emotional release. Eyes never leaving the task	Engrossed Involvement

Primary Subscripts

5:     Where there is strong emotion, laughing, smiling, frowning, but the behaviours are in control.

6:     Where there is excessive emotional release, positive or negative, and where the behaviours are observed to be out of control, eg. hugging, jumping up and down, yelling.

V: Where physical violence is occurring.

N: Where observably negative behaviours are being used.

G: Where the individual is interacting in a group

Table 2   *IRG-III Results*

Category	Number of Observations	Percentage
VERBAL AND NONVERBAL	260	1.000
No Apparent Involvement	5	0.019
Distracted Involvement	39	0.149
Spasmodic Involvement	158	0.607
Engrossed Involvement	58	0.223
VERBAL	133	0.512
No Apparent Involvement	0	0.000
Distracted Involvement	17	0.127
Spasmodic Involvement	73	0.549
Engrossed Involvement	43	0.323
NONVERBAL	127	0.488
No Apparent Involvement	5	0.039
Distracted Involvement	22	0.173
Spasmodic Involvement	85	0.669
Engrossed Involvement	15	0.117

In analysing the data obtained, it was concluded that unlike the engrossed involvement behaviours of the singular being, dyads exhibit spasmodic involvement due to the various pastoral behaviours. (The IRG-III results appear in Table 2). The researchers noted that over 60% of all behaviours during dyadic interaction were of the involved (3-13) nature. The percentage was somewhat lower in the verbal mode (approximately 55%) and higher in the nonverbal mode (approximately 67%).

These results clearly illustrate a dilemma facing physical education teachers in the classroom. While trying to provide individualized attention to students, they must constantly be aware of the various other conditions happening within a gymnasium even with assistance from undergraduates. It is also interesting to note that engrossed dyadic behaviour was the second most prevalent behaviour obtained in the total observation (0.223) and in the verbal segment (0.323). However, the fact that the teacher was nonverbal (spasmodic 0.173) illustrates the distraction that is inherent within this situation. The psychophysiological data yielded no significant peaks or valleys with a mean rate of 80.73 beats per minute.

4   Discussion

The findings of the study provide researchers with a viable measurement in the exploration of teacher-student dyadic behaviour in the gymnasium. The conflict that a teacher feels when attempting to form expressive relationships within a class was evident in the measurement results. Most teachers realize that the more positive a model they are to their class, the better the children tend to learn. McAuley (1985) found a direct relation to learning sport skills with modelling. Students who are taught by higher status models perform better than those who learn from low status models (McCullagh, 1986). Teachers of physical education are faced with this problem of intimacy with their classes. In most school physical education settings, classes are larger than in the other academic disciplines. How can the physical education teacher assess the whole class while performing the individual teaching (and pastoral) duties that establish the expressive relationships? How many potential athletes feel invisible in large gymnasiums, lacking dyadic or even small group encouragement and instruction? The spasmodic behaviour displayed in the experiment is an initial indication that the subject sought to control the teaching environment to suit the needs of the students. Teacher-student dyadic interaction in the physical education gymnasium is not something that has to occur at every moment, during every class or even once in an entire unit. In instances where teacher-student dyadic behaviour is appropriate, options should exist for this type of learning to proceed more effectively.

5   Recommendations for Further Study

In light of the findings of this study, it is the author's wish that continuing research explore the following areas:

(a)   Make valid and reliable other descriptive measures relating to dyadic behaviour in the physical education classroom.
(b)   Compare teacher-student dyadic interaction in 'academic' disciplines with the physical education field.
(c)   Study the 'teacher-aide' concept for physical education teachers. Will more adult supervision free teachers for small group and dyadic interaction?
(d)   Continue researching links between the interrelated concepts of social learning and modelling, dyadic interaction and physical education.

6   References

Bandura, A. and Walters, R.H. (1963) **Social Learning and Personality Development.** Holt, Rhinehart and Winston, New York, NY.

Chazan, Barry (1985) **Contemporary Approaches to Moral Education: Analyzing Alternative Theories.** Teachers College Press, New York, NY.

Cheffers, J.T.F., Mancini, V. and Martinek, T.J. (1986) **Interaction Analysis: An Application to Nonverbal and Verbal Activity, 2nd Edition.** Amidon Press, St. Paul, MN.

Crowley-Sullivan, E. (1990) Inside and outside: Involvement levels of pre-schoolers at play. Paper presented at AIESEP World Conference, Loughbourgh, England.

Goodman, S. (1989) Analysis of behaviour and emotional involvement of spectators during pro-hockey games. Unpublished doctoral dissertation, Boston University, Boston, MA.

Greedorfer, S.L. and Lewko, T.H. (1978) Role of family in sport socialization of children. **Research Quarterly,** 49, 146-152.

Martinek, T. and Johnson, S. (1979) Expectant levels of achievement: Effects on interaction and self-concept in elementary age children. **Research Quarterly,** 50, 60-70.

McAuley, F. (1985) Model and self efficacy: A test of Bandura's model. **Journal of Sport Psychology,** 7, 283-295.

McCullagh, P. (1986) Model status as a determinant of observation learning and performance. **Journal of Sport Psychology,** 8, 319-331.

Nastasi, R. (1989) Dyadic behaviour and influences during the social set of the sports crowd. Unpublished doctoral dissertation, Boston University, Boston, MA.

Simmel, Georg (1955) **Conflict and the Web of Group Affiliation.** Collier MacMillan, New York, NY.

RELATIONSHIP OF INSTRUCTOR AND STUDENT VARIABLES TO ACHIEVEMENT IN VOLLEYBALL SKILLS

J.L. GUSTHART AND I. KELLY
University of Saskatchewan, Saskatoon, Canada

Abstract
The purposes of the study were to: (a) establish a volleyball database of videotapes on instructional process behaviour, motor skill achievement data, selected presage and context data; (b) investigate the correlates of presage and context variables to student product learning in volleyball skills. Nine teachers and two hundred and twenty two eighth grade students were the subjects. Teachers were tested on technical knowledge and skill ability in three volleyball skills. They developed and taught a volleyball unit focused on the forearm pass, overhand pass, and underhand serve. All lessons were videotaped for future analysis. Student data on motor skills and technical knowledge from pre-test to post-test were obtained. A dependent t-test was calculated to determine if significant learning had occurred. Multivariate regression analysis were conducted to determine which student behaviours and presage variables were related to student skillful achievement. For the total student group significant learning did occur. Few strong relationships between teacher variables and student learning were found. A much stronger relationship was evident when student variables and learning was analysed.
Keywords: Student Achievement, Student Characteristics, Teacher Variables, Teacher Effects.

1   Introduction

A primary aim of school physical education has been to contribute to student learning in the cognitive, affective and psychomotor domains. Student product learning in these domains has come to be associated with programme effectiveness. Research in school physical education has identified a number of factors which have been studied in relation to student learning. Variables such as presage, context and process have all recently become a focus as they relate to student product achievement. Brophy and Good (1986) suggest that such research which was commonly referred to as 'school effectiveness' might be more accurately described as school effects research. They describe school effectiveness research in the broader view as requiring a definition of what constitutes the total programme success with identifiable instruments to measure student gains over an extended period of time.

A major focus of process research on teaching physical education has been mostly descriptive in nature (Werner and Rink, 1989). Much interesting data has been collected which attempts to provide rich descriptions of the teaching process. However, these descriptions of what physical education teachers behaviours might be, are not totally complete. An in-depth investigation of the process variables, when studied with the outcomes or products of instruction, may help establish a more detailed foundational base. A number of difficulties (such as obtaining good product measures and time limitation for student learning) have developed in attempts to relate learning to instructional behaviour. In addition when measures are available the research seems to suggest that teachers, in general, find student enjoyment a more appropriate goal than student achievement (Veal, 1988).

In the paper 'The Impact and Implications of Research on Teaching and Teacher Education in Physical Education', Bain (1990) makes the point that physical education research must move beyond descriptions of teaching behaviours and programmes to study the impact of an array of variables on student learning. She suggests that whatever research paradigm is selected, the trend is toward research that examines various context as well as instructional behaviours. Silverman (1988) has proposed that for coaches and teachers to completely understand certain aspects of motor skill learning, an awareness of the interrelationships of presage, context, process and product variables must be developed. Researchers are at the initial stages of their understanding the relationship of these variables with student achievement in physical education (Gusthart and Sprigings, 1989).

This paper is the initial phase of a multidimensional investigation of the correlates of student product learning in a select area of volleyball skills. The purposes of the present study were to: (a) establish a volleyball data base of videotapes on instructional process behaviour, motor skill achievement data, selected presage and context data, (b) to determine if learning did take place, (c) investigate the correlates of presage and context variables to student product learning in volleyball skills. The intent was to ascertain whether significant learning was evident and to determine what teacher and student variables were related to student achievement.

The student dependent variables chosen for investigation were the volleyball motor skills of underhand serve, forearm pass and overhand pass. These variables were selected because they reflect critical skills developed and refined at the eighth grade level in the school district. These three skills were stated as requirements in the Provincial Physical Education Curriculum. Furthermore these three skills have been the focus of several research projects in physical education (Gales and Gusthart, 1989; Graham, 1987; Rink, Werner, Hohn, Ward, and Timmermans, 1986; Silverman, 1988, 1990).

The independent variables chosen for investigation were: (a) Student pre-test psychomotor scores for each of the underhand serve, overhead serve and underhand pass, (b) Pre-test composite student cognitive technical knowledge of the three skills, (c) Sex of student, (d) Instructor technical knowledge of the three skills, (e) Instructor total motor score skills for each of the three skills, and (f) years of teaching experience. The rationale for selecting these independent variables was largely based upon the theoretical model developed by Yerg (1986). Her generic model of research in teaching physical education addressed the factors of presage variables, context and the interactive teaching phase. Silverman (1988) has more recently found that some types of student characteristics and teacher presage variables were related to student achievement and others were not. This study was an attempt to isolate some of these variables more specifically.

2   Methodology

2.1 *Subject*

Nine elementary school teachers and their intact classes of eighth grade students from nine discrete schools were chosen for this study. Two hundred and twenty-two students were enrolled in the physical education classes. Piéron (1984) has suggested that intact classes maintain the ecological validity of the instructional setting. All schools were selected from the same general socioeconomic class (middle class suburban) and from the same school district. The teachers were selected by the Research and Development Division of the local school board in consultation with the physical education consultant. A wide variety of teacher attributes were requested. These teachers had from one to twenty-seven years of teaching experience and ranged in age from twenty-seven to forty-eight. Eight of the teachers were male and one female. The school system had established strict guidelines regarding research in the system and these were concurred with through the study. Nine of the ten nominated teachers agreed to participate in the study. One teacher was uncomfortable with the project and withdrew at the very beginning. The project was explained to the teachers and consent was obtained. It was made clear that the teachers could withdraw as the project developed. No teachers withdrew. The curriculum for the school jurisdiction was prescriptive and supervised by a central office physical education consultant. A standard procedure in the school system is to provide all physical education instructors with unit outlines and suggested lesson plans. Individual teachers are free to follow the plan or modify as the situation requires.

2.2 *Instrumentation*

Psychomotor skill testing. Skill testing was conducted for eight of the nine schools at the university. Students and teachers were transported to the university testing station where all testing was conducted by a test team. Six intervarsity volleyball players were trained on test administration and conducted all psychomotor tests. Scheduling difficulties required that one school be tested in the home school. The test team conducted this testing in a similar facility to the university test location and with the university equipment.

Teachers were tested for skill on the forearm pass, overhand pass and underhand serve. The tests, reported below, were similar to those the students would take. Only the number of trials varied. The three skill tests had previously been developed and validated in the university volleyball programme (Tennant, 1989). Trial administrations were conducted to determine if the tests were appropriate for the subjects in the current study. In addition to providing a presage measure, the teachers were made aware of skills taught and testing procedures. The instructors were tested once prior to the unit of instruction.

Students were pre-tested and post-tested on the forearm pass, overhead pass and underhand serve. Pre-test was administered just prior to instruction in the volleyball unit and the post-test, the class period after the unit.

Technical knowledge of skills. Demographic information and a written technical knowledge test was administered at the time of instructor skill testing. The test was developed by a Level Five Certified National Volleyball coach. Both the Level 1 and 2 Canadian Volleyball Association Instructor Manuals (1986) were used as a reference for item selection. Items were then approved by the Provincial Volleyball Association. The final instructor test consisted of true and false items; 35 on forearm pass, 26 on underhand pass and 35 on overhead pass. Total score was determined by number items correct. The student test was comprised of 60 items. Readability checks were conducted prior to commencement of the study.

3   Data Analysis

For instructor effect studies to have meaning, learning must be evident. To test if a statistically significant increase was evident, dependent t-tests were computed on pre-test to post-test scores for each of the three skills. A second procedure was to perform a multivariate multiple regression between the three motor dependent variables: post serve scores, post forearm pass scores and post overhand pass scores to identify which student and presage variables were related to them. The multivariate multiple regression involved three standard multiple regressions on the same independent variables. The student independent variables considered were the following: pre-serve scores, pre-forearm pass scores, pre-overhand pass scores, pre-cognitive test scores and sex. The teacher independent variables considered in the analysis were: total motor skills scores, technical knowledge scores, and years of teaching experience. Analysis was performed using BMDP-6R with assistance from SAS programmes in evaluation of assumptions.

4   Results

Results are presented in two categories, those that deal with student product learning and those that relate to the correlation of presage and context variables.

4.1   *Pre-test to Post-test Learning*

On all three motor performance skills students made statistically significant gains from pre-test to post-test. The t-tests were conducted for all students together. For the serve, $t(221)=4.84$, $p<0.001$, the forearm pass, $t(221)=2.27$, $p<0.007$ and overhand pass, $t(221)=5.74$, $p<0.003$, change was evident.

4.2 *Correlation of Presage and Context Variables with Student Product Learning*

The correlations between all of the variables considered in this study are displayed in Tables 1a and 1 b. In terms of the presage variables two findings were evident. Teacher technical knowledge of the skills is related to their ability to perform the motor skills [r=(0.700), p<0.01]. Overall, teacher motor performance also correlates with the number of years teaching [r=(0.304), p<0.01]. In other words, the longer the teaching experience, the greater the skill level. This may be accounted for in the continual inservice opportunity provided by the school board or to the practice effect which may come with continued application. In terms of the student variables considered, it was evident that entry level skill behaviour on all three pre-motor scores correlate with a variety of other student variables. For example, pre-serve scores correlate with how well students do on the pre-overhead pass [r=(0.368) p<0.01] and pre-forearm pass [r=(0.370), p<0.01]. This finding is also consistent with post-test scores. Students highly skilled in any one skill tend to also be proficient in the other skills studied. The skillful performance as measured by the motor skill tests were constant.

An examination of Table 2 indicates that each of the dependent variables is related to one or more of the independent variables. Each of the overall f-statistics are highly significant (p<0.01). In addition, the multiple correlations (R²) indicate the portion of the variance of the dependent variable due to the independent variables together. In the case of student post-serve scores, differences in student scores on the pre-serve, pre-forearm pass, pre-overhand pass, sex, cognitive test scores and presage variables together explain 56% of the variation in post-serve scores. In the case of the two pass final scores (post-scores) the same independent variables account for about a third of the variation in final scores.

Table 1a.   *Correlation Matrix for Student Variables*

	Student Variables				
Variables	Pre-underhand Serve	Pre-forearm Pass	Pre-overhand Pass	Sex	Pre-Cognitive Score
Pre-serve	1.000				
Pre-forearm pass	0.370Δ	1.000			
Pre-overhand pass	0.368Δ	0.210Δ	1.000		
Sex	0.237Δ	0.242Δ	0.228Δ	1.000	
Pre-cognitive total	0.323Δ	0.180Δ	0.066	0.069	1.000
Motor total	0.409Δ	0.122	0.024	0.007	0.228Δ
Cognitive total	0.374Δ	0.167*	0.019	0.018	0.133
Years teaching	0.054	-0.050	0.044	-0.004	-0.024
Post-serve	0.673Δ	0.398Δ	0.0463Δ	0.220Δ	0.260Δ
Post-forearm pass	0.369Δ	0.469Δ	0.330Δ	0.191Δ	0.138
Post-overhand pass	0.367Δ	0.254Δ	0.485Δ	0.155*	0.105

   *   p<0.05   Δ p<0.01 (two-tailed) Df = 220

Table 1b. Correlation Matrix for Presage and Dependent Variables

Variables	Presage Variables			Dependent Variables		
	Motor Score	Cognitive Score	Years Teaching	Post-underhand Serve	Post-forearm Pass	Post-overhand Pass
Pre-serve						
Pre-forearm pass						
Pre-overhand pass						
Sex						
Pre-cognitive total						
Motor total	1.000					
Cognitive total	0.700Δ	1.000				
Years teaching	0.304Δ	0.158	1.000			
Post-serve	0.324Δ	0.346Δ	0.152	1.000		
Post-forearm pass	0.254Δ	0.214*	0.115	0.402Δ	1.000	
Post-overhand pass	0.004	0.011	0.042	0.374Δ	0.402Δ	1.000

   * $p<0.05$ Δ $p<0.01$ (two-tailed) Df = 220

Table 2.   Correlations for Dependent Variables

Dependence Significance Variable	R^2	F-statistic	(p less than)
Post-serve	0.56	33.17	0.000Δ
Post-forearm pass	0.33	12.74	0.000Δ
Post-overhand pass	0.30	11.33	0.000Δ

   Δ $p<0.01$

Table 3.   Standardized Regression Coefficients for Variables

	Dependent Variable		
	Post-underhand Serve	Post-forearm Pass	Post-overhand Pass
Student Variables			
Post-serve	0.460	0.085	0.245
Post-forearm pass	0.148	0.372	0.108
Post-overhand pass	0.250	0.206	0.375
Sex	0.012	0.034	-0.014
Pre-cognitive total	0.059	-0.004	0.014
Teacher Variables			
Motor skills	-0.037	0.145	-0.114
Cognitive total	0.144	0.003	-0.037
Years teaching	0.113	0.075	0.058

Table 3 provides information on which independent variables are strongly related to the post-scores. The standardized regression coefficients (or beta weights) indicate how much a variable is contributing to successful prediction of the dependent variable. The larger the (absolute) value of the beta weight of a variable compared to another variable the more it contributed to the dependent variable. In each case, as one might expect, the variable most strongly related to the post-scores is the pre-score on the same variable. For example, the pre-serve student score is most strongly related to the post-serve scores.

It is interesting to note that the pre-overhand pass seems to be related to all three dependent variables (post-serve, $\beta3=0.250$; post-forearm pass, $\beta=0.206$; and post-overhand pass $\beta=0.375$). This may suggest that the overhead pass may include some general movement skills which may lead to successful performance in the forearm pass and serve as well as overhead passing ability. This finding merits further investigation. It was also interesting to note that post-serve scores were strongly related to teacher technical knowledge ($\beta=0.144$) and years of teaching ($\beta=0.113$).

5   Summary

The data from this study indicate that on all three psychomotor skills learning did occur from pre-test to post-test. This learning was evident in a relatively short eight lesson span. These results are consistent with Silverman's (1988) findings and support the position that opportunity to participate in an instructional volleyball programme can produce significant psychomotor improvement. The finding that learning was evident allowed further investigation of presage and context variables.

In terms of student characteristics there were significant relationships between student entry level and eventual skill performance for all three skills. It was of particular interest to note the beta weights indicated that students who are highly skilled on the overhand pass are also highly skilled on all other dependent variables. This finding may serve as a focus of further investigation. It may be that this skill is the most complex (for this age group) skill investigated. Mastery may indicate the previous two skills have also developed. To determine the extent to which this may be so, it would be necessary to investigate the sequence of task presentations for the teachers.

In terms of the teacher variables studied no strong relationships were found with student learning. However, it was of interest to note that teachers' technical knowledge of the skill was related to their ability to perform the skills well. The most knowledgeable teachers were also the most skillful. It is of interest to note that in this study neither of these variables were strongly related to student performance. It would, however, be premature to conclude that the impact of the teacher variables were not in any way related to student performance. It may be plausible to suggest that over a longer period of time (term or year) these same variables of technical knowledge and skill may be evident on student skillful performance. Such teacher characteristics may be cumulative and not evident in such a short period of time as was considered in this study

This study was an initial attempt to understand some of the relationships which may accrue with student product learning. A large database was established which will facilitate future study of presage, context and process variables.

6   References

Bain, L. (1990, April) The impact and implication of research on teaching and teacher education in physical education. Presented at annual meeting of the American Educational Research Association, Boston.

Brophy, J.E. and Good, L.T. (1986) Teacher behavior and student achievement. In **Handbook of Research on Teaching** (ed M.C. Wittrock), (3rd edition), Macmillan, New York, pp. 328-371.

Canadian Volleyball Association. (1986) **Coaches Manual Level 1 and 2 Volleyball.** Ottawa, Ontario, C.V.A.

Gales, H. and Gusthart, L. (1989, June) Instructional behavior and student achievement. Paper presented at AIESEP World Conference Movement and Sport, Jyvaskyla, Finland.

Graham, K. (1987) A description of academic work and student performance during a middle school volleyball unit. **Journal of Teaching in Physical Education,** 7, 22-37.

Gusthart, L. and Sprigings, E. (1989) Student learning as a measure of teacher effectiveness in physical education. **Journal of Teaching in Physical Education,** 8(4), 298-311.

Piéron, M. (1984) Analysis of research based on observation of the teaching of physical education. **FIEB Bulletin,** 54(314), 39-42.

Rink, J., Werner, P.H., Hohn, R.C., Ward, D.S. and Timmermans, H.M. (1986) Differential effects of three teachers over a unit of instruction. **Research Quarterly for Exercise and Sport,** 57, 132-138.

Silverman, S. (1988) Relationship of selected presage and context variables to achievement. **Research Quarterly for Exercise and Sport,** 59, 35-40.

Silverman, S. (1990, April) Validity of Cheffers adaptation of Flanders interaction analysis system. Paper presented at the annual meeting of the American Education Research Association, Boston.

Tennant, M. (1989) **Development of volleyball skills test.** Unpublished manuscript, University of Saskatchewan, College of Physical Education.

Veal, M.L. (1988) Pupil assessment perception and practices of secondary teachers. **Journal of Teaching in Physical Education,** 7(4), 327-342.

Werner, P. and Rink, J. (1989) Case studies of teacher effectiveness in second grade physical education. **Journal of Teaching in Physical Education,** 8(4), 280-297.

Yerg, B. (1986) Research on teaching in physical education: An interactive model in operation. In **Sport Pedagogy** (eds M. Pieron and G. Graham), Human Kinetics, Champaign, Illinois, pp. 49-55.

A CONTENT ANALYSIS STUDY OF THE NON-SUCCESS FEATURES OF PRE-SERVICE TEACHERS' SWIMMING LESSONS AS PERCEIVED BY PRE-SERVICE TEACHERS AND SUPERVISORS

COLIN A. HARDY
Department of PE & Sports Science, Loughborough University, England

Abstract

The researcher extracted the non-success features (Placek and Dodds, 1988) from evaluation reports written by pre-service teachers and supervisors on actual swimming lessons taught by pre-service teachers. The statements were sorted and placed in one of twenty-three non-success categories. The ninety-six reports of the thirty-two pre-service teachers and the fifty-eight reports of the nine supervisors provided 337 and 411 non-success statements respectively. Apart from the occasional report with no statements and one supervisor's report with eighteen, the range of non-success statements was from one to twelve, with each pre-service teacher providing three reports and each supervisor between five and eight. The largest group of responses for both the pre-service teachers (47.78%) and the supervisors (89.05%) was teacher-centred. The largest individual categories for the pre-service teachers were pupil-centred, and these were non-compliance (17.80%) and difficulty with task (14.24%). With the supervisors the two largest individual categories were teacher-centred, and these were presentation of material (20.92%) and professional skills (14.84%). In general, pre-service teachers were more aware of the non-success features associated with the swimming environment and prior conditions than were supervisors, and they were more likely to see the cause of the non-success lying with the pupils. The difference in emphasis placed on the various non-success categories indicate that there could be conflict between the two groups unless supervisors initially try and match their comments to the pre-service teachers' levels of concern.

1   Objectives

(a)To understand what pre-service teachers see as salient features of their own non-successful teaching of swimming.

(b)To understand what supervisors see as salient features of pre-service teachers' non-successful teaching of swimming.

2   Method

The pre-service teachers' reports were based on swimming lessons taught during the year 1988-89, and the supervisors' reports were based on all swimming lessons seen between 1984 and 1988. The swimming lessons were taken by post-graduate pre-service teachers at Loughborough University in their final eleven week practicum.

Once the non-success features of the swimming lessons had been reliably extracted, each statement was recorded on an index card. A classification system was established and piloted and then the non-success statements were categorized independently by the researcher and a second coder. Inter-coder and intra-coder agreements for both sets of statements were checked using Scott's Pi Coefficient of Reliability; the pi value ranged from 0.89 to 0.92. Statements that had resulted in inter- and intra-coder disagreement were re-assessed by the researcher and the second coder. The statements were not always resolved in favour of the researcher. Frequencies and percentages were then calculated for the categorized card clusters.

3   Results

3.1 *Pre-service Teachers' Self-Evaluation Reports (Fig.1)*

(a)   Teacher-centred response categories made up the largest group of responses although no one category accounted for more than twenty-six responses (7.72%). The pre-service teachers recognized that they had made errors in choosing and organizing material, in presenting material and in judging lesson time. They acknowledged that they had some difficulties with managing and controlling pupils, and that their professional skills could be improved.

(b)   The two pupil-centred response categories of non-compliance and difficulty with the task accounted for 108 (32.04%) of the pre-service teachers' responses. The pre-service teachers acknowledged that their pupils had difficulty with swimming tasks and that they misbehaved at times, but the pre-service teachers did not seem to feel that they were responsible for these problems.

(c)   The remainder of the non-success responses centred around the environment and prior conditions. The pre-service teachers recognized that the general acoustics in a swimming pool and some unanticipated activity could affect the success of their swimming lessons.

Figure 1   *Pre-service teachers' statements of the non-success features of their swimming lessons in categories*

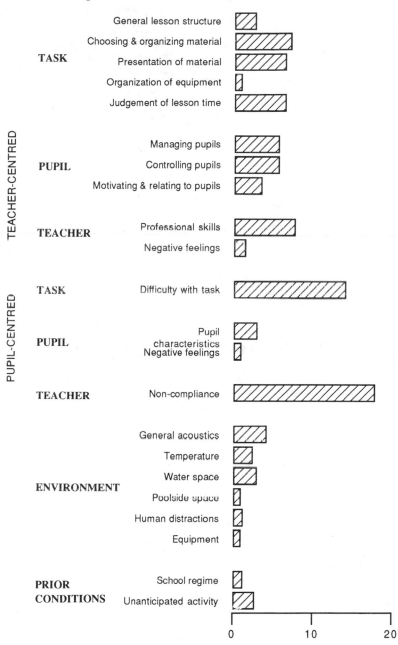

Figure 2.   *Supervisors' statments of the non-success features of pre-service teachers' swimming lessons in categories*

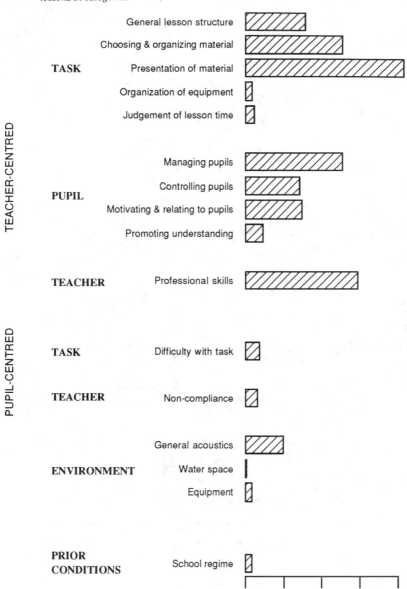

3.2 *Supervisors' Evaluation Reports (Fig.2)*

(a) Teacher-centred response categories made up the largest group of responses by far, with four categories accounting for 253 (61.56%) of responses. The supervisors felt that many of the pre-service teachers'errors were in their presentation of and their choosing and organization of material, in their managing of pupils and in their general professional skills. In addition, the pre-service teachers' general lesson structure and their inability to motivate and relate to and control pupils were also seen by the supervisors as factors affecting the success of swimming lessons.

(b) Apart from some attention to the general acoustics of a swimming pool, responses centred around the pupil, environment and prior conditions were seldom seen by the supervisors as factors affecting the success of swimming lessons.

4   Conclusions

(a) Teacher-centred response categories made up the largest group of responses for both the pre-service teachers and the supervisors. However, whereas this type of response dominated the supervisors' responses, the pre-service teachers also centred many of their responses around the pupils, environment and prior conditions.

(b) The differences in emphasis placed on the various non-success categories by the two groups indicate that conflict could occur between them unless they try and understand each other's perspective.

(c) If pre-service teachers are to benefit from the observations of supervisors, the latter's comments should initially match the pre-service teachers' level of concern, and then, with this basis of mutual understanding, the supervisors can help the pre-service teachers to understand the relationships between teaching behaviours and pupil learning.

5   Classification Definitions with Examples

Key   (P) - Pre-Service Teachers;   (S) - Supervisors

(a) General Lesson Structure
Any comment on the overall pattern of the lesson with reference to such features as balance, pace, perspective and variety, and to the overall organization of tasks within the lesson.
(P) 'I need to vary my tempo more. It's getting very predictable, e.g. No.1, No.2.'
(S) 'In a 50 minute lesson you need to think of symmetry to keep interest.'

(b) Choosing and Organizing Material
Any comment on the appropriateness of the material chosen, the organization of practices and the omission of practices.
(P) 'I don't think I should have extended to lunge dive as the quality from the kneeling dive was not sufficiently attractive. They still had their heads up.'

(S)   'Try to get the elbow up was probably enough - entry was little too advanced.'

(c)   Presentation of Material

Any comment about how the teacher communicated the material to the pupils with reference to choice of language, technical accuracy, the use of instructional cues and the use of demonstrations.

(P)   'In teaching arm actions, one teaching point at a time only! I tended to give one, then join on with another.'

(S)   'Back crawl task: One width **thinking** about your legs. Thinking about what?'

(d)   Organization of Equipment

Any comment relating to the provision, setting up or placing of equipment.

(P)   'I did not have the rubber bricks on hand and had to ask the Supervisor to go and get me 3.'

(S)   'Equipment - always bring floats with you - they are very useful, often needed and a safety aid.'

(e)   Judgment of Lesson Time

Any comment relating to judging time for a task, a series of tasks or for a whole lesson.

(P)   'I think my plan was a bit overambitious as I under-estimated the time it would take to get through backstroke and start.'

(S)   'You moved through your progressions rather too quickly.'

(f)   Managing Pupils

Any comment relating to managing or organising the pupils before, during or after the task.

(P)   'Might have brought everyone into the middle section before giving figures on diving accidents.'

(S)   'There was a delay in your coming through to the pool - don't send students through until you are ready. Deal with multigym, valuables, doors, etc. first.'

(g)   Control of Pupils

Any comment relating to disruption, disobedience or inattention which is not dealt with adequately by the teacher.

(P)   'I am guilty of being too soft, I had one child out of the pool for not doing as I had said. However, I let him back in about 5 minutes when I might have left him longer to think about things.'

(S)   'Keep your eye on the behaviour of the large fellow - you did speak to him but he needed attention before this.'

(h)   Motivating and Relating to Pupils

Any comments about motivating or relating to pupils as individuals or as a group.

(P)   'I didn't pay enough attention to the couple of pupils who were struggling.'

(S)   'If you can, add smiles, nods as they complete each width.'

(i)   Promoting Understanding

Any comment relating to promoting pupil understanding of the basic principles of swimming.

(S) 'He needs to appreciate action - opposite reaction - direction of kick to direction of drive.'

(j)   Professional Skills

Any comment relating to presentation of self with regards to voice, appearance, behaviour, mannerisms. Any comment relating to basic skills such as observing, positioning and gesturing.

(P) 'I tend to wander into group and lose sight of edges.'

(S) "Position yourself and then give your information - avoid 'walk and talk'."

(k) Negative Feelings

Any comment concerning negative feelings about self or about lesson or teaching in general.

(P) 'I was pretty apathetic."

(l)   Difficulty with Task

Any comment relating to pupils' difficulty with the task or failure to achieve the objective. The assumption is that reasonable efforts have been made by the teacher in the planning and presentation stages.

(P) 'They didn't quite grasp the spin turn for the backstroke.'

(S) 'Their breast stroke leg-kicks were still quite weak; a number still had screw kicks.'

(m) Pupil Characteristics

Any comment on characteristics of individuals or groups such as level of ability.

(P) 'One non-swimmer in group causes problems.'

(n) Negative Feelings (Pupil)

Any comment suggesting a general dislike of swimming or PE by pupils.

(P) '...two lacked enthusiasm for swimming.'

(o) Non-Compliance

Any comment where pupils disobeyed instructions, failed to pay attention or generally misbehaved. In this category the blame is laid on the pupil; the teacher is not held responsible for failing to assert control.

(P) 'I had a problem with the boys. They wouldn't hold hands with the girls.'

(S) 'Concentration and commitment to task poor - they are hard work.'

(p) General Acoustics

Any comment relating to the acoustics or general background noise of the swimming pool.

(P) '...noisy, echoey. Voice projection difficult again.'

(S) 'Because of air conditioning and heater noise I was unable to decipher much of your instructions.'

(q) Temperature
     Any comment relating to the termperature of air or water in the swimming pool.
     (P) 'Conditions extremely difficult - very hot.'

(r) Water Space
     Any comment relating to the shape, size or depth of the swimming pool.
     (P) 'I had 22 children with enough space for 9 comfortably.'
     (S) 'Feet off the bottom is virtually impossible in your pool - the same limitation of long throws, etc. can be achieved with one shoulder in the water.'

(s) Poolside Space
     Any comment relating to the shape or size of the poolside space available.
     (P) 'It is difficult because we are enclosed by the bottom and top groups and this prevents me being at one end so I can see all the boys.'

(t) Human Distractions
     Any comment relating to distractions to pupils' attention in the swimming pool.
     (P) '...public session, therefore distractions around pupils.'

(u) Equipment
     Any comment relating to the adequacy or suitability of equipment.
     (P) 'There were no half bricks, only blow-up arm bands and no light sinkable objects.'
     (S) 'Were there any more floats available?'

(v) School Regime
     Any comment relating to the regulations and restrictions imposed by the school regime.
     (P) 'At times I got groups that were on the large side and others which were very small.'
     (S) 'This was quite a short lesson which raises the issue of what to teach given the time.'

(w) Unanticipated Activity
     Any comment relating to a change in composition of class or length of lesson time that could not reasonably be foreseen.
     (P) 'I did not expect 9 children and of these there was 1 new girl which had not attended before, 2 new boys, and 2 boys which did not attend last week's session.'

6   References

Placek, J.H. and Dodds, P. (1988) A critical incident study of pre-service teachers' beliefs about teaching success and nonsuccess. **Research Quarterly for Exercise and Sport, 59** (4), 351-358.

THE PSYCHOLOGICAL FACTORS UNDERPINNING THE 'TEACHING FOR UNDERSTANDING GAMES' MOVEMENT

ROD THORPE
Department of PE & Sports Science, Loughborough University, England

This paper was designed to accompany a practical workshop.

1   Introduction

In the December, 1989, AIESEP newsletter, Magill and Pieron discuss the need for the areas of Sport Pedagogy and Motor Learning to work more closely together. Whilst at times it might be difficult to replicate exactly the laboratory experiment in the field, it is surely naive to ignore the findings from such kindred disciplines when developing a teaching approach. Indeed it is suggested here that the findings from the fields of Sports Psychology and Motor Learning provided the impetus for the development of what has become known, in Britain at least, as 'The Understanding Approach to Teaching Games' (or Games Centred Games).

Despite the fact that two of the central figures in the development of the approach (the author and David Bunker), work in the areas of Sports Psychology and Motor Learning, the psychological underpinning has not been adequately articulated. Explanations for this omission are quite clear, the exploration of this emerging idea demanded close scrutiny of content together with the appropriate progressions for representing the development of a game. This was seen as important because the team involved in the project recognized the need for a more adequate knowledge base for teachers. Put simply, teachers wanted to assess the effectiveness of the approach rather than discuss the psychological theory underpinning it.

At the functional level the development of the approach, 'teaching games for understanding', was a direct result of the observations we had made of our students and practising teachers presenting games using a skills[1] dominated approach. We realised that the intrinsic motivation of the children to play the game was subjugated to the teacher's desire to give them better techniques. An intrinsic desire to learn the techniques was rarely fostered. How could we resolve the dilemma that, as we taught Motor Learning and Sports Psychology, we stressed the importance of

---

[1]   This form of lesson might be more accurately called 'technique' dominated approach in that the movement practised was rarely in the context of the game

enhancing 'intrinsic' motivation, yet when we moved into the 'methodology area' we persisted with an approach which we felt had the opposite effect? Other considerations, not least, the outcomes we expected from a games education, directed our thinking. The following extract from 'A Changing Focus in Games Education' (Thorpe and Bunker, 1989) outlines the approach.

> Throughout the 1970s an approach to teaching games was formulated which placed the emphasis on ensuring that children understood the games they played while capitalizing on the intrinsic motivation most youngsters bring towards playing the game.

It is interesting to note that we use the phrase 'playing the game' but we do not use the phrase 'playing athletics' or 'playing swimming'. The problem seems to have been that a number of teachers found it difficult to resolve the relationship between the game and game skills.

Clearly to play a game well the skills have to be well-practised and it is logical to give children as much skill practice as possible. The major problem with this approach is that we (and many teachers we discovered later) realized that for many children the time available in the curriculum was insufficient to perfect or even reach adequate levels with many of the games skills, particularly if the teacher was always teaching the average child. Of course, teachers taught through the game and conditioned practices, but, by their own admission, did not really have a clear philosophy or framework within which to work. This problem seems to be international if the comment made in the introduction to our article, presented in the South Australian PE Bulletin in 1984, is typical:

> . . the idea of progressing from tactics to skills, or from Why? to How? rather than vice versa, is not new, but its organization and application has not previously been made coherent.

The model we proposed passes through the following stages in order

    (a)   Game
    (b)   Game Appreciation
    (c)   Tactical Awareness
    (d)   Making appropriate decisions
          - What to do
          - How to do it?
    (e)   Skill execution
    (f)   Performance

The typical games lesson of Introduction, Skill, and Game is rejected (Thorpe and Bunker, 1983).

Discussion in this paper will focus on competitive games and examples will be taken from games in the British culture. This is not to deny the attractiveness of the approach for helping children develop their own games, which could, if so desired, be essentially cooperative. It is, however, our view that part of our role is to help children realize that, for example, rules are arrived at by cooperation to make the game a better competition, and also that much competitive sport is played between friends.

2   Evaluating the Approach against a Psychological Framework

2.1 *Intrinsic Motivation*

It is essential to return to the underlying problem. 'How to capitalize on and enhance the 'intrinsic' desire to play games?' It is our finding, supported by several hundred teachers (Almond and Thorpe,1988), that this desire is very common in children, particularly when they are protected from embarrassment or perceived danger. Equally, it is our observation that it is those people that enjoy playing games that have well developed game skills. It is naive however to think that everyone entering a games teaching or coaching situation does so with the desire to play games. Many adults play games and understand games; they come to the lesson for technical assistance. A recent study (McPherson and French, 1989) reported that college students enrolling for tennis, learned better when skills were taught before tactics than others taught with a tactics first approach. In a group with knowledge of the sport and the intrinsic motivation to become better at the techniques of the sport, the teacher/coach might move quickly to technique work. It is our finding in schools, however, that most children wish to start in the game, using the relatively limited skills they have to hand; after a little while, some youngsters may ask for help with the skills - they are ready and we must help them.

In some ways this distinction between the pupil committed to performance improvement and the pupil committed to involvement for other reasons may illustrate why 'coaching procedures' may not be appropriate for the PE lesson.

2.2 *The Incentives of Playing Games*

Accepting that the teacher should use the intrinsic motivation of the child seems logical, it follows that the teacher must surely be aware of the incentives that might be operating in this situation. The extensive work on 'incentive systems' operating in sport, which developed from the work of Alderman and Wood (1976), has led to a general acceptance that **affiliation** (social interaction, social reassurance, making friends, etc.), **achievement** (in the sense of doing something well or better), **stress** or perhaps the less emotive term **sensation** (which might embrace excitement, being active, appropriate nervousness, etc) and **self direction** are central to involvement in sport. (Whilst we might debate differences between games in the PE programme and sport, children will surely consider they are playing a sport.) Such a list must only be used as a guide because as Whitehead (1988) suggests the incentives list may require modification for younger children.

Whitehead presents 6 goals for success; showing ability, task mastery, social approval, victory, breakthrough and teamwork.

2.3 *Affiliation*

Because the 'understanding approach' stresses the game and 'guides' children to discover and develop the game, it capitalizes on the incentive of affiliation in a number of ways.

(a) The rules necessary to play the game are developed by the children - which involves discussion with the 'opposition'.

(b) The approach challenges children to work out the ways to arrive at appropriate tactics - which necessitates cooperation with their own team-mates.

(c) Skill is practised individually or in small groups - anticipating that children will work with others, independent of the teacher.

Teachers may have to work for tolerance, equity, etc but the approach provides a situation in which this can happen.

2.4 *Achievement*

The idea of doing something well and/or better can be accepted merely as an incentive which can be utilized to increase participation in the sport. This is, of course, failing to recognize the wealth of evidence tieing outcome to self esteem. It was the observation of 'traditional' games lessons, in which teachers worked hard to teach the techniques necessary to play the game, that caused us to question whether, with mixed ability and mixed motivation grouping and limited time, many children were achieving anything when 'technique' was the focus. Skilful children were being taught techniques they had mastered earlier, less able children were finding yet new techniques to fail at. Because the skill was the central component of the lesson, the obvious conclusion to be drawn was that failure to produce the skill meant failure in games. For those teaching the early primary/elementary age range it is important to recognize that because failure at a task is attributed to lack of effort, rather than lack of ability in the younger child (Roberts, 1990) failure at a task may not generalize to failure to play games. Games based around technical skills may be appropriate at this age, these games are usually less tactically complex (see Thorpe et al, 1984).

Unlike activities such as track and field, gymnastics and swimming, in which time/distance/form are essential measures, the outcome of games are always relative to the opponent. It is possible to play a 'good' game, with 'poor' techniques. We would like to think that we have helped teachers realize that to develop some of the skills needed to play the adult forms of some games (field hockey, soccer, tennis, etc) may be impossible within the PE programme, but it is possible to help children succeed. If motivation is enhanced and opportunity provided, children may wish to commit the necessary time outside the PE programme to improve all elements of their games. Success might therefore be measured in continued commitment to sport rather than short term performance changes.

A unit for badminton was proposed by the author (Thorpe and Bunker,1982), which stressed the development of knowledge to exploit the long-short nature of the game. The better youngsters might hit much longer and use disguise, but less able youngsters can still move their opponent to open up the spaces. The teacher first watches for good use of space rather than for technical proficiency. Teachers who tried the approach often remarked that they found themselves saying positive things to all the children, including the less physically able. (Coventry teachers 'Action Research Project', in Almond and Thorpe, 1988). The use of the phrase 'good try' to mean 'you cannot do what I ask but you are staying on task', disappears. The value of a positive climate in the teaching situation has been stressed by behaviourists and humanists alike; it is most gratifying that teachers report an increase in positive statements.

2.5 *Sensation/stress*

'Doing something well' in games can take many forms; some children might be quite satisfied with exploiting the spaces, might work hard to beat an opponent on an individual point but do not 'at this time' wish to 'keep score'. Others will wish to place themselves into competitive situations, they will welcome the additional stress, they may well be a little nervous, they will probably work harder physically and enjoy the sensation of a good 'work out'. Despite the fact that generations of PE teachers have been introduced to concepts like 'need to achieve/ need to avoid failure' and more recently the differential effects of competitive stress on individuals, a badminton lesson will often include a mini-tournament for everyone. The recognition that some people enjoy playing 'competitive' games but consider the score irrelevant must influence the way the teacher uses competition and would seem to indicate that a tournament be introduced with care, perhaps as an option to continued practice. In lessons based on team games (particularly those with many people in a team) it is often difficult to meet the needs of the individuals within them, in such situations children are forced into the game intensity of the majority. This may be a contributory factor in the reported tendency (Murdoch, 1987) for young people in Britain to move toward the individual sports.

2.6 *Social Facilitation*

The idea of doing something well and feeling competent cannot be separated from issues of self-confidence, which in turn are central in multi-dimensional approaches to anxiety assessment. Lack of ability in itself may not be a problem, but the public exhibition of that lack of ability is. The lesson in which the children do the same thing, at the same time, and are shown how to identify the possible faults in the performance, can be investigated against a framework of 'social facilitation' findings. The key phrases in this theory are;

(a) that an 'evaluative' audience is necessary for the social facilitation effect; note that the teacher has developed this 'evaluative capacity' by giving all the children the ability to identify shortcomings and recognize 'good' and 'bad' technique,

(b)   that less well learnt skills are detrimentally affected by the presence of the evaluative audience.

Thus the less able children have poor skills to start with and the learning environment ensures that this lack of skill can be clearly recognized by their peers. We should not be surprised, therefore, that the skill deteriorates. Further we should not be surprised when these children take no part in or disrupt the activity, bring notes or absent themselves from the lesson. Placing skill in the background to be dealt with at the individual level might overcome this.

Clearly what is needed are activities the children can do and privacy to practise the things they cannot do. Again the badminton example might help.

As a 'coach' with a small group of well motivated and confident youngsters, I might well work on the overhead clear (an overhead action not dissimilar to the tennis service or smash) to the back of the court with the whole group. As a Physical Education teacher I would not use the same approach with a typical class of children simply because I know many would be unable to produce an action to either replicate the 'form' of the technique or to send the shuttle to the back of the court. Many would fail and be seen to fail. I might however take a 'whole class' session to help them all understand the flight path for the slow drop shot (a shot dropping steeply close to the net), because I have found from experience that this can be achieved with the very basic push of the less able, with the well formed action of the intermediate child and with the late deception necessary at high levels. All children can succeed and improve in the task irrespective of quite large differences in physical skill. When it is not possible to present skill in a way that all can succeed (for example with the overhead clear), technique teaching occurs in small groups of pupils with like needs. The rest of the class do not need to know what is happening and will continue with their game or practice. Privacy is achieved because the attention of the class is elsewhere.

A key factor in the teaching for understanding approach is that children play with equipment that allows them to think within the game, i.e. the skill demand is not taking all the attention capacity (see later). This can mean that the most appropriate equipment for many children in a tennis game might be a short handled racket and a sponge ball, but others might be capable of using the faster tennis ball. This could cause the better children to comment that the less able "are not good enough for the 'proper' equipment". Teachers who have used modified equipment have had most success when all children have the option of all equipment and can change equipment in their own time. The fact that the better players do play with the easy equipment sometimes - when they wish to have long rallies and move into the net - and the less able youngsters try the 'proper' equipment occasionally - perhaps in a cooperative game - breaks down the most obvious evaluative comparisons.

It is this author's opinion that physical ineptitude is far more embarrassing to children than lack of mental ability, if only because it is so much more obvious. We should not try to disguise these differences in physical ability but we need not make them the central component of our games lessons.

2.7 Self Direction

The teaching for understanding approach does not claim to make excellent performers in games, it does attempt to produce individuals who realize that whatever their ability (or disability) they 'can' play games and there is much to learn about games. Because the approach recognizes individual differences, it encourages teaching approaches that require individual responsibility. Children are presented with problems they have to solve. The recognition that in some situations leaving children to practise alone may be beneficial;

(a) for the retention of motor skills even when immediate performance is degraded (Schmidt et al, 1987, Wright and Thorpe, 1990),

(b) as a means to generating responsibility for play and practice beyond the lesson,

(c) as a means of moving the authority and power from the teacher.

Such procedures depend on the children wishing to continue to play and practise and so we return to intrinsic motivation. It must be noted that some psychologists see the element of self-determination as crucial in this intrinsic motivation.

> Intrinsically motivated behaviours are ones which a person engages in so that he may feel competent and self-determining in relation to his environment. (Deci, 1975)

2.8 Perception, Decision Making, Response.

Games, perhaps more than any other area of Physical Education, embrace equally the three components of a perceptual-motor skill; perception, decision making and response. The evidence from the skill acquisition, teaching and coaching literature is that the response element dominates our thinking. Only recently have researchers tried to tease out the perceptual components of games (reviewed by Abernethy, 1987) or coaches tried to unravel the decision making components of a given sport (eg Greenwood, 1986). The teaching for understanding approach places the perceptual problem first, seeks a solution and only then tries to find a response to match. If the child cannot strike a ball, the child might still play a tennis-like game by throwing the ball. The perceptual and decision making components of 'throw' tennis are almost identical to those of 'hit' tennis. Once one acknowledges that there are things to be learnt about perception and decision making, one is forced to examine the logic in which this information is presented to children; in Britain at least, there is no logic to the order. The first structured games that children meet are soccer and netball; as team invasion games the perceptual and decision making problems they pose are several times more complex than games like tennis. There is of course a reason for this order. As adults the simpler the game perceptually and in decision making terms, the more difficult should be the response component if we are to perceive a challenge. This response difficulty excludes children, but if we change the response demand we can open up the game. Mini games do this but they may also retain the complexity of the tactics. The idea of guiding children through games with increasing perceptual/decision making complexity has been discussed elsewhere. (Thorpe and Bunker,1989).

2.9   *The Limited Concentration Channel*

The idea of the human as a limited information processor has been with us for half a century. The implications of this limitation to a teaching for understanding approach may be best served by using the model proposed by Stallings (1982) who suggests a limited concentration channel that must be shared between

(a)   perceptual analysis,
(b)   choice of action plan,
(c)   attention to motor control.

Returning to the badminton example, the children are playing singles on a long/narrow court, all the children can manage to hit the shuttle back and forth, with greater or lesser success, in a cooperative rally. The teacher now poses the basic questions;

(a)   how do you win a point?
(b)   where is the space to hit into?
(c)   how can you best cover the space on your court?

The answers are slow in coming from the game, and there is little movement to show understanding. The Stallings model prompts us to ask if enough 'concentration' can be applied to the questions. Personal experience, supported by many teachers, is that if the rackets are placed aside for a few minutes and a game of underhand throw badminton is played with a volley ball, the pupils soon provide the answer. They have time to think about the problem, the ball is held and attention is not drawn to the response component. Once the perception and appropriate decision have been thought through return to the racket produces a change. The response may not be perfect even by individual standards but in terms of the model 'what to do' has been resolved, 'how to do it' may take a little longer.

The skill of the teacher is to recognize where attention might be placed at any time. We would suggest using striking implements like hockey sticks for a considerable time in tactically simple games before moving into the tactically complex game of hockey. At times a cooperative feeder or a tee in games like cricket, baseball, rounders is used to overcome the striking problem. We use cooperative feeders when the skill is quite well learnt to ensure that the limited concentration channel can be placed on how to beat the field rather than on how to hit the ball.

2.10   *Schema theory*

The idea that children need to learn the rules by which motor programmes might be modified to meet particular demands which underlies schema theory, supports the anecdotal evidence provided by teachers that children with a varied activity experience early in life seem best able to cope with the new situations which arise throughout their games education. A games education should allow children to use a range of skills in a variety of situations. By breaking the tendency to use certain skills only in the game form observed in the adult game, particularly in the primary/elementary school, teachers might go some way to providing this skill education. The skill of throwing can be practised and 'generalized' by playing different forms of games. Throw tennis played on small courts with an underhand two handed throw of a large ball, will produce a slightly different response to a one hand under arm pitch with a 'softball' but are there common 'rules' operating. Children like games, the skill of the teacher is to give a reasonable variety of games which embrace different skills contingent with the development of the child (a logic for the choice of games has been discussed elsewhere, Thorpe et al. 1984). For a fuller account of the relationship between Schema Theory and the Teaching for Understanding Approach see Piggott (1982).

3   Summary

These few examples might indicate how a psychological framework can provide a structure against which we might reflect about both the aims of our games lessons and the outcomes. Time does not allow for a complete analysis but hopefully this presentation has indicated that whilst there may be a need to replicate specific laboratory experiments in the field, there would seem to be an even greater need to examine our teaching behaviours against the larger framework of Motor Learning and Sports Psychology theory.

4   References

Abernethy, B.(1987) Anticipation in Sports: a review. **Physical Education Review**, 10, 1, 5-6.

Alderman, R.B. and Wood, N.L. (1976). An analysis of incentive motivation in Canadian Athletics. **Canadian Journal of Applied Sports Sciences.** 1, 169-176.

Almond, L. and Thorpe, R.D. (1988). Asking teachers to research. **Journal of Teaching in Physical Education,** 7, .3, 221-227.

Bunker, D.J. and Thorpe, R.D., 1982. A model for the teaching of games in the secondary schools. **The Bulletin of Physical Education.** 18, 1, 9-16.[2]

Greenwood, J.T.(1986) Think Rugby, A Guide to purposeful team play. London; A&C Black.

Lawton, J. (1987) A comparison of two teaching methods. Unpub. M.Sc. dissertation. Loughborough University.

McPherson, S. and French, K.E. (1989) Changes in cognitive strategies and motor skills in tennis.**Psychology of Motor Behaviour Abstracts.** NASPSPA.

Murdoch, E., (1987). Sport in Schools. **Desk top study commissioned by the Departments of Education and Science and of Environment.**

Piggott, R.E. (1982) A psychological basis for new trends in games teaching. **Bulletin of Physical Education,** 19, 17-22.

Roberts, G.C. (1990) The importance of the study of children in sport: an overview. In Lee, M. (ed) **Children in Competitive Sport.** Whiteline Press.

Schmidt, R.A., Shapiro, D.C., Suinnen, S. and Young, D.E. (1987) Optimising summary knowledge of results for motor skill learning. In D.Goodman and I.Franks (eds) **Psychology of Motor Behavior and Sports.** Vancouver;Simon Fraser.

---

[2]   Reproduced in Thorpe, R.D., Bunker, D.J. and Almond, L. (1986) Rethinking Games Teaching. London:Esmonde Press.

Thorpe, R.D. and Bunker, D.J. (1982) From theory to practice. **The Bulletin of Physical Education,** 18, 1, 17-22.

Thorpe, R.D. and Bunker, D.J. (1983) A new approach to the teaching of games in the Physical Education Curriculum. In Teaching Team Sports. **AIESEP Congress Proceedings, pp.**229-238.Rome:Coni.

Thorpe, R.D. and Bunker, D.J. (1989) A Changing Focus in Games Education. In Almond, L. (ed) **The place of physical education in schools,** London: Kogan Page.

Thorpe, R.D., Bunker, D.J. and Almond, L. (1984) A change in the focus for the teaching of games. Sport Pedagogy. **Olympic Scientific Congress Proceedings,** 6, 163-169. Illinois:Human Kinetics.

Whitehead, J. (1988) Why children choose to do sport. **Proceedings of the annual conference of the Northern Ireland Institute of Coaching.**

Wright, H.C. and Thorpe, R.D. (1990) The effect of different knowledge of result regimen on the learning of a motor skill in a school situation. **Physical Education Review,** 12, 164-167.

PART TWO

SPECIAL POPULATIONS

CURRENT INTERNATIONAL TRENDS IN RESEARCH IN ADAPTED PHYSICAL ACTIVITY

K. P. DEPAUW
Department of Physical Education, Sport & Leisure Studies,
Washington State University, USA

Abstract
Physical activity and sport opportunities for individuals with disabilities have
increased substantially over the past 40+ years. Concomitantly, research on adapted
physical activity evolved. Prior to the 1970's, the research tended to be descriptive
in nature and focused upon the effects of fitness/exercise or descriptions of the
growth and development of persons with disabilities. Current sport research has
become sport specific, disability specific, discipline-oriented, and performance
related. The adapted physical education research has focused upon (a) effective
teaching and learning of individuals with disabilities, (b) effects of integration, (c)
assessment techniques, and (d) effective programmes. Programmes of physical
activity for individuals of varying ability, classification (e.g. elderly, anorexic, mild
to severely impaired) and content (psychomotor, fitness, development etc.) have
been studied throughout the world. Although some differences exist internationally,
research tends to support (a) effectiveness of instruction/training/programmes, (b)
improvement in performance, (c) positive change in attitude, (d) benefits of
integration, and (e) similarity more than difference.
Keywords: Research, Adapted Physical Activity.

1   Introduction

In today's society, increasing emphasis has been placed upon the health and well
being of individuals around the world. As a result, more attention has been paid to
the physical activity needs of individuals with disabilities. To adequately address the
topic of adapted physical activity requires an acknowledgement of the benefits of
physical activity/exercise, a brief review of research, discussion of selected research
findings, and identification of research trends. For the purposes of this presentation,
physical activity/exercise will include many types such as: physical education,
recreation and leisure pursuits, sport, fitness programmes, therapeutic exercise
programmes and more; individuals with disabilities will refer to persons of all ages
with permanent or temporary impairments.

2   Benefits of Physical Activity/Exercise

Physical activity, or exercise, is generally accepted as being beneficial to all
individuals including those with disabilities. Many benefits of participating in
physical activity and/or exercise have been reported in the literature. Applicable to
both disabled and able-bodied individuals, the benefits of physical activity include
(taken from DePauw, 1988b):

(a) **Physical** benefits such as increased mechanical and physiological efficiency;
     increased fitness, flexibility and strength; decrease in resting heart rate;
     increased life expectancy; maintenance of motor skills throughout one's life;
(b) **Mental** benefits including reduction of stress, lessened anxiety, increased
     alertness, continued intellectual stimulation, creativity;
(c) **Social** benefits including improved social interaction, increased self
     confidence in social situations, social acceptance;
(d) **Psychological** benefits such as improved self concept and self esteem,
     inner sense of calm, increased self motivation;
(e) **Vocational** benefits including the positive effects found with performance at
     work such as improved productivity; increased job satisfaction, and
     decreased absenteeism;
(f) **Functional** benefits, specifically self sufficiency and motor function for
     taking care of the activities of daily living (ADL);
(g) **Recreational** benefits occurring from participation such as increased
     performance in recreation/leisure activites, improved motor skills, increased
     enjoyment, interest and success in physical activity.

3   Historical Overview of Research

Most of the benefits of physical activity/exercise identified above have been
supported by research throughout the twentieth century. Since the early 1900's, the
specific topics, research designs, the grouping of persons studied, and the
conditions under which individuals were studied have changed drastically. These
changes have been influenced by changes in society's awareness and attitude toward
disabled persons (DePauw, 1986; Pyfer, 1986).

Research prior to the 1970's tended to be descriptive in research design and
concentrated in three primary areas: (a) identification of motor-related problems, (b)
effects of fitness or exercise, and (c) description of the growth and development of
those with impairments. Although some of the specific topics such as menstrual
cycle deviations and postural disorders are not necessarily thought to be a part of
adapted physical education or disabled sport research today, the groupings were
logical for the early to mid 1900's.

The initial research investigations between 1900 and the 1930's included topics
such as the physical growth and motor development of mentally retarded individuals,
motor ability of deaf individuals, and resocialization of those with mental illness. In
addition, postural disorders were described relative to variations in posture, flat
footedness, and spinal curvatures. Also studied were the benefits of corrective

exercise for heart problems and hypertension. Menstrual problems were studied and even the relation between strength and dysmenorrhea.

Little research was reported during the 1940's. The specific motor related research that was undertaken included research on the relation between motor performance and academic functioning, motor learning of 'feeble-minded' girls, and play of mentally retarded individuals. In addition, the more health-related topics of social hygiene, dysmenorrhea, and foot disorders were investigated.

During the 1950's, research was continued on the health related topics of posture, specifically spinal malformations, dysmenorrhea, and cardiovasular conditions. Whereas previous research addressed the physical growth and development of those with specific impairments, investigators undertook research to identify the motor characteristics of mentally retarded, deaf, and visually impaired individuals. In addition, the effects of conditioning upon mentally retarded individuals was studied for the first time.

The research of the 1960's was influenced by two factors: (a) the gradual change in the type and design of research, and (b) the proliferation of categories of impairments studied. With this proliferation came specific research studies in which the motor characteristics were described for deaf, mentally retarded, asthmatic, cerebral plasied, emotionally disturbed, autistic, visually impaired, obese, and learning disabled individuals. Research topics included fitness, strength, flexibilty, improvement in motor performance, and the relation between perceptual-motor/sensorimotor and performance.

More and varied research topics were investigated in the 1970's. As a result of US federal legislation, some research was focused upon the legal mandates and their implications for physical education programmes. Specifically studied were programme effectiveness, performance evaluation, effects of mainstreaming, behaviour management approaches, and early intervention programmes. There was also increased specificity and refinement in the research investigations with exercise physiology, biomechanics, and motor learning/information processing of individuals with disabilities.

In as much as sport opportunities for disabled individuals increased as a result of the legal mandates, research on disabled sport increased. Two primary areas were investigated in the 1970's; exercise physiology and biomechanics (DePauw, 1988a). The disabled athlete's level of conditioning and response to exercise were studied by exercise physiologists; wheelchair propulsion was studied by biomechanists.

A substantial increase in research activity occurred during the 1980's. The research designs became more varied and sophisticated; the topics were more varied as well. Innovative intervention strategies that were studied included school-based programmes (e.g. reverse mainstreaming), community-based and home reared. Systematic research effort was devoted to understanding the scientific bases of performance, physiological as well as mechanical. Psychological and sociological factors (e.g. state anxiety, motivation, socioeconomic factors, sport socialization) affecting individuals with disabilities were studied for nearly the first time. Many studies were undertaken in the area of assessment of motor performance and the development of appropriate assessment instruments. The application of technology to the motor performance of disabled individuals took the form of research on movement efficiency through wheelchair design, adapted equipment, and prostheses. Sport has been studied in terms of the effects of training, selection and training of coaches, sociological/psychological aspects of sport, application of technology to sport, and application of physiological and biomechanical principles to sport performance.

4   Selected Research Findings

Generalizations about the results of research in physical activity or exercise for disabled individuals should be avoided, or at least, interpretated cautiously, due to the individualistic and preliminary nature of some of the research and the diversity found among disabled individuals. On the other hand, a synthesis and summation of such research could provide the essence of that which is known about physical activity for individuals with disabilities. For a synthesis of the sport research, the reader is referred to DePauw (1988a).

After a review of the recent research literature, the research findings about exercise/fitness of individuals with disabilities were grouped into the following areas: (a) Scientific Basis of Motor Performance, (b) Effects of Physical Activity including Sports Medicine and Rehabilitation (c) Teaching/Learning of Physical Activity, (d) Influences upon Physical Activity.

The following statements constitute a summary of the research findings reported in the literature of the past decade. Specific references are not cited but the reader is referred to the references for selected citations (Broadhead, 1986; DePauw, 1986, 1988; Dunn, 1987; Pyfer, 1986; Shephard, 1990; Stein, 1983) and recent issues of scholarly journals (e.g. Adapted Physical Activity Quarterly, Research Quarterly, Medicine and Science in Sport and Exercise, Physical Education Review, Sportwissenschaft, and more).

4.1 *Scientific Basis of Motor Performance*

Much of the research on understanding the scientific basis of motor performance has occured in the areas of physiological functioning and mechanical efficiency. The findings include:

(a) Fitness levels of disabled persons were found to be both similiar and different when compared to able-bodied individuals. Even those with the same impairment, variable performances on fitness assessment were found. Selected examples include no differences between deaf and hearing individuals nor between mentally retarded cerebral palsied and non-mentally retarded cerebral palsied persons, but higher energy costs of walking and running for blind adolescents.

(b) The fitness levels of mentally retarded persons have been frequently investigated, again with variable findings. Five different assessment tools have been recommended for use including 1.5 mile run, cycle ergometry, Rockport Fitness Walking Test, Canadian Step Test, and treadmill assessments. High and variable heart rates were found with mentally retarded individuals during the run test and with severely multiple-impaired individuals during both gross and fine motor activity. Although differences in measures of cardiovascular endurance of mentally retarded persons have been reported, only a few studies have provided evidence of actual physiological differences among those with mental retardation. Motivation remains a critical factor in the accurate assessment of cardiovascular endurance.

(c) Wheelchair propulsion for movement efficiency has been studied in terms of rim diameter, stroke frequency, seat height, technique, speed, level of impairment, and event (sprint vs. distance). No concise results can be reported because of the complexity of the interaction of the variables mentioned above in conjuction with the human factor. Computer simulation/modelling could assist this interdisciplinary research effort. Efficiency is related to habituation, age, training, etc.

(d) Differences in movement efficiency were found due to functional muscle mass and extent of physical impairment. For example, different cardiovascular adjustments were found with quadriplegics, specifically the hypokinetic circulatory syndrome. Decreased energy needs and metabolic cost of exercise were found with spinal cord injured individuals. Maximum oxygen intake is limited with increasing physical impairment, age, and sedentary lifestyle. Aerobic power found in cerebral palsied individuals may appear low; this is due to an increase of cell water and a reduced body mass.

(e) Body composition is affected by wasting of muscle tissue, amputation, and osteoporosis in paralysed limbs; lean body mass is restricted thus complicating the prediction of ideal body mass.

(f) Handgrip force is not substantially increased by wheelchair confinement but strength of shoulder and elbow muscles is greater than in able-bodied persons.

(g) Aerobic power of lower-limb disabled persons is assessed through arm ergometry, or wheelchair ergometry. During wheelchair exercise, effort expended against ground friciton and ascent of slope is proportional to body mass.

(h) In general, balance ability was not found to be different between able-bodied individuals and those with mental retardation, learning disabilities, deaf, and visually impaired. Specific differences were found based upon the aetiology of deafness and dynamic balance with blind individuals.

4.2 *Effects of Physical Activity*

Many studies were undertaken to examine the effects of various programmes upon the performance of individuals with disabilities. Other researchers examined the benefits of physical activity and the injuries which can occur. Among the findings are the following:

(a) The benefits of participation in physical activity (physical education, sport, therapy) were found to include improved fitness, flexibility, strength, social interaction, and self-concept.

(b)   Different intervention programmes work; but the results tended to be specific to the type of programme. Improved fitness, strength, conditioning may result but are dependent upon the specific programme. Improvement in self-concept and social interaction were found after a psychomotor therapy programme with anorexic and psychiatric patients. Specific health benefits were found among elderly individuals after participation in physical activity programmes.

(c)   Normal-speed wheelchair propulsion does not provide adequate training stimulus for young wheelchair athletes; training thresholds vary with age and habitual activity.

(d)   The injuries found among athletes with disabilities were similar to those found with able-bodied athletes. The frequency of specific types of injuries was related to the unique conditions surrounding the athlete (e.g. blisters with wheelchair racing). Conditioning programmes were found to prevent injury.

(e)   Training improves performance. Therapeutic horseback-riding was found to improve balance. Adaptive seating/position/stability increases performance. Although the regimens for training vary, athletic performances were improved as a result. Many disabled persons are capable of achieving high levels of fitness.

(f)   Physical activity was found to decrease the aggressive behaviour and hyperactivity of autistic individuals.

4.3   *Teaching/Learning Physical Activity*

The research in this area was rather diverse including such topics as practice, peer tutors, time-on-task, and selected aspects of motor learning and pedagogy. The following are among the findings:

(a)   Very little time of the total allocated for instruction was time during which the student was motor engaged (on the average less than 33%). Thus, there is a need for maximizing the time spent on teaching/learning.

(b)   With equal practice, motor tasks were learned with no differences between mentally retarded and able-bodied persons. Distributed practice and extra stimulus were found to enhance the performance of autistic individuals.

(c)   With training/instructional programmes, skills can be mastered by most everyone including the most severely impaired.

(d)   Peer tutors increased the time of task behaviour and motor performance of mentally retarded individuals

(e)   There was a similarity between mentally retarded and non-retarded individuals on co-ordination but not necessarily motor control. This and other studies of interference, transfer and retention and encoding indicate possible differences in the processing of information of mentally retarded persons.

4.4 *Influences upon Physical Activity*

This section includes research conducted on those factors which could influence physical activity such as attitude, integration, psychological and sociological factors. Examples include the following:

(a) The inclusion of disabled individuals with able-bodied individuals enhances motor performance, increases appropriate behaviour, and improves social interaction. These studies were conducted with autistic, mentally retarded, blind, and physically disabled persons.

(b) Attitudes toward disabled individuals are generally positive and can be changed. The acceptance of those who are disabled is directly related to one's attitude. Those who feel more competent held more positive attitudes toward disabled persons. Practica were found to be effective in changing attitudes.

(c) Disabled athletes (wheelchair, cerebral palsied, blind) were found to hold similar perceptions, cognitive behaviours, and psychological profiles as able bodied athletes. Self-concept was found to be variable and dependent upon one's level of physical ability.

(d) Coaches of disabled sport were found to have varied backgrounds and expertise; many sports had coaches only on a short term basis and mostly volunteer.

(e) Providers of physical education for disabled students in rural areas were found to be primarily physical therapists or special education teachers. Trained adapted physical education specialists are the primary service providers in urban areas.

5   Summary

Physical activity and exercise is known to be of benefit to individuals with disabilities. Physical activity/exercise programmes for individuals with disabilities have increased in number, scope and content over the past 40+ years in both quality and quantity. With this increase has come the research effort to understand not only the scientific bases of physical activity/exercise for individuals with disabilities but application as well.

Prior to the 1970's, research on adapted physical activity was descriptive in nature and focused upon fitness/exercise or growth and development of disabled persons. More recently, research has focused upon the effects of physical activity programmes, teaching and learning of disabled individuals, benefits of integration, techniques for assessing performance and/or fitness, and sport medicine and rehabilitation. Programmes of physical activity for individuals of varying ability and/or classification (e.g. elderly, anorexic, mild to severely disabled, psychiatric patients) and content (psychomotor, fitness, development, physical education, sport skill training, etc.) have been studied throughout the world. Although some differences exist internationally, research tends to support (a) specificity and effectiveness of instruction/training programmes, (b) improvement in performance,

(c) positive change in attitude, (d) benefits of inclusion/integration, and (e) similarity more than difference.

Adapted physical activity is a multi-disciplinary field. Professionals across disciplines/fields such as sociology, engineering/design, psychology, physiology, mechanics, materials, education/training, computer technology, rehabilitation, sport, and exercise should form interdisciplinary research teams to investigate human movement (physical activity) and individuals of varying ability. Professionals should be able to use these results in understanding the parameters around which programmes of physical activity can be developed and implemented for the benefit of all individuals including those with impairments.

6   References

American Alliance for Health, Physical Education, Recreation & Dance, (1975). **Annotated Bibliography in Physical Education, Recreation and Psychomotor Function of Mentally Retarded Persons**. Washington, D.C.: K. DePauw.

Broadhead, G.D. (1986). Adapted Physical Education Research Trends: 1970-1990. **Adapted Physical Activity Quarterly**, 3, 104-111.

DePauw, K.P. (1986). Research in Adapted Physical Education. Presentation for the Scientific Congress of the Pan American Wheelchair Games, October, Puerto Rico.

DePauw, K.P. (1988a). Sport for Individuals with Disabilities: Research Opportunities. **Adapted Physical Activity Quarterly**, 5, 80-89.

DePauw, K.P. (1988b). The Need for Technology to Enhance and Create Recreational and Leisure Experiences. Proceedings of the ICAART 88 Symposium. Montreal, Canada.

Dunn, J.M., (1987). The State-of-the-Art of Research Concerning Physical Education for Handicapped Children and Youth. Proceedings of the Civitan - I'm Special Network International Conference on Physical Education and Sport for Disabled Persons. Tampa, Fl: University of South Florida.

Pyfer, J.L. (1986). Early Research Concerns in Adapted Physical Education. **Adapted Physical Activity Quarterly**, 3, 95-103.

Shephard, R.J. (1990). **Fitness in Special Populations**. Champaign, IL: Human Kinetics.

Stein, J.U. (1983). Bridge over Troubled Waters - Research Review and Recommendations for Relevance (pp. 189-198). In Eason, R.L., Smith, T.L., & Caron, F. (eds). **Adapted Physical Activity**. Champaign, IL: Human Kinetics.

ASSESSMENT ISSUES IN CARDIORESPIRATORY FITNESS TESTING OF ADULTS WITH INTELLECTUAL IMPAIRMENTS

P. RINTALA, J.M. DUNN, J. McCUBBIN
Oregon State University, Corvallis, Oregon, U.S.A.

Abstract

Cardiorespiratory fitness is an important health factor for all people including those with intellectual impairments. Some professionals believe good fitness is perhaps more important for persons with intellectual impairments due to vocational implications (Moon & Renzaglia, 1982). It is well documented that the cardiorespiratory fitness level of persons with intellectual impairments is well below the normal population (Reid, Montgomery & Seidl, 1985; Schurrer, Weltman & Brammell, 1985). Assessment of cardiorespiratory fitness is of primary concern in the development and monitoring of programme effectiveness. However, instrumentation validity, reliability and feasibility are questioned due to the indiscriminant use of various protocols in assessing persons with intellectual impairments (Lavay, Giese, Bussen & Dart, 1987). Certain problematic issues, due to psychological and sociological learning characteristics of many persons with intellectual impairments, impede what is perceived as basic protocol in the assessment of cardiorespiratory fitness. These methodolgical issues have created concerns regarding the validity and reliability of previous descriptive research and generated the need for more research work regarding the reliability of cardiorespiratory fitness of persons with intellectual impairments. This paper reviews previous research and identifies protocol modifications that can be used successfully with this population. The discussion is directed to both field-testing methods as well as laboratory procedures.
Keywords: Intellectual Impairments, Assessment, Cardiorespiratory Fitness, Fitness Testing, Validity, Reliability.

1　Introduction

Physical fitness is as important for a child or an adult with intellectual impairments as it is for others (Moon & Renzaglia, 1982). Millions of people with intellectual impairments perform and compete daily in order to prove their worth and productivity in a society that values excellence. These persons should have adequate levels of physical fitness, not only to complete work tasks but also to enjoy and benefit from active participation in lifetime pursuits (Fernhall, Tymeson, & Webster, 1988). Physical fitness training may be even more important as the severity of impairment increases, since fitness training builds basic skills such as ambulation and fine-motor control (Wehman, 1979).

Adults with intellectual impairments have the right to participate in similar recreational and fitness activities as non-impaired adults, but they are frequently not self-directed enough to learn about these options (Day & Day, 1977). It may be difficult to enhance the physical fitness of adults with intellectual impairments to equal that of the non-retarded population since persons with intellectual impairments may not be initially motivated by such factors as weight loss, improved cardiorespiratory fitness, increased energy levels or other intrinsic benefits that encourage non-impaired persons to exercise. When preparing adults with intellectual impairments for community living, increased attention has been given to the potential value of exercise programmes (McCubbin & Jansma, 1987). Two reasons for this interest include a trend of the general population to recognize the value of improving health through exercise, and the potential benefits of exercise to various psychological variables (Moon & Renzaglia, 1982).

One of the primary problems of previous research with the intellectually impaired is the lack of valid and reliable instruments for assessing the fitness level of this population. Indeed, systematic validity studies are greatly needed and, as noted by Seidl, Reid, & Montgomery, 1987, determining a reliability estimate for the selected field measure should become an integral part of all research studies with this population. Therefore, the purpose of this paper is to review previous research on cardiorespiratory fitness with the intellectually impaired and identify protocol modifications that can be used successfully with this population. The discussion will focus on laboratory procedures as well as field-testing methods.

2　Cardiorespiratory fitness of the intellectually impaired

Cardiorespiratory efficiency is considered an essential component of health-related fitness. It is an important health factor for all people, including those with intellectual impairments. All individuals must meet a minimum level of fitness to live a healthy and productive life. According to Fernhall and Tymeson (1988), persons with intellectual impairments may be more dependent on their level of cardiorespiratory fitness than their non-retarded counterparts. For individuals with intellectual impairments, success or failure in employment can often depend upon their ability to efficiently sustain long periods of moderate physical activity. Moreover, an adequate level of cardiorespiratory fitness could help vocational transition and allow these individuals to successfully participate in vigorous leisure activities.

In the following section, descriptive laboratory and field studies of cardiorespiratory fitness for intellectually impaired adults will be reviewed.

2.1 *Laboratory studies*

Several laboratory investigations of cardiorespiratory fitness in adults with intellectual impairments have been undertaken. However, a variety of testing protocols and various subjects have been used. There are some studies where the results of cardiorespiratory fitness testing are uniform (Andrew, Reid, Beck, & McDonald, 1979; Cressler, Lavay, & Giese, 1988; Fernhall & Tymeson, 1988; Fernhall, Tymeson, Millar, & Burkett, 1989; Pitetti, Fernandez, Pizarro, & Stubbs, 1988; Schurrer, Weltman, & Brammell, 1985). These studies show considerably lower levels of cardiorespiratory fitness among adults with intellectual impairments compared with non-impaired adults. The VO_2 max values for the intellectually impaired ranged from 25 to 38 $ml·kg^{-1}·min^{-1}$.

Nordgren (1970) found no difference in cardiorespiratory fitness levels between subjects with and without intellectual impairments. However, considering that some reasons for non-completion were consistent with poor fitness (i.e., localized muscle fatigue, general fatigue), it is possible that only the more fit subjects were included in the Nordgren sample. In a recent study, the high level of cardiorespiratory fitness of intellectually impaired subjects reported by Nordgren was supported; Rintala (1990) reported a mean peak VO_2 value of 40 $ml· kg^{-1}·min^{-1}$ (n=19) which is considerably higher than the previous studies and slightly below the values for the non-impaired.

2.2 *Field studies*

Data from descriptive field studies of adults with intellectual impairments are almost non-existent (Fernhall et al., 1988). The largest cardiorespiratory fitness field study (n=184) was conducted by Reid, Montgomery, & Seidl, (1985) (see also Montgomery, Reid, & Seidl, 1988) with educable intellectually impaired and trainable intellectually impaired sheltered workshop employees. The cardiorespiratory fitness test was a modified step test, with a prediction of maximal capacity based on submaximal results. The results indicated that the subjects exhibited low levels of cardiorespiratory fitness compared to non-impaired peers.

Beasley (1982), using the Cooper 12 min run-walk test, showed that adults with intellectual impairments (educable and trainable, age range 16-50 yrs) exhibited low levels of cardiorespiratory fitness. Similar results were reported by Corder (1966) and Giles (1968) using the 600-yard run-walk test and Coleman & Whitman (1984) using the 300-yard run test.

Cardiorespiratory fitness field tests (run-walk) used with persons with intellectual impairments have ranged in distance from 300 yards to 1.5 miles, and included the 12-minute Cooper run. Different field tests have been used to assess the effect of training on subjects with intellectual impairments. In general, field studies with adults with intellectual impairments indicate these subjects exhibit low levels of cardiorespiratory fitness before involvement in a training programme (Fernhall et al., 1988).

There appears to be a need for more investigations using direct measures of oxygen consumption during maximal exercise (Seidl et al., 1987). At the same time more valid field tests are needed for practical reasons. However, both types of tests, laboratory and field tests, have their own methodological problems.

3   Assessing cardiorespiratory fitness

Special physical education instructors are faced with the dilemma of choosing an effective measure of cardiorespiratory fitness for individuals with intellectual impairments (Lavay, Giese, Bussen, & Dart, 1987). Although proper assessment procedures are necessary in order to provide programmes of physical activity effectively to persons with intellectual impairments (Werder & Kalakian, 1985; Wessel & Kelly, 1986), tests of cardiorespiratory fitness that have established norms, reliability, and validity for the general population have been used indiscriminantly with individuals who are intellectually impaired (Bundschuh & Cureton, 1982). Without tests that are reliable and administratively feasible, proper assessment procedures and, consequently, appropriate programmes of physical fitness for persons who are intellectually impaired cannot be fully achieved (Cressler et al., 1988). In the following section, testing issues such as variation in test methodology, cadence adherence, termination point, efficiency, learning, and motivation will be discussed.

3.1   *Variation in test methodology*

Seidl et al. (1987) reviewed the cardiorespiratory fitness tests used with persons with intellectual impairments. The tests have ranged from field tests such as the 300-yard walk-run to maximal treadmill walking and running protocols. The variety of tests employed makes comparisons difficult.

With the non-impaired population, it is widely accepted that cardiorespiratory fitness is best measured as VO_2 max; this is defined as the ability of the body to take in, transport, and utilize oxygen during maximal exercise. Although maximal treadmill protocols have been used in seven studies with adults with intellectual impairments (Andrew et al., 1979; Fernhall & Tymeson, 1988; Fernhall et al., 1989; Rintala, 1990; Schurrer et al., 1985; Tomporowski & Ellis, 1984a, 1985), only five of these (Andrew et al., 1979; Fernhall & Tymeson, 1988; Fernhall et al., 1989; Rintala, 1990; Schurrer et al., 1985) included direct measurements of oxygen consumption.

Field tests and submaximal laboratory protocols have been used with the intellectually impaired. However, since these methods have been shown to be population-specific, there is a need to establish their validity (Seidl et al., 1987). The 300- and 600-yard walk-run tests have been popular, and have been justified for persons with intellectual impairments on the grounds of subject motivational status. However, these field measures are not considered to be a valid means for evaluating cardiorespiratory fitness in non-impaired persons. Thus, one must question their validity with persons with intellectual impairments (Seidl et al., 1987).

The only field test that has been suggested to be valid with an intellectually impaired population is the 1.5-mile run-walk (Fernhall & Tymeson, 1988). The test was a valid indicator of cardiorespiratory fitness for men (r=0.88), but not for women (r=0.55) (Fernhall et al., 1988).

Kline et al (1987) investigated the potential of walking as an evaluative tool and concluded that a one-mile walk test protocol was a valid sub-maximum assessment for VO_2 max estimation among 30 to 69 years old non-impaired persons (n=343). This study led to the development of the Rockport Fitness Walking Test (RFWT) (1986/1987). After experimenting with the RFWT with adults with intellectual impairments, DePauw et al (1990) recommended the test for the assessment of fitness levels of intellectually impaired individuals. Rintala (1990) found the finishing time of one-mile walk and the weight of men with intellectual impairments accounting for 85% of variance in an equation predicting the peak VO_2 values of the subjects. In addition, Rintala (1990) reported that the one-mile walk test was reliable (R=0.97) for subjects with moderate intellectual impairments.

3.2 Test termination and cadence adherence

Ten studies listed by Seidl et al. (1987) to predict the cardiorespiratory fitness of adults with retardation used various procedures. Only three of them (Nordgren, 1971; Reid et al., 1985; Tomprowski & Jameson, 1985) commented on the applicability of the selected mode of exercise and protocol used. Nordgren (1971) encountered difficulty with 16 of 63 subjects with mild and moderate intellectual impairment in determining physical work capacity on a cycle ergometer. Problems included the inability of subjects to follow the required cadence and difficulty in completing more than one work load, which made extrapolation difficult. Lavay et al., (1987) and Cressler et al. (1988) confronted similar problems.

Bicycle ergometer tests and step tests present a similar administrative problem in maintaining a steady cadence. Reid et al. (1985), using a step test, reported a loss of 36 of 220 subjects with mild and moderate intellectual impairments. Many of them experienced difficulty in attaining and maintaining required stepping cadences. Moreover, 45% of the subjects stopped prior to reaching target heart rate.

Tomporowski and Jameson's (1985) study provides further support for the notion that persons with intellectual impairments experience difficulty in maintaining predetermined cadences. Behavioural data on 19 adults with severe and profound intellectual impairments revealed that few subjects were able to maintain a regular cadence while exercising with cycling and rowing ergometers. Physical prompting might be a useful method to maintain cadence and promote test adjustment (Tomporowski & Ellis, 1984b).

Studies using the treadmill with adults with intellectual impairments have not identified any apparent problems with the protocol because the cadence is mechanically determined (Seidl et al., 1987). The treadmill moves at a set speed and allows precise control of pace and ensures continuous exercise. Therefore, it is not surprising that some investigators believe a motor driven treadmill to be an excellent way to assess cardiorespiratory fitness (Rintala, 1990; Tomporowski & Jameson, 1985). However, previous practice is necessary for this population to feel comfortable while walking/running at different speeds and elevations on the treadmill (Cressler et al., 1988). A common problem with this population during treadmill walking is using the handrails for support (Lavay et al., 1987).

3.3 *Motivation, learning and physiological efficiency*

Reid et al. (1985) noticed that despite individual testing and encouragement, their intellectually impaired subjects were not sufficiently motivated to perform the step test to their potential. In contrast, Tomporowski and Jameson (1985) stated that '... perhaps the most important observation made during the course of training was the high level of motivation exhibited by subjects during exercise sessions' (p. 204).

If subjects are familiar with the test apparatus, repeated tests of cardiorespiratory fitness using a given protocol should result in similar scores (Seidl et al., 1987). However, Andrew et al. (1979) reported VO_2 max values ($ml \cdot kg^{-1} \cdot min^{-1}$) of two control subjects who decreased their cardiorespiratory functioning over 12 weeks from 43.5 to 25.7, and 50.5 to 40.0. Conversely, Schurrer et al. (1985) indicated that one of their five subjects showed an increase in VO_2 max from 20.6 to 42.3 $ml \cdot kg^{-1} \cdot min^{-1}$ as a function of the exercise programme. It is difficult to attribute such changes to physiological mechanisms and one must question if the tests were providing valid indicators of cardiorespiratory fitness for these individuals. Such extreme fluctuations in scores may more accurately represent changes in motivation rather than physiological functioning (Fernhall et al., 1988; Seidl et al., 1987).

Learning is undesirable, in the testing context, because it confounds the internal validity of the study. Seidl et al. (1987) recommend that when examining the validity of cardiorespiratory tests with persons with intellectual impairments, investigators should assess the extent of learning over several administrations of the test.

Attention has not been directed to physiological efficiency in studies of persons with intellectual impairments. However, indirect tests which predict oxygen consumption from work performance or heart rate assume a constant efficiency (Seidl et al., 1987). Poor efficiency, or a greater energy expenditure for a given work demand, can be attributed to such factors as poor co-ordination or lack of experience with a task or piece of equipment. Seidl's (1986) study lends support to previous reports of early test termination with increasing work and suggests that persons with intellectual impairments are not efficient exercisers compared with non-impaired persons (Seidl et al., 1987).

4   Conclusion

The above-mentioned aspects (variation in test methodology, test termination, cadence adherence, motivation, learning and physiological efficiency) can undermine the validity of the cardiorespiratory measures and cast doubt on studies, which depend on accurate and precise measures to determine the effectiveness of an exercise programme (Seidl et al., 1987). Researchers should carefully chronicle the characteristics and selection criteria of the subjects as well as the techniques employed to facilitate adjustment to the test methodology. Thus, it remains unclear whether the observed scores are entirely due to poor cardiorespiratory fitness *per se* or to the inability of subjects to perform optimally on the test. Therefore, it seems that studies investigating the relationship between a cardiorespiratory field test and direct measurement of oxygen uptake with adults with intellectual impairments are warranted.

5 References

Andrew, G., Reid, J., Beck, S. and McDonald, W. (1979) Training of the developmentally handicapped adult. **Canadian Journal of Applied Sport Science**, 4, 289-293.

Beasley, C.R. (1982) Effects of a jogging program on cardiovascular fitness and work performance of mentally retarded adults. **American Journal of Mental Deficiency**, 86, 609-613.

Bundschuh, E.L. and Cureton, K.J. (1982) Effect of bicycle ergometer conditioning on the physical work capacity of intellectually impaired adolescents. **American Correctional Therapy Journal**, 36, 159-163.

Corder, W.O. (1966) Effects of physical education on the intellectual, physical, and social development of educable intellectually impaired boys. **Exceptional Children**, 32, 357-364.

Cressler, M., Lavay, B. and Giese, M. (1988) The reliability of four measures of cardiovascular fitness with intellectually impaired adults. **Adapted Physical Activity Quarterly**, 5, 285-292.

Day, H.M. and Day, R. (1977) Leisure skills instruction for the moderately and severely retarded: A demonstration program. **Educationally Trainable Mentally Retarded**, 12, 128-131.

DePauw, K.P., Goc-Karp, G., Bolsover, N., Hiles, M. and Mowatt, M. (1990) Fitness of intellectually impaired individuals as assessed by 12 minute run, cycle ergometry and Rockport Fitness Walking Tests, in **Motor Development, Adapted Physical Activity and Intellectual impairments** (ed A. Vermeer), Karger AG, Basel.

Fernhall, B. and Tymeson, G.T. (1988) Validation of cardiovascular fitness field tests for adults with intellectual impairments. **Adapted Physical Activity Quarterly**, 5, 49-59.

Fernhall, B., Tymeson, G., Millar, L. and Burkett, L. (1989) Cardiovascular fitness testing and fitness levels of adolescents and adults with intellectual impairments including Down Syndrome. **Educationally Trainable Mentally Retarded**, 24, 133-138.

Fernhall, B., Tymeson, G.T. and Webster, G.E. (1988) Cardiovascular fitness of intellectually impaired individuals. **Adapted Physical Activity Quarterly**, 5, 12-28.

Giles, M.T. (1968) Classroom research leads to physical fitness for retarded youth. **Educationally Trainable Mentally Retarded**, 3, 67-74.

Kline, G.M., Porcari, J.P., Hintermeister, R., Freedson, P.S., Ward, A., McCarron, R.F., Ross, J. and Rippe, J.M. (1987) Estimation of VO_2 max from a one-mile track walk, gender, age, and body weight. **Med. Sci. Sports**, 19, 253-259.

Lavay, B., Giese, M., Bussen, M. and Dart, S. (1987) Comparison of three measures of predictor VO_2 maximum test protocols of adults with intellectual impairments: A pilot study. **Mental Retardation**, 25, 39-42.

McCubbin, J. and Jansma, P. (1987) The effects of training selected psychomotor skills and the relationship to adaptive behavior, in **International Perspectives on Adapted Physical Activity** (eds M. Berridge & G. Ward), Human Kinetics, Champaign, IL, pp. 119-125.

Montgomery, D.L., Reid, G. and Seidl, C. (1988) The effects of two physical fitness programs designed for intellectually impaired adults. **Canadian Journal of Applied Sports Science**, 13, 73-78.

Moon, M.S. and Renzaglia, A. (1982) Physical fitness and the intellectually impaired: A critical review of the literature. **Journal of Special Education**, 16, 269-287.

Nordgren, B. (1970) Physical capabilities in a group of mentally retarded adults. **Scandinavian Journal of Rehab. Medicine**, 2, 125-132.

Nordgren, B. (1971) Physical capacity and training in a group of young adult intellectually impaired persons. **Acta Paediatric Scandinavian Supplement**, 217, 119-121.

Pitetti, K.H., Fernandez, J.E., Pizarro, D.C. and Stubbs, N.B. (1988) Field testing: Assessing the physical fitness of mildly intellectually impaired individuals. **Adapted Physical Activity Quarterly**, 5, 318-331.

Reid, G., Montgomery, D.L. and Seidl, C. (1985) Performance of intellectually impaired adults on the Canadian Standardized Test of Fitness. **Canadian Journal of Public Health**, 76, 187-190.

Rintala, P. (1990) **Validation of a Cardiorespiratory Fitness Test for Men with Intellectual impairments.** Unpublished doctoral dissertation, Oregon State University, Corvallis, OR.

Rockport Fitness Walking Test. (1986/1987) Manual. The Rockport Walking Institute, Marlboro, Massachusetts.

Schurrer, R., Weltman, A. and Brammell, H. (1985) Effects of physical training on cardiovascular fitness and behavior patterns of intellectually impaired adults. **American Journal of Mental Deficoency**, 90, 167-170.

Seidl, C. (1986) **A Comparison of the Stair Stepping Efficiency Between Intellectually impaired and Non-Handicapped Adult Females.** Unpublished master's thesis, McGill University, Montreal, Canada.

Seidl, C., Reid, G. and Montgomery, D.L. (1987) A critique of cardiovascular fitness testing with intellectually impaired persons. **Adapted Physical Activity Quarterly**, 4, 106-116.

Tomporowski, P.D. and Ellis, N.R. (1984a) Effects of exercise on the physical fitness, intelligence and adaptive behavior of institutionalized intellectually impaired adults. **Applied Research in Mental Retardation**, 5, 329-337.

Tomporowski, P.D. and Ellis, N.R. (1984b) Preparing severely and profoundly intellectually impaired adults for tests of motor fitness. **Adapted Physical Activity Quarterly**, 1, 158-163.

Tomporowski, P.D. and Ellis, N.R. (1985) The effects of exercise on the health, intelligence and adaptive behavior of institutionalized severely and profoundly intellectually impaired adults: A systematic replication. **Applied Research in Mental Retardation**, 6, 465-473.

Tomporowski, P.D. and Jameson, L.D. (1985) Effects of a physical fitness training program on the exercise behavior of institutionalized intellectually impaired adults. **Adapted Physical Activity Quarterly**, 2, 197-205.

Wehman, P. (1979) Toward a recreation curriculum for developmentally disabled persons, in **Recreation Programming for Developmentally Disabled Persons** (ed P. Wehman), University Park Press, Baltimore, pp. 1-13.

Werder, J.K. and Kalakian, L.H. (1985) **Assessment in Adapted Physical Education.** Burgess, Minneapolis

Wessel, J.A. and Kelly, L. (1986) **Achievement-based Curriculum Development in Physical Education.** Lea & Febiger, Philadelphia.

MOT '87, A MOTOR SKILL TEST FOR CHILDREN FROM 4 TO 12 YEARS OF AGE: THE RELIABILITY OF THE TEST

J.H.A. VAN ROSSUM AND A. VERMEER
Free University, Faculty of Human Movement Sciences, Amsterdam, The Netherlands

Abstract
A study of the test-retest reliability of a motor skill test is reported. The test has been developed in the context of a research project on the effects of Motoric Remedial Teaching (MRT). MRT consists of extra classes of physical education, given to primary school children with a motor delay. The aim of the test is to assess the motor delay of children of elementary school age. In order to determine the reliability, first to fifth year pupils were tested twice with an interval of about a month. The test yielded reliable scores. Age differences can be determined well with the test, while the compilation of the test effectively prevented the occurence of sex differences.
Keywords: Motor Skills, Test, Primary Schools.

1   Introduction

A research project on the effects of Motoric Remedial Teaching (MRT) has been carried out in a middle-sized town in The Netherlands for the last four years. MRT consists of extra classes of physical education to be given to children with a motor delay in the primary school. In this project 17 teachers of physical education with special training in MRT in 26 primary schools are involved (Van Rossum and Vermeer, 1990). In the context of this research project a motor skill test has been developed (APPENDIX). The test has two versions, one version for years 1 to 4, and another version for years 5 to 8. The aim of the test is to assess the motor delay of children of elementary school age. The test is based on a test for children of 4 to 6 years of age developed by Zimmer (Zimmer, 1981; Zimmer and Volkammer, 1984).

The research executed with respect to this test until now showed that the test fulfills the following criteria:
(a)   The internal consistency of the test is high, in other words, all items measure the same factor.

(b) The test is not expensive, requires only 10 minutes preparation, and only about 20 minutes execution time.

(c) The test has a proven empirical validity: children with a motor delay, selected by the teacher of physical education for MRT, have lower scores than 'normal' children (Van Rossum et al., 1987; Vermeer et al., 1988).

In this contribution an account of the test-retest reliability of the test is given. Furthermore, we investigated whether the test is dependent on sex and age differences within the two versions of the test. It is supposed that older children perform better than younger children. This hypothesis is supported by a lot of research (Haywood, 1986; Keough and Sugden, 1985; Thomas, 1984; Williams, 1983). It is more difficult to formulate a hypothesis with respect to sex-differences. Differences in motor performance between boys and girls seem to be dependent on age (Corbin, 1980; Gallehue, 1982; Zaichowsky, Zaichowsky and Martinek, 1980) and the specificity of the motoric task. Boys are better in motoric tasks requiring strength, velocity and endurance (eg. throwing, jumping, running), while girls are better in tasks in which pliancy and co-ordination (balance, hopping) play an important role (Van Rossum, 1987).

In earlier research with this motor skill test we did not find differences between boys and girls in years 5 and 7, while we did find statistically significant differences between years 5 and 7 (Van Rossum, 1988).

2   Design

Children of years 3, 4, 5, 6 and 7 of four primary schools were tested twice. Year 7 consists of two classes from two different schools (Table 1).

The period between the two tests was 34 or 35 days. The children were tested during school time. Children were tested by the same researcher during both the test and the retest. Both researchers tested the same number of children in the different years.

Table 1.   *Number of pupils of years 3 to 7 in test and retest, age in months*

year	test 1	N pupils test 2	mean	Age s.d.	range
3	30	28	78.8	4.7	73-93
4	25	25	96.9	7.0	86-113
5	24	21	107.6	6.5	97-121
6	29	29	117.5	5.1	109-134
7a	27	24	132.7	5.8	122-145
7b	19	17	129.5	8.4	123-159
total 3-4	55	53	87.3	10.8	73-113
total 5-7	99	91	121.5	11.6	97-159

3 Results

First we analysed the mean scores per age level and sex during the first test. The scores for years 3 and 4 and for 5 to 7 are measured by means of different versions of the instrument. Therefore we investigated whether older children have higher scores than younger childrern and whether there are differences between the score of boys and girls.

Next we reported the correlations between the scores of the test and the retest. This coefficient is considered as an indicator of the reliability of the test.

3.1 *Group Comparisons*

YEARS 3-4. The results of 53 children (23 boys and 30 girls) were used (Tables 2 and 3). The scores are analysed by means of a 2(year) by 2 (sex) ANOVA. The main effect 'year' is significant (p=0.001). Younger children scored significantly lower than older ones. The main effect 'sex' and the interaction 'year by sex' is not significant (p=0.38; p=0.37).

YEARS 5-7. The results of 91 children (43 boys and 48 girls) were used (Tables 2 and 3). The scores are analysed by means of a 3 (year) by 2 (sex) ANOVA. The main effect 'year' is significant (p=0.001). By means of a post-hoc test (Duncan's test, p=0.05), it was established that the mean score of year 5 differs significantly from those of years 6 and 7, and that the mean score of year 6 differs significantly from the mean score of year 7. Older children scored higher than younger ones. The main effect 'sex' and the interaction 'year by sex' is not significant (p=0.30; p=0.83).

Table 2. *Group comparisons*

year	N	mean	s.d.
3	28	22.4	9.0
4	25	32.7	4.8
5	21	27.7	6.7
6	29	32.1	5.9
7	41	35.3	5.7

Table 3. *ANOVA and Duncan's test on year, sex and sex by year*

years 3-4	F	df	p
year	25.22	1.49	0.001
sex	0.79	1.49	0.38
year/sex	0.84	1.49	0.37
years 5-7			
year	11.09	2.85	0.001
sex	1.01	2.85	0.30
grade/sex	0.19	2.85	0.83

3.2 *Reliability*

YEARS 3-4. The product-moment correlation coefficient between the scores of the test and the retest of 53 children was established. The correlation was 0.87 (p=0.001). The correlations regarding boys and girls do not differ very much (Table 4). Similar results were reported for the two researchers (Table 5). Also the mean score on test and retest did not differ very much (Table 6).

   YEARS 5-7. The test-retest correlations between the scores of 91 children was established. The correlation was 0.77 (p=0.001). There are also no great differences with respect to boys and girls, the two researchers and the mean scores (Tables 4, 5 and 6).

   The test-retest correlations are about equal for all the years, except year 4 (0.65). It appeared that this result is strongly influenced by the score of one of the two researchers (res. 1: 0.46; res. 2: 0.74). And this score was caused by the scores of two children, who showed great differences between test and retest (9, respectively 11 points). If we eliminate these scores, the test-retest correlation of this researcher is 0.84.

Table 4.   *Test-retest reliablity of scores of the children*

year	m	N	f	m	rs	f	p
3		28			0.89		0.001
4		25			0.65		0.001
5		21			0.72		0.001
6		29			0.73		0.001
7a		24			0.70		0.001
7b		17			0.82		0.001
total 3-4		53			0.87		0.001
	23		30	0.90		0.82	0.001
total 5-7		91			0.77		0.001
	43		48	0.82		0.75	0.001

Table 5.   *Test-retest reliablity of scores of the two researchers*

	1	n	2	1	rs	2	p
years 3-4	26		27	0.83		0.89	0.001
years 5-7	47		44	0.79		0.73	0.001

Table 6   *The mean scores of the test and the retest*

	1	mean	2	1	s.d.	2
years 3-4	27.3		29.9	8.9		8.2
years 5-7	32.5		33.4	6.7		6.9

4   Conclusions

From the results of this research we conclude that a reliable motor skill test for years 3 to 7 is available. The results support the conclusions of earlier research with respect to age and sex differences.

5   References

Corbin, C.B. (ed) (1980) **A Textbook of Motor Development.** W.C. Brown, Dubuque (2nd edition).
Gallehue, D.L. (1982) **Understanding Motor Development in Children.** Wiley, New York.
Haywood, K.M. (1986) **Life Span Motor Development.** Human Kinetics Publishers, Champaign.
Keough, J. and Sugden, D. (1985) **Motor Skill Development.** MacMillan, New York.
Thomas, J.R. (ed) (1984) **Motor Development during Childhood and Adolescence.** Burgess, Minneapolis.
Van Rossum, J.H.A. (1987) **Motor Development and Practice.** Free University Press, Amsterdam.
Van Rossum, J.H.A. (1988) **Voortgangsrapportage III: MRT-docenten en de selectie van proefpersonen voor de proef effect studie** (Pilot Study of Effects of MRT). Free University, Amsterdam (Internal publication).
Van Rossum, J.H.A., Vermeer, A., Van den Born, S., Deelstra, H. and Van der Kolk, W. (1987) Het competentie begrip en motorisch gedrag: een toepassing in de Motorische Remedial Teaching (The concept of competence and motor behaviour: an application pertaining to Motoric Remedial Teaching). **T Orthopedagogiek,** 13, 515-524.
Van Rossum, J.H.A. and Vermeer, A. (1990) Perceived Competence and Motoric Remedial Teaching. **Int. J. Disability, Development and Education,** 2 (1), (accepted).
Vermeer, A., Van Rossum, J.H.A. and Bolk, J. (1988) MRT in de basisschool (MRT in the primary school). **Lichamelijke Opvoeding,** 76, 572-575.
Williams, H.G. (1983) **Perceptual and Motor Development.** Prentice-Hall, Englewood Cliffs.
Zaichowsky, L.D., Zaichowsky, L.B. and Martinek, T.J. (1980) **Growth and Development: The Child and Physical Activity.** C.V. Mosby, St. Louis.
Zimmer, R. (1981) **Motorik und Personlichkeitsentwicklung bei Kindern im Vorschulalter.** Verlag Karl Hofmann, Schorndorf.
Zimmer, R. and Volkamer, M. (1984) **Manual Motoriktest fur vier-bis sechsjährige Kindern, MOT 4-6.** Beltz Test Gesellschaft, Weinheim.

6   Appendix

The items of the test in the order of execution:

1. jumping in and out of a horizontal hoop
2. toe-to-heel walking in forward direction (twice : second time standing on one leg)
3. making dots on paper with pencil
4. picking up a handkerchief using the toes (twice: preferred leg, non-preferred leg)
5. jumping repeatedly sideways across a rope
6. catching a dropped stick (twice: preferred hand, non-preferred hand)

7. shuttle run
8. toe-to-heel walking in backward direction (twice: second time standing on one leg)
9. underarm toss for accuracy (twice: preferred hand, non-preferred hand)
10. picking up matches and putting in box
11. step through a vertical hoop (twice)
12. one-legged jump into a hoop (twice: preferred leg, non-preferred leg)
13. catch a rubber-ring (twice)
14. astride jumping with rebound with arm-clapping above head ('jumping jack')
15. standing jump over a rope (twice: two heights)
16. body rolling along vertical axis (twice: back-front-back, front-back-front)
17. jumping in and out of a horizontal hoop while making successive 90 degree turns (twice)
18. standing broad jump
19. throwing and catching a ball vertically while clapping the hands (twice: tennis ball, gymnastic ball)
20. step over a stick held horizontally with two hands
21. hopping (twice: preferred leg, non-preferred leg)
22. clapping the hands in front and behind the body (twice: second time with hopping)

Item one is a warming-up item and does not count for the score. A child can get 0, 1 or 2 points for each item, and for some items 0, 2 or 4 points. The maximum score for the two versions of the test is 48 points.

FRAMEWORK FOR CONDUCTING PEDAGOGICAL RESEARCH IN TEACHING PHYSICAL EDUCATION TO INCLUDE DIVERSE POPULATIONS

K.P. DEPAUW AND G. GOC KARP
Department of Physical Education, Sport & Leisure Studies, Washington State University, USA

Abstract

Research conducted by adapted physical education specialists over the past 40+ years has led to a greater understanding of the motor performance of individuals with disabilities but only a few adapted physical education specialists have attempted research utilizing a pedagogy framework. Similarly only a few sport pedagogists have conducted research with individuals with disabilities. A review of recent 'pedagogy' research (Journal of Teaching Physical Education, Adapted Physical Activity Quarterly, Physical Educator, Physical Education Review) during the last ten years was undertaken. Through this review, (a) a sparsity of studies that identified, recognized or even included disabled individuals in a physical education setting and (b) a lack of collaboration on studies of integrated physical education settings and factors influencing teaching and learning were identified. In order to conduct adapted pedagogical research, a framework was developed under the assumptions that: (a) pedagogists should identify and/or include disabled individuals in their studies, (b) adapted physical education specialists should adopt a pedagogical framework for their investigations of effective teaching/learning, and (c) specialists in both fields should collaborate on studies of integrated physical education settings and factors influencing teaching/learning. Through this framework, researchers will be able to identify (a) variables/factors pertinent to studying diversity in the physical education setting, and (b) strategies for establishing collaborative research efforts between the subdisciplines.

Keywords: Adapted pedagogical research, Research framework.

1   Introduction

In as much as pedagogy research has been conducted in, and about, the physical education setting for years, many authors have offered descriptions about 'what's going on in the gym' (Anderson & Barrette, 1978). Among others, these descriptions have been reported by physical educators, specifically sport pedagogists.

Perhaps it all started with 'Pygmalion in the Classroom' (Rosenthal & Jacobson, 1968); the first to bring our attention to the seriousness of the interaction between the student and teacher in the classroom. This work soon spread to the 'gym' and the systematic study of sport pedagogy evolved. Early studies (pedagogy) provided the basis for that which is known about teaching/learning in the physical education setting.

In the past 15 years there have been studies conducted regarding teacher expectations, teacher personalities, interaction analysis, teacher preparation, teacher and student time management, teacher concerns, sex equity issues, student engagement and success rates, and several presage-product and process-product relationships (Metzler, 1989). From these studies, we have learned that the teaching/learning act is complex and influenced by the context in addition to other factors.

Since the early 1900's, research has been conducted utilizing individuals with disabilities. Research prior to the 1970's was descriptive in research design and concentrated in three primary areas: (a) identification of motor-related problems, (b) effects of fitness or exercise, and (c) description of the growth and development of those with impairments (DePauw, 1990). Since then, research has become focused in the following four areas: (a) scientific basis of motor performance, (b) effects of physical activity and effectiveness of physical activity programmes, (c) teaching/learning of physical activity, and (d) factors influencing physical activity. Research conducted to date supports the following concepts: (a) similarity more than difference, (b) effectiveness but specificity of instruction/training, (c) positive change in attitude toward disabled persons, (d) benefits of integration settings/inclusion, and (e) improvements in motor performance.

2   Pedagogy research and disability

In order to assess the status of pedagogy research related to individuals with disabilities, a review of selected journals was undertaken. Research articles published in Journal of Teaching Physical Education, Adapted Physical Activity Quarterly, The Physical Educator, and Physical Education Review over the last ten years provided the basis for understanding sport pedagogy and individuals with disabilities.

The review revealed a sparsity of pedagogy research that specifically identified individuals with disabilities. More specifically, the studies that have been conducted can be categorized in the following manner:

(a)   Studies in which there was no mention of individuals with disabilities,
(b)   Descriptive studies in which specific disability groups are identified; e.g.

DePaepe (1985)	ALT-PE	MR
Jeltma & Vogler (1985)	Contingency	Behav. Dis
Webster (1987)	Peer tutors	MR
Rizzo (1984)	Attitudes	PH & LD

(c) Descriptive studies comparing disabled and able-bodied populations in a mainstreamed setting, e.g.

Auferhide et al(1982)	Individualized instruction
Gauthier (1980)	Teacher-student interaction
Karper & Martinek (1985)	Integration

(d) Descriptive studies comparing segregated and integrated programmes for specific disability groups,

| Titus & Watkinson (1987) | Participation & social | MR |

As can be discerned from these categorizations, the studies are influenced by the way individuals with disabilities are perceived or the contextual nature within which the population resides. The researcher can choose to ignore the presence of the disabled student in a study, include them without recognition, or choose to study disabled persons as a special group by itself or in comparison with other groups. All of the examples cited above were obviously influenced not only by the purpose of the study but by the way the teacher and/or researcher traditionally view individuals with disabilities.

Historically, individuals with disabilities have been viewed as a separate group, a 'special' population, as opposed to being considered as part of a continuum of populations that exist in the teaching setting. This segregation notion is evidenced by research studies (disability specific groups, group comparison studies) as well as in practice (separate classes, schools). In addition, the pedagogy research focused upon disabled persons has been conducted primarily by adapted physical education specialists with an interest in pedagogy while very few sport pedagogists have taken an active role in conducting research that acknowledges individuals with disabilities.

If we are to look, and we must, at pedagogy that includes or acknowledges diversity then we need to be examining not only what, how and to whom teachers teach but the why. There must be an understanding of the interaction of the individual(s) and the environment within the educational setting which involves an analysis of teachers' and students' beliefs and expectations, teacher and student behaviours as well as interpretation within the culture of the school and context of society.

3   Research Framework

To enhance the understanding of effective teaching/learning and the significance of the interaction of teacher and learner within the context of society, Dunkin and Biddle's (1976) model was adapted. The framework appears in Figure 1. The framework is based upon the premise that learning (or change) is the result of the individual-environment interaction. Pedagogical variables associated with presage, context, process and product are included. When compared to Dunkin and Biddle's model, greater emphasis is placed upon the process variables (interaction of variables) and both student learning and teacher change occur.

Of importance to understanding the framework are the two sides or 'frames' of the model. Understanding of the teaching/learning process requires the interpretation of pedagogy variables as influenced by socio-cultural and historical factors. That which occurs in the educational setting should not be examined in its own vacuum; so much of that which occurs in education does so because of external forces or societal influences. Socio-cultural and socio-historical (historical) factors include among others forces such as politics, economics, social mores, cultural values, legal mandates, and traditions. These in turn influence attitudes, beliefs, expectations, motivation, etc. of those who enter the teaching/learning setting; teachers and students alike. Examples include the following:

(a)   Investigation of teachers' belief in a continuum of abilities and their behaviours which increase positive feelings, tolerance, acceptance, pride, etc.
(b)   Equity in education in terms of quality of student-teacher interaction
(c)   Curricular content and its effect upon those of differing cultural, ethnic, socio-economic status, disability, gender etc.

Diversity exists in the classroom (and gym). Research on diversity within this setting must examine the variables that impact diversity from a multi-dimensional construct which naturally includes the socio-cultural and historical perspectives.

Disability represents one such example of diversity. In much the same way as gender (Griffin, 1989), disability must be reframed as a social construction. Disability should be studied in relation to the structure of physical education in a male-dominated, able-bodied society. As stated by Griffin (1989):

> The inclusion of a diversity of voices in the ongoing research dialogue will bring all of us to a deeper understanding of physical education and its relationship with the rest of our lives as members of a diverse and dynamic culture (p. 231).

4   Concluding Comments

Early adapted pedagogical research was more product oriented rather than process oriented and conducted on segregated settings. Due to the inclusion of disabled persons in physical education (integration or mainstreaming), research investigations relating to instruction should now be designed to systematically investigate factors influencing the teaching and learning of all children.

In preparation for the 21st century, current research must extend beyond the boundaries of the physical education setting to the broader societal context. Research which has emphasized categorisation, separation, and isolation/exclusion must now be replaced by a careful examination of characteristics not categories, inclusion not exclusion, and societal influences upon the individual-environment interaction. Diversity in the 'gym' exists and will continue.

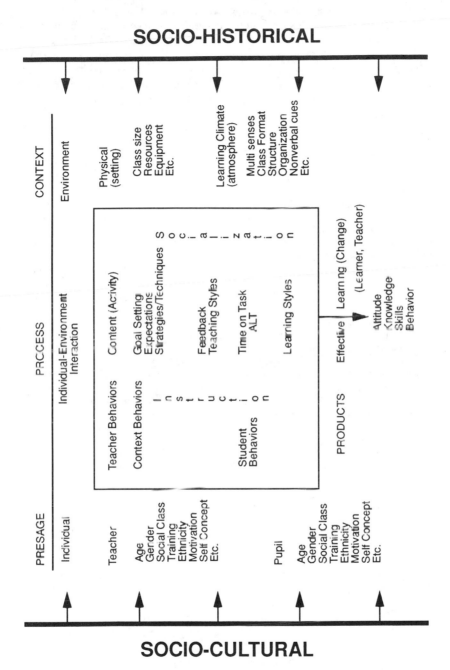

Figure 1

Through a model which includes pedagogical variables (process, presage, context, product) framed within socio-cultural and historical context, researchers will be able to identify variables/factors pertinent to studying diversity in the physical education setting and will develop strategies for establishing collaborative research efforts between the pedagogists and adapted physical education specialists. Collaborative research between pedagogists and adapted physical education specialists can facilitate the process of inclusion and acceptance of diverse populations within the physical education setting.

5   References

Anderson, W. and Barrette, G. (1978) What's going on in the gym. **Motor Skills: Theory into Practice**, Monograph 1.

Auferhide, S.K., McKenzie, T.L. and Knowles, C.J. (1982) Effect of individualized instruction on handicapped and nonhandicapped students in elementary physical education classes. **Journal of Teaching Physical Education, 5**, 34-41.

DePauw, K.P. (1990) Teaching and Coaching Individuals with Disabilities. **Physical Education Review, 13**, 12-16.

Dunkin, M.J. and Biddle, B.J. (1976) **The Study of Teaching**. Holt, Rinehart and Wilson, New York.

Gauthier, R.A. (1980) A descriptive-analytic study of teacher-student interaction in mainstreamed physical education classes. Abstract of Research Papers, AAHPERD, Reston, VA.

Griffin, P. (1989). In Templin, T.J. (ed). **Socialization into physical education: Learning to Teach**. Benchmark Press, Indianapolis, IN.

Jeltma, K. and Vogler, E.W. (1985) Effects of an individual contingency on behaviorally disordered students in physical education. **Adapted Physical Activity Quarterly, 2**, 127-135.

Karper, W.B. and Martinek, T.J. (1985) The integration of handicapped and nonhandicapped children in elementary physical education. **APAQ, 2**, 314-319.

Metlzer, M. (1989) A review of on-time in sport pedagogy. **Journal of Teaching in Physical Education, 8**, 87-103.

Rizzo, T.L. (1984) Attitudes of physical educators toward teaching handicapped pupils. **APAQ, 1**, 267-274.

Rosenthal, R. and Jacobson, L. (1968) Pygmalion in the Classroom in **Teacher Expectations and Pupils' Intellectual Development**. Holt, Rinehart, and Winston, New York.

Titus, J.A. and Watkinson, E.J. (1987) Effects of segregated and integrated programs on the participation and social interaction of moderately mentally handicapped children in play. **Adapted Physical Activity Quarterly, 4**, 204-219.

Webster, G.E. (1987) Influence of peer tutors upon academic learning time-physical education of mentally handicapped students. **Journal of Teaching in Physical Education, 6**, 393-403.

CLUMSY AT SIX - STILL CLUMSY AT SIXTEEN: THE EDUCATIONAL AND SOCIAL CONSEQUENCES OF HAVING MOTOR DIFFICULTIES IN SCHOOL

E. KNIGHT* , S.E. HENDERSON, A. LOSSE, M. JONGMANS
Department of Educational Psychology, University of London Institute of Education, London, England
**also PE Advisory Service, Hertfordshire Education Authority*

Abstract
It is now acknowledged that there are physically normal children in our schools who have exceptional difficulty with tasks requiring motor co-ordination and fluent movement. These children are commonly described as 'clumsy'. The problems of such children are of interest not only because they are directly distressing to the children concerned but also because they are thought to be associated with a high incidence of learning difficulties, school failure, and psychological and adjustment problems. One teacher who has first-hand experience of such children is the PE teacher. The question of whether problems of motor co-ordination encountered in early childhood recede with age has rarely been addressed. This paper reported the findings from a follow-up study of sixteen children identified by their teachers as having poor motor co-ordination around the age of six. At age sixteen, these children plus their matched controls completed a battery of assessments. The results suggested that the majority of children still had difficulties in the motor domain, had a poor self-concept and were not doing as well in school as their performance at six suggested they might. Such children continue to be poorly provided for. The implications of this are discussed.
Keywords: Motor Difficulties, 'Clumsiness', Poor Co-ordination, Special Needs, Adapted Physical Education.

1   Introduction

The purpose of this paper is to demonstrate that mild to moderate motor difficulties in early childhood should be a matter of serious concern to all professionals involved in the education and development of children - but in particular to the Physical Education Specialist. Our research has shown that the effects of being 'clumsy' are apparent right into the teenage years and manifest themselves not only in the motor domain but also in other spheres. In what follows, we describe the findings from our study in brief and consider the implications for those involved in the provision of physical education for **all** children.

Our study began ten years ago when one of the present authors examined a group of sixteen children from mainstream schools, selected by their teachers as 'having poor motor co-ordination for their age' (Henderson & Hall, 1982). This group of six year olds, then labelled 'clumsy', were compared with matched controls from the same classrooms. A number of medical and psychological assessments were made which confirmed the teachers' views that the children were equally competent intellectually but substantially less able than their peers in the motor domain.

Two years ago we traced the same two groups of children. By then they were between fifteen and seventeen years old. We managed to obtain data on all but one child. For each participant, five assessments were undertaken which focused on neurodevelopment status, general motor competence, intelligence, self-concept and leisure interests. In addition, we consulted as many of the children's school records as were available. As space restrictions prevent a detailed analysis of the results of the study, in this paper we have concentrated on the aspects that are educationally most relevant, (full details of the study appear in Losse, Henderson, Hall, Elliman, Knight, Jongmans, 1990).

2   Motor Competence

In our study, we used two 'motor' tests each tapping different aspects of performance, a neurodevelopmental assessment administered by a paediatric neurologist and a standardized test of motor competence, the TOMI (Stott, Moyes & Henderson, 1984). Both tests revealed that those teenagers who had been designated 'clumsy' at age six, continued to perform well below their controls at age sixteen. (See Table 1).

In order to determine whether the problems we had detected on the standardized tests were evident to the teachers who saw the children every day, we also examined each subject's last available school report. So that we could compare reports from different teachers and different schools, it was necessary to devise a rating system which could be applied universally. For both effort and attainment each child was

Table 1.   *Summary of Performance on the Neurodevelopmental Test (NDT) and Test of Motor Impairment (TOMI); high scores indicate poor performance; on NDT total possible is 1.0*

		Clumsy	Control
NDT	Mean	0.52	0.21*
	SD	0.26	0.16
TOMI	Mean	3.16	0.13*
	SD	2.43	0.35

* Difference statistically significant

Table 2.   *Physical Education teachers' ratings for effort and attainment for the two groups of subjects*

Attainment +	Clumsy	Control
Good	0	11
Average	6	3*
Poor	8	2
Avoids Participation	3	0
Effort		
Good	4	9
Average	5	6 (NS)
Poor	4	2

+ unequal numbers due to missing data;
* difference statistically significant;
NS not significant

rated as good, average or poor. Non-participants were also noted. The results of these ratings are shown in Table 2.

In most instances it was abundantly clear that the teachers shared our perspective. Although the content of the reports was often inadequate we had enough evidence to show that the level of attainment of the clumsy children was significantly below that of their controls. For example, eight of the clumsy children were rated as poor by their PE teachers compared to only two of the control children. None of the clumsy children were rated good and three failed to take part at all. Despite their lack of competence, however, many of the clumsy children tried just as hard as their peers, a finding which teachers should find encouraging.

In addition to examining the PE teachers' reports we also scanned all other subject reports with a view to identifying instances where classroom teachers noted the teenagers' motor difficulties. In the case of the 'clumsy' group, thirteen children were noted to have problems with handwriting and in subjects like Art, Craft Design and Technology (CDT), Practical Science and Domestic Science. No child in the control group had such difficulty.

3   Other Aspects of Development and Attainment

In addition to the motor assessments at 16, we looked at four further aspects of the development of these children, their academic attainment, their behaviour in school, their self-concept and their leisure interests.

3.1 *Academic Attainment*

When the teenagers' school reports were examined in more detail we found that the children with motor difficulties were also doing less well academically, than those children in the control group. In this case the clumsy teenagers were viewed by their teachers as not only achieving less than their peers but also making less effort. We rated the subjects as consistently good across all subjects, good but slightly variable,

Table 3.   *Teachers' Ratings of Attainment and Effort in Academic Subjects*

Attainment	Clumsy	Control
Consistently Good	0	2
Good - Variable	2	3*
Average	2	8
Poor - Variable	10	3
Consistently Poor	3	0
Effort		
Consistently Good	2	4
Good - Variable	5	6*
Average	6	4
Poor - Variable	4	1
Consistently Poor	0	1

* Difference statistically significant

average, variable but tending towards poor and consistently poor. These ratings are shown in Table 3. Since these two groups of children had comparable IQ's at age six this outcome is particularly disturbing.

3.2 Behaviour in School

In addition to under-achievement, there was another aspect of the teenagers' reports which struck us forcibly. Among the motor impaired group the teachers seemed to note a whole variety of behaviour problems. These were not always major problems. They were often small things which nevertheless seemed to interfere with the subjects' progress in class. The extent of the difference is illustrated in Table 4. While the majority of the control subjects had no mention of any behavioural or emotional problems, in the clumsy group 6 subjects were thought by their teachers to be lacking in confidence, 7 were described as shy, timid or withdrawn and 7 were reported to have personality and social problems (including lack of friends). The most frequently reported difficulties in the clumsy group were problems of concentration, distraction and forgetfulness.

3.3 Self Concept

Although we were unable to investigate the childrens' behaviour problems in as much detail as we would have liked, we did include one direct measure in our study which bears some relation to the observations we have just described. Each subject completed the Harter Scale of Perceived Competence (Harter, 1982), which is a multi-dimensional measure of self concept designed as an alternative to those yielding a single global score. Four domains of behaviour are examined: academic, social, physical and general self. On this scale we found that the clumsy group rated themselves significantly more poorly than the controls on all components on the scale but the differences were only statistically significant on the Physical and Social Components. The scores on this assessment are shown in Table 5.

Table 4.   *Incidence of behavioural and emotional problems encountered by the teenagers - as noted by teachers in school reports*

Type of Problem	Clumsy	Control
Stealing/in trouble with the law	2	1
Aggressive/lacks self control	2	0
Lacks effort/underachievement	3	2
Disorganized/gets lost	3	1
Low self-esteem/anxious depressed	4	0
Poor attendance/truanting	5	2
Picked on/bullied	5	0
Lack of confidence	6	1
Shy/won't ask for help/timid	7	1
Personality & social problems/no friends	7	0
Poor concentration/easily distracted/forgetful	8	2
No problems	3	9

3.4 School and Leisure Interests

The final assessment took the form of a questionnaire (adapted from Nias, 1975). This, combined with a semi-structured interview, gave us an insight into the subjects' likes and dislikes regarding school, leisure and sport. We have space to mention just one measure we obtained for the questionnaire, the percentage of activities that the teenagers said they enjoyed. (See Table 6).

Table 5.   *Teenagers scores on the Harter Scale Of Perceived Competence*

	Clumsy Children	Control Children
Cognitive	2.66	2.89 NS
Social	2.70	3.18*
Physical	2.23	3.06*
General	2.73	3.0 NS
Total	2.58	3.03*

* Statistically significant

Table 6.   *The percentage of activities the subjects enjoyed in each category of this on the questionnaire*

	Clumsy Children	Control Children
Sport	61.40%	73.20%*
	(36-100%)	(38-100%)
Leisure	65.27%	74.20%*
	(36-95%)	(44-95%)
School	49.67%	57.40% NS
	(7-94%)	(24-82%)

* Difference statistically significant

One of the interesting findings from the questionnaire itself was that the clumsy group actively participated in fewer sports activities than their controls. Moreover, of those that they did participate in, they actually enjoyed a smaller proportion. This data was brought to life by the remarks that some of the teenagers made during the interview. Some commented that they disliked sports because they were no good at them, they found them too rough, too tiring or too difficult. One frequent comment was that they disliked the sports because they got no help from their teachers. It is also depressing to note that one or two childrens' dislike of PE had resulted in total avoidance - they evolved strategies for getting out of it. 'I wasn't very good at it and refused to do it'.

3.5 *Summary*

To summarize our findings so far, the results of our study have shown that, contrary to common belief, children described as 'clumsy' in the early years do not simply grow out of their motor difficulties. In addition, we have shown that many of these children are now doing rather less well in school than their early performance indicated and may also be suffering emotional and behaviour problems. It is not, of course, possible to demonstrate that the motor and other difficulties these children have experienced were causally related but it is our tentative conclusion that they are intertwined in a complex way.

4   A Case Study

In order to emphasize the role of the school in the success and failure of children with this sort of difficulty we now turn to a case history. In the case chosen, it is our contention that the school system failed the child. We are not, of course, claiming that all children have the same experiences or that the system is generally flawed. We simply want to point out that we are still failing **some** of these children by not offering them help at the right time.

In Table 7 we provide a very brief outline of some of the data we collected on Alice at age 6 and 16. In what follows we will try to elaborate a little.

Alice was a child whose motor difficulties have been evident to her parents from a very early age. Over the years her mother had tried several times to get her doctor to consider her problems seriously but his response was to tell Alice's mother that she would grow out of it and that she must stop fussing. As a consequence, therefore, Alice's parents received no professional help in the pre-school years, either direct or indirect.

When Alice began school, her motor difficulties were apparent to her teacher. However, because she was doing so well in the 'academic' aspects of school, and socially was viewed as well adjusted, she saw no reason to seek additional help for her. Here was a happy, charming child who seemed exceptionally bright and was popular with both her peers and other adults. Why be concerned about her being unable to dress herself, use a knife and fork, ride a bicycle or catch a bean bag?

Table 7.   *Case study: Alice at six and sixteen*

	Age 6	Age 16
Type of School	Mainstream	Mainstream
Motor Difficulties	Noted by her teacher but not accompanied by suggestion of referral	Noted by many teachers but ignored Rated poor by PE teacher
	Lowest rank on TOMI Lowest rank on neurodevelopmental	Lowest work on TOMI Lowest work on neurodevelopmental
Intellectual Ability and Academic Attainment	Teacher considers her a bright child making excellent progress	Teachers reports variable, some reporting good ability but lack of effort, many noting decline in effort
Social/Emotional Status	Highly motivated, a charming child, popular with teachers and peers	Depressed, isolated, few friends, makes friends with other 'odd' children in the school

When she was identified as a subject in our initial study, Alice's verbal IQ proved to be 121 and her reading age was 9.5. When tested on the Test of Motor Impairment she was the lowest ranking child of the sample and failed to pass any of the test items. In addition, the paediatrician was very concerned about her performance on his neurodevelopmental test but after further investigation could find nothing medically wrong with Alice.

Because of our concern for her, however, we arranged for Alice to take part in a brief intervention programme which we ran as part of our research project. Although this resulted in a considerable improvement in her motor competence, the period was too short for it to be long-lasting and it was not followed up in her school.

Throughout her school career it seemed clear that teachers generally took her difficulties as 'something she had to live with'. There was no failure to acknowledge the child's motor problems but an omnipresent view that there was nothing to be done about it. Even her severe difficulty with handwriting did not seem to engender any action on the part of the school. We can only assume that Alice's sunny personality, motivation and interest in school and her 'attractiveness' as a model pupil were viewed as adequate compensation for her problem and justification for failing to intervene.

Our view that the strategy adopted by Alice's teachers was misguided, was confirmed when we saw Alice again at age sixteen. In contrast to one or two other children in our study she had stayed in mainstream school and, initially, had done well at secondary level. However, by the time we saw her in the fourth year, she seemed to have run into difficulties.

There was no doubt that her motor co-ordination remained exceptionally poor. She obtained the lowest rank work on the Test of Motor Impairment, the second lowest on the neurodevelopmental test and was rated as poor by her PE teacher. She still had problems with handwriting and generally recording material in written form e.g. CDT and maths. However, what was more significant was the change in other aspects of her performance and behaviour. She was now described as lacking

Table 8.   *Alice's likes and dislikes in sport*

	Comment
Dislikes PE	'I wasn't any good at it and I never had any help from teachers.'
Dislikes team sports	'Everybody is taller than me.' 'I couldn't hit the ball.' 'Too rough.' 'No comment.' 'I got out of it.'
Also Dislikes	
Jogging	'I couldn't keep going.'
Swimming	'I can't co-ordinate my arms and legs.'
Cross-country running	'I got out of this.'
Gymnastics	'I couldn't do it.'
Likes	Fishing, walking, horse riding, ten pin bowling, snooker, dancing, table-tennis, But Prefers watching sport on TV!

in effort and seemed to be achieving less than in earlier years. For example, her marks in German remained at A for 3 consecutive years then plummeted to D. Socially, too, she seemed to have changed and now had few friends. In fact, the school Special Needs teacher had noted that Alice tended to make friends with other 'odd' pupils and those who had personal problems of one kind or another.

To complete this case history, we present some of Alice's comments during the interview with the first author. These are shown in Table 8.

Of the many questions that arise from the results of our study there is one which is critical - Would the lives of these teenagers have been different if they had received a well planned intervention programme in the early years?

5   Some Practical Implications

The practical implications that can be derived from our study are numerous and relevant to many different professionals. In this paper we have room to deal briefly with only some of those which are directly relevant to PE teachers.

5.1   *Motor Difficulties - A Special Educational Need; The Continuing Battle to Increase Awareness*

As we have shown in our study, teachers do **notice** children with movement difficulties. Although there are some children who go completely unrecognized because they have become expert at hiding their difficulties, such instances are relatively rare. What is usually the problem is that teachers don't know 'how bad is bad' and what the consequences of ignoring the problems are.

Over the last decade, there have been some significant changes in the Physical Education field which has improved the situation somewhat. For example, there is now more literature on the topic available to teachers. More important, however, have been the broader changes in education universally.

In many countries of the world, PE teachers have become familiar with the more extreme cases of movement difficulty in children. This is mainly because many more children with physical impairments are integrated into mainstream schools. In the UK, the Warnock report (Warnock, 1978) and ensuing 1981 Education Act caused this to happen.

More recently, the introduction of a National Curriculum in the UK has led to further discussion about the way PE should be provided for all children. As PE is a foundation subject, schools will be required to re-examine their philosophy, their methodology and their expectations of children. The Act has compelled all teachers to consider the needs of individual children rather than teach 'the subject'. For example, curriculum planning will involve objectives like 'functional skills for a healthy life style' rather then the specific skills required to play hockey, football etc. In addition, these objectives will be discussed with other colleagues in a whole school context rather than in isolation.

Another change that is likely to emerge from better curriculum planning is improved recording of children's progress. The sort of school reports we consulted in our research project will not suffice. It will not, for example, be acceptable to write 'tries hard' without commenting on competence at the same time.

In spite of these changes for the better there are still some problems. For example, the procedures for identifying and referring children with motor difficulties are still unclear. Also, there are too few teachers in the primary sector with a good knowledge of motor development (this is mainly due to inadequacies in initial training). As a consequence many lack skill and confidence in teaching PE in general and helping children with difficulties in particular.

For the PE professional, there is a clear role to play in raising awareness about children with motor difficulties. They are the ones who can back up the classroom teacher who wants to seek help for a child; they are the ones who can help with intervention within the school system; and, most importantly, they can argue the case for recognizing that just like reading difficulties 'clumsiness' is a 'Special Educational Need'.

5.2 Service Provision

It is all very well to argue that children with motor difficulties should be identified within the school system as early as possible and that a referral should be made but when faced with the question of how the provision of intervention should be organized, many new and difficult questions arise, and to some of these it must be conceded that answers are not yet possible.

One of the major difficulties we face in relation to provision for the young child with motor difficulties is that of overall responsibility. In particular, there is genuine uncertainty among professionals as to how the process of referral should be organized. Although the school doctor or paediatrician may only be able to rule out the possiblity of a rare progressive disorder or the early signs of a more serious condition, the importance of doing so should never be underestimated. Once this has been done, the question that then arises is whether an educational specialist of some sort should take over or whether an occupational therapist or physiotherapist should be brought in. At present, we find that different school systems function quite differently in this respect and to some extent it is not through conscious planning but more as a result of interested professionals influencing higher level decion making. However, it is an issue that needs careful consideration so that clear procedures be documented and made available in the form of local or even national guidelines.

In an ideal world, all children with special needs would have access to as much help as they need, for as long as they need it. In reality, it is often the case that provision is limited both in time and amount. Among the many questions that arise in relation to the most productive way of organizing intervention, one of the most important concerns the communication between the professionals involved. Whatever the model adopted, be it advice to the teacher from an advisor, assistance from a therapist or school helper, or extra-curricular input in the form of a 'gym club', the need to keep very detailed records of what the child can and cannot do, has or has not learned etc. is critical. This is essential throughout the child's school career not just at the time of intervention. In the records to which we had access, it gives us no pleasure to note that these were totally inadequate. No new teacher receiving Alice, for example, into her classroom or PE lesson would have had any idea how severe her motor difficulties actually were. Although it is admirable and understandable that a child who tries hard should be acknowledged for doing so, this should not deter the teacher from documenting the problem. In whatever school system we function, professionals must be provided with clear guidelines on the assessment instruments to use and the means whereby the information they yield should be translated into an intervention programme.

There are many other points of discussion we could pursue in this paper but our final objective is to add a cautionary note. There are many different approaches to intervention for children like Alice. Some of these are exclusively undertaken by therapists, others are school based. Whatever their provenance and whatever their methodology, the hard fact is that we have very little evidence that intervention works. To be sure, we can all find instances where a child, parent or teacher is convinced that what they were offered, helped, but what is sadly lacking is solid research evidence on which to base decision making. Many PE teachers feel strongly that they are the right people to help such children. In recent years, they have been given training, they operate within the school system and they have direct contact with the other teachers concerned with the children. If they are to take on this important role in the future, they must now undertake research to demonstrate how effective they can be, not only in terms of helping children to acquire better motor competence in the short term but also in terms of the longer consequences.

We often talk of every child's entitlement to a broad, balanced, relevant and differentiated curriculum. There is some way to go before this becomes a reality.

6   References

HMSO. Education Act 1981, London. HMSO.
Harter, S. (1982) The perceived competence scale for children. **Child Development**, 53, 87-97.

Losse, A., Henderson, S.E., Elliman, D., Hall, D., Knight, E., Jongmans, M. (1990) Clumsiness in children - do they grow out of it? A ten year follow-up study. **Developmental Medicine and Child Neurology.**

Nias, D.K.B. (1975) Personality and other factors determining the recreational `interests of children and adults. PhD Thesis, University of London.

Stott, D.H., Moyes, F.A. & Henderson, S.E. (1984) **The Henderson Revision of the Test of Motor Impairment.** San Antonio, Texas, London, England: The Psychological Corporation.

Warnock, M. (1978) Special Educational Needs: HMSO.

MILDLY DISABLED AND NON-DISABLED PUPILS' PHYSICAL ACTIVITY AND LEARNING BEHAVIOUR IN PE CLASSES

P. HEIKINARO-JOHANSSON
Department of Physical Education, University of Jyväskylä, Jyväskylä, Finland

1   Introduction

A physical education teacher is responsible for teaching movement to all children, including those with special needs. This is a demanding task because the number of pupils participating in regular PE classes is high and there are only two PE lessons weekly. Further, teaching conditions vary widely. It happens only occasionally that teachers can expect assistance from other staff, such as persons specializing in assistance for children with disabilities or from other teachers.

There are only a few studies dealing with the behaviour of disabled and non-disabled pupils in physical education classes (Auferheide *et al*, 1982; Shute et al 1982; Silverman *et al*, 1984). In one study by Shute *et al.* (1982) time-on-task was the same for both disabled and non-disabled pupils. However, teachers were not able to direct disabled pupils' behaviour to get them to perform the various tasks successfully, with the same frequency as pupils without disabilities.

The Research Project on Physical Education for Disabled and Chronically Ill Children was begun it the Department of Physical Education of the University of Jyväskylä in 1984. The aim of the project is to acquire information about the situation of mainstreamed disabled children at comprehensive school and at upper secondary school. The investigation focuses on the teachers' readiness to instruct pupils belonging to special groups, and the pupils' physical activities and their experiences of physical education lessons and instruction.

The present paper is concerned with a description of physical education classes attended by disabled pupils, and with an analysis of the relationship between teacher education and the teacher attitudes on the one hand and the physical activity and behaviour of the pupils as well as the general atmosphere which prevails during lessons on the other.

2   Methods

During the school year 1985-86, a total of 138 physical education teachers were interviewed. From these were chosen 22 PE teachers who voluntarily participated in the next step of the research in the autumn of 1986. Pupil activities were observed during a total of 47 physical education lessons. Both disabled pupils and non-disabled pupils were observed, in comparison, during each lesson. After the lesson the observers evaluated the general atmosphere which prevailed during lessons.

3   Results and Discussion

The pupils observed in the course of the study had chronic illnesses or disabilities of very different types, and with highly varying degrees of severity. They varied from mild health-impaired conditions, such as overweight or asthma, to severe conditions such as spinal cord impairments.

During physical education lessons, both disabled and non-disabled pupils were observed for a total of 30 minutes. Pupil behaviour was observed and categorized in terms of a system of five categories based on 6-second time units. The intensity of the pupils' physical activity was assessed using a five-point scale. In addition the number of times pupils performed a given task was counted. In other words, the number of times pupils, for example, touched the ball in a volleyball game, or performed a movement in apparatus gymnastics were counted. On average, performing a task took half of the lesson time. Half of the time was taken up in organizing the pupils, positioning apparatus, etc., following instructions, and waiting for one's turn to engage in a task. The activities of disabled and non-disabled pupils did not differ to any significant degree. In Auferheides et al. (1982) study, organizing the various tasks similarly took about half the class time.

The physical activities of the disabled pupils were less intense than those of non-disabled pupils. During physical education classes disabled boys and girls exercised, to a statistically significant degree, less than did non-disabled boys and girls. A PE class in the gym typically lasts for about 37 minutes. Out of this time disabled pupils were active for about 16 minutes and non-disabled pupils were active for about 18 minutes. In addition all pupils moved with a very low intensity. In Figure 1 the mean of the pupils' physical activity is shown.

One third of teachers thought that the presence of disabled pupils made teaching more difficult. In those cases, the pupils had more severe disabilities than the average. The presence of disabled pupils in regular classes gave the teachers more work, for example in planning and implementing the lessons. According to teachers the rejections by other pupils of disabled pupils was seen mainly in game and competition situations.

There is a great deal of research comparing the effects of co-operative, competitive and individualistic learning. According to Johnson and Johnson (1984) co-operative learning situations create positive attitudes towards the acceptance of classmates, regardless of their disabilities, more than competition or individualistic teaching does.

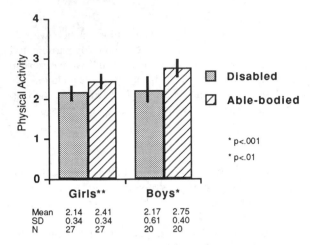

Figure 1.   *Physical activity of disabled and non-disabled children shown according to sex*

Only seldom did teachers change the way they organized their work because of a disabled pupil. There were only five lessons out of a total of 47 where disabled pupils were given individualized tasks; in addition there were two lessons in which a group of pupils, which included a disabled member, was given an individualized task. The periods of differential training were so short, about 10-15 minutes of lesson time, that there were no differences in pupil behaviour and physical activity between lessons where differential training was used and ordinary lessons.

In other words, although pupils need differential treatment, there is little differentiation in methods of instruction or according to pupils' abilities. The learning situations are the same for everyone and they are those most suited to the average pupil.

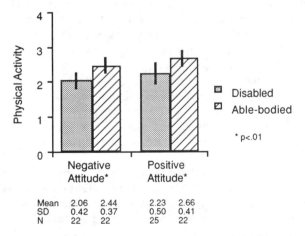

Figure 2.   *Physical activity of disabled and non-disabled children shown according to teacher attitude*

Teachers were divided into two groups according to their professional education and training in special education and adapted physical education. In the lessons of those teachers who had studied special education, more time was spent in organization and less devoted to time-on-task than in the lessons of teachers without any experience.

However, there were more activities performed in the lessons of experienced teachers. It seems that although organization takes more time, once the performance starts it is more effective quantitatively. No difference was found between disabled and non-disabled pupils behaviour according to teacher education. In both groups disabled children moved statistically significantly less than non-disabled children during PE lessons. No difference in the behaviour of disabled, as opposed to the non-disabled, pupils' behaviour was found to result from the amount of professional training the teacher had received.

The atmosphere which prevailed during a lesson was evaluated after each lesson: firstly, whether the atmosphere was positive, stimulating and encouraging or critical and inhibiting. Secondly, who made the decisions taken during the lesson; whether this was mainly the teacher, or both teacher and pupils, or mainly the pupils. Both atmosphere and authority were assessed according to a 5-point Likert scale.

Comparison of the means shows that the atmosphere was more positive in those lessons conducted by teachers who had studied adapted PE. There were no differences in decision making between the two teacher groups.

Teachers were also divided into two groups on the basis of how positive or negative their attitudes were as they were shown in the factorial analysis. There were no differences in pupil behaviour according to teacher attitudes. Disabled pupils moved significantly less both in the classes taught by those teachers with positive attitudes as well as those with negative attitudes.

The atmosphere was significantly more critical in the lessons of those teachers who had more negative attitudes to teaching students with disabilities, or who did not take so favourable a view of integration. Teachers with negative attitudes generally made all decisions on their own. By contrast, teachers with positive attitudes gave pupils more opportunities to make their own decisions.

Table 1   *Teacher's approach in PE classes shown according to degree of qualification*

	Teacher qualification	
Teacher's approach (and associated emotional climate)	no formal qualification %	qualified %
very critical	28	
critical	28	32
neutral	27	23
supportive	16	18
very supportive	4	18
total %	100	100
lessons	25	22

x=2.40; SD=1.19   x=3.32; SD=1.13   t=-2.70, p<0.01

Table 2.   *Teacher's approach in PE classes shown according to teacher attitude*

	Teacher attitude	
Teacher's approach (and associated emotional climate)	negative %	positive %
very critical	32	
critical	46	16
neutral	9	36
supportive	5	36
very supportive	9	12
total %	100	100
lessons	22	25
x=2.14; SD=1.21	x=3.44; SD=.92	t=4.20, p<0.001

Table 3.   *Decision-making in PE classes according to teacher attitude*

	Teacher attitude	
Decision-making	negative %	positive %
completely teacher	50	8
mostly teacher	32	56
both teacher and pupil	9	20
pupil	9	16
total %	100	100
lessons	22	25
x=1.77; SD=.97	x=2.44; SD=.87	t=2.48, p<0.05

4   Conclusions

Every physical education teacher sometimes has to teach disabled or chronically ill pupils. A teacher should know enough about pupils' physical condition and special needs to enable him or her to plan and implement the teaching which best suits a given individual. At present, PE lessons are carried out too much in the same form for everyone. Teachers too seldom practice individual goal setting, class content is usually based on the specific event, and teaching styles are mostly the typical ones, for example the command style and practise style.

Besides this there is a lot of competion in PE classes. In a large research project called 'Research Project on School Physical Education' half of all observed periods were competitive (Varstala, Telama & Heikinaro-Johansson, 1987). School games can be very competitive, because typically points are awarded and the teacher announces which team has won. The disabled pupil can put their team at a disadvantage. The team may lose because it contains a disabled pupil and this can be a reason why classmates ignore him or her. That is why teachers should be very cardful in the use of competitive games, and in making up teams in PE lessons.

Teachers should also be better instructed in how to stream their pupils. If teachers could use different methods, it would not be necessary to emphasize integration so much, at least when we are speaking of mildly disabled pupils.

The results of the study show that teacher attitudes toward teaching disabled pupils affects the atmosphere which prevails during lessons and also, to some extent, pupil behaviour. Teachers with negative attitudes are more authoritarian and spend more time in teaching. It depends on the pupil's own mind, how energetically he or she moves. It seems that in a stimulating atmosphere, pupils are more ready to move.

Successful integration or mainstreaming demands the following procedures: teacher education and in-service training should be developed so that instead of putting the main emphasis on knowledge and skills, teacher creativity and positive attitudes to individual differences and one's self should be emphasized. There are no ready-made solutions in adapted physical education but teachers must be able to consider pupils' different needs. In addition, collaboration between the various people responsible for pupil welfare is important. Collaboration is very important for PE teachers, because otherwise they will be unable to utilize additional resources and specialists in teaching.

5   References

Auferheide, S., Knowles, C. and McKenzie, T. (1982) Individualized teaching strategies and learning time: implication for mainstreaming. **The Physical Educator**, 1, 38, 20-25.

Johnson, D.W. and Johnson, R.T. (1984) Classroom learning structure and attitudes toward disabled students in mainstream settings: A theoretical model and research evidence. In R.L. Jones (ed) **Attitudes and attitude change in special education: theory and practice**. The Council for Exceptional Children, pp.118-132.

Shute, S., Dodds, P., Placek, J., Rife,F. and Silverman, S. (1982) Academic learning time in elementary school movement education: a descriptive analytic study. **Journal of Teaching in Physical Education** 1, 2, 3-14.

Silverman, S., Dodds, P., Placek, J., Shute, S. and Rife, F. (1984) Academic learning time in elementary school physical education (ALT PE) for student subgroups and instructional activity units. **Research Quarterly for Exercise and Sport** 55, 4, 365-370.

Varstala, V., Telama, R. and Heikinaro-Johansson, P. (1987) Koulun liikuntatuntien sisältötutkimus, menetelmäraportti. The Research Project on School Physical Education Classes: a Report of Methods. **Jyväskylä: Foundation for Promotion of Physical Culture and Health, 52.**

CLINICAL APPLICATION OF WHEELCHAIR DANCING

Y. HUTZLER[1], T. SHEFFI-MACHURO[2] AND B. ZUR[2]
[1]The Zinman College of Physical Education, Wingate Institute, Israel
[2]The Levinstein Center for Medical Rehabilitation, Raanana, Israel

Abstract

Wheelchair dancing has a tradition of at least 20 years. It evolved as a social leisure time activity in the United States, Great Britain, Scandinavia and West Germany and during the last decade, it also appeared as a competitive activity. However, few studies have been reported so far concerning the application of wheelchair dancing in clinical settings. About a year ago a specific programme was developed in the paraplegic department of the Levinstein Medical Rehabilitation Center in Raanana, Israel. This programme utilizes dance and instructed movement activity as an important therapeutic modality. It is a group activity of an hour per week which is guided by a specialized physical education teacher and supervised by a social worker. The patients participate in the activity on a voluntary basis during the time usually devoted to visits of the family. Staff and family members are encouraged to participate. The programme emphasizes improving personal and social efficacy and competence. Its main features include: (a) activation through musical stimuli; development of personal efficacy through creative and dance performance; development of self concept; and development of social contact and interaction with partners and group members. Preliminary evaluation of the programme proceeds by means of questionnaires administered to the patients and clinical observations.

1   Introduction

For physically disabled individuals, especially those in wheelchairs and those using crutches for daily mobility, dancing in a wheelchair can be a thoroughly rewarding and motivating experience. It allows one to enjoy fully a beautiful form of expressive communication, to gain self esteem and social acceptance. For these reasons, wheelchair dancing has expanded during the last 25 years in the American and European continents, and during the last two years in Israel. Manuals for wheelchair dancing have been written for instance by Hill (1976) and Krombholz and Zimer (1986), and reports on experimental activity have been published in the literature. Of these, it seems important to mention the work of Hecox and colleagues (1975) who were pioneers in this field while working at St. Luke's Hospital in New

York city; the work of Rivka Feldmann - a music therapist who reported on her experience at the beginning of the 80's at the Alyn Hospital for crippled children in Jerusalem; the numerous presentations made by Krombholz (eg. in English with Zimmer, 1986) and more recently, the creative work done by Boswell (1989).

As already mentioned, the development of wheelchair dancing in Israel is fairly new and started two years ago (Rosenthal, 1989). Today there are four active groups which have already gained some performing experience. These groups dance mostly for fun, for the social value of dancing, for the joy of expressive movement, etc.

During spring 1989 one further group was created, at the Levinstein medical rehabilitation center in Raanana. The main aim of activity in this group was, and still is, therapeutic.

2   Intention

Therapy means some kind of action intended to provoke a change in the situation of a sick or disabled person. To be medically approved, this activity must be carried out by appropriate and evaluated means.

Though Hill (1976) and Krombholz (1986) refer to physiological benefits of wheelchair dancing such as muscular strength, muscular endurance, flexibility and cardio-respiratory endurance, it seems that, at least clinically, the psychological gains are much more relevant.

Based on her experience, Feldmann reported that she felt she had helped 'to alleviate some of the students' complexes, resulting from their invalidity, by providing them with the opportunity to demonstrate their talents, and affording them the possibility of performing before an audience who would look at them - not with pity but with admiration'.

Dancing is also considered a splendid medium in which 'physically disabled persons learn about their bodies, find outlets for their emotions, and consequently can develop more positive attitudes toward themselves' (Hill, 1976:6).

The actual dance and movement programme was developed according to a model of personal development outlined by Hutzler (1990). This model utilizes the theoretical concepts of **self efficacy** (Bandura, 1977, 1982) and **competence** (Harter, 1978, 1982), and regards physical activity as a mediator for changes of psychological traits, such as self confidence, self concept, social acceptance and activity level.

3   Self Efficacy Theory

Efficacy expectations refer to the conviction of an individual regarding his or her ability to execute successfully an action necessary to master a desired task. These convictions significantly influence the individual's future action process: his or her selection of actions for the situations and of the coping efforts in which he or she would persist until success. On behalf of the theoretical and empirical evidence, Bandura (1982:126) claims that '**enactive attainments** provide the most influential source of efficacy information, because it can be based on authentic mastery experiences. Successes heighten perceived self efficacy; repeated failures lower it'.

Other sources of efficacy information include **vicarious experiences** (peer modelling), **verbal persuasion** and **emotional arousal** while facing a specific situation.

Dance experience is a socially accepted physical activity which is associated with positive values of beauty, agility and vitality. It seems logical, therefore, that disabled persons, who already consider themselves unable to do many things and suddenly master dancing exercise, get a mental boost of great magnitude. These feelings of **competence** tend to be broadly generalized to other situations in which other action settings are necessary.

4   Therapeutic Dance Experience

The dancing activity is conducted 1 hour weekly at the paraplegic department of the Levinstein Medical Center. It is instructed by a PE teacher who has specialized in sports for the disabled and in movement therapy. It is located in the social room of the department which is not ideal for dancing but it is very near to the patients.

The main problem confronted during this experience is how to **motivate** and **activate** the patients. This is done through all kinds of efficacy information: **Enactive attainments** are achieved through very popular musical stimuli, which also raises **emotional arousal**. The latter is also referred to through the sexual role play provided in partner dancing. **Verbal persuasion** has been achieved through very close collaboration with the social worker and the nurses in the department, and finally **vicarious experience** was achieved several times through individuals and groups of wheelchair dancers from outside the hospital who came to motivate and to activate the patients.

The next issue in the clinical application of dancing is the systematic development of personal perceptions of efficacy. This is achieved, for example, through exercises in which the patients are asked to perform and to let their partners follow them as a mirror. Other exercises are specifically designed to initiate positive reactions towards the impaired body and to enhance social contact through hand-grappling, dancing the rondo and group specific tasks, such as holding a balloon or a ball in the air during a certain piece of music.

5   Clinical Observations and Verbal Reactions of Group Members

No systematic evaluation of the dancing activity has been conducted yet. There exists, however, some qualitative information gathered through clinical observations made by the movement therapist and by a social worker. Group members were encouraged to reflect verbally on their perceptions during and after participation in the programme. Utilizing this information a number of cases can be described:

(a)   A young paraplegic man who suffered from suicidal thoughts, changed his emotions radically during and after engagement in the dancing activity. Some time after release from hospital he joined a sports centre for the disabled where he could continue his dancing practice.

(b) A middle-aged paraplegic woman who had also lost her leg, used to say that dancing makes her feel active and valuable again. After a number of sessions, she started to use make-up, to use lipstick and to dress elegantly prior to the activity.

(c) A young tumor-operated woman with quadraparesis used to dance before onset of disability. At the time she participated in the clinical activity, her husband was in the process of separating from her. The dancing was apparently one of the major resources for her mental strength. Once she mentioned that dancing taught her that 'there is life after.'

Some further evidence for the value of wheelchair dancing activity in building up positive perceptions of self efficacy and self concept come from comments of recreational wheelchair dancers.

(a) ELIAHU was a folk dancer as a youngster. After onset of disability he lost contact with dancing. 'Now', he said, 'I can continue more or less the way I used to'.

(b) NATI reports on a party he was invited to recently. 'This time', he said, 'instead of looking at the dancers as before from the chair, I suddenly found myself asking somebody to dance with me. Now I feel myself **less frozen, less stiff** and **I'm simply not ashamed any more**'.

(c) SHAI and KIKY met each other during the dancing activity of the recreational group and are now rehearsing to do a solo-tango at their wedding.

(d) ADA mentions that now she dances actively with her children at nursery school parties, while previously the nursery school teacher had to dance with her children.

6   Conclusions and Final Remarks

Dancing seems to be a very useful activity for enhancing self-efficacy and self-concept of individuals with locomotor disabilities. The comments gleaned from the participants indicate that the activity provides some generalizable effects. These reflect in applying efficacious action patterns used during the therapeutic activity to other situations (a party, a wedding, etc.).

Certainly this notion must be studied further by more accurate means, such as the physical self-efficacy scale developed by Ryckman et al. (1982). Wheelchair manufacturers, however, have already noticed that dancing may be an important factor for sales promotion, as observed in the following commercial:

'Our customers tell us our Rigid Chair is the quickest, fastest, most danceable chair they have ever owned! Originally designed for tennis and basketball, the sleek, functional design and tight turning radius of the Shadow Rigid works equally well on the dance floor, at lunch, or in competiton'.

7   References

Bandura, A. (1977) Self-efficacy toward a unifying theory of behavioral change. **Psychological Reviews,** 87, 7, 191-215.

Bandura, A. (1982) Self-efficacy mechanism in human agency. **American Psychologist,** 37, 2, 122-147.

Boswell, B. (1989) Dance as a creative expression for the disabled. **Palaestra** (Fall), 28-30.

Feldman, R. **Wheelchair ballet.** Unpublished paper.

Harter, S. (1982) The perceived competence scale for children. **Child Development, 53,** 87-97.

Harter, S. (1978) Effectance motivation reconsidered - toward a developmental model. **Human Development,** 21, 34-64.

Hecox, B., Levine, E. and Scott, D. (1975) A report on the use of dance in physical rehabilitation: Every body has a right to feel good. **Rehabilitation Literature,** 36, 1, 11-16.

Hill, K. (1976) Dance for physically disabled persons. Reston, Va: **Physical Education and Recreation for the Handicapped:** Information and Research Utilization Center.

Hutzler, Y. (1990) The concept of empowerment in rehabilitative sports, in **Adapted Physical Activity: An Interdisciplinary approach** (eds. G. Doll Tepper, C. Dahms, B. Doll and H. von Selzam), Heidelberg: Springer Verlag.

Krombholz, G. and Zimmer, M. (1986) Theory and practice of a new concept - Integrative wheelchair dancing, in **First European Congress on Adapted Physical Activity Proceedings** (eds. J.C. DePotter and H. Levarlet-Joye), Presses Universitaires de l'Universite Libre.

Rosenthal, N. (1989) Dances for disabled in wheelchairs. Paper presented at the Maccabiah International Congress in Sports and Training Sciences. June 30th, held at the Wingate Institute, Israel.

Ryckman, R.M., Robbins, M.A., Thornton, B. and Cantrell, P. (1982) Development and validation of a physical self-efficacy scale. **Journal of Personality and Social Psychology,** 42, 5, 891-900.

PHYSICAL FITNESS AS A DRIVING FORCE TO ENHANCE PSYCHOLOGICAL WELL-BEING IN DEPRESSED PATIENTS: RESEARCH HYPOTHESIS

H. VAN COPPENOLLE, E. NEERINCKX AND J. KNAPEN
Institute of Physical Education, K.U. Leuven, Belgium

1 Introduction

In the literature, more and more evidence is reported that many psychiatric disorders should be regarded as expressions of a deep-rooted experience of impotence (Garber & Seligman, 1980; Watzlawick, Beavin & Jackson, 1967). Patients feel they are not able to meet the requirements that, either really or allegedly, are demanded of them. Patients do not feel that they are in control of their existence and that they can organize it according to their own values and needs.

The psychic symptom, in this case depression, is then regarded as a manifestation of this experience of impotence. The forms of treatment that are associated with this line of thought focus on creating oportunities for individuals to test and evaluate their hypotheses about themselves as to how they relate to the world so that they can try to identify and change their maladjusted views and dysfunctional ways of interpreting events in their environment (Beck, 1967).

This study focuses on the formulation, within this theoretical background, of a research hypothesis about using physical activity in the treatment of depressive disorders. Indeed, quite a number of authors claim that physical activities such as jogging, give good results in the treatment of physiological disorders (Blue, 1979; Greist et al., 1979; Van Andel & Austin, 1984; Raglin, 1990). Models that account for these effects are most often developed within physiological frames of reference (Folkins & Sime, 1981; Weinstein & Meyers, 1983; Dishman, 1986). Cognitive models are referred to only sporadically. But, following Dishman (1986), we believe there may be useful leads in the latter:

> None of the biochemical or social psychological speculations for the anti-depressant effects of exercise have been confirmed, but it appears likely that the effects depend largely on graded mastery and feelings related to competence, self-control and symptom distraction or substitution. (Dishman, 1986).

We will attempt to provide the theoretical foundation of this line of thought as follows:

First, we give a brief review of the symptomatology and the cognitive-behavioural model of depression, on which the parameters used in our research project are based.

Second, we present some recent results of research on the effects of physical exercise in depressives.

Finally, we will attempt to formulate our research hypothesis and outline the research design.

2   Depression

2.1 *Symptomatology*

Clinically, patients with depression almost always experience more than one of the following psychological or somatic symptoms and behaviours:

(a)   depressed mood characterized by reports of feeling sad, low, blue, despondent, hopeless, gloomy;
(b)   inability to experience pleasure (anhedonia);
(c)   loss of energy, fatigue, lethargy, anergy;
(d)   retardation of speech, thought and movement;
(e)   change in appetite, usually weight loss;
(f)   sleep disturbance, usually insomnia;
(g)   bodily complaints;
(h)   agitation (increased motor activity experienced as restlessness);
(i)   decrease in sexual interest and activity;
(j)   loss of interest in work and other activities;
(k)   feelings of worthlessness, self-reproach, guilt and shame;
(l)   diminished ability to think or concentrate, with complaints of 'slowed thinking' or 'mixed-up thoughts';
(m)   anxiety;
(n)   lowered self-esteem;
(o)   feelings of helplessness;
(p)   pessimism and hopelessness;
(q)   thoughts of death or suicide attempts;

In this summary the depressed mood, negative body attitude, lowered self-esteem and feelings of helplessness will receive our further attention.

2.2 *Cognitive-behavioural model of depression*

According to Beck et al. (1969) cognitive factors are essential in the development and the persistence of depression. Crucial are the negative expectations of depressed people about themselves, their current situation and their future. In close relation with these negative expectations, they estimate their self-efficacy (Bandura, 1981) as very low and this dulls initiative. Depressives interpret the outcomes of their activities in a specific way. This difference in attributional style is an important predisposing and perpetuating factor in depression; even more than the amount of stress they may be exposed to or the skills in which they may fail. This is the starting point for the reformulated learned helplessness model of depression (Abramson, Seligman and Teasdale, 1978).

Observations of behaviour in experimental animals that were exposed to unavoidable negative stimuli, had already led Seligman to state that (reactive depression) is essentially 'learned helplessness'. Depression would be caused by the experience of uncontrollable events.

This concept of learned helplessness was reformulated on the basis of attribution theory which advances the following:

When a person is exposed to events with uncontrollable outcomes, he generates attributions which vary in three dimensions:

(a) the person attributes the outcomes to himself or to somebody or something outside himself;

(b) the person attributes the outcomes to causes which are long-lived or short-lived;

(c) the person attributes the outcomes to causes which are, or are not, considered to occur across situations.

Usually these dimensions are indicated with the three following pairs of terms: internal-external, stable-unstable, and global-specific.

Undesired events which are perceived to be uncontrollable lead to four depression related symptoms: dysphoria, lowered motivation, inability to learn 'response contingencies' and lowered self-esteem.

The combination of these symptoms with the above mentioned attribution dimensions gives the following picture. Generally, it can be stated that depressive people attribute negative events to internal, stable and global factors and successful outcomes to external, specific and unstable factors.

In a therapeutic view of the disorder Andersen et al. (1983), following Weiner (1979), add a fourth dimension to these three, namely 'controllability'. They state that a change in expectance for future success is primarily dependent on the extent to which people assume the cause of an outcome to be modifiable by themselves. Indeed, when a negative outcome is attributed to a controllable factor, the expectancy as to similar future situations will not be adversely affected.

Conversely, we can expect, - and this is the first basic assumption of our hypothesis - that individuals changing their perception about the uncontrollability of a factor, in this case performing physical activities, can constitute an important turning point for them. Whereas depressive patients, as mentioned before, attribute successful outcomes to external specific and incidental factors, a progressively developed training programme, so a successful one can be a starting point for a shift of attribution of success to internal factors (I have realized this; I am able to achieve something).

And here we come to the heart of the problem. Indeed, from research on depression it has become clear, especially, that the experience of uncontrollability together with the 'internal locus' are the two most important dimensions. By successful training, the global uncontrollability attributed to internal factors is broken down: depressive patients are confronted with the experience that they have regained control of a specific part of reality by means of their own capacities.

3   Physical Fitness as a Driving Force

If we adopt the foregoing hypothesis, there is a question of why we opt for physical activity. Why do psychomotor therapists think they can contribute to the treatment of depressive patients? The reason is twofold: favourable effects can be expected both on the physiological and on the psychological level.

From the physiological point of view, Morgan (1969) as well as Martinsen (1990) notice a strongly reduced physical work capacity in depressed patients. Pulmonary function is normal, so the depressed patient can be considered as physically sedentary. Already the health risks involved in this life style are sufficient reason for adding physical condition; we opted for aerobic training in our study. In this context, one would expect to act not only on the therapeutical level but also on the level of medical prevention (Raglin, 1990).

But there is more because for twenty years studies have reported that physical activity is correlated with changes in psychological variables; such as mood improvement. Older studies have only a relative importance due to their methodological defects, but more recent studies partially confirm the findings. Table 1 gives a survey of the most recent research.

In spite of the rather heterogeneous research designs all results confirm the depression-reducing effects of aerobic physical training. About the type of activity,

Table 1

AUTHORS	EXP. GROUP	CONDITION	RESULTS
McCahn & Holmes (1984)	43 women 'depressed'	aerobic exercise (1h 2x/week) relaxation training (20' 4x/week) Waiting list 23 weeks	all groups decreased depression aerobic group significantly greater decrease
Klein (1985)	74 outpatients 'major or minor'	aerobic exercise (1h 2x/week) meditation relaxation (2h 1 x/week) Group psychot. (2h 1x/week)	all groups signif. decreased depression after 9 months better outcome for exercise and meditation group
Freemont & Craighead (1987)	49 individuals 'elevated BDI scores'	aerobic exercise (20' 3x/week) cognitive therapy (1 session/week) aerobic exercise + cognit. therapy	no differences between groups. Significantly decreased depression scores
Martinson (1987)	49 inpatients 'major depression'	control group = occup. + milieu +1 or 2 session of individual psychotherapy training group = 3x/w occ. ther. substituted by aerobic exercise for 1 hour	significant increase in physical work capacity in training group significant decreased depression scores for both significantly greater decrease in training group

duration and intensity, however, no conclusions can be drawn. There is also a lack of clarity with the models that can account for the effects. We expect our study will shed some light on these problems.

4   Research Hypothesis

According to the foregoing discussion we have arrived at the following hypothesis:

(a)   Depressive patients are characterized by
- bad physical fitness
- negative body attitude
- negative perception of physical skills
- negative feeling of general competence
- lowered self-esteem.

(b)   A significant improvement of physical fitness leads to improvement of mood, a noticeably more positive body attitude and perception of physical skills.

(c)   A cognitive-behavioural model of depression can account for these changes. Physical training promotes a transformation or disruption of the maladaptive cognitive set a person has previously used to face the world. Physical exercise results in the formation of a more positive, internal attribution of achievement, which then restructures the individual's hierarchy of self-perceptions and self-evaluations.

(d)   This process increasingly reinforces an awareness that success and mastery are linked with goal achievement and self-competence through effortful, purposive behaviour. Consequently, maintaining physical fitness (through sustained training) leads to a significant improvement of the feeling of self-efficacy and of self-esteem.

5   Research Design

The subject group of this study will consist of hospitalized patients who, in the DSM III-R, are classified under 'depressive disorders' with subcategories 'major depression' (296.2X and 296.3X) and 'systhymia' (300.40; both the primary and the secondary type).

First the base-line of the subjects will be determined:

(a)   somatic: cardiovascular endurance (by means of the ergometer cycle; maximum muscular strength and endurance (by means of the multigym station).

(b)   psychological: profile of Mood States (POMS, McNair et al., 1971)
Tennessee Self-Concept Scale (Fitts, 1965)
Perceived Body Skills Scale (Bosscher et al., 1987)
Self-efficacy Scale (Sharer, 1986)
Body Attitudes Scale (Baardman, 1989).

Subjects are then given a training programme (4 hours/week during 12 weeks) according to which, in consultation with the patients, a standardized exercise schedule will be followed as a means to improve physical fitness and motivate the patient.

Evaluations are planned during treatment, on discharge from the hospital, and 6 months and 1 year after discharge. These will be evaluations both of the patients who will have kept on training and of those who will have stopped.

Beside the experimental group a control group will also be evaluated as well as a group who will be provided with a number of non-physical activities taking an equal length of time.

6   References

Abramson, L.Y., Seligman M.E.P. and Teasdale, J.D. (1978) Learned helplessness in humans: critique and reformulation, **Journal of Abnormal Psychology** 87, 49-74.

American Psychiatric Association (1987) **Diagnostic and statistical manual of mental disorders**, 3rd ed. Revised version, APA, Washington DC.

Anderson, C.A., Horowitz, L.W. and French, R. (1983) Attributional style of lonely and depressed people. **Journal of Personality and Social Psychology** 45, 127-136.

Baardman, I. (1989) **Ingebeelde Irlijkheid**, Free University Press, Amsterdam.

Bandura, A. (1981) Self-referent thought: the development of self-efficacy, in: Flavell, J.H., Ross, L.D. (eds) **Development of social cognition,** New York: Cambridge University Press.

Beck, A.T. (1967) **Depression: clinical, experimental and theoretical aspects**, Harper & Row, New York.

Beck, A.T., Rush, A.J., Shaw, B.F.and Emery, G. (1969) **Cognitive therapy of depression**, Guildford Press: New York.

Blue, F.R. (1979) Aerobic running as a treatment of moderate depression. **Perceptual and motor skills**, 48, 228.

Bosscher, R., Krommert, M., Pennings, J., Rebel, J., Steggink, D., van Veldhuizen, T. and Vroon, R. (1987) Gepercipieerde lichamelijk competentie: gemeten en gewogen, **Bewegen en hulpverlening** 4, 291-310.

Bosscher, R. and Baardman, I. (1989) Waargenomen competentie bij psychiatrische patienten, **Bewegen en hulpverlening** 4, 312-322.

Dishman, R.K. (1986) Mental health, in Seefeldt V (ed), **Physical activity and well-being,** American Alliance for Health, Physical Education, Recreation & Dance, 306-338.

Fitts, (1965) Manual for the Tennessee Department of Mental Health Self-concept Scale, **Counselor Recordings and Test**, Nashville, Tennessee.

Folkins, C.H. and Sime, W.E. (1981) Physical fitness training and mental health, **American Psychologists** 36, 373-389.

Garber, J. and Seligman, M.E.P. (eds), (1980) **Human helplessness: theory and applications**. Academic Press, New York.

Griest, J.H., Klein, M.H., Eischens, R.R., Faris, J., Gurman, A.S. and Morgan, W.P. (1979) Running as treatment for depression. **Comprehensive Psychiatry**, 20: 41-54.

Martinsen, E.W. (1990) Benefits of exercise for the treatment of depression. **Sports Medicine**, 9 (6): 380-389.

McNair, D., Lorr, M. and Droppleman, L. (1971) Manual: Profile of Mood States. Educational and Industrial Testing Service, San Diego.

Morgan, W.P. (1969) A pilot investigation of physical working capacity in depressed and non-depressed psychiatric males. **Research Quarterly**, 4: 859-861.

Nicholi, A.M., Jr. (1988) **The New Harvard Guide of Psychiatry**. Belknap Press of Harvard University Press, Cambridge, Massachusetts and London.

Raglin, J.S. (1990) Exercise and mental health. **Sports Medicine**, 9 (6): 323-329.

Sherer, M., Maddux, J.E., Mercandante, B., Prentice-Dunn, S., Jacobs, B. and Rogers, R.W. (1982) The self-efficacy scale: construction and validation. **Psychological Reports**, 51: 663-671.

Van Andel, G.E. and Austin, D.R. (1984) Physical Fitness and Mental Health: a review of literature. **Adapted Physical Activity Quarterly**, 1: 207-220.

Watzlawick, P., Beavin, J.H. and Jackson, D.D. (1967) **Pragmatics of human communication**. W.W. Norton & Company Inc., New York.

Weiner, B. (1979) A theory of motivation for some classroom experiences. **Journal of Education Psychology**, 71: 3-25.

Weinstein, W.S. and Meyers, A.W. (1983) Running as treatment for depression: is it worth it? **Journal of Sports Psychology**, 5: 288-301.

PSYCHOLOGICAL IMPLICATIONS OF PHYSICAL ACTIVITY IN INDIVIDUALS WITH PHYSICAL DISABILITIES

ELIZABETH BENSON[1] AND GRAHAM JONES[2]
[1] *British Sports Association for the Disabled, Sutton Coldfield, England*
[2] *Loughborough University, England*

Abstract
This paper provides a brief overview of recent research and developments in physical activity patterns and relationships with psychological well-being in individuals with physical disabilities. A number of issues are addressed under the following headings: The Psychological Implications of Disability, which discusses major components of the stress process and their relationships with physical disability. Particular emphasis is placed on chronic disability as a potential source of stress, and how this may be related to variables such as self-esteem and mastery; Physical Activity for Individuals with Physical Disabilities: A Rationale, which considers the historical development of sport for the disabled and discusses research which has examined the benefits of participation in physical activity; Research on the Psychological Benefits of Participation for Individuals with a Physical Disability, which examines research that has focused on the factors which may be influential in determining psychological well-being in individuals with physical disabilities.

1   Introduction

During the past decade or so society has witnessed a revolution in its concept of exercise and health. Health professionals have argued that regular exercise, in addition to having well-established physical health benefits, can be effective in both preventing the onset of emotional problems and in treating mental health problems once they have arisen. Whilst the positive health convictions of exercise developed there was a simultaneous increase in the number of individuals with a disability involved in sport. Knowledge of the rehabilitation benefits of exercise and the development of competitive sport for people with physical disabilities has been instrumental in fostering research in the area. This research, however, has predominantly considered the physiological effects of exercise, with the psychological implications left relatively under-developed. However, research into the psychological health benefits of physical activity for people with a disability is gaining impetus. This paper discusses three areas which provide an insight into this development: the first section discusses physical disability within the context of a model of stress which encompasses the sources, mediators and outcomes of stress; the second section addresses the development and benefit of physical activity for people with physical disabilities; and finally, psychological research on physical activity in individuals with physical disabilities is considered.

2   Psychological Implications of Physical Disability

To gain an insight into the possible psychological implications of physical disability the work of Pearlin et al. (1981) on 'The Stress Process' is considered. This provides an appropriate starting point since exercise has been shown to be influential in reducing stress, leading to a reduction in anxiety (Berger and Owen ,1987; Raglin and Morgan, 1987), a reduction in depression (Greist, 1987) and also an increase in self-esteem (Gruber, 1986). The structure of Pearlin et al.'s stress model allows for the effective analysis of research in the area of individuals with physical disabilities. These authors proposed that the stress process comprises three major components:

(a) sources of stress,
(b) mediators of stress;
(c) outcomes of the stress process.

Each of the components are now considered in relation to physical disability.

2.1 *Sources of Stress*

Sources of stress were stated by Pearlin et al. (1981) to arise from two broad circumstances; discrete events and chronic strains. They proposed that persistent role strains may act as a continual reminder of individuals' own failures, lack of success and proof of their inability to alter the unwanted circumstances in their lives. It is under these conditions that Pearlin et al. felt that individuals could become vulnerable to loss of self-esteem and to the erosion of mastery. Physical disability can be viewed as a source of stress due to its permanency, with the assumption that the greater the physical limitation then the greater will be the chronic strain.

2.2 *Mediators of the Stress Process*

Pearlin et al. (1981) considered two types of resources mediating stress; social support and coping. The findings from Turner and Noh's (1988) longitudinal study suggested that by improving social support and/or mastery then it may be possible to reduce the risk of depressive symptomatology. The most favourable method of coping according to Pearlin et al. (1981) is to deal with face to face relations rather than directing coping strategies at problems residing in formal organizations and authority. Van den Bout et al. (1988) examined the coping behaviour of 22 severe spinal cord injured (16 men and 6 women). The results appeared to show different coping behaviour tendencies between recently and long term disabled individuals. Specifically, it was found to be more adaptive for individuals disabled for a long time to be concerned with the cause of the accident and how it could have been avoided, but it was found to be maladaptive for recently disabled individuals to be concerned with these factors. Van den Bout et al.'s research appears to support Pearlin et al.'s suggestion that, for long-term disability, the most favourable method of coping is to deal with the factors which an individual can personally control.

2.3 *Outcomes of the Stress Process*

Pearlin et al. (1981) considered the consequences of stress by using depression as a global indicator. Their work suggested that self-concepts were not symptoms of stress but sources of it. The implications of this when considering individuals with a physical disability is that if they do not perceive their disability as affecting their self-esteem and mastery then their disability itself may not cause them to be depressed. This implies, therefore, that a functional abnormality may not be linked in a direct or simple way to psychological consequences. This is supported by Wright (1983) who proposed that:

> a somatic abnormality as a physical fact is not linked in a direct or simple way to psychological consequences. Instead, factors that pertain to intrapsychic events in the person and to external forces in the situation must be considered in accounting for variable effects of disabilities. (p.243).

Whilst acknowledging that a physical disability may not directly result in depression, research has shown that physically disabled people may be at risk to symptoms of depression. Turner and Noh (1988) conducted a two-wave longitudinal analysis over a four year period of physical disability and depression. The results showed that there was a reciprocal relationship between mastery and depression. Turner and Noh suggested, therefore, that either the level of mastery or a change in it could exert effects on levels of depression, and that a prior level of depression may indicate mastery levels. The results also suggested that physical disability is associated with an increased risk to depression regardless of age and gender.

The following sections examine the possible effectiveness of physical activity as an important factor in determining the outcome of the stress process in people with physical disabilities.

3   Physical Activity for People with Disabilities: A Rationale

After the Second World War, major medical advances and increased knowledge of the deteriorating effects of inactivity caused vigorous physical activity to be implemented in rehabilitation programmes (Brandmeyer and McBee, 1984). The aim of these programmes was to prevent the degenerative process characteristic of the sedentary lifestyle of the physically disabled population (Compton et al., 1989). Active leisure has developed with a dual purpose for people with a physical disabilty. Firstly, rehabilitation specialists view active leisure as therapeutic exercise that challenges a patient not to accept physical obstacles as inevitable limitations (Jackson and Davis, 1983), and secondly, active leisure, in the form of sport, can be seen as a means of pursuing excellence which may culminate ultimately in National and Olympic competition (Guttman, 1976). Sherrill (1984) interviewed 300 elite cerebral palsied (CP) athletes to assess their motives for participating in sport. The results suggested that some used sport as a means of affirming their competence to the able-bodied community, helping to focus attention on their ability rather than their disability. It appears, therefore, that sport may act as an agent in displacing the negative halo which some of the able-bodied community place around people with a physical disability (Horvat et al., 1986; Sherrill and Rainbolt, 1988).

According to Compton et al. (1989), physical activity is required by people with a physical disability for optimal body functioning and also to help act as a preventative strategy to secondary disorders which individuals with a physical disability have a tendency towards; for example, cardiovascular disease, obesity, diabetes and osteoporosis. Individuals with a physical disability need to take part consciously in physical activity because their physical disability can limit their movement, resulting in deconditioning and a lower capacity for daily living activities (Compton et al., 1989).

4   Research on the Psychological Benefits of Participation in Physical Activity for Individuals with a Physical Disability

Various studies have attempted to assess the psychological benefits which individuals with a physical disability may gain from participating in physical activity. Szyman's (1980) study involved 75 subjects (45 male and 30 female) with a wide range of physical disabilities, including traumatic quadraplegia, traumatic paraplegia, CP and poliomyelitis. All of the subjects participated in physical activity. The aim of the study was to assess whether participation caused certain psychological consequences, or if personal disposition caused them to participate. The findings suggested that individuals' leisure attitudes and well-being caused them to participate, whereas self-concept was equally divided on causing an individual to participate and being affected by participation. This type of study has far-reaching implications for the physically disabled population regarding the development of public policy and facility provision, culminating hopefully in increased levels of participation (Zoerink, 1988).

Henschen et al. (1984), Horvat et al. (1986) and Canabal et al. (1987) have all used McNair, Lorr and Droppleman's (1981) Profile of Mood States Questionnaire (POMS) to examine the mood states of athletes with a physical disability and then compared them with able-bodied norms. POMS identifies six mood states; tension, depression, anger, vigour, fatigue and confusion. All three studies reported that athletes with a physical disability manifested an iceberg profile on POMS similar to that reported for able-bodied atheletes (i.e. above average scores on vigour and below average scores on the other moods). The studies of Henschen et al. (1984) and Canabal et al. (1987) reported higher anger scores than mean scores recorded for able-bodied athletes, but they were still within the normal range. Furthermore, Henschen et al. (1984) found both state and trait anxiety in wheelchair athletes to be lower than adult and student norms and similar to those observed for able-bodied athletes.

The effect of athletic activity on the psychoneurotic components of physically disabled individuals was considered by Monnazzi (1982). The sample of 41 paraplegics had similar lesion levels and similar times of disability onset and consisted of 22 active and 19 non-active individuals. The Middlesex Hospital Questionnaire was used to assess the psychoneurotic components of anxiety, phobia, obsession, somatization, depression and hysteria. The results indicated that the inactive group were higher than the active group on all factors. The results of the athletes with a physical disability were compared to a group of able-bodied athletes and found to be very similar. The inactive physically disabled group had higher scores on all psychoneurotic factors when analyzed in relation to an inactive able-bodied sample. Monnazzi (1982) concluded:

> While paraplegia increases the psychoneurotic aspects of personality, the practices of sports attenuates them considerably giving them an expression comparable to that of individuals without handicap.(p. 93)

Hopper (1984) further investigated the influence of physical activity by inspecting self-acceptance on Rosenberg's (1965) Self-Esteem Scale. This study of 87 individuals who were either spinally paralysed or amputees illustrated that self-esteem increased the longer an individual had participated in sport, but that no relationship existed regarding success in sport. Spouse and career plans were proposed as other influencing factors on self-esteem. This is supported by Nelson and Gruver's (1978) study of self-esteem and body image in paraplegics. The results from Hopper's (1984) study also showed a relationship between self-esteem, severity of disabilty and age of onset of disabilty; the more severe a disability the lower was an individual's self-esteem, and the later in life a disability onset the higher the individual's self-esteem. Finally, Sherrill and Rainbolt (1988) examined the self-actualization profiles of male able-bodied and elite CP athletes. A sample of 265 able-bodied athletes and 30 CP athletes completed Shostrom's (1964) Personal Orientation Inventory. The results showed elite CP athletes and able-bodied inter-collegiate athletes to have similar self-actualization profiles.

5   Conclusions

The findings discussed in the previous section offer general support for the proposal that participation in physical activity for individuals with a physical disability can have psychological as well as physical health benefits. It is important to emphasize, however, that the evidence discussed tends to be associative rather than causal, and there has been a distinct lack of well-controlled longitudinal studies. Nevertheless, the current situation is encouraging in that the positive aspects of physical activity operating within the stress process for people with a physical disability appear to be established.

6   References

Berger, B. and Owen, D. (1987) Anxiety reduction with swimming: relationships between exercise and state, trait and somatic anxiety. **International Journal of Sport Psychology**, 18, 286-302.

Brandmeyer and McBee (1984) Social status and athletic competition for the disabled athlete: The Case of Wheelchair Road Racing. The 1984 Olympic Scientific Congress Proceedings, Vol. 9, **Sport and Disabled Athletes** (ed Sherrill, C. 1986), Human Kinetics Publishers Inc.

Canabal, M.Y., Sherrill, C. and Rainbolt, W.J. (1987) Psychological mood profiles of elite cerebral palsied athletes. In **International perspectives on Adapted Physical Activity** (eds Berridge, M.E. and Ward, G.R.), Human Kinetics Publishers, Inc. Champaign, Illinois.

Compton, D.M., Eisenman, P.A. and Henderson, H.L. (1989) Exercise and Fitness for Persons with Disabilities. **Sports Medicine**, 7, 150-162.

Greist, J.H. (1987) Exercise intervention with depressed patients. In W.P. Morgan and S.E. Goldston (eds), **Exercise and Mental Health**. Washington: Hemisphere.

Gruber, J.J. (1986) Physical activity and self-esteem development in children: a meta-analysis. In G Stull and H. Eckert (eds), **Effects of Physical Activity on Children.** Champaign, Illinois: Human Kinetics and American Academy of Physical Education.

Guttman, L. (1976) **Textbook of Sport for the Disabled.** H.M. & M. Publishers Ltd.

Henschen, R., Horvat, M. and French, R. (1984) A visual comparison of psychological profiles between able-bodied and wheelchair athletes. **Adapted Physical Activity Quarterly**, 1(2), 118-124.

Hopper, C.A. (1984) Socialization of Wheelchair Athletes. The 1984 Olympic Scientific Congress Proceedings Vol. 9. **Sport and Disabled Athletes** (ed Sherrill, C., 1986), Human Kinetics Publishers, Inc.

Horvat, M.R., French, R. and Henschen, R. (1986) A comparison of the psychological characteristics of male and female able-bodied. **Paraplegia**, 24, 115-122.

Jackson, R. and Davis, G. (1983) The value of sports and recreation for the physically disabled. **Orthopedic Clinics of North America**, 14, 301-315.

McNair, D.M., Lorr, M. and Droppleman, L.F. (1981) **Manual Profile of Mood States.** Educational and Industrial Testing Services, San Diego, California. 92107.

Monnazzi, G. (1982) Paraplegics and Sport: A psychological survey. **International Journal of Sport Psychology**, 13, 85-95.

Nelson, M. and Gruver, C.G. (1978) Self Esteem and Body Image Concept in Paraplegics. **Rehabilitation Counselling Bulletin**, 21, 108-113.

Pearlin, L.I., Lieberman, M.A., Menaghan, E.G. and Mullan, J.T. (1981) The Stress Process. **Journal of Health and Social Behaviour**, 22, 337-356.

Raglin, J.S. and Morgan, W.P. (1987) Influence of exercise and quiet rest on state anxiety and blood pressure. **Medicine and Science in Sports and Exercise**, 19, 456-463.

Sherrill, C. and Rainbolt, W. (1988) Self-Actualization profiles of male able-bodied and elite CP athletes. **Adapted Physical Activity Quarterly**, 5, 108-119.

Sherrill, C. (1984) Social and Psychological Dimensions of Sports for Disabled Athletes. The 1984 Olympic Scientific Congress Proceedings, Vol. 9. **Sport and Disabled Athletes** (ed Sherrill, C. 1986), Human Kinetics Publishers Inc.

Szyman, R.J. (1980) The effect of participation in wheelchair sports. **Dissertation Abstracts International**, 41, 804A-805A. (University Microfilms No. 8018209).

Turner, R.J., Noh, S. (1988) Physical Disability and Depression: A Longitudinal Analysis. **Journal of Health and Social Behaviour**, 29, 23-27.

Van den Bout, J., Son-Schoones, N., Schipper, J. and Groffen, C. (1988) Attributional cognitions, coping behaviour and self esteem in inpatients with severe spinal cord injuries. **Journal of Clinical Psychology**, 44, 17-22.

Wright, B.A. (1983) **Physical Disabilities: A psychological approach**. New York: Harper and Row.

Zoerink, D.A. (1988) Attitudes toward leisure: persons with congenital orthopedic disabilities versus able-bodied persons. **Journal of Rehabilitation**, April/May/June, 54(2), 60-64.

SPORT AS A MEANS OF SOCIAL INTEGRATION OF UNDERPRIVILEGED YOUTH

MARC THEEBOOM, PAUL DE KNOP AND PAUL WYLLEMAN
Higher Institute of Physical Education, Vrije Universiteit Brussel, Brussels, Belgium

Abstract
Sport seems to be a good activity in working with underprivileged youth. Apart from being a meaningful leisure activity, sport can be used to work towards an improvement of the social integration of these youngsters who are confronted with a multitude of problems. This paper discusses the role of a school sports programme for underprivileged youth in Antwerp (Belgium). The programme was evaluated through an inquiry of the youngsters, through interviews with teachers and sports instructors and through observation. Results showed that the youngsters were very interested in the programme. Absenteeism clearly decreased, there was an improvement of the relationship between pupils and their teachers and sport became also an interesting subject during other courses. Many youngsters showed great interest in continuing practising sport at school as well as in their leisure time. However it is necessary to point out that this programme can only be seen as an initial step towards a more integrated strategy to stimulate participation in sport among these youngsters.
Keywords: Underprivileged Youth, School Sports Programme, Social Integration.

1   Introduction

It is difficult to give a good definition of underprivileged youth because of their heterogeneity. However, they have one characteristic feature in common: they are all confronted with a multitude of problems (at school, at home, at work, during leisure time, with the police, ...). Youth welfare workers and teachers often have great difficulties in motivating these youngsters to take part in organized activities. Dealing with rules, standing by agreements and taking responsibility are some of the main problems involved.

Since participation in sport seems to be an appropriate way to attract many of these youngsters, it is used more and more while working with this group. Apart from being a meaningful leisure activity, sport also has, according to many, an educative character which can be of use to improve the social integration of underprivileged youth (Adolph-Volpert et al. 1984, Bergmann 1986, Böck 1986, Harms 1984,

Meiburg 1985, Middleton 1982, 1984, Nickolai 1982, Ruottinen 1982, Theeboom et al. 1989, 1990a-b, van Ancum and Meiburg, 1987, van der Gugten 1988, van Dijck 1987). Sports often help teachers and youth welfare workers to get in contact with these youths. It can improve their relationship with these youngsters, which is necessary in order to start working at their difficult situation.

Youngsters can take up sports activities through different institutions (sports clubs, community sports services, schools, youth welfare work, ...). However, since underprivileged youth does not frequently take part in organized activities, they are not likely to participate in sports on a regular basis. Many of them take up organized sports activities only through school. This paper discusses the effects of an intensive school sports programme on the attitude of these youngsters towards sports.

2   Method

During the first four months of the school year 1988-1989, an intensive school sports programme was organized in two Antwerp municipal schools by the Youth Advisory Centre for Sports of the Free University of Brussels (V.U.B.) and the local school sports federation. Through this programme, which was sponsored by the King Baudouin Foundation (Konig Boudewijnstichting), a co-operation with different local organizations was set up including:

(a)   the municipal education service
(b)   the municipal sports service
(c)   some sports clubs.

2.1 *Population*

127 pupils between the ages of 12 and 18 took part in the programme. These youths can be described as 'underprivileged'. 58.3% of them were children of immigrants (Morocco, Turkey). One school was situated in a typical socially neglected neighbourhood of Antwerp (poor housing, high percentage of ethnic minorities).

The other school was involved in an experiment for alternate learning (part time schooling/part time working). These pupils, aged 16 and older, can also be considered as underprivileged youth. They are usually not interested in school, but are forced to go because of the legislation of compulsory education.

2.2 *First inquiry*

By means of a written questionnaire at the start of the programme, the youngsters were asked to indicate their views on sports and sports participation in general. The purpose of this inquiry was not to compare these youngsters with other youths, but to get a general insight into their views on sports and sports participation.

2.3 *Participant observation, interviews and second inquiry*

During the study there were 16 sessions (5 hours each) in which pupils were offered a variety of different sports. Sports teachers and coaches were in charge of the technical sports guidance. Although the other teachers were invited to take part in the activities, not all of them did. The activities took place during, as well as after, school hours (Wednesday afternoon).

Youngsters were also informed about the existing possibilities to practise sports on a regular basis (addresses of local sports clubs, regular school sports programmes, etc.). The programme was evaluated.through participant observation, interviews with sports instructors and teachers and a second inquiry after the initial sessions.

3   Results

3.1   *Views on sports and sports participation*

The results showed that almost all youngsters have a positive attitude towards sports in general and that they like to practise sports. The male immigrant children, especially, seemed to be very fond of sport.

The pupils mentioned a variety of sports disciplines in which they take part. As Dequeecker (1988) has already indicated, Belgian pupils participated in a larger variety of sports disciplines compared to their Moroccan and Turkish class mates. It seems that the latter have fewer possibilities to get in contact with different sports. Or do immigrant children have fewer differences in interest than Belgian pupils? After all, immigrant boys almost unanimously indicated martial arts and soccer as their favourite sports.

The sports that were practised most were soccer, swimming and martial arts (judo, karate, boxing, wrestling). When they were asked what sports they would also like to practise, a majority again referred to the martial arts. Diving and power training also seemed to be attractive to them. The most common reasons why they did not take part in these activities were because of 'a lack of time', 'no possibilities in the neighbourhood' and 'high financial costs'.

According to a majority of the boys they became interested in sports through their friends, while girls said they usually took activities up through school. In a similar way, boys indicated they practised sports on the street or in a sports club with friends, while girls practised mostly at school.

Because of the age differences in our population, we looked for possible characteristics within the age groups. For example, the majority of pupils who said they did not like sports and also almost all youngsters who claimed not to participate in sports activities, were situated in the older age group (over 16 years). Can we therefore conclude that the older pupils are less interested in sports?

It is also interesting to note that the school seems to play a minor role in the sports participation of pupils of the older age group compared to the younger group; especially concerning its importance in the introduction of new sports and organization of activities. This finding seems logical taking into account the fact that youngsters of this group usually show little interest in any school activity and sometimes even have a so-called 'anti-school' mentality.

3.2 *Response to the programme*

Firstly, it is worthwhile to mention that, apart from some minor porblems, the co-operation between the different partners that were involved during the preparation, as well as during the organization of the programme, can be considered as a success.

Although the enthusiasm among the pupils was high, it soon became clear that some sports were more appreciated than others. The well-known and often practised sports disciplines, especially, were very popular; such as soccer for boys and girls. Pupils showed, also, a great interest in more spectacular sports such as diving and power training. Sports activities that required certain technical skills (and therefore some patience) were not very popular (eg. mini-tennis). The same can be said for sports disciplines with less-known rules (eg. badminton and baseball) and sports that require a certain amount of perseverance (eg. long distnce running). However, the latter only applies to the older pupils.

By using recreational sporting equipment several sports became more interesting (eg. hockey). In general, pupils usually responded better when a form of competition was organized. However, for some sports activities they were also interested in the development and improvement of their skills (diving and several track and field events).

Regarding the behaviour of the pupils during the activities, remarkable age related differences were observed. The youngest among them clearly responded very enthusiastically, boys as well as girls. Sometimes it was even necessary to gently calm them down. It was obvious that these pupils were enormously attracted by sports activities. As was suggested by one of their teachers, through sports the youngsters are able to attain some personal success, which is unlikely to happen during normal school activities.

Although the older pupils seemed to be more relaxed, they were also very enthusiastic about the activities, since almost all of them were present at all sessions. Furthermore it is interesting to note that there was a lack of a 'competition mentality' during team sports activities. It often occurred that the losing team was unwilling to 'fight' back. According to several of the accompanying teachers this attitude is not unusual, since most of these youngsters 'are used to losing every time'.

3.3 *Response to guidance*

Although almost all youngsters responded well to the advice of the sports instructors, it is necessary to indicate that there was a distinct difference between the two age groups among the youngsters. While the younger ones required more appreciation and attention for their achievements, the older pupils needed more support and stimulation from the sport instructors. This kind of approach for the latter group was also more relaxed and focused on encouragement rather than on an improvement of technical sports skills.

3.4 *Evaluation by the youngsters*

While the above described responses were based on participant observations and interviews with sports instructors and accompanying teachers, a second questionnaire for pupils was used after the programme.

The pupils were asked to indicate what they thought of each activity and whether or not it was the first time they had participated in it. In general, these findings correspond with the previous results from the participant observations.

The initiation in power training was found to be the most popular activity, immediately followed by the diving session (Figure 1). Although there was also a positive response for the other sports disciplines that were organized, there were distinct differences among various groups. For example, baseball and soccer were particularly popular among young immigrant pupils, while the younger girls, in general, were more fond of badminton, athletics and mini tennis.

More than half of the pupils (57.6%) indicated that they wished more sports were included in the programme (such as horseback riding, martial arts and ice skating/ice hockey), which clearly indicates the usefulness of this kind of school sport initiation.

Furthermore, most youngsters (77.8%) stated that they were interested in participating in several of the sports in this programme on a more regular basis.

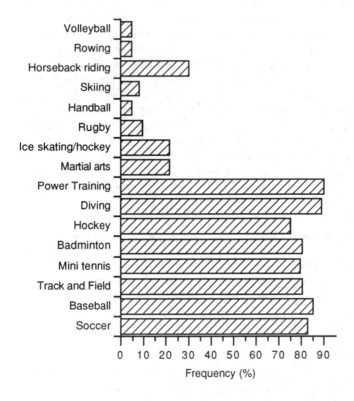

Figure 1.   *Popularity of different sports*

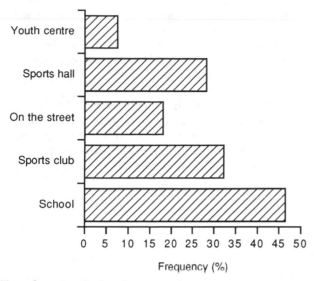

Figure 2.   *Localization of sports practice*

Several kinds of sport participation were indicated (sports clubs, with friends in a sports centre or swimming pool) (Figure 2). It is interesting to note that girls, especially, considered the school as a perfect way to practise sports regularly.

A vast majority of pupils (73.7%) hoped to see more similar sports programmes organized in the near future, because they expect it would improve their health. There were also several youngsters who said they considered this kind of programme as a better alternative than most of the other regular school subjects.

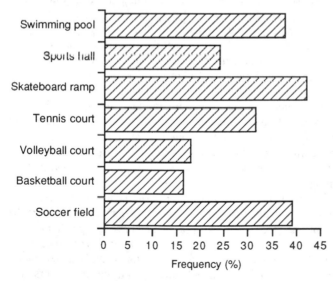

Figure 3.   *Sports facilities*

According to previous interviews with teachers and youth welfare workers one of the major problems in the organization of sports activities for underprivileged youth is the lack of available local sports facilities. Therefore, when the pupils were asked what kind of other sports facilities they would like to have in their neighbourhood, a number of possibilities were suggested (skateboard ramp, soccer field, swimming pool, tennis courts, etc. See Figure 3).

Finally, the youngsters were asked if their attitude towards sports and sport participation in general had changed after this programme. According to one third of the pupils (35.4%) it did, especially because of the fact it motivated them to practise more sports and it had brought them into contact with new sports disciplines. However, a large proportion of the youngsters (43.5%) said their (mostly positive) idea had not changed, since they were familiar with most of the sports that were organized.

4   Discussion

The results from the first inquiry indicated differences in the level of sports participation within the age groups. The younger pupils (- 16 years), especially, were more attracted to the activities than the pupils from the alternate education system (part time schooling/working). These differences also became clear during the study; where the younger pupils required attention and appreciation, the older ones needed to be motivated and supported by teachers and sports instructors in a more active way.

Furthermore, some sports were clearly more popular than others. Apart from the well-known disciplines (especially soccer), the more sensational sports (eg. diving and power training) were also practised with great enthusiasm. Sports with less-known rules (eg. badminton) or that require some basic technical sports skills (eg. mini tennis) were less appreciated. Still, it would be incorrect to say that there were sports in the programme which pupils did not like at all. The younger pupils, especially, were very much attracted by all sports activities. Apart from their enthusiastic participation, a majority of them indicated that they would like to practise these sports on a regular basis and explicitly asked for similar sport programmes in the future.

According to the pupils, school can play an important role in the organization of these programmes. As reported earlier, it is often the only way for young immigrant girls to come into contact with sports. Also the limited variation in the number of practised sports by young immigrant children, compared to their Belgian school-mates, can be considered as an argument to emphasize the importance of a varied school sports programme.

Furthermore, school sports activities can help to diminish the aversion older pupils often have for school. Results showed that sport can be a way to improve the relationship between pupils and their teachers, because they have an opportunity to get to know each other in a more informal way. One of the principles Quensel (1982) formulated in working with underprivileged youngsters is that teachers or youth leaders should try to build up a 'normal' relationship with the youngsters, without behaving as a superior, all-knowing example. Through practising sports activities together it is possible to build up such a relationship, because it will often reveal that teachers also have their weaknesses (for example, they lose a game or have poor sports skills). They might even learn something from their pupils. Teachers as well as pupils indicated this phenomenon.

The study showed that it is possible to get the attention of the pupils for the technical aspects of some sports disciplines, such as diving. After this sports programme aspects related to sport were introduced during the normal theoretical courses (physics, biology) at the request of the pupils.

And finally, there was also a clear demand for accessible sports facilities in their neighbourhood, where the youngsters have an opportunity to practise sports after school hours. Therefore we can conclude that the stimulation of sports participation of underpriviliged youth is a responsibility of several institutions and organizations (community sports services, schools, youth welfare work, etc.). Furthermore, we should note that it is almost impossible that a programme like this, which is limited in time, should have a distinct influence on the behaviour and attitude of these pupils. And yet our results already indicate that school sport programmes for underprivileged youth can be meaningful in a number of ways. The fact that a school sports programme has the potential to reach a large number of youngsters makes it an important phase in a sports policy for this target group. Others (such as sports services and clubs) can try to co operate with schools and determine their specific role in facilitating sports participation for underprivileged youth.

5 References

Adolph-Volpert, H. et al. (1984) Sport ohne Grenzen - oder wie die Integration ausländischer Mitbürger zur Realität werden kann. **Olympische Jugend**, 2, 10-13.

Bergmann, B. (1986) Der Stellenwert des Sports im Freizeitverhalten türkischer Jugendlicher. **Sportunterricht**, 35, 138-145.

Böck, F. (1986) Sport Ohne Grenzen: über die Möglichkeiten des Sports bei der sozialen Integration ausländischer Migrantenkinder. **Sportunterricht**, 35, 146-149.

Dequeecker, G. (1988) Sport en vrije tijd van veertienjarigen: vergelijkende studie bij jongeren uit een begunstigd en achtergesteld milieu. **Sport**, 3, 17-20.

Harms, H. (1984) Die soziale Zeitbombe ist noch längst nicht entschärft: Zur möglichen Funktion des Sports bei der Integration der ausländischen Arbeitnehmer und ihrer Familien. **Olympische Jugend**, 12, 6-16.

Meiburg, H. (1985) Twee sportprofecten met Rotterdamse randgroepjongeren. **Landelijk Contact**, 5, 16-17.

Middleton, C. (1982) Uphill Work: the story of the professor who stops crime with cricket. Sport and Leisure, 23, 14-15.

Middleton, C. (1984) Settled out of court: Chris Middleton visits a scheme aimed at channeling young offenders into sports. **Sport and Leisure**, 25, 54-55.

Nickolai, W. (1982) Sport und Sozialpädagogik mit Randgruppen, in **Sport in der sozialpadagogischen Arbeit mit Randgruppen** (eds W. Nickolai et al.), Lambertus-Verlag, Freiburg im Breisgau, pp. 41-47.

Quensel, S. (1982) Eine alternative Pädagogik für sozial behinderte Jugendliche - Prinzipien und Hindernisse, in **Sport in der sozialpädagogischen Arbeit mit Randgruppen** (eds W. Nickolai et al.), Lambertus-Verlag, Freiburg im Breisgau, pp. 13-39.

Ruottinen, E. (1982) Olympic experience teaches how to become best: programme led by champions for disadvantaged minority youth instills positive attitudes. **WLRA Journal,** 24, 20-23.

Theeboom, M., De Knop, P. Bollaert, L. (1989) Sportstimulering voor kansarme jongeren te Antwerpen. **Sport,** 3, 26-33.

Theeboom, M., DeKnop, P., Bollaert, L. Kansarme jongeren en sport: mogelijkheden voor maatschappelijke integratie, **Handboek voor de lichamelijke opvoeding** (in print)

Theeboom, M., DeKnop, P., Gittenaer, M. (1990a) Schoolsport-initiatieven voor kansarme jeugd: een experiment te Antwerpen. **Sport,** 32, 10-15.

Theeboom, M., DeKnop, P., Wylleman, P. (1990b) **Underprivileged youth: a forgotten target group within a sports policy?** Brussels, paper presented at International Congress 'Youth, Leisure and Physical Activity (May 20-25).

Van Ancum, R., Meiburg, H. (1987) Doelgroepenbeleid: zoekt en gij zult vinden? - Randgroepjongeren en sport. **Recreatie,** 25, 8-11.

Van der Gugten, M. (1988) De sport als aangrijpingspunt voor criminaliteitspreventie. **Justitiële Verkenningen,** 14, 86-112.

Van Dijk, J.J.M. (1987) **De rol van sportbeoefening bij de preventie van criminaliteit.** Paper werkconferentie: Sport, agressie en vandalisme: bestrijdend? bevorderend? Landelijke Contactraad, Noordwijk aan Zee.

EXCELLENCE - THE FUTURE OF SPORTS FOR ATHLETES WITH DISABILITIES

R. D. STEADWARD
Rick Hansen Centre, Edmonton, Canada

1   Introduction

The use of the word 'sport' by organizers, participants and spectators in the field of physical activity is as varied as the activities it brings to mind. It is not surprising that the term is so confusing when it is used to describe, on the one hand, what Wayne Gretzky does on the ice and on the other hand, a group of young children playing a game of street hockey.

Sport, according to Smith (1974), is a generic term with such scope that in order to render it manageable it must be identified or classified according to some unique elements. One useful method of classifying sport is to do so on the basis of participant objectives and expectations. Smith (1974) identifies three levels of excellence.

At one end of this sport classification spectrum, recreational sport can be described as having, as its primary objective, the enjoyment of the participant. For the most part, those who engage in recreational sport will do so on their own terms rather than on the terms of organizers or leaders. Rules, team size, equipment and playing area may be modified in recreational sports and in general, officiating, where applicable, is either on an honour system or by peers rather than trained officials.

Those who participate in competitive sport have as their primary objective a personal desire to compete. In doing so, they may be required to meet minimal performance standards and to accept required limitations and imposed conditions. Competitve sport experiences may range from high school basketball team participation to national level competition in track and field and may include the wide variety of activities, both individual and team, and competitive levels that fall within this range.

Participants at the sport excellence level generally engage in sport to fulfill an intense personal desire to excel and to reach their personal limits. In doing so, they achieve high standards of performance accompanied by appropriate personal, physical, intellectual and emotional qualities. At this level of participation, there must be a willingness to accept the required external conditions imposed by coaches, officials and others.

Others who participate in sport with a desire to excel can succeed at one or two different levels of excellence (Smith, 1974). When performance approaches the current limits of the individual, this individual is said to have achieved a personal level of excellence. A young child first learning to walk exemplifies personal excellence as does the high jumper who has just surpassed his or her own personal best performance. When performance, on the other hand, is compared to external standards and approaches the highest of these standards, the athlete is said to have achieved objective or external excellence. Athletes who participate at any sport level may achieve personal excellence but it is the elite athlete alone who must excel at the objective level as well as the personal level. The Olympic athlete must be the best both internally and externally.

In an effort to provide the elite athlete with a forum for excellence, the Olympic Movement has declared four basic aims including the promotion of the development of those qualities which are the basis of sport; the education of young people through sport in a spirit of better understanding between each other and of friendship thereby helping to build a better and more peaceful world; the teaching of Olympic principles throughout the world thereby creating international goodwill; and finally the bringing together of athletes of the world in the great four-yearly sport festival, the Olympic Games (International Olympic Committee, 1989).

Since the mid 1940's, athletes with disabilities have been engaging in one or more levels of 'sport'. It is the purpose of this paper to address several questions related to this participation. Firstly, do sport classification models such as the one presented by Smith (1974) accommodate athletes with disabilities? That is, can these athletes be categorized into the same or similar levels of participation based on the same objectives and expectations? Secondly, is sport excellence for athletes with disabilities synonymous with sport excellence for those without disabilities? And finally, does the athlete with a disability have the same opportunities for excellence in competition and the same recognition as his or her able-bodied peers?

2   The Paralympic Movement

Prior to World War II there was little or no evidence of organized efforts to develop or promote sport for individuals with disabling conditions. Following the Second World War, however, medical authorities were prompted to re-evaluate traditional methods of rehabilitation which were not satisfactorily responding to the medical and psychological needs of the large number of soldiers disabled in combat.

Recognizing that a problem existed, the British Government in 1944 opened the Spinal Injuries Centre at Stoke Mandeville Hospital in Aylesbury, England. Under the direction of Dr Ludwig Guttman, sport was introduced to the patients as a form of recreation and it was these efforts that moulded perhaps the most significant event in the history of sport for those with paraplegia.

Early forms of sport practised at the Stoke Mandeville Centre included punch ball exercises, rope climbing and wheelchair polo. With the success experienced by Dr Guttman and his staff, the incorporation of sport into the medical rehabilitation of the war-injured soon spread from Great Britain to other countries.

Since its inception as a rehabilitative tool, sport for those with disabilities has experienced rapid growth in a number of areas. Whereas in the early years, 'sport' included such activities as punch ball and rope-climbing, today's participants have the opportunity to engage in basketball, track and field, swimming, skiing, weight-lifting, archery and racquetball to name only a few sports. For the most part, present-day individuals with disabilities are unlimited in their choices for sport participation. The growth in the number of sports or events available to the disabled population has been tremendous.

The growth of sport for those with disabilities has also been made evident through the variety of disability groups currently participating in one or more sports. Although those with paraplegia, amputation and other orthopedic impairments were the first to benefit from organized sport, great strides have been made in recent years to promote sport for other disability populations. Today, sport opportunities for those with visual and auditory impairments, mental handicaps, cerebral palsy as well as amputations, spinal cord injuries and other orthopedic disabilities are commonplace.

Undoubtedly, the most impressive growth within the Paralympic Movement has been in terms of sport excellence. Whereas in 1944 sport for those with disabilities was considered solely for its therapeutic and recreational values, today, individuals with disabilities may choose to participate in a variety of sports and at a level of participation that suits their personal objectives and expectations. While recreational sport opportunities remain available for those who are interested in engaging in sport for their own personal enjoyment, competitive sport experiences are similarly available for those seeking this level of participation. This may include local, regional, provincial and national competition.

The Paralympic Movement has not, however, limited its involvement in sport to recreational and competitive levels as defined by Smith (1974). Highly motivated athletes whose objectives are to excel and reach their personal limits may participate in a wide range of international competitions. At this level, sport is practised for reasons beyond those of rehabilitation, prescribed exercise and recreation. Sports participation, for this group, stands on its own as an end in itself (Hansen, 1988). Today, sport excellence has no different meaning for the athlete with a disability than it does for the athlete without a disability.

3   Paralympic versus Olympic Competition

Just as the International Olympic Committee has as one of its aims the bringing together of athletes of the world in the great four-yearly sport festival, the Olympic Games (International Olympic Committee, 1989), the International Paralympic Committee similarly has such an objective. While both the Olympic and Paralympic Movements are concerned with providing a forum for excellence within their respective disciplines, there are some major differences between Olympic and Paralympic competition.

Because such a small percentage of the total athletic population is disabled, the number of athletes competing in the Paralympic Games is considerably smaller than the number competing in the Olympics. In the same light, many countries have yet to experience the advancements made by some in the area of sport excellence for disabled populations. Consequently, fewer countries are represented at Paralympic as compared to Olympic competition.

Further adding to the problem of relatively low athlete numbers in Paralympic competition is the need for athlete classification based on the nature and degree of disability and/or the degree of function of each athlete. Present-day Paralympic competition may include as many as twenty-seven separate classification categories for the variety of disability groups involved: seven for spinal-cord injured athletes, nine for athletes with amputations, eight for cerebral palsied athletes and three for visually impaired athletes. The result of such a classification system is a need for an unusually high number of medals awarded. In fact, summer Paralympic competition currently results in roughly three times as many medal presentations as summer Olympic competition, while the athlete participation numbers are 15,000 and 3,000 respectively.

With these statistics in mind, one cannot help but question the depth of competition in the Paralympic Games. While the aim of the Paralympics is to provide competition of the highest level for athletes with disabilities, the presence of current classification systems diminishes the amount of competition within each classification level. In fact, some Paralympic events may be contested by only a handful of participants. Although these participants certainly meet the sport excellence criteria, they are not being afforded the same degree of competition as their able-bodied counterparts.

Perhaps the most important difference between Olympic and Paralympic competition lies in the amount of public recognition and acceptance given to each. While the Olympic Games recognize the best in athletic ability through millions of dollars in ticket sales and numerous hours of media coverage, the Paralympics are still struggling to attract a mere portion of the public's recognition. The fact is , that for many, the Paralympics still elicit a feeling of pity within the spectator. Although the athletes are admired for their determination and accomplishments, Paralympic competitors, particularly those with high degrees of disability, will never attract the number of spectators enjoyed by Olympic competitiors. Although the basic goals and philosophies of the Paralympic and Olympic Movements are the same, the differences between the four-yearly competitions in terms of the number of athletes and countries represented, the depth of competition and the degree of public recognition afforded the athletes outweigh the similarities. Therefore, Paralympic and Olympic competition cannot be equated.

4   Integration

The issue of integration within the area of sport for those with disabilities has been a long standing one. Prior to 1976, all competition was segregated. Those with spinal-cord injuries competed separately from those with amputations and visual impairments. In 1976, for the first time in the history of the Paralympics, Toronto, Canada, hosted the first tri-disability Games but while spinal-cord injured, amputee and blind athletes competed within the same festival, they were restricted to competition within their own disability groups. Since the Toronto Games, the concept of integration within the Paralympics has met with mixed reviews. With the exception of 1984 Paralympics, however, which saw the spinal-cord injured competing in a separate venue, the integration of disability groups within Paralympic competition has grown to include four separate groups. The 1988 Seoul Summer Games, for example, included spinal-cord injured, amputee, blind and cerebral palsied athletes.

The advantages of integrating athletes with different disabilities into Paralympic competition are obvious. For any given event, the need for numerous classifications within that event would be diminished and the participant numbers would be increased. For example, while in the past the 100 metre sprint might have been contested up to twenty-seven times to accommodate all classes within each disability group, current functional classification systems allow athletes from many of these classes to compete together thus increasing the number of athletes competing for one gold medal and decreasing the total number of medals awarded.

The final outcome, of course, would be greater depth of competition for the athlete with a disability and greater athlete credibility in the eyes of both the spectator and the financial supporter. There is no question that any spectator would prefer to watch a race in which a dozen or more, rather than a handful of athletes were in contention for one gold medal. Similarly, both corporate sponsors and government officials are more likely to lend financial support to the athlete who succeeds in outperforming a large rather than a small contingent of athletes in a particular event.

Just as the Paralympics have been successfully integrating athletes with different disabilities within recent competitions, the International Olympic Committee has similarly responded to the growth and needs of these athletes by sanctioning their inclusion into both Summer and Winter Olympic Games. In 1984, the Winter Games in Sarajevo staged a demonstration downhill skiing event for amputee skiers while the Summer Games in Los Angeles hosted two demonstration wheelchair races. In February of 1988, two exhibition events for disabled skiers were held during the Olympic Winter Games in Calgary and most recently, two demonstration wheelchair races were again chosen for inclusion in the 1988 Summer Olympic Games in Seoul. While these competitions were not medal events, they did demonstrate the International Olympic Committee's growing support of the integration of athletes with disabilities into Olympic competition. As well, they demonstrated to the public, the skills and athletic abilities of these athletes.

Without question, athletes with disabilities are pleased with the progress that has been made to date. The demonstration events included in the past four Olympic games have certainly stimulated both public and athlete interest. The goal, however, of the athlete with a disability extends beyond participation in demonstration events alone. For this athlete, as well as any elite athlete, the ultimate experience in competitive sport is the quest for Olympic triumph (Hansen, 1988) and access to this opportunity, via full medal events, should be a natural progression of the advancements that have been made to date.

In 1989, the International Paralympic Committee was formed and while it is no stranger to the problems inherent in the integration process, it is the driving force behind the ultimate integration of athletes with disabilities into the Olympic Games. In justifying the inclusion of sports for athletes with disabilities into Olympic competition, it can be argued that these athletes truly do fit the 'excellence' mould used to describe the Olympic athlete who does not possess a disability. Both groups of athletes are highly motivated with an objective to excel both personally and in comparison to external records or standards. The elite athlete, whether disabled or not, is interested in competition at the highest level possible.

Some may argue that the International Paralympic Committee should be responsible for providing its own athletes with the appropriate level of competition. While this, in principle, may be true, the existence of classification systems designed to provide fair and equitable competition for athletes with disabilities, makes it all but impossible. Although today's trend in Paralympic competition is toward fewer classes as well as classes that combine different disabilities, the fact is that there will always be a need for some amount of classification within the Paralympics. The low number of athletes combined with the high variability in the types and degrees of disability makes a totally open classification system an impossibility. While the Paralympics are essential to the continuing development of sport for athletes with disabilities, however, those who are worthy should have the opportunity to experience Olympic triumph.

It is certainly recognized that inclusion in Olympic competition cannot encompass all disability groups and all sports/events pracised by those with disabilities. Worthiness of this inclusion must be based on a number of criteria.

First and foremost, any event practised by those with disabilities seeking inclusion in Olympic competition must exemplify athletic skill. That is, the event must be one that displays superior athletic abilities on the part of the athletes involved and provides a high degree of audience or spectator appeal. It must be a high visibility, technically advanced event that does not generate a great deal of undue sympathy for the participating athletes.

As well, the event in question must not distinguish between different classes within a given group. For example, a 1500-metre wheelchair race must allow competitors from a number of disability groups (i.e., amputee, cerebral palsy, spinal-cord injured) to qualify. Only the best, regardless of disability, would be eligible then for Olympic competition. Those events that lend themselves to multi-disability competition would therefore be the most desirable in terms of inclusion in the Olympic Games.

For the most part, athletes with disablities would be seeking the inclusion of specific events, as opposed to sports or disciplines, in the Olympic Games. As outlined in the Olympic Charter (International Olympic Committee, 1989) 'an event is a competition included in a sport or in one of its disciplines...Only events practised in at least twenty-five countries and three continents both by men and/or women may be included in the programme of the Games of the Olympiad and Olympic Winter Games'. Undoubtedly, this criterion would be all but impossible for a Paralympic event to achieve due to the relatively low number of countries practising Paralympic as opposed to Olympic events. It is hoped, however, that this would be an area in which the International Olympic Committee would grant the International Paralympic Committee some leeway by still enforcing a significant depth of participation but reducing the number of countries necessary to define this significance.

5   Summary and Conclusions

Over the years, the goal of Olympism has been clear and unchanging. According to Raymond Gafner (1989: 4), IOC member and administrator, the Olympic movement can be compared to a ship steering through a sea full of reefs. The start of the Voyage generally begins with a clearly set destination but during the journey, various hazards necessitate circumnavigation and the re-establishment of the initial course.

While the goals of the movement have been clear from the outset, obstacles have frequently presented themselves thus resulting in quick manoeuvering on the part of those in command yet, at the same time, adhering to the established goals. For example, issues such as the inclusion of the female athlete and Third World nations in Olympic competition, the inclusion of new sports in the Olympic programme, the boycott of the 1980 Moscow Games, the budgeting problems of the 1976 Montreal Games and most recently, the use of performance enhancing drugs in Olympic competition all represent hazards or obstacles that were dealt with and/or overcome without jeopardizing the clearly defined goals of the Olympic movement. As Robert Pariente (1989: 21) explains, 'in order to survive, we must be able to adapt'. In the past, the Olympic Movement has indeed adapted and in the process, has done more than survive - it has grown.

The issue of integrating athletes with disabilities into Olympic competition is yet another reef in the Olympic sea. While it may force Olympic leaders to manoeuver around or change the path of the Olympic Movement, it does not threaten, in any way, the intended destination or goal. 'The characteristic of a movement', according to Pariente (1989: 21), 'is that it need not come to a halt'. The inclusion of athletes with disabilities into Olympic competition would not only provide these athletes with a forum for sport excellence but it would also contribute to the growth of the Olympic Movement. While the course may, at first glance, appear difficult, the results would undoubtedly be rewarding for both parties.

6   References

Gafner, Raymond (1989, March) Prologue. **Olympic Message**, p.4.

Hansen, R. (1988) Response to a challenge: A draft proposal for the inclusion of athletes with disabilities at the Olympic Games. Unpublished manuscript.

International Olympic Committee (1989) **Olympic Charter '89.**

Pariente, Robert (1989, March) On the threshold of the XXIst Century. **Olympic Message**, p. 21.

Pound, D. (1987, April) Interview with Rick Hansen and Dick Pound: Inclusion of Disabled Athletes in the Olympics. Unpublished interview.

Smith, M. (1974) A preliminary case for classifying sports environments by participant objectives. **Journal of the Canadian Association of Health, Physical, Education and Recreation,** September-October, 27-30.

DEVELOPMENT OF AN INNOVATIVE THROWING PATTERN FOR DISABLED ATHLETES - THE SPIN TURN IN A WHEELCHAIR

ALAN BROWN
University of Newcastle upon Tyne, England

Abstract
Improvements in performance by cerebral palsied athletes have resulted from technological improvements in wheelchair design, increased physical fitness and improvements in the development of individual technique. Research in these areas has been well documented by Brown (1975), DePauw (1984), Sherrill (1986) and DePauw (1990). The scientific principles underpinning the study of human movement are exactly the same when applied to people with disabilities although adaptation may be necessary in applying them to special populations. The application and adaptation of this principle to the coaching of disabled athletes has led to the development of many highly individualized throwing techniques. In almost all cases these throwing techinques have taken place from a fixed and stationary wheelchair. The purpose of this experiment was to investigate the possibility of developing an 180° spin turn in a wheelchair, leading to increased momentum in the club and discus events. The increased momentum across the throwing circle led to a 12.5% improvement in performance and two world records in the 1988 Seoul Olympic Games.
Keywords: Wheelchair Athletics, Club Throw, Cerebral Palsy, Spin Turn.

1   Introduction

Innovations in athletics techniques have usually developed from either improvements in the technology of equipment manufacture, or from a radical change in the movement pattern of the performance. The fibreglass pole and the aerodynamic javelin are good examples of technology affecting performance in field events where changing technique resulted in startling improvements in world records. On the other hand, world records have been greatly influenced by the development of a new technique that conforms more efficiently to the mechanical principles governing the event, as in the Fosbury Flop.

The same principles apply in the coaching of disabled athletes and coaches are constantly seeking the help of technology or the development of different techniques appropriate to the particular abilities of each individual athlete. Improvements in times for wheelchair track events have been markedly affected by improvements in wheelchair design, better training programmes and sound analysis of wheelchair cranking styles. The individually tailored sports wheelchair is now commonplace at National and International events, with lightweight frame, cambered wheels, variable axle plate, and adjustable handrims. By altering any of these variables the disabled athlete now has a multifunctional vehicle adaptable for several sporting purposes.

Provided that the athlete has an appropriately adapted wheelchair the situation in field events is rather different. Improvements in performance tend to result from modified techniques which have been adapted to suit the strengths of the athlete. Initially the coach can not begin teaching an athletics throwing event holding a preconceived idea of the best technique for that event. The range of physique, skill, and level of disability within the same class may be so widely ranging that there may have to be as many varying techniques as there are athletes in the class. Coaching is strictly on an individual basis and the coach must modify his or her ideas according to the, often, weird movements presented. Techniques which are accepted as being the most efficient methods of performance in the conventional events may be of no value to the athlete who can not reproduce the desired pattern of movement. Even in this relatively enlightened age in the United Kingdom we have coaches of quality in a particular activity who do not understand the specific problems of a disabled athlete, and on the other hand we have many enthusiastic and dedicated teachers and physiotherapists who fully comprehend the nature of disability, but do not have the necessary technical knowledge of the sport.

In the development of throwing techniques for disabled athletes we need to understand the mechanical principles governing performance and balance this against the known limitations imposed by disablity on the use of muscular power.

In any throwing event, the greater the distance, and, therefore, the time, over which momentum is developed, the greater the momentum possible. The longer that force is applied to the implement, then the greater the force imparted. In addition to the speed of release of the implement, the distance thrown will be controlled by the angle of release, and this can be a major problem for a wheelchair athlete.

The application and adaptation of these principles to the coaching of disabled throwers has led to the development of many highly individualized throwing techniques over the years. There are three basic movement patterns used for throwing; overarm, sidearm, and underarm. Cerebral palsied children often can not perform the whiplike action of the overarm pattern as they throw with the arm only, can not produce the body action, and allow the elbow to drop close to the side of the body, thus causing a pushing action to occur.

The underarm throw is mechanically inefficient from a wheelchair, in achieving speed or distance, since both the backswing and body rotation are more restricted.

The sidearm throwing pattern allows for the use of body rotation and, therefore, a longer backswing. Since a longer backswing is possible and more muscles contribute to the throw, more force is generated by a wheelchair athlete than from the other types of throwing action.

For more severely disabled athletes with restricted mobility it has been found that a backward overhead throw from a rear-facing position greatly enhances the range of movement and throwing performance. The principles of developing individualized throwing techniques for severely disabled children have been reviewed by Brown (1987).

These same principles apply to the elite Olympic athlete. Efforts to increase throwing power from a wheelchair have been based on the need to increase the range of movement over which the athlete can exert muscular power from a static wheelchair. Once the most effective throwing pattern for the athlete has been determined by practice, then we need to experiment with the position of the wheelchair relative to the direction of the throw. Most Class 4 international athletes throw the club with a sidearm action from a wheelchair placement at 90° to the line of throw. This allows the athlete to lean sideways out of the chair, away from the line of throw, utilize a strong body extension and rotation, and deliver the club in discus fashion. The momentum generated from a powerful athlete produces strong forward motion from the throw and it is vital that provision is made to either hold down or tie down the chair. A common variation on this technique is to rotate the wheelchair backwards into a starting position some 135° to the rear of the direction of throw and release the implement above the forward non-throwing shoulder at a high angle. Each of these techniques are performed from a fixed and static wheelchair.

Thirty years ago, Broer (1960), indicated that for able-bodied athletes approximately 50% of the velocity of a throw resulted from the body rotation and step, and the total distance achieved was reduced by this amount when the legs were immobilized, though in a standing position. This underlines the problems for disabled athletes who can not add any forward movements to add force to the throw. The transference of weight by a run, shift or turn all give the body added momentum which is transferred to the throwing arm and thus to the object to be thrown.

In 1988, prior to the Seoul Olympics, two Class 4 International athletes experimented at the Percy Hedley Centre, Newcastle upon Tyne, to see if it was possible to add wheelchair momentum to the club throw. Both athletes were mature males, spastic paraplegic, highly skilled in upper body control, hugely muscular and weighing more than 105 kilos. Aged 35 years and 23 years, the athletes had previously broken world records in several field events. Both athletes used sports wheelchairs with cambered wheels for stability, and without brakes or armrests.

2   Objectives

(a)   To develop optimum wheelchair momentum across the throwing circle.
(b)   To control and maintain body balance throughout the movement.
(c)   To establish an efficient body and chair position at the end of the turn, from which maximum power would be developed.

3   Problems

(a)   To develop optimum speed and retain control of the wheelchair.
(b)   To develop a firm grip on the club and yet use both hands for the drive.
(c)   To discover the maximum range of wheelchair rotation and finish in a good throwing position.
(d)   To develop momentum in a straight line across the circle despite the rotating turn.
(e)   To keep the wheelchair within the constraints of the circle and avoid overbalancing.

Following discussion and a great deal of practice it was decided to use a 180° turn as this kept the application of force on the wheels within a straight line across the circle.

4   Technique (illustrated by video tape)

(a)   The athlete takes up position at the rear centre of the circle, rear facing.
(b)   The club is held between the first and second fingers, leaving the thumb and first finger of the throwing hand free to manipulate the wheel.
(c)   The athlete leans forward and grips the wheel tyres and handrims as low as he can comfortably reach, leaving the club trailing on the ground at its base (see Phase 1, Figure 1).
(d)   A two-handed drive backwards pulls the wheelchair straight to the centre of the circle. This is a single cranking action.
(e)   The left hand shifts forward to a low position on the wheel and performs a single pull drive to rotate the chair on its axis forwards.
(f)   Simultaneously the right hand is removed from the wheel into a backswing ready for the throwing action from a sidearm position (see Phase 2, Figure 1).

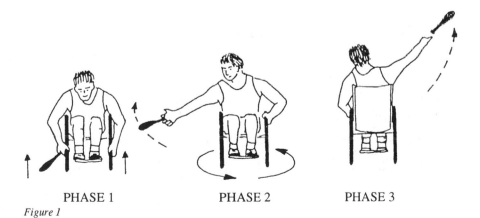

PHASE 1   PHASE 2   PHASE 3

Figure 1

(g)   As the wheelchair spins into a forward-facing position, the club is released with a sidearm whippy action at a release angle of $45°$ (see Phase 3, Figure 1).

(h)   The wheelchair is allowed to continue rotating after the club is released so that the athlete remains within the circle.

This particular movement pattern replicates the run around the circle technique of an able-bodied discus thrower. Improvements in performance were almost immediate with increases of 2-3 metres on previous best performances. Both athletes commented on increased confidence to apply full body force as they felt the movement of the wheelchair helping them into a good throwing position.

Throughout the development period the greatest problems were in learning the sequence of movements and co-ordinating the sequence of force patterns. In addition it was difficult to sequence the left hand controlled spin with the need to draw back the throwing arm in readiness for the throw. The stages of learning are well illustrated on the video. Initially the cognitive aspects are seen as the athlete consciously sequences the movements in slow motion as he works out the pattern. A long period of practice at normal speed, with and without the club, is seen as flaws are smoothed out. Finally the autonomous stage is reached as the athlete prepares to throw in the Olympic Games.

The athletes won gold and silver medals at Seoul and both broke the existing world record. It is estimated that the new technique of a spin turn was worth an increase of approximately 12.5% on their previous best throws.

Attempts to develop the same technique for throwing the discus failed. The need to use thumb and forefinger in holding the discus meant that only the little finger could be used to drive the right hand chair wheel. This was not strong enough to develop sufficient wheelchair speed to compensate for an inefficient final throwing position.

The club event has now been withdrawn from Class 4 events; not the first time that innovation in an athletics throwing event has come to an untimely end.

5   References

Broer, M.R. (1960) **Efficiency of Human Movement.** W.B. Saunders, London.

Brown, A. (1975) Review: Physical fitness and cerebral palsy. **Child: Care, Health and Development**, 1, 143-152.

Brown, A. (1987) **Active Games for Children with Movement Problems.** Paul Chapman Publishing, London.

DePauw, K. (1984) Kinematic analysis of wheelchair cranking of paraplegics. In **Adapted Physical Activities.** (eds. A. Brown et al). Proc. IV I.F.A.P.A. Symposium, London, pp.114-132.

DePauw, K. (1990) Teaching and coaching individuals with disabilities: Research findings and implications. **Physical Education Review**, 13:1:12-16.

Sherrill, C. (1986) **Adapted Physical Education and Recreation.** Third Edition. Wm. C. Brown, Iowa.

MOTIVATION FOR SPORTS ACTIVITY AMONG TOP SITTING VOLLEYBALL PLAYERS

RAJKO VUTE
Pedagoska Akademija, University of Ljubljana, Yugoslavia

Abstract

This research attempts to establish the structure of motivation for sports activity of players of sitting volleyball. The sample comprised 102 players of ages 19-46 that have taken part in the Open European Championship in sitting volleyball in Sarajevo in 1987. All were members of the national teams. With the help of factor analysis 10 factors were isolated as important for wanting to participate in sports activity among the physically disabled players of sitting volleyball.

Keywords: Competitive Sport, Physically Disabled, Motivation.

1   Introduction

Elite competitive sport is probably the most disputable part of the whole sport sphere regarding the physically disabled and their participation. The demonstration of power and abilities is common in sport generally and specifically in the sport of the disabled. When the intrinsic experience of sport is analysed it is noted that the physically disabled also wish to prove themselves; they have an intense desire for achievement; they want to attract attention, etc.

The Open European Championship in sitting volleyball, held in Sarajevo in 1987, offered a good opportunity to get some information from the players who represent the elite level in their chosen sports activity, which in this case is sitting volleyball.

Physical disability is often expressed in terms of limited mobility. From the need and a wish to introduce volleyball to people with disabilities a new game was created - sitting volleyball. It is one of the forms of volleyball. It is a team game with a ball that is played over a net and one of its characteristics is that even though there is no direct contact between the players of the two teams, the game is very dynamic and attractive. Sitting volleyball is a multipurpose game that is suitable for men and women, children and adults. It is important as a recreational activity and as a competitive sports activity.

2   Methodology

The sample of the study comprised physically disabled male subjects, aged 19-46. The majority of the disabilities were a variety of amputations of lower extremities and some cases of poliomyelitis, cerebral palsy and congenital deformations. The number of players taking part in the study was 102, drawn from the national teams of Norway, USA, Finland, Holland, Sweden, West Germany, Switzerland, Austria, Great Britain, Hungary and Yugoslavia. . The data were collected at the Open European Championship in Sarajevo (Yugoslavia) in June 1987 using a modified questionnaire which included questions on motivation for participation, sports activities and physical disability.

With the help of factor analyses 10 factors were isolated as important for participating in sports activity among the physically disabled players of sitting volleyball.

These isolated factors were named with the intention to grasp the meaning of internal motives.

3   Isolated factors

F 1 - *Way to success*

The most significant statements which co-determine the first factor are:

M 28 - to overcome different barriers
M 36 - my friends also take part
M 32 - a chance to distinguish myself
M 23 - I like the coach's way of training

Overcoming different barriers is a general characteristic of sports activities. Each sports activity has its own special barrier. It might be time, distance, number of points (score), etc. In sitting volleyball the barrier is the opposing team. Testing one's strength and abilities is a challenge for the players. Significant elements in team sports are understanding, co-operation and friendship.

We found that ties of friendship in the team are a strong motive for participating in sports activities. Good co-operation with the coach is also needed for success in sport. The coach leads the player and helps him to fulfill his ambitions. For the success of the team it is often necessary to subsume personal ambitions, but at the same time each player gets an opportunity to distinguish himself individually and as a member of the team. In the team, players share the experience of victory and also of defeat.

We can say that the above mentioned elements represent a part of the way to success and they seem to be significant for the physically disabled sportsmen - players of sitting volleyball and their active participation in sport.

F 2 - *Healthy man*

The most significant statements which determine the second factor are:

M 41 - improve physical fitness
M 27 - more needed than for able-bodied
M 04 - help to improve health
M 29 - test my physical abilities

Even though we had a highly selective sample of players we noticed a very strong reason for participation in sports in order to achieve better general all-round fitness and improve health. For the competitors in sitting volleyball we can say that their desire for better physical fitness directly influences their better competition performance. Many times we declare and advertise competitive sports activities as a certain desire for health but for the top competitive sport this is not necessarily always true.

Sport in which people with physical disabilities take part - at least at the elite level - is still not on such a level that the processes of training would lead to over-exhaustion of one's organism; other pressures like the pressure of the audience, pressure of the press, etc. are not yet detrimental. Although competitions are of a moderately good standard we can say that competitive activities are still on the level that could be recognized as health beneficial.

The statement that sports activities are needed more for individuals with physical disabilities than for those who are able-bodied shows that disabled sportsmen are aware of the fact that certain disabilities reduce or take away a particular ability. Knowledge of the fact that it is worthwhile to develop and strengthen only those abilities that exist shows the essence of the problem with which people with physical disabilties are confronted.

An exaggerated interest in a healthy life is common to all statements of this factor. Individuals can participate in many fitness activities where the goal is to motivate each individual to pursue a more active sports life without any element of competition. Healthy man is the name of the isolated factor.

F 3 - *In the footsteps of the successful*

The most significant statements co-determining the third factor are:

M 06 - know successful athletes
M 04 - better health
M 12 - they recognize I am not able
M 19 - enjoy the fight

The finding that the competitors participate in sport because they know successful athletes shows how important the experience of others is for people with physical disabilities, regardless of whether the successful athlete is able-bodied or disabled. Able-bodied sport idols are important to people with physical disabilties in spite of the fact that their disability is a limitation. On the other hand, the performance of these sport idols is unapproachable even for a great majority of the able-bodied.

Is the experience of a physically disabled top competitor, therefore, close to that of able-bodied elite athletes? A comparison of abilities and the assessment of one's capacities is not difficult and it is possible for people with physical disabilities to be successful, to become famous and a model to others. Therefore it is of major importance to develop this field of sport as it may have a great influence on the motives for participation in sports activity among people with physical disabilities. This is reason enough to organize international sport competitions for people with physical disabilities, eg. European, World and Olympic championships. The positive experience of others is connected with the usefulness of sport for the health of individuals and with the fact that one can be successful in sport in spite of a physical disability. To achieve this, assiduity and endeavour is necessary as one may be confronted with less pleasant experiences.

This factor was named 'In the footsteps of the successful' as it shows that a good example always has followers.

F 4 - *Everything for success*

Significant statements which determine this factor are:

M 22 - often achieve success
M 11 - more successful than my friends
M 18 - awards stimulate
M 24 - my name in news media
M 30 - people admire me

Statements determining the fourth factor show that success is an important incentive for participating in sport. It is present everywhere, especially in competitive sport. This is also true for sport in which one can be successful merely by taking part. A particular sport seems to be more attractive if success in it can be achieved more frequently. When one achieves success it is necessary to train even harder as there are many waiting to replace him. To be better than the others is an important idea in competitive sport. Different kinds of diplomas, trophies, medals, awards, and titles - eg. European, World or Olympic champions - also stimulate participation.

We know that different media - newspapers, radio, television pay attention only to winners. His name in the newspaper is something special for the disabled sportsman because we all know that for such attention one must work very hard. When reporters write about sports events or competitions where people with physical disabilties participate then a large number of people are informed about such activities.

In this study a highly selective sample of sportsmen proved that their motives for participating in sports activities which are based on achieved success exist; they are real. Sport in which people with physical disabilities participate shows that sport is just sport; it doesn't matter if the protagonists are disabled or not. It has recognized rules and behaviours which achieve victory and success. These are real and respected in sport in general.

F 5 - *For relaxation*

The most significant statements that determine this factor are:

M 31 - relaxation
M 35 - satisfaction and pleasure
M 34 - contacts with opposite sex
M 30 - people admire me
M 24 - my name in news media

Tense situations, so common in competitive sport, call for relaxation periods. The sample of sitting volleyball players in this study indicated that relaxation is not only important after exciting sports contests but is also necessary for current daily living conditions. The pace of living is extremely high and is increasing according to the development of the society and our environment. Sport offers possibilities for relaxation, it can give satisfaction and enjoyment.

For sport for people with physical disabilties it is often said that the activities are meant to bring health, satisfaction and pleasure. But we find it to be only partly true. The other part of the truth is that competition in this field has already taken deep roots. Nevertheless, success, proving one's quality and contacts with the opposite sex are not the most important things sport can give. For some it is really the activities which they truly enjoy because they feel relaxed at the same time. This is interesting as the sample consists of elite sitting volleyball players. We presume that it is possible to take part in competitons for different reasons not only because of a tendency to achieve success.

F 6 - *To attract attention*

The most significant statements which determine this factor are:

M 01 - have better figure
M 34 - chance for contacts
M 21 - forced by others
M 08 - more success with the opposite sex

When we speak about people with physical disabilities a desire for a good appearance is not insignificant. Having a good looking figure is one of the changes gained through sports activities as we know that sport develops musculature, helps to build a better physique, improves posture, etc. To attract attention, especially of the opposite sex, is one of the strongest motives for participating in sport activities but we don't like to admit it. Sport offers opportunities where we can show what we know and also what we look like. The population on which this research is focused is aware of this fact.

In a team game like sitting volleyball, a group impression is also very important. The team gives a player a chance to be exposed when he wants to make an impression but he can also be covered by the others when he doesn't want to stand out. In individual sports activities the pressure put on each individual is much stronger since all of the attention is focused only on one person. The element of pressure is also present in one's social environment. It can originate with parents or friends, for example, who put pressure on a person with a disability when they suggest or even demand that he starts doing sports in order to introduce himself into society.

The successfulness of integration into society is measured also by an ability of communication and here the opposite sex plays an important role. Being in the company of girls and women is a mark of the success of integration and we should bear this in mind when we speak about sitting volleyball players. We can say that contacts or relations with girls or women mean a great deal to a male with a disability and they are very important for the growth of his self-confidence.

We can sum up these ideas with the statement: sportsmen with physical disabilities can be attractive with the help of sports activities and can catch the attention of others.

F 7 - *Joy in sport*

The most significant statements which determine the seventh factor are:

M 35 - satisfaction, pleasure
M 14 - admire great sportsmen
M 42 - forget problems
M 33 - I like the sport I chose

The inner satisfaction which sportsmen feel during sport performance represents an important stimulus for participating in sports activities. We have achieved a lot if participants like the sport they have chosen and feel satisfaction and pleasure while practising it. For competitors this is a good basis on which we can build. We know that the processes of training and competitions do not bring only moments of pleasure but they bring unpleasant experiences as well. This enables them to understand their problems more thoroughly and they appreciate much more the efforts they put into sports activities. One's own experiences are most valuable but the experiences of others, especially of already well known and famous athletes, also count. It is also possible that through our emotional engagement we can push worries and everyday problems away and this is evident with people with physical disabilities as well.

With competitors the emotional component is even stronger because the situation is full of tension and excitement. Changes are a basic part of competitive sport and they call for the full engagement of both the physical and mental capacities.

F 8 - *Empty space*

The most significant statements which determine this factor are:

M 05 - otherwise bored
M 16 - easiest way to achieve success
M 20 - chance to have company
M 03 - forget my disability

We learned that it is a necessity of life for sitting volleyball players to be active in sport. Without sports activity there would be an empty space in their lives. Sitting volleyball is a game in which they can play on the national team for a relatively long period. Experience gained during the years of playing successfully replaces some losses of physical abilities. In sitting volleyball it is not uncommon to see some excellent players who are 30 years old or more.

The existence of an empty space which comes at the end of active playing for the national team can give one of the possible answers to the question why it is so difficult for many players to say farewell to the national uniform. With the delaying of withdrawals they put obstacles in the way of youngsters trying to make it onto the team. For a fair replacement the new, younger players must, of course, be good enough. However, playing on the team also means company, an opportunity to fill in one's free time with quality and to forget many unpleasant moments of everyday life.

It seems that for people with physical disabilities one of the easiest ways to obtain success is through sport and this is achieved more easily if participants like their sport.

F 9 - *Need for adjustment*

The most significant statements which determine this factor are:

M 17 - put forward my own ideas
M 18 - awards stimulate
M 16 - easiest way to achieve
M 06 - know extremely successful people

Statements which determine the ninth factor have a negative connotation. The competitors call attention to the fact that it is necessary for them to adjust to team mates, coaches etc. A competitor knows how it is if he wants to put forward his own ideas. In the opinions of some respondents they have almost no chance to put forward their ideas in their teams. Players are only supposed to carry out the instructions which are given to them by their coaches. Performing exactly as they are asked, listening to, adjusting themselves completely to the team are demands which don't stimulate and encourage individuals towards better sport achievements.

Is the motive for sports activity then in experiencing sport in general? Knowing and taking into consideration that there are rules and regulations in competitive sport demands that each member submit, to follow instructions and listen to the coach. The success of the team requires giving up the player's own ideas and that is why some of the players interviewed think their ideas are completely neglected. Sport is certainly not a field where it is easy to achieve success and sportsmen prove that awards are not an equal stimulus for everyone. Some even deny the incentive in the form of awards at all. Even though engaging in sport is optional according to one's wishes there are some compulsory actions to which the players must adjust themselves and take them into consideration.

F 10 - *Privileges*

The most significant statements which determine this factor are:

M 02 - benefits
M 26 - more liked
M 10 - make my life easier
M 09 - feel pushed away

It's a fact that from their sports activity sportsmen with disabilities also expect some benefits, especially because the sample for this study consists of top players in a particular sport. Sport gives players an opportunity for joy, entertainment, they have a chance to prove themselves, etc. and they also gain other benefits. These are a chance to travel, getting to know new places and people and there are also some small material rewards such as, for example, sports equipment. In sport for people with physical disabilities the advantage is to participate in big international contests like the Olympic games, World championships etc. For such an opportunity a player has to work very hard but being a member of the national team means to be recognized and well known in the area where they live. However, proving that sport for disabled is already at a high level of quality is a permanent need because the non-disabled society doesn't recognize them as their equals. Besides the small privileges, which are a kind of stimulus for their sports activity, people with physical disabilities want and expect more. They think that their sport efforts should be recognized as real sports achievements and count as such. Their achievements, too, are the result of their abilities, efforts and knowledge.

4   Conclusions

In this paper the population of elite players in sitting volleyball have been the focus of attention.

(a)   They master the game at the elite level but if we take into consideration other things like their methods of training, their approach towards obligations, material benefits, etc. we can't say that all this is limited only to the elite level. We found that for the interviewed players success is a very important aspiration. This is a leading motive for participating in sport.

(b)   Victory and the title of champion are becoming more and more important in the competition of people with physical disabilities.

(c)   A desire for psycho-physical balance is also an important incentive for participating in sports activity. Many of these are seen as 'healthy' activities where the level is that of recreation but some competition is also present.

(d)   Emphasizing the importance of success is reflected in clear expectations of some benefits that are possible through sports activities.

(e)   A significant reason for participating in sports activities is the spontaneous experience and enjoyment of sport and, after all, this is the hidden essence, that indispensible quality of participation in sport, which is recognized as such by people with physical disabilities.

(f) It seems that participating in team games, including sitting volleyball, demands an adjustment by the individual to the group but at the same time it presents an incentive for sports activities. Sports activities fill in one's free time, they are becoming a part of the life-style of an individual and also they provide an opportunity to escape boredom.

(g) Besides the physical, technical and tactical preparations it is also important in sport to know the psychological relations. Motivation is a crucial aspect of this preparation.

This study has attempted to answer the basic question: what is the reason for an individual participating in sports activities? The conclusions are valid for players of sitting volleyball, but we can also use findings on other sportsmen with physical disabilities. Moreover, the applicability of the results is not limited to competitive sport only but it is also applicable at the recreational level and in physical education.

Knowing the motives of those whom they guide and train is undoubtedly indispensible information for coaches and others who are involved with sports for the disabled. More knowledge and more information on motives mean better possibilities for success. The development of sports activities is also based on scientific findings. With this piece of work by focusing on people with physical disabilities and their sport activity, we would like to contribute to a more complete picture of sport. The international scope of the study should be noted as the players were representing 11 European countries and the USA. We hope that this research will contribute even though in a small way to the enrichment of knowledge in the field of sport and especially in the field of sport for people with physical disabilities.

5   References

Beard, G.J. and Ragheb, M.G. (1983) Measuring leisure motivation. **Journal of Leisure Research,** third quarter, 219 228.

Fulgosi, A. (1979) **Faktorska analiza.** Skolska knjiga, Zagreb.

Momirovic, K. (1972) **Metode za transformacijo i kondenzaciju kinezioloskih informacija.** Institut za kineziologiju, Zagreb.

Petri, H. (1981) **Motivation: theory and research.** Wadsworth Publishing Company, Belmont, California.

Scanlon, K.T. (1982) Motivation and stress in competitive youth sports. **Joperd,** 36, 27-28.

Vute, R. (1985) **Struktura stalisc, motivov in preferenc sportnih panog telesno prizadete moske mladine v odnosu do kinezioloskih dejavnosti in razlike v staliscih, motivih in preferencah glede na mobilnost te mladine.** Fakultet za fizicku kulturu Zagreb, Zagreb.

GET ACTIVE. A LOOK AFTER YOUR HEART CAMPAIGN. POWERJOG 50 AND PEDAL POWER 50.

J. BARTLEY[1]
Superintendent Physiotherapist, Royal Albert Hospital, Lancaster, England.

Abstract

Lack of exercise is one of the major risk factors for Coronary Heart Disease. Motivation to exercise presents problems for many people including those with a Mental Handicap, who may be unable to understand the benefits to their health that taking part in regular exercise will bring. A 'Get Active' twin exercise package developed for residents of a Lancaster Hospital for people with a mental handicap offers a simple, effective and objective practical programme for such clients to initiate and maintain exercise participation. Motivation to exercise is further reinforced by staff involvement, and programmes, suitability for home, leisure and Day Centres further enhances the positive integration of such individuals within the community.

Keywords: Exercise, Coronary Heart Disease, Motivation, Mental Handicap.

1   Introduction

While it is encouraging that there is seemingly an increasing trend amongst the public to pursue personal health and fitness activities, it is nonetheless disturbing that heart disease is the highest killer in the United Kingdom and one of the most preventable.

Although not a complete panacea, the adoption of exercise as a means of developing a healthy heart via personal health and fitness would undoubtedly diminish this unacceptable coronary statistic. Fitness and health of course must never be treated as a 'fad' but as a formula to be embraced by the nation as effort well worth expending to gain fitness for life. Such aims, of course, require positive attitudes and motivation to initiate and maintain fitness programmes. Although some people seem naturally blessed with a high degree of discipline and self-motivation to acquire fitness and health levels the majority of the population finds such motivation problematic. Even amongst those who do exercise, relatively few will persist, with the majority discontinuing exercise programmes within the first few months.

[1]   The Author wishes to acknowledge the support given by Lancaster District Health Promotion Unit and Management and Secretarial Staff of Royal Albert Hospital.

Motivation to initiate and maintain exercise activity presents even greater problems for people with a mental handicap who may be unable to understand the benefits to their health that taking part in exercise will bring. Exercise task complexity, behaviour characteristics, communication and physical handicap are other common factors mitigating against encouraging and sustaining positive exercise behaviour.

Despite such factors if people with a mental handicap, and indeed the population at large, are to appreciate the physical and mental health benefits that exercise and fitness brings then they must be active.

With such concerns in mind and as a contribution to the National Look After Your Heart (LAYH) campaign aimed at a variety of institutions and organizations (i.e. schools, the National Health Service and community organizations) an activity package, appropriately titled 'Get Active', was developed for the residents of the Royal Albert Hospital in Lancaster. This is a hospital for people with a mental handicap.

'Get Active' consists of two achievement orientated programmes 'Powerjog 50' and 'Pedal Power 50'. Both were structured to achieve the following **Aims** and **Objectives**.

2   Aims

(a)   To promote and encourage people with a mental handicap to become involved within a reward orientated programme that will not only enable cardio-vascular fitness but enhance motivation to exercise within a structured and progressive framework.

(b)   Promote positive integration.

(c)   Enhance the normalization process.

3   Objectives

(a)   Provide a structured and progressive success-orientated exercise programme that establishes rewards towards the target of accumulating either 50 miles upon a treadmill (Powerjog 50) or 50 hours upon a static bike (Pedal Power 50).

(b)   Such involvement within a programme that can be applied to any setting (eg. home, day leisure centres) will only enhance positive integration within the community.

(c)   The programme can be used by the population at large thus encapsulating the concept of normalization.

4   Strategy

4.1 *Powerjog 50*

The initial programme concept was established around the use of a 'Powerjog' motorized treadmill machine within the Physiotherapy Department of the Royal Albert Hospital, Lancaster. From this author's experience the treadmill offers an opportunity for a most effective mobility and cardio-vascular exercise activity for those with a mental handicap. It moves at a set speed and can be matched to the pace of the individual's ability level. Continuous exercise is ensured for participants with the minimum of prompting, and there is minimal task complexity which is often a major factor that hinders the effective functioning of these individuals in exercise programmes. Such enhancing factors have thus allowed an opportunity for clients with additional disabilities such as spasticity, diabetes, visual impairment, or challenging behaviour to participate positively and enjoyably within exercise programmes.

The high level of motivation exhibited by these clients during exercise sessions created the atmosphere to provide a structured and progressive success orientated exercise programme that offered staged rewards in the form of certificates at 5, 15, and 25 miles. A specifically designed Powerjog 50 T-Shirt is awarded on completion of 50 miles. This mileage is based on the accumulation of distance covered in each exercise session on the treadmill. Awards of such cheerful, possessable items not only encourages and rewards participation but also promotes the 'FUN' aspect of exercise activity.

4.2 *Pedal Power 50*

Although the treadmill has many advantages it is not widely available. The Pedal Power 50 programme was thus developed to compliment the Powerjog programme and counter a lack of access to treadmill machines.

Pedal Power 50 utilizes a static bike. Although this equipment is not as effective in ensuring on-task behaviour as the treadmill, it is nonetheless readily available, inexpensive and widely utilized as an exercise activity. Pedal Power 50 maintains the same theme and structure as its Powerjog counterpart, but time accumulated rather than distance is rewarded, with certificates at 5, 15 and 25 hours. The Pedal Power 50 T-Shirt is awarded when 50 hours are complete. Time rather than distance was chosen because it allows a static bike to be used independently of an odometer and also it serves to exphasize the **little and often** conceptual approach to exercise activity.

The introduction of Pedal Power 50 thus enables more widespread use of the 'GET ACTIVE' programme within hospitals, appropriate centres and also at home.

5   Target Groups

Both Powerjog 50 and Pedal Power 50, although primarily aimed at people with a mental handicap, was nonetheless intended to appeal to both client and staff alike. The integrative nature of this client/carer involvement creates an important social support structure that serves to reinforce motivation and develop positive attitudes towards exercise activity.

6   Client Case Studies

Since the inception of 'GET ACTIVE' within the Royal Albert Hospital many clients and staff have actively participated. All involved in these programmes are success stories. Here are just a few examples:-

(a)   'Enjoy the Action'
Gwen, although asthmatic and with hemiplegia, has happily embarked upon the treadmill. Gwen has taken 300 sessions at an average speed of 1.2km/hr to gain her Powerjog 50 T-Shirt. In that time Gwen has learned to operate the machine herself and is totally independant in its use. Gwen is now living within the community and has embarked upon the Pedal Power 50 within her own home.

(b)   'Active With A Little Help From Friends'
Keith, although wheelchair bound, was one of the first to request to use the Powerjog treadmill. His bilateral spasticity will only allow a walking speed of 0.9km/hr but with the support of staff at each side he's getting there.

(c)   Or Alternatively 'Get There By Bike'
Keith, who has a gross hearing impairment, certainly communicates his enjoyment for the Static Bike. Indeed it is difficult to get him off it. He has already gained a 50 mile T-Shirt with Powerjog, but he is peddling so fast to his second target that a Pedal Power 250 and 500 will be needed!

Such examples, although emphasizing those with more severe disabilities, hopefully highlight the simplicity and effectiveness of such programmes. Those with visual impairments are able to walk/jog independantly. Others have been trained via Powerjog 50 and Pedal Power 50 to represent their community, and indeed Country, in the Special Olympic Games, and as we say in Special Olympics - 'Everyone Is A Winner'.

7   Outcomes

7.1   *Hospital Based*

Since the official introduction of 'Get Active' in May 1990, some 30% of Hospital-based clients have embarked upon Powerjog 50 and Pedal Power 50 programmes. The degree of associated disability determines the pace of progress with major targets taking months to years.

A significant number of staff have also embarked upon both programmes.

7.2   *Community Based.*

Few opportunities arise within the community for widespread implementation of Powerjog 50. Pedal Power 50 in particular, however, is proving a practical and popular activity that is now established within Hospital Wards, Community Day Centres and indeed at the homes of clients and staff.

The interest shown at this early stage by many Health Promotion Units throughout the United Kingdom for the 'Get Active' package also bears a hopeful sign that other interested parties will become activated towards exercise.

8   Evaluation

The following methods of evaluation represent the range of objectives identified for this twin exercise activity package.

(a)   The number and proportion of clients taking up the project is the first indicator. Some 120 clients and 45 staff have embarked on programmes within the first 3 months of 'Get Active' introduction.

(b)   The numbers reaching Powerjog 50 and Pedal Power 50 set targets. All of these have been attained by some clients and staff and requests are in for a furtherance of targets.

(c)   The take up by other bodies is also an indicator. Physiotherapy staff have established 'Get Active' within the Day Centres and homes of this client group within the Lancaster District. Fifteen Health Promotion Units within the United Kingdom are already promoting the scheme.

(d)   Improvement in fitness is revealed by preferred exercise variables eg. time, speed, resistance, utilized within each programme.

(e)   Increased mobility and reduced obesity are readily measured.

(f)   Eventually, repeat cardio-vascular fitness surveys will reveal the extent of success.

9   Summary

While it may be fair to state that people without a mental handicap face difficulties in achieving the motivation to embark upon health and fitness training programmes, experience and research have shown that those people with a mental handicap in general terms have a greater difficulty involving themselves in activities structured towards short and long term goals, eg. fitness.

The factors determining such motivation are varied and complex and apply to the handicapped and non-handicapped alike. The focus of 'Get Active' upon establishing an award-based programme structured around two basic but effective exercise components attempts to address such constraining factors. The twin programmes of Powerjog 50 and Pedal Power 50 have certainly helped many clients and staff of the Royal Albert Hospital to 'Get Active', with all participants framing their certificates and wearing their T-Shirts with pride. 'Get Active' continues to attract more support and more participants throughout Lancaster District and indeed within the United Kingdom at large.

The suitability of the programmes for the population at large and their use within different settings also provides an active contribution to the positive integration of such a client group within the community. The concept of 'normalization' is thus built into the programme.

There are, of course, numerous activities that benefit health and fitness. The 'Get Active' package nonetheless is simple, objective and effective and offers just one small practical attempt to motivate and enable individuals to take the first and many steps to activity, fitness and health.

We are all handicapped to some degree in motivating ourselves to appreciate the value of health and fitness, this project will hopefully diminish that handicap.

PHYSICAL EDUCATION CURRICULUM FOR PUPILS WITH SEVERE LEARNING DIFFICULTIES

M.J. ALCOTT
Green Hedges School, Cambridge, England

Abstract

This paper describes a Physical Education curriculum that has been designed to meet the needs of pupils with severe learning difficulties who attend a special school in Cambridge, England. The age range of the pupils is 3-19 years. The curriculum is based on the Objectives Model. Its design, delivery and evaluation are covered. Areas for further development are suggested.

Keywords: Physical Education, Curriculum, Pupils, Severe Learning Difficulties.

1 Introduction

First, a few words about the terminology of UK special education. In 1987 a major educational document was produced - the Warnock Report. This government-initiated report introduced a new range of terms to describe pupils 'handicapped by disabilities of body or mind'. The concept of 'special educational needs' (SEN) was created. Along with it came the concept of **learning difficulty.** Pupils may have **moderate learning difficulties** (MLD) or **severe learning difficulties** (SLD).

Behind these innovations lay the desire to remove restrictive and degrading labels from children - such concepts as **sub-normal** and **severely sub-normal**, for example, did nothing to enhance the self-esteem of the labelled person and even suggested that the person was an inferior being.

The new terminology did not change the children. It did change attitudes to them and expectations of them. They were accepted as full members of the human race who had difficulty in learning. The new terminology also brought these young people into the full embrace of British society. At least in theory.

Not quite, in reality. The integration of pupils with learning difficulties into mainstream schools, encouraged by the government through the 1981 Education Act, has so far only been implemented in a patchy way. The majority of pupils with severe learning difficulties are educated in segregated special schools.

2 The School

Green Hedges School, Cambridge is one such special school for pupils who have severe learning difficulties. There are 45 pupils, male and female, ranging in age from 3 to 19 years.

In 1984 the school governors decided to appoint a specialist PE teacher who would create and deliver a PE curriculum to all pupils in the school. The hypothesis behind this appointment was simple enough: if the pupils had access to a well-designed PE curriculum their needs would be met more effectively and they would make valuable educational gains. For the UK, this was an unusual and exciting innovation. The provision of PE was (and still is) woefully inadequate in schools for pupils with severe learning difficulties.

3 The Pupils

Number: 45. Age range: 3-19 years

This population included pupils who have psychological, physical and sensory impairments often combined in tangled complexity. Some had profound and multiple disabilities. Whilst some of the pupils had been diagnosed clinically for such conditions as Down's syndrome, autism and cerebral palsy, many defied diagnosis, their conditions noted as being of 'unspecified aetiology'.

Whatever the aetiology of their condition, the population shared a number of characteristics of importance when considering their PE curriculum:

(a) limited cognitive ability
(b) low level of fitness
(c) motor difficulties/delays
(d) limited experience of play
(e) limited range of physical experiences
(f) small/non-existent repertoire of sports skills
(g) low level of self-esteem
(h) limited language of physical activity

This group of pupils, with this range of shared characteristics and, in some cases, additional disabilities such as sensory impairment, multiple handicaps, were to be the population sample for pupils with severe learning difficulties. The challenge was to design and deliver a Physical Education curriculum that would address and meet their needs.

4 The Curriculum Model

The Objectives Model of the curriculum seemed to offer a workable basis for curriculum development. Based on observed changes in behaviour it provided a clear structure. It did have its limitations, especially in the area of affective development. However, it provided a good starting point for a PE curriculum. After all, the education of the physical is much concerned with observable changes in motor performance.

The major blocks of this curriculum were:

AIMS   CONTENT   ORGANIZATION   METHODS   EVALUATION

4.1 *Some Aims of the PE Curriculum*

To develop and maintain:

(a)   fitness (health-related)
(b)   motor skills
(c)   sports skills
(d)   experience of a range of physical activities
(e)   self-help skills
(f)   health knowledge

Through Physical Education to develop and maintain

(a)   enjoyment in physical activity
(b)   a sense of achievement and success
(c)   enhancement of self-esteem
(d)   confidence
(e)   positive social interaction
(f)   language and number skills
(g)   integration into the community

4.2 *Content of the PE curriculum*

A number of CORE areas were selected to form the main structure of the PE curriculum.

> Fitness (health-related)
> Motor Skills
> Body Management
> Movement
> Aquatics
> Games
> Athletics
> Outdoor Pursuits
> Recreation
> Health & Hygiene
> Self-Help
> Competition
> Spectator

4.3 *Components of the PE curriculum*

Activities that formed the components of each core area were identified. This gave the following total curriculum content:

(a)   FITNESS
    Cardio-respiratory fitness, flexibility, strength, muscular endurance, body composition, fitness tests

(b) MOTOR SKILLS
Gross Motor
Pre-walker: lying, rolling, sitting, kneeling, crawling, standing
Walker: walking, running, hopping, skipping, jumping, balance, climbing
Fine Motor
Hand-eye co-ordination, foot-eye co-ordination

(c) BODY MANAGEMENT
Posture, body parts, body awareness, spatial awareness, direction, laterality, relaxation

(d) MOVEMENT
Music & movement, dance, gymnastics, trampoline/rebound therapy, Sherborne movement, yoga

(e) AQUATICS
Pre-swimmer
Water play, entries, exits, propulsion, flotation, breathing, retrieval, hygiene, self-help
Swimmer
Entries, exits, strokes, flotation, retrieval, survival, endurance, rescues, self-help, theory

(f) GAMES
Preliminary
Ball skills, small games
Invasion games
Soccer, rugby, hockey, basketball
Net games
Volleyball, badminton, tennis
Striking games
Rounders, cricket
Co-operative games
Parachute, various

(g) ATHLETICS
Track
Sprints, middle distance, hurdles
Distance
Jogging, cross country
Field
Long jump, high jump, ball throwing, shot put

(h) OUTDOOR PURSUITS
Walking, hiking, climbing, cycling, riding, orienteering, skiing, camping, backpacking, youth hostelling, canoeing, sailing

(i) RECREATION
Outdoor
Small toys, trike, skating, putting, bowls, archery, playground apparatus, adventure playground, golf
Indoor
Bowls, snooker, darts, table tennis

(j)   HEALTH
      Diet, clothing, anti-smoking, body care
(k)   SELF HELP
      Washing, showering, grooming, dressing, toileting, first aid
(l)   COMPETITION
      Within school, between schools, Special Olympics
(m)   SPECTATOR
      By visit or video
      Other classes, other schools, local clubs, national & international events

4.4   *The Organization of the PE curriculum*

The curriculum was then organized for delivery. The aim was to create a
progressively unfolding curriculum that, however adapted, could be offered to all
pupils according to their needs and abilities. A developmental, sequential
progression for all components of the curriculum was then written out.

Next, each component was taken apart following the process of task analysis.
That is to say: a target behaviour with conditions and criteria was defined. Smaller
steps for the attainment of the target behaviour were used but not written down.
Here is an example from Aquatics.

Core	Aquatics
Component	Propulsion
Target Behaviour	Swim breast-stroke
Conditions	10m in deep water without stopping or touching sides of pool
Criterion	Performed on 3 occasions (this is arbitrary)

The breast-stroke was then broken down into a number of familiar steps - arms
and leg actions, body positions, breathing, co-ordination. Each can be learned
independently and then combined.

With the PE curriculum organized in a progressive manner and with each
component anlaysed then the delivery had to be considered.

4.5   *Delivery of the curriculum*

Grouping the pupils for PE sessions was not a straightforward matter. In broad
terms, they were grouped according to age and ability. Each group was timetabled
for two PE sessions a week. A PE session was 90 minutes long for the senior
pupils and 40 minutes long for the youngest. In addition to these sessions, all pupils
had additional swimming time, with pony riding once a fortnight and an unspecified
number of recreational periods scattered through the week.

4.6   *Lesson Design*

In order to try to meet the many needs of the pupils and achieve the aims of the
curriculum, each lesson was designed to address a range of needs. Every lesson
included aspects of the following:

SELF-HELP	FITNESS	MOTOR SKILLS
SPECIFIC SKILLS (SPORT ETC)	RELAXATION	

Through the activities of each lesson other aims of the PE curriculum were pursued - eg, enjoyment, achieving success, developing confidence.

5   Methods

A wide variety of methods were used. Some are used in mainstream Physical Education, others have been developed by special educators to overcome the learning difficulties of pupils with severe learning difficulties. Here are some of the methods that were used to deliver this PE curriculum:

> whole-part-whole
> part-part-whole
> demonstration/modelling
> individual exploration
> group teaching (direct)
> individual coaching (direct)
> peer tutoring
> chaining
> shaping

In addition, many activities were adapted in a variety of ways (equipment, playing area, rules), prompts were used (physical, gesture, verbal), positive reinforcement was given where appropriate.

6   Evaluation of Pupil Progress

Records of progress were kept, detailing mastery of skills and pupil participation in a range of activities such as hikes, camps, riding. The records show that in many instances pupils acquired new physical skills.

In May 1990, 10 students who had taken part in the PE curriculum for 6 years were selected for close examination. To what extent had they attained the aims of the PE curriculum? What had they gained from their experiences in Physical Education? Precise, quantitative data were not collected but the records, observations of staff and parents gave a broad indication of their attainments.

6.1 *The Sample*

Total - 10,   Males - 6   Females - 4

Age range now: 15 - 20 years

All have shown some improvements in fitness (especially cardio-vascular endurance) and motor skills; a variety of sports skills have been acquired (eg swimming strokes, trampoline moves, hockey, rounders and simple basketball skills). They have experienced a very wide range of activities, including simple gymnastics, trampolining, invasion/net/striking and co-operative games, jogging, cross-country, simple athletics, hiking, camping, backpacking, youth hostelling, swimming, skiing, sailing, canoeing, riding.

With regard to self-help skills, participation in PE lessons twice a week has helped with dressing, showering, personal hygiene and general mobility around the community. It has also provided occasions to deliver health knowledge in practical circumstances.

Most of the students appear to have enjoyed activities most of the time. Some have grown immensely in self-confidence through successfully facing numerous challenges. There have been many occasions for positive social interaction - in team games, co-operative games, camping, sailing and canoeing. They have all extended their vocabulary through PE and frequently had to face simple number tasks.

Finally, integration into the community. By this is meant participation in physical activities with other members of the community. Here, success has been limited. Activities have gone on alongside other people - as in the public swimming pools or on the ski slopes. But so far there has been only limited interaction with members of the general public through participation in physical activities.

This generalized summative evaluation is based on observations by the school staff and study of the PE records. Continuing in a qualitative way, here are the comments of a school welfare assistant on one student (we'll name him David).

6.2   *Welfare Assistant's comments on David, a 19 year old who has Down's Syndrome.*

'PE has helped David's fitness a lot. His stamina has greatly improved. His motor skills have developed a lot with fine motor skills showing steady improvement. He enjoys physical activities a fair amount. At one time he was apprehensive of descending steps/stairs but has overcome this fear. He has achieved a lot of success through PE - in general fitness, confidence, social interaction and personal development.

PE has done a lot for David's self-image. He shows obvious pleasure when succeeding with an activity. For example, in skiing, after many, many attempts at trying to 'plough', therefore stop, on a downward run he was absolutely delighted with his success. I think PE has contributed a fair amount to his language development. When working in a team situation, although he doesn't initiate ideas he does have verbal interaction and this has improved. His sense of humour shows through too.

I also think PE has helped David's integration into the community a lot. He swims at Cambridge City pool, he has done sailing and canoeing at an outdoor centre, camped, backpacked and hiked.

Working with David in PE changed my attitude to him. As I became aware of David's increased confidence and sense of wanting to achieve I found my attitude more positive and I encouraged him to reach his goals and beyond. I have known David for sixteen of his nineteen years and I feel the structured PE curriculum has been one of the greatest benefits of his education and his overall development'.

Now, to add another dimension, here are the views of David's father.

6.3   *Father's comments on David*

'PE has helped David's fitness a lot. He is very fit. He has made a very good improvement in running and jumping. His balance has improved a lot and he is in control of himself and thinking ahead. His climbing has improved a lot. Four years ago he had problems climbing stairs. Today he skiis down some of the highest mountains.

David now shows a lot of interest in sports - gym, skiing, indoor hockey, canoeing, swimming, horse riding, Olympics and darts. He watches sport on TV with a fair amount of understanding. He likes PE a lot. He joins in sport with other people in the community - gym and skiing and outward bound courses.

PE has helped his development a lot. He has learned many new skills from many people. He takes to challenges. He has turned out to be an upfront man with the social skills to go with it.

Canoeing has led to him being picked to go to Sweden, one of six out of all East Anglia. Skiing - what do you say? Three times to the Swiss Alps, Scotland, TV, Daily Mail Ski Show. And Dad skis too now. David comments 'Me and you, Dad. What a team!'

All David's sports opportunities have started at Green Hedges School'.

7   Future Developments

There are a number of areas for further exploration and study. Here are some of them:

(a)   This objectives-based model is very teacher-directed. It would be worth exploring ways of developing self-directed learning.

(b)   It would be interesting to examine the processes of the Objectives Model.

(c)   Assessment. We need simple instruments to assess pupils who may have profound and multiple handicaps.

(d)   Recording. Different methods of recording, related to records of achievement, need to be tested.

(e)   Integration. More integrated activities to be stimulated.

(f)   Parental involvement. Ways of increasing parental involvement to be explored.

(g)   Pre-school and post-school provisions in Physical Education for this special population to be developed.

(h)   Teachers and administrators in Local Education Authorities to be persuaded of the great value of PE for all pupils with special needs.

8   Conclusion

A broad, varied PE curriculum based on the Objectives Model and founded on the development of fitness, motor skills, sports skills and extending the range of experiences can contribute much to the quality of life of young people who have severe learning difficulties.

EVERY BODY ACTIVE PROJECT

M.F. TUNGATT
Sports Council, Manchester, England.

Abstract
Every Body Active is a major partnership project sponsored by the Sports Council to develop and implement schemes to increase sporting and recreational opportunities for young people with disabilities. The project has developed partnerships with leisure providers, local authority decision makers, school teachers, disability groups, sports coaches, sports administrators and voluntary sports clubs. The promotion of activities in education, community sport, performance sport and countryside activities have all featured in the programme. The Sports Council believes the schemes offer excellent 'models' for others to replicate to ensure a more positive sporting experience is available to all young people with disabilities throughout the country.
Keywords: Sport, Education, Partnerships, Disability, Integration, Opportunities, Action, Involvement.

1 Introduction

The Every Body Active project is one of a series of National Demonstration Projects supported by The Sports Council to forge new partnerships to increase participation in sport. The Sports Council has identified the need to support sports development and facility-based programmes aimed at young people with disabilities. However, in its 1988 Strategy Review, the Council noted that 'the needs of the market are not fully understood and further experiment and policy development will be required'. (Sports Council, 1988 a)

The project began work in 1987 with a one-year research phase during which time a range of questionnaire surveys were carried out in North East England by the Project Team, which comprised lecturers and researchers from Sunderland Polytechnic, Newcastle Polytechnic and Durham University together with three full-time project staff. The research focused on the project's three primary aims:

(a) to promote increased participation amongst sensorially and physically disabled young people (aged 11 years and above) in mainstream physical education

(b) to promote increased participation among sensorially and physically disabled young people (11-24 years) in community sport and recreation

(c)   to promote increased involvement among sensorially and physically disabled young people in coaching, officiating and administrative roles in sport and recreation.

2   The Research Phase

The research concentrated on three broad areas:

(a)   physical education for people with disabilities in mainstream schools in North East England
(b)   physical education for people with disabilities in special schools in North East England
(c)   community provision for sport and active recreation for people with disabilities, focusing on Sunderland Metropolitan Borough.

The detailed results of the research were to underpin the development of a series of implementation schemes and the nature, processes, issues and initial conclusions from the five schemes eventually included in the project form the basis of the remainder of this paper. The Research Results were reported in a series of Working Papers (Williams, 1988) and summarized in the Sports Council's Phase 1 Monitoring Report (Sports Council, 1988 b)

The research confirmed many of the previous experiences of the Project Team. In mainstream schools most teachers cannot cope with the one or two pupils thrust into their PE lessons and require more knowledge of disabilities. Teachers and non-disabled pupils in mainstream schools tended to hold pejorative attitudes towards pupils with disabilities and, as a result, individual disabled pupils were acutely aware of their lack of skill and were apprehensive about participating.

As far as the Special Schools were concerned, the research revealed that all of the schools responding exhibited some deficiencies in the provision of PE. The majority emphasized physical recreation, not physical education. The practice of exclusion was common, with all but two schools excluding wheelchair pupils from field and sports hall games. The Project Team concluded that Special Schools contributed to inequalities in community sport and recreation by restricting the capacity of school leavers to make informed choices. Although transport, lack of facilities, and lack of specialist equipment were all factors, the Project Team concluded that the most important factor was the lack of expertise amongst the teachers taking PE lessons.

Within the community, most sports and recreation organizations in Sunderland have little or no involvement of people with disabilities and several felt their sport was 'unsuitable' or that there was a need for potential disabled participants to be assessed because of perceived risks. This confirmed the Project Team's impression that the capabilities of disabled people were often underestimated before they even had a chance to get involved.

Moreover, physical access and transport were major barriers. The design and structure of many of the facilities deny access to people with disabilities. In short, the notion of structural inequality was massive and widespread, especially in the casual use of sport and recreation facilities. To the disabled individual, 'dropping-in' to a facility was not undertaken lightly and the whole process of participation became a serious business, demanding time, effort and resources. Nevertheless, it was undoubtedly made more difficult than it needed to be by many of the attitudes and constraining factors outlined above.

3   The Implementation Phase

The underlying philosophy behind the five schemes was that they should build on the professional strengths of the individual members of the Project Team and that Every Body Active would function both as a catalyst in partnership with external organizations and as an agency of direct intervention. In order to give strength to the notion of self-help groups, each scheme would operate autonomously under the direction of a 'scheme manager'. In each case a small 'scheme team' would be set up to advise on the development of the work. These teams would involve disabled participants and practitioners from partner organizations.

The Project Team identified five key areas from the research which the implementation schemes needed to address:

(a)   the fundamental need emerging from both PE research and the community surveys for an increased capacity for individuals to make informed choices about their participation

(b)   the need to match the aspirations of young disabled people for casual participation in sport facilities with the management practices and programming encompassing special needs in such facilities

(c)   the urgent need to improve the quality of the physical education experience for pupils with disabilities in both mainstream and Special Schools

(d)   the need to match the structure of special programmes for swimming, popular in Special Schools, to general community swimming programmes

(e)   the need to develop management policies and action plans for coach education programmes to enable disabled sports players to coach and receive coaching at an appropriate level.

The five schemes developed in each of these key areas for the implementation phase are outlined briefly below together with an initial assessment of their impact. A full monitoring report is available from the Sports Council (Sports Council, 1991).

4   Life and Leisure Scheme

4.1   *Background*

The Life and Leisure Scheme is attempting to expand the capacities of young people with disabilities to make leisure time choices and to extend their horizons. The scheme is a partnership with the Fieldfare Trust[1] and the Salters Lane Special School in Darlington, with some involvement from two adjoining schools (Glebe School and Mayfair School) that cater for pupils with moderate and severe learning

---

[1]   The Fieldfare Trust is a charitable trust set up to promote countryside and outdoor pursuit activities for people with disabilities.

difficulties. The main approach throughout the scheme's life has been working with individuals in counselling them with regard to their leisure interests. A seven stage model has been developed to carry out this 'sports counselling' process:

4.2 *Stage 1*

First a profile of the individuals is drawn up by discussion with the individual. This includes all aspects of the individuals' leisure patterns and more general features of their lives; mobility, income, interests, social contacts.

4.3 *Stage 2*

A profile of the individuals is developed which identifies where there may be barriers to participation: not just those resulting from disability. There would be little point in addressing physical mobility difficulties in the countryside if an individual were never properly going to be able to afford the transport cost to get there.

4.4 *Stage 3*

A personal programme of activities is negotiated with each individual. The starting point for this is the determination of what interests the individuals have. In many cases introductory activities are set up to provide those that have had limited experiences on which to base their preference with a firm basis for choice.

4.5 *Stage 4*

The next stage involves the development of the skills and confidence that will be needed to pursue chosen activities. These are not always activity based and may involve breaking away from parental protection, developing personal mobility or acquiring some specific skill such as map reading for orienteering.

4.6 *Stage 5*

During the first activities support is provided to ensure that any problems are resolved and the basis for continued independent participation is established.

4.7 *Stage 6*

The next stage sometimes involves an introduction to a community-based activity club. The scheme counsellor accompanies people to the club in order to facilitate their introduction and in many cases allay the unfounded fears of club members that the involvement of people with disabilities will in any way detract from their leisure opportunities.

4.8 *Stage 7*

The final stage is the gradual withdrawal of support. This is done at a rate and in a way which ensure there is as much chance as possible of individuals remaining involved with their chosen activities but independently of support from the scheme.

4.9 *Conclusions*

The efforts of the Life and Leisure Team have identified the opportunities that can be developed and, at the same time, the constraints that remain if independent participation is to be truly achieved. Firstly, the importance of breaking down the stereotypes which are often applied to people with disabilities is paramount. Too often recreation providers and, indeed, volunteer helpers consider the constraints inhibiting a person with disabilities as always associated with his or her impairment. The evidence from the Life and Leisure scheme is that there can be a whole multitude of other reasons, just as there may be for other members of the community. Accordingly people need to be supported as complete individuals and not as 'disabled participants'. There is little point, in sports development terms, in focusing on the disability if the other constraints are still going to inhibit participation.

Secondly, the importance of spending time getting to know the individuals involved in this type of work cannot be over-emphasized. Leisure counselling is a slow, time-consuming process, but its value in building confidence and trust is enormous. It is by getting to know individual disabled participants and their personal circumstances (eg family, friends) that the superficial problems highlighted by their disability can be placed in the wider context of their overall lifestyles. Only when this is achieved will sustainable, independent participation ever seem a likely proposition for participant and 'counsellor' alike.

Finally, the scheme has encountered some resistance among community recreation providers, statutory and voluntary, to accept people with disabilities into the mainstream. This rarely manifests itself as overt discrimination, but two aspects of the 'resistance' have been common:

(a)   suggestions that the individuals involved in the scheme would be better served by going to specialist segregated programmes
(b)   a series of apparently logical problems for not being able to provide equal opportunities

The Life and Leisure scheme has proved that with some effort in creating awareness, providing sensitive counselling to encourage people with disabilities to identify their abilities, and establishing contact between the providers and individual disabled participants, these attitudes tend to be overcome. The key, once again, is in ensuring that within all leisure programmes people with disabilities are regarded as complete individuals, and not merely as people with impairments which require special attention.

5   Every Body for Leisure Scheme

5.1 *Background*

The Every Body for Leisure Scheme has been established in partnership with Crowtree Leisure Centre and Sunderland Borough Council with a view to providing a flexible range of services to enable people with disabilities to enjoy leisure pursuits of their choice at the Centre. In order to cement the relationship between the Project Team and Crowtree Leisure Centre, the Deputy Manager was asked to become the Scheme Leader with management responsibilities for the work.

The scheme aimed to facilitate independent integrated participation and group segregated sessions by close consultation with disabled participants and potential participants. In addition the Centre Management hoped to identify effective Leisure Management practices to precipitate participation.

5.2 *Methods*

A team of outreach workers were recruited to conduct market research and outreach work within the community. Segregated sessions were established and a co-ordinator appointed to assist the disabled participants in organizing their own activities. Precise action plans were agreed with the participants, encompassing the activities on offer, the extent and range of the programme, the specific needs of each participant and the publicity needed to develop the scheme. Management awareness training and a disability awareness day were organized to give the Centre staff the confidence to identify the necessary refinements in management practices and a range of short, medium and long term adaptions to the Centre's facilities were identified and either implemented or, where capital expenditure was needed, added to the planned development programme and budget. After 18 months the participants were given advice on how to set up their own leisure club and organize their own activities.

5.3 *Conclusions*

The scheme has succeeded in establishing a new young people's leisure club from scratch, has encouraged the young people to develop their own support systems, both financial and constitutional, and has been instrumental in enabling the participants to be far more outward looking in their leisure expectations. Confidence building, trust and a genuine involvement in the organization of the club have been important factors behind this success. However, it must be stressed that the success was only achieved by ensuring that the initial outreach work was conducted in a sensitive manner and that sufficient staff were available to reach the disabled community.

Perhaps the most telling conclusion from the scheme is the need to establish a 'community-based' leisure club that is segregated before developing any notion of independent use or individual links with able-bodied clubs. Attempts to achieve the latter too early in the scheme's life were not successful. Only by allowing the young people to feel confident in their surroundings on their own terms has independent use begun to develop.

In this context the scheme has re-affirmed that for people with disabilities, the surroundings are more than the bricks and mortar. Whilst it was encouraging that the Centre Management were able to begin to implement the adaptations, the more important factors have been the staff awareness training, the active involvement of the leisure centre staff, at all levels and grades, and the outreach work. Talking and listening, promoting a consumer-led philosophy and involving the young people in planning and promoting their own programmes have been vital factors. Crowtree does not run a disability leisure club; the participants operate **their** club at Crowtree and use its facilities, and others in the Borough and beyond, in the same way as any other group of able-bodied sports players.

6   Physical Education Scheme

6.1 *Background*

The Physical Education Scheme is seeking to enhance the quality of the PE programme for people with disabilities and to encourage positive attitudes amongst able-bodied and disabled pupils to one another, to the PE programme and to participation outside the formal curriculum. The scheme staff worked in partnership with the staff of Pendower Hall School in Newcastle which is a Special School for children with physical disabilities. The main issue which the Project Team had to address was the pupils' lack of skill and enthusiasm. Furthermore, the difference between sport or physical recreation and Physical Education had to be appreciated by the staff who taught on the activity programme.

6.2 *Major Work Areas*

An awareness and understanding of what constituted a sound scheme of work and lesson structure in PE had to be inculcated through discussion and the scheme staff had to become directly involved in the **practical** delivery of the PE sessions. Initially the staff were involved as observers or helpers in order that the existing programme could be assessed. As the scheme staff became more familiar with the pupils they began to teach and supervise sessions and to integrate the disabled pupils with pupils from a nearby Comprehensive School. As well as developing the programme of dry-slope skiing, swimming and games skills, the scheme staff attempted to broaden the pupils' horizons. An integrated residential weekend was held at an outdoor activities centre, links between PE and Health Education were re-inforced through a health leaflet. A community resource booklet was produced identifying local leisure opportunities and links were set-up with local sports clubs.

6.3 *Conclusions*

Although the Scheme Leader feels the work tried to achieve too much, too quickly, especially in relation to integration, the successes were gratifying. The links with mainstream schools and community clubs have provided a good starting point for further integration, but much more work in terms of personal contact and strengthening these relationships is required before real 'success' can be claimed.

In this respect, the Scheme Leader feels that several opportunities to develop the work were missed. Firstly the scheme staff ought to have developed more of a dialogue with the pupils themselves. As with the Life and Leisure scheme, the concept of leisure counselling, building-up trust and confidence, and then gradually withdrawing support, has a lot to offer. The Scheme Leader feels that there are many factors to take into account for disabled participants. Getting to know them better, taking individual values into account, matching the development of the PE programme more closely to their perceived ability and simply listening to their views could all have improved the scheme's success. In his own words, 'we were a bit mechanical about it all and too detached from the human element'.

In terms of developing 'activity for life' the Scheme Leader also felt they had missed an opportunity to involve the pupils' parents. For able-bodied pupils, any PE programme ought to be geared to encouraging post-school participation. A disability programme should be no different. However, for pupils with disabilities the support of able-bodied friends and their parents is vital. The involvement of parents in the physical education of their children while still at school might be an important factor in developing post-school opportunities.

Despite these missed opportunities the scheme's experiences are a useful model for other schools to build upon. The leaflets, brochures and workshop/seminar papers represent an invaluable source of resource material for both Special Schools and for mainstream PE teachers attempting to deliver PE to pupils with disabilities.

7   Every Body Active Swimming Scheme

7.1 *Background*

The Swimming Scheme was set up with a view to encouraging more young people with disabilities to continue swimming after leaving school and to alleviate the apprehension of some teachers, coaches and parents in working with disabled swimmers. The scheme's work has been concentrated in the Sunderland area, initially developing new opportunities at the pools at Barbara Priestman Special School, Sunderland Polytechnic, and Crowtree, but eventually the scheme hoped to offer sessions at the outlying pools within the Borough (Hetton, Washington and Boldon) to avoid the problems of transport faced by many of the potential participants.

7.2 *Major Work Areas*

As independence was an aim of the scheme exclusive transport was not organized, but information on transport availability was provided. Access problems were identified and suggestions for adaptations and flexibility in the use of facilities were made. Additional pool equipment was provided at the three main centres. Disability awareness courses were set up and a series of progressive teacher training courses were run. Polytechnic students became a useful source for paid and voluntary help. Informal visits were made to schools and centres and publicity through leaflets, local press and T.V. was organized.

Regular segregated sessions were set up at the Special School. Times were arranged at the leisure centre when help would be available as an introduction to using this community pool. For the more competent swimmers a regular integrated session with Sunderland Swimming Club was provided. Opportunities to participate in the planning and running of the swimming scheme and to attend basic teaching courses were organized where appropriate to the disability.

7.3 *Conclusions*

Despite some successes with Sunderland Swimming Club and an evident wider awareness of the need for special sessions or special attention to cater for people with disabilities, the Scheme Leader feels the work has served, once again, to highlight the problems that face disabled swimmers. Conventional swimming lessons, traditional public swimming sessions and existing coaching or training opportunities were rarely appropriate for disabled swimmers or disabled participants wishing to learn to swim. Moreover, co-ordinating the efforts of swimming teachers, pool managers and club coaches who had the desire and/or the qualifications to offer opportunities were fraught with practical difficulties. Pool availability, access problems, availability of appropriate equipment, and sufficient numbers of volunteer helpers all impinged on the scheme's programmes.

Even with the resources of the Every Body Active project, the Scheme Leader felt that they had never been able to create the full range of opportunities necessary for a coherent performance structure for disabled swimmers, nor to provide appropriate participation opportunities. Building on the abilities of the coaches, the teachers and disabled swimmers themselves had taken much longer to achieve than had been anticipated. An important lesson in itself for the future development of **any** integrated sports development programme for people with disabilities. A start has been made for swimmers in Sunderland, but there remains a long way to go.

8   Every Body Active Coaching Scheme

8.1 *Background*

The Coaching Scheme is a response to the fact that previous attempts to generate coherent policies towards coaching people with disabilities had relied on the skills and initiatives of a few individuals. The Scheme Team hoped to develop a pro-active response to the development of general coach education policies, the preparation of a detailed action plan and the promotion of basic coach education programmes. Following discussions with several Tyneside local authorities, a partnership scheme has been developed between the National Coaching Foundation (NCF) and the Metropolitan Borough of North Tyneside who had recently begun to develop a disability policy statement, led by the Director of Leisure and Tourism, although there was broad support from both the Social Services and the Education Departments.

8.2 *Major Work Areas*

The scheme worked closely with the local authority officers in developing policies specific to the needs of people with disabilities and jointly prepared an 'action plan' which recognized, and would underpin, approved policies. A sports specific data base was established containing detailed information on coaching opportunities for people with disabilities.

The scheme encouraged coaches, administrators and officials to adopt a positive policy towards disabled people and assisted in the production of basic coach education programmes by adapting and refining the existing NCF Coaching Award courses. A video was produced which focused on the systems of support required by disabled people.

Finally, the scheme addressed sports specific coaching practices in six sports and produced method statements which could be used by clients and contractors in the Compulsory Competitive Tendering (CCT) procedures to ensure that suitable opportunities were provided for **all** people with disabilities.

8.3 *Conclusions*

Although the work has successfully developed a range of resource materials for adapted NCF courses and established the concept of method statements to promote the development of individual sports, the scheme highlighted three issues which affect the development of coaching programmes for people with disabilities:

    (a) policies need to be reviewed and continuously adapted to changing circumstances. The introduction of CCT offers the opportunity to review existing or proposed method statements as future contracts are prepared for renewal

    (b) schemes which require local authorities to co-ordinate activities between departments and with outside agencies do not fit easily into the current structure for providing for people with disabilities. Therefore, there is a need to consider carefully the appropriateness of the existing structures

    (c) there is a concern that the arrival of CCT may restrict the opportunities which are made available to people with disabilities, particularly through mainstream local authority recreation programmes. It is imperative that this is not allowed to happen.

These issues aside, the scheme has produced a valuable input into the coaching 'system' for people with disabilities. However, the full implementation of this type of work requires a long-term commitment by local authorities to the preparation, implementation and evaluation of the schemes. The NCF course adaptations proposed have been well received and the draft method statements welcomed by those local authorities who have been sent pilot copies. The Scheme Leader is hopeful that the policy statement developed can now be widely adopted as the basis upon which other local authorities can build their own local policies.

9   Summary and Conclusion

The Every Body Active team feel that many useful lessons have been learnt as the implementation phase has developed. However, they believe **five fundamental concepts** need to be applied to all programmes aimed at people with disabilities. These five 'keywords', and the associated areas of action, are briefly summarized below.

The first, and most important, is **TRUST.** Developing positive attitudes, negotiating with disabled people through sensitive discussion, and breaking stereotypes in providers' minds, including social stereotypes, are all vital first steps. Establishing public policy statements that demonstrate the political will to put plans into action is also paramount.

The second concept is **CONFIDENCE.** Working with complete individuals through a life counselling approach has been fundamental to all the schemes. Developing motivational programmes to break down the apathy, amongst both disabled people and providers, has been a significant aspect of the counselling. Developing the 'I can do it' approach and fostering independence is also a major factor in the confidence building process, but this undoubtedly takes time. Confidence cannot be built up overnight.

Thirdly, providing **OPPORTUNITIES** to take part which are appropriate to people with disabilities. Identifying restrictions, developing knowledge and awareness, providing support services and transport and, most important of all, ensuring positive experiences are common factors in any sports development programme. For people with disabilities they assume even greater importance.

The fourth keyword is **POSITIVE ACTION.** The preparation of Action Plans and method statements, the provision of staff awareness training, coach education programmes, and sensitive outreach work are all examples of this approach. However, the most fundamental lesson from Every Body Active is the need for a long term commitment to such programmes. Provision for disability has often been one-off pieces of action, rather than part of an integrated development programme.

Finally, the **INVOLVEMENT** of the people with disabilities themselves. Involvement in planning, in reviewing requirements and in the organization of activities. Listening and talking and adopting a consumer-based approach that involves friends and families as well. In short, getting away from the position where able-bodied people make all the decisions.

In conclusion, it is evident that all too often in the past programmes for people with disabilities have tried to go from OPPORTUNITIES straight to INVOLVEMENT and have been disappointing as a result. Every Body Active has shown that success has to be built on developing the TRUST, building the CONFIDENCE and ensuring that POSITIVE ACTION involves people with disabilities in the decision-making process. Only then will the reality live up to the expectations for both the service providers and the people with disabilities themselves. The Sports Council believes the schemes offer excellent 'models' for others to replicate to ensure that the reality of a positive sporting experience is available to all people with disabilities throughout the country.

10   References

Sports Council (1988a) **Into the Nineties**. Sports Council, London.

Sports Council (1988b) **Participation Demonstration Projects: Every Body Active.** Sunderland Polytechnic, et al. Phase 1 Monitoring Report. Establishing the Scheme and the Research Phase. Sports Council, Manchester.

Sports Council, (1991) **Participation Demonstration Projects: Every Body Active.** Sunderland Polytechnic, et al. Phase 2 Monitoring Report. Implementing the Schemes, Sports Council, Manchester.

Williams, T. (1988) (Editor) **Working Papers of the Every Body Active Demonstration Project**. Sunderland Polytechnic, Sunderland.

PART THREE

HEALTH RELATED EXERCISE

EXERCISE, EXERSENSE, EXERSCIENCE AND EXCELLENCE

B.H. ROSS

School of Physical Education, University of Otago, Dunedin, Aotearoa (NZ)

Keywords: Aerobics, Exercise Science, Formal Exercise, Physical Education, Research, Swedish Gymnastics, Work Physiology.

Punchy music, designer gear, classy expensive gymnasiums, chromed exercise machines, computer printouts, glossy books - aerobics, has colonized our thinking about, and practice of exercise. Many schools now run aerobic classes as part (and sometimes all) of their physical education programmes. Images of the lean, tanned sexy exercisers (nearly always white women) constantly flicker across our TV screens to **sell** anything from softdrinks to 4 wheel drives. But does **exercise** as a commodity actually utilize knowledge from **science** to encourage **sensible** physical activity which may assist individuals to attain **excellence** in health or happiness?

Exercise to music is not new. Those of us not old enough to actually remember have never-the-less heard the stories or seen the photographs showing children performing **physical drill.** These regimented, formal, stereotyped exercises lead by authoritarian instructors appear to be mindless physical jerks and as such appear to have no place in today's physical education programmes. But are they less mindless or less authoritarian than **aerobics**?

This paper comments on the crucial role that formal exercise has played in the development of physical education as a core school subject by outlining the original function of Swedish Gymnastics. It also argues for an acceptance of formal exercise as the essential unique component of physical education by critiquing **aerobics** and the role of **work physiology research** within physical education.

Per Henrik Ling (1776-1839) was a fascinating man. Founder of the Central Institute of Gymnastics in Stockholm in 1814 he served as its Director until 1839. A fencing master, a poet and an expert on Norse mythology he taught medical and military gymnastics where he devised a system of formal exercises for both women and men (Georgii, 1854; Westerblad, 1909). His gymnastics arose out of his experience in teaching soldiers and his intimate knowledge of current scientific and medical beliefs. He believed that formal gymnastics were an important educational tool which could help develop and maintain the health and well-being of ordinary people. The effectiveness and popularity of Ling's form of exercise led to its adoption in English primary schools in the late 1800's (McIntosh,1968) and the establishment by Madam Bergman-Osterberg of a physical education training college for women in 1884 (Fletcher, 1984). The English experience subsequently influenced the physical education programmes in the developing pakeha school system in Aotearoa.

Ling's Swedish gymnastics were a carefully structured form of deliberate exercise. They are perhaps best characterized by Thulin's (Stothart,1974) description:

> By gymnastics we mean systematically arranged bodily movements which aim at educating, developing and maintaining the physical and psychical qualities of the individual.

Thulin in his Gymnasic Hand-book and its accompanying Gymnastik Atlas (Thulin, 1945) expanded, collated and systematized Ling's system of Swedish Gymnastics. Ling was very clear about the purpose of formal exercise. These aims have been formalized by Thulin (Thulin, 1947):

Gymnastics should aim at:

(a)   maintaining and eventually improving the functional efficiency of the internal organs, especially those of circulation and respiration and respiration and the nervous system;
(b)   maintaining and eventually improving the normal mobility of the joints and functional efficiency of the muscles;
(c)   promoting a good and aesthetically pleasing posture;
(d)   paying due attention to the demands of practical life and promoting an appropriate, labour-saving style of movement and rest; both by means of the applied exercises which develop strength, quickness and endurance and also the qualities of mind which promote capability of action (such as the correct estimation of ones own powers and self-control, courage and energy), all this with as little expenditure of energy as possible;
(e)   furthering the formation of character and personality, preserving balance of mind, cheerfulness and pleasure in work by giving the exercises an interesting and purposeful content and making them arouse a feeling of happiness (psychical influence).

Perhaps few of us[1] would quarrel with these aims if they were applied to physical education. They make intuitive sense and fit very well with the so-called **learning**

---

[1]   I'm not sure who 'us' are; physical educators seem to be a dying breed giving ground to 'kinesiologists, exercise or work physiologists, ergonomists, biomechanics, psychomotor-psychologists, sports scientists' and the like. See Smithells (1964) 'A Plethora of Terms.' PAS's Lecture Notes in Principles of Exercise Study and Resource Manual. B.H. Ross (Ed.) School of Physical Education, University of Ontago pp. 9-12. 1981.

outcomes listed in the 1987 Physical Education Syllabus for Aotearoa. But how were these ideals to be implemented through Swedish gymnastics? What was (or is, or should be) the function of formal gymnastics? Ling in his book 'Menneskeorganismens Lagar' ('The Laws of the Human Body'), (Groner, 1939), written between 1820 and 1839 states his **rules** for formal gymnastics:

(a) The object of gymnastics is to develop the body by the help of certain exercises which must be correct.

(b) These exercises are said to be correct when they are based on the constitution of the body to be developed.

(c) The body is said to be correctly developed when all its components are in as perfect harmony as the aptitude of the person in question permits.

(d) The human body cannot develop further than the natural aptitude of the individual in question permits.

(e) The constitutional qualities of the human being may be concealed, but not destroyed by incorrect exercises.

(f) These innate qualities may be prevented from making their appearance because of incorrect exercises, or by exercises which have not any special aim. A wrong exercise may thus more injure than improve the harmonious development of the body.

(g) Unilateral exercises are more difficult both to learn and retain than bilateral which make everything seem easier and simpler.

(h) With most people, stiffness and immobility of certain parts of the body is usually the result of an exaggerated development of one part of the body which is always accompanied by corresponding weakness in other parts of the body.

(i) By distributing the exertions evenly, the super-strength of a certain component can be toned down, to the advantage of weaker parts of the body, which will then be strengthened.

(j) Personal strength or weakness is not determined by the surface-area of certain parts of the body, but by the relations between them.

(k) All real and growing strength is a concentration of the ability of the different components to react. This concentration must, therefore, take place at the same moment if a maximum of power is to be attained.

(l) Health and strength are thus interdependent. Both depend on the different components of the body being in harmony.

(m) If the novice commences his gymnastics with the most simple exercises, he may proceed step by step to the most difficult ones without the slightest danger because he knows his power and what he (sic) is doing, and is also aware of his (sic) abilities.

Remember these rules were written more than one hundred and fifty years ago! Where today can you find such an extensive set of **rules or principles** for an exercise programme? Certainly the 'Fitness Leader's Exercise Bible' (Egger et al, 1987) as an example of a recent exercise text shows no such wisdom. No clear reasons for exercise are given in this widely used aerobics manual and the 600 exercises described include 158 weight training exercises and 153 stretching exercises as well as a series of exercises for various areas of the body. Although lip service is given to progression and variation and potentially dangerous exercises[2] are carefully described this book contains no clear objectives for each exercise and gives little guidance on individual physical activity needs. In a sense it is a catalogue of exercises which have no meaning as they have no immediately obvious purpose. This type of exercise book is rather like a recipe book which just lists some ingredients and then presents them as a satisfactory cook book!

Although this 'Fitness Leader's Bible' is much better than most of the popular exercise literature it still illustrates, I think, the mindlessness of our present day preoccupation with 'aerobics' or drill to music! Contrast the 'Fitness Leader's Bible' with Thulin's thorough collation of Ling's exercises. This classic collection of some 6,000 carefully graded exercises all illustrated with both line drawings and photographs details the purpose of each exercise and provides clear anatomical and physiological explanations for each set of exercises. Certainly not a mindless catalogue of exercises but rather a scholarly documentation of exercises based on sound anatomical and physiological principles. This collation is rather like a recipe book which lists ingredients along with an explanation of how each ingredient can be used in different dishes but it leaves the construction of the meal to the individual teacher/exerciser. Thulin's compilation of his and Ling's work stresses form, grace, individuality, joy and skill all of which are clearly missing from the 'Fitness Leader's Bible'.

Thulin also makes it abundantly clear that Ling believed that formal gymnastics should meet individual physiological needs and not become a dull regimented series of physical jerks by quoting a basic principle propounded by Ling (circa 1834-40): 'Gymnastic movements must be founded on the needs of the human organism and its laws'.

It is also obvious that Ling believed that his system of formal gymnastics should undergo constant revision as science was used to study medicine and human function.

> ..then, within a few generations, the newly-born gymnastics will die unless it be scientifically nourished by physicians and gymnasts, but I beg to God that coming doctors and educationalists will gradually extend and improve these experiments of mine.

Has current physical education lived up to Ling's hopes with respect to research on exercise? I know that aerobics are not what everyone teaches today in physical education. But after 20 plus years of teaching in a University School of Physical Education I find that the general public still views physical educators as a group of super-fit individuals who teach people physical jerks. So I believe our present identity is created by the media image of aerobics whether we like it or not. And to me aerobics have not resulted from the research which Ling hoped would improve and adapt his gymnastics.

---

2   The evidence for so-called **dangerous exercises** is scant, equivocal and open to criticism. The attention that physical education pays to this 'Sports Medicine' approach to exercise and research highlights the paucity of our imagination and the timidity of our professionalism.

If we look again at Ling's 'Laws of the Human Body' we find that medical, or physical education research has not added much to Ling's insight about the nature of beneficial exercise. We know from the work of Christensen (1933), Hill (1927) and Dill (1974) that two basic 'laws' govern human response to repeated exercise. These are the **law of overload** and the **law of diminishing returns**. That is physiological function (strength, endurance or suppleness) improves dramatically at first in response to a rather light intensity of training. However as improvement occurs the intensity of the exercise must increase but the magnitude of the improvement is then proportionally smaller. Recent studies (Astrand and Rodahl, 1986) have verified these two laws and provide numerous examples of cardiovascular responses to increasing training stimuli. There are fewer studies on muscle function (DeLorme, 1945) but these too show that the **law of overload** and the **law of diminishing returns** still apply even though the data supporting them comes from experiments involving, mainly, men doing intense aerobic or strength exercise (Astrand and Rodahl, 1986). But let's be honest, even these principles did not originate from the investigations of work physiologists. Milo the 6th Century BC Greek athlete supposedly lifted a calf every day until he could lift a fully grown bull!

Interestingly, few studies exist which attempt to look at the physiological responses to formal exercise. What studies do exist are mainly in the area of physiotherapy (Wessell & Van Huss, 1974) and these do not provide clear evidence of the benefits of formal exercise programmes but rather try to assess the clinical effectiveness of particular exercises used for therapy. It is interesting to note that we have a whole profession based on the idea that exercise is good therapy yet the nature of the 'hard science' evidence supporting this idea is obscure, fragmentary and often contradictory. But what is humbling to me as a physical educator is the realization that work physiology research in physical education has had little or no direct effect on my understanding of the benefits or effectiveness of formal exercise. Certainly we have a lot of detailed information about the physiological responses of the human body to and during vigorous exercise. But this information has not provided us with principles, theories or laws about the practice of exercise which improve on those proposed by Ling. As an academic physical educator with a specialized knowledge in neurophysiology I am dismayed at how little of my specialized research and knowledge is applicable to the teaching, practice or understanding of exercise. For example my specific research interest is human motor unit recruitment (Thomas, Ross & Stein, 1986) which means I know a great deal about the activity of human motor units in a small hand muscle but I cannot explain how a baby puts her thumb in her mouth or how Jacqueline du Pres produced magical music.

As physical educators we have to be brave as we face the next century. We have to counter the madness of exercise as a commodity, we have to stand up to the 'sports scientists', 'work physiologists' and other 'researchers' in supposedly academic physical education by demonstrating the inadequacy of their 'normal science incremental encyclopedic' approach to scientific research (Nelson, Megill & McCloskey, 1987). What we have to do is dream a future where physical educators are not ashamed of exercise as the focus of our skill, expertise and knowledge; we have to dream a future where physical educators take pride in helping people to take control of their own bodies by enabling them to understand how their bodies work; we have to dream a future where physical educators are artists in the way they encourage people to learn to creatively use and experience their bodies; we have to dream a future where research on exercise is holistic, people centered, open ended and imaginatively striving for useful principles; we have to dream a future where physical educators can awaken people to the joy of simple movement.

Perhaps in dreaming our futures we can use exersense and exerscience to fulfill Philip Smithells'[3] dream of excellence in physical education.

> The teaching of exercise is one of the most difficult and underrated tasks which the physical educator undertakes. It requires elaborate and thorough preparation, skilful execution and continuous personal vigilance. It is also the only unique skill of the physical educator, and it is a field which takes many years of application and practice to perfect.

References

Astrand, P.O. and Rodahl, K. (1986) **Textbook of Work Physiology.** McGraw-Hill. N.Y. Chapt. 10.

Christensen, H. (1933) **Arbeitsphysiologie**, 4:128-202, 453-502.

DeLorme, T.L. (1945) **Journal of Bone and Joint Surgery** 27:645-667.

Dill, D.B. (1974) **Science and Medicine of Exercise and Sport.** W.R. Johnson & E. Burskirk (ed) 2nd Edition. Harper & Row, N.Y. pp. 37-41.

Egger, G. et al (1987) **The Fitness Leader's Exercise Bible.** Kangaroo Press, Kenthurst, Aus.

Fletcher, S. (1984) **Women First. The Female Tradition in English Physical Education 1880-1980.** Athlone Press, London.

Georgii, A. (1854) **A Biographical Sketch of the Swedish Poet and Gymnasiarch,** Per Henry (sic) Ling. H. Bailliere, London.

Groner, S. (1939) **Lingiaden Stockholm 1939 Kongressen.** p. 170.

Hill, A.V. (1927) **Living Machinery.** G. Bell & Son Ltd, London.

Ling, P.H. **General Principles of Gymnastics** (circa: 1834-1840). Cited by Maja Carlquist, Lingiaden Stockholm Kongressen 1939, p. 61.

McIntosh, P. (1968) **Physical Education in England Since 1800.** Camelot Press Ltd, Southampton.

Nelson, J.S., Megill, A. & McCloskey, D.N. (eds) (1987) **The Rhetoric of the Human Sciences.** The University of Wisconson Press, Wisconsin.

Stothart (1974) **The Development of Physical Education in New Zealand.** Heinman Educational Books, Auckland.

Thomas, C.K., Ross, B.H. & Stein, R.B. (1986) Motor-unit recruitment in human first dorsal interosseous muscle for static contractions in three different directions. **Journal of Neurophysiology.** 55:1017-1029.

Thulin, J.H. (1945) **Gymnastikatlas.** Sydsvenska Gymnastikinstitutet, Lund.

Thulin, J.H. (1947) **Gymnastic Hand-book.** South Swedish Gymnastic Institute, Lund. p.22.

Wessell, J. & Van Huss, W. (1974) **Science of Exercise Medicine and Sport.** pp. 439-454.

Westerblad, C. (1909) **Tidscrift I Gymnastik.** 4:1000-1053.

---

3   Professor Philip Smithells (1910-1978) founded the School of Physical Education at the University of Otago in 1947. He served as Director of the School until 1975. Quotation is from his personal lecture notes dated (1974).

ATTITUDES AND HEALTH-RELATED EXERCISE: REVIEW AND CRITIQUE

R. ANDREW SMITH[1] AND STUART BIDDLE[2]
[1]*Kerland Sports Services and Physical Education Association Research Centre*
[2]*Physical Education Association Research Centre, University of Exeter, Exeter, England*

Abstract
It is common for those promoting the adoption and maintenance of physical activity and exercise to suggest that changes in attitude are a necessary, even sufficient, precursor of changes in behaviour. However, research in social psychology has revealed a complex interaction between attitudinal and social factors in the prediction of health behaviour change. This paper reviewed and critiqued selected attitude models that have been tested, or have relevance, for the adoption and maintenance of health-related exercise. In particular, reference was made to Fishbein & Ajzen's 'Theory of Reasoned Action', Ajzen's 'Theory of Planned Behaviour', as well as models proposed by Triandis ('Theory of Social Behaviour') and Rogers ('Protection Motivation Theory'). These approaches were reviewed and critiqued with a view to providing directions for research and interventions in education and public health policy.
Keywords: Attitude, Behavioural Intention, Health-Related Exercise, Perceived Behavioural Control.

1   Introduction

It is suggested that changes in attitudes towards exercise are necessary, even sufficient, precursors of change in exercise behaviour, and a number of public health strategies have focussed on trying to change peoples' attitudes. However, research in social psychology has revealed complex interactions between attitudinal and social factors in the prediction of health behaviour change.

This paper, therefore, will review and critique key attitude models from social and health psychology, question their use in health promotion, and make suitable applications, where appropriate, for the adoption and maintenance of health-related exercise.

2   Theory of Reasoned Action

The Theory of Reasoned Action (TRA; Fishbein & Ajzen, 1975) has been one of the most influential attitude models in social psychology.

2.1 *The model*

Fishbein & Ajzen (1975) postulate that behaviour can be predicted from behavioural intention, attitudes, and social norms. The model is shown in Figure 1.

A central feature of the model is the concept of correspondence. This states that the components of the model must be directly related to the behaviour under investigation. If that behaviour is jogging, for example, questions must relate to jogging rather than general exercise programmes if jogging behaviour is to be predicted with any confidence.

2.2 *Research*

Riddle (1980) found a strong relationship between behavioural intention and jogging behaviour ($r=0.82$) and a significant difference in the beliefs of adult joggers compared with non-exercisers. Olson & Zanna (1982) also found support for the TRA in predicting adherence to a health club exercise programme. Less supportive of the model are the results of Godin & Shephard (1986). When compared with Bandura's (1986) Social Cognitive Theory (SCT), Dzwaltowski (1989) found that the TRA was less predictive of exercise patterns for college students.

2.3 *Critique*

Insufficient attention has been paid to the measurement of the behaviour under investigation. Without an accurate measure of the behaviour, the principle of correspondence cannot be applied. This casts doubt on some of the research just reviewed as Riddle (1980) used self-reports of jogging behaviour, Godin & Shephard (1986) measured only intentions and not behaviour itself, and Dzweltowski (1989) used several different exercise modalities. The definition of the behaviour and its measurement presents particular problems for the study of exercise adherence.

2.4 *Application*

The TRA reminds educators that attitude theories recognize a broad definition of attitude. The TRA not only considers attitude, but also social norm beliefs and behavioural intention. The belief structures underpinning the direct measure of attitudes can also help to steer exercise promotion campaigns. The TRA has shown the importance of spouse support and also the need to emphasize that exercise need not take up a great deal of time.

3   Theory of Planned Behaviour

The Theory of Planned Behaviour (TPB; Ajzen, 1985) is an extension of the TRA.

3.1 *The model*

The TPB is the same as the TRA with the exception of the additional variable 'perceived behavioural control' (PBC). Ajzen (1985) claims that PBC is similar to Bandura's concept of self-efficacy. The TPB is shown in Figure 1.

Ajzen suggests that the TRA is sufficient when investigating behaviour that is under volitional control. In situations where control over the target behaviour is incomplete PBC is required. PBC is defined as the belief concerning how easy or difficult performing the behaviour is likely to be. This concept of control may be particularly relevant in an exercise setting.

3.2 *Research*

The TPB has not been tested as much as the TRA and is only now being used to investigate exercise. Gatch & Kendzierski (1990) found that PBC significantly increased the prediction of intention to attend an exercise class over and above that of attitude and social norm, although no measure of actual exercise behaviour was taken.

3.3 *Critique*

The concept of PBC requires further clarification. It has still to be demonstrated that it is the same, or similar to, self-efficacy. Standardized measures of PBC have not been used when testing the TPB and this has hindered comparisons across studies.

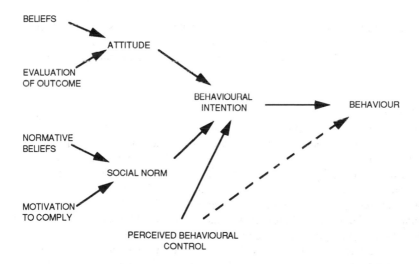

Figure 1.   *Theories of Reasoned Action and Planned Behaviour. TRA excludes the variable 'perceived behavioural control'.*

3.4 *Application*

Paradoxically, this attitude theory shows the importance of other psychological perspectives when attempting to promote complex behaviours such as exercise adherence. Campaigns which focus purely on attitude change are in danger of ignoring control and confidence factors deemed important within the TPB.

4   Theory of Social Behaviour

The Theory of Social Behaviour (TSB) is attributed to Triandis (1977). It is a similar formulation to the preceding models.

4.1 *The model*

Triandis suggests that behaviour is a function of prior behaviour (habit), intention, and facilitating conditions. Volitional control is thought to decrease as habit increases. Behavioural intention is thought to be related to social factors, emotional reaction to the behaviour, and value of the perceived consequences.

4.2 *Research*

Less research has been reported on the TSB compared with the TRA. However, Valois et al. (1988) compared the Triandis model with the TRA in predicting exercise intention and behaviour. Although they found that the TSB was a better predictor of intention, the two models were equally successful in predicting actual exercise behaviour.

4.3 *Critique*

The quantity of research using the TSB in health-related contexts is low, thus there are a number of measurement and conceptual issues that remain unclear. When studies have been conducted, they have not always included a direct measure of behaviour.

4.4 *Application*

The TSB does point to the importance of a number of factors likely to lead to exercise. However, the applications at this stage must be tentative due to the paucity of specific research. However, Valois et al (1988) concluded that community exercise promotion should account for the fact that exercise does require volitional thought and is not likely to become a subconscious habit. This suggests that the intensity of exercise, and other perceived barriers to exercise such as time constraints, must be reduced. Valois et al. found that their subjects viewed exercise as hard work; this perception has to be reduced or changed. Related to this, they suggested that greater emphasis needs to be placed on exercise enjoyment as they found that intention was related to the emotional aspects of exercise.

5   Protection Motivation Theory

Protection Motivation Theory [PMT; Rogers (1983)] is a conceptual model based on the role of 'fear appeals' or 'health threats' in health behavioural change.

5.1 *The model*

Protection motivation is the motivating force resulting from a number of cognitive mediating processes which centre on two appraisals: the threat appraisal and the coping appraisal. The threat appraisal is determined by the relative strengths of perceived vulnerability to a health problem and its possible severity, and the intrinsic and extrinsic rewards attached to the health behaviour. The coping appraisal is determined by feelings of efficacy or confidence, and the costs of making a response.

5.2 *Research*

Wurtele & Maddux (1987) found that exercise intention was increased by appeals based on vulnerability and self-efficacy, whereas threat appeals were ineffective. Robberson & Rogers (1988) found that appeals to disease prevention could be effective in promoting exercise intentions.

5.3 *Critique*

PMT uses concepts, such as self-efficacy, which have been found to be powerful predictors of behaviour in other situations. However, the model was developed to study health decision-making in the context of health threats. The extent to which sedentary habits are perceived as health threats by such people has usually been questioned.

5.4 *Application*

The main strength of the PMT is that it contributes to the understanding of the processes effecting persuasion and persuasive appeals. Public health campaigns are based on the belief that 'appeals' can change behaviour. PMT research does suggest that perceptions of vulnerability and feelings of self-efficacy can influence health-related intentions, including exercise.

6   Discussion

The common assumption that positive attitudes change behaviours is too simplistic for effective public health interventions. However, it would be wise for those involved in the promotion of exercise to be aware of attitude research in health and exercise. In summary, the following could be said to be 'known':

(a)   attitude measures will predict behaviour more strongly when the measures are specific to the behaviour in question, but

(b)   other factors will predict behaviour, such as social norms, thus leading to attitude-behaviour relationships that account for relatively small amounts of behavioural variance;

(c)   behavioural intention is more reliably predicted than exercise itself;
(d)   intentions are necessary, although not sufficient, to predict exercise.
The following require further research:
(e)   the nature of the attitude/social norm interaction for different groups;
(f)   the role of persuasive appeals in attitudes and exercise adoption;
(g)   the relationship between intention and action in both supervised and
       unsupervised exercise settings, and for different groups.

7   References

Ajzen, I. (1985) From intentions to actions: A Theory of Planned Behaviour, in **Action Control: From Cognition to Behaviour** (eds J. Kuhl and J. Beckmann), Springer-Verlag, Berlin, pp. 11-39.

Bandura, A. (1986) **Social Foundations of Thought and Action: A Social Cognitive Theory**. Prentice-Hall, Englewood Cliffs, NJ.

Dzewaltowski, D.A. (1989) Toward a model of exercise motivation. **Journal of Sport & Exercise Psychology**, 11, 251-269.

Fishbein, M. & Ajzen, I. (1975) **Belief, Attitude, Intention, and Behaviour: An Introduction to Theory and Research**. Addison-Wesley, Reading, Mass.

Gatch, C.L. & Kendzierski, D. (1990) Predicting exercise intentions: The Theory of Planned Behaviour. **Research Quarterly for Exercise & Sport**, 61, 100-102.

Godin, G. & Shephard, R.J. (1986) Psychosocial factors influencing intentions to exercise of young students from grades 7 to 9. **Research Quarterly for Exercise & Sport**, 57, 41-52.

Olson, J.M. & Zanna, M.P. (1982) **Predicting Adherence to a Programme of Physical Exercise: An Empirical Study**. Report prepared for Ontario Ministry of Tourism and Recreation, Toronto, Canada.

Riddle, P. (1980) Attitudes, beliefs, behavioural intentions and behaviours of women and men toward regular jogging. **Research Quarterly for Exercise & Sport**, 51, 663-674.

Robberson, M.R. & Roger, R.W. (1988) Beyond fear appeals: Negative and positive fear appeals to health and self-esteem. **Journal of Applied Social Psychology**, 18, 277-287.

Rogers, R.W. (1983) Cognitive and physiological processes in attitude change: A revised theory of protection motivation, in **Social Psychophysiology** (eds J. Cacioppo and R. Petty), Guildford, New York.

Triandis, H.C. (1977) **Interpersonal behaviour**. Monterey: Brooks/Cole.

Valois, P., Desharnais, R. & Godin, G. (1988) A comparison of the Fishbein and Ajzen and the Triandis attitudinal models for the prediction of exercise intention and behaviour. **Journal of Behavioral Medicine**, 11, 459-472.

Wurtele, S.K. & Maddux, J.E. (1987) Relative contributions of protection motivation theory components in predicting exercise intentions and behaviour. **Health Psychology**, 6, 453-466.

HEALTH BASED PHYSICAL EDUCATION AND THE HEALTH IN PRIMARY SCHOOLS PROJECT[1]

D. COLQUHOUN
School of Education, Deakin University, Geelong, Victoria, Australia

1   Introduction

Cardiovascular disease, principally atherosclerotic coronary heart disease, is a major problem still facing the western world. Evidence suggesting that, in this case, Australian children are not immune to the problems of coronary heart disease, is profound and well documented. Indeed, the clinical disease becomes manifest in adult years but there is evidence to suggest that the problem has its origins in childhood. Clearly, schools are an important focus in attempts to combat the disease before risk factors promote the development of indices of morbidity.

Most preventative strategies incorporate several aspects along the structural and behavioural dimension continuum. In health promotion generally there is a tension between these two dimensions and in particular, where the emphasis should lie. For example, are structural modifications to the food production chain from the farmer/grower through to the processor and finally onto the consumer, more beneficial in improving health than simple behaviour changes? And what are the long term implications of such modifications (or to use the currently in-vogue question 'How is health **sustainable?**')?

2   The Health In Primary Schools (HIPS) Project

To attempt to address this problem of sustainable health for children, a research and development project has been developed in Victoria, Australia, by Monash University and Victoria College, Burwood. The project is attempting to promote an awareness of the need for health and fitness programmes in particular, which are first of all achievable, and secondly which are sustainable and enduring. By this, the project means behaviours (and other health enhancing activities) which will enable children to maintain and improve on their health over several years. It is this 'futuristic perspective' which is a major problem for health education. Indeed, it is a

[1] This project is funded for three years by The Victorian Health Promotion Foundation. I would like to thank the Board of Management of HIPS Project for their generous support which enabled the development of this presentation.

slippery and elusive concept which is difficult to grasp or address, especially in the school setting.

The Victorian Health Promotion Foundation (VHPF) was recently established by the State government of Victoria by the Tobacco Act (1987) to promote health and prevent disease in Victoria. The Tobacco Act provides for the VHPF to distribute funds raised by a levy on the wholesale of tobacco products. Last year the levy (5%) was about $25 million. The VHPF has five major programme areas:

2.1   *The Replacement of Tobacco Sponsorship*

The relationship between smoking tobacco, health and sport is a major concern to the VHPF. With this in mind they have initiated a campaign to buy out tobacco sponsorship of sporting events, teams, and locations. Most major sporting teams now carry the logo of 'QUIT' somewhere on their uniforms and the QUIT emblem can be instantly recognized at most major sporting venues. Indeed, some of you may be aware of the public and political debate over the location of the Australian Grand Prix for motorcycle racing. There was a degree of controversy over the present site (in Victoria) and the cyclists' right to promote their sponsors' names and logos both on their uniforms and on their bicycles. It is expected that QUIT will eliminate tobacco sponsorship of sport over the next five years. Approximately 20% of the VHPF's funding will be devoted to the replacement of tobacco sponsorship.

2.2   *Sport Sponsorship*

All types of sporting bodies are eligible for funding from the VHPF, ranging from competitive to non-competitive sports. In particular, the VHPF prefers to fund those sports which can overtly exhibit a relationship between their activities and the enhancement of health in the community. Disadvantage and social justice are two key elements of this funding. About 30% of the VHPF's funding will be devoted to the sponsorship of sport.

2.3   *Sponsorship of the the Arts*

The VHPF will sponsor a diverse range of art and cultural projects which encourage excellence in their field. Again, preference is given to those artistic endeavours which promote health in the community. Dance groups, theatre groups, family projects, and structures are just some of the areas of funding. At least 7% of the VHPF's funding will be spent on the arts.

2.4   *Health Promotion*

Major health promotion organizations as well as community based groups can all apply for funding to the VHPF. Health promoting campaigns also receive funding for activities such as promoting specific prevention and illness awareness strategies. At least 30% of the VHPF's funding is devoted to this category.

2.5 *Research*

Public and charitable organizations will be supported by the VHPF in their research endeavours. In particular, biomedical, behavioural and public health research activities will be funded. Often the research projects submitted to the VHPF will be assessed internationally for their credibility and worth.

3   Structure of the HIPS Project

The HIPS project has been funded for three years commencing in 1989 (July). The project is divided into three distinct stages - approximately one stage per year (apart from the initial establishment time needed to initiate the project in the first instance):

3.1 *Stage 1*

In this first stage (July 1989 - January 1991) 14 lighthouse schools from the state, Catholic and independent systems are working on and developing their own school based strategies which will operate across each school. These schools were selected on the basis of their submissions to the HIPS Board of Management and each school received approximately $8,000 to support their activities which included: teacher in-service, teacher release, funding school canteen staff, weekend camps, equipment, capital expenditures such as food processors, running tracks, exercise stations and so on. These submissions attempted to capture the uniqueness of the given school and what each school could offer the project. Schools were not given a programme to teach. In some schools the proposals were developed largely by individuals, say the physical education teacher, but in most schools groups of teachers formed communities and co-opted parents and local community representatives from various bodies.

3.2 *Stage 2*

This second stage (January 1991 - April 1992) will be the pilot stage and will involve approximately 25 schools. These schools are being sought with support from the local school support centres and the health education consultants for the region. These schools, which will only receive about $1,000, will initiate the findings and developments of the lighthouse stage. It is hoped and anticipated that the lighthouse schools will still be operating their programmes but they will not be receiving any financial support from the HIPS project.

3.3 *Stage 3*

This stage will involve a culmination of all the evaluations and reflections of the people involved in the project. In particular, system advice will be given to the Ministry of Education (Victoria), the Catholic Education body, the independent school system, the Department of Health (Victoria), the Australian Council for Health, Physical Education and Recreation (ACHPER), and of course, the VHPF. Policy recommendations and costings will be made to the relevant authorities so that the findings of the project can be implemented state-wide.

3.4 *Objectives of the HIPS Project*

The project has three major aims which focus on the health status of Australian primary age school children:

(a)   To promote healthy and sustainable lifestyles which will continue into adult life.
(b)   To develop a programme of health related fitness which incorporates regular exercise and related studies in human biology and nutrition.
(c)   To develop an integrated approach to improving lifestyles encompassing all aspects of the school's educational programme.

Clearly, nutrition and exercise have been targeted by the HIPS project in an attempt to give the schools a focus. All the schools have taken these two aspects on-board to varying degrees. There are already many existing packages and materials available for schools to modify, translate and develop in the areas of nutrition and exercise. For example, the National Heart Foundation of Australia has published a widely used resource 'The Heart Health Manual' which is largely a classroom based programme aimed at reducing coronary risk factors in children. Several schools have developed, or are in the process of developing, a 'Daily Fitness' programme which the children will experience each day. Some schools have been particularly innovative in their approach to the HIPS project. I will just report briefly on a few of them.

3.5 *The RED Programme (Recreation, Exercise and Diet)*

Geelong East Primary school is in a low socio-economic area and so decided that access to recreational facilities would be a major problem for its charges. The school has initiated a support scheme for children to experience a variety of activities in the locality of the school. The local council has also supported the programme with funding for capital expenditures - this has allowed the school to divert funds to supporting the recreational aspects of the programme. In addition, the school has also focused on daily fitness and the notion of a healthy canteen. It is encouraging to note that so far not one school has reported a downturn in profits from orientating their canteen towards more 'healthy' foods.

3.6 *Grovedale Families Fit Together*

In one of the most innovative projects Grovedale primary school has targetted the family in an attempt to encourage the concept of sustainable healthy practices. Families exercise together three times per week and then meet on one weekend per month for a special health related excursion. All the family activities are linked to classroom lessons. So far the themes have included a surf carnival and a 'how to surf' afternoon, canoeing, hiking and bushwalking. Because of the success of the school's project, the school has attracted funds from other sources including the local council and school support centre.

3.7 *CATCHES - Children Actively Teaching Children Health and Exercise Strategies.*

Beechwood primary school has developed this peer teaching programme so that grade 6 children teach grade 2/3 children a whole range of activities in the personal development, nutrition, exercise and health areas. CATCHES is based on the premise that peer pressure has a very strong influence on children. Indeed, since health education may be seen to be about establishing positive attitudes, decision making and lifestyles, then positive peer support in this direction may be an effective tool in promoting healthy behaviours. In addition to the CATCHES programme Beechworth have also initiated a whole string of ideas including: fitness testing, daily fitness, a gross motor programme for the younger grades, a dramatic change in the foods sold in the canteen, links with other health promoting agencies in the Beechworth locality, aerobics for parents, a school physical education uniform, a specialist personal development teacher for 1990, staff and parent professional development, and finally, a Tryathlon-Lapathon fund raiser for the whole school.

3.8 *Food to Go, Grow and Glow*

Billanook primary school began their HIPS project with a week of activities aimed at improving the nutrition available to the pupils at the school. A local nutritionist spoke on the benefits of healthy eating and the canteen now has creative suggestions for the children to try as well as a healthy eating cookbook which the entire school has been involved in producing.

3.9 *PEACH - Personal Exercise and Community Health*

Riddells Creek primary school has made a concerted effort to establish links with its local community. Sporting clubs have been established with the community in the areas of table tennis and volleyball where enjoyment and participation are emphasized. The management of the school's programme also involves members of the local community.

These schools have been deliberately selected because each of them exhibits a particular strength of the HIPS project. Even though the focus of the overall HIPS project is on fitness and nutrition, it is apparent that the schools take these two areas of focus and modify them to suit their own particular setting or circumstances. For instance if we have a close look at one school, Our Lady Star of The Sea school in Ocean Grove, it is clear that they have placed their emphasis on a broad list of topics which include: fitness tests, prevention education, food and nutrition, asthma, surf, stress and relaxation and special needs. Ocean Grove is a small rural town on the Bellarine Peninsula and has what have been called the best and safest beaches in Victoria - hence the emphasis on surfing. Also, the incidence of asthma amongst children on the Peninsula is alarmingly high. The special needs section of the project involves the development of a perceptual motor programme for the younger grades and the school has also emphasized the aspects common to many schools - the canteen and daily fitness. Again like the other schools, attempts are made in the classroom to integrate the HIPS project throughout the curriculum.

4   Key Issues for Curriculum Development

Below is a list of five key issues which are highly related, and yet when we consider them in isolation it is clear that we know very little about health, exercise and their role in the school curriculum. In Australia at least, because the awareness of health and environmental issues and the re-conceptualization of the relationship between the individual and his/her environment, the social and cultural climate is facilitating the interrogation of some of these issues at both the conceptual and practical levels.

4.1   *The Concept of Sustainable Health*

Health is a dynamic and transient process and not a monolithic product. We are constantly striving to attain health as if it were an entity which we could grasp and hold dear. Unfortunately, health is more elusive than we often perceive. Perhaps the following list of questions might lead us to some sort of answer where we can come to grips with some of the gaps in our knowledge:

(a) just how do individuals perceive health?
(b) are there differences in our perceptions in terms of say, exercise and nutrition?
(c) what factors change our perceptions over time?
(d) do we perceive of our bodies differently over time? If so how does this manifest itself?
(e) are physical health measures (fitness) enough of an indicator of overall health on a longitudinal basis?
(f) what structural factors need to be attended to to facilitate sustainable health?
(g) what role can schools really play in encouraging sustainable health?

4.2   *School and Community Relationships*

In the past we have often thought of schools as islands in a sea of community. There was very little interaction between the school and the community and when there was interaction it was usually a one-way process; schools needed something from the local community. This manifests itself in fundraising activities such as door knocks, appeals, gifts from local businesses and so on. Clearly, schools are part of the community and need to reflect this in their practices from pedagogy, curriculum and management. We need to re-think what it is to be a community and what features of a community do we wish to promote. One important issue raised by the HIPS project is just how insular we are in the way we rationalize and operationalize school community links. For example, many schools in the HIPS project have built up excellent relationships with the local Rotary, Apex or health centre yet not one school has approached feminist groups (to say, look at the medicalization of women in the curriculum), environmental groups (such as Greenpeace), trade unions (to look at health and safety at work) and so on.

Quite often how we encounter exercise and fitness in terms of community links has been through 'mapping' exercises where schools simply get the children to literally 'map' out the facilities in their locality. Do not get me wrong - this is an important exercise. However, we have to ask the question 'why stop there?'

Surely, we could use this simple exercise to look at, say, inequalities in provision and access to exercise facilities at the very least.

4.3 *Children, Teachers and Advocacy*

This concept of advocacy is central to the new and emerging health and environmental consciousness. Basically, what it refers to is how and should teachers and/or children initiate social action into issues which they consider to be important to the future of both themselves and their communities. At the heart of the concept of advocacy are the two notions of social justice and equality. Perhaps the problematic nature of advocacy can be best illustrated by an example:

Teacher X works in a school in a suburb where there are plans to build a new chemical factory. Some members of the community are pleased because of the prospect of new jobs and a better infrastructure with more money to build squash courts, football and hockey pitches, and so on. However, the chemicals are carcinogenic and this particular chemical company has an appalling health and safety record and has been banned from operating in some countries. Some of the teacher's pupils could be employed in the factory next year.

The problem - what does the teacher do? what can the teacher do? what can the children do? what has traditionally been the case?

Clearly, this is but one example. Many other examples could just as easily have been used: the local swimming pool is closing down and the teacher's pupils will have to cross four busy roads to get to the next one; the local council is stopping the subsidy for single income parents for entry into the local sporting complex; local parents are being disadvantaged because the new sporting facilities to be built by the multi-national do not have child minding facilities...

The concept of advocacy by both teachers and children (perhaps are two separate issues?) is a major problematic when we consider the potential use and abuse of social action. What the concept does however, is to enable us to recognise that knowledge is not neutral and that there are vested interests and political interests in teaching and the process of schooling. In addition, it highlights the fact that some school subjects have in the past, attempted to get children involved in deliberating 'controversial' issues by initiating them in social action, whereas some subjects like health and physical education have clearly not, as Aronowitz and Giroux (1985) have suggested, made the 'political pedagogical and the pedagogical political'. However, in Australia at least, this trend is changing with a move towards what has been called a 'critical health education' or 'emancipatory health education' (Colquhoun, 1989).

4.4 *The Socio-cultural Construction of Knowledge in Health*

It is widely recognized that the curriculum reflects powerful dominant vested interests. These powerful individuals or groups in society are able to define what is and is not legitimate knowledge (either directly or indirectly) to be taught in our schools. Clearly, the way we teach health for example, reflects influences which have impinged on the curriculum over time. The socio-cultural determinants of the health education curriculum for instance, can be recognized as the development of scientific medicine, dominant perceptions of the human body, and finally, the emergence of the new public health. We ought to examine each of these three determinants to identify the dialectical relationship between each of them and the curriculum and to trace how they influence the curriculum in their various guises. Instances of transformation, refraction, and contradiction are crucial in attempts to understand the curriculum. By recognizing that the curriculum influences and is influenced by these key socio-cultural determinants we are recognizing the fallacy of value neutrality in terms of the social construction of knowledge. Simply **describing** what is happening in schools through thick descriptions of our research is inadequate. I would argue that we should raise the political agenda of our research so that we are indeed attempting to transform 'educational practices, the educational understandings and educational values of those involved in the process, and the social and institutional structures which provide frameworks for their actions' (Carr and Kemmis, 1986).

4.5 *Biography and Curriculum*

We all know that our pedagogy and curriculum are largely shaped by our own biographies and experiences. Sport, physical education and health are just three obvious examples of this. However, what is often neglected in our attempts to research this thing called curriculum, is that as researchers we too have biographies and experiences which shape our responses to, and in fact the instances we are researching. The reflexive nature of researching the curriculum needs to be addressed more seriously by researchers of health and physical education if we are to avoid what Gitlin and colleagues (1989) call the 'realist' position. For example, if we are researching perceptions of the human body within the process of schooling then we need to recognise and account for our own bodies and the perceptions which individuals will have of them. Taking this further, the responses we would get from teachers and children to questions about the body (and related topics such as nutrition, exercise, sexuality) would be completely different (or would they?) if the researcher exhibited a different body 'type' to that of the teacher, the children or even their perceived 'ideal'. My own research for example, is focused on people with physical disabilities and their perceptions of their bodies, health, exercise and sport. I contend that the responses I would glean would be different if I too were physically disabled, or indeed, obese or very thin.

5   Conclusion

The HIPS project has been a major initiative in primary schools in Victoria, Australia. With its focus on sustainable health and school community links, the project is developing key insights into the teaching of health related aspects. The project, because it is school based, is encountering many important issues which can be translated into their broader context. In the next few years the HIPS project will be significant in influencing the development of the school curriculum in Victorian primary schools towards health based issues.

Even though the HIPS project has only been underway for one of its three years, it has still nevertheless encountered several problematics which need to be addressed.

At this point five key issues have been recognized as needing attention by researchers associated with the project; the concept of sustainable health; school-community links; children and teachers as advocates; the socio-cultural construction of knowledge in the curriculum; and finally, the relationship between biography and curriculum. Essentially, and simply, these problematics revolve around the construction and possibilities of the curriculum (and schooling) for initiating social change, the improvement of social justice and amelioration of inequalities.

6   References

Aronowitz, S. and Giroux, H. (1985) **Education Under Seige**, RKP: London.

Carr, W. and Kemmis, S. (1986) **Becoming Critical: Education, Knowledge and Action Research**, Falmer Press: London.

Colquhoun, D. (1989) Emancipatory Health Education and Environmental Education: The New Public Health, **Australian Journal of Environmental Education**, September, 5, 1-8.

Gitlin, A., Siegel, M. and Boru, K. (1989) The Politics of Method: From Leftist Ethnography to Educative Research, **Qualitative Studies in Education**, 2, 3, 237-253.

AN ANALYSIS OF THE TYPICAL ELEMENTARY SCHOOL TIMETABLE: A CONCERN FOR HEALTH AND FITNESS

G.J. FISHBURNE[1] AND D.A. HARPER-TARR[2]
[1] *University of Alberta, Edmonton, Canada*
[2] *Caldew School, Cumbria, England*

Abstract
Research evidence is cited to provide a profile of the typical elementary school timetable in effect in the Province of Alberta, Canada. It is demonstrated that Language Arts dominates the elementary school curriculum. Literacy figures are used to offer support for the opinion that the heavily dominated language curriculum is, in fact, failing to meet the educational needs of the vast majority of school children. In addition, statistics emanating from research on health and fitness levels of children are cited to demonstrate that the typical elementary school timetable is also failing to meet children's needs in these major developmental areas. If the developmental needs of school children are to be realized, then changes need to occur in elementary school curricula. Initial steps to help resolve the problem are forwarded. Finally, a comparison is made between the Alberta elementary school timetable and the Infant and Junior School timetables typically employed in the British school system.
Keywords: Timetable, Elementary School, Curriculum, Health, Fitness, Development.

1   Introduction

In Alberta, Canada, a publication entitled: 'Program of Studies for Elementary Schools' (1988) is published by the Provincial Government and forms the cornerstone for the policy of education in Alberta elementary schools. This Government document formally states the goals of education and the goals of schooling for Alberta. The public school curriculum for Alberta is charged with achieving the goals of schooling and contributing toward the goals of education. The school curriculum is divided into discrete subject areas. The rationale for discrete subject area delineation is based on the educational value of each separate area; each discrete subject area must contribute toward achieving the goals of schooling and education. For example, Physical Education claims a place in the curriculum since it directly addresses one of the specific goals of schooling, which is to provide children with a means to 'acquire knowledge and develop skills, attitudes and habits which contribute to physical, mental and social well-being' (p.v). What better area is there than Physical Education to develop the 'physical' side of children?

The 'Program of Studies' goes on to identify the purpose of the elementary school. Of the three school levels of elementary, junior-high, and high-school, it is the elementary level which is singled out for special consideration since:

> ...the elementary school probably has the greatest impact on the child since it occurs during the early stage of development. This is a time when children learn rapidly, when they may be characterized as eager and curious. In the elementary school begins the task of formalizing a child's learning experiences. Here the foundation is laid for later learning. (p.vi)

Thus, Alberta Education formally recognizes the importance of the elementary school. The mission or purpose of the elementary school is summarized into five statements. The elementary school consists of providing opportunities for students to:

(a)   Develop an appreciation for learning.
(b)   Acquire fundamental learning skills which will enable them to progress to more difficult learnings.
(c)   Acquire requisite knowledge in the physical, intellectual, and personal functioning areas.
(d)   Acquire the requisite social skills which will enable them to function effectively both in school and in the community.
(e)   Develop certain desirable attitudes and commitments towards themselves, their peers and the world as they know it. (p. vi)

All five statements are reproduced here to make the point that elementary schooling is **not** merely the three R's. In fact, the three R's are not formally mentioned at all in any of the five statements which constitute the mission or purpose of the elementary school. Neither are any of the five mission statements priorized in order of importance. The degree of importance occurs when subject area time allocation is stated.

2   Subject-Time Allocation

The decision to recommend minimum times for the various subject areas included in the elementary school curriculum is based on several factors. One of the reasons cited is to 'provide some indication of the importance to be attached to the various components of the Elementary School Program' (p.vii). Fishburne (1989a) has written elsewhere on the fallacy of such reasoning. For example, the Alberta Government would find it difficult to defend that Mathematics is 2.6 times more

Table 1.

Subject Area	Grades 1 - 3	Grades 4 - 6
Language Arts	35%	30%
Mathematics	13%	13%
Social Studies	7%	10%
Science	5%	7%
Music	5%	5%
Art	5%	5%
Physical Education	6%	6%
Health	4%	4%
Undefined	20%	20%

important than Science for children in grades 1 and 2. Or, further, that learning to read is much more important than developing strong and healthy bones. Such fallacious reasoning has resulted in the following breakdown of minimum subject area time allocation being mandated by the Alberta Government (see Table 1).

As can be seen, if the 20% of undefined time is allocated by the school or teacher to Health and Physical Education, it is possible to have 30% of the school timetable given over to these areas. However, in reality the 20% undefined time is rarely used in this way (Fishburne, 1989a).

3   Typical Elementary School Timetable

Fishburne (1989a) surveyed elementary school timetables in Alberta's provincial capital city of Edmonton, and in school districts of the immediate surrounding area, and found that a great similarity in timetables existed. The following grade 1 timetable was drawn at random from a sample of 40 grade 1 and grade 2 timetables surveyed in the Fishburne (1989a) study, and represents a typical grade 1 timetable in use in the Edmonton area. It should be noted that a matrix layout is the usual method for presenting school timetables, and is the one most commonly employed by school and teaching staff. However, the matrix layout makes it difficult to assess the allocation of subject area time through visual inspection alone. Hence, the typical grade 1 timetable presented here has been reduced to percentages of total time to allow for easy comparison with the recommended minimum times advocated by the Provincial Government (see Table 2).

Inspection of the grade 1 timetable reveals that the 20% undefined time has been allocated to the basic three R's (66%) together with Social Studies and Science (18%). Also, in this timetable both Music & Art and Physical Education & Health **fail** to meet the minimum required times of 10% for each of these combined areas.

Table 2.

Subject Area	Actual Time	Recommended Minimum Time
Language Arts	50%	35%
Mathematics	16%	13%
Social Studies	10%	7%
Science	8%	5%
Music	4%	5%
Art	4%	5%
Physical Education	6%	6%
Health	2%	4%
Undefined Time	0%	20%

3.1 *Typical grade 5 timetable*

The following grade 5 timetable (Table 3) was chosen at random from a sample of 80 grade 3,4,5 and 6 timetables surveyed in the Fishburne (1989a) study. This particular timetable consisted of a 6-day programme and included the subject areas of Religion, Computers and Library. When reducing the matrix timetable formation to percentages of total time, a decision was made to add Library time to Language Arts and to add Computer time to Mathematics. A slight error may have been introduced here since Computer time may have included areas other than Mathematics. However, the majority of elementary school computer software programmes are in the areas of Mathematics and Language Arts, so allocating Computer time to the basic three R's was more than likely a valid decision.

Inspection of the timetable reveals that the 20% undefined time has been allocated to Religion (6.3%) and, in the main, to the basic three R's which still account for over half of the curriculum time (54.2%).

Table 3.

Subject Area	Actual Time	Recommended Minimum Time
Language Arts	37.5%	30%
Mathematics	16.7%	13%
Social Studies	8.3%	10%
Science	8.3%	7%
Music	6.3%	5%
Art	6.3%	5%
Physical Education	6.3%	6%
Health	4.2%	4%
Religion	6.3%	-
Undefined	0%	20%

3.2   *Reality of the typical elementary school timetable*

When you consider that Social Studies, Religion, Science, and Health require children to read and write when these subject areas are taught, and Science may also require some form of Mathematics (e.g., measuring), then the result is a typical elementary school timetable which allocates over 80% of time to Reading, Writing, and basic Mathematics.

4   Back to Basics

The real question to be answered by educators is that if children spend in excess of 80% of the normal school day on the basic three R's, why is there an illiteracy problem in Canada? According to the Southam Literacy Survey (1987) almost one quarter (24%) of the Canadian adult population is illiterate. In the Southam survey 'illiterate' refers both to adult Canadians who can barely read and write, called 'basic illiterates', and also to those whose reading and writing and numbers skills are not sufficient to get by in everyday life, called 'functional illiterates'. The research survey found 8% of the adult population to be basically illiterate and 16% functionally illiterate, for a total of 24% illiterate. An additional 9% could be classified as only marginally literate.

To counter the illiteracy problem it might be suggested there is nothing wrong with children spending in excess of 80% of the school day on the basic three R's; the illiteracy problem stems from those adults who failed to complete many years of schooling and/or completed schooling many years ago when there was less of an emphasis on basics and at a time when schools were not blessed with modern technological support. Had these adults had the opportunity to complete their schooling today and experience the 80% plus emphasis on the basics, they would not be functionally illiterate. However, such an argument has difficulty countering a recent research finding in Alberta where 52 adults formed the subjects for an illiteracy study. These adults were reading about a mid-grade 5 level. The mean age of this group was only **25 years** and the average number of years of school completed for each adult was **eleven** years (Fagan, 1988).

When illiteracy figures are quoted there is usually a call from politicians and educators alike for a greater emphasis to be placed on the 'basics' at school. After spending in excess of 80% of a typical school day on the basic three R's - for 200 days per year - for 12 years of schooling - there is still an illiteracy problem! And the solution tendered is to give the basic three R's a greater emphasis in the elementary school! Clearly, there is no other area in society that would be continually funded so many millions of dollars to produce a product where one in every four (24%) is functionally defective, and this is after 12 years on the production line working continuously with professionally qualified personnel.

5   The Typical School Timetable

For many children the typical timetable does not work. The Canadian illiteracy figures are only one measure on the barometer of ineffective schooling. In the USA over one million children are on a daily dose of the drug methylphenidate (Ritalin) because they do not fit into the expectancy of learning in the traditional timetabled school. Comparative figures for Canada are unavailable but many Canadian children are on stimulant drug therapy programmes in an effort to increase their school learning (Fishburne, 1989b). David Elkind (1986) makes the point that in the last 20 years Attention Deficit Disorder (ADD) has become the leading form of learning disability in our schools. Many students have difficulty attending to the tasks set, especially hyperactive children. The word 'hyperactive' includes 'active', yet educators timetable a typical school day to include little or no physical 'activity'. With the majority of a 5 hour school day requiring sedentary inactive seatwork, is it surprising to find that normal active children easily get distracted? Any child exhibiting any of the vague criteria associated with Attention Deficit Disorder (ADD) is likely to be diagnosed as suffering from a chemical imbalance in the brain that needs to be corrected through stimulant drug medication (Fishburne, 1989b). The solution appears to lie with nature and not nurture; to tamper with a child's brain via neurochemical drugs is to manipulate nature. Apparently, educators within our school systems are prepared to accept the latter (tampering with nature) as a possible remedy for the ineffective learning which occurs in our schools. Changing the typical timetable (nurture) is not a considered solution.

6   Historical Design of a School

Historically, school timetables were based on a vague knowledge of brain development. It was clear that a newborn baby could not talk, manipulate numbers or portray any scientific knowledge. The human brain was therefore judged 'empty' and in need of education. In order to 'fill' the brain's empty faculties with appropriate knowledge, it was ruled necessary to school the brain in a variety of separate disciplines. This brought about the birth of 'discrete' subject areas, with each area chosen to educate (fill) a particular faculty of the brain. Such a notion of brain development had nothing to do with the body. As a result, the body had nothing to do with education, and so formed no part in the early school curricula.

A second major influence on the design of schools was the pragmatics associated with 'mass' education. In order to educate an entire population, organizational decisions had to be made. Chronological age was chosen as the organizing factor and not individual differences based on development. Each year the mass of students would all move on to the next level based on their chronological age.

The historical design outlined above is the legacy we have been left with and resembles the schools of today. The education of the brain had nothing to do with the body. Hence, Physical Education failed to gain entry into the early traditional timetables.

Physical Education eventually made its way into the timetable through a concern for the health and fitness of children. For example, in the late 1800's there was a concern in Britain for the physical condition of the men conscripted to the armed forces. They were in such poor physical condition the British Government declared these conscripts were not 'fit' to defend their country. Hence, they charged the schools with responsibility for maintaining the physical condition of its students. The teaching profession declined, since the body had nothing to do with educating the brain. They believed physical education had no place in a school curriculum. Further, the teaching profession claimed they had no training in the instruction of physical fitness since they were educators. To solve the problem, the Government furnished the schools with PTIs (Physical Training Instructors) from the armed forces. These instructors were immediately ostracized by the teaching profession since a child's body was judged to be incidental to the process of learning and, hence, played no part in the education process. The armed forces approach of regimental drill and physical training (PT) was now part of the school but not part of the real curriculum.

Physical training (PT) eventually gave way to Physical Education (PE) as educators began to realize the educational aspects associated with movement and that fitness (PT) was only one area of developmental concern.

Today, brain research is still in its infancy, but we do know much more about the intricate processes involved in the human brain. We now know much more about the processing differences between the left and right hemispheres than did educators when the first notions of curriculum programme planning occured. Fishburne (1984a) has written elsewhere on the hemispheric differences of the human brain and the intricate relationship between brain and body in child development (Fishburne, 1983b). Suffice to say that the brain and body should not be viewed as being separate and that a complementary view should be taken in education if the 'whole child' approach to learning is to be realized. Today, Physical Education is part of the school curriculum but its true potential and the intricate link it holds with development is realized by so few (Fishburne, 1984b). For this reason, this subject area is abused in schools and is given little credibility as a subject area that contributes towards a child's learning and development.

7   A Concern for Health and Fitness

Why do we need Physical Education in the school curriculum? Space does not allow for a full review of literature on the benefits of Physical Education for school children. Instead, a brief summary of major research findings will highlight some of the concerns educators have regarding the physical well-being of children in today's schools. All of the following statements emanate from research studies conducted in Canada and North America:

(a)   60% of Canadian children do not meet average fitness standards.

(b)   Children today expend 4 times less energy than did children 40 years ago.

(c)   Children in Canada watch, on average, 6-1/2 hours of TV per day (Forbes, 1987).

(d)   Todays children are prime targets for cardiovascular disease - the number one killer of North Americans.

(e)   Approximately 40% of Canadian children already have at least **one** risk factor for heart disease - reduced fitness due to an inactive lifestyle.

(f)   In Grade Two one child in four cannot touch toes.

(g)   76% of elementary school girls and 26% of boys cannot do **one** chin up.

(h) 1/2 of all teenage boys and 3/4 of all teenage girls cannot walk up and down stairs for longer than 6 minutes without straining their cardiovascular system.

(i) Only 5% of youth are active enough to reap the rewards of good health from an active lifestyle.

(j) Only 9% of boys and 3% of girls 10-19 years of age play a sport once a week.

(k) Canadian enrollment in high school PE courses has dropped to 30% today from 80% in the early 1970's. (In Alberta, only 17% take PE in Grade 12).

(l) Experts say a daily dose of Physical Education is necessary with 150-300 minutes per week as the minimum.

(m) 1987 CAHPER survey showed that at the elementary school level only **2** Provinces have the recommended minimum time of 150 minutes. Not a **single** Canadian Province recommends daily Physical Education.

(n) Only about 1/2 of all Canadian children, including teenagers, know how to swim - yet, over 70% of all recreation activities in Canada take place on or next to water.

(o) 12 year old children drink an average of 2-1/2 cans of pop daily and the average child eats one of three meals away from home.

(p) In North America 40% of 5-8 year old children can be classified as obese.

(q) The North American diet today contains 31% more fat and 43% less complex carbohydrates than it did in the year 1900.

(r) Children do 75% less exercise today compared to children in the year 1900.

(s) An obese preschooler has a 25% chance of becoming an obese adult. An obese teenager has a 75% chance of remaining obese for life.

(t) Diabetes - 3 times more likely in obese people. Hypercholesterolemia - 2 times more likely in obese people.

(u) Hypertension in obese 20-45 year olds is 5 times that of normal weight people.

(v) Risk of sudden death is over 1200% greater in those people who are 40 lb. overweight.

(w) Between 1960-1980 obesity rates in the US for children 6-11 years of age rose 54%. Super obesity rates rose 98%.

(x) Obese children face health risks including: Hypertension, psycho-social damage, respiratory and orthopedic problems, etc. In fact, everything from flat feet to cancer is more likely in obese people.

In addition to an illiteracy problem, Canada also has an incredible number of children and adults who could be classified under the heading 'physically illiterate'. From these research statistics, it is obvious that schools are neglecting their responsibility to provide for the physical well-being of children. In fact, it has been suggested by members of the medical profession that it is a form of child abuse to allow young children to develop the disease of obesity because of sheer neglect (Fishburne, 1989a). Clearly, Canadian schools are neglecting their responsibility to physically educate children.

It has been shown that the typical elementary school timetable employed in Alberta does not put much emphasis on Physical Education, and from the statistics reviewed, it would appear this situation is widespread across Canada and North America. It is beyond the scope of this article to make a comparative study of different education systems, but a recent survey of British elementary school timetables does provide for an interesting comparison.

8   Elementary School Timetables in Britain

Harper-Tarr (1990) conducted a survey of elementary school timetables currently in use in a small sample of Primary schools in England. The survey was limited to 18 schools in the North of England and so it would be inappropriate to generalize beyond this sample. The survey results are presented here to represent a profile of the 18 British schools and to compare subject time allotment with Alberta elementary schools. The average percentages of time allocated to subject areas in the 18 British Infant and Junior schools were as follows (Table 4):

Results of the survey confirm a very similar distribution of subject area time between the Infant and Junior schools. The typical weighting in favour of the 'basic' areas is present but not to the same degree that was noted in the Alberta timetables. The British schools allocated slightly less than half the curriculum time to the basic three R's (46.25% Infant and 44.5% Junior), whereas the timetables presented earlier from Alberta gave more than half of the curriculum time (66% grade 1 and 54.2% grade 5) to the three R's. What is of interest here is a comparison with the recommended minimum subject area times advocated by the Provincial Government of Alberta. The recommended minimum time for the three R's is 48% for infant grades and 43% for junior grades, which is very similar to the actual percentages of time allocated in the British schools in the Harper-Tarr survey. The real difference is the decision by Alberta schools to use their 20% undefined time on the basic three R's instead of sharing this time with other subject areas.

Although the British schools would seem to be better off for Physical Education and Health Education, in reality this may not be the case. Teachers freely admitted in the Harper-Tarr survey that Physical Education did not always take place each week

Table 4.

Subject Area	Infant (Grades 1 - 2)	Junior (Grades 3 - 6)
Language Arts	28.125%	27.000%
Mathematics	18.125%	17.500%
Social Studies	5.250%	7.000%
Science	16.750%	16.182%
Music	6.687%	7.125%
Art	8.312%	6.937%
Physical Education	9.000%	10.000%
Health	2.750%	2.750%
Religious Education	3.187%	4.187%
Undefined	1.810%	1.250%

Due to a lack of facilities and/or lack of inclination on the part of the teacher, Physical Education did not always occur. Obviously, a lack of accountability in the school system allows Physical Education to be abused in this manner.

8.1 *British school children: Health and fitness concerns*

The lack of accountability for administering a sound Physical Education curriculum in elementary schools has, more than likely, had a significant impact on the health and fitness of British school children. The colossal work by Armstrong and his colleagues at Exeter University confirm the poor physical condition of many British school children and the health risks they face (see Armstrong, 1984; Armstrong & Bray, 1986; Armstrong & Davies, 1980a, 1980b, 1982, 1984).

8.2 *Coronary heart disease*

Approximately 180,000 Britons die annually from atherosclerotic coronary heart disease. Although this clinical disease becomes manifest in adult life, Armstrong and his colleagues cite evidence to suggest the disease is of paediatric origin. Autopsy studies have revealed fatty streaks in the aorta of many children less than 3 years of age (Armstrong & Bray, 1986). The build up of fatty streaks in the inner lining of the arterial wall is the first step toward coronary heart problems. Childhood would therefore appear to be the appropriate time to commence the fight against cardiovascular heart disease (Armstrong, Balding, Gentle and Kirby, 1990).

In order to demonstrate that coronary heart disease has its origin in the early years of life, Armstrong (1989) has shown that although **young** children in Britain are, in fact, fit, their inactive life style throughout their school years and beyond contributes to a severe decline in fitness as they get older. Such a pattern of physical inactivity is one of the risk factors associated with coronary heart disease. To alleviate such a risk factor, it is obvious that children need a solid foundation in Health and Physical Education during their elementary school years. Unfortunately, current evidence would suggest this is not happening.

Children need to develop the habit of an **active** life style. They need to be **educated** toward an active life style - something which becomes a natural part of their daily routine. However, in order to be successful in the physical endeavours in which they partake, children must possess the necessary motor skills and motor abilities. It is of paramount importance that Primary schools provide the environment to develop children's motor skills and motor abilities (Fishburne, in press). For, without motor proficiency, children will find it almost impossible to achieve real success in the many physical and sporting endeavours available, and necessary, to develop an active life style. A lack of success, and hence enjoyment, will result in a move toward an **inactive** life style. This must not occur, for the life span of many children may very well depend upon their level of physical activity. Hence, the major goal of the school Physical Education programme should be to achieve what Armstrong (1989) terms 'activity independence'. When the extrinsic motivation of the teacher is removed, children need to possess the intrinsic motivation to continue to participate regularly in physical activity pursuits. Clearly, from the evidence presented in this article, this is not happening at the present time.

9   Creative Timetabling

From the sample of British and Canadian elementary school timetables reviewed, it has been shown that Physical Education is not a prominent feature in the elementary school curriculum. Unfortunately, without significant changes to elementary school education, the situation is unlikely to change.

In general, educators suffer from the idea that 'more is better'. If statistics demonstrate that after 12 years of schooling there is still a chronic illiteracy problem, then the usual solution tendered is that children need more - a greater emphasis needs to be placed on the three R's. To suggest that children need **less** would be illogical. How could anyone suggest that 'less' might produce 'more'? The problem, however, does not really revolve around 'more' or 'less', but is due to a traditional timetable that does not reflect a child's natural development and penchant for learning. We have seen that a typical elementary school timetable emphasizes the three R's. Such an emphasis draws heavily on the processing of information in the left hemisphere of a child's brain (Fishburne, 1984a). In contrast, Music, Art, and Physical Education are de-emphasized in the elementary school - areas which require a majority of processing in the right hemisphere of the brain (Fishburne & Haslam, 1986). If the total development of the 'whole' child is desired, then an educational environment must provide for optimum brain and body development. Producing an environment which caters mainly to the left hemisphere of the brain, one that provides little stimulation for the right hemisphere, and almost totally neglects bodily movement, could hardly be described as an environment that caters to the entire (whole) development of the child. Such is the typical elementary school timetable.

Eastern countries have realized for some time that a balance in life is necessary for harmonious living. The T'ai-Chi symbol representing the complementary relationship between the polar opposites of 'Yin and Yang' signifies the balance inherent in the eastern philosophies. It is suggested here that a similar balance is necessary for the optimum development of children. There is research evidence to suggest that children's academic standing improves when Physical Education time is increased and academic core time is decreased (Fishburne, 1983a). Intuitively, this might seem odd, especially since the usual educational practice is to give an even greater emphasis to the basic academic areas when children exhibit learning problems. However, there is sufficient research evidence to indicate that large gains in overall performance can be expected with school timetables which allocate as much as one-third of curriculum time to Physical Education (Fishburne, 1983a, 1984b; Forbes, 1987; MacKenzie, 1980; Neff, 1987). With such a timetable, the problems of illiteracy and poor health and fitness can be addressed at the same time.

10   Educators are Slow Learners

Evidence of the benefit of quality daily Physical Education has been well documented for many years. Such evidence is data backed and has been replicated many times throughout the world. Yet, educators are slow to respond to this research evidence and continue to shy away from a curriculum that emphasizes a balance in subject areas. The 'complementary' nature of development plays very little, if any, part in today's school curricula. If anything, recent trends indicate a move even further away from the complementary balance advocated in this article. Todd (1988) cites Otto Jelinek, the former Canadian Federal Minister of State for Fitness and Amateur Sport, as saying that his fight for daily Physical Education in schools was the single most frustrating experience of his job. He lobbied Provincial Governments to do something about the 'disgraceful lack of Physical Education programs' (p.152). He even offered to provide money to allow quality PE to be part of the school timetable. Not one Province took him up on his offer. The reason cited by the Provinces for not going ahead with daily PE - not enough time in the school schedule. In other words, nobody was prepared to change the traditional timetable or even to allocate the 20% undefined time in the Alberta curriculum, to Physical Education. In the Provincial Governments' view, the three R's must maintain their dominance since 'less' would clearly result in 'less'.

11   What Can Be Done to Solve the Problem?

Creating change in education is difficult. Perhaps a new theory of education is needed whereby the development of the whole child (mind and body) forms the basis for curriculum development and teaching methodology. To achieve this, curriculum theorists will need to be cognizant of the latest findings in brain research. They must also be cognizant of individual differences and aware of the 'complementarity' aspect of natural development.

11.1   *Teacher educators*

Teacher educators must refrain from being driven by the outdated view of the basics being the three R's. Movement is basic to life and is intimately connected to human development. All subject areas play a basic part in a child's development. Teaching institutions must emphasize the benefits of Movement and not de-emphasize the areas of Physical Education, Art and Music.

Teaching institutions must also provide teaching practices with 'role models'; models which emphasize areas other than Language Arts and the three R's. Further, they must provide instruction in long-term planning - planning which makes creative use of the flexibility built into the elementary school curriculum (e.g. 20% of undefined time in Alberta).

11.2   *Student teachers*

For those students entering into programmes of teacher education, they must take courses to alleviate weaknesses in their educational background. Courses and programmes which will give them a well rounded view of education - not a view dominated by Language Arts.

New teachers must be educated so as not to be driven by existing school timetables when they enter the profession. They must be educated and encouraged to experiment with the traditional timetable.

11.3   *Different approaches*

Although some of the studies which adopted a one-third Physical Education timetable (e.g. Vanves study) have recently come under some criticism (Kirk, 1989) from a research experimental design point of view, they have, nevertheless, demonstrated the tremendous benefits to be gained when a more balanced and complementary approach to the elementary school curriculum is employed.

12   Creating Change

Creating change is not easy! Obviously changes in attitude and educational policy must take place at all levels. All the way from Government agencies and Teacher Education Institutions, to Education Authorities, School Administrators, Teachers and finally parents.

Even with these suggested changes, there is no guarantee that change will occur. Senior administrators in education hold the real power for change and it is often their poor role model that perpetuates the myth that the mission of the elementary school is to spend 80% of the day emphasizing the basic three R's. For example, in an article published in 'The Executive Educator', an outlet for articles written by senior education administrators, Lowe and Gervais (1987) wrote on how to handle desperation budget cuts without despair. The intent of the article was to show other administrators how to cut budgets without affecting the quality of the educational process. They wrote:

> Eliminate specialist positions... Consider eliminating specialists in elementary school Art, Music, and Physical Education... The key is to cut away the excess, not the core of the program (p.19).

What a limited view of education! To view Movement, Art and Music as nothing more than extras in the school curriculum shows a poor understanding of how children develop and learn. Perhaps David Elkind (1986) was right when he stated that at the present time, decisions made regarding children 'derive more from the needs and priorities of adults than from what we know of good pedagogy for young children' (p.636).

Despite the difficulty involved in creating change, every effort must be made by those educators who truly understand the vital role that movement plays in child development. Changes in curriculum and teacher preparation must occur if we are to make any impact on the frightening statistics highlighted in this paper. School administrators must also play their part and support timetables which reflect a balance between mind and body - timetables that are **not** dominated by the three R's. The effectiveness of our schools depends on it.

13   References

Armstrong, N. (1984) Why implement a health related fitness program? **British Journal of Physical Education,** 15, 173-175.
Armstrong, N. (1989) Children are fit but not active! **Education and Health**, 7(2), 28-32.

Armstrong, N., Balding, J., Gentle, P. and Kirby, B. (1990) Estimation of coronary risk factors in British schoolchildren: a preliminary report. **British Journal of Sports Medicine**, 24(1), 61-66.

Armstrong, N. and Bray, S. (1986) The role of the physical education teacher in coronary prevention, in **Trends and Developments in Physical Education** (eds B. Wright and G. Donald), E. & F. Spon Ltd, London, pp. 346-352.

Armstrong, N. and Davies, B. (1980a) The prevalence of coronary risk factors in children, **Acta Paediatr. Belg.**, 33, 209-217.

Armstrong, N. and Davies, B. (1980b) Coronary risk factors in children - the role of the physical educator. **Bulletin of Physical Education**, 16, 5-11.

Armstrong, N. and Davies, B. (1982) High density lipoprotein cholesterol and physical activity patterns in children. **Australian Journal of Sport Medicine,** 14, 53-59.

Armstrong, N. and Davies, B. (1984) The metabolic and physiological responses of children to exercise and training. **Physical Education Review**, 7, 90-105.

Elkind, D. (1986) Formal education and early childhood education: An essential difference. **Phi Delta Kappan,** 67, 631-636.

Fagan, W.T. (1988) Concepts of reading and writing among low-literate adults. **Reading Research and Instruction,** 27(4), 47-60.

Fishburne, G.J. (1983a) Is reading more important than physical education? **Elements: A Journal for Elementary Education**, 15(1), 3-5.

Fishburne, G.J. (1983b) Explaining the mystery of movement. **Elements: A Journal for Elementary Education**, 15(1), 18-21.

Fishburne, G.J. (1984a) Hemispheric differences in the human brain. **Elements: A Journal for Elementary Education**, 15(2), 18-23.

Fishburne, G.J. (1984b) Muscular Christianity in the twentieth century. **Ethics in Education**, 4(2), 5-6.

Fishburne, G.J. (1989a) The link between mind and body: Implications for curriculum planners, in **Issues in Teacher Education** (eds G.J. Fishburne and D.J. Sande), Faculty of Education Pub., University of Alberta, Edmonton, pp.24-43.

Fishburne, G.J. (1989b) Stimulant drug therapy and children with Attention Deficit Disorder: An ethical issue. **McGill Journal of Education**, 24(1), 55-68.

Fishburne, G.J. (In Press) Motor and physical development during early childhood, in **Teaching Health and Physical Education in the Early Childhood Classroom** (ed L. Read), Alberta Teachers' Association Pub., Edmonton.

Fishburne, G.J. and Haslam, I.R. (1986) The functional organization of the human brain. Effect of brain research on curriculum development, in **Trends and Developments in Physical Education** (eds B.Wright and G. Donald), E. & F.N. Spon Ltd, London, pp.431-437.

Forbes, W. (1987) (Producer) Flabby kids. **MIDDAY**, Canadian Broadcasting Corporation, Toronto.

Harper-Tarr, D.A. (1990) Survey of British infant and junior school timetables. **Unpublished data.**

Kirk, D. (1989) Daily physical education research: A review and critique. **Physical Education Review**, 12(1), 21-30.

Lowe, R. and Gervais, R. (1987, January) How to handle desperation budget cuts without despair. **The Executive Educator**, 18-19.

MacKenzie, J. (1980) The Vanves experiment in education. **Runner**, 18(3), 17-20.

Neff, C. (1987, October) The CAPE of good hopes. **Sports Illustrated**, 84-88.

Program of studies for elementary schools (1988) **Alberta Education** (Provincial Government), Edmonton.

Southam Literacy Survey (1987) **Southam News**, Ottawa.

Todd, P. (1988, October) Out of action. **Homemakers**, 144-156.

BODY AS MACHINE AND BODY AS SELF IN TEACHING PE

MARGARET E.WHITEHEAD
Bedford College of Higher Education, Bedford, England

Abstract

The argument that underpins this paper is the view that our body plays a significant role in existence **not** principally as a consciously manipulated, highly sophisticated mechanism, but rather as an integral part of our personhood or 'human being'. In this context it is not necessarily advisable to highlight our bodily dimension and treat it as if it is an inanimate machine. The point is made, however, that we **can** view both our own embodied dimension and that of others from a variety of standpoints. These range from seeing this dimension as an object or tool, to accepting the dimension as integral to the individual concerned. The implications of adopting these different views is considered. The treatment of an individual's embodiment as an object or a tool, against that person's inclinations is discussed with particular reference to the consequences that this incongruence of views can bring about. It is proposed that one outcome can be a rejection of one's own bodily dimension. The work in physical education which stresses health related fitness is singled out as tending to treat the bodily dimension as a machine, and therefore being in danger of alienating the individual from participation in all forms of physical activity.
Keywords: Teaching, Existentialism, Phenomenology, Sartre, Merleau-Ponty, Body Modes.

1   Introduction

As the title of this paper suggests the nature of our bodily form or embodiment is ambiguous. This ambiguity gives rise to a range of views, typically those of dualism and monism, and these views are not simply the province of the layman's debate, they can be seen to initiate high level enquiry and research. So for example phenomenologists and existentialists are, through their philosophical study, revealing the nature of existence as essentially relying on a monist perspective; while at the same time others such as scientists are revealing daily the minutiae of the mechanical workings of the body as an object, that is, working from a dualistic view. That different perspectives can be taken on our embodiment is irrefutable, however what is to be resolved is the role our own embodiment plays, for each one of us, in the totality of our existence. It was by working through one proposal concerning this role that I found a possible explanation to one of our problems in physical education (Whitehead, 1987). The particular problem to which I am referring is the love/hate attitude many pupils seem to have towards physical education. This is an attitude that seems to become entrenched and often results in a similar view being held throughout life to physical activity. I find it surprising that this situation has attracted little attention and seems to have been accepted with a degree of fatalism by physical education teachers. In this short paper I would like to show how a mismatch between the views on the body could give rise to this situation.

The arguments that underpin this proposal arise from the work of existentialists and phenomenologists such as Sartre and Merleau-Ponty. Not only do these philosophers tend to support monism and perceive the individual as essentially one integrated whole, they also have a sincere respect for the body - seeing it as playing a pervasive and influential part in life as we know it. Our bodily dimension has central significance in being the form of our presence in the world, our access to the world, and the medium through which we make contact with our surroundings. It is thus a major contributor in giving meaning to the world and to existence. In their view the bodily dimension is not simply a concrete material structure or an intricately functioning mechanism - but is identified as having a range of key roles on different levels of our existence. The body as an object is seen as of less importance than the fact that we are by nature embodied. More than this in fact - both philosophers predict that in certain circumstances less than ideal outcomes can be the result of views taken of the body (or embodiment) which focus on it as an object or a mechanism. These outcomes can be in the form of an alienation from the body and/or of a rejection of those situations where the body is so viewed. Given that in physical education, not least in those aspects of the subject concerned with health and fitness, we spend a good deal of time helping pupils to become aware of the mechanical or instrumental capacities of their embodiment, this observation is somewhat alarming. The situation is, however, complex as there is a whole range of ways in which we and Others can view our embodiment. What appears to be the crucial issue is the congruence of the views adopted by the individual mover and significant Others in a situation. The variety of ways in which the body can be viewed needs to be explained first before this important relationship can be appreciated.

2

The notion that a range of perspectives can be taken on the body was proposed by Sartre (1943) and supported in many respects by Merleau-Ponty (1942). Sartre in 'Being and Nothingness' identifies three body 'modes'. The 'body-for-self', the 'body-for-Others', and the 'body-for-Others-as-perceived-by-the-self'. His example of the experiences of a mountaineer is most commonly used to illustrate these modes. In this Sartre describes a climber whose goal is to complete a difficult ascent. In preparation he pays attention to all he will need to achieve the challenging task ahead - his equipment, his clothing, his own fitness, and his ability to execute the necessary movement techniques. However once he starts the climb all these separate items and concerns merge into his single minded attempt to reach his goal. He no longer concentrates on specific movement patterns he must perform, but is totally absorbed in his task. His embodied dimension is lived to the full but not contemplated. It is 'passed by in silence' (Sartre, 1943). It is an element of his total endeavour. This is the lived embodiment or the 'body-for-self'.

The second body mode comes into being when an observer watchers the climber. The onlooker sees him simply as a body/instrument - reaching, holding, stepping, easing, heaving. This mode of embodiment, Sartre's 'body-for-Others', is essentially an object or mechanism. The final mode, the 'body-for-Others-as-perceived-by-the-self', comes into being, Sartre proposes, when the climber himself realizes that someone is watching him. Through feeling this 'look' directed towards himself the mountaineer is drawn to contemplate his embodiment as it is seen by the onlooker. He becomes acutely, and Sartre suggests, unnaturally, aware of his embodiment as an object/mechanism. He feels exposed and vulnerable, and readily adopts a self critical attitude towards this aspect of himself. Furthermore as an outcome of this situation the mountaineer is prone to fumble, trip or lose his footing.

Both Sartre and Merleau-Ponty are quite clear in their view that in everyday circumstances and for the majority of the time we live our embodiment in the first mode. This is the 'natural' mode. We do not have to stop, start, or direct our embodiment. In all our dealings with our surroundings we simply presume on its involvement, its capacities and the appropriateness of its response. In addition both philosophers see the acquisition of new movement patterns as an almost unconscious response by the individual to the situation in the world as it presents itself. Merleau-Ponty's view of learning a movement skill is thought provoking. He says that in learning nothing new is acquired but a new ability is revealed, and again that 'nothing new is achieved - rather stimuli acquire the power to initiate a response' (Merleau-Ponty, 1942). Our embodiment he claims works, as it were, without need of conscious direction, in an ongoing relationship with the environment. It answers our needs almost automatically. This view is not dissimilar to some of Tim Gallwey's ideas in his books on the 'Inner Game' (Gallwey, 1975). Here he urges us not to over-intellectualize the body but to leave it to respond to the situation itself. It will, he proposes, fulfil our requirements far better if we take our concentration off it.

Sartre would certainly agree with this and goes to some length to underline the disturbing experience that can result if we contemplate our embodiment from the standpoint of the Other, that is as an object. He proposes that the Other is responsible for bringing into being the 'object' form of the body. In fact, he continues, it is a form that we cannot create for ourself. In a sense, then, the Other 'owns' my body as an object. It is not truly 'my' body but the formulation by the Other of my embodiment. As such it is alien to me and any contemplation of this perspective of my embodiment tends to highlight the separateness of 'my' body and can promote a rejection of it and maybe a desire to dissociate myself from it. This is an unnerving experience that is not an unknown phenomenon. For example, R.D. Laing (1960) talks of schizophrenics having an experience of being divorced from their embodiment and of the totally disorientating and disturbing effect this has.

Sartre warns, then, that if we are drawn to adopt an object perspective to our embodiment - probably on account of experiencing another's 'look' - we may firstly withdraw our attention from our surroundings and, as the mountaineer, stumble; and secondly feel alienated from our embodiment to the point of trying to dissociate ourself from it. In addition to the Other's 'look' Sartre identifies two further factors that he feels make us particularly susceptible to being caught up uneasily in viewing our embodiment as an object. Firstly the sensing of anything critical or negative in the attitude of the onlooker, and secondly our being more scantily dressed that usual. It is not difficult to see how the situation Sartre describes could occur in physical education. One of our jobs in teaching is to observe pupils and identify and correct errors in their movement, and of necessity pupils do wear briefer clothes than usual. Sartre's perceptions could maybe help to explain why some pupils persistently absent themselves from our lessons. However they are perhaps overly pessimistic and leave little room to explain why some pupils love rather than hate our subject. This is, I feel, because they do not tell the whole story. He suggests that there are two attitudes we can adopt towards our own embodiment and one that Others can adopt. This, while being a valuable insight, rather oversimplifies the situation.

3

There would seem at least four perspectives that I can take on my own bodily dimension. First, I can consider it purely as an object when, for example, I take regular measurements of it during a course of slimming. Alternatively, I can consider it as an instrument when maybe I am concerned to develop a new pattern of co-ordination in order to master a particular technique. Thirdly, I can view it as one of the means by which I am, or am about to be, involved in a particular environment. In this mode my bodily aspects are just one consideration in my thoughts rather than the focus of my attention. I adopt this attitude when, for example, I am debating if I have time to run to the station to catch the train or when I am wondering if I will be too nervous to play the cello as well as I might in a forthcoming examination. In both cases I am incorporating my bodily capacities in my thoughts - among other features relevant to the situation. Finally, I can just live my embodiment unreflectively, incorporate it into my perception of myself and in a sense, take it for granted.

Sartre would only seem to recognize fully the last of these perspectives. His notion of the first two is that they only arise as a result of someone else adopting this view on our embodiment and that they always result in a feeling of alienation from that dimension of ourself. This is surely wrong. I can decide, myself, to adopt an object or instrument view on my body in the interests of a particular goal. And in these cases there will be no grounds on which to reject my body as I shall be considering it as essentially 'mine'. Sartre himself hints he might concede the point as in his discussion of the mountaineer he alludes to the idea that the climber may have given some attention to his embodiment in his preparation for the ascent. In situations such as this I would be focusing on my embodiment to achieve a personal objective - to conquer the mountain, to slim, to get fit, to improve my ice skating.

In a not dissimilar way an Other can take a number of perspectives on my bodily aspects. For example, an Other can view my body as an object/mechanism - as a doctor or dentist may do. Alternatively he may view it as a tool, a means towards achieving his own end. There is a whole range of degrees of this particular attitude ranging from the extreme example of mediaeval peasants being used to tread a mill wheel to an ambitious football manager bent on achieving success for his team solely for his own prestige. The third perspective is when an onlooker views my bodily capacities as a vehicle of my intentions. This view is normally adopted by someone who is either concerned to understand me and/or what I am doing, or who is attempting to help me to achieve a goal. For example, he may be watching me busy in a yacht and be considering what part I am playing in its handling; or he may be observing me as I try to open a door while carrying a pile of heavy packages. In these cases there is an effort to identify with the person observed and his objective, and possibly an interest to help him use his capacities to reach his objective.

A final perspective the Other could take on my embodiment is one where it is almost disregarded, is not dwelt on as a separate entity, is simply incorporated into his total perception of me.

4

If it is the case, contrary to Sartre's view, that an Other can view my embodiment in all these ways, I would argue that the results of an Other's attention need not always be unnerving. Certainly the last two perspectives would seem to offer no threat as they are entirely supportive of the individual and tend to pass over the embodied dimension in the interests of a more all embracing consideration of the individual. The first two perspectives do, however, bring with them potential problems. In the first though, there would seem no danger if, in the interests of a particular goal, an individual asks an Other to pay attention to his embodiment as object or mechanism. For example, I may well request the doctor, the dressmaker or the fitness expert to view my embodiment in one of these ways.

The problem would seem to arise when an Other views my embodiment in one of these ways against my wishes. It is in these cases that I can feel most uncomfortable. If I do not wish to be measured or tested I shall not enjoy the experience and in an attempt to withdraw from the situation I may try to divorce myself from my embodiment. A similar situation may be the result of an Other forcing me to use my embodiment as a tool to further his own end or an end with which I cannot identify. He may seem to have no regard for my feelings, wishes or intentions and simply manipulate me in a comparatively unfeeling way. Again I may well try to dissociate myself from my embodiment and experience the disturbing effect of this effort.

It would seem that the potentially unsettling and disorientating experience Sartre identifies could be a real possibility in situations where the view of the individual and the observer are at odds. Where the observer is endorsing a goal adopted by the individual, however, there is little problem. These possibilities are perhaps the key to understanding what can occur in physical education.

5

In this context tasks are often set that require pupils to focus their attention on the 'instrument' capacities of their bodily dimension. If a pupil understands and identifies with the purpose of the task he will usually readily adopt an instrument perspective on his body and work through the task to achieve whatever objective has been set. However, if a pupil can see no point in the task he will resist adopting an 'instrument' attitude and do so only reluctantly, feeling himself being, in a sense, manipulated in order to achieve someone else's ends. He will feel all the more uneasy if his bodily capacities are not reaching the required standard. The situation may be made all the worse because his body is clearly visible to others, dressed as he is in brief sports kit. He may feel ashamed of this aspect of himself, feel alienated from it and attempt to disown it. In respect of one's embodiment this effort can be profoundly disturbing. This is because we 'are' our body, and there is no way that we can separate ourself from an aspect of our very nature. The whole unhappy situation can add up to one that the pupil will dislike, fear or even dread.

Situations of this nature would seem to have the potential to develop a strong antipathy towards physical education and could help explain why there is such a dichotomy of views among pupils towards this subject. Lessons focused on health-related fitness are particularly prone to this danger as work here is very often quite specifically concerned with measuring and testing the body as a mechanism. The rationale for the lessons is usually spelled out in terms of clearly quantifiable attributes of the body as object. The teacher and others may need to touch the mover's body in order to carry out the testing, and this could exacerbate the situation.

For the involved, interested, assured pupil there appear few problems. He happily identifies with the goal set by the teacher. This goal, relying heavily on the appropriate use of the body-as-instrument for its achievement, will carry no threat of alienation from his embodiment as he will be freely adopting this perspective. He will tend to interpret the teacher's attention and comments positively as helping him reach his goal. Presuming that the pupil feels that the goal is within reach there will be an element of confidence in his approach to the work. The pupil will not be ashamed of his performance and will not feel vulnerable on account of his efforts being so visible to his peers. In this situation pupil and teacher will work together and progress is likely to be made.

For the apprehensive, less confident or uninterested pupil, however, the situation could be very different. This pupil is unlikely to identify with the teacher's goal but may have to work towards it for fear of reprimand or punishment. In this situation the pupil feels manipulated and goes through the motions only to fulfil the teacher's demands. He experiences his body as a mechanism almost under another's control and this tends to make him want to reject it. The teacher's attention and comments are interpreted as critical and negative. The pupil feels exposed, vulnerable and open to ridicule in his half hearted fumbling. He begins to dislike his body and cannot wait to cover it up and forget about it. The thought of this whole pattern of exposure, manipulation and humiliation is extremely unpleasant and he will do all he can to avoid the situation in future.

If this is a feasible explanation of the situation, the question needs to be asked how negative experiences in physical education can be avoided. The answer seems to rest squarely with the teacher, who is responsible for creating the working context and climate of the lessons. The choice of content and method are crucial, but so is the nature of the interaction between teacher and pupil. In planning the work the teacher needs to be able to identify with the pupils - to start from where they are, to set relatively short term goals that they can understand, accept as their own and achieve. There needs to be an atmosphere in the lessons of encouragement, understanding and shared endeavour - not only between the teacher and the pupil but also between pupils. The teacher could well avoid too much stress on the mechanical or instrumental use of the embodiment and might focus more on the goal than the detailed bodily manipulation. The teacher's knowledge of the functioning of the body as a mechanism - probably acquired in initial training - should be referred to sparingly, if at all.

Our bodily capacities are very much part of us and positive attitudes to these readily pervade our view of ourself as a whole. Regrettably negative attitudes are also pervasive and we, as teachers, would do well to avoid any such developing wherever possible. We need to be supportive and encouraging, and to treat pupils as people not 'mechanisms'. In this way we can, hopefully, avoid pupils developing a dislike of their body and of physical education, and guard against contributing to a lessening of self esteem.

Above all we have to see the situation through the eyes of the pupil. This is the key - but perhaps the most difficult thing for us to do. We have never been the clumsy child last to be picked for a team; we have never been the only one not able to do a forward roll or the one who repeatedly fumbles the ball. We have lived our embodiment with pride and developed our self esteem in situations where this dimension of ourself has been central. We have never been where so many of our pupils are - but it is perhaps where we should try to go more often. If we can do this we can perhaps use Sartre's insights to promote our work, rather than just to explain our problems.

6   References

Gallwey, T. (1975) **The Inner Game of Tennis**. Jonathan Cape.

Laing, R.D. (1960) **The Divided Self**. Penguin.

Merleau-Ponty, M. (1942) **The Structure of Behaviour**. Methuen 1965.

Sartre, J-P, (1943) **Being and Nothingness**. Methuen University Paperback 1969.

Whitehead, M.E. (1987) Unpublished PhD thesis 'A study of the views of Sartre and Merleau-Ponty related to embodiment, and a consideration of the implications of these views for the justification and practice of physical education'.

Whitehead, M.E. (1988) Dualism, Monism and Health Related Exercise in Physical Education. **Newsletter 19, Health and Physical Education Project**, Loughborough University, p.4.

Whitehead, M.E. (1990) Teacher/Pupil Interaction in Physical Education - the Key to Success. **The Bulletin of Physical Education** Vol. 26 No. 2, Summer 1990, 27-30.

THE COMPLEXITIES OF SELF-ESTEEM PROMOTION IN PHYSICAL EDUCATION AND SPORT

K.R. FOX

Physical Education Association Research Centre, University of Exeter, England

Abstract

The association of self-esteem with mental well-being and positive achievement behaviour has prompted its promotion as a primary educational objective. However, clear guidelines regarding curriculum design for self-esteem enhancement have not been forthcoming, apparently because of a lack of understanding of the psychosocial mechanisms involved. Recently, there has been an upsurge in self-esteem research and several interesting theories and models have emerged which have relevance to the educational setting. Self-esteem appears to be multidimensional in nature with self-perception within the physical environment playing an important contributory role. There is evidence that dimensions are hierarchically arranged with increasingly specific and differentiated perceptions existing at lower levels. The normative content of this hierarchical structure appears to be determined by societal values which change by age. Individuals also have the capacity to customize their self-esteem structures by discounting their inadequacies and attaching increased importance to domains in which they perceive success. Additionally, unconditional social support and style of achievement orientation may have a significant impact on the development of youngsters' self-esteem. Some implications of these concepts to physical education are briefly presented.

Keywords: Self-esteem, Self-perception, Physical education, Social support, Achievement orientation.

1   Introduction

There are two reasons why self-esteem may be of interest to physical educators and sport coaches. First, self-esteem is probably the most frequently used indicator of mental well-being, and sport and exercise may be important vehicles for its promotion. Second, an individual's drive to seek out and experience self-esteem may direct choice and persistence in behaviours such as sport and exercise. Thus, increased understanding of self-esteem theory should help teachers and coaches produce happier and more active youngsters. It is not surprising, therefore, that self-esteem promotion emerges consistently as a prime objective in educational curricula.

Progress in self-esteem research has been limited by a confusion of overlapping terminologies and instrumentation. Recently, there appears to have been agreement on some major definitions. Self-esteem is best defined as 'the awareness of good possessed by oneself' (Campbell, 1984, p.9). It is an evaluative declaration of personal worth dependent on what the individual values and defines as worthwhile. As will be discussed, these contributing fields of 'good', such as academic ability, physical appearance, or popularity among peers, will be largely determined by societal values. However, individuals may also be empowered to modify or opt out of their societal straightjacket and personalize the content of their self-esteem structure.

2   Normative self-esteem structures

It is clear that self-esteem is the outcome, at least partially, of self-judgement in several different domains of life. We judge ourselves differently according to the life setting. This multi-dimensionality can be identified throughout the lifespan from early childhood (Harter, 1988; Marsh & Shavelson, 1985) with content becoming increasingly diverse with age. The normative content of these dimensions is likely to differ by age, gender, social-economic background and culture, charged fundamentally by group values. Some subgroups may set up radically different indicators of success, which might include behaviours which would normally be seen as antisocial, but which may still provide content for self-esteem promotion. An example would be the football hooligan who prides himself and achieves group status through bravado or expertize in vandalism.

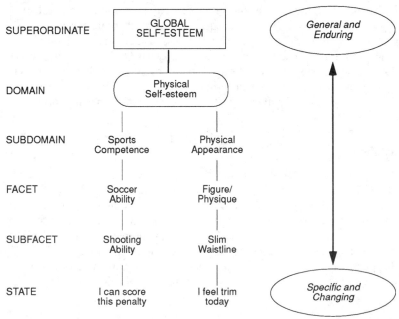

Figure 1   *Levels of physical self-perception*

Some researchers have cast this multidimensionality of content into a hierarchical framework (see Fox, 1988), with global statements of worth forming the apex and increasingly specific aspects constituting the more numerous roots. The physical domain seems to be well-represented at all levels with physical appearance and ability elements dominating. For example, Figure 1 shows two aspects of the physical domain which might be fractioned into perceptions at increasingly specific and less stable levels of experience. This structure provides a possible route by which repeated single exposures in related activities such as sports may eventually give rise to a more global self-statement of sports competence, dependent on the degree of success experienced.

The content of the physical domain within this hierarchy has been studied in greater depth (Fox, 1990; Fox & Corbin, 1989). With a young adult population in the United States, elements of sport competence, physical attractiveness, physical strength and physical condition have been identified as contributors to a global construct of physical self-worth (see Figure 2). The hierarchical relationship among these constructs and global self-esteem has been supported with several samples of subjects, with physical attractiveness emerging as the most salient of the subdomains for both genders.

This line of research has revealed that distinct self-esteem content both within and outside the physical domain can be identified for populations of similar background and age. Further research is needed so that important self-esteem content in children can be fully identified. However, some immediate implications for physical educators are apparent:-

(a) the physical domain is not the only vehicle through which self-esteem promotion can be achieved. Other areas where self-appraisal might occur in the curriculum, such as in maths or music, may be equally important. The PE curriculum is likely to have its greatest impact through its influence on physical self-worth. Much of this development may occur in children outside the curriculum through play. Physical self-worth is also dominated by perceived physical appearance over physical abilities by adulthood and perhaps should be as much a consideration of physical educators.

(b) the degree to which physical education has potential for influencing what becomes the salient content of physical self-perceptions in children has yet to be established. Health-related fitness, for example, may be an important curricular objective, but may not be constructed in the minds of young children. Simpler, more public attributes such as height or the ability to run fast may be more pertinent. This would suggest that educators have to consider children's perceptions, values and stage of understanding before some attributes become a sought after commodity.

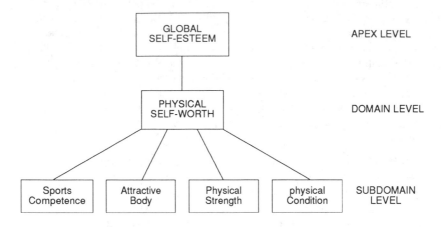

Figure 2.   *Content and structure of physical self-perceptions*

3   Personalized self-esteem structures

Although self-esteem content may be largely determined by societal values, mechanisms have been identified through which an individual might personalize their self-esteem structure. The question might be asked 'do youngsters suffer low self-esteem if they come to believe that they are poor performers in sport (low perceived sport competence)?' There is evidence to show (Fox, 1990) that although many young adult females rate themselves low in sport competence, they also attach a low importance weight to sport and tend to avoid it. In effect, they discount sport and its potential source of failure from their self-esteem structures in order to preserve their self-esteem. At the same time, they may attach a high importance and become attracted to other areas outside the physical domain where they perceive competence. Harter (1988) has shown that those children who are most successful in operating these self-serving mechanisms are more likely to experience high self-esteem and this has also been replicated within the physical domain (Fox, 1990).

Additionally, some youngsters may experience success in activities which are not typical of their group as a whole, such as ice skating or orienteering. The sense of competence achieved may then be incorporated into their personal self-esteem pool.

It is interesting to note that discounting one's inadequacies appears to be most difficult in areas where societal pressure for success is at its strongest. Females' self-rated physical attractiveness is similar to males. Many males, however, who perceive low attractiveness are able to discount its importance. The majority of females experience a high discrepancy between their desired and perceived attractiveness and this is associated with low self-esteem. Conversely, the physical self-worth of obese adult males is quite low but this is unrelated to their global self-esteem (Fox, Mucci & Dirkin, 1990), suggesting that they have discounted the importance of the physical domain and and looked elsewhere for their sense of achievement.

Discounting would seem to represent a sensible and healthy mechanism for maintaining and enhancing mental well-being. It raises a number of issues for physical educators:-

(a) to what extent should discounting of areas such as sport competence be discouraged or encouraged? On the one hand, it may be a buffer for self-esteem preservation. On the other, it may result in avoidance behaviour in that subdomain.

(b) to what extent should physical educators intervene and encourage discounting and self-acceptance in the area of physical attractiveness? Should physical education take on board the responsibility of counteracting those societal pressures which it may consider to be unhealthy?

(c) how can physical educators maintain interest in areas such as sports when it is clear that a range of physical abilities will always exist?

4   Achievement orientation

Related to this last question is an area of research which has recently emerged through the work of Nicholls (1984) and Duda (1987). Achievement orientation is concerned with the goal perspectives adopted when attempting to demonstrate competence. Nicholls identifies two types of goal involvement. Task orientation involves the judgement of personal competence in an achievement setting by reference to successfully accomplishing a task or improving on previous efforts and/ or performance. Perceived competence therefore arises through **self** reference in relation to mastery of a task. Ego orientation on the other hand focuses on judgement of one's own ability through comparison with the performance of others. It is therefore essentially **externally** referenced.

By the time youngsters enter adolescence, they are capable of using either of these approaches but tend to be dominated by one or the other. In the public environment of sport participation, it is difficult for youngsters to avoid judging their own abilities by comparison with others. While confidence is high and comparisons with others favourable, this will result in high perceived sport competence and motivation will continue. However, for a variety of genetic, maturational and environmental reasons many will not compare well, and this is likely to result in low perceived competence and a tendency towards discounting and avoidance in the sports domain.

It would seem that an emphasis on task mastery, goal setting and personal improvement as the major source of competence information is more likely to sustain involvement and commitment throughout adolescence and beyond. The question remains as to how much physical educators are prepared to take this issue on board and how best it can be achieved.

5   Unconditional social support

To this point, discussion has been restricted to self-esteem which is conditional upon personal abilities and attributes. The traditional route in education to self-esteem enhancement has been through competence building along these lines. On this basis we might assume that an individual who comes to perceive few competencies has little foundation on which to build high self-esteem. Although this has been partially supported, there is increasing evidence (Harter, 1988) indicating that perceived social support may be equally important in determining self-esteem levels, particularly with young children. There are also suggestions that this type of support is most effective when it is **unconditional** and separate from judgements of an individual's abilities and attributes. For example, Harter's research has indicated that the suicidal thoughts of depressed teenagers are more related to the conditionality of their parental support than its quantity.

Much more research is required in this area but there may be an underlying self-esteem requirement by individuals to feel that they are valued regardless of their achievement successes and failures. This would suggest that in addition to competence development, teachers may have an important pastoral function to perform in the self-esteem equation. It would seem that the quality of the teacher/student relationship is the key here, and a balanced philosophy of teaching/coaching is required which does not allow the trading of a child's dignity and sense of worth for the sake of a competent performance.

6   Summary

Although the importance of self-esteem promotion in physical education is reflected in numerous national reports and statements, the means by which this is best achieved are not clear. This inadequacy may be reflected by the fact that only weak evidence exists showing that physical education programmes can make a difference (Gruber, 1985). This paper has attempted to raise awareness of the complexity of the self-esteem issue and provide some initial insight into the state of our understanding of the mechanisms involved in its promotion.

7   References

Campbell, R.N. (1984) **The new science: Self-esteem psychology.** Lanham, MD: University Press of America.

Duda, J.L. (1987) Toward a developmental theory of achievement motivation in sport. **Journal of Sport Psychology**, 9, 130-145.

Fox, K.R. (1988) The self-esteem complex and youth fitness. **Quest**, 40, 230-246.

Fox, K.R. (1990) **The Physical Self-Perception Profile Manual**, DeKalb, IL: Office for Health Promotion, Northern Illinois University.

Fox, K.R. & Corbin, C.B. (1989) The Physical Self-Perception Profile: Development and preliminary validation. **Journal of Sport and Exercise Psychology**, 11, 408-430.

Fox, K.R., Mucci, G.W. & Dirkin, G.R. (1990) Exercise psychology of obese adults attending clinical treatment: An ongoing longitudinal study. **Journal of Sport Science**, 8,(1), (conference communications).

Gruber, J.J. (1985) Physical activity and self-esteem development in children: A meta analysis. **American Academy of Physical Education Papers**, 19, 30-48.

Harter, S. (1988) Causes, correlates, and the functional role of global self-worth: A lifespan perspective. In J. Kolligian and R. Sternberg (eds) **Perceptions of competence and incompetence across the lifespan.** New Haven, CT: Yale University.

Marsh, H.W. & Shavelson, R. (1985) Self-concept: Its multifaceted hierarchical structure. **Educational Psychologist,** 20, 107-123.

Nicholls, J.G. (1984) Achievement motivation: Conceptions of ability, subjective experience, task choice, and performance. **Psychological Review,** 91, 328-346.

EMANCIPATORY HEALTH EDUCATION AND THE POTENTIAL AND LIMITATIONS OF HEALTH BASED PHYSICAL EDUCATI0N

D. COLQUHOUN
School of Education, Deakin University, Geelong, Victoria, Australia

1   Introduction

It is clear from the attention Health Based Physical Education (HBPE) has received in professional physical education journals and elsewhere, that it has been a major focus for the efforts of physical educators in recent years. A brief scan of the British literature alone shows that HBPE has been prominent since the early nineteen eighties. Perhaps now, almost ten years on since the early publications of Almond (1983) and Whitehead and Fox (1983), it is opportunistic and timely to reflect critically on the brief history of HBPE even bearing in mind, of course, that what was an innovation ten years ago may still have a significant potential ahead of itself.

   In this paper I will outline the potential and limitations of HBPE from within a critical perspective. In other words, I will suggest that until we do take a critical stance to HBPE we will not really see its full potential. We must engender the ideas bound within the notion of a 'socially critical curriculum' (Kemmis et al, 1986). Failure will mean we will be dogged by our myopia and a reliance on a dominant discourse which does nothing to enhance the true potential of HBPE as a curriculum subject in whatever form it takes. Indeed, HBPE will be presented as an area which could significantly influence the development of physical education as a part of the curriculum. To be possibilitarian and by reconceptualizing what we mean by HBPE and its instrument, the body, we will be able to expand the terrain of physical education to go beyond what has traditionally been its major focus - the discourses of performance and technocratic rationality (see Tinning, 1990). Only by fulfilling this task can we break free from the major limitations of HBPE which for the purposes of this presentation, can be seen to be bound up within the problems of the ideology of healthism.

2   HBPE and health education: Identifying the dominant ideology

The dominant ideology of health education has been identified by numerous researchers working in different contexts and settings (Colquhoun, 1990a; Colquhoun et al, 1990; Combes, 1989; Riska, 1982; Vertinsky, 1985) to be that of healthism (Crawford, 1980), individualism (Naidoo, 1986) or what has even been called lifestylism (Rodmell and Watt, 1986). Briefly, healthism involves the promotion of self-responsibility for health over and above all other methods for improving health. Of course, healthism fits neatly into the rhetoric of the State and of the 'me' or 'now' generation - a rhetoric reinforced by a moral majority and a blame the victim mentality. Healthism operates in school (and the community) by making it appear 'natural' and 'given' that individuals take responsibility for their own health and by so doing depoliticizes health education so that broader perspectives are marginalized or ignored. Healthism also denies the individual agency in which to influence the factors detrimental to health and well-being. The problems with healthism are several and include; first, the concern with the emphasis on the individual at the expense of other, possibly more plausible, explanations of ill-health - what Crawford (1984) calls 'the politics of diversion'. A second problem is the fact that it assumes free choice for individuals to actually be able to change their behaviours or to be able to choose a more healthy lifestyle. Clearly, this is problematic for many. Third, healthism legitimates the status quo since because of its individualistic nature broader questions are not engendered. Social, cultural, economic and political questions are rarely asked by health educators yet we know these are serious factors in promoting ill-health.

2.1 Manifestations of healthism in the school curriculum

Healthism is so pervasive within our practices at the primary, secondary and tertiary levels that it is relatively easy to identify once we engage the idea of critical thinking (Carr and Kemmis, 1986), problematization (Freire, 1970), or what Burnard, (1989) calls 'reflective scepticism'.

First, much of what passes as health education (and therefore HBPE) involves a reductionist and atomistic perspective. This is probably a legacy of the historical development of medicine, and in particular, anatomy. Diseases were located in the individual body so therefore the treatment was also located within that same body. Technology has allowed us to forage deeper and deeper into the human body - into areas which not too long ago were thought to be inaccessible. Also, health education's close relationship in the curriculum to other subjects such as Biology, Sex Education and Physical Education in particular, whose brief is, and always has been , 'the physical'. This of course, is represented in the simplistic man-machine (sic) metaphors which prevail in HBPE (see Colquhoun, 1990a). It will be clear from this paper that this 'physicality' of physical education has been a major stumbling block to the potential of HBPE to foster anything close to emancipation or a socially critical perspective.

The second point follows on from the first because not only is health education often reductionist but in many instances it is factual. Gammage (1988), in her analysis of sexuality (sex education) as a school subject, has called this 'the flight to facts'. Many teachers feel more comfortable with dealing with facts, particularly in perceived 'controversial' areas such as sexuality. The reliance on the factual also reinforces the legitimacy of a certain type of knowledge - that of the scientific (and therefore often medical) at the expense, say, of the experiential or the aesthetic. This reliance on factual knowledge is related to the nature of knowledge in traditional health education programmes. Most contemporary health education practices are based on the health belief model (see Figure 1). The provision of information leads to changes in attitudes and beliefs, which in turn lead to decision making and which finally leads to the selection of positive behaviours. Now clearly, this is an ideal representation, but it does reflect the kinds of processes inherent in health education. HBPE for example, may actually start at practical behaviours such as skipping (and enjoyment of), this will then lead children to actively seek more information (knowledge) of the topic. The problem with the health belief model is that it doesn't work (French and Adams, 1986; Naidoo, 1986) and that the links between the various strands of the model are tenuous at best.

Again, the third point is related to the previous two. Health education often has decision making at its core. The idea that we as health educators only need to enable individuals to weave their way through the decision making process, is pervasive, so much so in fact, that it often seems the *raison d'être* of health education. The 'Say No' campaign in the U.S.A. is a good example of this. The justification of the emphasis on decision making is that children are often susceptible to peer pressure and that the ability to withdraw from health threatening behaviours and contexts is seen as important - often the most important aspect of health education. Drug education in Australia is a prime example where decision making has taken over. Broader issues in drug education are rarely tackled.

Fourth, if the emphasis in health education isn't on decision making then it tends to be on self-esteem. Often self-esteem appears to be the 'catch all' because it is also important in the problems of girls and schooling (Kenway and Willis, 1988) and in particular, the relationship between sporting success and failure:

> The lack of recognition of female sporting success and physical potential has implications not only for girls' general physical fitness but also for their self-esteem and perceptions of their own capacities. (Schools Commission, 1984, p.30)

I am sure that most of you have seen or at least heard of the very popular texts 'Self-esteem: A Classroom Affair - 101 Ways To Help Children Like Themselves' (Borba and Borba, 1978), and '100 Ways To Enhance Self-concept in the Classroom: A Handbook for Teachers' (Canfield and Wells, 1976). These two

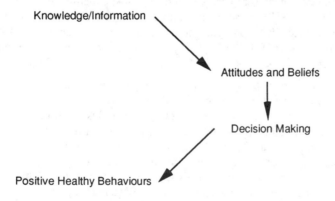

Figure 1.   *The Health Belief Model*

books are among many on the topics of self-esteem and self-concept which can be found in almost any Australian primary school. With this in mind, health education is often characterized as 'touchy feely' - an attempt to get children to become 'warm fuzzies' and not 'cold pricklies'.

Fifth, according to Hyland (1988), health educators are a profession of 'fence sitters' who constantly strive for value neutrality and objectivity. This denies the recognition that knowledge is socially constructed by powerful individuals or groups who have vested interests in health and that health knowledge has a history which is often presented as 'Whig history' - a legitimation of the (usually) great men of medicine.

These are the obvious or overt representations of healthism but it also permeates policy (both at the school and broader community levels) in various guises. For instance, I have recently suggested (Colquhoun, 1990b) that at the policy level the dominating discourse is one of economic rationalism, cost cutting and belt tightening. This shift in overall funding from expensive, highly charged curative medicine to prevention has occurred in a general fiscal crisis, of which the health care costs are simply compounding. Taking this economic rationalism in with a moral imperative to abstain and work hard at your health and we have a pressure to become healthy based on the utilitarian perception that the individual's health is intimately linked to the health of society. In other words, by working hard on your health you are saving your country money. Clearly, this is an important tool in the justificatory rhetoric of many health policies.

Obviously, self-esteem, decision making and health facts are all important in the health education curriculum. What I am suggesting however, is that there is too great a reliance on these issues at the expense of a broader agenda. **Real** causes of health and disease are often marginalized in the curriculum or simply not encountered at all.

3   The potential of health based physical education

The potential of HBPE has been couched in the idea that coronary heart disease (mainly) is a paediatric problem which can be affected in childhood by intervention in the areas of exercise and nutrition programmes. The amount of evidence for this is quite startling and is accumulating almost daily. Risk factors such as blood pressure, blood lipids, and obesity have been identified as major problems, in particular, for children in Western developed countries such as Britain, U.S.A., Canada, and Australia. Reasonable though these claims obviously are, and after all, they have the moral pressure of the emotive subject of children's' health, I would argue that we need to focus our attention on a critical perspective which would enable us to challenge the rhetoric and practice of HBPE wherever and however it appears.

3.1 *What do we need to do to foster a critical approach to HBPE? A ten point plan!*

A critical approach to schooling has, according to Sultana (1989), a three pronged base; it draws on what we know about the social construction of knowledge and its production, legitimation and distribution; it recognizes that school knowledge is now value free but reflects dominant vested interests; and, a critical perspective has a transformative and emancipatory aim in favour of visions of social justice and equality. In particular, a critical perspective on schooling raises the political agenda - an agenda which so far has been lacking in representations of HBPE. To foster a critical edge to HBPE I suggest, following earlier work on emancipatory health education (Colquhoun 1989), a ten point plan which could be taken up at the school and tertiary education levels.

(a)   We need to identify and challenge healthism wherever it exists at both the theoretical and practical level.

(b)   We need to question the taken-for-granted assumptions about HBPE which at the moment dictate our practice.

(c)   We need to reflect critically on our practices both individually, but preferably collaboratively.

(d)   With this in mind we need to build links with other teachers (and communities) in the same field.

(e)   We need to equip ourselves, our children and their parents with the necessary skills to move beyond the traditional apolitical presentation of physical education.

(f)   We need to make the 'pedagogical political and the political pedagogical' (Aronowitz and Giroux, 1985).

(g)   Accept the need for a socially critical curriculum which has emancipation, social justice and equality at its core.

(h)   Recognize that there is no such thing as 'value free knowledge'.

(i)   Break free from the 'teacher as technician' perspective which sees teachers implementing 'expertly' produced curriculum packages.

(j)   Identify and support the role of agency in resistance, refraction and transformation.

4   A possible starting point? Cultural contradictions, consumerism and reconceptualizing the body

Shapiro (1988) suggests that critical theorists can begin their task by identifying and interrogating the cultural contradictions which we are all exposed to day in and day out:

> These contradictions center on the demand for a Protestant work ethic in the area of production, for a demand for pleasure and play in the area of consumption ... The cultural contradictions of capitalism confront the modern consciousness with a bewildering set of conflicts and moral dilemmas: authority vs freedom, restraint vs indulgence, satisfaction vs denial and so on. (Shapiro, 1988; p. 428-429)

In addressing these contradictions and their significance for physical education, and more specifically HBPE, we can access the debate through what Featherstone (1983) has called 'consumer culture'. This involves:

The impact of mass consumption on everyday life which has led to the gearing of social activities around the accumulation and consumption of an ever increasing range of goods and experiences. New modes of cultural representation ensure the proliferation of images which saturate the fabric of social life with a melee of signs and messages which summon up new expressive and hedonistic definitions of the good life. (Featherstone, 1983; p.4)

Consumer culture is largely involved in the analysis and decoding of messages which bombard the individual's consciousness, messages which ultimately lead to the consumption of consumer goods and the production of profit. To do this, consumer culture induces self-improvement and self-expression by focusing on idealized representations of lifestyle, the body and health:

Consumer culture latches on to the prevalent self-preservationist conception of the body, which encourages the individual to adopt instrumental strategies to combat deterioration and decay... and combine it with the notion that the body is a vehicle of pleasure and self-expression. Images of the body beautiful, openly sexual and associated with hedonism, leisure and display, emphasise the importance of 'the look'. (Featherstone, 1982; p.18)

Clearly, consumer culture is a rich source and data bank for the physical education profession. Images and messages saturate our consciousness in almost every conceivable way. What we need to do as a profession with a mission of developing a socially critical curriculum, is to tap into this resource of the media and consumerism so that we can indeed begin our task of striving for emancipation, social justice and equality. Aronowitz and Giroux (1985) are worth commenting here:

A programmatic alternative... might begin by recognising that if the task is to penetrate the apparently opaque 'mind set' of students, then the spectacle in which they are caught must be deconstructed... Many of them (students) live for the spectacle of the television show, the rock concert, the record party and other mass cultural activities...deconstruction of mass audience culture is the first priority. We mean that writing could consist in the first place in analysis of TV shows of the most popular variety, critical interrogation of popular music, and close scrutiny of film genres that approximate mass culture... In other words the job of the teachers is to legitimate mass audience culture in order to criticise and transcend it , or to discover whether legitimate expressive forms are repressed within it. (Aronowitz and Giroux, 1985; 52)

Later, Giroux (1988) suggests that critical curriculum theorists have two main tasks; first to 'analyze how cultural production is organised within asymmetrical relations of power in schools', and second they need to 'construct political strategies to fight for schools as democratic public spheres' (p. 201). This second point, that schools are inherently political, has also been recognized by Ilona Kickbusch of the World Health Organization who has suggested that one of the major goals of health education today is to, through the emerging New Public Health, locate health on the political agenda (both little 'p' and big 'P') (see Colquhoun and Robottom, 1990a).

To fulfil what Giroux (1988) calls 'cultural politics' we could embark on analysing three fields: 'the discourse of production, the discourse of text analysis and the discourse of lived cultures'. Briefly, what Giroux is referring to by the discourse of production is the examination of how structural forces outside schooling and in the public sphere have shaped how schools function in society. We could investigate instances of domination, construction and representation.

By examining the discourse of text analysis Giroux highlights how messages and meaning penetrate the curriculum and how cultural forms are reproduced in practice. Michael Apple (1982) perhaps is the most popular theorist who has analysed curriculum packages, whilst Williamson (1978) has written a classic piece on decoding advertisements. Indeed, a variety of texts have been examined mainly of issues such as sexism - such as **Thomas the Tank Engine** (Carrington and Denscombe, 1987), and racism - **Little Black Sambo** (Lloyd, 1984). My own research, which can be broadly classed as 'The Politics of Health' allows me to focus on the individual human body and how it is presented in childrens' story books, and also in childrens' cartoons (How can we understand the popularity of 'The Teenage Mutant Ninja Turtles', or 'Transformers' or 'Masters of the Universe' for example?), and also on popular music videos which are specifically aimed at adolescents. What is clear is that sexism and racism are rife in childrens' texts but what I want to examine is the prevalence of healthism in these same childrens' texts. Early explorations in the area (Colquhoun, 1990b) show that healthism is just as pervasive as other forms of bias and distortion.

The discourse of lived cultures, according to Giroux (1988), refers to what Touraine (1977) calls 'self-production'. In other words, how do we give meaning to our various daily experiences given that we live in a complex social, cultural and political world. In this regard, Colquhoun and Robottom (1990b) have suggested that in the health area we need an investigation into the perceived meanings which individuals ascribe to the various categories of existence such as 'health' and 'environment'. Simply, we need to examine what exactly does 'health' **mean** for individuals and perhaps more important, we need to elaborate on the social and cultural conditions which determine the form and content of our perceptions. Building on the work of Gregory Bateson (1972), Kickbusch suggests that we need to develop coherent and plausible theories of health behaviour which take in to account individuals' meaning and context. Individuals are not mere reactionaries to pre-ordained stimuli, we all take into account the context of our behaviours and actions. Because of this we as investigators need to interrogate the relationship between meaning and context to discover, as Kickbusch suggests, the patterns or meta-patterns of health behaviour which serve to reflect the inter-connectedness and the dialectical nature of meaning and context. If you like - the cause and effect chain of human behaviour is so long and complex that we need to study the context of the behaviour and the ascribed meaning by the individuals concerned. Only then will we be able to theorize adequately individuals' health behaviour. In addition, and of crucial importance, is that we as researchers must recognize the reflexive nature of our biographies in terms of the dialectical relationship between our biographies and the object or subject under investigation.

4.1 *Reworking the body*

It is clearly evident that physical education presents a functional corporeality. The body is to be trained, serviced, maintained and manipulated through various sets of exercises if we are to avoid ill-health in the future. We only need to conduct a brief content analysis of some of the GCSE syllabuses in use in Britain at the moment to see how we present and rationalize the human body. The Northern Examining Association (NEA) Physical Education syllabus for 1989 for example has three major components:

(a) Physical Activities

(b) The Physical Basis of Practical Performance
   - the human body as a unit
   - the effects of physical activity on the body
   - physical fitness
   - factors affecting fitness
   - the effects of training
   - methods of training
     diet
   - injuries

(c) Organization of and Participation in Physical Activities
   - growth and development of sport and physical recreation
   - national organisations
   - local provision of physical activities
   - issues and values in sport and physical activities

On the face of it this is a reasonable and typical physical education syllabus. What I would argue, however, is that by focusing so much on the functional aspects of corporeality (fitness, biology, training, diet, injuries) as well as on an unproblematic encounter with the structure of sport at an institutional level, we are depoliticizing the body (Lock, 1988) just at the very time when we need to raise its political profile. Scientific rationality is the dominant discourse - a discourse which sets aside emotional and moral dimensions.

In contrast when we consider a broader perspective on the body we automatically enter debates about 'relationships between body and mind, culture and nature, self and society' (Turner, 1987; p. 218), as well as a phallocratic domination of women's bodies through the 'technical, political and ideological battle' over sexuality. To remain mute is to condone the depoliticized tendencies of how we think about the body.

Being more optimistic we could take the lead from one Australian school curriculum - VCE (Victorian Certificate in Education) Health Education which is equivalent to the British 'A' levels. The VCE Health Education is organized around four areas of focus; health for youth, health for all, issues in health, health in a changing society. Underpinning the VCE course is a belief that while many health problems are related to personal behaviours and could be prevented by action at the individual level, it is often too easy to blame the sufferer of the disease. The starting point for improving health is to recognise how our ways of life are dependent on the social, cultural, economic, physical and political environment. (VCE Draft Study Design, 1988)

For each of these units the students are expected to complete selected work tasks, one of which is a media analysis of a given health issue, the purpose of which is to

assist students to critically analyse a health issue presented in the media and to reflect on the role of the media in providing information on aspects of health and in contributing to community attitudes and behaviours in health matters.

Clearly, one area of focus could be the presentation of the human body in the media (and texts). What images, messages and meanings are associated with these presentations and how do these messages manifest themselves in our daily practices? Issues encountered might include; representations of personality types and body shape/size, sexual stereotyping, using the body to sell consumer goods, how exercising the body/sport is related to consumer goods, how is the unhealthy body presented in the media?, how is the 'disciplined' body presented in the media, the moral imperatives which are associated with the body, how we polarize the body in terms of positive and negative poles (Levin, 1985), how weight loss or diminution is presented in the media, the idealized images tp which we are exposed, the bodily metaphors (for example, the body/machine metaphor) that exist, and so on.

Isn't it amazing! For a profession dealing with the body we know surprisingly little about it ! Tinning (1990) has mentioned recent leanings towards postmodern thought and how this may affect pedagogy in physical education. Postmodernism may also have significant repercussions for how we operationalize the body and how we think about health and illness. In one of the few articles on postmodernism, health and fitness, Glassner (1989) suggests for example, that with modernism dualities such as the inner and outer bodies, male and female, work and leisure are the order of the day. However, within postmodernism thought 'contradictions and complexity prevail'. I would urge however, that just as we develop our postmodern insights into the body, health and fitness, we also investigate the body from a broad frame of reference. For example, we can pursue what Levin (1985) calls phenomenological psychology, 'embodiment', and 'humanization' and also 'archeological' studies of the body such as the classic by Onians (1988) as well as the sociological and phenomenological (Howes, 1989). In addition, we can examine the socio-cultural and historical roots of our thinking about the body by investigating how the great philosophers such as Neitzche, Merleau-Ponty and Heidegger see the body.

5   Conclusion

In this short paper I have attempted to present the limitations and possibilities of health based physical education (HBPE) first of all by outlining the dominant ideology of health education and thus, HBPE, and secondly by suggesting that the future of HBPE is secured if it takes on board a critical perspective which has emancipatory intent and social justice at its core. Healthism can be identified in various guises in the curriculum ranging from an emphasis on reductionism and the factual through to a heavy reliance on self-esteem and decision making. A critical pedagogy would foster a collaborative and supportive approach to curriculum. By having popular culture as a focus of study it would be possible to fulfil what I consider to be a necessity; a broadening of our perceptions of the body. By examining the reconceptualised body and how it is presented and operationalized, we can move beyond the traditional boundaries and discourses of physical education.

6   References

Almond, L.. (1983) A rationale for health related fitness, **Bulletin of Physical Education, 19,** (2) 5-10.

Apple, M. (1982) **Education and power,** ARK: London .

Aronowitz, S. & Giroux, H. (1985) **Education under siege.** RKP: London.

Bateson, G. (1972) **Steps to an ecology of mind,** Ballantine Books: New York.

Borba, M. & Borba, D. (1978) **Self-esteem: a classroom affair - 101 ways to help children like themselves,** Winston Press: Minneapolis.

Burnard, P. (1989) Developing critical ability in nurse education, **Nurse Education Today, 9,** 271-275.

Canfield, J. & Wells, H. (1976) **100 ways to enhance self-concept in the classroom: a handbook for teachers and parents.** Prentice Hall: New Jersey.

Carr, W. Kemmis, S. (1986) **Becoming critical: knowing through action research,** Deakin University Press: Geelong, Australia.

Carrington, B. & Denscombe, M. (1987) Doubting Thomas: reading between the lines, **Childrens' Literature in Education,** 18, (1) 45-53.

Colquhoun, D. (1989) Emancipatory health education and environmental education: the new public health, **Australian Journal of Environmental Education,** August, (5) 1-8

Colquhoun, D. (1990a) **Healthism and health based physical education,** Unpublished Ph. D. thesis, University of Queensland, Australia.

Colquhoun, D. (1990b) Images of healthism in health based physical education, In: Kirk, D. & Tinning, R. (Eds.), **Physical education, curriculum and culture: critical issues in the contemporary crisis,** Falmer Press: London.

Colquhoun, D. Kelly, P. & Stevens, L. (1990) Individualism and school health education: a case study of alcohol education in a Victorian primary school, **ACHPER National Journal.**

Colquhoun, D. & Robottom, I. (1990a) Health education and environmental education: toward a shared agenda and a shared discourse. **Unicorn,** 16, (2), 109-118.

Colquhoun, D. & Robottom, I. (1990b) **Action research and adolescents' perceptions of health and environment.** NH&MRC research proposal.

Combes, G. (1989) The ideology of health education in schools.. **British Journal of the Sociology of Education,** 10, (1), 67-80.

Crawford, R. (1980) Healthism and the medicalization of everyday life, **Int. J. of Health Services,** 10, (3), 365-389.

Crawford, R. (1984) A cultural account of "health": control, release and the social body. In: J.B. McKinlay, (Ed.), **Issues in the political economy of health care,** Tavistock: London.

Featherstone, M. (1982) The body in consumer culture, **Theory, Culture and Society**, 1, (3), 4-9.

Featherstone, M. (1983) Consumer culture: an introduction, **Theory, Culture and Society**, 4, 55-70.

Freire, P. (1970) **Cultural action for freedom**, Penguin: Harmondsworth.

French, J. & Adams, L. (1986) From analysis to synthesis: theories of health education, **Health Education Journal**, 45, (2), 71-74.

Gammage, S. (1988) The teaching of sexuality, In: Carrington, B. & Troyna, B. (Eds.), **Children and Controversial Issues**, The Falmer Press: London.

Giroux, H. (1988) Critical theory and the politics of culture and voice: rethinking the discourse of educational research, In: Sherman, R.R. & Webb, R.B. (Eds.), **Qualitative research in Education: Focus and Methods**, The Falmer Press: London.

Glassner, B. (1989) Fitness and the postmodern self. **Journal of Health and Social Behaviour**, 30, 180-191.

Howes, D. (1989) Re-figuring the body. **Sante, Culture and Health**, VI, (1) 73-81.

Hyland, T. (1988) Morality, individualism and health education, **Journal of the Institute of Health Education**, 26, (2) 80-83.

Kenway, J. & Willis, S. (1988) **Hearts and minds: self-esteem and the schooling of girls**. DEET: Canberra.

Kemmis, S., Cole, P. & Suggett, D. (1986) **Orientations to curriculum and transition: towards the socially critical school**, Victorian Institute of Secondary Education: Melbourne.

Kickbusch, I. (1989) Self care in health promotion, **Soc. Sci. Med.**, 29, (2), 125-130.

Levin, D.M. (1985) **The body's recollection of being: Phenomenological psychology and the deconstruction of nihilism**, RKP: London.

Lloyd, E. (1984) Little black sambo, **Dragons Teeth**, 20, 4.

Lock, M. (1988) Introduction, **Biomedicine examined**, Kluwer Academic: London.

Naidoo, J. (1986) Limits to individualism, In: Rodmell, S. & Watt, R. (Eds.), **The politics of health education: raising the issues**, RKP: London.

Onians, R.B. (1988) **The origins of European thought about the body, the mind, the soul, the world, time and fate**. Cambridge University Press: Cambridge.

Riska, E. (1982) Health education and its ideological content, **Acta Sociologica**, 25, Supplement 41-46.

Rodmell, S. & Watt, A. (1986) **The politics of health education: raising the issues**, RKP: London.

Schools Commission, (1984) **Girls tomorrow: the challenge for schools.** The report of the commonwealth schools commission working party on education for girls. AGPS: Canberra.

Shapiro, S. (1988) Beyond the sociology of education: culture, politics and the promise of educational change, **Educational Theory**, 38, (4), 415-430.

Sultana, R.G. (1989) Are there any critical educators out there? Perspectives on teachers and transformation. **Critical Pedagogy Networker**, 2, (4).

Tinning, R. (1990) Pedagogy in teacher education: dominant discourses and the process of problem setting, **AIESEP**, Loughborough University.

Touraine, A. (1977) **The self production of society**, University of Chicago Press: Chicago.

Turner, B.S. (1987) The interdisciplinary curriculum: from social medicine to postmodernism, **Sociology of Health and Illness**, 12, (1) 1-23.

Vertinsky, P. (1985) Risk benefit analysis of health promotion: opportunities and threats for physical education, **Quest**, 37, 71-83.

Whitehead, J. & Fox, K. (1983) Student centred physical education, **Bulletin of Physical Education**, 19, (2), 21-30.

Williamson, J. (1978) **Decoding advertisements**, Marion Boyars: London.

THE SYSTEMATIC DEVELOPMENT OF FITNESS SKILLS FOR PRIMARY SCHOOL CHILDREN: A PLANNED INTERVENTION

A. TAGGART
Curtin University of Technology, Perth, Australia

Abstract

The importance of introducing preventative measures in childhood aimed at reducing the risk of cardiovascular disease in later life is now widely acknowledged. Such strategies are based on evidence that these risk factors are already operative at an early age in substantial proportions of populations of children of developed countries. Correction and possible reversal of these and other risks, by simple and readily acceptable life style changes, could potentially have a dramatic impact on heart disease in adult life. The study outlined here is designed to evaluate the short and long term effects of diet and exercise programmes for 11 and 12 year old children. The focus of this paper is to describe the development, field testing, piloting, implementation and monitoring of the fitness/exercise intervention. Earlier work had shown that although children can improve fitness skills with short, intense fitness programmes, the generalizability of the fitness skills for the children and teaching skills of teachers, specific to fitness instruction, were limited. Further features of curriculum innovation specific to the development, field testing and pilot study phases of the study are discussed. The paper will conclude with a description of the fitness/exercise activities that have been implemented during the first phase of the study. The effectiveness of the specified teaching strategies will also be discussed.

Keywords: Fitness, Children, Cardiovascular Disease, Daily Fitness, Teacher Effectiveness.

1   Introduction

The importance of introducing preventative measures in childhood aimed at reducing the risk of cardiovascular disease in later life is now widely acknowledged. At both international (World Heath Organization, 1990) and national (Better Health Commission, 1986) levels there has been a very strong emphasis given to the encouragement of physical activity as a central preventative strategy. Similarly, the need to address the prevention of cardiovascular disease through approaches based on quitting smoking and changes to diet patterns are now well documented in Australia (Baghurst et al., 1988), Scandinavia (Erhholm et al., 1982) and North America (Hubert, 1986).

Australian adults and children are typical of similar populations of western countries in having high dietary fat intakes (Jenner and Miller, in press), a factor which has been established as a cardiovascular disease risk factor for children (Webber et al., 1986; Pollastschek and O'Hagan, 1989). The relationship between cardiovascular disease risk and level of exercise has also been investigated with evidence demonstrating the reduction of risk factors such as blood pressure and body weight following exercise programmes (Haskell, 1984).

This study, now half way through its three year term, is a major Federally funded project where researchers from Medicine - epidemiologists, Health Promotion nutritionists, and Education - physical educationists have combined their knowledge and skills to evaluate the short and long term effects of diet and exercise programmes on 11 and 12 year old children. Interventions in adult populations have shown cardiovascular risk factors can be reduced by modification of diet and exercise patterns (Rouse et al., 1983; Sedgwick et al., 1988). It is expected that diet and exercise interventions with children would have similar results although limited data is available to support this assumption (Dwyer et al., 1983). Studies which target both diet and exercise with children have typically taken place at school and have shown positive results (Downey et al., 1987; Maynard et al., 1987).

Whereas this study is designed to examine the effectiveness of nutrition and physical activity-based interventions in reducing further cardiovascular disease risk in children, this paper will focus on the development, field testing, implementation and monitoring of only the fitness/exercise (school phys. ed.) intervention. The children in the study are in year 6 classes in State primary schools in the Metropolitan area of an Australian capital city. The study includes two separate 2 x 2 factorial experiments. The first experiment is designed to examine the effects of a school-based nutrition education programme, a school-based physical education programme and their combined effects relative to control group. (see below)

School nutrition + School phys. ed	School nutrition
School phys.ed	Control

The second experiment is designed to examine the effects of the same school-based nutrition education programme, a home-based nutrition education programme and the combined effects relative to a control group. (see below)

School nutrition	School nutrition + Home nutrition
Control	Home nutrition

Approximately 1,000 children have been randomly allocated, by school, to each of the six groups. Ten schools formed the school phys. ed. group. Dependent measures for each group in the study are categorized under the broad headings; Adherence to programmes; Knowledge, values and attitudes; Dietary assessment; Physical activity assessment; Physical fitness; Physical measurements; Biochemical measurements; Process measures of the validity of the independent variable.

2   Fitness/Exercise intervention

Fitness in schools is seen by some as a curriculum issue central to physical education (Blackwell, 1990), whereas by others, fitness-only programmes are critized because they don't or can't work and emphasize only the temporary attainment of physical fitness (Corbin, 1987), and, by others, a fitness emphasis for K-12 programmes is seen as too restrictive in terms of what quality physical education should provide for children (Metzler, 1990; Taggart, 1988). Tinning (1990) on the other hand believes that morning fitness sessions ' ... are at best window-dressing, and at worst a reinforcement of the values and assumptions of healthism which ignore the social and political context of health.' (p.88). The beliefs underpinning this study were that health related fitness for children, or health based physical education as it is often termed, is about developing an essential skill that all students should be encouraged to practice and hopefully achieve. With appropriate attention to behavioural shaping, reinforcement schedules and controlling environmental stimuli (that's what a behaviourist calls the social and political context) health related fitness can be achieved within school curriculum time. The fitness/exercise intervention is about having children huffing and puffing for 15-20 minutes, 4 or 5 times each week. It is about developing fitness behaviours, getting them to appear and then shaping them so that they generalize in the child's non-school environment. Good behaviour analysts, good fitness educators, and indeed good teachers plan on nothing less.

Although physical education has long advocated its contribution to physical health it can be argued that unless fitness-direct instruction is implemented (Taggart, 1985) it is unlikely that this advocacy can be justified. Physical education classes with a skill focus rarely achieve fitness gains. Motor skills are not learned without specific repeated practice. Fitness skills can be viewed as a subcomponent of motor skills and as such specific practice is essential if skill gains are to accrue. The exercise scientists tell us that this specific skill training, that is the practice of fitness skills, must occur frequently, three or four times each week, for a duration of 15-20 minutes at an appropriate intensity (heart rate greater than 150 beats/min). Most classroom teachers in primary schools can be introduced to and understand (verbalize) the concepts of specificity, frequency and intensity yet they rarely have the teaching skills and fitness content knowledge to implement these concepts in fitness sessions with a class of 30 pupils. The fitness/exercise intervention was directed at promoting effective teaching skills thus increasing the probability of children participating in fitness sessions that can make a physiological difference.

2.1 *Pilot study and field testing of the fitness intervention*

A pilot study was conducted in term 4 1989 with eight schools participating. The pilot study included an inservice programme which was designed to be interactive to ensure teacher input, yet informative enough to promote confidence in beginning the programme. A three hour session, consistent with established Ministry of Education formats, included goals and objectives of the programme, the principles of fitness improvement and maintenance for children, an outline of the knowledge based classroom programme and practical activities demonstrating some of the intended lessons of the fitness programmes. Objectives were developed for all aspects of the programme. The objectives focused on behaviour change specific to activity levels and performing fitness activities.

Discussions, interviews and observations of the teachers and pupils during this one term pilot study was enlightening. The results emphasized the need for knowledge based classroom materials to be very brief. The teachers could clearly build on and develop in-class activities that met the knowledge objectives of the classroom component. No teachers covered the content of the five lessons in the suggested time, and several teachers completed only two of the five lessons. The pilot study results emphasized the need for a high degree of structure in the fitness activity sessions. If the principles of intensity and progressive overload were to be even remotely adhered to, classroom teachers needed highly structured and prescribed lesson plans. Teachers could generally adhere to suggested time frames (lessons of 15-20 minutes) for the fitness sessions although the activities themselves were sometimes modified to meet the time allocation.

Teachers expressed concern about organization and management issues to promote high intensity activity. For example, starting and stopping the running activities incorporating the interval principle (and the organization of teams for relays) and also about their lack of knowledge in activities such as health hustles (exercise to music) and skipping (Jump Rope for Heart). The children compounded some of these issues by indicating their enjoyment in performing skipping and health hustle activities. This was particularly evident with the girls and emphasized by the teachers as a positive outcome for these students. Several changes to the testing protocol of the teacher controlled field tests (1.6km run and Leger Shuttle run) were also suggested and the need for skill instruction for skipping activities became clear.

2.2 *Development of materials for implementation*

Based on teacher and pupil feedback and the observations of the researchers the curriculum package was modified and support materials prepared. For example a video was prepared for the health hustle activities where a large sample of warm-up and up-tempo exercises were shown in isolation, then with music and then in a model health hustle lesson. Organization and management strategies for the teacher controlled field testing were also included in a video which became part of the teacher's materials.

The classroom knowledge based programme was designed as five 30-minute lessons so that pupils would be able to identify the components of physical fitness, the benefits of regular physical activity, the principles upon which an exercise programme should be based and that exercise, food intake and weight loss and/or gain are interrelated. The fitness activity programme was to be conducted four or five times each week and was designed to ensure that the intervention included four clusters of activities.

Table 1 *Sample weekly and term schedule for fitness activities*

Aims: To build on basic fitness levels established in term 1. To closely monitor intensity (heart rate) and improvement levels for a variety of fitness activities to ensure students are making gains in cardio-respiratory fitness

Week	Monday	Tuesday	Wednesday	Thursday	Friday
1	RUN	RUN	RELAYS	RUN	RELAYS
2	RUN	HEALTH HUSTLE	FUN RELAYS	RUN	HEALTH HUSTLE
3	RUN	HEALTH HUSTLE	RUN	LEGER SHUTTLE	HEALTH HUSTLE
4	RUN	HEALTH HUSTLE	RUN	LEGER SHUTTLE	HEALTH HUSTLE
5	RUN	HEALTH HUSTLE	* 1.6 Km RUN	LEGER SHUTTLE	* 1.6 Km RUN
6		JRFH or CHOICE	RELAYS	LEGER SHUTTLE	JRFH or HEALTH HUSTLE
7	RUN	JRFH or CHOICE	RELAYS	* LEGER SHUTTLE	JRFH or HEALTH HUSTLE
8	RUN	JRFH or CHOICE	RELAYS	RUN	JRFH or HEALTH HUSTLE
9	10 MIN CLASS RUN	JRFH or CHOICE	RELAYS	CLASS SESSION	JRFH or HEALTH HUSTLE
10	RUN	JRFH JUMP OFF	RELAYS	HEALTH HUSTLE	CLASS SESSION

* *Testing Session*

Individual Running, Relays, Health Hustles and Jump Rope for Heart/Skipping were allocated to a weekly and term schedule (see Table 1). Two half-day inservice programmes were provided for the teachers. The first inservice programme began five days before the programme was to begin and the second after week three of the programme. Teachers in the pilot study had stressed the need for a follow-up inservice to provide assistance with problems that occurred during the early phases of the programme.

2.3 *Fitness/exercise activities of the programme*

Individual Running was seen as the cornerstone of the programme for several reasons. Firstly it was an individual activity, where individual accountability is stressed; it required little equipment, few sophisticated management strategies and the principles of interval training could be readily implemented. Teachers also saw it as an 'ideal' activity to begin the week. As running is frequently a punishing activity for low fitness children a very low intensity, jog/walk interval training programme was initiated. It began (week four) with a 30-second jog/ 30-second walk regimen for a total of five minutes and by the end of term one (week ten) had progressed to a 60-second jog/30-second walk regimen for a total of 12 minutes. This represented a very controlled and systematic attempt to raise the level of aerobic fitness of low fitness children to a level that would promote the achievement of basic fitness skills. Running activities generally incorporate interval training, formal testing (1.6km run and Leger shuttle run), fun runs and a variety of activities that emphasize continuous individual practice.

Relays incorporated conventional running over short distances (10, 15, 20 metres) with the number of sets and repetitions at these distances being controlled in each lesson. This was to promote the maximum utilization of the allocated time for each lesson. File, shuttle, zigzag, Leger shuttle and novelty relays were incorporated during the programme. The need for up-tempo running and team sizes of four or five pupils were emphasized. Small teams allowed the physiological benefits of interval training, an inherent part of relays, to be optimized.

Health Hustles are a sequence of exercises performed to music. Each health hustle lasts for 15-20 minutes and has two parts, a warm-up (generally the first song) and an up-tempo work out (the remaining three or four songs). Both during the inservice programme and in the curriculum package (including a videotape) the aim of the health hustles was stressed. The aim was for all children to be actively engaged in whole body movements. The desirability of 'looking good' and moving in precise rhythm was de-emphasized. Contemporary music was selected and students were encouraged to bring their own favourite music during term two. During term three and four students were encouraged to design their own health hustles. Teachers were encouraged to periodically monitor the exercise heart rates of children during the health hustles. A target of 150 beats per minute was set for the up-tempo phase.

Jump Rope for Heart/Skipping, a programme developed by the National Heart Foundation, added to the variety of fitness activities traditionally incorporated in fitness sessions. Schools were provided with ropes for each child and the Jump

Rope for Heart instructional booklet. Classroom teachers or physical education specialists were requested to teach a skills unit on skipping prior to introducing a fitness session based on skipping. Prior monitoring of lessons had indicated that skills levels often determined the intensity of the workout, that is, low skills-low intensity. Initially the programme incorporated basic jump variations and a timed interval training approach moving from eight to 12 minutes of interval skipping. Skipping to music was also encouraged and children are encouraged to choreograph the skipping sequences.

Leger Shuttle Run. The Leger Shuttle run (Leger et al., 1984) is a field based test used to measure maximal aerobic capacity of children. A set cadence is played on a tape recorder, and the children are required to repeatedly cover a distance of 20 metres commencing at a slow jog and then at a gradually increasing tempo. The shuttle run was used as a test of maximal aerobic capacity but was also modified in the form of relays and interval regimes as part of the daily fitness sessions. The intensity level of the activity was structured to promote adherence to intensity and duration principles.

Each fitness lesson was based on a lesson plan. Sample plans for each activity from term 2 are given in Table 2.

Table 2   *Sample lesson plans for fitness activities*

Monday	Tuesday	Wednesday	Thursday	Friday
RUN	JRFH or CHOICE	RELAYS	LEGER SHUTTLE	JRFH or CHOICE or HEATH HUSTLE
Warm-up	**Warm-up**	**Warm-up**	**Warm-up**	
Student led (four stretches)	Heel-toe (30 secs) Calf stretch Rope swings (no jumping)	Stretches calf hamstrings shoulders	as Wednesday	JRFH - as Tuesday Health Hustle select new or repeat an earlier health hustle
Activity	**Activity**	**Activity**	**Activity**	Choice - student teacher to choose activity
6 min jog/ 1 min walk - 14 min total	JRFH: Basic jump: - 30 sec skip / 30 sec rest - 6 sets	Relays - teams of 4 Zig-Zag file relay	7 mins max rest (Set shuttle target of 60 laps)	
(this is 2 sets of jog-walk)	This is 12 mins interval skipping	.5 .10 .15 .20 - x 5 at 15m - x 5 at 10 m	* Students who stop before 7 min continue to jog-walk once results recorder	
* Target of 1100-1200 metres in 6 minutes	Choice - student or teacher to choose activity	File relay: Pass baton/ball /beanbag - x 5 at 15m - x 5 at 10	* Partners record lap	

All fitness sessions are conducted outdoors four or five days each week and are preceded by a very brief, two or three minute warm-up. The brief warm-up was initially teacher controlled but gradually becomes the children's province. The pupils were not required to change clothes for these activities although appropriate footwear and head attire were encouraged. Teachers maintain a weekly log of the fitness activities indicating the duration of the session, a brief description of the activities and any comments of significance. To this stage teachers have indicated concerns about asthmatics and sore feet, problems with motivating both low and high fitness students, over-zealous runners who don't want to stop, and girls who plan health hustles in maths classes, to name but a few.

3   Monitoring the independent variable

It appears that although physical educators often claim the health values of physical education, most research has typically been of the pre-test and post-test variety with little if any of monitoring of the quality of the independent variable. Given the complex and diverse nature of children in relation to fitness attitudes and skills it is essential that researchers identify the quality of the physical education and/or fitness sessions children partake in. The quality or amount or time spent actively engaged in fitness sessions and more specifically fitness activities that are likely to bring about fitness benefits, that is, heart rates around 150 beats/min for 15-20 minutes, need to be monitored.

This study, through the combined use of a modified Academic Learning Time - Physical Education (ALT-PE) instrument (after Siedentop, Tousignant and Parker, 1982) (see Table 3) and a heart rate meter (Sports Tester PE 3000 which records heart rate during activity) closely monitored the quality of the fitness sessions. The heart rate meter has a memory function which allows for heart rates to be monitored and recorded every five or 15 seconds thus allowing for a correlation to be established between the child's heart rate and the interval-by-interval recording of the modified ALT-PE instrument. A 'new' ALT-PE category labelled Activity-fitness

Table 3.   *ALT-PE (Fitness) Key student behaviour*

Management	(M)	related to class business, unrelated
Transition	(T)	managerial and organizational activities related to instruction
Activity	(A)	engaged in motor skill activity, motor activity specific to warm-up, cool down or non-locomotor exercises
	(AF)	high intensity cardiorespiratory activities (> 140 beats/min)
Waiting	(W)	completed at task, period of no activity and no movement between activities
Knowledge	(K)	listening to instructions, watching a demonstration, questioning, discussing
Off Task	(O)	not engaged in assigned activity, misbehaviour, talking when teacher is explaining

Table 4.   Student time spent in ALT-PE (fitness) activities

ACTIVITY	M	K	T	W	O	A	Af
Run	0.0	0.6	5.1	6.2	0.0	23.7	64.5
Relay	0.4	1.0	14.1	50.1	0.0	7.3	27.0
Health Hustle	0.2	3.8	7.7	5.7	0.5	50.3	31.9
JRFH	0.4	4.3	16.0	28.0	0.0	31.2	20.4
Leger Shuttle	1.4	0.0	3.4	24.5	0.0	31.2	40.4
Mean	0.5	1.7	9.3	22.9	0.7	23.7	41.5

(Af) has been defined to objectively describe physical activities likely to elicit a heart rate response greater than 140 beats/minute.

Preliminary data from direct observation of fitness sessions (see Table 4) indicates that running activities provided high intensity exercise (Af) for 64.5% of the allocated time. Relays provided the lowest levels of high intensity exercise (Af) at 27.0%. Given that physiological benefits accrue during the rest phase of interval training (W - Waiting; 50.1%) fitness gains may still occur as a result of relay sessions.

The relatively low levels of Management (M) and Transition (T) behaviours suggest that the students are engaged in the intended activity for a substantial period of the allocated time. Mean levels of Activity time (A and Af) indicate that the fitness sessions have the potential to impact on the cardiovascular risk factors of children if indeed school based fitness activities are in themselves a powerful enough factor in reducing the early onset of cardiovascular disease. The data collected at the end of this study should in part verify or disprove this claim.

4   Conclusion

It is anticipated that with further data collected and with refinements of the instrumentation, that teachers will be able to identify with some degree of reliability if their students are working at levels likely to make a fitness difference, i.e. the heart is working hard. It is important that teachers be able to see that students are working at appropriate levels in a fitness session. There seems little point in calling a part of the school curriculum daily fitness if it is not likely to promote fitness gains.

This interim report suggests that the planned fitness intervention has the potential to make a difference to the fitness levels of children. Whether this difference will generalize to reducing cardiovascular risk factors remains to be seen.

5   References

Baghurst, K.I., Crawford, D.A., Worsley, A. and Record S.J. (1988). The Victorian Nutrition Survey intakes and sources of dietary fats and cholesterol in the Victorian population. **Med. J. Australia**, 149, 12-20.

Better Health Commission (1986). **Looking forward to better health. Vol 1**. AGPS, Canberra.

Blackwell, E.B. (1990). Physical Education is a central curriculum issue. **Journal of Health Physical Education and Recreation**, 61(1), 18.

Corbin, C. (1987). Physical fitness in the K-12 curriculum. **Journal of Education, Recreation and Dance**, 58 (7), 49-54 .

Downey, A.M., Frank, G.C., Webber, L.S., Marsha, D.W., Virgilio, S.J., Franklin, F.A. and Berenson, G.S. (1987) . Implementation of 'heart smart' . A cardiovascular school health promotion program. **J. School Health**, 57, 98-104.

Dwyer, T., Coonan, W.E., Leitch, D.R., Metzel, B.S. and Baghurst, R.A. (1983). An investigation of the effects of daily physical activity on the health of primary school students in South Australia. **Int. J. Epidemiol**, 12, 308-313.

Erholm, C., Huftuner, J.K. and Pietinen, P. (1982). Effect of diet on serum lipoproteins in a population with a high risk of coronary heart disease. **N. Eng. J. Med**, 14, 850-855.

Haskell, W.L. (1984). Health benefits of exercise, in **Behavioural Health** (eds J.D. Matarazzo, S.M. Weiss, J.A. Herd, and N.E. Miller), Wiley, New York.

Hubert, H.B. (1986). The importance of obesity in the development of coronary risk factors and disease: the epidemiological evidence. **Ann. Rev. Public Health**, 7, 493-502.

Jenner, D.A. and Miller, M.R. (in press). Nutrient intakes of 12 year old Western Australian children. **Australian Journal of Nutrition and Dietetics**.

Leger, L., Lambert, J., Goulet, A., Rowan, C. and Dinelle, Y . (1984) Aerobic capacity of Quebecois aged 6-17 in the 20 metre shuttle run test with one minute stages, **Can. J. Appl. Sport Sci.**, 9, 64-69.

Maynard, E.J., Coonan, W.E., Worsley, A., Dwyer, T., and Baghurst, P.A. (1987). The development of the lifestyle education program in Australia, in **Cardiovascular Risk factors in Childhood: Epidemiology and Prevention** (eds B.S. Hertzel and G. S. Berenson) . Elsevier, Amsterdam, pp 123-150 .

Metzler, M. (1990). A questionable leap of faith. **Journal of Physical Education. Recreation and Dance,** 61 (4), 4-5 .

Pollatschek, J.L. and O'Hagan, F.J. (1989). An investigation of the psycho-physical influences of a quality daily physical education programme. **Health Education Research**, 4 (3), 341-350.

Rouse, I.L., Beilin, L.J., Armstrong, B.K. and Vandongen, R. (1983). Blood pressure lowering effect of a vegetarian diet in a controlled trial in normotensive subjects. **Lancet**, i, 5-10.

Sedgwick, A.W., Davidson, A.H., Taplin, R.E. and Thomas, D.W. (1988). Effects of physical activity on risk factors for coronary heart disease in previously sedentary women: a five year longitudinal study. **Aust. NZ. J. Med**, 18, 600-605.

Siedentop, D., Tousignant, M. and Parker, M. (1982). **Academic learning time - Physical education 1982 revision coding manual**. The Ohio State University, Columbus, Ohio.

Taggart, A. (1985). Fitness direct instruction. **J. of Teaching in Physical Education**, 4 (2), 143-150.

Taggart, A. (1988). Physical education: then endangered species revisited. **ACHPER National Journal**, 121, 34 -36 .

Tinning, R. (1990). Physical education as health education: Problem setting as a response to the new health consciousness. **Unicorn**, 16(2), 81-89.

Webber, L.S., Freedman, D.S. and Cresanta, J.L. (1986). Tracking of cardiovascular disease risk factor variables in school age children, in **Causation of Cardiovascular disease risk factors in children,** (ed G.M. Berenson), Raven Press, New York.

World Health Organization. (1990). **Prevention in childhood and youth of adult cardiovascular diseases: time for action**. World Health Organization, Switzerland.

STRATEGIES FOR SCHOOL FITNESS CURRICULAR MODIFICATION: AN INTEGRATIVE MODEL UTILIZING THE SUPERORDINATE GOAL THEORY

R.S. FEINGOLD, C. ROGER REES AND G.T. BARRETTE
Adelphi University, Garden City, New York, USA

Abstract
This paper presents strategies used in the implementation of new, innovative school fitness curricula, focusing on a conceptual approach to fitness knowledge, and taught within a positive framework. This particular curricular reform strategy required the co-operation of the classroom teacher and the physical education teacher in the planning process. The paper discusses the use of the superordinate goal theory in the establishment of a co-operative environment, and the development of a multi-disciplinary/integrative/co-operative model (MIC), the effectiveness of the model, and some of the curricular revisions that have begun as a result of the project. Issues and problems are identified with current school fitness programmes, difficulty in curricular reform, and the utility of the (MIC) Model, utilizing principles of superordinate goal theory as a model for future curricular reform.

1 Introduction

Numerous studies in the United States have shown significant decreases in the fitness level of its children and more importantly a significant decrease in their activity. Cardiovascular disease, once considered to be a geriatric problem, is now largely becoming recognized as a pediatric problem (Fixler and Pennock, 1983; Gabbard and Crouse, 1987). Overall, younger children weigh more and have more body fat than they did twenty years ago (Ross, et al., 1987). And the fitness levels of youth have significantly declined (Blair, 1985). Television, video games, computers, and advanced technology have often been noted as the major contributors to the decrease in the activity level of children (Raithel, 1988). In 1987, the American Academy of Pediatrics highlighted the problem in the school itself. They noted that 'schools should decrease the time spent teaching skills and team sports ... and support school programs promoting lifelong habits of health-related exercise' (Amer. Acad. Ped., 1987). The American College of Sports Medicine, the following year, prepared a position paper in support of ' ... training programs to be developed ... to provide school teachers with the knowledge and skills to help their students achieve cognitive, affective, and behavioural skill objectives associated with exercise, health and fitness. Teachers also need assistance in ways to integrate other aspects of health promotion (good nutrition and not smoking, for example) into instruction about exercise and physical fitness.' (ACSM, 1988). In the same year, the American Heart Association placed as its first priority the School Site, and for the first time noted prevention to be a viable alternative to adult heart disease (AHA, 1988). And prior to the recent position papers, others have strongly recommended that exercise behaviour must be learned during early childhood in order to develop healthy lifestyles (Kraft and McNeil, 1986), (Steinhardt and Stueuk, 1986), (Fraser, et al., 1983).

Although the American Academy of Pediatrics, American College of Sports Medicine, the American Heart Association, as well as (AAHPERD) American Alliance for Health, Physical Education, Recreation and Dance through its 'Physical Best Project' all endorse greater emphasis be placed on the teaching of health-related concepts in the schools, the Physical Education Profession in the United States has yet to fully endorse such a curricular perspective for the schools. Curricular content issues continue to be debated, specifically the teaching of skills and team sports versus health-related fitness (Simmons-Morton, et al, 1988), and an issue, this time, in regard to those who are in favour of fitness is the development of fitness, itself, versus the teaching of health-related fitness concepts and behaviour change. Other more peripheral issues relate to the testing of fitness, norm-referenced vs criterion referenced, what specific test items, and how the results of fitness tests are to be used (Fox and Biddle, 1988). Even though there is some movement towards a more conceptual approach (Parcel, 1987), (Corbin, 1987), (Gabbard, 1990), (Petray, 1989) there has been little discussion on the integration of fitness and health-related knowledge as part of a comprehensive and co-operative programme throughout the school day, i.e., integration with other subjects.

While higher education, as endorsed by NAPEHE and AIESEP mission and goal statements, has become more concerned with an integrative model, more specifically in the study of the 'whole child', the intellect, the psychology, as well as the physiology of the person, there has been a surprising lack of an integrative direction in the planning for health-related knowledges from a more multi-disciplinary, comprehensive direction.

1.1 *Typical School Fitness Models*

Typical school fitness models currently found in the schools have been summarized by Gabbard, (1990):

(a) Fitness Assessment Model typically assesses fitness at the start and end of each school term;

(b) General Activity Model assumes all sport and play activities contribute to fitness;

(c) Introductory Warm-Up Model places emphasis upon the five to ten minutes of calisthenics prior to each class;

(d)   Comprehensive Model relates fitness concepts as taught in the gymnasium to healthful life-long activity patterns - often times, health service and food service personnel are included.

In addition two models not noted by Gabbard, include

(a)   No Pain, No Gain Model that places strict discipline, training, and hard work as prerequisites to getting into shape, and

(b)   Comprehensive, Multi-disciplinary/Integrative, Co-operative Model, known heretofore as the (MIC) model, and the preferred model, emphasizes a conceptual and comprehensive approach to fitness concepts taught, and as in the comprehensive model includes health and food service personnel, but also includes the classroom teacher in addition to the physical educator. By including both the classroom and physical education teacher, the concepts are reinforced both in the gymnasium as well as the classroom.

2   Model for Multi-Disciplinary/Co-operative Workshop

With the above models and needs in mind, a model for an in-service training workshop utilizing such a multi-disciplinary/integrative/co-operative approach to curricular reform in the schools was developed with the following assumptions. The most basic, of course, is the assumption that the promotion of positive attitudes in children can foster a healthy lifestyle (Kraft and McNeil, 1986), Steinhardt and Stueuk, 1986), (Fraser, et al., 1983). Others that follow from the first assumption, include:

(a)   It is best to fight heart and cardiovascular disease by developing positive attitudes towards physical activity, exercise, nutrition and smoking while in the elementary school (Blair, 1985) (AHA Board, 1988).

(b)   Teaching of health-related concepts requires the co-operation of the physical educator and classroom teacher, so that concepts are appropriately reinforced.

(c)   Positive feelings about physical activity will occur more through positive experiences than through negative experiences.

(d)   Testing and evaluation is a means of providing feedback on how well one is doing, rather than to be used as a means of comparison to others (Fox and Biddle, 1988).

Thus in an effort to enhance health-related fitness knowledge and develop positive attitudes in children, a full-day workshop on teaching concepts was established. The significance of the presentation is not that the workshop was held, nor that 97% of the one hundred teachers that attended wished to come back on their own time, nor the prospective changes in the schools that developed, but instead the model used, specifically the co-operation of the physical educator and the classroom teacher in the integration of health related fitness knowledge, and the use of superordinate goal strategy in providing the co-operative environment for curricular change.

Therefore, in order to gain this multi-disciplinary perspective and to gain the co-operation and communication necessary for change to occur, we devised the following strategy for the workshop. Space available for the workshop was limited to one hundred participants or fifty elementary schools each with a physical educator and a classroom teacher. In order to ensure that they would bring the two as a team, the American Heart Association instructional kits and materials, valued at $75, were given to them, but only if they came as a team. In fact, because of limited space available, a school could not be represented unless there were two faculty team members in attendance. The funding for the materials, luncheon, and speakers came from a local bank. Also of interest was the make-up of the committee and sponsorship of the workshop. The committee was chaired by myself and included a school nurse, a hospital critical care nurse, two school teachers, a school superintendent, a director of physical education for one of the school districts, and two faculty (curriculum/pedagogy and psycho/socio specialists) from Adelphi University. Sponsorship came from the American Heart Association, the organization primarily responsible for running the workshop, Adelphi University, NYSAHPERD (their local president was on the committee), School Superintendent's Association, whose representative was on the committee, and EAB Bank who were funding the workshop.

3   Superordinate Goal Theory

Although a strong believer in integration, utilization of the sub-disciplines, and the use of superordinate goal theory or shared responsibility in the achievement of goals, it was not the original intended strategy of this project. Not until one of the teachers on the committee indicated that she did not want someone telling her what to do, nor how to teach, did I realize that utilization of superordinate goal theory format or shared responsibility may be appropriate. To further substantiate the workshop format, a few months later, long after it was decided to bring the classroom teacher and physical educator together, one of the committee members, who was to be a presenter at the workshop, indicated that she would present the physical education perspective. That comment was followed by the nurse who indicated that classroom teachers would not be interested in listening to a physical educator, and that comment was followed by the Superintendent who indicated that the classroom teacher was not allowed to teach physical education anyway, so why not separate them so that the physical educator can have more time at the workshop with physical education and the classroom teacher can have more time on what the classroom teacher does. Obviously, they missed a critical point in regard to the multidisciplinary/ integrative/ co-operative, model. After some fairly forceful discussion, it was reinforced that one of the major goals of the workshop was to get the physical educator and classroom teacher together as a team in order to communicate. to work together, to break down stereotypes, and to reinforce what each was doing in each other's class. That was why they were being brought together in the first place. That was, of course, a major goal of the workshop.

The superordinate goal theory, originally developed by M. Sherif in his study of the interaction between eleven and twelve year old boys in summer camp (Sherif, 1958), are goals which cannot be achieved without co-operation of potentially competing groups or individuals. In his classic study, Sherif and colleagues observed as animosity between two groups of boys increased and then tried to find ways to reduce the friction. While it is worth noting that competitive sport provided the context for the development of this conflict, the principle finding of the study was that common goals developed by these competing groups did not decrease the tension. Only when the experimenters introduced superordinate goals in which the two groups had to co-ordinate their actions to attain success was tension reduced.

Superordinate goals concept has also been suggested as way of reducing tensions in which stereotypes are reinforced (McClendon and Eitzen, 1975). In this case, it was not sport as in their study, but the stereotype of the physical educator and the classroom teacher. Rees (1985) has suggested that superordinate goals are essential in promoting peace and harmony, and in another study Parlebas (1986) found more positive feelings among groups in which interaction was necessary for the successful completion of the goal.

Within the structure of the workshop, besides promoting interaction, communication, and co-operation on the part of the team (two teachers from each school), the organizers of the conference deliberately emphasized a 'working together' rather than a telling 'how to do it' approach. Both the organizers and school teachers (team members) were to be equal partners in the superordinate goal of making the school experiences more enjoyable and meaningful for their students. Key elements in the planning for the workshop followed a similar format and structure that myself, Rees and Barrette (1989) had developed in working with youth sport coaches, as reported on last in Finland. They include:

(a) Emphasis on working together
(b) Shared ownership
(c) Maximum interaction
(d) Integration of concepts across disciplines
(e) Obtain feedback on how it worked
(f) Reinforce that their opinion and experiences are valued.

4 Workshop Outline

The structure of the workshop is presented in outline form in order to save time.

(a) Presentation on the need for fitness in our children, and the need to develop positive attitudes through innovative approaches to teaching health-related concepts, reinforced both in the gymnasium and classroom
(b) Introduced to American Heart Association Material (teacher)
(c) Application of material for the gymnasium and classroom, (classroom and physical education teacher)
(d) Introduced to basic principles on curriculum development, (university professor)
(e) At Lunch the participants were given Heart Association materials to work with team member
(f) Also during the lunch break they were given a chore, a concept, whereby they were to develop a creative way to teach the concept in the gymnasium and the classroom

(g) Evaluation techniques on how do you know that programme changes are benefitting children (university professor)

(h) Each were given the responsibility to work with the materials and develop an innovative, creative unit on health-related fitness, anywhere from a two week unit to complete curricular reform, utilizing parent education and/or school health and food service personnel.

Although we will not meet formally again until next autumn, some of the feedback that has been received so far have been significant, including:

(a) Three school districts applied for and received grants on curricular reform,

(b) Development of exercise physiology unit with equipment to be joined with the study of exercise in the gymnasium,

(c) Many districts have incorporated activity units studying the heart and nutrition, e.g., running through the cardiovascular system, the heart, picking up balloons of oxygen in the lungs and dropping them off in the muscles; picking up other balloons of carbon dioxide and dropping them off in the lungs,

(d) Combining with social studies as they run across their county, State or country, or foreign lands (utilize cycling and running at home to accumulate homeroom mileage - parent must sign off,

(e) Development of a unit called 'Heart Healthy Halloween Snacks'

(f) Combined with Math

(g) Combined with special events and outings

5   Conclusion

The significance of the project and the multi-disciplinary/integrative/co-operative model lies in the communication between the classroom teacher and physical educator. Many for the first time realized that physical education really does have an importance in a child's life and the school curricula, not only in the games and play, but also in the concepts learned. Although we are just in the beginning stages of school curriculum reform, we have seen some important successes and we offer it as a viable alternative for future curricular reform and modification.

6   References

ACSM (1988) Position Statement of Youth Fitness. **Medicine and Science in Sport and Exercise,** 20(4), 422-423.

AHA (1988) American Heart Association position statement presented at New York State Affiliate Board meeting, Saratoga Springs, New York.

Amer Acad Pediatrics (1987) Physical Fitness and the Schools. **Pediatrics,** 80(3), 449-450.

Blair, S.N. (1985) A total health fitness lifestyle. In Cundiff, D. ed., **Implementation of Health Fitness Exercise Programs,** AAHPERD, Virginia, pp.7-13.

Corbin, C.B. (1987) Physical fitness in the K-12 curriculum;: some defensible solutions to perennial problems. **JOPERD,** Sept, 49-54.

Fixler, D.E. and Pennock, L. (1983) Validity of mass blood pressure screening in children. **Pediatrics,** 72(4), 459-464.

Fox, K. and Biddle, S. (1988) The Use of fitness tests: educational and psychological considerations. **JOPERD**, Feb, 47-53.

Fraser, G., Phillips, R.L., Harris, R.L. (1983) Physical fitness and blood pressure in school children. **Circulation**, 67(2), 405-412.

Gabbard, C. (1990) Health-Related Fitness curricular formats for elementary physical education. **Strategies**, Jan, 14-18.

Gabbard, C. and Crouse, S. (1987) Children and exercise: myths and facts. **Physical Educator**, 45(1), 35-43.

Kraft, R.E. and McNeil, A. (1986) An aerobic program for children's physical education. **Physical Educator**, 43(1), 18-22.

Lieberman, E. (1974) Essential hypertension in children. **Clinical Symposia**, 30(3), 3-43.

McClendon, M.J. and Eitzen, D.S. (1975) Interracial contact on collegiate basketball teams: a test of Sherif's theory of superordinate goals. **Social Science Quarterly**, 55, 926-938.

Parcel, G. (1987) School promotion of healthful diet and exercise behaviour: an integration of organizational change and social learning theory intervention. **Journal of School Health**, 57(4), 150-156.

Parlebas, P. (1986) L'interaction sociale en education physique. Paper presented at the AIESEP World Convention, Heidelberg, Germany, August.

Petray, C.K. (1989) Classroom teachers as partners teaching health-related physical fitness. **JOPERD**, Sept, 64-66.

Raithel, K.S. (1988) Are children really fit? **Physician and Sports Medicine**, 16(10), 146-154.

Rees, C.R. (1985) The Olympic dilemma: applying the contact theory and beyond. **Quest,** 37, 50-59.

Rees, C.R., Feingold, R.S. and Barrette, G.B. (1989) Perspectives for improving intervention strategies for youth sport coaches. Paper presented at the AIESEP World Conference, Jyvaskyla, Finland, July.

Ross, J., Pate, R., Corbin, C., Delpy, L. and Gold, R. (1987) What is going on in the elementary physical education program? **JOPERD**, 58(9), 78-84.

Simmons-Morton, B., O'Hara, N., Simons-Morton, D. and Parcel, G. (1988). Children and fitness: a public health perspective, reaction to the reactions. **Research Quarterly for Exercise and Sport**, 59(2), 177-179.

Sherif, M. (1958) Superordinate goals in the reduction of intergroup conflict. **American Journal of Sociology,** 63, 349-356.

Steinhardt, M.A. and Stuenk, P.M. (1986) Personnel fitness: a curriculum model. **JOPERD**, 57(7), 23-29.

EXERCISE AND HEALTH IN A SPANISH PE CURRICULUM: A MODIFIED PROGRAMME OF 'THE EXERCISE CHALLENGE'

J. DEVIS AND C. PEIRO
IVEF & IB Generalitat Valenciana, Spain

Abstract
In this paper is described the implementation of a 'health related exercise' programme into a Spanish PE curriculum. The evaluative end of our study leads us to look at the main aims of the programme: the involvement and participation of students, and the introduction of a critical thinking to them in the context of health and exercise. Through observations, interviews and document analysis, four areas of interest were identified (contextual problems, student engagement and participation, gender differences and improvement, and prevention and lifestyle) in order to analyse the information in such a way that allows a posterior discussion and conclusion of this evaluative study, according to the main pursuits of the programme. A primary conclusion is that in addition to participation and engagement of students in their monitoring process, more attention should be paid to encourage them to appraise and understand broad socio-cultural issues related to exercise and health.
Keywords: Health Related Exercise, Physical Education, Educational Evaluation, Implementation.

1   Introduction

During the last decades fitness has been an important focus within Spanish physical education curriculum oriented to develop the basic components of fitness (speed, endurance, power and flexibility). It presents no connection with a health concern and has been taken as a set of physical tests that teachers consider valuable in themselves. These tests have become the plea to fill the PE lessons, neglecting and wasting the precious time of the current short timetable (Devis, 1990).

Although there is an increasing PE professional attention to health issues in contemporary society (see Colquhoun and Kirk, 1987), and the last regulation of Spanish PE programmes (B.O.E., 1987, Order 18 September) for High Schools (ages from 14 to 18) introduces a health concern, the above-mentioned aspects have not changed very much. As Almond (1983a) argues, there is a lack of coherent rationale to develop that idea in schools. In this sense, these facts have promoted a general confusion in the Spanish profession that has fed the maintenance of a focus on fitness as it were an innovation without change (Sparkes, 1989). This fitness focus is associated with a constant search for physical improvement, and viewed as a preparation for the efficiency and high performance in sport since it follows the principles of training (Almond, 1988).

However, in this paper is described the implementation of a programme which attempts to link exercise and health into a PE curriculum in the first course of a Spanish high school (Institut de Batxillerat). It is close to a 'health related exercise' (Almond, 1988) focus as an Innovative idea which moves away from high performance and allows participation, and satisfies the needs and interests of the majority of the pupils. The programme is a modification of 'The Exercise Challenge', developed by Sonia McGeorge (1988) at Loughborough University within the Health and Physical Education Project. The description will help to evaluate its implementation, since the involvement and participation of students in the learning process, and the introduction of a critical thinking to them in the context of health and exercise, were the two main pursuits of the programme.

2 Procedures

2.1 *School context, subjects and programme*

This study was conducted at the 'Tirant School' (pseudonym), located in a town near Valencia from January to April 1989. Four first year groups aged 14-15 (1E,1F,1K and 1L) were selected. They were required to do physical education twice a week and the classes were mixed with an average of 35-40 pupils each.

The teacher was a high school physical education specialist with two years experience. She was one of the few teachers interested in a health concern within the PE curriculum. It was her first year teaching at this school and also the first time she had put the programme into practice. She explained the programme to the other two teachers of the PE Department, but they showed no interest in it.

The modified programme takes into account the following aspects:

(a) Pupils should write and monitor their own plans considering their individual possibilities and limitations.

(b) The role of the teacher in this situation was not central, she didn't control strictly pupils' decisions on plan making, her function was to advise, give basic guidelines and review the plans.

(c) The teacher had to give a final qualification to students because PE is an examinable subject in the Spanish educational system.

(d) The material given to the pupils consisted on a series of photocopied cards in order to follow the development of their own plan. They were also handed out a newspaper article about the polemic between exercising and heart disease called 'El Infarto y el Ejercicio Fisico' (Diario 16, 1984) for comment.

2.2 *Data collection and method*

We have opted for a qualitative (Bogdan & Biklen, 1982) or naturalistic (Lincoln & Guba, 1985) research methodology because we consider it the best way to describe and understand in depth a particular event, as the implementation of the health programme in a particular situation and setting. We used informal interviews, observations and documentary analysis for gathering data. When a particular setting is chosen and the focus is centred on the perspectives and experiences of the participants, the qualitative researcher can deal with what participants think and feel as significative realities that facilitate an understanding of behaviour in context. Rather than collecting data to test preconceived hypotheses, a qualitative researcher analyses data inductively and searches for patterns and themes emerging from the data (Glasser and Strauss, 1967).

Since the qualitative or case study tradition has little resonance in the Spanish PE field, this study represents one of the first within the school setting and it was conducted for an evaluative end (Goetz and LeCompte, 1984; Merriam, 1988). In accordance with Stufflebean, 'The purpose of evaluation is to improve, not to prove', suggesting that it implies judgments of what constitutes value or worth (in Rohs, 1988, p.113).

We especially used data gathered from different perspectives: informal interviews from students, teacher observations of the teaching process, students notes and diaries as well as Official Department Acts were analysed.

3   Analysis

Data analysis reveals specific areas of findings to present the information. They are linked to the main pursuits of the programme but described according to the following areas:

(a)   Contextual problems or limitations
(b)   Student engagement and participation
(c)   Gender differences and improvement
(d)   Prevention and lifestyle

3.1 *Contextual problems or limitations*

Most of these problems were determined by the particular contextual conditions and characteristics of the 'Tirant School', its structure and schooling.

One of the main limitations or problems appeared in relation to the PE curricular timetable and its distribution within the total school curriculum. The timetable for the physical education lesson is officially two hours per week. Some schools can reduce the length of every curricular lesson from one hour to 55 minutes per class, due to school peculiarities for adjusting the total curriculum timetable, and this is the case of the 'Tirant School'. Therefore, the PE lessons, like the other subjects, have five minutes less per lesson and although it is not really significant for a subject with five lessons per week, it is a shortcoming for the PE subject which has two lessons per week. We must add some other problems due to the distribution of the PE timetable within the total structure of the school curriculum, since PE lessons must be taught in any hour possible between other academic subjects and after lunch time. It shows little attention to the PE subject because it is assumed that within class time students must get changed at the beginning and have a final shower before then going immediately to another lesson. Therefore, the real activity time is reduced from 55 to 40 minutes at best. This represented a great limitation for the students to develop their plans, as appeared repeatedly in the teacher's observations and pupils' notes. It made students and teacher react and find a solution. Although the teacher had in mind to suggest the use of time outside the school curriculum, some students expressed their intention in doing so:

> 'We haven't got enough time to finish what we had planned for today, but we'll finish it after school.'

Some others decided to take the last part of the morning break to start exercising when their PE lesson was taught after the break. The timetable structure also showed another important problem from a health point of view when the lesson took place immediately after lunch, as a student critically wrote:

> 'If we are referring to exercise as health, I think the first thing that should be done is to avoid PE lessons directly after lunch.'[1]

A second notable difficulty was related to indoor and outdoor spaces. In this sense the facilities to carry out the health programme were reduced to two narrow gyms and two small courts with a surrounding area full of stones, pebbles and holes which constrained the possibilities of exercising, especially stressed when PE teaching coincided at the same time. This situation created a lot of complaints from the students, particularly when they were running around the small playground. This basic problem was discussed in Department meetings (Acts of 88-89 school year) and was referred to the Head of the schools. Waiting for the playground to be repaired, the poor condition of the area surrounding the small courts was impossible to remedy during that school year. The use of alternative spaces like the local beach or the athletics track was refused because they were quite far away and there were no school curricular timetable changes which made it possible.

Due to these problems the teacher negotiated with the students to practise outside school time at least one day per week to complete the programme. This fact was criticized by some students at the beginning of the implementation, viewing it as a way of cheating the teacher or as a sort of obligation:

> '...it cannot be proved whether every pupil practises the activities proposed in his/her own plan.'

> 'You had to do it either outside school or on Saturdays and Sundays...'

---

[1]   Attention should be drawn to the fact that Spanish lunch is heavier and takes a longer time than other European countries.

3.2 *Student engagement, choice and participation*

One of the most significative things students liked was the fact of it being they themselves who made the decisions about their personal plan and established their own goals, although they perceived it in different ways. Some students saw it as a sign of independence or autonomy,

> 'This is quite a good programme since it allows you to have independence in programming your work'

> 'You can exercise to your own style, you don't follow the rhythm of the rest of the class...'

And others considered it as a personal commitment, becoming responsible for carrying out their own activity,

> '...you are responsible for reaching the goals established by yourself'

> 'By controlling yourself you feel more responsible and as you can establish your goals, you try to reach them and you can get the better of yourself'

Students were also fond of choosing and practising activities they wanted to do,

> 'I do like the freedom to practise what you want without anyone interfering in your work'

> 'I like it because we had the opportunity to choose'

They frequently referred to the aspects they most like by comparing the programme lessons with the lessons of years before:

> 'I think these lessons are better than the traditional ones because they let you do what you want, although you commit yourself to reach the goals established by yourself'

> '...the exercises are much more varied [now] than before. The lessons were dedicated to only one thing'

> 'I like it because I have done what I ...had proposed but not what someone obliges me to ... I didn't like physical education before, but now I like it more and I practise it more easily and longer without getting bored and without feeling forced to do it'

Moreover, this health programme facilitated the participation of all students, the skilful ones and the less skilful, the overweight and the slim, as students' opinions and teacher's observation reveal:

Student:

> '...this programme applies to every person, the most and least able, because before, a few years ago, teachers demanded a unique goal for everyone, and now you can establish your own goal and reach it. And this can be adapted to everybody'

Teacher:

'...the overweight are more accepted in class now. Comparison with the 'privileged' students [skilful] does no longer suit with this programme'

3.3 *Gender differences and improvement*

The analysis shows that although the PE lessons were mixed, the activities students planned revealed some general predilections according to gender differences.

From the observations and comments, male students showed an insistent demand towards sportive activities (preferably football and basketball games) that in the beginning were no part of the programme. 'They only want to play sport', said the teacher. Due to this interest in games, the teacher decided to include them in the programme, but establishing some limitations. She determined to give the students the opportunity to choose one day for practising games, but only during 10-15 minutes and a maximum of six pupils, so they could also have time to practise some other activities. Despite this solution, some students disagreed with that short time dedicated to sportive activities. In contrast to the boys' demands, girls showed a special disposition towards individual activities, although practised in groups of friends, as the teacher pointed out,

'Girls tend to jog and do mat or floor exercises (stretching, sit ups, etc)...it's been a success - the formation of groups to exercise during the weekend, either cycling or jogging'

Their reference to personal improvement was seen as a challenge, and many of them were astonished by their achievement, but it mainly denotes a low level of physical activity,

'In my case, I began to run for 5 minutes, and the other day I was able to run for 40 minutes, and I feel so happy!'

'I do like this programme because I have done exercises that I thought I could have never done by myself'

'The truth is that, at the beginning, I found it very hard to get used to it, but now after exercising outside school and in the PE lessons, not only have I improved my physical abilities, but also it has been very pleasing to feel the improvement in my physical condition...it was impossible for me to run without stopping and now I've run for 45 minutes...'

Speaking in a general sense, the personal improvement refers to the monitoring procedures students realized. They were administered as a motivational ingredient and as a reference to organize and adjust the plan at the beginning and in the middle respectively, as the teacher stated:

'...they (monitoring procedures) can be used as a means by which the students can check out whether they are progressing adequately or need to vary the plan once it is advisable to use the monitoring procedures in the middle of the programme'

But the monitoring procedures were also administered at the end of the programme to prove the total improvement of the students. They were used as an important element to take into account when the qualifications had to be given. This fact introduced indirectly some critical points from the students, particularly in terms of the lack of relation between the realization of the activities they had been engaged in and the outcomes of the monitoring procedures:

> 'I think to perform a prior and posterior trial is the best way of checking the accomplished improvement, it depends too much on a single thing'

> 'I consider it an inconvenience that we had to pass some exam-trials, since they don't really reflect all your effort, particularly in cardiovascular'

Students were in agreement in their complaints, especially when referring to the cardiovascular monitoring procedure. The Multistage Shuttle Run was introduced because the teacher thought it was a new exercise and would be very motivating, and it was in fact, but it proved very disappointing when the pupils passed it at the end of the programme and found that they had hardly improved. Moreover, it should be added that they had been practising jogging frequently during the programme, so they discovered a lack of connection between their low outcomes in the Multistage Shuttle Run and the results in jogging. A student's opinion clearly expresses this point:

> 'In my opinion, the 'bips' trial is not the best to check out our cardiovascular endurance because we have been practising jogging at the same rhythm and in this trial you are to increase the rhythm constantly and it's very hard and you get tired immediately'

3.4 *Prevention and lifestyle*

The links between exercise and health were especially appraised as a prevention to heart disease and as lifestyle. It is shown by the students' and teacher's statements:

Students:

> '...to do physical exercise regularly protects you from a heart attack'

> 'I think that exercise is very important both for preventing heart disease...(and) for a healthy life'

Teacher:

> 'It is more important to highlight a change in their lifestyle...'

Regarding heart disease, students were critical about the place exercise occupies, when commenting on a newspaper article,

> 'This article pretends to change some 'taken for granted' concepts about the relation between heart disease risk and physical exercise'

> 'Many people think that by doing physical exercise they are immune to heart attack. Exercise is only an aid to prevention, not a remedy'

On the other hand, lifestyle is usually perceived as a means to create exercise habits which ensure health for the rest of their life, and even as a way of self-control, as one student commented,

Students:

'This programme is very hard, but very important since it creates a habit now at our age, and it will help us to live a healthy life during all our life'

'I think this is a very positive activity...since if it (the exercise) is well controlled and done regularly, a habit to do physical activity is created, which is beneficial for your `health'

'...the moment we begin exercising is like a relief, and one doesn't have in mind bad things and problems'

Teacher:

'...it is attempted that they (students) are aware of the consequences that a sedentary life produces in adults, and that they have the opportunity of preventing that, by creating the habit of physical exercise...for all their life'

This is probably the reason why the health programme is generally viewed as a method, technique or way of exercising which gives them support to know how to do it and what for,

'I am going to continue this programme. It has been the introduction to teach us how to make and follow a plan of exercise'

'By making my own programme I've learnt a method of work'

'I have learnt new techniques and ways of exercising'

'I think that before I didn't know the use of the exercises I used to do, but now I have learnt what each exercise is used for'

Only a few students considered the programme to be a way of feeling good,

'But now (after the programme) I am feeling better'

'I have realized that doing exercise, almost daily, I feel much better...'

Nevertheless, at a general level the health programme is regarded as something different from what students were used to, which contributes to the progress and improvement of PE curriculum,

Students:

'Physical education lessons have always been very superficial, I have never done anything in particular. This year we have practised everything, we have learnt'

'I think this programme is a good solution to give the physical education subject the importance it didn't have before'

Teacher:

'I think this programme gives the PE subject another 'touch'...It breaks the monotony of the fitness lessons which are directive and without sense, that is to say, which are outside of an educative context'

4   Discussion and conclusion

The modified programme implemented by the teacher is an attempt, in a Spanish context, to link exercise with health into a PE curriculum although altered by important contextual constraints. The timetable and its distribution within the total school curriculum, the problems with the small school spaces for activity, as well as the teacher's isolated innovation attempt, are important elements if we want to discuss an evaluative perspective in this experience. These are seen as serious difficulties if change is to be promoted (see e.g. Griffin, 1985; Sparkes, 1988) and were only balanced by the teacher-students negotiation, although some students criticized them at the beginning of the programme. Moreover, the presence of contextual limitations at 'Tirant School' reflects an evident problem of the low status of PE as a subject that the teacher and students perceive as being liable to improvement by programmes like the one put into practice.

One must stress the extensive participation and involvement of students in the process of implementation which can be an approach either to democratize physical education or to shift away from the sports-oriented elitism (Almond, 1983; Kirk, 1988). The girls' preference for individual activities, as appears in our study and in other Spanish studies (see Buñuel, 1986; Puig, 1987; Serrano, 1989), and the boys' demand for sportive activities support the argument of a male competitive discourse. As Carrington and Leaman (1986) suggest, a physical education approach to health is more likely to equalize opportunities between males and females than a competitive one and it considers socialization differences, though it does not solve all the different gender opportunities.

Students have the opportunity to choose activities and make decisions about their own plans, constituting a different way of teaching from the directive fitness style. The health programme also introduces them to ways of exercising and monitoring their activities, especially addressed to the aspects of heart disease prevention and learning a new lifestyle.

However, recent critical contributions (see Colquhoun, 1988; George and Kirk, 1988; Kirk, 1988; Sparkes, 1989) demand more questioning and critical understanding of the underlying values and assumptions of the health and exercise movement. Under this perspective, the above-mentioned notions of responsibility, habit, self-control and feeling good have wider social and ideological relationships which have been considered here in a positive and unproblematic way. Besides contextual limitations, only a few matters associated with monitoring procedures and students comments from the newspaper article appear as problematic. The lack of connection between the improvement in some activities students were engaged in during the programme and the outcomes of the monitoring procedures, is a problem that requires specificity in practising the trials in order to improve them successfully.

Moreover, the importance the teacher gives to the improvement as a means to qualify students emphasizes the monitoring procedures results and a constant improvement that the modified programme wanted to challenge. These things must question how far the monitoring procedures are from the fitness scores of traditional tests.

With the newspaper article the teacher tried to challenge the beliefs and practices which consider that any type of physical activity is good for health being the panacea of all modern diseases. But this assumes, from a technical-rational view, that information will change behaviour, when in fact the assumption needs to be supported by experiences and activities relevant to it.

The discussion induces a suggestion that in the future more attention should be paid to social and ideological underpinning of the health programme, particularly if it tries to involve students in a critical thinking about health and exercise. In addition to participation of all the students in different physical activities and the engagement in their monitoring process it is necessary, as Kirk (1988) and Sparkes (1989) point out, to encourage students, through practical, theoretical and reflective experience, to appraise and understand different issues about exercise and health as closely linked to broader cultural and socio-economical patterns and processes.

5   References

Almond, L. (1983a) A rationale for health related fitness in schools. **Bulletin of Physical Education,** 19(2), 5-10.

Almond, L. (1983b) Health related fitness. **British Journal of Physical Education,** 14(2), 35 and 37.

Almond, L. (1988) Translating an innovation from theory to practice, in **Essays in Physical Education, Recreation Management and Sports Science** (ed. LUT), Loughborough University, Loughborough, pp.1-13.

B.O.E. (1987) number 228 of 23 September, Order 18 September.

Bogdan, B. and Binklen, S. (1982) **Qualitative Research for Education: An Introduction to Theory and Methods.** Allyn and Bacon, Inc., Boston.

Buñuel, A. (1986) Imagen, comportamientos y actitudes frente al fenómeno social de la gimnasia recreativa y femenina. **Revista de Investigación y Documentación sobre las Ciencias de la Educación Física y del Deporte,** II, 2, 35-56.

Carrington, B. and Leaman, O. (1986) Equal opportunities and physical education, in **Physical Education, Sport and Schooling** (ed. J. Evans), The Falmer Press, pp.215-226.

Colquhoun, D. (1988) Health as an issue in the physical education curriculum: a questioning of assumptions. Invited Lecture, School of Education, University of Exeter, November.

Colquhoun, D. and Kirk, D. (1987) Investigating the problematic relationship between health and physical education: an Australian study. **Physical Education Review,** 10,(2),100-109.

Devis, J. (1990) Renovación pedagogica en la educación física: dos alternativas de acción I. **Perspectivas,** 4, 5-7.

Diario 16 (1984) 'El infarto y el ejercicio físico'. 18 October.

George, L. and Kirk, D. (1988) The limits of change in physical education: Ideologies, teachers and the experience of physical activity, in **Teachers, Teaching and Control in Physical Education** (ed. J. Evans), The Falmer Press, pp. 145-155.

Glasser, B. and Strauss, A. (1967) **The Discovery of Grounded Theory.** Aldine Pub., New York.

Goetz, J.P. and LeCompte, M.D. (1984) **Ethnography and Qualitative Design in Educational Research.** Academic Press, London.

Griffin, P.S. (1985) Teaching in an urban, multi-racial, physical education program: the power of context. **Quest**, vol. 37, 154-165.
Kirk, D. (1988) **Physical Education and Curriculum Study. A Critical Introduction.** Croom Helm, London.
Lincoln, Y.S. and Guba, E.G. (1985) **Naturalistic Inquiry.** Sage Publications, London.
McGeorge, S. (1988) **The Exercise Challenge.** LUT. Loughborough.
Merriam, S.B. (1988) Doing case study research in education, in **Qualitative Research in Education: Substance, Methods, Experience** (eds. Goetz, J.P. and Allen, J.), The University of Georgia, Athens, pp. 84-90.
Puig, N. (1987) El proceso de incorporación al deporte por parte de la mujer española (1939-1985), in **Ponencias del Seminario 'Mujer y Deporte'** (ed. Instituto de la Mujer), pp. 83-89.
Rohs, F.R. (1988) The qualitative researcher as evaluator, in **Qualitative Research in Education: Substance, Methods, Experience** (eds. Goetz, J.P. and Allen, J.), The University of Georgia, Athens, pp. 113-118.
Serrano, J.A. (1989) Consideraciones acerca de la práctica de actividad física en el horario extraescolar en alumnos de enseñanzas medias. **Apunts**, 16-17, 129-136.
Sparkes, A.C. (1988) The micropolitics of innovation in the physical education curriculum, in **Teachers, Teaching and Control in Physical Education** (ed. J. Evans), Falmer Press, pp. 157-177.
Sparkes, A.C. (1989) Health related fitness: An example of innovation without change. **British Journal of Physical Education**, 2, Summer, 60-63.

VALIDITY AND RELIABILITY OF FITNESS TESTING IN PRIMARY SCHOOL CHILDREN

C.A. MAHONEY AND C.A.G. BOREHAM
Health and Physical Education Unit, The Queen's University of Belfast, Northern Ireland, UK

Abstract

The purpose of the study was to establish the reliability and validity of selected tests of physical fitness on primary school children, aged 7 to 11 years, and to establish baseline normative data. A sample of 113 children of both sexes and from three age groups (7, 9 and 11 years) were involved in a test-retest reliability study using the following tests from the Eurofit test battery; hand grip, sit and reach, standing broad jump, 10 x 5 metre sprint, sit-ups completed in 30 seconds and the 20 metre endurance shuttle run (20MST). To ascertain test-retest reliability, the tests were repeated within one month under controlled conditions. All tests were shown to be significantly reliable (p<0.005). However reliability was generally poorest in children under 8 years. A subsample of 50 children of mixed sex and ages were run to exhaustion on a treadmill to determine peak oxygen uptake. These scores were correlated with their 20-MST scores to establish the validity of this field test using a one-tailed Pearson product-moment correlation. Although a moderate correlation was achieved (r = 0.56) results were highly significant (p<0.001). Baseline normative data from these tests was subsequently established for Belfast children, by testing 670 primary schoolchildren, aged 7 to 11 years, taken from four Belfast schools. This study has shown that the Eurofit tests of physical fitness are reliable when administered to primary schoolchildren. The tests are all easily administered and require limited equipment and experience. The 20-MST has been shown to be a valid and reliable measure of cardiorespiratory fitness and appropriate for use as a field test to be used in primary schools with a 20 metre gymnasium.

Keywords: Primary Children, Fitness, Eurofit.

1   Introduction

An understanding of the development and assessment of physical fitness in children is particularly important in the light of evidence relating contemporary lifestyle patterns to hypokinetic disease. There are a number of initiatives operating in Northern Ireland aimed at increasing community awareness of the benefits of exercise and activity. Recent studies have investigated the fitness and activity levels (Riddoch, 1990) and prevalence of coronary risk factors (Primrose et al, 1990) in Northern Irish secondary schoolchildren. This concern for the youth of Northern Ireland has arisen from the extremely high adult incidence of coronary heart disease within the country, and has been recognized by the Health Boards who have instigated a variety of initiatives to promote health and fitness in the community.

Although several other national studies have investigated the physical fitness of secondary schoolchildren (Australia, 1986, New Zealand, 1988), very few have included data on children of primary school age, and none have been published which used the 'Eurofit' battery of fitness tests (Eurofit, 1988) with this population. The 'Eurofit' tests were originally devised to provide a low-cost but acceptable test battery for general use with European schoolchildren.

The aims of the project were to determine the reliability and validity of the 'Eurofit' test battery on primary schoolchildren, and to provide normative data for Belfast schoolchildren based on these tests. The components of fitness measured in the study included strength, speed, power, endurance, flexibility, co-ordination, agility, anthropometric factors and cardio-respiratory endurance.

2   Materials and Methods

2.1 *Pilot Study*

A total of 113 children completed both test and retest of the fitness battery. This group consisted of three year groups - Primary 7, Primary 5 and Primary 3 (11, 9, 7 years respectively), with each group consisting of approximately equal numbers of boys and girls. Table 1 describes the sample population.

Details of the test battery are shown in Table 2. All tests, with the exception of the vertical jump, were taken from the Eurofit test battery. Where appropriate, the best score from two trials was recorded for subsequent analysis.

Testing Testing was carried out in a gymnasium associated with the pilot school. The tests were carried out in the same order during both test and retest within one month of each other, and measured at the same time of day. Anthropometric measures were not assessed on retest.

Table 1.   *Sample Population.*

	Boys' Class			Girls' Class		
	3 n=17	5 n=20	7 n=21	3 n=17	5 n=19	7 n=19
Age (yrs)	7.2	9.1	11.5	7.1	9.4	11.3
±SD	0.3	0.4	0.5	0.4	0 3	0 3
Height (cm)	120.7	133.6	141.0	121.9	131.5	141.1
±SD	4.5	4.9	4.6	6.0	7.0	7.6
Weight (kg)	21.6	30.5	35.0	22.9	30.4	36.5
±SD	2.5	4.2	4.5	3.1	6.7	8.5

Table 2.   *Test-Retest Test Battery*

1.	Age
2.	Sex
3.	Height (mm)
4.	Weight (kg)
5.	Body Composition (% body fat)
6.	Flexibility - sit and reach (cm)
7.	Muscular Strength - hand grip (kg)
8.	Muscular Endurance - sit-ups/30 secs
9.	Muscular Power
	(a) Broad Jump (cm)
	(b) Vertical Jump (cm)
10.	Speed/agility - 10 x 5m sprint (secs)

The validity of the 20-MST as a test of aerobic endurance was established by comparison with peak VO_2 measured in the laboratory. This was completed on 50 subjects representing the age and sex range present in the pilot study.

Peak VO_2. To validate the 20-MST against a standard test of cardio-respiratory fitness, a sample of children from each year group and each school, underwent a test of maximal aerobic endurance in laboratory conditions. Because of the difficulty in getting young children to work maximally, the test of cardio-respiratory fitness in the laboratory has been defined as peak VO_2, rather than VO_2 max. Peak VO_2 was measured on a treadmill following the Bruce protocol (Bar-Or, 1983). This followed habituation of the subject to walking, running and dismounting from the treadmill, as well as the safety procedures for stopping the treadmill. ECG was recorded throughout the test, using sternum, dorsal apex and ventral apex electrode placement. The test was terminated according to BASS guidelines for the assessment of peak VO_2 (BASS, 1988), ie two or more of the following:

1. Heart rate within ± 5 of age related maximum
2. Respiratory quotient in excess of 1.10
3. A plateau occurring in oxygen uptake despite an increased workload
4. Voluntary exhaustion

2.2 *Main Study*

The subjects were selected from four schools within the Belfast area. The schools were selected to provide a representative sample of the cultural and socio-economic backgrounds which commonly exist within Northern Ireland. In each school the Primary 3, Primary 5 and Primary 7 groups were tested. Every pupil within these classes in each school was included in the potential sample population; thereafter, written informed parental consent was sought. Only pupils whose parents refused consent, or who were ill, absent, or had medical contraindications were excluded from the eventual test sample. In total only 5% of the subjects who were selected withdrew from the testing for any reason.

Administration The children were tested in groups of 25 taken from the same class and age groupings. Children were required to wear sports clothing. The battery was completed in the same sequence for each of the groups tested. The more strenuous tests, the 10 X 5 metre sprint and the 20-MST, were completed last.

The Tests Personal details (eg name, date of birth, sex) were taken from the school roles. Thereafter the results were recorded for each subject at the completion of each test. The protocols used were similar to that found in the Eurofit test battery, with appropriate instructions given to the younger age groups to facilitate understanding of the task required.

Aerobic Endurance This was measured with the 20-MST outlined in the Eurofit test battery, using the modified protocol shown in Table 3. Subjects began running at 8 km/hr for the first minute with the speed increasing by 0.5 km/hr each subsequent minute. The number of laps completed was the score recorded for the subject's aerobic endurance.

Table 3.   *20 Metre Shuttle Test Protocol*

Stage	Speed (km/hr)	Time per Lap (sec)	Laps per Stage (number)	Cumulative (laps)
1	8.0	9.0	7	7
2	8.5	8.47	7	14
3	9.0	8.0	8	22
4	9.5	7.58	8	30
5	10.0	7.2	8	38
6	10.5	6.86	9	47
7	11.0	6.55	9	56
8	11.5	6.26	10	66
9	12.0	6.0	10	76
10	12.5	5.76	10	86
11	13.0	5.54	11	97
12	13.5	5.33	11	108
13	14.0	5.14	12	120
14	14.5	4.97	12	132
15	15.0	4.8	12	144
16	15.5	4.65	13	157
17	16.0	4.5	13	170
18	16.5	4.36	14	184
19	17.0	4.24	14	198
20	17.5	4.11	15	213

2.3 *Statistical Analysis*

The purpose of the pilot study was to assess the reliability and validity of the proposed test battery for use with primary schoolchildren. Mean, standard deviation, correlation (Pearson's r), and differences (paired t-tests) were calculated. A correlation between 20-MST and peak VO_2 was completed to assess the validity of the field test as a measure cardiorespiratory performance. For the production of normative data with the larger population, simple statistics providing means and standard deviations were calculated.

3   Results

3.1 *Pilot*

Correlation coefficients between test and retest were generally high throughout the test battery, indicating that the tests will differentiate between subjects on first application. In fact, correlation coefficients in this study were frequently higher than those reported from the test-retest reliability study applied to secondary school children. Paired t-tests between test and retest results, showed all tests were within acceptable mean variations and were within appropriate levels of significance. The results of the test-retest reliability are summarized in Table 4 and show few significant differences between the means. It can be seen however that differences did occur between test and retest for the males in the sit-up test, and between flexibility, standing broad jump, sit-ups and 10x5m sprint for girls. However in every instance the variation between the test and retest, although marginally significant, was negligible in size and did not warrant the test being dropped for all three age groupings.

The majority of the tests had adequate test-retest reliability, with high coefficients of correlation, and appropriate levels of significance from paired T-tests to accept the null hypothesis, that variation in means between test and retest were not significant. Generally, there seemed little to preclude large scale testing of primary school children.

The purpose of the peak VO_2 test was to validate the 20-MST. Using a one-tailed Pearson Correlation test, a correlation of r=0.56 was obtained with a significance of

Table 4.   *Test Retest Reliability (paired T-test)*

| TEST | Boys Class | | | Girls Class | | |
| | 3 | 5 | 7 | 3 | 5 | 7 |
	n=17	n=20	n=21	n=17	n=19	n=19
Flexibility	ns	ns	ns	ns	p<0.05	ns
Standing Broad Jump	ns	ns	ns	p<0.05	ns	ns
Grip Strength (R)	ns	ns	ns	ns	ns	ns
Sit-ups	ns	ns	p<0.05	ns	p<0.05	ns
10 x 5m Sprint	ns	ns	ns	ns	ns	p<0.05
Vertical Jump	ns	ns	ns	ns	ns	ns

Table 5.   Peak VO$_2$

CLASS		Boys	Girls
Primary 3	Mean	48.5 (10)	46.1 (7)
	SD	7.3	5.1
Primary 5	Mean	51.2 (12)	46.1 (8)
	SD	9 5	7 7
Primary 7	Mean	52.2 (7)	50.2 (6)
	SD	4.5	4.9
		(n=29)	(n=21)

p<0.001. The regression equation calculated from the subjects who completed both the 20-MST and the peak VO$_2$ test is:

Males: VO$_2$ = 41.41 + 0.17 x 20-MST

Females: VO$_2$ = 38.67 + 0.21 x 20-MST

3.2 *Main Study*

In a study such as this the results tend to be descriptive rather than statistical. The purpose of the main study was to provide baseline normative data for the fitness levels of primary schoolchildren. Table 6 outlines the age groups used in the main study, while Table 7 has a summary of the entire population used for the production of Belfast primary schoolchildren norms.

6   Discussion

Studies by Boreham et al 1985, Farrally et al 1983 and Watkins et al 1983, have all assessed the fitness and activity levels of secondary aged children. The limited number of studies related to primary children tended to concentrate on a specific component of fitness, such as aerobic endurance, (Krahenbuhl et al 1978, van Gerven et al 1984, Zwiren 1989). Studies including the New Zealand Health and Fitness Survey (University of Otago, 1988), the Australian Health and Fitness Survey (ACHPER, 1986), a study of Hungarian youth by Barabas (1986) and a study of Flemish boys and girls by Lefevre et al (1990) have all assessed components of children's fitness in the 7-12 year age group, and have used some

Table 6.   *Age in Years*

AGE	FREQUENCY	%
6-6.9	60	8.8
7-7.9	144	21.1
8-8.9	95	14.0
9-9.9	141	22.2
10-10.9	107	15.7
11-11.9	124	18.2
TOTAL	671	

Table 7.   *Belfast Population Norms*

	Boys' Class			Girls' Class		
	3 n=91	5 n=109	7 n=94	3 n=93	5 n=95	7 n=105
Height (cm)	122.4	132.4	141.6	119.9	131.1	142.4
±SD	5.7	6.1	6.1	4.7	5.9	7.4
Weight (kg)	25.6	29.3	34.5	24.1	29.2	35.4
±SD	6.5	5.5	7.0	5.2	5.3	7.8
Body Composition (%fat)	16.3	16.8	17.0	19.5	19.9	20.6
±SD	3.6	4.9	4.6	4.7	5.6	5.7
Grip strength (kg)	10.5	14.3	16.4	9.7	13.5	15.9
±SD	2.7	2.9	2.9	2.3	2.8	3.6
10 x 5 metre sprint (secs)	28.4	24.7	23.6	28.5	25.2	23.9
±SD	3.2	2.1	2.1	3.1	2.2	2.0
Situps in 30 seconds (no.)	14.5	18.9	21.6	13.8	17.9	20.6
±SD	3.5	4.6	3.3	3.7	4.6	4.2
Sit and Reach (cm)	17.5	16.0	15.3	18.9	16.9	17.4
±SD	4.9	5.4	6.0	5.1	5.5	7.0
Standing Broad Jump (cm)	110.4	132.2	144.8	105.5	124.4	141.0
±SD	17.6	17.4	18.0	16.6	20.5	19.1
20-MST (laps)	32.0	45.8	62.2	29.3	41.3	52.6
±SD	13.9	17.4	18.0	12.0	16.7	19.1

comparable tests with this survey. No studies have been published, however, that describe the fitness of primary schoolchildren using the Eurofit test battery.

It is apparent from the Pilot Study that younger children required adapted instructions, responded more effectively to demonstrations of test performance, and took longer to complete the tests. However, it was still possible to maintain full test protocols throughout.

Peak VO_2 values in this study compare favourably with those obtained by van Praagh et al (1989). The French study reported VO_2 max values of 47.0+ 5.8 ml/kg/min with 7 year old boys in the laboratory. The values in the current study were 48.5± 7.3 ml/kg/min for the same age and sex group. Other studies of aerobic power in young children are in agreement with the results achieved here (Krahenbuhl et al 1978, Zwiren 1989, Shephard 1988). The peak VO_2 values obtained in this study were correlated with the 20-MST scores to obtain a measure of the validity of the 20-MST test with primary schoolchildren. The high level of significance (p<0.001), with a moderate correlation (r=0.56) is not too dissimilar to other validation studies involving the 20-MST against known tests of aerobic power in older children (Boreham et al, 1990 (r=0.87), van Mechelen et al, 1986 (r=0.76) and Leger and Gadoury, 1989 (r=0.87)).

The study of Flemish boys and girls by Lefevre et al (1990) and the ACHPER (1986) study, include tests and results which offer comparability with this survey. In comparable tests, there appears to be little difference between the three groups.

Belfast children are shorter in all age and sex groups (2-3 cm), and their weight is lower by 2-3 kg. Conversely, the standing broad jump test produced better results for the Northern Ireland study. Flexibility measured by the sit and reach test showed the closest comparative results.

The results clearly show that changes do occur with increasing age within the three age groups chosen for the Primary survey. A relatively linear increase in both height and weight occurs for both boys and girls. Body composition or predicted body fat differed consistently by about 10% between girls and boys, and increased by appoximately 2% between Primary 3 and Primary 7.

Flexibility declined with increasing age in boys, while flexibility increased in girls. This is in agreement with previous work (ACHPER 1986, Lefevre et al 1990). For the tests of strength and power, standing broad jump, grip strength, sit ups in 30 seconds and the vertical jump, boys performed better than girls. Finally with speed and agility, assessed by the 10x5 metre sprint, boys performed better than girls, while both sexes showed improvement with age.

7   Conclusions

The Eurofit tests used in this study have been shown to be reliable for use with primary schoolchildren. Provided the instructions are described carefully to the participating children and follow closely the correct protocols, little difficulty will be experienced with the administration of these tests to primary children.

Correlation of the 20-MST test with the peak VO_2 test on the treadmill, produced a highly significant level of confidence, but a moderate coefficient of correlation. This may be taken to reflect the difficulty of motivating very young children to complete a maximal activity that takes considerable effort and time.

The results have provided a group of tests which are reliable for use with primary aged children, which are easily administered and cost effective in terms of equipment required. The baseline normative data also provides a reference point for those concerned with the current levels of fitness amongst primary schoolchildren.

8   References

ACHPER, (1986) **Australian Health and Fitness Survey**. Australian Council for Health Physical Education and Recreation Inc. Parkside, South Australia.

Barabas. A. (1986) Selected factors of physical performance in the Hungarian youth. **Anthrop. Kozl**. 30, 233-242.

Bar-Or, O. (1983) **Pediatric Sports Medicine for the Practitioner**. Springer-Verlag, New York.

BASS. 1988. Position Statement on the Physiological Assessment of the Elite Competitor. **British Association of Sport Sciences.** White Line Press, Leeds.

Boreham, C.A.G., Paliczka, V.J. and Nichols, A.K. (1986) **Fitness Testing of Belfast Schoolchildren**. 5th Eurofit Symposium, Council of Europe, Strasbourg.

Boreham, C.A.G., Paliczka, V.J. and Nichols, A.K. (1990) A comparison of the PWC_{170} and 20-MST tests of aerobic fitness in adolescent schoolchildren. **The Journal of Sports Medicine and Physical Fitness.** 30(1),19-23.

Borms, J. (1986) The child and exercise: an overview. **Journal of Sports Sciences**, 4(1), 3-20.

Council of Europe. (1983) **The Eurofit Test Battery - Provisional Handbook**. Council of Europe, Strasbourg.

Durnin, J.V.G.A. and Rahaman, M.M. (1967) The assessment of the amount of fat in the human body from measurements of skinfold thickness. **British Journal of Nutrition**, 21, 681 - 689.

Farrally, M.R., Watkins, J. and Ewing, B.G. (1983) **The Physical Fitness of Scottish Schoolboys aged 13, 15 and 17 years**. Jordanhill College of Education, Glasgow.

van Gerven, D., Vanden Eynde, B. and Peerlinck, G. (1984) Influence of activity and age on the working capacity of boys and girls aged 8-12 years. **Children and Sport**. Edited by Ilmarinen, J. and Valimaki, 1. Springer-Verlag Berlin Heidelberg.

Krahenbuhl, G.S., Pangrazi, R.P., Petersen, G.W., Burkett L.N. and Schneider, M.J. (1978) Field testing of cardiorespiratory fitness in primary school children. **Medicine and Science in Sports**, 10(3), 208-213.

Lefevre, J., Claessens, A., Beunen, G., Renson, R., Simons, J. and Vanreusel, B. (1990) **Provisional norms for Flemish boys and girls**. Institute of Physical Education, Catholic University, Leuven.

Leger, L. and Gadoury, C. (1989) Validity of the 20m shuttle run test with 1 minute stages to predict VO_2max in adults. **Canadian Journal of Sport Science**, 14(1), 21-26.

van Mechelen, W., Hlobil, H. and Kemper, H.C. (1986) Validation of two running tests as estimates of maximal aerobic power in children. **European Journal of Applied Physiology**, 55, 503-506.

van Praagh, E.V., Bedu, M., Fellmann, N. and Coudert, J. (1989) Laboratory and field tests in 7-year-old boys. **Children and Exercise XIII**. Editor Oseid M. Human Kinetics Publishers, New York.

Primrose, E.D., Savage, J.M., Boreham, C.A.G., Strain, G.W. and Siralii, J.J. **Coronary risk factors in Belfast schoolchildren**. Submitted for publication 1990.

Riddoch, C. (1990) **The Northern Ireland Health and Fitness Survey**. A report by the Division of Physical and Health Education, Queen's University of Belfast.

Shephard, R.J. (1988) Required physical activity and child development. **The Australian Journal of Science and Medicine in Sport**, 20(2), 3-9.

University of Otago. (1988) **The New Zealand Fitness Test Handbook**. University of Otago, New Zealand.

Watkins, J., Farrally, M.R. and Powley, A.E. (1983) **Anthropometry and Physical Fitness of Secondary Schoolgirls in Strathclyde**. Jordanhill college of Education, Glasgow.

Zwiren, L.D. (1989) Anaerobic and aerobic capacities of children. **Pediatric Exercise Science**, 1(1), 31-44.

HEALTH-RELATED PHYSICAL FITNESS PATTERNS OF BRAZILIAN CHILDREN (CITY OF VIÇOSA, STATE OF MINAS GERAIS, BRAZIL)[1]

M.T. SILVEIRA BÖHME AND E. MYOTIN
Universidade Federal de Viçosa, Viçosa, Minas Gerais, Brazil

Abstract

In view of the need for measurement and evaluation in Physical Education, the importance of determining the state of growth and physical fitness in children and the absence of standard reference tables for such measurements in Brazilian schoolchildren, research was conducted involving a sample of 1500 pupils of both sexes between the ages of 7 and 17 in the city of Viçosa, central Brazil. Its objective was to elaborate standard reference tables in percentiles of each measurement related to aspects of health-related physical fitness to be used by physical education teachers in the region in the evaluation of their pupils. The following measurement standards were elaborated: weight; height; abdominal and arm circumferences; subscapular, triciptal and abdominal and arm skinfolds; abdominal, arm and leg strength; trunk flexibility and aerobic capacity.

Keywords: Evaluation, Health-related Physical Fitness, Children, Patterns, Kinanthropometry.

1   Introduction

The evaluation is part of a dynamic cycle in the educational process; to facilitate understanding it is divided into diagnostic, formative and summative evaluations. Diagnostic evaluation is made to assess the initial condition of the pupil in relation to the physical education programme to be developed; formative evaluation is made during the educational process, the purpose being to assess how learning is progressing and to be used as feedback in the revision of the proposed objectives; the summative evaluation is made at the end of the teaching unit, in order to grade the pupils.

[1]   This research was supported by the Conselho Nacional de Pesquisas - CNPq - and the Fundaçao de Amparo a Pesquisa de Minas Gerais - FAPEMIG. The authors are grateful to the examiners.

In the process of evaluation the physical education teacher makes use of tests and measurements with the following objectives:

(a) to determine the individual condition of the pupils
(b) to elaborate a physical education programme with appropriate aims
(c) to classify and to encourage pupils
(d) to group the class in a homogeneous manner
(e) to evaluate the development of the programme
(f) to observe if pupil growth and development is normal or not.

Evaluation comprises different forms of comparison; for example: to compare with his/her own achievement or with a norm or standard. One of the most frequently invoked criteria of evaluation by comparison in physical education is the standard reference table in percentiles (Eckert, 1974; Johnson and Nelson, 1979; Kirkendall et al., 1980; Mathews, 1980). Brazilian literature includes patterns of height and weight, (Marques et al., 1982) which are used by pediatricians, and patterns of health-related physical fitness (Barbanti, 1983), which were elaborated in Sao Paulo, another Brazilian state.

The selection of the tests as well as the criteria of evaluation which should be used in the physical education evaluation process, depend upon the aims of the programme and are determined by the physical education teacher.

The development of health-related physical fitness is fundamental to every physical education programme. This is one reason why the physical education teacher needs to have patterns of health-related physical fitness of the pupils.

This study addresses the need for measurement and evaluation in Physical Education, the importance of determining the state of growth and physical fitness in children and the existence of few standard reference tables for such measurement in Brazilian schoolchildren. Its objective is to elaborate standard reference tables in percentiles of each measurement related to aspects of health-related physical fitness from children between 7 and 17 years, in the city of Viçosa, central Brazil, to be used by physical education teachers in the region in the evaluation of their pupils.

2   Methodology

2.1   *Subjects*

The children attended eight schools in the county of Viçosa, State of Minas Gerais, Brazil. The data was collated in 1987/1988. The random sample of 10% from each age of the school population was determined.

The age of the subject was determined by rounding up to the nearest whole year if an incomplete year measured 0.6 or over and rounding down to the nearest whole year if an incomplete year measured 0.5 or under; for example, a pupil aged 11.6 or over or 12.5 or under was considered to have an age of 12.

2.2 *Measurements*

The data for each child included:

Anthropometry: weight, height, abdominal and arm circumferences, tricipital, subscapular and abdominal skinfolds.

Physical performance tests:

(a) Sit-up

Starting position: child lying on back with knees flexed and feet on floor; arms crossed on chest with hands on opposite shoulders.

Procedure: the child, by tightening his/her abdominal muscles, curls into the sitting position touching wrists to thighs and returns to the starting position.

Scoring: the score is the number of correctly executed sit-ups completed in thirty seconds, as described by Simons et al., 1983.

(b) Standing broad jump

Starting position: standing behind starting line with feet parallel.

Procedure: the child should jump horizontally as far as possible and land straddling the tape measure attached to the floor.

Scoring: the score is the best of three attempts as described by several authors (Barrow and McGee 1978; Fetz and Kornexl, 1976; Johnson and Nelson, 1979; Litwin and Fernandex, 1977; Mathews, 1980; Kirkendall et al., 1980) in centimetres.

(c) Throw of medicine ball (1kg)

Starting position: child sitting on floor with back straight against a wall, legs together and knees straight; arms extended upward holding medicine ball with both hands.

Procedure: the child throws the medicine ball as far as possible across the test area where a tape measure has been placed.

Scoring: the score is the best of three attempts, as described by Johnson and Nelson (1979), in centimetres.

(d) Sit-and-reach

Starting position: child sitting on floor, knees fully extended; feet placed at the 50cm mark of a measuring tape attached to the floor; arms extended upward.

Procedure: the child extends arms forward with palms down.

Scoring: the score corresponds to the farthest point reached; when reach extends beyond toes the score is greater than 50cm and when reach falls short of toes the score is less than 50cm.

This study used the test described by Kirkendall et al. (1980), with the scoring in centimetres.

(e) Nine-minutes distance run

Starting position: standing behind starting line.

Procedure: the child runs as far as possible during the nine minutes; walking is allowed in case of tiredness, as described by Barbanti (1983).

Scoring: the score is the distance covered during the nine minutes, in metres.

The measurements were made in the school, during the physical education lessons. Three lessons were used in each class: the first for anthropometry measurements; the second for the strength and flexibility tests and the third for the endurance test. The measurements were collected in circuit by eight trained examiners, and recorded in individual achievement charts.

3   Results

The elaborated standard references tables in percentiles of each measurement from each age and gender are shown in Tables 1-4.

4   Interpretation and Conclusion

Generally, the greater the obtained percentile, the better the child's result. It follows, therefore, that:

(a)   between the 1st and 25th percentiles - development is lower than normal;
(b)   between the 25th and 75th percentiles - development is normal;
(c)   between the 75th and 99th percentiles - development is above normal.

Table 1.   *Percentiles of height(cm) - Girls and Boys*

Perc.				Years						
	7	8	9	10	11	12	13	14	15	16	17
10 F	114	119	123	130	129	139	144	148	150	151	156
10 M	116	119	124	128	133	137	143	149	157	164	163
25 F	120	122	127	134	138	144	148	152	157	155	158
25 M	120	122	127	132	137	141	147	154	161	165	170
50 F	124	127	132	128	142	148	153	156	161	160	162
50 M	123	126	131	135	142	147	152	161	165	171	173
75 F	126	131	137	144	146	153	160	160	164	165	166
75 M	127	131	137	141	147	152	157	165	171	174	177
90 F	129	135	141	148	153	157	165	164	168	167	169
90 M	134	136	144	145	151	157	165	174	176	181	180

Table 2.   *Percentiles of weight(kg) - Girls and Boys*

Perc.				Years						
	7	8	9	10	11	12	13	14	15	16	17
10 F	19	21	23	25	25	28	35	37	42	41	44
10 M	19	21	23	24	28	29	32	36	42	43	51
25 F	20	23	25	28	28	33	36	40	47	46	47
25 M	22	23	25	27	30	32	35	41	47	49	53
50 F	23	26	27	32	33	38	42	47	51	51	52
50 M	24	25	27	29	34	37	41	45	53	56	59
75 F	25	29	31	37	38	42	48	53	55	55	60
75 M	26	29	31	34	40	45	50	54	59	68	65
90 F	28	32	38	43	44	47	59	58	60	62	65
90 M	33	35	38	37	46	53	56	63	72	76	75

Table 3.   *Sit and reach(cm) - Girls and Boys*

Perc					Years						
	7	8	9	10	11	12	13	14	15	16	17
10 F	41	42	39	39	33	40	41	39	40	39	37
10 M	41	41	40	38	35	33	36	36	37	38	34
25 F	44	46	44	43	43	46	47	46	46	42	49
25 M	46	46	44	41	38	39	41	43	43	43	40
50 F	50	50	50	51	48	53	53	50	52	50	52
50 M	49	50	48	47	44	47	46	49	49	46	50
75 F	53	54	54	55	53	57	58	55	60	56	56
75 M	54	54	52	50	48	50	50	52	54	52	59
90 F	59	58	57	60	57	60	64	61	64	62	63
90 M	58	58	56	54	52	53	54	60	61	54	61

Table 4.   *Nine minutes distance run(m) - Girls and Boys*

Perc.					Years						
	7	8	9	10	11	12	13	14	15	16	17
10 F	852	808	893	946	1006	990	985	995	1071	1215	1252
10 M	850	926	980	1160	1058	1104	1202	1151	1291	1197	1397
25 F	971	977	1046	1053	1099	1150	1134	1176	1298	1305	1347
25 M	985	1055	1164	1236	1245	1220	1371	1358	1533	1575	1706
50 F	1046	1078	1150	1176	1207	1275	1323	1310	1374	1392	1460
50 M	1148	1176	1287	1349	1365	1424	1549	1639	1710	1826	1877
75 F	1224	1236	1264	1295	1315	1489	1389	1457	1549	1553	1653
75 M	1260	1347	1407	1470	1467	1567	1659	1767	1854	2128	2148
90 F	1556	1299	1394	1372	1432	1609	1543	1589	1758	1655	1759
90 M	1357	1441	1495	1581	1599	1706	1785	1883	2062	2224	2265

4.1 *Some care must be observed*

Weight and Height The percentile of weight must always be compared with the percentile of height, because it can occur that:

(d)   the child has a normal development with similar percentiles of weight and height, between the 25th and 75th percentiles;

(e)   the child shows a weight development above the 75th percentile, while the percentile of height is normal between the 25th and 75th percentile. This can mean that the child has a weight above normal, and probably tends toward obesity. It indicates that she should control her nutrition and increase her physical activity;

(f)   the child shows a weight development below the 25th percentile, while the percentile of height is normal ie. between the 25th and 75th. This can mean that the child is in a meagreness process, or even subnutrition. It indicates that she should improve her nutrition and she should not do intensive physical activity;

(g) the child shows a development above or below the normal for her age with similar percentiles of weight and height. This is probably a consequence of hereditary factors.

Skinfolds and Circumferences Some aspects may be considered in the evaluation of skinfolds and circumferences:

(h) above the 75th percentile - development above normal indicates that the child tends to obesity. She should be oriented in her nutrition and practice more physical activity;

(i) below the 25th percentile - development below normal indicates that the child tends to meagreness or even subnutrition; she should improve her nutrition and not engage in too intense physical activity;

Muscular strength, flexibility and endurance

(j) between the 25th and 50th percentiles - the child should be stimulated to improve her performance;

(k) below the 25th percentile - the child should be given more individualized physical activity to reach normal levels.

By the percentual result of the different measurements, the physical education teacher will be in a position to:

(l) evaluate if the growth and development of the child is below normal, normal or above normal;

(m) elaborate a programme consonant with the needs of the class;

(n) test again and evaluate at another time his pupils and conclude if the development work considered the programmes' objectives or not.

5   References

Barbanti, V. (1983) **Aptidao Fisica relacionada à saude. Manual de testes.** SEED-MEC, Itapira.

Barrow, H.M.G. and McGee, R. (1978) **A practical approach to measurement in physical education.** Lea and Febiger, Philadelphia.

Eckert, H.M. (1974) **Practical measurement of physical performance.** Lea and Febiger, Philadelphia.

Fetz, F. and Kornexl, E. (1976) **Tests deportivo motores.** Editorial Kapeluz, Buenos Aires.

Johnson, B.L. and Nelson, J.K. (1979) **Practical measurements for evaluation in physical education.** Burgess Publishing Company, Minnesotta.

Litwin, J. and Fernandez, G. (1980) **Medidas evaluacion y stadisticas aplicadas a la educacion fisica y el deporte.** Editorial Stadium, Buenos Aires.

Kirkendall, D.R. et al. (1980) **Measurement and Evaluation for Physical educators.** Wm. C. Brown Company Publishers, Iowa.

Marques, R.M. et al. (1982) **Crescimento e desenvolvimento pubertario em crianças e adolescentes brasileiros. II Peso e Altura.** Editora Brasileira de Ciencias, Sao Paulo.

Mathews, D.K. (1980) **Medida e avaliacao em Educaçao Fisica.** Interamericana, Rio de Janeiro.

Simons, J. et al. (eds) (1983) **Evaluation del'Aptitude motrice.** Rapport du seminaire de recherche european sur l'evaluation de l'aptitude motrice. Institute d'education physique de la K.U. Leuven, Belgique.

THE HEALTH RELATED FITNESS OF STUDENT NURSES

N.J. WALTERS AND D. MICHAELS
Human Performance Laboratory, Polytechnic of Central London, London, England

Abstract
The health related fitness of female students entering the basic foundation programme of a college of nurse education was examined by means of standard physiological tests. Aerobic power, lung function, total cholesterol and % body fat measurements were made on 151 students (mean age=20.3 yrs). Mean values were: aerobic power, 36.1 ml/kg/min; forced expiratory volume (1 sec), 3.5L; total cholesterol, 3.76 mMol/L; % body fat, 27. The results show that the average student entering the nursing profession was of generally healthy status but improvement to aerobic power and body fat would reduce the incidence of early fatigue at work.
Keywords: Health Related Fitness, Student Nurses, Physiological Tests.

1   Introduction

The high rates of premature death due to coronary heart disease (CHD) in western countries have resulted in various attempts to identify the causes of this condition. Consequently the identification of the so-called 'risk factors' has meant a clearer view of the problem has been made possible. A recent growth area of research has been into the early detection of features which, given time, will often be likely to develop into coronary heart disease. Screening for these features is now relatively commonplace with many health organizations offering a range of simple tests designed to pick out those individuals at risk.

The origins of many of these tests lie within the area of physical education and therefore have been the subject of many studies into their accuracy and reliability with respect to predicting or measuring fitness (Mathews, 1974). As a result many studies have established values for various ages and levels of ability ranging from the sedentary to elite athletes (Astrand, 1960; Fox and Biddle, 1986). Comparisons can therefore be made with most groups of individuals. In addition to PE based tests, health related fitness assessment requires the inclusion of tests which traditionally have been found in the clinical area. Such tests as those of lung function and cholesterol are now seen to be essential in order that as complete a profile as possible can be made.

As part of a programme of study to explore the theoretical background to CHD, all students entering the basic foundation studies course at a London college of nurse education experience the nature of these screening tests at first hand. The purpose of this programme is to establish baseline values in the student population, to illustrate the nature of the assessments and to allow personal experience of the assessment situation by those who may at some point in their career be involved in assessment of patients or clients.

2   Method

2.1 *Subjects*

In the course of a twelve month period, 151 female student nurses (mean age 20.3 yrs) attended the laboratory in a post absorptive state. A pre-test questionnaire was completed by all subjects in order that the existence of any contra-indicating conditions might be known prior to testing.

2.2 *Assessment Tests*

The following tests were carried out on each student: Aerobic power was measured by using a modified Astrand 6 minute test (Astrand and Ryhming, 1954). A Monark 864 cycle ergometer and Cardionics 275 Cardiometer were used in conjunction with a BBC Micro-computer. The computer used software which acted as a time-clock and estimated the maximal oxygen uptake (ml/kg/min) from the heart rate data.

Lung function ($FEV_{1.0}$, FVC & FER) was observed by means of a MicroLoop flow volume transducer producing a flow volume loop.

Total cholesterol was determined by the analysis of 50 μl of whole blood obtained from a finger prick incision using an Analox Instruments LM3 analyzer and appropriate reagents.

Estimates were made of % body fat by means of the infra-red interactance technique using the Futrex F5000 Body Composition Analyzer.

Risk factor profiles were constructed using a modified scoring system prepared by Farquhar et al of the Stanford Heart Disease Prevention Programme.

3   Results

Descriptive statistics for the parameters studied are presented in Tables 1-3. The anthropometric data shown in Table 1 reveal that the population studied showed a typical profile for the age range and sex. Table 2 illustrates the range of values obtained from the cardio-respiratory tests. The relatively high standard deviation seen in the aerobic power test (9.1 ml/kg/min) is indicative of the large range of work capacity shown by this group. The range of values in the tests chosen to examine coronary heart disease risk factors are shown in Table 3. Body composition values reveal a large range but a relatively low standard deviation, indicating the majority of the values lie close to the mean.

Table 1.   *Anthropometric data (n=151)*

Index	Height (cm)	Weight (kg)	Body Mass (kg/m^2)
Mean	1.65	60.1	21.9
Standard Deviation	0.06	8.4	2.8
Maximum	1.79	90.0	32.3
Minimum	1.44	43.5	16.7

Table 2.   *Cardio-respiratory data (n=151)*

	Aerobic Power (ml/kg/min)	F.E.V.$_{-1.0}$ (L)	F.V.C. (L)	F.E.R. (%)
Mean	36.1	3.1	3.5	90
Standard Deviation	9.1	0.4	0.5	5
Maximum	67.6	4.2	4.5	99
Minimum	14.0	1.9	2.2	75

Table 3   *Coronary risk factor data (n=151)*

	% Body Fat	Total Cholesterol (mMol/L)	RISKO
Mean	27.0	3.7	6.8
Standard Deviation	3.5	0.7	2.0
Maximum	33.4	5.2	16.0
Minimum	11.8	1.0	1.0

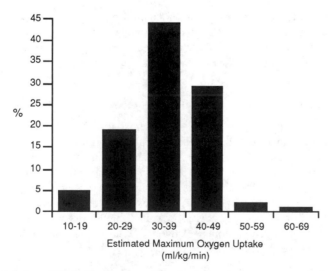

Figure 1.   *Distribution frequency for estimated maximum oxygen uptake (ml/kg/min) (n=151)*

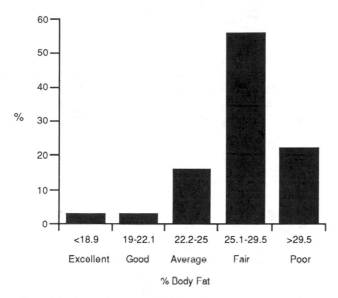

Figure 2. *Distribution frequency for % body fat (Metropolitan Life % Body Fat Categories)*
(n=151)

Figures 1-3 represent distribution frequency histograms for the aerobic power test
(Fig. 1); the data on % body fat (Fig. 2) and the coronary risk factor profiles (Fig.
3). Distribution in terms of percentage is displayed above the bars for each of the
appropriate categories.

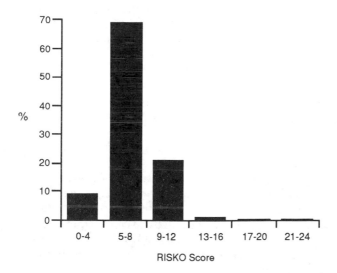

Figure 3. *Distribution frequency for coronary risk factor profiles (Stanford Heart Programme*
Risk Factor Score) (n=151)

4   Discussion

4.1 *Anthropometric data*

The mean age (20.3 +/4.6) is typical of that of a student population, body weight and body mass are in the acceptable range for general health purposes. A body mass index greater than 25 being considered to be possibly deleterious to health. A number of studies have shown that variance in body weight is not a simple function of adiposity but reflects the basic morphology of the individual (Martin et al., 1986; Ross et al., 1987).

4.2 *Cardio-respiratory data*

The test for aerobic power estimates the maximum oxygen consumption from heart rate data. This and other similar tests have been widely used for screening of large populations (Siconolfi et al., 1982). The values obtained in this study are, for the age of the students, lower than that which might be expected. Astrand (1960) considered that average values for female students 20-29 years should be in the range 35-43 ml/kg/min. 44% of the students had aerobic capacities in the range 30-39 ml/kg/min. This range is indicative of a population which is relatively inactive, a feature borne out by negative answers to the question 'do you exercise regularly' (3-4x per week) in the pre-test questionnaire.

The lung function data obtained from a flow-volume loop indicates that the population studied had adequate pulmonary capacities. The onset of lung disease is perhaps best characterized by patterns of change in the parameter known as the one-second forced expiratory volume ($FEV_{1.0}$). $FEV_{1.0}$ loss is a typically slow process and the value at age 25 years is often used as a benchmark with which to compare declines later in life. The group population age is just under this value and therefore we would not expect the lung function to be below average. The ratio of $FEV_{1.0}$ to Forced Vital Capacity (FVC), the Forced Expiratory Ratio (FER) is normally in the range 85-95% (Fletcher and Peto, 1977), this study shows average FER values to be 90+/- 5% and are therefore in concordance with other studies.

4.3 *Coronary Heart Disease Risk Factors*

Body fat levels (a reflection of obesity), total blood cholesterol and a risk factor profile were chosen as suitable parameters to examine in relation to coronary heart disease.

The mean % body fat was, by age and sex classification, found to be in the 'fair to poor' category (Metropolitan Life Assurance Co.). Nearly 80% of the group had body fat levels of 25% or more. This is not unexpected as the exercise frequency of the group was very low, additionally many of the subjects admitted to regular ingestion of convenience foods (ie. those with a high refined sugar and fat content). It was a little surprising therefore to find that the total blood cholesterol value was low. This is well below the 5.2 mMol/L value used as a 'cut off', above which individuals of 20 years or less are recommended to take specific dietary measures to reduce it (Ashton and Davies, 1986).

The Stanford Heart Disease Prevention Programme risk factor profile takes into consideration smoking habits, blood pressure values, cholesterol levels, a self rating of stress/personality and tension, body weight and level of physical activity. The scores obtained for the group were consistently low (mean = 6.8). An interpretation of this value is that the risk of a heart attack or stroke is about one quarter of the national average. A number of individuals (21%) were in the category above the mean, here the risk doubles to that of half the national average risk (Ashton and Davies, 1986); a regular smoking habit was the main cause of appearance of students in this category.

5 Conclusions

In summary, the variables studied show that the students can be considered to be generally fit on a health related basis, however with their chosen vocation in mind a reduction in body fat by 2-3% and an improvement in aerobic power by 15% would be of long term benefit. These changes could be achieved by participation in a regular exercise programme. Fentem et al (1988) indicate, in their review of the role of exercise, that the evidence for beneficial effect on preventative diseases such as heart disease is now even more clear than in their earlier review (Fentem and Bassey, 1978).

6 References

Ashton, D. and Davies, B. (1986) **Why Exercise?** Basil Blackwell, Oxford.

Astrand, I. (1960) Aerobic work capacity in men and women with special reference to age. **Acta Physiol. Scand.**, 49, (Suppl. 69).

Astrand, P.-O. and Ryhming, I. (1954) A nomogram for calculation of aerobic capacity from pulse rate during submaximal work. **J. Appl. Physiol.**, 7, 218.

Fentem, P.H. and Bassey, E.J. (1978) **The case for exercise**. Sports Council Research Working Papers, No.8, London.

Fentem, P.H., Bassey, E.J. and Turnbull, N.B. (1988) **The new case for exercise**. Health Education Authority, London.

Fletcher, C.M. and Peto, R. (1977) The natural history of chronic airflow obstruction. **Br. Med. J**, 1, 1645-1648.

Fox, K. and Biddle, S. (1986) Health related fitness testing in schools: introduction and problems of interpretation. **Bull. Phys. Ed. U.K.**, 22, 3, 54 64.

Martin, A.D., Drinkwater, D.T., Clarys, J.P. and Ross, W.D. (1986) The inconsistency of the fat-free mass: a reappraisal with implications for densitometry in **Kinanthropometry III** (eds T. Reilly, J. Watson and J. Borms), Spon, London, pp. 92-97.

Mathews, D.K. (1974) **Measurement in Physical Education**. W.B. Saunders, Philadelphia.

Ross, W.D., Martin, A.D. and Ward, R. (1987) Body composition and aging: theoretical and methodological implications. **Coll. Anthropol.**, 11, 15.

Siconolfi, S.F., Cullinane, E.M., Carleton, R. and Thompson, P.D. (1982) Assessing VO2max in epidemiologic studies: Modification of the Astrand-Rhyming test. **Med. Sci. Spt. Ex.** 14, 335-338.

PART FOUR

COACH EDUCATION

COACH EDUCATION IN THE 21ST CENTURY: A LOOK INTO THE FUTURE

SUE CAMPBELL
Director, National Coaching Foundation, Leeds, England

Abstract

With more and more countries using sport as a means of increasing national pride, developing international relations and as a form of foreign policy, many challenges face coaches in general and coach educationalists in particular. This paper focused on the changing demands modern sport was placing upon the coach. It was noted that the quest for higher and higher sporting achievements would require coaches to have a greater width of knowledge and the ability to work closely with experts from the fields of Sports Science, Sports Medicine and other related areas. It was suggested that alongside this increase in standards, there would be increased pressure to 'win at all costs'. As a result of this pressure to win, the need for coaches to protect their performers, themselves and their own profession was seen as paramount. It was argued that coaches' associations would emerge to guide and regulate their members and enforce codes of practice where necessary. A continued increase in community sport was predicted. It was envisaged that coaches would, in order to meet the diverse needs of the community, require specialist knowledge of particular groups, such as the elderly. Finally, the increased demand for full-time and part-time coaches was seen as providing the ideal opportunity to implement local and national strategies for the training and deployment of coaches.

1   The Role and Function of Coaches

Before attempting to look at the future of coach education, it may be worth reviewing what we understand by the word 'coach'. In the past the word has been used liberally to describe a variety of people involved in a range of tasks and it has never clearly been defined. Sports coaches come from many different backgrounds and enter sport for various reasons - they may be ex-athletes themselves; they may wish to work with young people or they may be interested parents of young performers. At one end of the scale coaches can be described as an enthusiastic army of volunteers and at the other a dedicated group of top professionals. Coaches possess many qualities but perhaps the three that should be given top priority in any coaching education programmes are the three 'C's' - CARING, COMMITMENT and CRAFT.

(a)   CARING involves not only nurturing the talent of each performer, but also having an overall concern for their well-being as individuals.
(b)   COMMITMENT is about time, money and above all a willingness to seek out knowledge and develop new skills.
(c)   CRAFT involves knowing every aspect of the 'job' and being able to use all the tools of the trade effectively.

There is no doubt that coaching is a very complex business. Coaches work in many different situations with a wide variety of people of all abilities and ages. If talent is to be nurtured and developed in a systematic manner then it is important that there are well educated coaches working at all levels of sport.

Throughout the world there is a growing recognition of the need to co-ordinate effort among various agencies to develop national strategies for coaching.

'Not all kids are born athletes, but many are naturals. With help they will be world beaters. But someone has to give them the help. That's where coaches come in ... and like athletes, coaches are not just born ... they're trained. But there aren't enough coaches and there aren't enough training courses. One of the reasons is the lack of career prospects for coaches.' (Australian Coaching Council).

Coach educators in Britain have been attempting to define the role and function of coaches working with different groups so that training needs can be more clearly identified and some degree of standardization achieved across sports. They have considered the needs of people taking part in sport under four headings: Foundation; Participation; Performance and Excellence. These groupings are considered to form a continuum which people enter and leave at various points - how far they go along the continuum is determined by their level of ability and their desire to succeed.

1.2 *Foundation - 'Physical literacy'*

Most young children are naturally active. It is an expression of their inquisitiveness and their need to learn. They learn through play which initially is unstructured but gradually becomes more directed as they grow. It is generally accepted that Play is a social, recreational and educational activity, voluntarily undertaken by children and young people. Play can be a method of acquiring social skills and a mechanism for the acquisition and practice of cultural and physical skills. Play is a medium through which a child may gain some understanding of social values. It is therefore inherently creative. Play is an expression of identity and an opportunity to explore limitations, both social and physical.

The prime responsibility for laying this foundation rests with physical education teachers and parents. Coaches play some part in this process but require special training to carry out this role effectively.'

It is important that coach education programmes in the 90's ensure that any coach working at this level has a child centred approach to what they do rather than a sports centred approach. The experiences gained at this level must provide a rounded, enjoyable and safe physical experience. The major element of coach education programmes at this level should include ethics (fair play), safety, ways of adapting games, the improvisation of equipment and an understanding of the child's body and mind. People working at this level should be encouraged to provide children with a wide range of experiences and not focus on one particular sport.

2   Participation

Coaches or sports leaders working in participation will be involved with people of all ages 'having a go' at particular sports or activities. They will probably be working in community based sports facilities on a voluntary or part-time basis. Their aim will be to provide an enjoyable and safe introduction to the skills and techniques of a particular sport or activity. In the past novice performers have usually found themselves in the hands of novice coaches. Perhaps we now need to re-think this approach. Coaches working at these early stages of learning should have a clear understanding of how skills are successfully introduced as well as an in-depth knowledge of the developmental stages children go through. Additional training and incentives to retain good coaches at this novice performer level may be needed. In the 90's, it will become increasingly important to ensure that highly trained coaches work at all levels and that status is not attached only to those coaches working with elite performers.

Another aspect of the participation level of sport which has implications for coaching is the great range of people (ages and abilities) entering sport. In the past coaches have had little or no training in dealing with particular sections of the community - the elderly, women, ethnic minorities, disabled people, young children - which has meant they have been inadequately prepared to face certain groups. People have often regarded coaches as only wanting to work with 'the best' rather than having an overall concern for everyone involved in sport. In the future, educational programmes which allow coaches to get a better understanding of the needs and expectations of the whole sporting population must be developed.

3   Performance

The development of performance is where the majority of coaches will be working. Performers can be defined as those young people or adults with a long term or medium term commitment to improving their performance. They tend to be training and competing inside a regular formal structure through sports clubs, university teams, school teams, or local authority sports centres. Their aim is to get better at what they do so coaches working with them need to be able to devise progressive training programmes. As well as requiring a sound knowledge of the techniques, tactics and strategies of their sport, coaches will also require an in-depth understanding of the minds and bodies of their performers. Unless they are given this knowledge they will work through 'mimicry' rather than through applying sound principles to a particular individual or group they are coaching. The various sports science disciplines - physiology, psychology, biomechanics and sports medicine - have much to offer coaches. It is no longer necessary to run athletes over the sand dunes until they are sick, sensible physical conditioning programmes can be devised based on understanding rather than trial and error. There is also much more that can be done to help players prepare mentally for competition, so they do not 'blow it' during the game. In those sports where there are complex physical movements clear analysis to assist the coach understand the principles which underpin a successful performance can be provided. It is through this type of understanding that coaches can begin to be innovative and create their own solutions to the questions posed by performers.

Performance standards are rising at all levels of sport and young aspiring champions are involved in intensive training programmes. It is important that coaches do not become so focused on success that they sacrifice the performer's well-being. Those coaches working with younger children need to have clear ethical guidelines -- athlete first; winning second. It is the responsibility of all coach educators to ensure that coaches are a positive influence on their performers and uphold the values of sport.

Performance development is a continuous process and as such will pass through a number of stages. Coaches need to be trained to deal with the various levels of performance -- novice, intermediate, advanced -- and to understand the various developmental progressions necessary to help performers fulfil their potential.

4   Excellence

Excellence as defined here means working with performers of national and international standard -- coaching elite sportsmen and women. This role requires special training and is not one that has been clearly understood or supported in the past. The elite performer will usually be highly self motivated and willing to commit time, money and energy to reach the top. He/she will have a limited life span at this level and time will therefore be of the essence. In a paper recently published by Frank Dick, Director of Coaching for the British Amateur Athletics Board, a number of areas were highlighted as being of special importance for the top achievers.

Lifestyle Management	Time Management, Stress Management, Money Management, Professional/ Personal Skills Training
Performance Management	Access to facilities/equipment, Special camps - altitude/warm weather Preparation Programme Planning, Physiological testing and monitoring, Biomechanical analysis, Nutrition Analysis/Advice
Medical Management	Medical Insurance Specialist referral, Rehabilitation, Local Medical Support

If all these factors are essential to high performance then it is vital that the coach understands the value of each facet and can draw on the relevant expertise to create an effective training programme. There is no doubt that at this level the coach becomes a facilitator, mentor and manager of resources for his or her performer(s).

Coaches working with elite, high performance athletes will require a special education programme. It will also be important to improve the coaching environment in which these top coaches work. The demands and pressures of high performance sport are very great. There is a need to define a philosophical basis for involvement at this level and then critically analyse the policies, programmes and services that are provided. A code of practice will be essential to help with the evaluation of coaches' behaviour and to set standards for the monitoring and control of coaches.

5 Considerations when designing a Coaching Education Programme

Coaching education schemes of the future will be designed with the following considerations in mind:-

(a) the nature and content of the NGB award schemes already in existence
(b) the amount of time and resources that coaches working on a voluntary and professional basis have available
(c) the different needs of the various sports
(d) the different levels of coaching expertise and experience needed to service sport in the community and at international level
(e) the type of delivery best suited to the geographical spread of the population and the type of adult learning programmes already accepted in the country -- courses, home based learning, etc.
(f) the quality control mechanism needed to ensure that standards are maintained across the country
(g) the degree of flexibility possible to make sure services are as widely available as possible
(h) the need for the accreditation of individual coaches or NGB schemes to ensure that there is equality between sports and a career pathway for coaches
(i) the type of support programmes needed for coaches once they have qualified -- in-service training, information service, research programmes, travel grants, etc.

6 Content of Coach Education Programmes

So what do coaches need to know if they are going to help people improve and achieve their potential? There are many aspects to a fully rounded coach education programme and not all elements are relevant to all coaches. However they can be summarized in six sections:-

(a) Sports-specific knowledge (techniques, tactics, strategies)
(b) Ethics and philosophy (code of behaviour/practice)
(c) Performance related knowledge (fitness, nutrition, mental skills, movement analysis)
(d) Management/vocational skills (planning, managing time, managing people)
(e) Teaching/Coaching Methodology (communication skills, organization and presentation)
(f) Practical coaching experience

The balance of these six aspects and the relative importance placed on each will depend on the particular needs of the sport and the level at which the coach operates.

In the future, each area will need to be presented as a series of modules allowing the coach to 'pick and mix' appropriate units to satisfy their own particular needs. It will be a 'CUSTOM BUILT' approach to the education of coaches. It is vital that the content of the units are jointly developed by academic experts and sports coaches. Much academic knowledge fails the 'so what?' test. Coaches do not need to know complex scientific facts but they do need to understand the implications for their performers and their sport.

An example of this 'custom built' approach can be seen in the NCF's Diploma in Sports Coaching. The Diploma has two main components:-

(a)   Supporting Studies Units - these are distance learning modules which enable the coaches to study in their own time and place, at their own pace. Coaches are required to study certain modules but are afforded the opportunity to select others in accordance with the demands of their sport and their own interest/expertise.

(b)   Coaching Studies which is a series of two day workshops with all coaches reviewing the application of knowledge to the coaching process, this includes a Sports-specific Study - a study into the coach's own particular sport on a topic agreed between coach, tutor and NGB.

Each coach registers centrally and is allocated to a host institution close to his or her home. It is envisaged that the majority of coaches enrolled will study in their own time and take a minimum of two-and-a-half years to complete the Diploma.

This Diploma which has equivalent status to other professional awards will help to establish a new level of qualification and training for coaches. This more formalized certification process may extend to other levels in the 90's. It will be the responsibility of the British Institute of Sports Coaches to ensure that the content and delivery of such programmes meet the requirements of coaches. The responsibility of the coach educators will be to meet the academic standards necessary to give the awards appropriate standing and status in the community at large. How much time volunteer coaches should spend on training is difficult to determine. It is finding a balance between the ideal programme in terms of education and the amount of time available to a volunteer who has so many other demands on his or her time. The 90's will see the need to lay down minimum standards of training for all voluntary and professional coaches. The diverse developments across sport in coach education and certification in the past have made it difficult to evaluate the relative levels of competence. Some form of standardization and accreditation across sport is necessary. If coaching is to become credible in the eyes of the public then it must offer a 'guaranteed' service.

7   How is Coach Education to be Delivered?

At the present time in Britain, coach education is presented by NGBs through courses held throughout the country combined with modules of study offered by the National Coaching Foundation through its network of National Coaching Centres. A modular approach to education is becoming more important as the coach finds himself or herself in an expanding and complex sporting environment. Coaches will need initial training to achieve minimum standards of competence and then on-going opportunities to up-date and expand their knowledge. In the future there will be a broader range of modules available to coaches to cover all the various areas needed to deliver an effective service to the customers at foundation, participation, performance and excellence levels.

The other significant change in the future will be the development of distance learning packages so that coaches can learn 'at home'. This approach has already been developed by the NCF and will continue to expand. There will, of course, be a need to support these distance learning programmes through appropriate tutorials and other support structures. Delivery of the right programmes to the right people is vital and will require close co-operation between NGBs and other agencies. There is no doubt that it is becoming increasingly important to provide a semi-professional or professional infra-structure for coaching at local level. Coaches need to work with performers; train other coaches; and help to manage and organize coach education programmes.

8 Quality Control of Coach Education

There are a number of ways of ensuring quality control of the education process and this will become even more vital as the modular approach is developed further. The essence of coach education courses is tutoring, so the appointment and training of tutors becomes a vitally important factor. At the moment in Britain, tutoring of the sports-specific (NGB) element is conducted by senior coaches and the tutoring of core information is largely done by personnel from within the Institutions of Higher Education according to their relevant academic expertise and their close contact with coaching. In the future, it is anticipated more coaches will be involved in the tutoring of **all** elements of the coach education programme (sports-specific and core). It is the **application** of the knowledge to practice based on a sound understanding of theory which is central to the education of coaches. Too often in the past coaches with limited understanding of theory have made even simple ideas sound complex. The presentation of information and method of delivery to sports coaches need special training. Tutor training should also be provided for everyone involved in the coach education process to exchange knowledge and share expertise. Just as it is wrong to assume that a good performer will become a good coach it is equally wrong to assume that a good coach will necessarily be a good coach educator.

Resource material to support courses should be designed to supplement the tutored programmes. These provide a basis of common understanding and a useful reference once the course is over. It is essential that these are developed by experts in the particular discipline working with coaches. Updating and refining these packs is also important but this requires both human and financial resources which is often lacking in NGBs. Some support structure to assist NGBs develop the appropriate materials is needed at national level if a 'quality' service is to be provided.

Monitoring and evaluation should be carried out annually on all courses to assess the effectiveness of the coach education programme. It should focus on the following key areas:-

  (a)   Recruitment of coaches including the publicizing of course, how and to whom courses are promoted, links with the regional and national bodies, assessment of those sports responding to the scheme and reasons for co-operation.

  (b)   Consideration of the specific needs of the regions of the country.

  (c)   Timing, structure and location of courses.

  (d)   Assessing the reception and perceived effectiveness of courses in the eyes of the coaches.

  (e)   The effectiveness of the information given on the courses, curriculum content level and 'pitch' of information, presentation, practical/theory, general versus specific approach, relevance to particular sports.

It is important that all NGB coach education programmes should demonstrate a coherent, systematic and realistic approach to coach education.

9   Coaching Support Services

Coach education is a continuous process and it is important that once coaches have qualified there are services available to support them in their work. Some countries have already developed extensive information and advisory services. The bibliographic and audiovisual databases which exist provide coaches with access to the latest technical and scientific information. This information is made available to coaches through the production of current awareness bulletins, technical monographs and periodicals. In Britain the network of 16 National Coaching Centres provides coaches with a local information point which they can contact for advice or information on a range of topics including fitness advice, psychological preparation, match analysis or the availability of education courses. At national level the NCF is developing two major databases for coaches - a bibliographical database and an audio-visual database. It is also producing a series of current awareness bulletins. At present there is a general bulletin, called 'Coaching Update' and sports-specific versions on athletics, racket sports, team sports, swimming and health-related fitness.

9.1   *In-service Training*

In the future, in-service training of coaches will become more crucial. Many coaches in the past have taken qualifications and then remained in the 'wilderness' with no further contact from their NGB and no opportunities to update themselves. This has lead to 'old-fashioned' practice or even bad practice. In-service training opportunities will need to be built into all future coaching education programmes at a number of levels. Certainly professional, senior coaches should be required to attend regular review days or seminars with other top coaches. Re-certification is becoming more crucial as the body of knowledge required to support performance development becomes more extensive. Research in Sports Science and Sports Medicine is helping to push forward the frontiers of knowledge on a wide range of topics and coaches at all levels need to be aware of the implications of this 'new' knowledge if they want to provide the best possible environment for their performers.

Another form of in-service training for coaches at intermediate or novice level is to work as an 'apprentice' to a senior coach. This type of scheme already exists in some countries and will become more widespread in the future. The selection of the 'master' senior coach is crucial if the experience is to be worthwhile. The 'apprentice' needs to watch and learn but he or she should also be encouraged to think for him or her self. No two coaches are the same, each must develop their own unique style. However, much can be learnt from observing and analysing effective coaches at work.

Top level coaches may also wish to work alongside the 'best'. In their case this could mean travelling to another country or inviting a top overseas coach to work with their own performers. It is likely in the future that scholarships for coaches and money to 'buy in' overseas experts will be made available by many countries throughout the world. Hopefully, this will lead to a much greater exchange of information and expertise than has previously been known.

9.2 *Sports Science and Sports Medicine*

Another aspect of coaching education is research or problem solving. In the past sports scientists and others decided on their research topics often with little consultation with the actual sport. Much of the research therefore produced answers to questions no-one had ever asked or needed to ask! As coaches become more knowledgeable in the various disciplines, they learn to identify the problems in their sport more accurately. With assistance from the appropriate experts these coaches are often the best people to 'research' the problem. Britain has established a research programme for coaches and there are a number of projects being funded through the National Coaching Foundation and the Sports Council to assist various top level coaches with particular 'problems' in their sport.

Sports science and sports medicine provide essential support for the development of sport at all levels. Fitness testing, relaxation techniques, injury prevention and the analysis of performance are just some of the ways sports science and medicine interface with today's sportsmen and women. The coach needs to understand the role and function of these other experts and to learn to work alongside them successfully. Coaching education must include an in-depth knowledge of the type of contribution that these experts can make. The coach may not always wish to use all these experts directly with their performers but the coach does need to appreciate what support he or she can call on. The present NCF Sports Science Education Programme funded by the Sports Council has assisted 23 sports to link their elite performers to a sports science support programme. These projects providing physiological testing, psychological counselling and biomechanical analysis are providing top performers with essential support. They are also providing material and information to assist with the development of coach education. In many cases it is this work which has been the spur to incorporate appropriate training modules into the coach education process for coaches throughout the sport.

10   Conclusion

Coaching education is being more widely recognized as a vital component of sports development. Coaches are important at all levels of sport and their training needs vary according to the age and ability of the individuals they are working with at any one particular time. Coaching education is an on-going process and a structured national programme of support is essential. All coaches should have an equal opportunity to access the latest information and to receive a high quality education suited to their own needs.

'Purposeful participation and improved standards of performance in sports are the product of a number of inter-related factors which include access to facilities, opportunities for appropriate competition and the availability of well trained coaches. Although coaching is only one element of the matrix it is essential to harness the increasing participation in sport and the apparent desire to improve standards by ensuring that all is done to provide the coaching resources required' (National Strategy for Coach Education and Coaching Development in Scotland - The Scottish Sports Council, April 1988).

There is no doubt that the winds of change are blowing in sport and that coaching is moving into a new era.

SYSTEMATIC COACHING BEHAVIOUR: AN INVESTIGATION INTO THE COACHING PROCESS AND THE IMPLICATIONS OF THE FINDINGS FOR COACH EDUCATION

J.W.B. LYLE
Moray House College, Edinburgh, Scotland

Abstract

Coaching is a process which involves a rational approach to the improvement of competitive performance through a planned and co-ordinated programme of preparation and competition. This process embraces both direct intervention strategies and the manipulation of contextual variables affecting player preparation and performance. This paper contends that a systematic approach to coaching, which co-ordinates and controls variables through goal setting, planning, monitoring and regulation, will result in achieving the performers' objectives more effectively and efficiently. An investigation is reported in which the self-reported behaviours of qualified and experienced coaches in swimming, athletics and volleyball (n=30) were collated and analysed. The results demonstrate that overall the coaches employed a systematic approach but that this was limited in terms of goal setting, loading factors, feedback, monitoring and recording. Coaches used a decision making process dependent upon intuition and the triggering of crises thresholds. This paper examines the implications of the findings for coach education. An explanation for intuitive decision making is offered which emphasizes the knowledge-in-practice of the coach and distinguishes this from ill-founded judgements. It is suggested that the artistry of the most successful coaches be incorporated into coach education.
Keywords: Coaching Process, Coach Education, Rationality, Systematic, Intuition, Decision Making.

1 Introduction

Coaching is a vocation which is widely practised and little understood. An emphasis on research into the performer has left far behind an appreciation of the coach's behaviour. This short paper attends to one specific issue. Do coaches operate systematically? Whatever the conclusion - what are coach educators to do about it?

There is a danger in any consideration of matters of theory of falling into the abyss between theory and application. Nevertheless, sports coaching is woefully short of the theoretical basis to enable praxis to take place. This paper is intended to stimulate thinking about the way coaches make decisions and to question the extent to which this ability is trained in current coach education programmes. In passing, reference is made to one of the hardy perennials of coaching: is it an art or a science?

2   The Coaching Process

Coaching is a process which involves a rational approach to the improvement of competition performance through a planned and co-ordinated programme of preparation and competition. To make this statement involves making a number of assumptions, a step which very few writers on coaching actually take. There will be little disagreement on the use of the terms improvement, competitive, performance, planned, co-ordinated, preparation and competition. These are the defining characteristics of the enterprise known as coaching. However, to assume a rational approach and to assert that coaching is a process require further elaboration.

Coaching is a process in that it consists of an integrated, interdependent and serial approach to the achievement of a single (albeit multi-faceted) goal. The coach therefore takes part in, or rather, directs a coaching process. To use the term coaching in any other way is inappropriate. In order that such a process actually occurs there are boundary considerations of duration, frequency, intensity and stability. The justifications for these assertions are based on personal experience and observation of the practice of 'coaches' who deal with committed athletes and teams.

Initially, the question of a rational and systematic approach is one of philosophy rather than observation. What characteristics 'ought' the coaching process have? It is unlikely that there would be a call for an irrational approach. Nevertheless, there are many other possible philosophies of how a process should be implemented. The argument underpinning the rational approach goes something like this. The ultimate goal of the coaching process is competitive success. In order to achieve this, the coach has to attempt to control, co-ordinate and manipulate the large number of variables impinging on the performance. To this end, the efficient and effective process will, of necessity, have sub-processes of analysis, planning and regulation (including monitoring and evaluation) and will be effected in a realistic context (goal setting, finance etc). In addition, the work will employ learning principles and training theory principles which follow systematic bodies of knowledge.

Such an argument justifies the rational, systematic approach. One difficulty in accepting this stems from the reluctance on the part of some individuals to apply such principles to human behaviour. However, this is partly a lack of familiarity with the knowledgeable application of theory from sports psychology and social interaction. This is the genesis of the mystique of coaching: the fallacy that an esoteric tradition of coaching skills lies awaiting the coaching initiate. Coach education, as with all education, is the process which shortcuts learning through trial and error. Two qualifying statements await another forum for discussion. Firstly, the rational, systematic approach does not preclude a personal philosophy of coaching which emphasizes particular forms of social interaction, outcomes or processes. However,

the relationships between theoretical principles and personal interpretations has not
been fully articulated. Secondly, any perspective is subject to critical analysis, and it
has to be recognized that a claim for a rational, systematic approach may be an
unquestioned concomitant of a taken-for-granted world which embraces science and
technology, industry and application, order and discipline, in a largely secular
society. A critical sociology of coaching is yet another neglected facet of coaching
theory.

3   An Investigation into Systematic Behaviour

In the pursuit of matters relating to the theory of coaching, the question arose 'to
what extent do coaches exhibit systematic behaviour in relation to their decision
making?'. For the purposes of this paper, some data has been extracted from a
larger study into the self-reported behaviour of coaches, conducted in 1988. This
data is presented in descriptive fashion and is intended merely to stimulate discussion
on how the coach's decision making qualities are trained.

A sample of very experienced sports coaches was given an extensive
questionnaire seeking both opinion and self reported behavioural data (Tables 1-3).
All had senior NGB qualifications, and had coached representative athletes.

Table 1.   *Characteristics and experience of coach sample*

Sport	Swimming	Volleyball	Athletics
Number	10.0	10	10
Average age	40.0	36.7	50.5
Number male	8.0	10.0	10.0
Average experience	13.2 yrs	10.8 yrs	19.0 yrs
Session/week	9.1	3.1	2.8
Hours/session	1.7	2.1	2.2
Weeks/year	47.0	40.0	47.0

Table 2.   *Rank order of process elements by sport*

Process	Swimming	Volleyball	Athletics
Physical conditioning	1	3	1
Technique development	2	1	4
Planning	3	4	2
Practice management	4	5	6
Psychological development	5	8	7
Contest management	6	6	9
Goal setting	7	7	5
Objective testing	8	11	8
Injury prevention	9	9	3
Tactical development	10	2	11
Social relationships	11	10	10

Table 3.   *Positive responses to planning elements by sport (%)*

Monitoring	Swimming	Volleyball	Athletics
Written plan for session	70	80	50
Written record of session	80	50	70
Workloads identified	90	40	80
Exercises based on testing	90	0	0
Programme sufficiently individualized	40	20	80
Recording in systematic form	90	40	40
Close monitoring of athletes' personal training	50	30	40
Potential estimated			
- constantly	10	50	30
- each session	30	50	30
- competition	90	80	80
- by objective tests	90	20	20
Sufficient information for goal setting	20	70	60

Coaches were asked to give their opinion on the relative weighting of a number of elements of the process. There were obvious sports specific differences but planning was rated highly. Goal setting was surprisingly lowly rated, along with objective testing.

Table 3 illustrates the responses to a selected number of items from the planning menu. The figures refer to the percentage who replied affirmatively to using each element of planning.

The data presented in Table 1-3 is highly selective. Nevertheless, it does offer support for the claim that coaching is perceived to be a systematic process although the reality of practice often falls short of the coach's knowledge and intentions. It is clear that a large percentage of those experienced coaches engaged in the planning process and attempted to monitor and regulate the process. However, there were a number of cautionary issues: very little was committed paper, there was little regulation of athletes working on their own, and testing of athletes appeared to have a low priority. It should be recognized that there were very significant differences between swimming, a major sport based on the stopwatch, and volleyball, a less well developed sport, in which performance analysis is perhaps more problematical.

Table 4 shows a further selection of responses from coaches. Some of the questions were designed to elicit a more detailed response about the criteria on which decisions were based. These provided more diverse replies. Only the swimming results are presented by way of illustration.

Although the coaches had no difficulty in responding to the questions, they produced very different answers. The point to be made there is not one of right or wrong. Coaches appear to have very different criteria to be employed for essentially similar tasks. The most significant feature of the data collected on the decision making processes, particularly those relating to immediate or crisis situations is that they appear to depend on the 'intuition' of the coach. Each set of criteria has a

Table 4.   *Responses by swimming coaches on threshold criteria*

Which criteria do you use to monitor progress?

Competition times (3)	Training performance (2)	Recent comp performance (1)
Competition results (4)	Test sets (2)	
Lactates (2)	Same point in previous season (1)	

How long would the non-achievement of training results be allowed to continue?

Session	less than 1 cycle	4 weeks	1 week
Quickly	immediate	2/3 days	
3/4 weeks	2/3 sessions	2 weeks	

How great would be the gap between potential and expected performance before you change expectations?

Significant (3)	Not much	Keep going until not possible
Leave as long as possible	Quite a lot	
Very small	Intuition when not achievable	

---

subjective rationality for that coach and by far the greater number depend on a judgement by the coach. This was evident in further examples related to the relationship between injury, progress and the initiation of new training cycles.

The general proposition, therefore, is that the planning stage of the coaching process is recognized to be a systematic process. Analysis, goal setting, periodization, unit planning and monitoring are perceived as parts of a rational, co-ordinated attempt to improve performance. On the other hand, the evidence from coaches themselves is that practice often takes a short cut, and very little recording takes place. This, however, is likely to be sport specific.

There seems to be little doubt, however, that the detailed implementation of the coach's intentions and the crisis management of the process is not approached in an overtly systematic fashion. Coaches take decisions based on feelings or intuitions. Such circumstances appear to apply to decisions as varied as individual exercise loadings (intensity, recovery), response to injury, performance expectations, and the timing of training cycles. Where change was required, coaches worked, not to a systematic monitoring of data but in response to the triggering of a crisis threshold. The thresholds depended on the coach's interpretation of the the crisis.

If the general proposition outlined above is the case, there are implications for coach education and it is to this that the latter part of the paper turns.

4   Coach Education

The absence of a coherent approach to coach education is a significant limitation to the achievement of professional status. Coach education programmes have often been equated with coaching award courses and have suffered, therefore, from the inadequacies of these courses. Sports specific technical content, even when bolstered by 'common theory' material continues to be presented as packaged discipline knowledge. It is difficult to claim that the skills of the coach are being enhanced when there is no consensus on what they are!

Following on from the proposition made earlier, it could be argued that there is no inherent difficulty in transmitting the sort of discipline knowledge on which planning is based. Planning itself, training theory, sports psychology strategy, etc, all have principles to inform the rational, systematic approach to the coaching process. However, it is obvious that decision making in circumstances of uncertainty or under pressure of time or even without complete knowledge is a skill required by the coach. How can this be developed?

At this point I want to refer to the work of Donald Schon (1983, 1987) and to suggest that he may be able to point coach educators towards some of the answers.

Schon draws a distinction between the technical rationality underpinning high status discipline based education for the professions and the competence required for day-to-day action. He poses a rigour-relevance dilemma for educators. His key words are knowing-in-action and reflection-in-action. With knowing-in-action, individuals cannot necessarily describe how the action is done, but they can do it. The knowing is in the action. The knowing forms an artistry which is the hallmark of those we recognize to be most competent in their vocation. Interestingly for this debate on sports coaching, Schon recognises that his wisdom or intuition 'eludes conventional strategies' (1987, p.13). However, he states quite clearly that 'it is not inherently mysterious: it is rigorous in its own terms' (1987, p.134).

Schon elaborates on reflection-in-action as thinking about what is being done whilst it is being done. This is a competence required for circumstances of uncertainty, uniqueness and crisis. Herein lies the message for coach educators. Can the competence required to deal with problem solving, the problem framing, improvisation and selection of alternatives, be transmitted to embryo coaches?

To continue with the analogy of educating to be reflective-in-action, it is necessary to ground the education of the coach in experience. This has a number implications: coaching must be clearly distinguished from instructing, animating and other forms of sports leadership; content must be problem-solving based, requiring case histories; 'coaches' will be required to assist the learner to evaluate decisions (interestingly Schon uses the word coach for this professional educator); master-apprentice schemes will be necessary; the need to study carefully the competences of those coaches recognized to be unusually good. None of this seems particularly radical, but to what extent are present coach education programmes based on experiential learning, structured around problem solving and underpinned by a support system which recognizes the gradual development of individual reactions to changing circumstances?

Schon sums this up.

> Professional education should be redesigned to combine the teaching of applied science with coaching in the artistry of reflection-in-action. (Schon 1987, p xii).

There is an interesting dichotomy here. It would appear that having recognized an intuitive, subjective decision making process in the coach, the suggestion is that this be trained. Is this the opposite of the systematic approach to coaching? The answer is the very opposite. The capacity for making apparently intuitive decisions is based on rational processes. With experience and learning, the intermediate processes are subconscious. Previous cases, recognition of variables, past experience, knowledge of the outcome of alternative courses of action are scanned immediately and subconsciously. The result is a process of knowing-in-action. The ability to deal with the unforseen, the crisis, in other words to reflect-in-action is a coaching competence, the education of which should be approached in a similarly systematic fashion.

5　Summary

Having examined the nature of the coaching process itself, and having asserted that the process was rational and systematic, the paper used selected data to illustrate this. The findings were that a systematic planning shell was often implemented in an intuitive, subjective way. It was then argued that Schon's work had some relevance in pointing to an interpretation of coaching behaviour and suggesting a basis for improved coach education.

In conclusion, coaching is neither an art nor a science. Without doubt there is a strong supporting structure of discipline based knowledge applied in a rational, systematic way. Coaching is not an art but there is a craft or artistry in the implementation of the process. A process that is not systematically designed and decision making that is not based on successful experience are dangers for the emerging profession.

There is a significant element of knowledgeable, experienced evaluation in decision taking. To say that it is intuitive is not to deny that it has a rigour. However, there is an element of artistry without mystique and not evolving from esoteric tradition that identifies the competence of the most successful coaches. Coach education has failed thus far to recognize this or to incorporate it into the systematic education of the next generation of coaches. In the drive to professional status such an omission is at our peril.

6　References

Schon, D.A. (1983) **The Reflective Practitioner.** Basic Books. New York.
Schon, D.A. (1987) **Educating the Reflective Practitioner.** Jossey-Bass Pub, San Francisco.

COACHING IN THE NINETIES

M. LASHUK
The University of Calgary, Calgary, Canada

Abstract
A three stage model was presented in an effort to enhance the sport experience for the performer. The needs, motives, and characteristics of the athlete serve to determine the characteristics, skills and behaviours of the coach as well as the type of delivery system appropriate at each stage. Congruency between the athletes' needs, the coaches' behaviours and the systemic features was predicted to result in more satisfied and talented athletic performers.
Keywords: Coaching, Sport Administration, Sport System.

The role of coaches in the athletic experience of individuals is varied and poorly defined. Expertise ranges from the professional coach to the volunteer parent coach. As the 1990's unfold, coaching is receiving increased scrutiny from various interest groups such as AIESEP. There are many diverse programmes, such as the coaching certification programme sponsored by the Canadian Coaches Association that have been developed to improve the sport experience. The purpose of this presentation was to propose a model which would result in more athletes achieving higher levels of accomplishment by marrying the behaviour and intentions of coaches and parents with systemic features in order to service the fulfilment of motives and needs of athletes at different stages of development. The role of the coach was discussed only in the context of the unified model rather than in a mutually exclusive manner.

The models' (Table 1) three stages of Romance, Precision and Generalization were originally proposed in the educational theories of Whitehead (1929). In 1985, Benjamin Bloom used similar categories of Early years, Middle years and Later years in describing his research on the development of elite performers in several fields of endeavour including athletics. While these three periods are labelled as discrete categories, it should be noted that as one period blends into another, it is impossible and undesirable to avoid a mix of the two categories. Further, no attempt was made to place specific chronological ages on the three stages because of variations in age of entry into various sports.

Rather than dealing with coaching, playing and administrative features as mutually exclusive features of the sporting experience, the proposed model centres on the athlete. The motives, needs and characteristics of the performer dictate which skills,

Table 1.   *Factors in the development of athletes*

Stages	Athlete needs, motives and characteristics	Coach characteristics, skills and behaviours	Programme and system features
Romance (Early years)	fun-participation, affiliation, self-esteem, self-confidence, challenge, excitement, curiosity, experimentation, variety	counselling skills, reqards participation not excellence, playful, rewards often (social, material), supportive, instruction is informal and personal, warm, enthusiastic, encourages lots of interaction between learners, friendly, encouraging, excellent model, creative, experimenting, master of general movement skills, earns the love of the learner, not a perfectionist, lots of smile, few judgements of skill 'right or wrong'	broad range of lead-up games and activities, clear statement of objectives to coaches (and parents and athletes), low level skill development, exposure to top athletes (models), high parental involvement, organization by school or immediate community, no travel for practice or competition, lots of small competitions, variety of activities, lots of laughter and noise
Precision (Middle years)	desire for skill mastery, control, achievement, identity development, eg. 'gymnast', individual recognition, goals are specified, breadth of activities are sacrificed, fun-mastery and achievement	technical expert, skills teacher, directive, detailed, more demanding, experts respect more than love, some technological expertise, rewards participation and outcomes	shift from participation to excellence, specialization begins, increased centralization of coaches and athletes and programmes, more formal competitions, some travel, support personnel are consultants, clear mission statement
Generalization (Later years)	excellence, fun-achievement, control, recognition, takes charge of training, concern with public image, focused	creativity, demanding of excellence, master teacher, master tactician, highly organized, shift from directive to sharing, skilled manager of support personnel, may change in the age of the applied sport scientist, technological expert	athletes move to centralized resources, much competitive and training travel to encounter peers who are excellent, many hands-on support personnel (physiologists, dieticians, psychologists, etc), coaching teams with specialization, financially expensive, clear mission statement

behaviours and characteristics are necessary for coaches to help the athlete achieve satisfaction and excellence at each developmental stage. Further, the programme and system features are also geared toward assisting athletes to satisfy their needs and achieve their motives at each stage. It is suggested that such congruence shall counter alarmingly high drop out rates in many sports. The socialization of athletes into the 'win at all costs' philosophy is often so rapid that performers are subjected to high skill demands before they can enjoy the romance stage. If athletes can fall in love with an activity before being drilled for high performance levels, they shall stay in the activity longer and seek higher performance levels in a proper developmental pattern.

With the athlete at the centre of the model, the practices and philosophies of the system, the coaches and the programmes are determined at each stage by the developmental needs, motives and characteristics of the athlete. This helps to overcome many current sport experience problems. Overzealous coaches often destroy performer satisfaction as they indulge in practices that are ego enhancing to themselves rather than being primarily concerned with the development of such characteristics as self-esteem in the performer. Similarly, sport administrators would become more interested in the development of individual characteristics rather than sponsoring stressful regional and national competitions before the athlete is prepared to handle such intensive competition.

At the first developmental stage, Romance, the athlete's motives are primarily to make new friends, have fun through participating and to develop self-esteem and self confidence through challenge, experimentation and a variety of activities. The coach at the Romance stage would have many of the characteristics of a model parent. Table 1 lists the skills and behaviours of the coach who is able to interact with the athlete in a manner that would result in the athlete achieving the motives and needs previously described. It may be that some people are best suited to coach at a specific level such as Romance due to personal characteristics and interests. Lastly, the programmes would be organized and administered solely with the developmental interests of the performer in mind. A variety of activities would be required, with only low levels of competition taking place with little or no travel for practices or competition. Perhaps most importantly, there would be a clear statement of programme objectives given to the athletes, coaches and parents. This would help overcome the current practice in many constituencies of coaches, administrators, parents and athletes having their own set of objectives which are often incongruent with each other resulting in dissatisfaction, poor development and high drop out rates.

After an indeterminate period of time, athletes wish to develop more proficiency in their activity and to compete more against their peers. This movement into the Precision stage is subtle and needs to be recognized in order that the type of coaching may change and new programmes be entered. As athletes develop through this stage, they begin to identify themselves as 'gymnast' or some other name, they begin to seek skill mastery, establish performance expectations and change their characterization of fun from participation to achievement and mastery. Athletes often change coaches upon entering this stage. They now have different needs and motives and thus seek out a coach who has different characteristics, skills and behaviours. The coach is now more of a technical expert, more directive and begins to socialize athletes into the competitive world of winning and losing. The system now begins to formalize competition, offer specialization and broaden the competitive world by introducing some travel for practices and/or competition. It should be noted that some individuals may choose to leave the competitive model being described at this point. A parallel recreational model could be proposed to service the needs and motives of this population but such a model is beyond the scope of this presentation.

The final change into the Generalization stage has athletes defining fun as achievement and taking control of many features of their sport experience.

Movement to a coaching 'guru' often occurs upon entry into this stage. The system now offers centralized training, extensive travel for competition and involvement of support personnel such as exercise physiologists, sport psychologists, etc. This is the world of the outstanding national and international athlete.

The intention of this presentation was to propose a model that would result in more satisfied athletes and more athletes that are satisfied. Further, it is suggested that the implementation of the features described would result in more excellent athletes and more athletes that are excellent. The role of the coach in such a process is determined by the characteristics, needs and motives of the athlete. It becomes obvious that the training of coaches for the proposed model would be quite different than current practice. The Romance stage coach would be a generalist with expertise in growth and development. The Precision stage coach would be a teacher with excellent analytical and technical skills. The Generalist stage coach would be an outstanding motivator, analyst, strategist and manager of support personnel such as applied scientists.

In the nineties, coaching roles are likely to undergo much change. This presentation has proposed one method of making the sporting experience more fulfilling for all involved parties.

References

Bloom, Benjamin. (1985) **Developing talent in young people**. Ballantyne.
Whitehead, Alfred North. (1929) **The aims of education**. Mentor Books.

'THE SHARP END' - COACHES' RESPONSES TO THEIR EDUCATION AND TRAINING COURSES

H. McD. TELFER
University of Lancaster, England

Abstract
The purpose of the study was to investigate drop out rates in the coach education programme of a governing body of sport. This study was a pilot for an in depth study of all coaches entering the system of one governing body of sport within the north west region of England. The method used in this pilot was a self completion questionnaire administered retrospectively which focused on (in addition to the general data on coaching frequency, level of operation, age group focus and contact formally and informally with the sport), four specific domains related to their coaching course. 'Personal commitment' was gauged by answers relating to time and course cost. 'Relevance' was charted by issues relating to personal coaching needs while 'Coaching Performance' was assessed by questions relating to the relationship between the technical (instrumental) content of courses and the communication skills (operational) content of courses. The final domain related to 'Delivery and Perceived Competence', assessing tutor-coach relationship based on coach perception of information relevance. The results show an imbalance in course structure towards the technical; a lack of clarity on 'how' to coach (communication skills) and a mismatch in delivery related to coach needs, expectations and the final product. Conclusions arising from the study show a large dissatisfaction with the 'process', a drop out rate in excess of 50% at first level supports this. The conclusion seeks to establish the links between non course completion, first stage registration and dissonance relating to the course experience, suggesting that the link between the course and the coaches' local reality is not made.
Keywords: Coach Education, Governing Body Of Sport, Coaching Course Content, Coaching Performance, Relevance, Drop Out.

1   Introduction

In his introduction to a 'A Total Statement' (The National Performance Plan 1989-1993), the Director of Coaching for track and field athletics in the United Kingdom, Frank Dick, commented that coaches must be 'equipped' to accept their responsibilities and that at the very least this must be the application of '. . .relevant

education and experience to teaching an athletic technique, training and tactics. . .'
(Dick, 1989, p.2).

In the aims and objectives of that document Dick gives as his second aim,

> To provide a service which will enhance the coach's capacity to apply his or her
> knowledge, experience and expertise to directing the athlete towards that
> (athlete's) statement. (Dick, 1989, p.4).

This study of Track and Field athletics investigated coaches' perceptions of their
experiences of their education process as prescribed by the governing body. For a
coach's capacity to apply knowledge and expertise to be enhanced, one must first of
all recognize that what is prescribed is of use.

In a previous study by the author of the relationship between theory and practice
in governing body award courses in track and field athletics (Telfer, 1986), the
responses of coaches indicated that while the technical content of courses was
considered to be of benefit, the content relating to 'how to coach' of methodology
(application), was not considered as having been adequately prescribed in course
content to influence in a significant way the individual circumstances of a substantial
number of coaches (Table 1). Further studies of coaches' perceptions of courses,
including 'Drop Out' in education courses within a regional structure of governing
bodies have been reported (Telfer and Simpson 1989, Telfer 1990). In all cases the
reasons for 'Drop Out' and the coaches' perceptions of their courses indicated a multi
dynamic works on coaching courses which is located in the coach's immediate
experiences of coaching and not necessarily in the prescribed way of course content.
Lack of congruity therefore leads to drop out since courses and local reality do not
appear to match needs.

Lyle, in his paradigm paper on Coach Education, comments on the nature of
coaching as eclectic with governing bodies variously emphasizing Eastern European
models of training theory in relation to performance with its resultant '...attendant
science based disciplines and modest input of didactics.' (Lyle, 1986).

Table 1   *Source: Telfer (1986) (n=135)*

	No Previous Coaching Experience (62.2% of Sample)	Professed Coaching Experience (37.7% of Sample)
Course helped in 'How to Coach'	53.5%	52.9%
Course was of no particular value in 'How to Coach'	41.6%	43.1%
Couldn't Evaluate	5.1%	5.0%

Table 2   *Source: Telfer (1990)*

Track & Field Athletics	1st Level Award	2nd Level Award
Course Attendances 1981-1989	1197	302
Registrations and Completions 1981-1989	534 (44.6%)	193 (63.9%)
Drop Out/Non Completion 1981-1989	663 (55.4%)	109 (36.1%)

The impression of coaching in the United Kingdom is one of infant taxonomical processes; sport located diversification leading to distinctive sport 'cultures' and a cafeteria notion for the client coach of choosing elements of the process which they perceive to be of value to them. The coaching systems appear to be outcome driven in justification rather than a synthesis of concepts, processes and outcomes. This study therefore is one which is underpinned by previous studies and has assumed the points previously made as a suitable detail base. The study examines coaches' responses to the process of education and training by extracting professed criteria from the coaches in relation to their experiences. It is therefore limited in scope but presents the raw responses to simple questions which provide possible direction for the future structure of courses and the nature of evaluation procedures.

2   Method

Using data from a previous study on skiing (Telfer and Simpson, 1989) a self completion, retrospective questionnaire was sent to a structured sample of course attenders at the first level award course in Track and Field athletics.

The structure of the sample was determined by course attenders who had (a) completed the course and further requirements and subsequently registered and (b) completed the course and failed to complete the other requirements of registration. In both groups, two year sampling blocks of course attenders was considered necessary since the record of course attendance in relation to registration commenced from 1981.

The questionnaire sought to derive responses in four key areas of

(a) 'Personal commitment' (time, course cost, convenience)
(b) 'Relevance' (personal coaching needs of event, facility, club, peers and coaching group)
(c) 'Coaching Performance' (related to the inter relationship between the technical and communication elements of course content)
(d) 'Delivery and Tutor competence' (examined the nature and content of delivery and the extent to which course staff sought to locate the information in the coaches' needs, i.e. information relevance)

2.1 *Personal Commitment*

The degree to which coaches commit themselves to coaching varies apparently with no logical underpinning theme. It did not always follow that those coaching at a higher level spent more time coaching. To this extent it was difficult to gauge responses to questions seeking to establish links with the coach's time spent coaching (and related activities - telephoning, schedules etc) and the course experience. Three distinct strands emerged however.

Lack of Awareness of the nature of course content aim and structure. For many coaches this left them disadvantaged in expectations and in their attempts to search for relevance in relation to their own local coaching experience whilst on course.

Cost was considered to be a major factor for a first level course of one weekend (two day) duration (the fee £10). One factor underlying responses was the feeling that as a 'volunteer' coach in a sport still professing an amateur ethos whilst making money overtly, the need to pay to do something which one can do without the rigours of course attendance, troubled some coaches.

Time was felt to be a valuable commodity. In trying to vie family, business and athletic commitments, coaches inferred that courses were to be tolerated as the price for inclusion in the system. While many did not like the one weekend, two day system, equally as many preferred not to be involved in a system of more but limited exposures. In this respect coaches appear undecided as to what system suits. For the Governing Body there appears to be a real need to encourage the notion that courses are not end products but facilitating processes which coaching holds central in its philosophy and that coaches should **expect** and **need** exposure to peers and experts within their coaching lifetime.

2.2 *Relevance*

Coaches clearly see the course as prescriptive, designed to give remedies which are instantly workable. This is to a degree at odds with the philosophy of the structure. Certain features of coaching needs were identified in the survey and while they are not exhaustive they are recognizable and to a degree predictable in the beginner coach of whom nearly all subscribed to the view.

The course was not specific enough in its technical content in relation to young athletes. Nearly all technical input was modelled on sophisticated performers.

Needs of coaches were primarily associated with, and identified as, dealing with issues surrounding the growing, child programme planning, injuries and practical coaching. These issues were claimed as deficient in the courses.

Nearly all professed disappointment with the lack of practical coaching in the course content.

The changing nature of clubs highlighted the response of the 'new wave athlete' belonging to jogging clubs. These are distinct from Harrier Clubs and the more established Track and Field athletic clubs. There is a need to address the ethos of these groups which lie essentially in taking part, in low level competition and social running.

Within the limitations of the questionnaire, coaches were primarily concerned to receive information **not** connected with strong event specific input, although they wished to retain this element.

2.3 *Coaching Performance*

Coaches responses were unanimous in relation to the link between their course and their ability to communicate their craft. In line with the findings of a previous study of the relationship between theory and practice (Telfer, 1986), the majority of respondents believed that more time needed to be devoted to communication in two ways.

Examples of good coaching practice needed to be seen with regard to good, relevant practices and drills. In essence they wanted to be shown how to link the theory to practice at a technical level. The skills enabling them to link the theory to practice appear to be unsophisticated at this embryonic coaching level.

Many believed that insights into how to present information, language and strategies in persuasion were necessary technical tools for the coach. Within this element responses in relation to motivation and communication skills were cited, as well as a greater need for sensitivity in pressurizing athletes and the need to emphasize, fun and perspective.

2.4 *Delivery and Tutor Competence*

Most responses were complimentary of course staff. There was a recognition that the staff could not undertake personal tuition but nevertheless there were responses which indicated a need for a closer focus on practical issues relating to real coaching environments.

It was felt generally that course tutors were helpful and that in this respect the respondents highlighted

(a)   The tutor was known as a coach
(b)   The tutor was from within the coaching region
(c)   The tutor knew examples from local athletes and could relate examples of 'real' problems to known local performers
(d)   Discussions with tutors meant that there was familiarity with the subject matter and
(e)   Offers of assistance outside of course time were more realistically given.

Balanced against this was the conviction that course time gave little opportunity for discussion, either with peers or staff.

3   Conclusion

Whilst this study was in itself not intended to derive conclusions but rather to indicate the direction for a further more substantial study, the implications are insightful.

Given the evidence of a drop out rate in excess of 50% subsequent to the initial exposure to the coaching process **during** the first level award there need to be explanations which indicate reasons.

This study indicates that courses may not materially affect the coaches' local experience of coaching. A sense of curiosity in course attendance rather than of deliberation is evident. The course seems to confirm technocratic approaches rather than strike a balance of a tripartite nature between what to coach, how to coach and the adaption to the needs of the particular coach/athlete partnership.

Too often the emphasis on courses is the leadership role rather than the coaching role of the coach (Lyle 1986), and there is a conceptual failure on the part of the Governing Body in understanding this is relation to the wider coaching context of the coach. Since literature of a technical nature is relatively accessible in Track and Field athletics, some coaches now use the role of the course as something different from that of a technical exposure. Coaches are now seeking answers to how they apply their knowledge rather than knowledge per se. Explanations as to the nature of coaches' responses are obviously varied but in a market where compulsion to attend does not exist, it behoves some Governing Bodies to examine their presentation. There is a growing sport literature, a greater awareness towards the professionalism of coaching and a reduction in the perception of the Governing Body as the purveyor of all wisdom and convention. Peer values and models seem to be important since it is in practical examples of proven worth that coaches feel secure. Additionally, it is important to consider that despite exposures to the lower level awards not all coaches coach at this level, nor are they without a degree of experience.

This summary of responses from the pilot study will hopefully indicate more clearly how to lower a drop out rate of 55% to one which reflects less of a comment on the nature of their education and training experiences to one of rather more pragmatic reasons.

4   References

Dick, F.W. (1989) **A Total Statement**. British Amateur Athletic Board, Birmingham.

Lyle, J. (1986) Coach Education - Preparation for a Profession in **Coach Education: Preparation for a Profession Proceedings of the VIII Commonwealth and International Conference on Sport, Physical Education, Dance, Recreation and Health**, E. & F.N. Spon, London, pp. 1-25.

Telfer, H. McD. (1986) A study of practice related to theory of the coach education system for track and field athletics in the U.K., in **Coach Education: Preparation for a Profession. Proceedings of the VIII Commonwealth and International Conference on Sport, Physical Education, Dance, Recreation and Health**, E. & F.N. Spon, London, pp. 316-321.

Telfer, H. McD. and Simpson, P. (1989) A study of ski instructors' perceptions of their governing body scheme of assessment with specific reference to Club Instructors and A.S.S.I.'s. Unpublished dissertation, University of Lancaster, England.

Telfer, H. McD. (1990) Drop Out in Coach Education in **Proceedings of the IX Commonwealth and International Conference on Physical Education, Sport, Health, Dance, Recreation and Leisure, Volume 2.** The New Zealand Association of Health, Physical Education and Recreation, Auckland, pp. 86-90.

PLANNING THE PSYCHOLOGICAL TRAINING SYSTEM: A GUIDE FOR COACHES OF DEVELOPING AND ELITE ATHLETES

I. R. HASLAM[1] AND G. J. FISHBURNE[2]
[1]*Faculty of Education, University of Western Ontario, London, Ontario, Canada*
[2]*Faculty of Education, University of Alberta, Edmonton, Alta., Canada*

Abstract
Planning training programmes for athletes is a decision making process. One way to analyse the decision making process is to view the needs of athletes in terms of the major systems of sport training. For example, most sports can be analysed in terms of a physical training system, a technical training system, a tactical training system which, at least in terms of soccer (and sports like soccer) can be organized around knowledge about creating space and closing space. Each training system has a conceptual framework that represents the important skills and knowledge to be coached at different levels. In recent years, mostly the last decade, a fourth major system of training has emerged and that is the psychological training system. Responsive decision making regarding the needs of athletes in any major training system requires a conceptual framework that systematically integrates and defines the parameters of the system. The purpose of this paper was to outline a conceptual framework for psychological skills training as it relates to the developmental characteristics of athletes from six years of age to adulthood and to the level of participation of the athletes.
Keywords: Coaching, Mental Practice, Soccer, Psychological Training System.

1 Introduction

A systems approach to planning a coaching programme is grounded in modern organizational theory and in that sense it is not a recent phenomena. It is, however, relatively new to coaching. A system can be seen as a set of related components that have been established so as to attain the ends for which the system was designed. The 'related components' of a sports programme include the technical, tactical, physical and psychological domains of training and the 'ends' of the sports programme are the goals that have been set for the athletes to be coached.

Coaching is a process of planning sport domains which are made up of a series of training continuums (one or more for each sport domain) developed, implemented and evaluated for a particular athlete or group of athletes. The training continuum is seen as an unbroken chain of experiences planned with and for the athlete or group of athletes throughout his or her contact with the programme. In the sport domain of physical training, for example, the training continuums would include the aerobic, anaerobic, strength and flexibility continuums. In the tactical sport domain the training continuum might include (for some sports) offensive and defensive awareness whereas in the technical sport domain the athletic continuum could include receiving, retaining or projecting skills (however they are defined in various sports). The psychological domain and associated training continuums have received considerable attention in recent years (Suinn, 1986, Orlick, 1986, Loehr, 1986) but from the diversity of theoretical interpretations of the area has emerged a confusing array of psychological functions and skills in sports coaching. The purpose of this paper was to introduce a conceptual framework for the psychological sport domain in soccer and to define the related training continuums for athletes from 6 years to adulthood and to the level of participation of the athlete.

2   A model for mental practice

The notion of mental practice and imagery use has received considerable attention in recent years. No single composite model seems to exist to embrace all of the possibilities of psychological training for sport. Some models emphasize the social possibilities of psychological domain of behaviour while others attend to the cognitive learning strategies of motor skill acquisition. In a recent search of the available literature an integrated framework of mental practice concepts was presented by Paivio (1985). It is on the basis of this model that the psychological domain of training for soccer is presented. Paivio (1985) conceptualized an analytical framework for imagery effects in which he describes the cognitive and motivational functions of imagery at both a general and specific level. His framework is based on research 'evidence that imagery mediates behaviour through either cognitive or motivational mechanisms, which effect specific or general response systems.' (p.225). Table 1 illustrates the psychological sport domain and the various training continuums of motivational and cognitive imagery of either a general or specific nature and is adapted from Paivio (1985). The following explanations and examples are from the sport of soccer but could also be applied up to a point to a variety of similar sports that are 'goal' oriented.

Table 1.   *The psychological domain of sport training based on Paivio's analytical framework for imagery effects*

	Motivation	Cognition
General	Are you nervous and fretful or tired and lethargic toward the game?	Can you see yourself creating space when attacking and closing space down?
Specific	Can you see yourself training hard or tracking an opposition player on a run?	Can you see yourself shooting for goal or controlling a pass?

2.1 *The motivational general function of imagery*

This aspect of the conceptual framework refers to 'the degree of physiological arousal' that an athlete experiences toward a performance. In the soccer example in Table 1 the question deals with perceived levels of game related activation from being bored and disinterested in playing the sport at one end of the continuum to being anxious and fretful about playing the sport at the other end of the continuum.

2.2 *Motivation specific function of imagery*

The motivational specific function of imagery has been defined by Paivio as 'goal oriented responses' (p.235) to particular events. In the context of soccer this could have to do with shooting and scoring a winning goal or making a superb save in a major championship game. It could also have negative connotations such as missing a penalty shot or making a bad tackle or getting injured on a play. Paivio notes that this type of imagery is likely to elicit various emotion which could serve as a motivational function.

2.3 *The cognitive general function of imagery*

This component of the conceptual framework relates to the covert rehearsal of spatial strategies of game play. In the broadest terms a player could concentrate on the offensive, defensive or transitional aspects of play. Offensively a player could imagine creating space for a team mate in a particular situation by intelligent running off the ball. Defensively, a player could visualize themself covering space behind a tackling player or guarding an opponent at a defensive corner.

2.4 *The cognitive specific function of imagery*

The final aspect of Paivio's conceptual framework is the covert rehearsal of specific technical skills. Learning or refining the shooting of a low drive to the corner of the opponents goal, or heading to clear a ball wide to a full back on the flank are examples of this type of imagery. At higher levels of skill development creative combinations and elaborations of skills can be visualized by players such as a striker taking a ball on the chest in the opposition's penalty area and turning and striking the ball for goal on the volley.

If Pavio's model is to be useful in planning the psychological domain of training the four training continuums must be further defined in terms of specific elements which are relevant to each of the four training continuums. The process of defining the elements of each of the psychological training continuums will result in a conceptual framework that systematically describes the training possibilities.

3   A conceptual framework for the planning of the psychological domain in soccer

A conceptual framework is a structure within which to select important training outcomes or coaching objectives. Each domain of training whether it be the physical, technical or tactical system will have a conceptual scheme that helps coaches to determine the objectives for athletes at different ages and at different levels of participation. Over the years a number of authors in the area of curriculum studies (Tyler, 1949; Taba, 1962; Jewett and Mullan, 1977) have consistently argued the importance of conceptual frameworks to the decision making process of educational planning. Table 2 illustrates the conceptual framework for the psychological domain in soccer.

4   Designing the psychological training programme

4.1 *The athlete*

Consideration of the characteristics of individual athletes is central to effective planning and in turn to successful coaching. The principal area of concern is the growth and development characteristics of the athlete. While the second area of consideration is the amount of practice time an athlete is willing to engage in during a single session and in terms of practices each week.

Four distinct periods of development are identified as the focus for organizing the psychological training domain, they are the period of childhood between 6 and 11 years of age; the period of early adolescence between 12 and 16 years of age, the

Table 2.   *A conceptual framework for the psychological training domain in soccer*

1. Motivational functions of imagery
    A   General motivation
        (i)   Relaxation: The ability to diffuse nervous tension and energy in the body.
        (ii)   Energizing: The ability to increase tension and energy in the body.
    B   Specific motivation
        (iii) Physiological capabilities: The ability to visualize and feel the most effective responses to specific physical performances in training or in competition.
        (iv)   Technical capabilities: The ability to visualize and feel the most effective response to specific motor skill behaviours in training and in competition.
        (v)   Tactical capabilities: The ability to visualize and feel the most effective responses to specific spatial problems in training and competition.
        (vi)   Behavioural capabilities: The ability to visualize and feel the most effective responses to specific interpersonal problems in training and competition.
2. Cognitive functions of imagery
    C   Cognitive general
        (vii) Creating space: The ability to visualize and feel the sport's offensive characteristics.
        (viii) Closing space: The ability to visualize and feel the sport's defensive characteristics.
    D   Cognitive specific
        (ix)   Retaining skills: The ability to visualize and feel moving with the ball under control.
        (x)   Receiving skills: The ability to visualize and feel controlling the ball.
        (xi)   Projecting skills: The ability to visualize and feel controlling the ball.
        (xii) Intercepting skills: The ability to visualize and feel tackling for the ball.

period of late adolescence from 17 to 20 years and adult athletes over 20 years of age. Explanations of the cognitive, emotional and physical characteristics of each group are beyond the scope of this paper. By deduction, however, it is not difficult to realize that the thinking skills, the emotional characteristics as well as the physical capabilities will vary radically from the 8 year old youngster to the 16 year old person. Similarly, the psychological training priorities will vary for each age group.

4.2 *Frequency and intensity of participation*

The frequency of participation in sport refers to the number of practices and the length of the athlete's season. Naturally, this will determine the amount of time available for practice of any of the systems of training whether it be the physical, technical or psychological aspects of the game. The intensity of participation refers to the relative seriousness or degree of importance that the sport has in the life of the athlete. A national level athlete would likely participate in the sport with that much more commitment than a recreational athlete in the same sport. Similarly, the frequency of practice and playing time would vary with the level of participation. In this regard, therefore, a distinction is made between the developmental and elite athlete in terms of the frequency and intensity of their involvement in the sport. This distinction can be applied to each age level through the participation cycle. There will be elite and developmental athletes at each age category from 6-11 years, to 12-16 years and to 17-20 years. In terms of adulthood there will be athletes at the beginning, intermediate and advanced stages of a sport.

4.3 *The vertical organization of psychological training*

The sequence of psychological training refers to the vertical organization of the motivational or cognitive aspects of the framework according to the athlete's age and level of participation. An emphasis chart depicting in percentage the amount of time to be devoted to the different training continuums can be used to determine the priorities of the training programme. In the following examples the percentage

Table 3.   *Percentage of time devoted to the psychological training continuums from 6 years to adulthood*

		Motivation		Cognitive	
Age	Level of participation	General	Specific	General	Specific
6-11 yrs	Developmental	5%	10%	15%	70%
	Elite	10%	15%	25%	50%
12-16 yrs	Developmental	10%	15%	25%	50%
	Elite	20%	30%	30%	20%
17-20 yrs	Developmental	10%	20%	20%	50%
	Elite	30%	40%	20%	10%
	Beginner	10%	30%	20%	40%
Adults	Intermediate	20%	30%	20%	30%
	Advanced	30%	40%	20%	10%

Table 4.   *Psychological training emphasis for advanced level adults*

| | Training continuums | | | |
| | Motivation | | Cognitive | |
100 hours total training time	General	Specific	General	Specific
Advanced adult player	30%	40%	20%	10%
Total time in each training continuum	30 hrs	40 hrs	20 hrs	10 hrs

amount of time was established through a questionnaire survey of soccer coaches (n=223) from the developmental to the elite level. Coaches were asked to complete a questionnaire priorizing the importance of the psychological training continuums according to age of the athlete and levels of ability of the athlete. This information was averaged and expressed as a percentage of time to be devoted to each training continuum.

4.4 *The emphasis chart*

Utilizing the emphasis chart requires that the coach determine the amount of practice time to be devoted to categories of imagery training over a season. This will include not only the actual practice time in training but also private training away from the practice site. If the index for the season were, for example, 100 hours, then in the case of the elite adult athlete the training time according to each general category of the conceptual framework would be according to Table 4.

Some of this time will occur during practice and would be conducted by a coach either by way of individual, small group or large group work. This might take the form of video sessions, relaxation procedures, tactical talks etc. When the coach has identified the objectives to be introduced in the regular practice situation the amount of in-practice and extra-practice time will be evident. If this amounts to 20 hours over the season then the athlete might have 80 hours of independent imagery training away from the practice site.

5   Children in sport - 6-11 years of age

5.1 *Developmental athletes*

Developing athletes tend to spend considerable time during practice on improving and developing their skills in the sport. In terms of mental practice and in relation to the often limited practice time the emphasis would be in the cognitive specific imagery. Athletes might be given imagery work sheets (rather like the competition and pre-competition coping strategy sheets used with elite athletes in the late 1970's, Rushall, 1978) with specific skills illustrated on them and asked to list the important coaching points of the skill or annotate on a diagram of the skill particular body parts that could be used in striking the ball ie. in shielding the soccer ball from a defender the player should remember some key teaching points. If each of the skills of the game were collapsed on to imagery practice sheets of paper and given to players for independent training the coach of the developing athlete would have almost unlimited resources for cognitive specific imagery training that would serve to support the technical training on practice days. At the same time, work sheets could be developed for strategical information about the game as players are encouraged to think about positions on the field and the various roles each position is required to play. Motivationally, players at this age should be asked to help with games at the warm up, to create mini games and be encouraged to play in a variety of positions.

5.2 *Elite athletes*

Elite athletes in this age range could have a similar imagery training programme with emphasis in the look and the feel of various skills of the game. As can be seen from the emphasis chart an increase in strategic information is encouraged because it is likely these players, particularly at 10 or 11 years of age, will be assigned to travel teams that tend to justify higher levels of play. At this level it would not be unreasonable to ask players to think about their specific strengths and weaknesses and be encouraged to engage in physical and mental practice to improve their skills. The specific motivational area could also involve imagery work sheets with visual and kinesthetic imagery activities. For example, list three words that describe how you feel when you have made your best effort in a training run; these could be, 'strong, powerful and determined'. Think about that training run every day and remind yourself of your three cue words by using them in relation to your training activities. Another example would be to design a mini game to play with their neighbourhood friends that helps develop a skill or combination of skills in a game-then play the game as often as possible between practices.

6   Early adolescents in sport - 12-16 years of age

6.1 *Developmental athletes*

Developing athletes at this level are also encouraged to work on their cognitive imagery of the sport. By definition many of these athletes continue to enjoy the recreational aspects of participation the quality of which might be improved with extra practice on the specific techniques of the game. If athletes in this category were interested with personal improvement in the sport then they should be encouraged to complete imagery work sheets especially on the cognitive imagery topics ie. basic skills and strategies.

6.2 *Elite athletes*

Elite athletes at this age are generally highly motivated to play and to improve and in that sense perhaps committed to extra practice away from the site. It is at this age that a marked increase in motivational imagery is evident. In the general motivational area selected relaxation procedures can be introduced such as breathing control, centring, autogenic training or meditation. Energizing activities would include the use of cue words, rapid tensing and relaxing of muscles and physical exertion. In the more specific area of motivational imagery training positive thinking, generally and then in relation to specific aspects of play, is important as is work on thought stopping and positive affirmations.

7   Late adolescents in sport - 17-20 years of age

7.1 *Developmental athletes*

If athletes at this age and in this general category of participation are interested in sport specific improvement then the emphasis should be on the cognitive imagery functions. The motivational imagery training should amount to about 30% of the time and would include controlling activation levels with breathing and progressive muscular techniques as well as the use of situation specific affirmation statements such as 'I feel confident about this penalty kick - I can see it go in the goal - I can feel the ball when I strike it'.

7.2 *Elite athletes*

This category of athlete could spend up to 70% of their time on motivational imagery work. For the most part the skills of the game are reasonably well refined and performance indicators are usually motivational rather than cognitive in nature. The motivational specific imagery area and particularly the behavioural imagery element might be especially important. Relationships with team mates, opposition, coaches and other game personnel become a feature of the training. Leadership contributions, team harmony, team specific roles and responsibilities are visualized with effective responses that lead to positive feelings of self worth. The cognitive imagery would be team specific expectations of each player's overall contribution to the team. As in the case of a player at the national level being asked to play out of position or in a system of play that they were not used to at the provincial or club level.

8   Adults in sport

This category of athlete is divided according to three sub levels instead of two. In one sense the relative emphasis of imagery training for sport improvement is similar to the three stages of developing and elite athletes in the previous three categories. The beginner would benefit from cognitive imagery training as new projecting, receiving, intercepting and retaining skills and spatial strategies are introduced and refined. The intermediate level athlete could strike more of a balance between the motivational and cognitive functions of imagery with probably increased emphasis on the specific motivational functions and the spatial strategies in the cognitive general categories. The advance level adult athlete would probably be wise to spend more time on the motivational functions of imagery such as relaxing, energizing, thought stopping and situation specific affirmation statements. At this stage it is likely that fundamental skills and game strategy are reasonably well understood and less time need be afforded these areas.

9   Summary and conclusions

Paivio's analytical framework for imagery effects served as a basis for the development of a conceptual framework for imagery training. Twelve purpose elements further defined the content possibilities of the psychological training domain for the sport of soccer. An emphasis chart for each age category by developmental stage and level of participation was formulated based upon a questionnaire survey of Canadian soccer coaches. The concept of a systems approach to planning training programmes would allow for a more organized and systematic implementation of coaching programmes. Fortunately, the scope and sequence of the physical and technical training systems are well established in many sports but the psychological training system tends to be piecemeal and fragmented if it is planned for at all in many programmes. It takes creative, organized coaches and self motivated, committed athletes to embrace the notion of complete preparation in sport to the fullest.

10 References

Jewett, A.E. and Mullan, M.R. (1977) **Curriculum Design: Purposes and Processes in Physical Education Teaching-Learning**. AAHPER. Washington, DC.

Loehr, J.E. (1986) **Psychological Toughness Training for Sport**. Stephen Greene Press. Lexington.

Orlick, T. (1986) **Coaches Training Manual to Psyching for Sport**. Leisure Press. Champaign, IL.

Paivio, A. (1985) Cognitive and motivational functions of imagery in human performance. **Canadian Journal of Applied Sports Sciences**, 10, 225-285.

Rushall, B.S. (1978) Environment specific behaviour inventories: developmental procedures. **International Journal of Sport Psychology**, 9.

Suinn, R.M. (1986) **Seven Steps to Peak Performance**. Hans Huber. Toronto.

Taba, H. (1962) **Curriculum Development: Theory and Practice**. Harcourt Brace and World Inc. New York.

Tyler, R. W. (1949) **Basic Principles of Curriculum and Instruction**. The University of Chicago Press. Chicago.

THE ROLE OF SPORT PSYCHOLOGY IN THE EDUCATION OF COACHES IN FLANDERS (BELGIUM)

P. WYLLEMAN[1,] M. THEEBOOM[2] AND K. DE MARTELAER[2]
[1]*Belgian Federation for Sport Psychology, Brussels, Belgium*
[2]*Higher Institute of Physical Education, Vrije Universiteit Brussel, Brussels, Belgium*

Abstract
In major sporting nations specific sport psychological units have been introduced into coach education programmes. Research shows that in Flanders sport psychology has only recently evolved and that it has been installed in only a few coach education programmes. Results of an inquiry held with the (assistant-) coaches of the Flemish Judo Federation (VJF) show that (1) almost 75% are interested in the field of sport psychology, (2) they indicate that sport psychological unit should direct its attention to the following topics: concentration, self-confidence, stress management, motivation, and the relation coach-athlete, and (4) the sport psychologist should have a specific task within the federation. Following these results a unit 'Sport Psychology' was introduced in the coach education programme of the VJF. This paper reports on how it was introduced, on its content and organization. In conclusion, reflections are made on the role of the sport psychologist in a sports federation, and criteria are formulated for optimizing the evolution of sport psychology in general, and for the introduction of sport psychology in coach education programmes in particular.
Keywords: Sport Psychology, Coach Education Programme, Judo, Psychological Guidance, Relation Coach-Sport Psychologist.

1 Introduction

1.1 *Coach education programmes*

Sports coaching, constituting the backbone of all levels of organized sport, has entered a period of increased recognition, development and provision (Johnston, 1986). Although it is debatable if sports coaching can be called 'a science and an art' (Lyle, 1986), it must be clear that coaches are primordial to the realization of sports performances. As such it is necessary that they have the knowledge required to guide and direct athletes towards specific sports related goals. Although this knowledge can be based on past experience (for example as an athlete), there is a growing consensus that sports coaches must be prepared (trained) in a more structured and formal way. Herein several factors play an important role: provisions for coach education, accreditation of coaches, coach education programmes, certification and regulation (Lyle, 1986).

In (major) sporting nations there is a distinct evolution towards developing specific coach education programmes (Table 1).

1.2   *Contents of a coach education programme*

Contents of coach education programmes have always (almost entirely) concentrated on technical and tactical information. It is only during the last decade that the need was felt for more, and general knowledge and information from disciplines such as psychology, physiology, principles of motor learning, and so on.

It is interesting to see that, following the rise in the importance of (international) elite sports and in the wake of the evolution of sport psychology, coaches are getting more and more interested in the psychological or mental aspects related to sports performances. Gowan et al. (1984) report on a survey the Coaching Association of Canada conducted of the National Sport Governing Bodies concerning the importance of different sport sciences. Results showed that sport psychology was seen as the most important sport science discipline.

This importance is on the one hand reflected in the many publications and articles directed towards coaches relating to this topic (for example Martens et al., 1981; Klavora and Daniel, 1984; Orlick, 1986), but on the other hand also in the above mentioned coach education programmes, which have recognized the growing need and demand for this specific sort of knowledge. A 'tour de horizon' of the coach education programmes of Australia, Canada and the United Kingdom shows us that topics related to sport psychology are being treated in units of 1.5 hours to 4.5 hours.

In the 'Trainerakademie' of Cologne, we find that sport psychology has been covered in a very extensive manner, with subjects such as 'motivation', 'group dynamics', 'mental preparation', 'the coach and mental guidance' (Deutscher Sportbund, 1986).

If we want to be able to highlight the role of sport psychology in the education of coaches, it is imperative to get a clear picture on the position of sport psychology. This paper reflects firstly on the presence and situation of sport psychology in

Table 1.   *Examples of coach education programmes or organizations which supply coach education programmes*

Australia	National Coaching Accreditation Scheme (NCAS)
Canada	National Coaching Certification Programme (NCCP)
FRG	Trainersakademie Koln
UK	National Coaching Foundation

USA	American Coaching Effectiveness Programme (ACEP)

Table 2.	*Topics related to sport psychology which are part of coach education programmes of Australia, Canada and the United Kingdom (Campbell, 1986; Gowan and Thomson, 1986; Pyke and Woodman, 1986).*

Mental Preparation in Sport	Communication Skills
Sport Psychology 'A' Motivation	Stress Control Techniques
Sport Psychology 'B' Competitive Anxiety	Mental Preparation for Competition
Identifying General Strategies for Mental Preparation in Sport	Motivating Athletes for the Long Term
Psychology of Sport	

Flanders in general. Secondly, attention is directed at the presence of sport psychology in coach education programmes in Flanders. As a example, a description of how sport psychology was introduced in the coach education programme of the Flemish Judo Federation is given. Finally, criteria are specified on how the introduction of sport psychology in coach education programmes in general can be optimized.

2   Status of sport psychology in Flanders

Sport psychology is a relatively new and young science. Especially in the large sporting nations (for example in the United States of America, the Federal Republic of Germany, Canada) sport psychology is evolving at a more rapid pace than in other nations. This is clearly reflected in the development of sport psychology consultancy services for top level - Olympic athletes in these countries (Nideffer, 1984). It is also clear that the evolution of the field of sport psychology in general, is determining the pace at which sport psychology is finding a specific place in the education of coaches.

In Flanders however, sport psychology has only evolved clearly during the last 3 to 4 years. Experience has shown that since in 1987 the Flemish Society for Sport Psychology was started by sport psychologists of the three major Flemish universities (in 1988 followed the Belgian Society for Sport Psychology), interest from the world of sport for sport psychology steadily increased. But although sport psychology in Flanders is moving forward, it is clear that there are still specific factors that have inhibited, and are still inhibiting, its evolution.

Firstly, the status of the field of sport psychology itself has been downgraded by four factors:

   (a)   sport psychology as a science has no specific profile

   (b)   there is almost no interest from the field of general psychology and little from the other sciences of sport (such as sportsmedicine, sports pedagogy)

   (c)   as a field that has evolved from general psychology, it is clear that sport psychology has done little to clarify the terminology it is using, and is therefore covering itself in a cloud of 'difficult', 'unclear', 'mystifying' terminology which forms a barrier between the sport psychologist, the athlete and/or coach

(d)   there is no official sport psychology education programme in Flanders (or Belgium).

Secondly, there are specific factors related to the sport psychologist that restrict a more swift evolution:

(a)   the link with the (especially clinical) psychologist and with expressions such as 'mental illness', 'psychiatric treatment', 'psycho-analysis'

(b)   the title of 'psychologist' has not yet been legalized in Belgium, contrary to neighbouring countries such as the Netherlands, so that everyone can use the title 'psychologist' in the context of a private consultancy service

(c)   psychologists who are involved in sport psychology have amazingly enough shown little (practical) knowledge, experience and /or empathy for sport, and especially for competitive sport - a factor which may clearly impede the relation sport psychologist - top level athlete - coach when it comes to psychological preparation and guidance towards top level competitions.

It is clear that sport psychologists must find specific solutions to optimize an active interaction with the world of sport. And yet, even when such a co-operation has come about, experience shows that the contribution of the sport psychologist is also influenced by specific factors

(a)   the expectations of athletes, coaches, board of directors, and so on towards the sport psychologist and his/her possible contributions

(b)   the support from specific persons within the sports federation (for example the national coach, the board of directors, the committee of coaches)

(c)   the interest and co-operation from the (top level) athletes

(d)   the personal contribution from the sport psychologist
   - experience and knowledge of, and empathy towards (competitive and top level) sports
   - willingness to participate in specific activities in the sports federation (for example special training sessions)
   - presence at national competitions, or specific activities, so that all present can easily and in an un-official manner approach the sport psychologist
   - flexibility in attending to questions and problems (Wylleman, 1989).

3   Coach education programmes in Flanders

In Flanders the Ministry of Culture and Sport of the Flemish Community is, by means of a Commission for Education and Formation (Landelijke Commissie Kadervorming or LCK) responsible for the coach education programmes of 55 different sports. For every sport there is a 'think tank' in which there are representatives of

(a)   the sports federation itself

(b)   the higher Institutes of Physical Education of the Flemish Universities

(c)   BLOSO (the Sports Department of the Ministry of Culture and Sport).

Table 3.   *Levels and goals of the coach education programmes of the LCK*

Initiator		initiating beginners (mainly youth) in the technical aspects of a specific sport
Trainer B	assistant coach	technical and tactical knowledge; training and developing the physical qualities of athletes - in preparation for possible participation in competition
Trainer A	coach	guidance of athletes towards participation in (senior level) competition at national level
Top-trainer	top level coach	guidance of elite-performers at international level

This 'think tank' is responsible for determining the contents and the profile of the coach education programme for their specific sport. In general a coach education programme consists of four levels (Table 3).

3.2 *Sport psychology in the coach education programmes of the LCK*

When we look at the coach education programmes provided by the LCK, we see that the topic of sport psychology is not represented in the same manner in the coach education programmes compared to the programmes of other countries (as exemplified earlier). Research shows that in the coach education programmes of 52 different sports, sport psychology is touched upon as a specific and individual unit in only seven sports (judo, mountaineering, rowing, squash, tae-kwondo, waterpolo and waterski). These units are captioned as 'Psychology', 'Sport psychology', 'Mental guidance' or 'Psychological preparation'. Time spent on these units varies between 1 hour to 6 hours. These units represent a total of 30 hours or 6% of the total time of the coach education programmes of these seven sports. Sport psychology is also indirectly touched upon in fencing, karate, table tennis, tennis and cycling. These results indicate that there is an interest in sport psychology, although this interest is not translated directly into the organization of related courses in all coach education programmes of the LCK.

3.3 *Sport psychology in the Flemish Judo Federation (VJF)*

In 1985 a study revealed that the members of the national judo team attributed on the average one quarter of their ever best performance to mental, psychological factors (Wylleman, 1985). Three world champions rated this influence as high as 40% to 50%. Although these elite judokas realized that mental factors had an influence on their performances, there was no planned training or guidance directed at enhancing these factors. At that point the national coach of the VJF asked the co-operation of a sport psychologist in order to optimize the preparation and guidance of the elite judokas (Wylleman,1989a). During the following years elite judokas were guided and prepared towards participation at European and World Championships as well as Olympic Games.

Throughout this period it became clear that the success of this psychological guidance and preparation was dependent upon several factors: the co-operation of the elite judokas themselves; and the assistance/support of not only the national coach but also of the coaches of the sports clubs of which these judokas were a member. It was clearly felt that by involving more the coaches of the federation, the co-operation between the sport psychologist and top level judokas could be enhanced. It was decided that the first step in strengthening this involvement should be informing and educating the coaches on the subject of sport psychology in general, and psychological guidance and preparation of athletes in particular.

3.4 *Inquiry on the co-operation between (assistant-) coaches and sport psychologist*

An inquiry was held to establish the wishes and the needs of the (assistant-) coaches for possible co-operation with the sport psychologist. A questionnaire was completed by assistant-coaches, coaches and referees on the following topics

(a)   their basic knowledge of sport psychology
(b)   their wishes and interest for the introduction of a unit 'Sport Psychology' in their education programme, and the contents of such a unit
(c)   the objectives of co-operation with the sport psychologist.

Respondents had an average of 22 years involvement in judo with approximately 10 years of international competition.

Knowledge on sport psychology   Results showed that 27% had never heard of sport psychology, 40% had heard about it and wanted to know more on the subject and 33% had taken the initiative to search for information or literature on sport psychology. This meant that for every four coaches, three coaches indicated an interest in sport psychology.

Sport psychology as part of the coach education programme   They stated that sport psychology should be introduced at all levels of the coach education programme. In the programme, sport psychology was ranked as the third most important subject (after sport pedagogy and sport physiology). Regarding its contents, 46% indicated that the emphasis should be on aspects of 'training', 46% wanted the emphasis to be on 'competition' related aspects and only 8% had a balanced interest in both. Although it was found that in general a majority wanted to be instructed at both a theoretical and practical level, there was also a large percentage (37%) who were only interested in the practical or applied side of sport psychology. Finally, (assistant-) coaches specified that the following topics should be part of the unit 'Sport Psychology': 'concentration' (24%), 'self-confidence' (21%), 'stress management' (20%), 'motivation' (15%) and 'the relation coach-athlete' (13%).

Co-operation with the sport psychologist   The final part of the questionnaire related to the necessity and the possible objectives of a co-operation with a sport psychologist. The (assistant-) coaches indicated that such a co-operation was

(a)   sometimes necessary with the judokas (62%) (for example personal problems, preparation of important competitions...),
(b)   mostly necessary with the coaches (35%) (for example information and knowledge regarding specific psychological topics)

(c) always necessary with the federation itself (58%) (for example as an Ombudsperson).

Regarding psychological guidance and counselling the (assistant-) coaches ranked as most important target group the top level judokas, followed by the sub-top level, the former top level and the other judokas.

Finally, it was interesting to see that the referees participating in this inquiry, indicated not only an interest in sport psychology, but also that they would like to learn special techniques as a function of their participation in international competitions. They found topics such as 'concentration' and 'stress management' of great interest.

The role of the sport psychologist Following these results, it was decided to develop the co-operation of the sport psychologist in two specific directions. Firstly, the sport psychologist should have a specific and permanent place in the federation itself. The sport psychologist was made a member of the Medical Commission of the VJF. This commission has as task furnishing guidance and treatment for the (top level) judokas (for example on international competitions), and advice and information towards the coaches of the federation.

Secondly the sport psychologist should have four specific tasks:

(a) psychological guidance and preparation of elite judokas
(b) education and formation of coaches
(c) functioning as an Ombudsperson
(d) supplying specific information regarding sport psychology.

3.5 *Sport psychology in the coach education programme*

Within the coach education programme of the VJF organized by the LCK, a unit 'Sport Psychology' was introduced. Its goal was to provide information and knowledge on sport psychology in general, and on psychological guidance and preparation of athletes in particular. The purpose of this unit was not to turn coaches into sport psychologists, but to supply them with (basic) knowledge on sport psychology, so that coaches will be able to optimize their coaching, and 'feel more at ease' when working together with a sport psychologist. It was directed at the level of Trainer A or coach and consists of two units:

(a) a 3 hours theoretical unit, which is aimed at providing information on a more general level on 5 specific subjects: anxiety, communication, competition, motivation and training
(b) a 3 hours practical unit, which is aimed at initiating and exercising techniques of stress management and communication.

Evaluation by candidates showed that 'communication' in relation to the organization of training sessions in their sports club, and 'anxiety' and 'stress management' in relation to preparation and guidance for competition, was most appreciated.

4. Discussion

4.1 *The role of sport psychology in coach education programmes*

Taking into account

(a) the parallelism between the evolution of sport psychology in general, and its introduction in coach education programmes

(b) the specific factors that are inhibiting an optimal evolution in the future

(c) the apparent lack of attention for sport psychology in the coach education programmes

it was clear that there was still a long way to go before sport psychology was automatically thought of as being an inherent part of coach education programmes.

In order to optimize this trend, it is important to acknowledge

(a) firstly that a sport psychologist can have two specific functions within a sports federation
- as an education oriented sport psychologist, involved in the coach education programme of the sport federation,
- as an applied sport psychologist, involved in the psychological preparation and guidance of (top level) athletes.

(b) secondly that sport psychology in general, and the education oriented sport psychologist in particular, must offer and develop specific units regarding sport psychology for coach education programmes. When developing these units one must acknowledge more in detail the following aspects:
- the target group for which the education programme is developed (for example assistant- or top level coaches)
- the goal of the education programme (for example theoretical or applied)
- its contents (specific subjects which relate to the goal that is put forward)
- the way in which it is organized (eg. class-teaching, clinics, ...).

It is also important to realize that, although in general 'Sport Psychology' can be introduced in the coach education programmes of all sport disciplines, there is a specificity which sport psychologists must keep in mind when developing education units for specific sports (for example individual and group sports).

Finally, attention must also be directed at the development of a unit specifically for referees.

4.2 *Future evolutions*

To go forward with the evolution and integration of sport psychology it is clear that several specific changes are required to optimize its future evolution

(a) legislation of 'psychology' and the use of the title 'psychologist'

(b) specific (post-) graduate programmes in sport psychology should be installed at the Universities and the Higher Institutes of Physical Education

(c) the contribution of sport psychology should be recognized
- in general by the other sport sciences,

- in relation to psychological guidance and preparation by the authorities responsible for top level sport (for example the Olympic Committee, the Flemish Bureau for Top level sport)
- in relation to its educational value by the authorities responsible for the instalment and organization of coach education programmes (for example the LCK) and by the Higher Institutes for Physical Education

(d) sports federations should be given the opportunities to work with a sport psychologist (for example financial support, a centralized sport psychology consultancy service).

There is a need for the introduction of sport psychology in the coach education programmes of all sports. As a first step a unit 'Introduction to sport psychology' should be organized in the ABO-course which is an obligatory unit for all Initiators who want to start level 'Trainer B'. This introductory course should be general and relate to all sports. In the following levels, units should be organized on sport psychology, which are more detailed and which should relate to the sport in question. Within these units attention should be paid in balancing theoretical and practical/applied topics.

It must be clear that only when the above stated criteria are realized, it will be possible to introduce on a more general scale sport psychology in the education programmes of coaches. And it is only when the authorities responsible for the organization of the coach education programmes, the Societies for Sport Psychology, the Universities and Institutes of Physical Education work together, that the appropriate climate can be created in which these criteria can be developed to an optimal level.

5   References

Campbell, S. (1986) State of the art, in **Coach Education: Preparation for a Profession** (eds Conference '86 Glasgow), E. & F. N. Spon Ltd, Glasgow, pp. 61-75.

Deutscher Sportbund und Verein Trainerakademie Köln e. V.(1986) **Curriculum für das Studium an der Trainerakademie Köln**, Deutscher Sportbund, Köln.

Gowan, G. R. and Thomson, W. G. (1986) The Canadian approach to training of coaches: matching the paradigm, in **Coach Education: Preparation for a Profession** (eds Conference 86 Glasgow), E. & F.N. Spon Ltd, Glasgow, pp. 39-60.

Gowan, G. R., Botterill, C. B. and Blimkie, C. J. R. (1984) Bridging the gap between sport science and sport practice, in **Coach, Athlete, and the Sport Psychologist** (eds P. Klavora and J. V. Daniel) University of Toronto, Toronto, pp. 3-9.

Hug, O. (1983) **Eine Informationsschrift über die Ausbildung zum staatlich geprüften Trainer.** Deutscher Sportbund, Köln.

Johnston, K. D. A. (1986) Introduction, in **Coach Education: Preparation for a Profession** (eds Conference '86 Glasgow), E. & F. N. Spon Ltd, Glasgow, p. xi.

Klavora, P. and Daniel, J. V. (1984) **Coach, Athlete, and the Sport Psychologist.** University of Toronto, Toronto, Ont.

Lyle, J. (1986) Theme discussion paper (paradigm paper) Coach education: preparation for a profession, in **Coach Education: Preparation for a Profession** (eds Conference '86 Glasgow), E. & F. N. Spon Ltd, Glasgow, pp. 1-25.

Martens, R. Youth sport in the USA, in **Sport for Children and Youths** (eds M. R. Weiss and D. Gould), Human Kinetics Publishers Inc., Champaign, pp. 27-33.

Martens, R., Christina, R.W., Harvey, J.S. and Sharkey, B.J. (1981) **Coaching Young Athletes.** Human Kinetics Publishers Inc., Champaign, Ill.

Nideffer, R.M. (1984) Current concerns in sport psychology, in **Psychological Foundation of Sport** (eds J.M. Silva III and R. S. Weinberg), Human Kinetics Publishers Incs., Champaign, Ill, pp. 35-44.

Orlick, T. (1986) **Coaches Training Manual for Psyching for Sport.** Human Kinetics Publishers Incs., Champaign, Ill.

Pyke, F.S. and Woodman, W.G. (1986) The education of sports coaches and sports administrators in Australia, in **Coach Education: Preparation for a Profession** (eds Conference '86 Glasgow), E. & F.N. Spon Ltd, Glasgow, pp. 29-38.

Wylleman, P. (1985) **Analyse van de psycho-sociale prestatiebepalende beïnvloedingsfaktoren (Analysis of the psycho-social factors that influence performance).** Unpublished dissertation, Vrije Universiteit Brussel, Brussels.

Wylleman, P. (1989a) A pre-Olympic mental preparation preparation and guidance program for the Flemish elite judokas, in **Proceedings of the IVth International Congress on Sport Psychology** (eds R. Vanfraechem-Raway and F. Van Dam), ATM, Braine-le-Chateau, pp. 333-343.

Wylleman, P. (1989b) De rol van de sportpsycholoog binnen een topsportschool (The role of the sport psychologist in a school for top level sport). **Sport,** 2, 40-47.

FAIR PLAY AND THE ORGANIZATION OF SPORT

DAVID P. JOHNS AND GLORIA ELDRIDGE
Sport and Exercise Sciences Research Institute, and Department of Psychology, University of Manitoba, Canada

Abstract
This paper attempts to analyse the responses of young children who completed a short questionnaire which related to the role of adults and the significance of fair play, winning and learning in their involvement in sport. The paper discusses the results of a survey conducted on approximately 590 children between the ages of 8 and 14 years. The results were derived from a broad sample of urban and rural children. A relatively equal distribution of male and female respondents were obtained. Preliminary results indicated that children preferred games which they organize themselves over those dominated by adults. In addition, playing fair was of considerable concern to children. This was discussed in relation to Webb's (1969) study which indicated that as children aged they learned to regard winning as an important aspect of competing. Children in this survey indicated that fair play was still an important feature of their play considerations.

1 Introduction

Modern youth sport, like its forerunner informal play, contains valuable opportunities for young athletes whose lives undoubtedly are affected by their involvement (Berryman, 1982; Berlage, 1982). Both sport forms possess inherent and positive qualities, including the joys of victory, the sense of satisfaction from acquiring a skill, the feeling of being part of a team, and the anticipation and recollection of play (Johns et al., 1990). Nevertheless, sufficient questions have been posed by Coakley (1990) and enough concerns have been reflected in the current research (Orlick, 1984; Chalip, et. al. 1984; Weiss and Gould, 1984) to indicate that while children's sports opportunities have improved, increasing amounts of adult intervention in the form of professionally trained personnel are required so that undesirable side effects do not reduce these opportunities.

The debate of whether adults really contribute to children's play continues (Scanlan, 1982, 1984; Passer, 1982; Smith and Smoll, 1982; Smith, 1984; and Orlick, 1986; Kleiber and Roberts, 1983; Deveraux, 1977, Johns et. al., 1990) while the interest in what is being taught is also of considerable concern to parents and youth sport organizers. Specifically, as children are encouraged through rationalization to play more effectively in competitive settings, there is a concern that they take on the professional values related to what Webb referred to as 'the ideology of the political economy of urban-industrialized society' (1969, p. 163). Webb's original study of the professionalization of children's sport was primarily concerned with the economic components 'endemic in Western urban thinking' (P.161), of skill, equity and victory, which are developed as a consequence of the emphasis which adult leaders place on the practice and playing of sport. Webb suspected that as children aged and continued to play, their priorities about what was important in the game might change. His rationale was more recently examined by Knoppers, Zuideman and Bedker Meyer (1989, p. 71), who questioned the validity of the Webb scale, suggesting that situational ambiguity and a unidirectional scale were less satisfactory in the evaluation of game orientation than their own 'Game Orientation Scale'. A more recent analysis of these two scales has been completed by Greer and Lacy (1989, p. 380-390), who conclude that both scales have equal merit in terms of their validity in measuring game orientation. Assuming that both are comparable, this study adopted the original Webb Scale to examine the orientation of young children who have been exposed to organized sport in schools and in the community.

2   Purpose and Method

The purpose of this paper was to examine the value orientation of children towards participation and to the sport organization in which they played. Differences in preferences by sex and by age were examined and the question of professional attitudes as defined by Webb (1968) were explored. A sample of 589 children between the ages of 8 and 14 were surveyed. A group of 14 year old boys was over represented with 19% of the sample while the other sex and age representation of groups ranged from 11% to 15.8%. A questionnaire was used to determine (1) the preferences of this sample with regard to adult or self organized games, and (2)

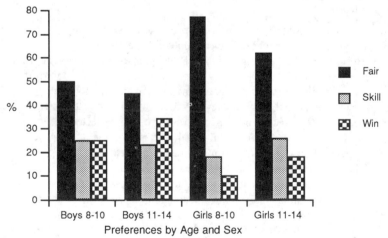

Figure 1

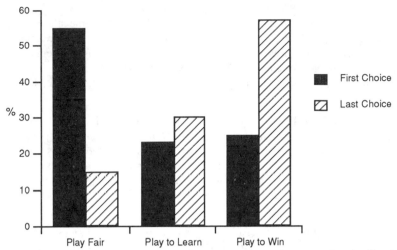

Figure 2

to determine the order in which the children would place the components of equity, skill or victory in the importance of participating in competitive sport.

A copy of the questionnaire was provided for each of the members of a sociology class who, as a part of the course methods section, were given instructions in conducting a survey. Each member of the class was asked to interview five children between the ages of 8 and 14 and to return the questionnaire. The sample was drawn from approximately 150 locations in urban and rural settings, and from a wide range of socio-economic backgrounds. The data were reduced, analysed by Systat and are presented in Figures 1-3.

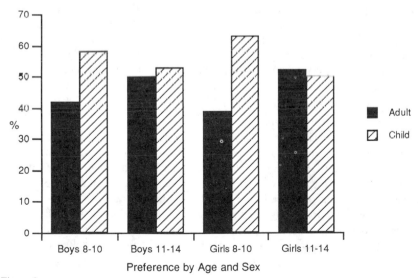

Figure 3

3   Results and Discussion

In a paper of this nature it is impossible to discuss all the findings of the study. Nevertheless, three figures have been selected to convey the broadest interpretation of the data. The first two figures are concerned with the children's assessment of the relative importance of equity, skill and victory in participating in sport. The third figure shows the preferences of the sample in terms of their association with adult-organized sport.

With regard to equity, skill and victory, these findings indicate that most children in the sample viewed fairness as the most important component of playing sports, while winning remains their last choice. This preference is consistent across the sexes and throughout the age range with girls indicating a slightly stronger concern with fairness than boys of similar age. Both Figures 1 and 2 indicate that skill acquisition is slightly more important than victory but does not rival the issue of fairness.

As shown in the third figure, there was no such clear indication of an overall preference for child vs adult-organized games. Older children tended to report no preference for either form of sport, while younger children tended to prefer child-organized games. In spite of the fact that children believe adults to display superior organizational ability, younger children at least prefer the independence of their own leadership when it comes to playing games.

4   Conclusion

While children's sport is increasingly managed by adults, the data in this study indicate that the recipients of this attention are not entirely appreciative of such intervention in what is essentially a child's domain. Instead of continuous interference, children prefer to be given the opportunity to manage and organize their own game forms from time to time. Such an opportunity is seemingly diminishing in a modern urban society where so-called 'discretionary time' is increasingly occupied, from an early age, by the regimentation and conscription of children for the ranks of organized sport.

While many have expressed concern for the lack of value training in sport it appears from the findings in this study that the moral judgement of children, with regard to fair play, has not been impaired by their exposure to organized sport. Unlike the original work by Webb, this study does not indicate a marked shift of values from equity to the desire for victory as children age and supposedly develop effective coping strategies for the ideology of the political economy of urban-industrialized society. However, it is interesting to note that older boys place somewhat more emphasis on the importance of winning relative to other children and that this may reflect greater exposure to or acceptance of competitive values in this group.

5 References

Berlage, G. (1982) Are childrens competitive team sports socializing agents for corporate America. **Arena Review** 6(1).

Berryman, J.W. (1982) The rise of highly organized sports for pre-adolescent boys, in R.A. Magill, M.J. Ash and F.L. Smoll, (eds), **Children in Sport**. Champaign: Human Kinetics Publishers Inc.

Chalip, L., Csikzentmihalyi, M., Kleiber, D. and Reed, L (1984) Variations of Experience in formal and informal sport. **Research Quarterly for Exercise and Sport** 55 (2). 109-116.

Coakley, J. J. (1990) **Sport in Society : Issues and Controversies**. Toronto: Times Mirror/Mosby.

Devereux, E.C. (1977) Backyard versus little league baseball: the impoverishment of childrens games in D. M. Landers (ed), **Social Problems in Athletics**. Chicago: University of Illinois Press.

Gould, D. (1987) Understanding attrition in childrens sport in D. Gould and M.R. Weiss (eds), **Advances in Pediatric Sport Sciences**. Champaign: Human Kinetics Publishers, Inc.

Greer, D.L. and Lacy, M. G. (1989) On the conceptualization and measurement of the attitudes towards play: The Webb scale and GOS. **Sociology of Sport Journal**. 6, 380-390.

Johns, D. P. (1987) Persistent problems related to adult intervention in childrens sport. **C.A.P.H.E.R. Journal**.

Johns, D.P., Lindner, K. and Wolko, K. (1990) Understanding Attrition in Female Competitive Gymnastics: Applying social exchange theory. **Sociology of Sport Journal**, 7 (2) 154-171.

Kleiber, D. and Roberts, G. (1983) The relationship between games and sport-involvement in later childhood: a preliminary investigation. **Research Quarterly**, 54(2) 200-203.

Knoppers, A., Zuideman, M. and Bedker Meyer, B. (1989) Playing to win or playing to play? **Sociology of Sport Journal**. 6, 70-76.

Orlick, T. (1984) Evolution in childrens sport in M. R. Weiss and D. Gould (eds), **Sport for Children and Youths**. Champaign: Human Kinetics Publishers Inc.

Orlick, T. (1986) **Psyching for Sport:Mental training for athletes**. Champaign: Human Kinetics Publishers Inc.

Passer, M. (1982) Psychological stress in youth sports in R. A. Magill, M. J. Ash, and F. L. Smith, (eds), **Children in Sport**. Champaign: Human Kinetics Publishers, Inc.

Scanlan, T. (1982) Social evaluation: a key developmental element in the competition process, in R. A. Magill, M. J. Ash, and F. L. Smoll, (eds), **Children in Sport**. Champaign: Human Kinetics Publishers Inc.

Scanlan, T. (1984) Competitive Stress in Children, in M. R. Weiss, and D. Gould, (eds), **Sport for Children and Youths**. Champaign: Human Kinetics Publishers Inc.

Scanlan, T. (1988) quoted in G. Gilbert Competition: is it what lifes all about? **Sports Illustrated**. May 16, 1988.

Smith, R.E. and Smoll, F. L. (1982) Psychological stress: a conceptual model and some intervention strategies in youth sports in R. A. Magill, M. J. Ash. and F. L. Smoll, (eds), **Children in Sport**. Champaign: Human Kinetics Publishers Inc.

Smith, R. E. (1984) Component analysis of athletic stress in M. R. Weiss, and D. Gould, (eds) **Sport for children and youth**. Champaign: Human Kinetics Publishers Inc.

Webb, H. (1969). Professionalization of attitudes towards play among adolescents. in Gerald Kenyon (ed). **Aspects of Contemporary Sport Sociology**. Chicago: The Athletic Institute.

Weiss, M. R. and Gould D. (1984) (eds) **Sport for children and youth**. Champaign: Human Kinetics Publishers Inc.

SOCIAL EXCHANGE IN THE PROCESS OF WITHDRAWAL FROM ADOLESCENT SPORT.

DAVID P. JOHNS AND KOENRAAD J. LINDNER.
Sport and Exercise Sciences Research Institute, University of Manitoba, Winnipeg, Canada

Abstract

While sport provides many positive contributions to the enrichment of young people in modern urban society, it also forms, upon close examination, a deceptively complex component of the life opportunities of young athletes. In a previous paper (Johns et al., 1990) the process of attrition in sport was examined through the theoretical conception of social exchange. In this paper we further examine the processes of withdrawal by presenting qualitative interview data from a small number of high performance gymnasts who have recently (in the past four years) retired. The interviews revealed that sports do not always generate negative forces and overwhelming degrees of stress for the elite performer. Instead, our research begins to suggest that sport becomes one of many activities in which active membership is difficult to maintain especially during the later stages of adolescence. These findings have particular relevance for those involved in training young adolescent athletes and some recommendations are offered to promote a longer and more productive sports career.

Keywords: Attrition, Withdrawal, Social exchange, Youth sport.

1   Introduction

Opportunities in youth sport, particularly in modern urban society, are considered to be plentiful according to the literature (Gould, 1987, Valeriote & Hansen, 1986). Nevertheless, when females reach adolescence they experience at least two significant social forces which limit their involvement in sport. The first of these is the perceived and often real limitation to participate in other sports as they drop out of the sports they so fervently played as younger children. Although women's sport has increasingly provided opportunities for participation (Coakley, 1990. p. 200), they still do not match those found in male sport. Females find themselves limited in choice with regards to the alternatives should they withdraw from competitive sport. The second significant influence on the lack of involvement of adolescent females in sport is that alternative status cultures (Johns, 1980) begin to emerge and exert considerable attraction on females during this stage of their development. It is during this adolescent period that newly discovered freedoms along with the quest for increasing independence reach a critical stage and sport, for many, becomes a secondary pursuit.

Not only does participating in sport present some difficulties for the adolescent female, it is also a factor affecting the coach. Few studies have addressed the relationship of these sociological pressures to coaching and no specific recommendations have been established to guide the youth leader through these difficult times in the coaching experience. What this paper sets out to do is to first, suggest that female adolescent sport is but one of the settings which consume the lives of youth, and second, to show how youth leaders must be sensitive to these pressures in order to encourage female participants to remain involved in what turns out to be a limited participatory opportunity especially at the highly competitive level of sport. These finding are based on a recent research project which set out to examine attrition in female competitive gymnastics (Johns, Lindner and Wolko, 1990). The use of interviews completed in that study and the examination of quantitative data through a social exchange theory provide evidence that youth participants are challenged with considerable problems as they face increasing obligations from home, peers and school.

2   The Theoretical Perspective

The Social Exchange theory has its roots in both psychological and economic theory and was first developed in 1961 by Homans (1974). In its widest sense, social exchange encompasses the view of the individual 'as a rational calculator of pleasures and pains, forever intent on maximizing returns and minimizing losses' (Coser, 1977, pp. 572). According to Blau (1975, p. 15), Homans viewed social structures as being 'rooted in psychological processes of individual behaviour, notably the rational choices of individuals in seeking to maximize expected rewards or utilities through their behaviour.' Exchange in this paper refers to the intangible or tangible rewards, such as: positive feelings about participation, or observed success in accomplishing skill, which interacting individuals seek to acquire through a relationship based on giving what is perceived as valuable in exchange for what is perceived as reward. To Homans, social activities continued until the social actors considered the rewards of their social efforts to be in decline, at which stage 'individuals will search for alternative activities so as to continually maximize their own social rewards' (Orenstein, 1985, p. 68).

3   Data Source and Procedures

A set of theoretical concepts suggested in Gould's (1987) model were selected, operationalized and included in a research instrument which was administered to 83 artistic gymnasts who had recently withdrawn from the sport. The research instrument was designed to gather information on (1) reasons for dropping out, (2) the experiences of gymnasts prior to leaving gymnastics, (3) what they did to replace the sport, and (4) if injured, questions were posed about the injury and its effect on participating. Most of the questions were answered on a 5-point Likert scale and the data were reduced and analysed with the assistance of the Statview program on a Macintosh computer. In addition to the questionnaire, ten of the gymnasts were also questioned in a structured interview and their responses were collated and transcribed for interpretive use. The return rate from the survey was 92% and provided the researchers with a representative group of gymnasts from different competitive levels. The performance levels of the gymnasts ranged from Provincial Level I (PI), in which the athlete was involved an average of six hours of training each week to National Elite (Nat), in which the gymnasts attended on average twenty two hours of weekly practices. The sample as a whole was on the average 14 years old, had 6.29 seasons experience in gymnastics and had competed at close to Provincial Level 3 before withdrawal.

4   Results

Ten athletes were selected to be interviewed and they represent the upper level gymnasts who had reached national level. This discussion focuses on their responses.

Reasons for dropping out of gymnastics can be divided into the following response categories:

(a) Interest.
'I wasn't interested anymore. I was tired of it.'
'At first I met a lot of new people, I went to Changes (a nightclub for teens under 18). I got a job which took up a lot of time and I spent more time on school work.'
'I didn't like gym that much. I liked other things better. I liked being with my friends more. Gym just wasn't that much fun after a while.'

(b) Injury.
40.8% of the group had sustained an injury during their career which had not prevented them from continuing, nevertheless, the occurrence had in some way affected their progress.
'My ankles were just too sore to continue training.'
'I was injured for the last six months before retiring. There was a chain of injuries one after the other. First, a broken finger, then a fractured wrist, a pulled hamstring, illness and finally the biggy, the dislocated elbow! Also, the coach and I did not get along well.'
'I had back problems and tendonitis in my ankles. It got painful and interfered with my workouts.'

(c) Other Pressures.
'Other reasons,' accounted for 23.7% of the responses given for withdrawal, included coaches' influence either through pressure or ignoring the athlete, attraction by another activity other than sport, mounting pressures in school through increased homework assignments, and demands of school life.
'My coaches pushed too hard and too fast. There was too much pressure on the team. Every other event was fine except I was afraid on the beam. The

coaches weren't very friendly or understanding and they were rather mean. They yelled if you didn't go for the move.'

'I didn't like the coaches, plus I did not like gym anymore. I wasn't getting a whole lot better.'

'It took too much time ... all my time. There was no time for school activities. Also, the coaches pushed too hard. I would just learn a new skill and they would demand another.'

(d)   Time.

Nearly 66% of the gymnasts gave time consumption as a reason for giving up.

'It got to be too much ... too much stress. I had not time for myself. My friends were doing other things and I felt left out.'

'Well, gym took up a lot of my time and I really didn't have time for myself or my friends. I was going into Junior High and I wanted to try all the new activities offered there.'

'Gym took up all my time. These activities (diving and piano) are only about once a week. The practices are not hard with the new activities and they are fun and there is no pressure at all.'

'Gym took up all my time. Without it I can do a variety of activities which are just for fun. No one was making you do the skills and you don't have to work as hard in school activities or sports.'

5   Discussion

Given these preceding comments, one begins to receive a clear message that not all youths retire from sport with a positive feeling about their experience. There is also an increasing realization as the athlete gets older that sport does not exist in a vacuum but is related to other life activities. This 'unfolding' realization has been noted by other sociologists who have studied careers of professional athletes (Hearle, 1975; Allison and Meyer, 1988). What has not been systematically accomplished in their analyses is an evaluation of the process which takes place as youths deliberate over the virtues of giving up the sport of their choice for other activities.

In this study, we set out to examine this process through the sociological perspective of social exchange which holds that the exchange between what the athlete is prepared to invest in the sport and what she receives in return have to be perceived to be in balance. If this is not the case and investments outweigh perceived returns, it is likely that the athlete will decide that the activity is not worthwhile and will consequently withdraw from the sport.

Several authors (Feigley, 1987; Gould, 1987; Massimo, 1984) have hinted at the possibility that loss of interest in the sport may be a natural aspect of social and cognitive development rather than the consequence of some negative qualities of the sport. It is tempting to view the fact that an overwhelming majority of the dropout studies cite 'other things to do' among the reasons provided (e.g. LeBlanc & Salmela, 1987; Narciso, Otto & Mielke, 1984; Gould & Horn, 1984; Pooley, 1981) as being in support of this notion. This paper suggests that perhaps there is a combination of influences taking place in the process of withdrawal. First, the sport experience for older youths becomes less rewarding and more demanding as they progress towards the complexity of international gymnastics making the experience more difficult to rationalize. Second, once the gymnast has suffered a temporary injury, she frequently discovers a new world of possibilities which include friends, time for other activities, and time for herself. It is in this region of personal debate with oneself that the notion of social exchange appears to help the explanation of what happens in the process of withdrawal. Therefore, the suggestion that attrition is a natural consequence of maturation is too simplistic and we are inclined to view the process as more complex.

Most certainly as athletes reach the adolescent stage, conflicting lifestyle alternatives begin to play an increasingly important role in the lives of youths in North American urban society. Most significantly and particularly in such individual sports as aquatics, ice sports and gymnastics, females (and probably males) find the competitive sport preparation to be too time consuming, especially those at the provincial and national levels. We note in our paper:

> Between school, part time work, extra curricular activities and the competing status cultures ... found among teenagers, time becomes precious and its expenditure is carefully considered. Belonging to a status culture that is rooted in the popular culture is an alternative that may well compete with the sport culture of the gymnasium, wherein the requirements of membership are more difficult to maintain (Johns, Lindner and Wolko, 1990 p. 167).

By carefully weighing the investment of time and energy devoted to the sport, the gymnast in her attempt to, at least, keep the payoff in balance must receive some form of reward for her effort. The question finally rests on the way the investment and rewards are perceived. If the gymnast perceives the output and the returns to be equitable then she will continue. On the other hand, if she perceives the output to be in excess of the returns she begins to question the effort. For the younger females entering the sport, the idea of exchanging effort for return was equitable. After several years of this effort the athlete gradually begins to evaluate her contribution and perceives it to be yielding less rewards. Other settings, which have gradually become options (such as, using public transport or going to the shops with friends etc.), can provide equally or more rewarding returns with far less output.

National gymnasts in particular, who were slightly older, found that withdrawal provided more time for their friends. While T. V. viewing did not appear to claim more of the athlete's time, there was an increase in shopping as the gymnasts got older and they were more likely to respond to the features of popular culture which included hanging out with friends and visiting the shopping malls (Johns et al., 1990). The response of more time to be with friends, to participate in hobbies and to go shopping, all point to the re-establishment of a more equitable social exchange for older athletes.

We also observed that the requirements for entry into a status culture required the knowledge of dress codes, speech, and behaviours which are readily acquired through association. On the other hand, membership in a gymnastic club required strict adherence to adult imposed rules. These rules included performance of highly complex movements, maintaining a high degree of specific fitness for the accomplishment of skills, large amounts of time away from the normal groups of peers, and maintenance of habits which promote good health including no smoking, going to bed at an earlier hour than the average teenager and adhering to a nutritional diet. In short, being an athlete required a great deal of self discipline upon which adults make ever increasing demands. Consequently, alternative cultures become more appealing. Some withdrawing gymnasts who had chosen alternate sport cultures expressed the need to divide their time between a sport interest and other cohort activities.

6   Relating the findings to Coaching Responsibilities

These findings have significance for youth coaches, particularly those who coach individual sports where the athlete is passing through the adolescent stage of development. In North American culture, the arrival of this stage of development is accompanied by an array of alternative status and sub-cultures for the growing male and female. They are encouraged through the powerful influences of media and commercialism to become involved. In addition, other interests naturally grow into the lives of youth and pressures to conform to ideal types in school, at home and in the accompanying status cultures all generate role conflict for the young athlete. Sport is not always central in their lives and has a tendency to become less important as other interests rise to prominence. Of course these choices are all based on how individuals view their investment and what they perceive the rewards to be.

If coaches want to reduce attrition, they have to respond to these influences by ensuring that the sport environment is one that can be perceived as equitable. Athletes require the rewards to not only balance the investment of their time and energy, but also to exceed it. Sport has to take place in a setting where satisfaction through accomplishment can be perceived to be accessible. For the retiring gymnasts, it was apparent that the intrinsic values of the sport they once enjoyed had become less significant in their lives and that alternative experiences were providing appropriate rewards.

One of the most notable characteristics of adolescent status culture is the absence of adult leadership. This lack of direct adult influence suggests that youths prefer to make many decisions themselves with regards to membership. Behaviour and other cultural norms are generally ascribed through membership concensus of the status culture. Such a characteristic has a strong message for competitive sport groups where the intervention of adults is profound. The following propositions are offered:

First, the findings suggest that adults should be present in the adolescent sport setting as a resource and facilitator rather than an authoritarian figure. This relationship can be established through the use of several strategies which include group goal setting where the members have a direct input into their own futures in the sport setting.

Second, coaches should be in the business of teaching leadership and independence. Therefore, athletes should be provided with the opportunity to take charge of their own training and to become more self reliant through reduced direct coaching and feedback and through increased self monitoring. Coaches should be attempting to reduce, not increase, the athlete-coach dependency and by so doing encourage young athletes to become more responsible for their own futures.

Third, greater efforts have to be made to make the practice session for all athletes a positive social experience. Rather than have gymnasts who compete against each other in the same gym, it would appear to be beneficial to have the athletes working together and even helping one another for the good of the whole group.

Fourth, better monitoring and understanding of the values of rest should incorporate practices which include a variation in intensity and volume of work to be accomplished. The athletes should be assisted in understanding the need for intense and regenerative cycles in training. Such a comprehension helps athletes to work to long term objectives through short term goals.

These very pragmatic steps are frequently overlooked by coaches whose focus is primarily on technique and the perfection of skills. Often coaches assume that the accomplishment of these factors is possible in isolation from all other factors which affect the lives of youths. The literature strongly indicates that performance is closely related to the entire social-psychological spectrum (LeUnes & Nation, 1989) of outside influences and must be considered before the athlete can fully benefit from the competing and practising experience. This is particularly significant for sports such as gymnastics whose ratio of practice to competition is relatively high. Practising is a large part of the sport and older athletes are sensitive to the exchange of their efforts and the returns. If the exchange question is settled by providing equitable conditions, it will be likely that the attrition rate can be reduced and athletes will be involved for longer and more meaningful sport careers in the sport.

7   References

Allison, M.T. and Meyer, C. (1988) Career problems and retirement among elite athletes: The female tennis professional. **Sociology of Sport Journal**, 5 (3) pp. 212-222.

Blau, P. (1964) **Exchange and Power in Social Life**. New York: Wiley.

Blau, P. (1975) **Approaches to the study of social structure**. New York: The Free Press.

Coakley, J.J. (1990) **Sport in Society : Issues and Controversies**. Toronto: Times Mirror/Mosby.

Coakley, J.J. (1983) Play, games and sport: developmental implications for young people. In J.C. Harris and R. J. Park (eds), **Play, Games and Sports in Cultural Context**. Champaign, Ill: Human Kinetics.

Coser, L. (1977) **Masters of Sociological Thought**. New York: Harcourt Brace Jovanovich, Inc.

Feigley, D. A. (1987) **Preventing psychological burnout**. In J. H. Salmela, B. Petiot and T.B. Hoshizaki (eds), **Psychological nurturing and guidance of gymnastic talent**. Montreal: Sport Psyched Editions.

Gould, D. (1987) Understanding attrition in children's sport. In D. Gould and M. R. Weiss (eds), **Advances in Pediatric Sport Sciences, Volume II**. Champaign, Ill.: Human Kinetics.

Gould, D. and Horn, T. (1984) Participation motivation in young athletes. In J. M. Silva and R. S. Weinberg (eds), **Psychological foundations of sport**. Champaign, Ill.: Human Kinetics.

Gould, D., Feltz, D., Horn, T. and Weiss, M. (1982) Reasons for attrition in competitive youth swimming. **Journal of Sport Psychology**, 5, 155-165.

Hearle, R. (1975) Career patterns and career contingencies of professional baseball players. In J. Loy and D. Ball (eds), **Sport and the social order** (pp. 457-519). Reading MA.: Addison Wesley.

Homans, G. (1974) **Social Behaviour: Its Elementary Forms.** New York: Harcourt Brace Jovanovich.

Johns, D. P., Lindner, K. and Wolko, K. (1990) Understanding Attrition in Female Competitive Gymnastics: Applying social exchange theory. **Sociology of Sport Journal,** 7 (2).154-171.

Johns, D. P. (1980) Status cultures in North American Schooling. In P. Klavora and K. Wipper (eds), **Psychological and sociological factors in sport.** Toronto: University of Toronto.

LeBlanc, M. and Salmela, J. H. (1987) Longitudinal time management patterns of elite persistent and dropout gymnasts. In J. H. Salema, B. Petiot and T. B. Hoshizaki (eds), **Psychological nurturing and guidance of gymnastic talent.** Montreal: Sport Psyche Editions.

LeUnes, A. D. and J. R. Nation. (1989) **Sport Psychology: An introduction.** Chicago: Nelson-Hall.

Massimo, J. (1984) The decision to quit! **International Gymnast.** 26, 77, January.

Murphy, P.J. (1989) Sport and Gender. In Leonard, W. M. (1988) **A sociological perspective of sport.** New York: MacMillan Publishing Company.

Narciso, M., Otto, S. and Mielke, D. (1984) An analysis of reasons for athletic dropout in youth soccer programs. **Soccer Journal,** 29, (39) pp. 33-34,

Orenstein, D. M. (1985) **The Sociological Quest: Principles of Sociology.** New York: West Publishing Company.

Pooley, J. (1981) Drop outs from sport - A case study for boys age group soccer. Paper presented at the meeting of the American Alliance for Health, Physical Education, Recreation and Dance, Boston.

Roberts, G. C., Kleiber, D. A. and Duda, J. L. (1981) An analysis of motivation in children's sport: The role of perceived competence in participation. **Journal of Sport Psychology,** 3, 206-216.

Valeriote, T., and Hansen, L. (1986) Youth sport in Canada. In M. R. Weiss and R. D. Gould (eds), **Sport for children and youth.** Champaign, Ill.: Human Kinetics.

VALUES OF YOUNG ATHLETES GOING TO THE SPECIAL SPORT SCHOOL

M. SUOMALAINEN, R. TELAMA AND K. HERVA
LIKES Research Centre and Dept of Physical Education, University of Jyväskylä, Jyväskylä, Finland

Abstract

As part of a more extensive research project the present paper studied young athletes' values and attitudes connected to their socialization. The questions addressed within the study were: 1. How did the young athletes in high school value certain aspects of life such as education, economy, sport achievement, health, peace and social relations as compared to other students in high school? 2. How did the values change during high school years? and 3. What differences were there between top level athletes and lower level athletes, and between athletes in individual sports and athletes in team sports? The subjects (aged between 17 and 19 years) were athletes studying in special sport high schools (SPE, N=43), athletes attending ordinary high schools (ORD, N=23), and non-athletic high school pupils (NON, N=27). For measuring the values a questionnaire including 13 Likert-type value statements and various background information was administered at the beginning of the high school and three years later at the end of high school. There were no differences between the studied groups in economic, social and basic values nor did these values change during the three senior high school years. At the beginning of the senior high, all groups valued school achievement equally but in the two athlete groups its value decreased over time. The same is true of valuing athletic performance.
Keywords: Athlete, Education, Special Sport School, Values.

1   Introduction

One of the great human problems of top athletics is the fact that the athlete may find it difficult to adapt to normal life after the active career is over. Schooling is becoming increasingly important in preparing for employment and the more inadequate the athlete's schooling the more likely are the adaptation problems.

Hahn (1980) has noted that society may have strong expectations for athletic performance but at the same time it is expected that the athletes cope with normal life, for instance, with school and studying without any special arrangements. This may create strong role conflicts and even psycho-social problems. Special arrangements, which are intended to harmonize sport and school, are becoming increasingly important for the athlete's socialization and personality development.

In socialization, the development of a world view is essential. A world view can be regarded as a hierarchy of a variety of schemata. Its central components are self-perception and values. Values reflect desired goals of action (Rauste-von Wright et al., 1984).

The values of modern top athletics partly coincide with those values that the school represents, e.g. the valuation of performance and achievements. At this time economic values also feature prominently in sport, and adopting them may help adaptation to the market economy. By contrast, certain humanistic values and basic values, such as health and family, may risk a conflict with the athletic values.

One way of solving the compatibility problem between schooling and athletics and thus facilitating an athlete's socialization is special sport schools. Their purpose is to organize a lot of athletic training and create flexible conditions for studying, for instance, by extending the time for study.

2   Purpose and problems

As a part of a more extensive Research Project on the Education of Young Athletes (Suomalainen and Telama, 1988) the present paper studied young athletes' values and attitudes connected to their socialization . The questions addressed within the study were: 1. How did the young athletes in special sport high school value certain aspects of life such as education, economy, sport achievement, health, peace and social relations as compared to the athletes in normal high school and to other students in high school? 2. How did the values change during high school years? and 3. What differences were there between athletes in individual sports and athletes in team sports?

3   Procedures

The subjects (aged between 17 and 19 years) were athletes studying in special sport high schools (SPE, N=43), athletes attending ordinary high schools (ORD, N=23), and non-athletic high school pupils (NON, N=27). For measuring the values a questionnaire including 13 Likert-type value statements and various background information was administered at the beginning of the high school and three years later at the end of high school. In addition to the questionnaire an unstructured thematic interview was carried out with smaller groups of subjects (SPE N=13, ORD N=13, NON N=14) in order to collect qualitative data about feelings and attitudes. The re-test correlations of value statements with the interval of ten days were on average 0.51.

The original scale contained 12 items (Rauste-von Wright et al. 1984). These were grouped as in Table 1. To these sport achievement was added.

Table 1.   *Source: Rauste-von Wright et al. (1984)*

Economic values	High standard of living
	Earning enough for life's necessities
Humane values	World peace
	Opportunity to make friends
	Opportunity to realize oneself
	Approval and respect by others
Basic values	Close and safe family relations
	Close and safe friendship relations
	Long life
	Health
School achievement	

4   Results

There were no differences between the groups (SPE, ORD, NON) in economic, humane or basic values. Nor did these values change significantly during the three senior high school years.

All groups valued school achievement equally. The valuation of school achievement decreased in the SPE and ORD groups (p<0.01; cf. Figure 1).

Also the valuation of sport achievement decreased during senior high in both sport groups, in the SPE group more (p<0.01) than in the ORD group (p<0.05). The SPE group showed consistently higher sport valuation than the ORD group (p<0.05; cf. Figure 2).

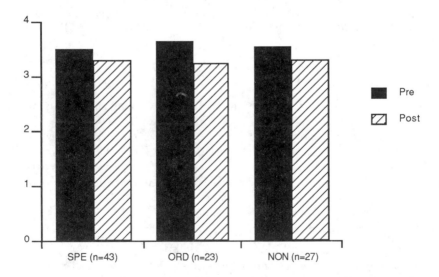

Figure 1.   *Pre- and post-test means of valuing school achievement in three study groups.*

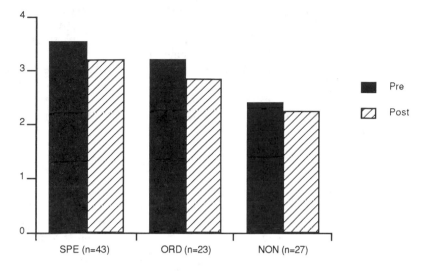

Figure 2. *Pre- and post-test means of valuing sport achievement in three study groups*

Those sport school (SPE) students who had decided to extend their school over the standard three years valued school achievement less and sport achievement more than those who had decided to complete the sport school in three years (p<0.05).

There were no differences in any values between individual and team athletes or between top and lower performance level athletes. For instance, the valuation of sport achievement diminished equally among top and lower performance level athletes.

When subjects were asked in an interview what they considered most important, good human relationships featured prominently in all groups. Athletes naturally regarded sport as very important as well. It was also found out that sport was valued not only in terms of achievement and success but also as a way of life, which would be valued, even if active careers were over. 'If I did not do sport, I don't know what I would be doing.' 'Perhaps I wouldn't know how to live without sport. I enjoy it and it gives meaning to my life.'

5   Discussion

Modern top athletics presupposes very strong commitment to sport and sport becomes a dominant factor in life. For this reason, it might be assumed that the values of a young athlete who has chosen an athletic way of life and decided to attend a special sport school might differ from those of an ordinary school youth. The results do not support this assumption. Young athletes and non-athletes value similar things in life, at least when values are measured by a questionnaire.

The only difference between the groups was in the valuation of sport achievement. The fact that the SPE group (sport school students) valued sport more than ordinary school athletes can, on the one hand, be taken as an indicator of the validity of the instrument and, on the other hand, as a reflection of a serious commitment to the career of a top athlete. It was interesting to note that those who were on a national or international level did not differ from those at a lower performance level in terms of valuing sport achievement. Nor did individual event athletes differ from team athletes. This may reflect the normative character of the questionnaire. All those interested in sport say that they value achievement. The difference is seen only when there is a clear situation involving decision about an athletic career, ie., choosing to attend a special sport school. The result may also reflect a situation of cognitive dissonance: the serious decision is motivated by displaying high valuation of sport and sport achievement.

The valuation of both school achievement and sport achievement diminished in both athletic groups during the three years of senior high school. This may be part of a more general developmental process in youth. The decline of valuation of sport achievement may also be connected with the fact that sport has become a way of life for young people, which means that they have a more comprehensive view of sport than just valuing it by the criterion of sport achievement. This interpretation was supported by the interviews. Those athletes who had to extend their study time beyond the normal three years in the sport school did not display any decrease in sport valuation but they had a very low view of the importance of school achievement. This shows again the link between values and concrete decision-making situations: athletic career is set clearly above schooling.

6   References

Suomalainen, M. and Telama, R. (1988) **Research Project on the Education of Young Athletes: A Survey of the Starting Situation**. Liikunta ja Tiede 25, 242-246. (In Finnish with English summary).

Rauste-von Wright, M., Niemi, P. and Nurmi, J-E. (1984) **Problems in the Empirical Study of Values: A Comparison of Different Methods**. University of Turku, Studies of the Department of Psychology n:o 72. (In Finnish with English summary).

THE DIFFERENCES IN COACHES' AND ATHLETES' PERCEPTION OF LEADER BEHAVIOUR OF FINNISH COACHES[1]

SIMO SALMINEN[2], JARMO LIUKKONEN[3] AND RISTO TELAMA[4]
[2]*University of Helsinki, Department of Social Psychology, Helsinki, Finland*
[3]*LIKES-Research Centre, Jyväskylä, Finland*
[4]*University of Jyväskylä, Department of Physical Education, Jyväskylä, Finland*

Abstract
Leader behaviour of coaches can be seen as an important factor affecting the emotional atmosphere of training sessions. The purpose of this study was to compare athletes' perception of leader behaviour in their coaches to the coaches' perception of their own leader behaviour. As a part of a larger project analysing coaching from an educational point of view, 97 coaches and 399 athletes answered the Leadership Scale for Sports (LSS). The results show, that coaches have a consistently more positive picture about themselves than the athletes do. Coach's gender and athletes' age have little effect on the athletes' perception of leader behaviour in coaches.
Keywords: Leader behaviour, Coaching, Coach evaluation

1 Introduction

Leader behaviour of coaches can be seen as an important factor affecting the emotional atmosphere of training sessions. Chelladurai (Chelladurai, 1980, 1984b) has presented a multidimensional model of leadership in coaching. According to the model, both situational factors and characteristic features of coach and athletes affect the coaches' leader behaviour. If these factors are congruent, athletes should be satisfied and perform well. This presumption has been empirically supported (Chelladurai, 1984a; Horne and Carron, 1985; Weiss and Friedrichs, 1986; Schliesman, 1987; Garland and Barry, 1988; Ho and Gordon, 1989).

For empirical examination of the theory, Chelladurai and Saleh (1980) have constructed The Leadership Scale for Sports (LSS) consisting of 40 items dealing

---

1   This study was supported by the Finnish Ministry of Education

with five dimensions of leader behaviour in coaching: training and instruction, democracy, autocracy, social support and rewarding behaviour. The psychometrical properties of the scale have proven satisfactory (Chelladurai and Saleh 1980; Chelladurai and Carron 1981; Dwyer and Fischer 1988). The LSS has also proven to be suitable for adolescent athletes (Chelladurai and Carron 1981).

Previous studies have shown that there are gender differences concerning athletes' expectations in leader behaviour of coaches. Males expected more autocratic leader behaviour than females (Chelladurai and Saleh, 1978; Terry 1984; Terry and Howe 1984). Males also expected more social support from coaches than females (Chelladurai and Saleh, 1978). Females, in turn, expected to be more active in decision making than males (Chelladurai and Saleh, 1978; Chelladurai and Arnott, 1985; Chelladurai, Haggerty and Baxter, 1989).

The age of the athletes has also been proven to affect their expectations of the coach. Mature athletes want more social support than novice athletes do, and expectations concerning training and instruction decrease by age (Chelladurai and Carron, 1983).

A few studies have compared athletes' preferences in coaching style with the coaches' perception of their own leader behaviour. Coaches proved to be more autocratic than the athletes wanted (Chelladurai, Haggerty and Baxter, 1989; Prapavessis and Gordon, 1989). Horne and Carron (1985) found that according to the coaches' personal evaluation of their leader behaviour, coaches were more informative, democratic, socially supportive and more rewarding, than according to athletes' evaluation of them.

The purpose of this study was to compare athletes' perception of leader behaviour in their coaches to the coaches' perception of their own leader behaviour.

2   Hypotheses

Based on previous studies, the following hypotheses were tested

   (a)   The coaches' perception of their leader behaviour is more democratic, socially supportive and rewarding than the athletes' evaluation of them.

   (b)   The difference is greater with female than with male coaches, because the majority of athletes are male, who prefer autocratic leader behaviour. Due to the fact that leader behaviour of male coaches is generally more autocratic than expectations of their athletes.

   (c)   The athletes' ability to assess leader behaviour of their coach should develop by age, so the differences between coach and athlete perceptions should decrease.

3   Subjects and methods

This study consisted of two different sets of data. The first included 97 coaches, 60 of which were men and 37 women. As a part of a larger project analysing coaching from an educational point of view, coaches answered the LSS self-evaluation version (Chelladurai and Saleh 1980), which was back-translated into Finnish.

Table 1.   *Evaluation of leader behaviour in coaches by coaches and athletes*

Dimensions	Coaches (N=97)		Athletes (N=399)		
	M	SD	M	SD	T-test
Instruction	3.98	0.43	3.82	0.56	p<0.01
Democracy	3.18	0.57	3.17	0.63	n.s.
Autocracy	2.43	0.44	2.87	0.63	p<0.001
Social support	3.55	0.45	3.09	0.64	p<0.001
Rewarding	4.37	0.47	3.95	0.70	p<0.001

Table 2.   *Evaluation of leader behaviour in male coaches by male coaches and athletes*

Dimensions	Coaches (N=60)		Athletes (N=264)		
	M	SD	M	SD	T-test
Instruction	3.96	0.44	3.81	0.54	p<0.05
Democracy	3.07	0.58	3.09	0.62	n.s.
Autocracy	2.44	0.46	3.04	0.57	p<0.001
Social support	3.49	0.44	3.04	0.64	p<0.001
Rewarding	4.30	0.46	3.97	0.69	p<0.001

The second set of data consisted of 399, 9 to 18 year old athletes, 264 of which were boys and 135 girls. These athletes answered the LSS version of coach evaluation, which was also back-translated into Finnish.

4   Results

As suggested in hypothesis one, coaches evaluated themselves more socially supportive and rewarding than athletes did. They also evaluated themselves more informative and less autocratic than athletes did (Table 1).

Female and male coaches considered themselves to be more socially supportive and rewarding than the athletes did. Male coaches also evaluated themselves less autocratic than the athletes did (Table 2), whereas no statistical difference was found between female coaches and their athletes in this area (Table 3).

Table 3   *Evaluation of leader behaviour in female coaches by female coaches and athletes*

Dimensions	Coaches (N=37)		Athletes (N=135)		
	M	SD	M	SD	T-test
Instruction	4.02	0.40	3.84	0.59	p<0.05
Democracy	3.35	0.50	3.34	0.62	n.s.
Autocracy	2.42	0.41	2.53	0.60	n.s.
Social support	3.65	0.46	3.20	0.64	p<0.001
Rewarding	4.49	0.47	3.92	0.71	p<0.001

Table 4   *Age group evaluation differences in leader behaviour of coaches by coaches and athletes*

Age groups	Coaches			Athletes			
	M	SD	N	M	SD	N	T-test
Training and instruction							
9-10	4.06	0.28	22	3.75	0.58	69	p<0.001
11-16	3.91	0.45	57	3.88	0.57	202	n.s.
17-18	4.08	0.43	13	3.63	0.61	31	p<0.01
Democratic behaviour							
9-10	3.21	0.63	22	3.12	0.77	68	n.s.
11-16	3.11	0.54	57	3.16	0.59	202	n.s.
17-18	3.30	0.46	13	2.97	0.63	31	p<0.05
Autocratic behaviour							
9-10	2.48	0.34	22	2.80	0.71	68	p<0.01
11-16	2.45	0.45	57	2.91	0.60	202	p<0.001
17-18	2.28	0.38	13	2.83	0.64	31	p<0.001
Social support behaviour							
9-10	3.61	0.46	22	3.04	0.68	69	p<0.001
11-16	3.50	0.41	57	3.13	0.63	202	p<0.001
17-18	3.62	0.46	13	2.78	0.64	31	p<0.001
Rewarding behaviour							
9-10	4.52	0.43	22	3.80	0.77	69	p<0.001
11-16	4.35	0.44	57	4.03	0.65	202	p<0.001
17-18	4.29	0.52	13	3.47	0.87	31	p<0.001

Results concerning the connection between the athletes' age and differences in the coach and athlete evaluations were not congruent (Table 4). Differences in instruction evaluations were found in youngest and oldest age groups, whereas differences in evaluations of autocratic and democratic behaviour increased by age.

5   Discussion

The first hypothesis, according to which the evaluation of leader behaviour differs between coach and athletes from each other, was supported. The differences corresponded with previous studies (Horne and Carron, 1985; Chelladurai, Haggerty and Baxter, 1989; Prapavessis and Gordon, 1989), where coaches considered themselves to be more instructional, socially supportive and rewarding, but less autocratic than the athletes perceived them to be.

According to the second hypothesis, the differences between coaches' and athletes' perceptions should be greater for female coaches. This hypothesis was not supported. There were three statistically significant areas of differences in females, and in males there were four. The 'extra' difference in males was found in autocratic behaviour, which strengthens the hypothesis that autocracy plays an important role in male coaching behaviour (Chelladurai and Saleh, 1978; Terry, 1984; Terry and Howe, 1984).

According to the third hypothesis, differences in coach evaluation, between coach and athletes, should decrease as the athlete matures. Results partially supported this idea. Differences did decrease in instruction, but increased in autocracy.

The simple interpretation could be the fact that people in general overestimate their own socially desirable features and underestimate undesirable ones. The crucial question is how much overestimation is 'normal' or 'acceptable'. One explanation could be that athlete's perception of coaching behaviour is narrow and restricted. However, if the difference between coach's and athlete's evaluation depends on athlete's perception, then it could be expected that the difference would decrease with age. In any case, more critical analysis of coaches' own coaching behaviour is recommended in coach education.

6   References

Chelladurai, P. (1980) Leadership in sports organizations. **Canadian Journal of Applied Sport Sciences,** 5, 4, 226-231.

Chelladurai, P. (1984a) Discrepancy between preferences and perceptions of leadership behaviour and satisfaction of athletes in varying sports. **Journal of Sport Psychology,** 6, 27-41.

Chelladurai, P. (1984b) Leadership in sports. **Psychological foundations of sport** (eds J.M. Silva and R.S. Weinberg) Human Kinetics Publishers, Champaign, IL, 329-339.

Chelladurai, P. and Arnott, M. (1985) Decision styles in coaching: Preferences of basketball players. **Research Quarterly for Exercise and Sport,** 56, 15-24.

Chelladurai, P. and Carron, A.V. (1981) Applicability to youth sports of the leadership scale for sports. **Perceptual and Motor Skills,** 53, 361-362.

Chelladurai, P. and Carron, A.V. (1983) Athletic maturity and preferred leadership. **Journal of Sport Psychology,** 5, 371-380.

Chelladurai, P., Haggerty, T.R. and Baxter, P.R. (1989) Decision style choices of university basketball coaches and players. **Journal of Sport and Exercise Psychology,** 11, 201-215.

Chelladurai, P. and Saleh, S.D. (1978) Preferred leadership in sports. **Canadian Journal of Applied Sport Sciences,** 3, 85-92.

Chelladurai, P. and Saleh, S.D. (1980) Dimensions of leader behaviour in sports: development of a leadership scale. **Journal of Sport Psychology,** 2, 34-45

Dwyer, J.J.M. and Fischer, D.G. (1988) Psychometric properties of the coach's version of Leadership Scale for Sports. **Perceptual and Motor Skills,** 67, 795-798.

Garland, D.J. and Barry, J.R. (1988) The effects of personality and perceived leader behaviours on performance in collegiate football. **Psychological Record,** 38, 237-247.

Ho, K. and Gordon, S. (1989) Leadership behaviour and the satisfaction of athletes. In **Proceedings of the 7th World Congress in Sport Psychology** (eds C.K. Giam, K.K. Chook and K.C. Teh). Singapore Sports Council, Singapore, 179-181.

Horne, T. and Carron, A.V. (1985) Compatibility in coach-athlete relationships. **Journal of Sport Psychology,** 7, 137-149.

Prapavessis, H. and Gordon, S. (1989) Coach-player relationships in tennis. In **Proceedings of the 7th World Congress in Sport Psychology** (eds C.K. Giam, K.K. Chook and K.C. Teh). Singapore Sports Council, Singapore, 181-183.

Schliesman, E.S. (1987) Relationship between the congruence of preferred and actual leader behavior and subordinate satisfaction with leadership. **Journal of Sport Behavior,** 10, 3, 157-166.

Terry, P.C. (1984) The coaching preferences of elite athletes competing at Universiade '83. **Canadian Journal of Applied Sport Sciences**, 9, 4, 201-208.

Terry, P.C. and Howe, B.L. (1984) Coaching preferences of athletes. **Canadian Journal of Applied Sport Sciences**, 9, 4, 188-193.

Weiss, M.R. and Friedrichs, W.D. (1986) The influence of leader behaviors, coach attributes, and institutional variables on performance and satisfaction of collegiate basketball teams. **Journal of Sport Psychology**, 8, 332-346.

PART FIVE

SPORT AND LEISURE

ACCESS TO SPORT AND LEISURE: THE WINNERS AND THE LOSERS

SUE GLYPTIS
Loughborough University, England

1 Introduction

The world of sport and recreation is a world of contrast. Much of this conference is concerned with contrasts in preparation for sport through different coaching systems, different pedagogical concerns, and different curricula. Much of it is concerned with contrasts in sports performance, and their scientific basis. My concern in this paper is to focus on two other areas of contrast: in participation and provision. In both respects, I believe, we can identify winners and losers - though not by any single or straightforward criterion.

2 Participation.

At first sight, we are all winners in a world of growing leisure. If time, money and mobility are the trappings of leisure, then we are rapidly becoming a leisured society. Over the past 30 years average holiday entitlement has increased substantially: in 1961 only 3 per cent of manual employees were entitled to more than two weeks holiday; now 99 per cent have four weeks or more (**Social Trends**, 1990). Add to this a trend towards earlier retirement, and increased life expectancy, and there is the prospect of a substantial block of largely free time at the end of a working life. Men reaching the age of 60 in 1990 can expect to live another 17 years, and women another 21 years (**Social Trends**, 1990).

The increase in free time has been accompanied by an increase in wealth. Disposable income per head has increased by 40 per cent over the past 15 years. Spending on many leisure-related items has risen dramatically: spending on television and video has increased by 142 per cent; spending on vehicle purchase by 109 per cent. Two-thirds of British households have a car and one in five have two or more cars (**Social Trends**, 1990).

Table 1.   *Sports participation in the UK (Source: General Household Survey)*

| | | % taking part in past month | | |
| | | Outdoor | | Indoor |
		excluding walking	including walking	
Men	1977	23	35	31
	1980	24	37	32
	1986	27	40	35
Women	1977	8	21	13
	1980	9	24	15
	1986	10	24	21

Against that backcloth, all bodes well for the world of participation. This is borne out by basic participation statistics. Successive **General Household Surveys** since 1977 have shown a steady rise in adult participation rates in sport and active recreation, with the sharpest increase occurring in indoor sports participation by women (Table 1). Sport, overall, however, is still a minority activity, and in Britain only 11 activities attract as many as 3 per cent of the population (Table 2). We should not forget, of course, that 3 per cent of the population amounts to 1.7 million people, a lot of activity, and a lot of expenditure of time and money. Nonetheless, compared to many other forms of leisure, sport is a poor relation - sport itself is a relative loser.

Participation is not only low, but socially stratified. The contrasts are lessening, but the basic distinctions remain. In sport for all terms, the winners - those most likely to take part - are male, young, white, car owners, and in white-collar occupations; the losers - those least likely to take part - are women, older people, ethnic minorities, non car owners, and people in blue collar occupations. If we simply take the social class effects the contrasts are clear (Table 3). The same contrasts apply, albeit in softer relief,

Table 2   *The most popular sports: % taking part, 1986*

Walking	23
Snooker	11
Swimming (indoor)	11
Swimming (outdoor)	7
Darts	7
Keep fit/yoga	4
Golf	4
Fishing	3
Football	3
Squash	3
Tennis	3
Cycling	3

Table 3   *Sports participation and social class (Souce: General Household Survey)*

	% taking part in past month, 1987	
	Professional	Unskilled manual
Swimming	21	5
Football	6	3
Golf	10	1
Cycling	12	6
Tennis	4	1
Squash	9	1
Badminton	7	1
Keep fit, yoga	9	3

to many other forms of leisure activity. Why some people take part and others do not is well documented, but not well understood. Clearly a complex mix of personal, social and structural circumstances comes to bear - and the effects that these have on participation will be examined in other papers in this conference by Wolf Brettschneider, Ken Roberts, and Tess Kay. Less prominent in the literature, but no less relevant to participation, are other dimensions which form the basis for this introductory paper, and which have to do with **providers**: they are prescription, perception, and provision.

3   Prescription.

Many of our leisure opportunities are provided by - or influenced by - public sector providers at national and local level. This is particularly true of sports opportunities. Public sector policy in Britain has long been underpinned by the promise (some would say the threat) of leisure opportunities for all - a promise derived from a mixture of motives, sometimes as a genuine contribution to social welfare and the quality of life, sometimes as a means of social control. The welfare motive was evident, for example, in the provision of parks for the urban poor in Victorian times, and in the concerns of the national parks campaigners of the 1930s and 40s to provide open air enjoyment 'for people of every class and kind'. It has underpinned the commitment of the Sports Council to the provision of opportunities for 'Sport for All'. It received its clearest government endorsement in the 1975 White Paper **Sport and Recreation**:

> recreation should be regarded as 'one of the community's everyday needs', and provision for it is 'part of the general fabric of the social services' (Department of the Environment, 1975, para.5)

Against that backcloth - of leisure as a right, of recreation for all - non-participation was interpreted not merely as a fact, but as a problem to be rectified. Non-participants were not merely just that; they were judged to be recreationally deprived. The diagnosis was not wholly benificent; it was prompted also by concerns for social control. As the

White Paper confidently put it, 'By reducing boredom and urban frustration, participation in active recreation contributes to the reduction of hooliganism and delinquency among young people' (ibid., para.13).

Non-participation, then, has been redefined as recreational deprivation, and many policy prescriptions have resulted, some addressed to deprived places, and some to deprived people.

In terms of place, recreational deprivation is generally seen as an inner city problem. In the inner city there is physical decay, poor and overcrowded housing, derelict land and declining industry. There is the maximum concentration of social stresses - of high density living, of lower socio-economic groups, of young people, of people on low incomes and unemployed, of single parent families, of ethnic minorities, and a transient community in which it is difficult to create and sustain social relationships and a sense of identity. Paradoxically, such areas tend to be closest to the greatest concentrations of commercial entertainments, cinemas, pubs, restaurants, discos and the like. However, accessibility is not just a matter of physical proximity, but of financial and social accessibility too. Few inner city residents can afford city centre restaurant and cinema prices, and the range and style of provisions offered are often more attuned to the tastes of tourists and the more affluent and mobile residents of the outer city.

The Sports Council responded to this mainly urban problem with a new category of grant-aid for projects in so-called Areas of Special Need. And the concern for inner city recreation opportunities has extended beyond leisure policy specifically, to urban policy generally. For some years, the Urban Programme, the government's programme for the revitalization of cities, has included funding for recreation provision. In 1986 - 7, 30 per cent (£65.7 million) of Urban Programme expenditure was allocated to 'social projects'. Of this, £19 million was spent on some 7,130 sport, recreation, play and community schemes (DOE,1987,p12).

Recreational deprivation is also seen as a problem of remote rural areas with dispersed and declining populations. Some villages have a range of community resources. But the populations of many villages and hamlets are inadequate to support even the most basic community facilities. Existing facilities, such as village halls and primary schools, fall into disuse and disrepair, and the people who remain have greater distances to travel to use facilities in towns, fewer means of doing so, and sometimes tortuous routes to negotiate.

However, the urban and rural stereotypes are being eroded and are no longer an adequate basis for planning. Approximately 20 per cent of the population resides in rural areas, but this proportion is rising rapidly, as early retirees, commuters and high technology industries are more free-floating, and are no longer tied to towns and cities. This 'counter-urbanization' brings to rural areas incomers who are affluent, mobile, articulate, and accustomed to urban standards of service provision. In terms of standard social indicators they are far from deprived, but they are moving to areas with little or no recreation provision. Another complication is that even residents in the remotest rural areas are not the isolated self-contained communities of the past; they have access to urban aspirations through the media. The urban way of life owes as much to awareness, attitudes and communications as to the simple fact of location.

Recreational deprivation, in any case, is not confined to urban and rural extremes. Other types of areas can be equally deprived. Many suburban council housing estates contain concentrations of social deprivation; many private housing estates are completely lacking in community recreation facilities. And many tourist resorts are surprisingly lacking in recreation provisions geared to the needs of local residents. When next visiting a seaside resort on holiday, and wondering what to do when it rains, spare a thought for the folk who live there all year round!

In the end, of course, if deprivation exists it affects people, not places. This is recognised in policies addressed to the needs of particular target groups, such as those of the Sports Council. In marked contrast to the 1970s, which was very much a decade of bricks and mortar, concerned with building facilities, the 1980s has been an era of people orientation, community orientation, with much greater attention to overcoming the barriers faced by particular target groups. This has been evident, for example, in special sports leadership schemes aimed at unemployed people, in the Action Sport community sports leadership projects, and in the Sports Council's Participation Demonstration Projects, all of which involved investing in leadership, in motivators, in people, working with target groups, and tailoring activities to their needs. Bob Laventure will be referring to one of those demonstration projects, Active Lifestyles, later in this conference.

Many of these projects have considerable success to report. Some have attracted high levels of use, and demonstrated that latent demand for sports participation has existed within the various target groups. Several have been disappointed about their longer term impact. The Leicester STARS scheme of the early 1980s is a case in point. Over a three year experimental period when registered unemployment in Leicester was approximately 20,000 the scheme attracted 6,400 users and over 30,000 attendances (Glyptis et al., 1986). The scheme hit its target - 98 per cent of those attending were unemployed people. Not only that, but the scheme succeeded in tapping latent demand - 40 per cent of users had never previously taken part in the activities they did at STARS, and even among the other 60 per cent, half had long since given up sport.

Once recruited or resurrected, however, involvement was hard to sustain. For a committed minority (about one in ten users) sport became a central interest. For most, however, it was something to taste, and perhaps to dabble in occasionally. Three-quarters of all STARS users attended five times or fewer. This is not necessarily a mark of failure, nor is it greatly at variance with the participation habits of young people generally. The scheme clearly provided an important opportunity for casual 'dropping in'. Most of the unemployed, it seems, are unlikely to become frequent sports players, but the fact that high levels of use were sustained throughout (and beyond) the three year period showed considerable demand for something to do on an occasional basis. But for the providers' judgement in creating opportunities, that demand would have remained unexpressed and unmet.

Providers in the UK, then, have diagnosed non participation as a problem. Prescriptions for tackling recreational deprivation have involved, in effect, positive discrimination - grants and provisions targetted at particular types of places and people, to try to ensure that those who are losing out are given the opportunity to take part. Linked with these prescriptions about who loses out, though, are issues to do with the perception of non participation.

4   Perception.

It is a truism to say that most recreation provision is conceived and supplied by professional providers. Indeed it is a proper exercise of professional judgement and specialist knowledge that providers should identify areas of need and seek to eradicate inequities. To exercise that judgement in isolation from the potential consumers, however, is to run many risks. One is stereotyping: assuming that all rural areas, or all unemployed people, face the same circumstances and constraints, and have the same interests and needs, and that blanket prescriptions will do. Another risk is paternalism - that the provider knows best: the risk of assuming that people must want that which they do not have, the risk of judging what is good and right and sufficient for people.

A third risk is stigmatizing: of offering special provision in such a way that people find it divisive or degrading, or embarrassing or offputting. One unemployed person involved in the STARS scheme felt that the very idea of 'special' provision created a form of stigma in itself:

> I feel that the ... scheme is an insult to a person's identity ... a bit like going on an outing for underprivileged kids, and everyone feeling sorry for you because you've never seen the sea before. Being unemployed is bad enough, without new stigmas being created.

Whether people see their needs as providers see them is only rarely put to the test. Recent studies in a range of rural and outer urban areas provide some illustrative insights (Glyptis 1987a, 1987b, 1987c). All of the studies were commissioned by providers who were concerned about recreational deprivation in these areas.

The five areas can be placed along a rural-urban continuum, with Swaledale the most remote, and Theale the most urbanized (Table 4).

Table 4   *Studies of recreational need*

Area	
Swaledale, North Yorkshire	5 people per km².
Ryedale, North Yorkshire	
Castle Donington, Leicesterhsire	
West Berkshire	
Theale, Berkshire	690 people per km².

Present participation patterns were similar in all five areas, but with some local variations. The most relevant of these for the present purpose is to note that in West Berkshire sports participation was higher than the national average, and in Theale it was higher still.

To examine the extent of recreational deprivation as perceived by the communities, five indicators of constraint were used. We asked people:

(a)   whether they had any difficulties taking part in their current leisure activities;

(b)   whether they had any difficulties using existing recreation facilities;

(c)   what they thought about the range of sport and recreation facilities currently available;

(d)   whether there were additional activities they would like to take part in but could not at present;

(e)   whether there were additional facilities they would like to have available locally.

There were few signs of massive deprivation. Most people had no difficulties doing the activities they currently took part in, and no difficulty using existing facilities. Most regarded existing facility provision as 'good' or 'very good'. Interestingly, complaints about provision were greatest in Theale. So too were aspirations for future participation and provision. Thirty seven per cent of people wanted to take part in additional activities, and 56 per cent wanted more facilities. By contrast, in remote Swaledale, only 28 per cent wanted extra facilities. In this, the most rural area, local residents were realistic enough to know that substantial facility provision was unlikely to be viable and, in any case, many were not keen on the idea of 'depending' on facilities, or having their leisure 'organized'. So, from the consumers' point of view deprivation appears to be less of a problem than from the providers'. There are several reasons for this. One is that residents' priorities are not necessarily geared to formal provision. Many people feel that a rural way of life and pleasant surroundings more than make up for a lack of facilities. Indeed, some specifically wanted to get away from facilities, and being provided for, or targetted:

'It is a most delightful, pleasant and scenic area.............and does not need spoiling by any more leisure opportunities.' (Ryedale)

Another reason for the relative contentment was that people were accustomed to doing things for themselves. Local voluntary initiative plays a strong part in supplying satisfying leisure opportunities:

'Our village hall is used nearly every night of the week, due to a very good village hall committee and support from the village.' (Swaledale)

'Swaledale is rich in activities of all kinds, culture, music making, crafts, etc. We are probably better off than most places in the country.' (Swaledale)

A third reason for the contentment was that some people simply did not wish to take part. The constraints, though, were not evenly shared. Those affected were disproportionately made up of four groups:

(a) **Women** - especially those without transport, particularly young mothers, teenage girls and elderly women.
(b) **Young people** - children and teenagers. For children, the main deficiencies were a lack of small, safe play areas, and a lack of play leaders. Teenagers (and their parent chauffeurs!) had great difficulties in using town-based facilities and in finding things to do during school holidays.

'Unless youngsters have parents who are willing enough (and rich enough) to run their children all around North West Leicestershire there is very little for them to do.' (Castle Donington)

'the village has no kiddies' playground, or any area for older boys to play football etc. At the moment they use the road, and the village bus shelter as a goal. This is totally unsatisfactory.' (Swaledale)

(c) **People without access to cars**.

'Very poor public transport. The nearest bus stop is approximately three and a half miles away.' (Swaledale)

'There is only one bus per week into Newbury, 10am on a Thursday, returning at 12.30pm. There isn't enough time to shop for food, let alone recreational activities.' (West Berkshire)

'Everything seems to take place somewhere else - not easy to get to during the week with two young children and a limited bus service.' (Theale)

(d) **Retired people** - especially non car owners, and those living alone.
(e) **Newcomers**. Generally, increasing length of residence in an area brings increasing familiarity and greater contentment, and to that extent deprivation diminishes with time.

Adjustment is harder, though, in the more 'urban' rural areas, where the majority of newcomers have relocated because of jobs. Interestingly, in most cases the newcomers already had much higher than average participation rates in sport and recreation. But participation is not an indicator of contentment: they wanted to take part still more. So some sectors of the community - especially in the more rural areas, including the original village of Theale - do little and want little. For others, abundantly represented in the new estates of Theale, the more they do, the more they want to do, and the greater their expectations that opportunities will be provided.

5   Provision.

I have indicated already that participation depends in large measure on provision. Discussions of recreational provision tend to focus on large scale purpose-built facilities or purpose-managed leisure resources, but this view is unjustifiably narrow. There is the use of the outdoor environment - for sports serene and not so serene.   And there is leisure provision that extends way beyond what is formally categorized as leisure services. Leisure providers who acknowledge this potential can be classed as winners. The winners are those who identify and effectively meet community needs. The losers are those who do not. Winners and losers can be identified at any scale and sophistication of provision, and in any sector of provision, be it the government, the commercial sector, or a voluntary initiative. The keys to success are consultation, commitment, resourcefulness and good management.

5.1 Consultation

Consultation is important both with the intended users, and with potential partners in provision. The most successful schemes have been developed **with** people, not imposed upon them, and with a commitment to consultation not as a mere formality, but as a way of finding out exactly what people think and need (Pack and Glyptis, 1989). In devising its Sports Motivation Project for unemployed people, for example, Middlesbrough Borough Council compiled a data bank of the interests of over a thousand local unemployed people, and it maintains a high profile by contacting people in shopping centres, Jobcentres, etc.

Leicester Kids Afloat, a voluntary organization which provides canal and river trips for inner city youngsters, has built and fitted out one of its narrowboats for use by disabled people. Before the work started local disabled groups were invited to view the new boat and advise on its internal design and fitting.

At the Walker Street Recreation Facilities in Hull, particular attention was given to the needs of young families and elderly people, so plenty of play equipment and seating were provided. Local residents were consulted about the initial design, and as a result of their comments the children's play area was moved nearer to the housing, and the surrounds to the site were planted with ground cover vegetation only, to deter potential muggers.

The winners recognize that consultation is not just a one-off gesture before a facility opens, and not just a matter of talking to users. Consultation with the users must not stop once the facility is opened. A recent survey in a Hertfordshire District with a considerable range of local leisure provision found that as many as 45 per cent of local residents were unable to name any sport, recreation or community facilities in their area. As well as consulting users, consultation with potential sponsors is crucial to the survival of many schemes, such as Centre AT7 in Coventry, which is run by a voluntary organization, the Coventry and Warwickshire Awards Trust. To help in its negotiations with sponsors the centre has prepared a list of sponsorship options, ranging from £75 to £250,000, including details of how the sponsors' name can be linked with each option.

5.2 Commitment

Many schemes have come about because of the driving force of key individuals. They tend to be people of vision, persuasiveness, energy and commitment. They are often well known and well connected locally - they have the contacts to generate support for their schemes. We cannot plan for such people, but we can seek them out and support them.

5.3 Resourcefulness

We need the vision to see new uses in unexpected places, the vision to turn liabilities into assets. This is happening, for example, at Port 86 in Birmingham, where in the heart of Handsworth, one of the most notoriously deprived and unstable communities in Britain, a disused port has been transformed into a multi-purpose recreation centre. It is happening at the Ackers Trust in Birmingham, where a disused industrial site is gradually being transformed into an outdoor adventure centre in the heart of the inner city. It is happening at the Wheels Adventure Park, located on a former rubbish tip. It is happening at the Liverpool Watersports Centre, which began on a very unprepossessing stretch of the Leeds - Liverpool Canal, and now uses some of the disused docks and dockside buildings as well. Some of the more unusual examples of resourcefulness include abseiling from disused railway bridges and viaducts, and the use of the external wall of a prison as a climbing wall!

5.4 Good management

Good management is not something that should be confined to the larger centres or the purpose-built facilities. We need proactive management and an active sports development policy for even the smallest of facilities. There is a temptation in low cost facilities to cast management into a purely caretaking role - open the building, switch on the lights, let the people come and go, sweep the floor and lock up the building. Management must be much more positive, high profile and proactive - so that managers are not merely caretakers but catalysts. To be otherwise is to diminish the community benefit of the facility. Many of our leisure centres are greatly underused. Kit Campbell Associates (1989), for example, examining the usage of the Small Community Recreation Centres, found that the main hall at the Markfield centre is used to only 32 per cent of capacity, that at Verdun Street, Sheffield, to 28 per cent, and that at Fleckney to a mere 17 per cent.

Management needs to adopt a flexible approach to meeting people's needs. The Ackers Trust, for example, operates a differential pricing system - in effect the Robin Hood principle - so that those who can afford to pay the going commercial rate for skiing pay that rate, and the income is used to employ more staff and to subsidize activities for the local community.

Good management also involves cultivating leadership and self-help. We need not only to take responsibility, but to **give** responsibility and support it. We need to recognize that facilities are not everything. They can help enormously, but they do not guarantee success. Only good management can do that.

We must recognize too that most of our leisure, and much of our quality of life, is beyond the direct influence of leisure providers, for the best used and most neglected leisure centre of all is the home. A recent time budget study showed that 74 per cent of all leisure activities took place at home but even home based leisure opportunities are not without their inequities (Glyptis, McInnes and Patmore, 1987).

In any case, overall leisure prospects are conditioned by broader life circumstances and daily routines - recreational opportunities relate both to the incidence of free time and to the degree of control over its use. Archetypal single persons, who can schedule their time as they please, have very different routines from those of busy mothers who may be continually 'on call' Recreational deprivation relates not only to lack of free time but to lack of freedom.

6   Conclusion

Overall, then, there are winners and losers. With regard to participation, the winners arc those who participate as they please - and those who choose not to participate. The losers are those who want to take part - or who want to take part more than they presently do - but who cannot do so. Among providers, the winners are those whose prescriptions take into account the perceptions and preferences of the community, and whose concept of provision is not confined to buildings and to purpose-designed facilities, but extends to people, to leadership, to the shared use of existing premises, and to the innovative use or adaptation of non-recreational facilities. In sport and leisure management, the real winners are those who work with people rather than for them, and those who have the resourcefulness to translate problems into opportunities.

References

Department of the Environment (1975) **Sport and Recreation.** Cmnd. 6200, HMSO.

Department of the Environment (1987) **The Urban Programme 1986/87: a report on its operation and achievements in England,** D77 NE, HMSO.

Glyptis, S., Kay, T.A, and Donkin, D. (1986) **Sport and the unemployed. Report on the monitoring of Sports Council schemes in Leisester, Derwentside and Hockley Port 1981-1984.** London, Sports Council.

Glyptis, S. (1987a) **Sport and recreation in rural area. A sample study of Ryedale and Swaledale.** Leeds, Yorkshire and Humberside Council for Sport and Recreation.

Glyptis, S (1987b) **Recreation in expanding residential areas. A study of West Berkshire and Theale.** Report to the Sports Council and Newbury District Council.

Glyptis, S (1987c) **Recreation and leisure in Castle Donington and District: statistical data.** Report to Castle Donington Parish Council, Castle Donington Community College and North West Leicestershire District Council.

Glyptis, S., McInnes, H. and Patmore, J.A. (1987). **Leisure and the home.** London, Sports Council and Economic and Social Research Council.

Kit Campbell Associates (1989) **Small Community Recreation Centres (SCRC) Monitoring Study. Background reports: Markfield: Verdun Recreation Centre. Sheffield: Fleckney Village Hall and Sports Centre.** Reports to Sports Council.

Pack, C.M. and Glyptis, S. (1989) **Developing sport and leisure. Good practice in urban regeneration.** London, HMSO.

ADOLESCENTS, LEISURE, SPORT AND LIFESTYLE

W.-D. BRETTSCHNEIDER
University of Paderborn, Germany

1 Introduction: some aspects of adolescent sport

Try to imagine for a moment the situation of an extraterrestrial, who by chance has the opportunity to observe and participate in those leisure time activities in which adolescents of the industrialized countries participate. Here are some of the scenes and images he or she may come across:

Some young people are sitting with their friends or with other members of the family in the living-room watching a sporting event on TV. Some are bored, others more or less interested. The volume has been turned down, as nobody seems to be taking much interest in what the commentator is saying. In the background you can hear the latest top ten chart hits, while the coke and the peanuts on the table are gradually consumed. There are youths - more boys than girls - who go to a sports club twice a week to train for a competition the following weekend, and who are proud to tell their family and friends all about it. He or she will find young people who are critical of these kinds of sporting activities, especially of professional and commercialized competitive sport, and who will point out the environmental dangers of sport. These young people, with their cultivation of the natural, the pure and the authentic might be members of therapy groups or muesli eaters who will fast one day, and jog the next - always trying to reach a higher level of self realization.

Then there are those who enjoy modern leisure pools with exotic music, wild water channels, slides and hot whirl-pools, which offer a mixture of enjoyment, excitement, relaxation and health related activities. Another - older - group of adolescents define themselves by their appearance. Always suntanned and dressed in a trendy outfit, these adolescents will use their body to increase their social prestige. Whether in a squash-court or during outdoor-activities it has to stay painless, the T-shirt indicates 'I'm the coolest'. These adolescents are actors of their own part which is in itself very much part of an elite sports-code.

The inhabitant of another planet will meet youths who are looking for risky, borderline situations. Bungie-jumpers for example, who are not afraid of the highest bridge or gondola, or 'underground surfers' who will spray their 'tag' on the outside of the windows of moving underground trains. He or she will see boys and girls on skateboards skating between the pedestrians in a zig zag course and jumping over dustbins. He or she will see young people racing each other on mountain bikes, surfing on lakes or playing beach volleyball.

But he or she will also meet youths from broken homes, often unemployed, and living on the fringe of society. These youths often train in bodybuilding studios where they try to find their own identity and gain recognition by exhibiting physical strength. The so called hooligans in European soccer stadia are representatives of this particular type of athletic subculture.

I am not sure whether an extraterrestrial would realize that these observations are related to each other in that they all reflect various facets of leisure time activities, which adolescents in many parts of the world refer to as 'sport'. I would even go so far as to say that not only would our extraterrestrial have problems grappling with the various manifestations of youth sport, but even many adults with a professional interest in adolescent sport would find it very difficult to understand the whole scope of sports activities.

This applies to researchers who are concerned with youth and sport; they have problems analysing this phenomenon because their own (adult) understanding of sport differs from the adolescents' understanding of sport. PE teachers too will have difficulties in understanding the various sporting activities of their pupils and students, firstly, because they will see adolescent sport from an adult point of view determined by their own process of socialization, and secondly, because their view will usually be restricted by the school gym and outdated curricula, while the developments outside of school, social changes in the youth culture, will often enough go unnoticed.

2 Guidelines for an analysis: Precise observation, interdisciplinary approaches and cross-national and comparative perspectives

But, as well-founded interventions and pedagogical measures in the field of sport can only be undertaken by someone who really knows and understands adolescent sport, the first step must be a precise analysis of the present juvenile sports culture.

Adolescent sports culture must be seen through a strong lens, and should be analysed from an international and comparative point of view, on the basis of an interdisciplinary approach.

In order to observe and understand adolescent sports culture we need a stronger lens, and sometimes a new camera, so that we can apply new approaches, paradigms and innovative methods. Only if we adopt new methods and perspectives will we be able to investigate adolescents' sports activities, their context-specific configurations of motives and their concepts of sport adequately. Researchers as well as PE teachers should be aware of the fact that they are in danger of producing cover versions of their oldies without realizing that the young generation has moved on to compact discs (cf. Büchner et al. 1990; Ferchhoff/Olk 1990).

It is high time to adjust the discipline-oriented approach to the analysis of youth and sport in favour of an interdisciplinary approach corresponding to the dynamic changes in the field of adolescence and sport. Strangely enough, in sociology, psychology and sport studies, sport and youth are still treated as unrelated phenomena. Nevertheless, I have reason to believe in the thesis that there is a process of mutual adaptation and differentiation underlying the changes presently affecting the sport- and youth culture. Sporting activities, sporting orientations and accessories of sport have become increasingly important elements within the pluralization of youth cultures. And vice versa: the great variety in adolescent sports culture is unmistakably a reflection of trends connected with present changes in the phase of adolescence. All in all, there is every reason to give reference to an interdisciplinary point of view.

My third desideratum would be that we should not stop at national borders when analysing the phenomenon of youth and sport. The economic, technical and cultural network between the industrial nations has, to a certain extent, led to an internationalization of the situation of adolescents. Dominant factors are the expansion of tourism, international information technology, the multinational music- and fashion scene, and especially the sports scene. Nowhere else is the 'world society' so real as in sport, in institutionalized sport, as well as in informal sport. European sports, Eastern movement forms, elements of African and South American dance cultures and outdoor activities from California or the Southern hemisphere can be found everywhere on the globe. Then there are international social and political initiatives such as conservation, or problems arising from the transition from school to working life, or simply the question of how to organize one's leisure time. Consequently, research must take into account cross-national and cross-cultural as well as comparative perspectives, whereby the focus of attention should rest not only on parallel developments, but also on national particularities regarding sport or youth cultures. The latter are met by national research traditions with specific concepts and methodical instruments.

3   Changes in sports culture and adolescence

My initial thesis is:

> *The present adolescent sports culture has many faces. In order to describe adolescent sports culture it is necessary to draw up an ethnography of cultural diversity. Its explanation calls for analysis of the social changes youth culture and sports culture are subject to.*

These changes become most apparent when seen with an eye to history. I shall not begin with Adam and Eve or ancient Greece. Neither will I concentrate my analysis on the entire period of time which has elapsed since the social invention of youth, that is since the time of Rousseau, who is understood to be the inventor of the phase of adolescence. And neither will I attempt to outline the genesis of modern sport, which in Europe is more or less synchronous not only with the period of industrialization, but also with the development of the social phenomenon of youth. It is not surprising that the young generation had a great influence on the development of modern sport. Not only from a biographical perspective, but also from a socio-historical point of view, there is a close link between youth and sport.

The terms are so closely related that they have almost begun to form a kind of social symbiosis.

I would like to concentrate not on the last 200, but merely on the past 30 years, as this will give me the opportunity to compare two generations. An additional advantage is that many of you will be reminded of your own youth and therefore will be able to judge by your own experience and memories to what extent the speaker's observations are valid, or whether he or she is simply talking nonsense. If you should arrive at this rather unfavourable opinion I would ask you to bear in mind, that in spite of all that the Western industrialized nations have in common, there are still national features which have a considerable influence on social developments and specific research traditions. And although I try to see things from an international and comparative point of view, my observations are of course closely attached to a German, or at least Central European context.

3.1 *Changes in sport*

I will begin by describing some of the changes in the sport of adolescents, and then go on to show some of the changes in the phase of life we refer to as adolescence.
My thesis:

Many modern industrialized countries are presently witnessing similar changes in adolescent sport. These changes do not occur in isolation and have to be seen in the context of social changes.

In the last 30 years the number of young people who participate in sport has increased enormously. Sport has a top position among the favourite leisure time activities of adolescents. Both informal and organized sport are on the winning side.

Table 1.   *Sports practised by adolescents in 1954 and 1984 (expressed as percentages). Source: Zinnecker, 1987.*

		Youth 1954 Age 15-24 N=1493	Youth 1984 Age 15-24 N=1472
Total		47	72
Gender	Male	60	75
	Female	35	69
Age	15-17	52	77
	18-20	48	73
	21-24	42	68
Status	Students	66	77
	Fully employed	45	66
Community	Less than 2000 inhabitants	35	68
	More than 2000 inhabitants	55	74

It is safe to say that sport has a strong appeal to all groups of adolescents. Again, you may find it interesting to remember for a moment your own past and present sporting activities.

With regard to the development of sex, age, social strata, economic and social status and their relevance for participating in sport, we are confronted with a rather recent phenomenon. In the course of the last 30 years we have witnessed a process that could be described as a gradual 'social levelling' in sport. Though the level of participation in sport still reflects sex differences, age trends, social strata effects, and the influence of living conditions in general, it can be stated that physical activities and sport have had the effect of a social catalyst among young people (cf. Zinnecker 1987).

Not only the number of active adolescents, but also the frequency with which sport is practised has increased. As impressive is the increase in the amount of time adolescents are willing to invest in informal and in organized sports activities. In this context I would like to mention the increasing amount of leisure time adolescents have at their disposal. In Germany the actual average weekly time adolescents spend practising sport is between 8 and 10 hours.

The change towards a greater availability of leisure time has also had an effect on the sports-market. When we look at the table comparing the young generation in the mid-fifties and the young generation today we recognize not only the enormous expansion but also the differentiation of adolescent sport culture (cf. Zinnecker,

Table 2.   *Sports practised by adolescents in 1954 and 1984 (expressed as percentages). Source: Zinnecker, 1987.*

	Youth 1954			Youth 1984		
	Total	M N=776	F N=717	Total	M N=725	F N=747
Soccer	13	26	0	16	31	3
Handball	3	4	2	4	5	3
Hockey	1	1	0	1	1	1
Basketball	-	-	-	2	2	2
Volleyball	-	-	-	7	7	7
Tennis	-	-	-	7	8	7
Badminton	-	-	-	2	1	2
Squash	-	-	-	5	6	4
Surfing	-	-	-	3	4	2
Jogging	-	-	-	21	20	21
Bodybuilding	-	-	-	5	6	3
Aerobics	-	-	-	3	-	5
Jazz-dance	-	-	-	2	-	4
Judo/Jiu Jitsu	-	-	-	1	2	1
Karate etc.	-	-	-	1	1	1
Swimming	13	13	15	20	16	24
Ski	4	4	3	6	6	7
Gymnastics	7	4	9	3	1	5
Track & Field	5	7	4	3	4	2

1989). Within the last 30 years the number of sports activities youth has participated in has doubled. There is a clear pattern behind the increasing number of sporting activities: On the one hand there are the institutionalized forms of ball-games such as tennis, badminton, volleyball and squash, which are characterized by a tendency to avoid physical contact with opponents. On the other hand there are new individual sports such as bodybuilding, jogging and surfing as well as the Eastern movement forms and the different forms of aerobic dancing. They are characterized by individualistic self-disciplined exercise, respectively by their tendency towards creativity and body maintenance techniques. This increase seems to correspond to three historical trends.

(a)   The direction of the increase may represent a long term tendency in the process of civilization as described by Elias (1987). Following his argument it can be stated that youth tends to favour those sports in which the participant must strictly control his or her behaviour (cf. Zinnecker 1987). Tennis, badminton or volleyball, with no physical contact and a net to separate the opponents, may serve as examples of this tendency.

(b)   These changes in contemporary adolescent sports culture could be seen as a reflection of the present Western experience, that ethnic and cultural pluralization may gradually replace the Eurocentric perspective. Whether it is the South American lambada, the Turkish belly dance, the martial arts and the meditative body techniques from Asia or the US-imported informal outdoor activities with their health-orientated hedonism - all these changes signal that adolescents in European countries are on the threshold of a dialogue between patterns of sport, reflecting the complexity of their society, and the decreasing homogeneity and diminishing hegemony of its system of values (cf. Featherstone 1987).

(c)   The changes mentioned above reflect another recent tendency in our society. It is no coincidence that the direction which the development of adolescent sports culture has taken corresponds to a trend, which in sociology has been termed 'collective individualization'. During the past several decades, people living in highly industrialized countries have experienced the dissolution of secure traditional ties, which were provided by affiliation with a rank or class in society, by the family or neighbourhood or by values such as religion or nationhood. These structural changes have contributed to the establishment of a social norm prescribing individual responsibility for the organization of one's own life. The trend not to stick to one particular sport, but to participate in various kinds of sport which exhibit a high degree of individualism, can be seen as a symbol of the new demands with which the young generation is confronted.

Today, adolescents regard many activities as sport which 10 or 20 years ago would have been considered to be non-athletic activities. In the eyes of the present young generation skateboarding, cycling or trekking are seen as sports. We are presently witnessing a cultural redefinition of sport. My argument is: adolescents no longer accept the institutional meaning of sport, but attach great importance to their subjective understanding of sport.

The sporting element is firmly established in youth culture. This is evident not only in the language used by advertising to appeal to adolescents, but also in the language of adolescents, in which terms relating to sport, body and fitness have become firmly integrated.

Tourism and the communication networks of the mass media, as well as the commercialization of cultural life have contributed to an internationalization of many of these tendencies. In the world of music and fashion as well as in sport we are presently witnessing the formation of a 'brave new world' of leisure culture.

3.2 Adolescence and social change

The changes I have so far pointed out are not limited to sport, and can only be explained by the changes modern differentiated societies are subject to. Focusing my attention on youth in the context of social change I will especially concentrate on those tendencies I believe are internationally relevant.

To begin with, we have to abandon a myth about youth. There is no such thing as 'the youth'. I would like to make it clear that there can be no general and uniform images of youth. On the other hand, the understanding that youth has many faces and shows a tendency towards differentiation should not mislead us to believe in a new myth: the myth of boundless individualization.

My thesis:

The present phase of adolescence shows signs of generalization and of an increasing level of homogeneity. On the other hand there is a trend towards an individualization and pluralization of life styles. Both processes run parallel and complement one another.

In the following I will describe some of the characteristic features of the structural change in the modern phase of adolescence, some of which are internationally relevant (cf. Krüger, 1990). For the purpose of clarification, allow me to draw some comparisons between adolescents of the fifties and adolescents of the eighties.

In the fifties, for the majority of adolescents, to be young was to be gainfully employed. Nowadays, the majority of adolescents are pupils. Adolescents today start to work at a much later date than 30 years ago.

Table 3.   *Educational and economic activities of 16 years olds (Great Britain).*
Source: HMSO (Eds); Social Trends 18 (1988) and 19 (1989)

	1975 %	1987 %
Full-time education	37	45
Youth Training Scheme	-	2
Unemployed	2	11
In employment	61	19

Recent data from our host country comparing the seventies and the eighties show that this is not only a German phenomenon (cf. HMSO 1989). As you can see, there has been a considerable prolongation of the time adolescents are at school and in vocational training. Table 3 shows that the proportion of 16 year olds who were in full time education rose from 37% in 1975 to 45% in 1987. Today about 27% are on the YTS, and 11% of all 16 year olds are unemployed. For our purpose it is not important whether the Youth Training Scheme, which exists not only in England, but in similar forms also in a number of other countries, is an efficient way of preparing adolescents for working life, or whether it is simply a means of camouflaging the problem of adolescent unemployment. In this context it is merely important to realize that education and adolescence have become parallel phases of life.

Families are changing. The families today are smaller than they used to be; in Germany one in three children grow up without a brother or sister, 50% grow up with only a single brother or sister. The General Household Survey 1986 confirms the same trend for Great Britain in the last decades, though the birth rate began to rise again at the beginning of the 1980s. Many former family responsibilities are passed on to the state, commercial socialization agencies or peer-groups. The family is losing the dominant supervisory responsibility for children, while the economic dependency of adolescents on their parents remains unaltered. This development too can presently be witnessed in many countries.

The increasing similarity between the roles of the sexes is a very important trend. Girls are equally represented in education, as well as in many leisure activities of peer-groups. Gender disparities still exist, but they are gradually disappearing. All in all, there is a trend towards a depolarization of male and female identities.

For a majority of adolescents youth is no longer simply a transitional phase between childhood and adolescence, a through station one wishes to leave behind quickly. Youth is an independent phase of life. This is why deferred gratification patterns are no longer accepted. The life of adolescents revolves very much around the present, which is why they want to have fun and enjoy themselves.

The gap between the generations is narrowing. The older generation is losing its monopoly on 'introducing adolescents to life'. The growing importance of technological developments diminishes the adult privilege of being the keepers of the Holy Grail of wisdom. There is mutual influencing between generations not only when dealing with computers, interactive video and other electronic equipment, but also through consumer behaviour in general. In the field of leisure - especially in fashion, music and sport - the enhanced status of health and fitness, and the omnipresence of youth in commercials have had the effect that the power balance between the generations is changing. Adolescents have become trendsetters for adults in many fields of everyday life. Adults who do bodybuilding or jogging, who try to keep up a youthful and sporty appearance at work and in their spare time are sufficient evidence of such a trend.

A comparison between the normal biography of an adolescent in the fifties and an adolescent of today will help to illustrate the present changes in the phase of adolescence.

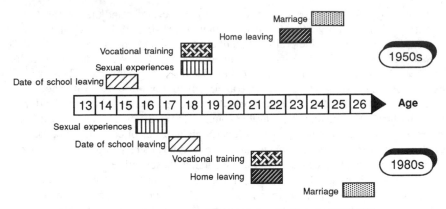

Figure 1   *'Normal' courses of life in the 50s and 80s (Source: Krüger, 1990, 118)*

As you can see, in the fifties the phase of adolescence was considerably shorter than today. You will also have noticed the order of the central experiences in the fifties: Leaving school, sexual experiences, vocational training, date of leaving home, marriage. On the other hand, the youth biography of the 80s shows inconsistencies and tensions: Sexual experiences before leaving school, leaving home in spite of economic dependency. All in all, the sharp differences between youth and early adulthood are disappearing (cf. Büchner et al. 1990; Ferchhoff/Olk 1990).

It is safe to say that in some Western countries the prolongation of education, the increasing leisure opportunities and the later entry into working life have led to a certain degree of homogeneity and standardization of the phase of adolescence. On the other hand, in contradiction to the fifties, this development is also paralleled by processes of destructuralization and individualization of this phase of life. In the course of the last three decades adolescents in many industrial societies have had to face the fact that they can no longer rely on secure traditional ties such as family, neighbourhood, religion or nation. Adolescents of today are, unlike the generation of their parents, called upon to be the producers of their own biography. As this is hardly possible at school, the motor of individualization runs on high revs in leisure time.

On the brighter side, the trend towards individualization results in a pluralization of life styles and a growing spectrum of biographical options for adolescents. On the darker side this trend is also a burden on young people, which leads to insecurities about how to build up an identity and find a specific and individual style of life (cf. Beck 1986).

4   Lifestyle

Lifestyle is the key term of my next analyses. It would seem that the same social processes underlying the changes in the phase of adolescence in the last few decades are also recognizable in sports culture. Apparently sport has become increasingly important in the context of adolescent everyday life beyond age, gender and social class. Therefore we should take a closer look at the connection between adolescent sports culture and style of life.

4.1 *Sport and lifestyle - theoretical reflections*

For two reasons it is dangerous to concentrate on the lifestyle concept. First, any reference to the term lifestyle exposes one to the risk of being accused of jumping on a bandwagon and of perpetuating terms that are as fashionable as they are irritatingly meaningless.

Secondly, there is such a variety of theoretical lifestyle approaches that a discussion on an abstract level would not only be complicated but also very tiresome. As we are living in a time of dynamic lifestyles, I cannot risk letting you fall asleep. Therefore I will not strive to clarify this umbrella concept in a detailed way. Except to say:

It is not my purpose to use the lifestyle concept to explain the effects of social disparities in adolescent sports culture. Although this theoretical perspective on the lifestyle concept is very interesting, it is not relevant to the point I am trying to make. I am more interested in the descriptive and diagnostic function of the lifestyle concept. I will therefore use it to describe new social developments and their continuation as trends, forms and styles of adolescent sports culture.

I understand lifestyle as the short and precise description of the fact that an individual as a member of a society is able to organize his or her life in a specific and therefore distinctive way. It is a kind of link between two requirements: on the one hand it is a means of securing one's individuality, on the other hand, lifestyle is also a means of signalling one's wish to belong to a certain social and cultural group, which wants to be different from other groups.

The main function of lifestyle is the preservation of one's personal and social identity. On the one hand lifestyle allows the development of everyday routines and the stabilization of subjective identity. On the other hand, lifestyles are also ways of presenting one's private sphere to others. These two demands of lifestyles manifest themselves mainly in leisure time. Therefore sports activities, the body concept and the orientation towards fitness and health, the wish to look good and feel great, the longing for youthfulness can all be seen as elements and symbols of lifestyles.

My thesis:

> *Sport plays an important role in modern lifestyles. There are two trends which supplement one another: Firstly, sport and the body have become important factors in the planning and shaping of lives, and secondly, there are also changes in sport regarding lifestyles.*

The significance of sport in lifestyles is evident in everyday life: in the trend to run about in trainers and trendy track suits, and all the other sporting accessories. These symbols express more than simply the desire to participate in sport. Whoever goes to funpools - modern temples of leisure - is looking for more than just water to swim in. In some sports studios the ambience and small talk at the vitamin bar are more important than the actual fitness gymnastics.

These last were examples of how leisure and sports culture present themselves as elements of lifestyle and how they affect lifestyle. But there are also examples of how lifestyle changes sport. For example, the norm 'to look good and feel great' which combines the present ideal of body and beauty, has led to the increasing popularity of outdoor-sports activities with a leaning towards a health-orientated hedonism. This 'renaissance of the body' as part of modern lifestyles is also evident in the trend towards body-maintenance techniques. The various kinds of activities are, although seemingly unrelated, phenomena of the enhanced status of the body. The fact that 'sport' is no longer determined by the interpretation of sports organizations, but more importantly by subjective meanings, is further evidence of the changes of sport in connection with lifestyles.

The impressionistic examples clearly show the connection between lifestyles and sport; they are at the same time proof that lifestyles are determined by concrete, expressive and symbolic activities, as to be found in the field of leisure, sports activities, body and clothing. The concentration on these aspects of lifestyle cannot obscure the fact that a detailed explanation of lifestyle differences must also account for structural changes such as sex, age, class, home as well as fundamental preferences, motivation and orientation patterns.

With this last remark I would now like to turn to the decisive question, and relate this question to adolescents: are there any findings to prove that there is a connection between sport and lifestyle, and what exactly do these findings suggest? Because please remember: there is a difference between the assertion of the effectiveness of individualization tendencies, or the assumption of a class influence on the sporting activities of adolescents on the one hand and the definite empirical findings in proof of such an assumption on the other hand. The success of a theoretical argument can be judged best on the basis of empirical research.

4.2 Sport and lifestyle - empirical findings

Are adolescents who go in for sport any different from adolescents who don't engage in sport or who are totally against sport? Do they have different lifestyles? Is sport involvement an adequate parameter for the differentiation of adolescent lifestyles? Are there any relations between the adolescent sport concept and sport-related elements such as body-awareness and health evaluations on the one hand and other components of lifestyles such as political and social orientations on the other hand? I will give an account of a few recent studies, which are representative for West-Germany.

The first step was to find out whether there was any difference between adolescents involved in sport activities and non-athletes so far as their general views on life, their attitude towards urgent political and social problems are concerned. Apart from the fact that adolescents interested in sport are generally more communicative than those who abstain from sport there are no significant differences between the two groups. The result is not surprising: Sport, with all its facets has become so much of a norm with adolescents that the question of 'adolescent sport involvement' is not an appropriate item for the differentiation of lifestyles (cf. Zinnecker, 1987; 1989).

A further study was carried out to ascertain differences between adolescents who participate in organized sports and who are members of sports-clubs and others who are members of youth associations such as the YMCA, Amnesty International, music bands, charity groups, fire brigades etc.. The results: again there were no significant differences between adolescents who participate in organized sport and the other social groups with respect to those elements which might be regarded as mainstream to their lifestyles (cf. Sack 1986).

Another study, however, is interesting. Body, sport and games as well as other elements of lifestyles are being expressed in a more differentiated way. Four groups of adolescents considered to be typical members of the young generation of this decade were compared with each other as to their dominant lifestyle pattern. (a) Adolescents who sympathize with protest movements; (b) adolescents who regard writing diaries, letters and poems as essential activities, (c) adolescents who like to perform things that are a little out of the ordinary, and (d) adolescents who emphasize body-stylization and strive to improve their bodies through aerobics/jogging/bodybuilding (cf. Fuchs and Fischer 1987).

Distinctive profiles become apparent. The resulting configurations suggest a close link between specific patterns of activity and lifestyles. Furthermore the results would seem to suggest that the common global thesis that the authenticity of experiencing one's body is a common focus during adolescence, is no longer valid. There is a clear connection between the wish to maintain or improve their bodies, signifying dynamism and fitness, and other elements characteristic of a certain 'type' of lifestyle.

In our own study of more than 4000 13-21 year olds structural variables such as gender, age and social stratum and variables of the sport- and body-concept were combined with variables referring to the adolescents' personality, their relationship to their parents, their pastime preferences, their views on health issues and general political and social orientations. It was our purpose to draw up a typology with the help of factor and cluster analyses. Groups should be found which differentiate individuals according to their patterns of attitude, considering the aspect of maximum potential homogeneity within the group and simultaneous maximum potential separation between the groups.

Again distinctive profiles become apparent. The resulting configurations suggest close links between adolescents' general orientation towards life, their attitude towards parents, adults and peers on the one hand, their sport concepts, their body image and their health evaluations on the other hand. We may say that the different types are characterized by a specific deep structure. Though the findings call for a detailed interpretation, let me make just a few comments on the types (cf. Brettschneider and Bräutigam, 1990):

Type 1: As far as the distribution of 'types' among the adolescents is concerned, the figure shows that there is a small group of adolescents, whose appreciation of sport is limited. They are interested in computers, in music or in other leisure time activities. Their (slightly overweight) body does not epitomize the actual body ideal, but they have no problems with their physical appearance. Their social network is intact, relations with friends and parents are equally harmonious. 5% of the population belong to this group, which may be called the 'no sports-group'.

Type 2: We find another small group of adolescents for whom sport activities are instrumentalized and for whom specific sports are the means of image promotion (4%). They are very much interested in body maintenance activities which are considered as means to enhance and display masculine virility. Their concept of life does not indicate clear plans for the future. They approach adults in a very reserved manner. Not parents, but peer groups and 'pals' are the major reference groups of everyday life. We may say that 'action' and 'motion' are the elements that characterize the lifestyle of this group.

Type 3: Almost one fifth of our sample belongs to a group whose lifestyle is influenced by a negative body concept (17%). Their well-being is impaired by delicate health and a general feeling of physical discomfort. There is a strong longing for a slim and athletic figure, which is thought to enhance personal attractiveness. Again there is a complex interaction between the sport concept, body image and self-concept and attitudes toward social and political affairs in the framework of adolescent lifestyles.

Type 4: Our next group (13%) is absorbed in a constant search for individuality and self-expression, always trying to promote the stylization of life, in fashion, leisure, music as well as in sport, the latter based on fun and good atmosphere rather than on training and performance. These adolescents are hoping to maintain or produce a fit and slim body; they are disposed towards a health-orientated hedonism. They do not care much about their future and their relationship to adults and their parents. Style and individualism are of top priority in this group.

Type 5: 61% of the population have a profile, the contours of which reflect the 'normal adolescent biography'. In this surprisingly large group of inconspicuous adolescents we find boys and girls, in whose biography the sport concept as well as the other facets of lifestyle are well-balanced. Achievement and fun, competition and spontaneous activities are not seen as alternatives, but as two sides of the same coin. In such an interpretation sport in all its variety is a commonly accepted element in adolescents' mainstream lifestyles. These adolescents are satisfied with their body image and their physical and facial attractiveness. They do not pay much attention to weight-control and they do not report health problems. They live on good terms with their parents and their peers. They have a positive outlook on life.

This proposed five cluster solution presents a typology which clearly shows the connection between sport and lifestyle. It is worthwhile mentioning in this context that the findings of our quantitative study are confirmed by our qualitative data, which was gained with the help of focused interviews - transcribed on 2500 pages. Nevertheless we should be aware of the limitations of typology studies. A major problem with research focusing on typologies is that they do not say anything about the stability, or the changes of the clusters through the course of adolescence and adulthood. Therefore it is safe to say that the value of our classification has primarily to be seen on a heuristic level.

5   Conclusion

We may summarize:

(a)   Sport is experienced by adolescents not as a homogeneous whole, but in all its various features and aspects. Its characteristics vary in different social groups, sports settings and situations. Sport environments cannot be treated as if they were alike. If we want to gain a deeper insight into adolescents' sports concepts, their involvement and its underlying orientations, we have to analyse the relevant contexts of the everyday life of adolescents.

(b)   Sport is not a sacrosanct place separated from everyday life and not the only context that reflects social values. It is therefore necessary to recognize that the dominant characteristics and values of a society pervade the adolescents' world as a whole. Therefore adolescent sport involvement must be studied in the broader framework of cultural contexts and historical developments.

(c)   Our findings suggest close links between the adolescents' general orientation towards life, their leisure patterns, their social relations, their sport concepts, their body image and their evaluation of health. Sport and body can be identified as suitable elements for composing specific adolescent lifestyles, the profiles of which are influenced by two seemingly opposite trends - by the trend towards homogeneity and standardization as well as by the trend towards individualization and pluralization.

It was not the purpose of this study to point out the consequences of our findings on sport, leisure and lifestyle for pedagogical interventions at school, for Physical Education curricula, for sports activities in clubs and other social contexts. Nevertheless I hope that our findings have contributed to the insight, that a rethinking of adolescent sport and education is inevitable.

6   References

Beck, U. (1986) **Risikogesellschaft**. Suhrkamp, Frankfurt.

Bourdieu, P. (1985) Historische und soziale Voraussetzungen modernen Sports. **Merkur**, 39, 575-590

Brettschneider, W.-D. et al. (eds) (1989) **Bewegungswelt von Kindern und Jugendlichen.** Hofmann, Schorndorf.

Brettschneider, W.-D. and Bräutigam, M. (1990) **Jugend und Sport**.

Buchner, P. et al. (eds) (1990) **Kindheit und Jugend im interkulturellen Vergleich.** Leske & Budrich, Opladen.

Elias, N. (1978) **The Civilising Process. The History of Manners.** Blackwell, Oxford.

Featherstone, M. (1987) Leisure, symbolic power and life course. In **Sport, leisure and social relations** (eds J. Horne et al.), Routledge & Kegan Paul, London/New York, pp. 113-138.

Featherstone, M. (1988) In Pursuit of the Postmodern. **Theory, Culture and Society**, 5, 195-215.

Ferchhoff, W. and Olk, T. (eds) (1990) **Jugend im internationalen Vergleich**. Juventa, Weinheim/Munchen.

Fuchs, W. and Fischer, C. (1987) **Körperstilisierung im Kontext von pragnanten Sinnmustern.** Hagen (Ms).

Fuchs, R. et al. (1988) Patterns of physical acitivity among German adolescents: The Berlin-Bremen-Study. **Preventive Medicine**, 17, 746-763.

Glassner, B. (1989) Fitness and the postmodern self. **Journal of Health and Social Behaviour,** 30, 180-191.

Hendry, L. B. (1988) Social perspectives of sport in Britian: Achieving the right blend? **Sportwissenschaft** 18, 270-283.

HMSO (eds) (1989) **Social Trends 19.** London.

Krüger, H.-H. (1990) Zwischen Verallgemeinerung und Zerfaserung. Zum Wandel der Lebensphase Jugend in der Bundesrepublik Deutschland nach 1945, in **Kindheit und Jugend im interkulturellen Vergleich** (eds P. Buchner et al.), Leske & Budrich, Opladen, pp. 113-124.

McCormack, J. B. and Chaplin, L. (1988) Sport as socialisation: A critique of methodological Premises. **The Social Science Journal** 25, 83-92.

Motilily, K. E. (1989) Meanings of recreation and leisure among adolesents. **Leisure Studies** 8, 11-23.

Mrazek, J. and Schafer, G. (1988) The meaning of 'sport' in the Federal Republic of Germany on the USA. **Rev. for Soc. of Sport,** 23, 109-122.

Roberts, K. (1983) **Youth and Leisure. Leisure and Recreation Studies 3.** George Allen & Unwin, London.

Roberts, K. et al. (1989) Leisure patterns, health status and employment status. **Leisure Studies,** 8, 229-235.

Sack, H.-G. (1986) Zur Bedeutung des Sports in der Jugendkultur, in **Sport und sportverein** (ed G. A. Pilz), Rowohlt, Reinbek, pp. 188-205.

Zinnecker, J. (1987) **Jugendkultur 1940-1985.** Leske & Budrich, Opladen.

Zinnecker, J. (1989) Die Versportung jugendlicher Korper bei Jung und Alt, in **Bewegungswelt von Kindern und Jugendlichen** (eds W.-D. Brettschneider et al.), Hofmann, Schorndorf, pp. 133-159.

LEISURE CONSTRAINTS[1]

GUY A.M. JACKSON AND TESS KAY
Loughborough University of Technology

1   Introduction

It is becoming a commonplace to remark on the recent growth in research into leisure
constraints - a growth which has both broadened the empirical base for the study of this
area, and increased the conceptual and theoretical sophistication of our attempts to
explain it. It is worth noting, however, that this achievement has been primarily a
Canadian and North American phenomenon. In Britain, study of restricting and
precluding factors has occurred mainly within detailed research into the leisure behaviour
of particular population sub-groups, research into women and leisure being the most
substantial example of this. With a few notable exceptions (Rodgers, 1977; Boothby,
Tungatt and Townsend, 1981), leisure studies researchers in Britain have not
concentrated on leisure constraints *per se*. This is the context for the work described
here.

The results presented in this paper form part of the findings of a broader study of
leisure constraints which was conducted in the city of Stoke-on-Trent, England, between
1982-1987. As little general data on leisure constraints was in existence, the first aim of
the research was to identify the range and scale of factors which restricted participation in
desired leisure activities by urban dwellers. The project was concerned, therefore, with
the category of constraints which Jackson (1990) terms 'intervening' constraints - i.e.
those which people are conscious of, which affect their ability to spend their leisure time
as they prefer. Less attention was paid to constraints in the form of underlying social
factors and influences, which have a major effect on the way in which leisure
participation patterns, but one which is unlikely to be identified by individuals.

In the initial stages of data analysis, emphasis was placed on identifying socio-spatial
patterns of constraints, through the use of a specifically constructed multivariate Social

---

[1]   This paper draws on material presented in 'Leisure Despite Constraint', Kay and Jackson, Journal of Leisure Research 23,
4, 301-313. 1991.

Area Analysis of Stoke-on-Trent. The emphasis placed on this aspect of the study's findings partly reflected providers' interests in charting the occurrence of constraints to leisure participation - a congruence of academic and practitioner interests that has also been noted by other writers on constraints research (e.g Goodale and Witt, in Jackson and Burton (eds), 1989). Subsequently, attention was given to examining how different constraints operate, the extent to which they affect individuals' leisure participation, and the circumstances under which they might be overcome. It is on this more recent work that this paper reports.

2   Method

An interviewer-administered questionnaire survey was implemented in areas of the city of Stoke-on-Trent selected to represent a wide range of neighbourhoods, social groups and housing types. The interview schedule, which contained more than 200 variables, included prompted and unprompted questions to identify the range of constraints experienced by respondents and the extent to which they affected leisure participation. Information was also obtained about respondents' current and past leisure participation. Sub-samples were filtered to more detailed questioning concerning the operation of the constraints which they said *most* affected their leisure participation; in addition, all respondents were asked about recent (previous weekend) occasions on which constraints might have occurred. Additional questions concerning leisure participation during the three years prior to the interview were included to identify influences on taking up and ceasing activities during this period. Finally, a comprehensive range of personal information was obtained, comprising conventional details of respondents' characteristics and, additionally, further information on household composition, family members, car ownership, and educational history.

The information obtained from interviewees was supplemented by the Social Area Analysis of Stoke on Trent referred to above. Detailed discussion of the rationale and procedures used in the development of this approach is given in Jackson and Oulds, 1985, in which the limitations of the method are also reviewed. In summary, the approach provides a multivariate summary of a range of social indicators through statistical amalgamation. This has the advantage of recognizing the concurrent existence of several social factors which may be influential on leisure behaviour. By using Factor Analysis, several forms of social and demographic characteristics are combined into a smaller, but representative, number of composite variables. This process identifies sub-samples which are socially different from each other but have high internal uniformity. Based on area-specific census information, the resulting data could also be mapped to show the spatial distribution of the distinctive social categories which had been identified. In this study, the Social Area Analysis categorization for each interview location was included in the survey variable list, and was used in the analysis of social variations of patterns of leisure participation and leisure constraint.

3   Results

3.1   *The extent of constraints to leisure participation*

A total of 366 completed questionnaires were obtained. Most respondents (59%) were female, while the age-profile showed some over-representation of the 25-34 age-group and a corresponding under-representation of the pre-retirement (45-64) group. The sample was generally more evenly distributed across the social class categories than the city's population, reflecting deliberate sampling strategy.

The survey sought to establish what, if anything, respondents felt constrained their leisure, and whether certain constraints were considered to be more severe in their effects than others.

Although one in every four respondents (26%) did not feel his or her leisure was constrained, by far the majority (72%) did feel that there were factors which prevented them from taking part in recreational activities as they wished. More than 80 different constraining influences were identified by unprompted questioning, which were amalgamated into 30 broader categories. 'Shortage of money'/'expense of participating' was by far the most frequently mentioned, affecting 116 people - more than half of those who felt constrained (55%), and more than a third of the sample as a whole (39%) (Table 1). Shortage of time was mentioned by 24% of the sample, while 13% said they felt restricted by family-related factors, 7% by the demands of work, and 6% by health considerations. Overall, the constraints which respondents considered to be major influences were overwhelmingly related to personal circumstances. Supply-related constraints were barely mentioned. Prompted questioning by means of a constraints checklist produced higher responses than the unprompted questions, but the results were similar in content and were once more dominated by matters of personal circumstance (Table 1).

Table 1   *Constraints categories affecting leisure participation unprompted*
and prompted responses (n=366; respondents could give more
than one answer)

Constraint	% of respondents	
	unprompted	prompted
money	39	56
time	24	45
family	13	27
work	7	33
health	6	13

Table 2   *The constraints most affecting respondents' leisure*

Constraint	respondents affected %
money	53
time	36
family	13
work	13
transport problems	12
health-related	7
lack of leisure facilities	7
household chores	6

When the relative importance of different constraining influences was taken into consideration, this pattern became even more marked. Asked to identify the constraints which they felt *most* affected their leisure (Table 2), respondents gave two main answers - 'money' (53%) and 'time' (36%) - and in all, 15 of the 18 types of response given were related to personal circumstance.

Comparison of constraints which were widely experienced by the sample, and those which were considered to be most influential, showed that there were differences between the two categories: although some constraints (such as 'money' and 'time') fell into both categories, others which affected large numbers of people had relatively little impact on them, while a third group were experienced by only a few, but were highly influential in determining the level of recreation possible for these people.

There were variations within the sample, with different types of people being affected most by different constraints. Although there was, for example, little difference in the overall proportions of men (74%) and women (72%) who thought their leisure was constrained, there was considerable variation in some of the constraints affecting them (Table 3). More women than men considered themselves constrained by the demands of their family, by feeling 'too tired', and by doing household chores - constraints which may be associated with traditional wife/mother roles. However, women also made more mention of external factors than men, a quarter (26%) mentioning transport difficulties, 20% saying that desired activities were unavailable, and 15% citing a shortage of facilities. This variation between the sexes was not, however, apparent in respect of money constraint, which affected 58% of women and a similar proportion (54%) of men.

Some of the largest variations within the sample were those between age-groups. The overall picture was complex (Table 4). Amongst younger people, more frequent mention was made of the constraints of money, transport problems and poor availability of

Table 3   *The constraints most affecting leisure participation, for males and females*

Males	%	Females	%
money	54	money	52
time	42	time	32
work	18	family	17
health	9	transport problems	14
transport problems	9	household chores	
family	7	work	6
household chores	4	health	4

activities than by older respondents, suggesting that the young were primarily constrained by practical barriers to participation. In contrast, the constraints which most often affected both the 25-34 year olds and, more acutely, the 35-44 age-group, related to the competing claims of other aspects of their lives: these included family and/or household factors, work, and a general shortage of time - which was uniquely ranked in first place by the 35-44 group. Such factors declined in importance for those aged 45-64, who were less affected by most of the listed constraints than the younger age-groups; however, age itself, and its physiolgical limitations, had begun to counteract their relative freedom.

Constraints were also found to vary between the social groups categorized by the Social Area Analysis. This had identified five socially distinctive classifications of sub-populations within the study area (Table 5), all of which were represented in the sample (Table 6). The questionnaire data was subsequently analysed to identify the extent, range and differential importance of constraints to leisure operating in each of the five main sub-samples. It was found that distinctive patterns of constraint were operating in each of the five social area categories.

Table 4   *The constraints most affecting age-groups*

	16-24 %	25-34 %	35-44 %	45-64 %	65+ %	all %
money	66	58	51	43	38	53
time	44	49	40	32	6	36
family	12	22	27	4	4	13
work	16	15	8	11	-	13
transport	13	6	8	12	22	12
health	-	1	-	6	16	7

Table 5   *The Social Area Analysis Categorization*

Category	Main characteristics of each category
Category 1	Local Authority Housing Areas. Areas of the inner city dominated by Local Authority housing. Mostly distinctive by their tenurial characteristics but also generally exhibiting low social status and other indicators of relative deprivation.
Category 2	Inner City Residual Areas Areas in the city dominated by older owner-occupied, often terraced, housing in the urban core; stable and old population profile, medium to low social status.
Category 3	Inner City Transitional Areas Areas of the inner city dominated by rooming house/bedsit/ sub-divided, often rented, accommodation; high proportions of young people and non-indigenous groups.
Category 4	Middle Class - Young Age Structure Suburban areas of the city, usually outside the urban core, dominated by groups of middle social status, often exhibiting a younger age profile than the city as a whole.
Category 5	High Status - Mature Age Structure Prestigious areas of the city dominated by groups of high social status and professional occupations. Low living densities, high car ownership, and a mature age structure.

In each type of area, the majority of respondents considered themselves to be constrained in their leisure. Leisure constraint was most widely reported by those from the 'transitional' inner city areas (Category 3; 80%), the council housing areas (Category 1; 77%), and the young middle class areas (Category 4; 76%). Less constraint was reported by those in the 'residual' inner city areas (Category 2; 67%) and the high status areas (Category 5; 63%). Even in the least constrained areas, however, almost two-thirds of the sample felt their leisure was restricted.

There were differences between the Social Area sub-groups concerning which of the constraints listed in the checklist most affected them (Table 7). Although the types of constraint affecting each social category varied considerably, differences in the overall level of constraint identified were, however, surprisingly small for sub-groups which differed so greatly in their demographic and socio-economic characteristics. The high level of constraint amongst the more affluent Category 5 is particularly noteworthy, for recreational disadvantage and barriers to participation are traditionally associated with

Table 6   *Representation of Social Area categories in sample*

Area classification		n	%
Category 1	Council housing	116	32
Category 2	Residual inner city	72	20
Category 3	Transitional inner city	50	14
Category 4	Young middle class	54	14
Category 5	Mature high status	71	10
	Unclassified	3	1

Table 7   *The constraints most affecting leisure in the social area categories*

Constraint	Category 1 %	Category 2 %	Category 3 %	Category 4 %	Category 5 %	All %
money	61	56	62	53	37	53
time	20	32	34	48	40	36
family	12	14	16	10	17	13
transport	13	14	22	9	6	12
work	4	7	10	18	10	11
health	11	7	2	4	4	6

areas of obvious deprivation. The data suggests that this is an exaggerated view, and that a baseline of constraint is universal. The variations which existed between categories stemmed from the types of constraint prevalent within them, and the relative importance of different constraints, rather than the extent of constraint.

These results show that although leisure constraint was widely experienced, there were considerable variations in the extent to which different types of people were constrained, and in the factors which most affected them. There were indications, too, that there might be variations in the way constraints operated. Five types of constraints had been pre-selected at the research design stage for detailed questioning in the latter part of the constraints questionnaire. Their selection had been based upon the evidence of previous research, and was subsequently confirmed by the survey's own preliminary findings, which indicated that four of the five (financial factors, time factors, commitments and transport problems) were widely and/or acutely experienced by the sample. The fifth (deficiencies of provision) proved to be of less significance to respondents, but was retained on the basis of its importance to providers. For the purposes of this paper, discussion is confined to the example of financial constraints.

3.2 The operation of constraints: financial constraints to leisure participation

The constraint of money was widely mentioned by the sample, especially by the younger age-groups and those of lower socio-economic status. In addition, four of the five social area categories ranked money as their most acute constraint, with only Category 5 relegating it to second place (cf. Table 5). More detailed questioning about the operation of financial constraints addressed the importance which interviewees attached to their leisure expenditure, their approximate weekly expenditure on activities, the way in which they coped with financial constraints on their leisure participation, and the practical effect which financial constraints had on their leisure participation.

Leisure spending. Respondents attached high priority to their leisure expenditure: most classed it as 'a very important (but not essential)' element of their total spending. More men than women attributed high importance to leisure expenditure, a quarter considering leisure to be their 'most important' form of expenditure compared to an eighth of women. The greater priority which men attached to leisure spending was illustrated by the amounts they spent, women apparently being more restricted in their leisure spending than men.

Among the Social Area sub-groups, the lowest level of expenditure was found, not surprisingly, among Category 1 respondents. The highest expenditure was amongst those from Category 3 - not, as might be anticipated, from the residents of the most affluent area, but amongst the relatively young inhabitants of the transitional zones. Categories 4 and 5, for whom financial limits were less acute, did however attach high importance to leisure spending, with 1/3 of those in Category 4 and 1/4 in Category 5 regarding it as their most important form of expenditure. This contrasted particularly strongly with Category 1, where only 1 in 50 said this. Leisure spending thus appeared to have lower priority in the less affluent areas, where general low income might be expected to make the essentials of life the dominant financial concern, and leisure relatively unimportant. The lower priority given to leisure expenditure by those in Categories 1 and 2 may also partly reflect these people's low level of activity, possibly accompanied by low aspirations for leisure; it is also possible, however, that this low priority reflected the characteristics of the leisure activities in which they are most likely to engage, which had few costs directly related to consumption (e.g. watching television, and other forms of home-based leisure). Members of the lower status groups were more likely than other respondents to adopt home-based leisure pursuits and purposeful, money-saving activities, although they also engaged in drinking and socializing.

Although respondents in Categories 4 and 5 appeared to give high priority to leisure spending, they did not appear to spend a much higher proportion of their income on leisure than respondents from other categories. The importance which Category 4 and Category 5 respondents attached to their leisure expenditure may be viewed in the context of their relative financial security. This may give leisure expenditure a greater apparent importance simply because more fundamental expenses are taken for granted, and met 'automatically', while leisure activities may be open to more deliberation, and expenditure on them made in a more conscious way.

The activities affected by financial constraints. Although there were variations in the extent to which cost influenced leisure participation for different types of people, there were some similarities in the types of activities which were affected. In Social Area categories 2, 3 and 4, cost most affected going out for drinks or meals, and going out to the theatre, cinema, or for general entertainment. Eating out and going to the theatre were also mentioned by Category 5 respondents. A number of activities did not appear to be affected by cost, including discos, bingo, going on trips, doing hobbies, and going shopping. Participation in sport did not appear to be affected by financial constraints.

The most distinctive difference between the Social Area categories in terms of the types of activities affected, was the low response by Category 1 respondents - for although they spent least on leisure and thus appeared most constrained by the cost of activities, they were least likely to mention specific activities which were constrained. Cost appeared to act as a general restriction, rather than one which frustrated specific leisure aspirations. It cannot be assumed from this data, however, that financial constraints were the most significant cause of low participation for this group, which was also likely to be influenced by factors such as 'leisure illiteracy' - i.e. lack of awareness and experience of forms of participation.

The impact of financial constraints. The interviewees who cited financial constraints as one of the two main restrictions on their leisure were questioned about the way in which they dealt with this problem.

The majority of this sub-sample said that financial constraints made them reduce their leisure participation below their preferred levels. More than half (57%) participated less frequently than they wanted to in some of their leisure activities, and another 11% did not participate in certain activities at all. More women (34%) than men (29%) were likely to reduce their participation because of financial constraints, and younger participants more than older: more than two-fifths of the 16-24 year olds did so, compared to a third of the 25-44 year olds, and a quarter of those over the age of 45. There were also variations between the Social Area categories, with higher proportions reducing their participation in Categories 1, 2 and 3 than in Category 4 and Category 5 (Table 8).

Almost one quarter of those questioned found ways of surmounting financial constraints. The most popular methods were to save up to participate (11%), or to find cheap ways of taking part (8%). Another 4% economized on other areas of expenditure to allow them to continue their leisure activities, and a further 10% mentioned a variety of other ways of dealing with this problem which did not involve reducing their level of participation. In total, about one-third of those affected by financial constraints were able to overcome them at least partially in these ways. As the majority took part in the activities which they wished to do, but less frequently than they would have liked, financial constraints appear to be an absolute barrier for only a small minority of those affected by them.

A number of activities did not appear to be affected by financial constraints. These were mainly informal activities, many of them home-based. They included watching television, visiting friends or entertaining friends at home, reading, gardening, taking

Table 8   *Social Area variations in methods of dealing with financial constraints (table shows number of interviewees)*

Response	Category 1	Category 2	Category 3	Category 4	Category 5	All
reduce participation	26	32	18	33	9	117
save up	7	-	4	10	2	23
not participate at all	7	4	5	4	2	22
find cheapest	2	1	2	9	16	
cut down	-	2	1	6	-	9

part in educational activities, taking exercise, and just 'staying in'. Financial constraints most affected going out for drinks (14%) or meals (14%), and going out for entertainment (11%). Other activities mentioned were sightseeing (5%), taking part in sport (4%), going to discothèques/nightclubs (3%), and taking part in hobbies (3%).

Financial constraints were experienced by people in very different financial circumstances, and varied in their overall effect on individuals' leisure. This diversity needs to be taken into account when conclusions are drawn about the nature and effect of leisure constraints.

4   Discussion

This study differs somewhat from previous work in Britain, in suggesting that the extent to which constraints are experienced across the population as a whole is probably greater than formerly believed. Earlier studies provided detailed information about specific sub-groups, but did not indicate how different sub-groups compare; in addition, such work usually concentrated on groups known to be recreationally deprived, in which a high level of constraint can be expected. The remainder of the population has therefore been relatively under-researched. It now seems possible that while high levels of constraint are experienced by deprived groups, constraints also affect the participation of those in other sectors of the community, and are not confined to demonstrably low-participant groups. Furthermore, constraints appear to be widely and acutely experienced across all groups, regardless of their demographic and socio-economic characteristics; they affect many individuals not considered among the 'problem' sub-groups by public sector leisure providers.

In many cases in this study, high levels of constraint were perceived by the sub-groups which also had high levels of participation in out-of-home activities. This apparent contradiction was further substantiated when comparable inconsistencies were found at a more detailed level in the operation of individual constraints. In several cases those who demonstrated the highest propensity to undertake a course of action felt most constrained in doing so. Examples of this type were found in relation to transport constraint, which was experienced most acutely by the young, Category 3 respondents, who travelled most, and concerning time constraint, most-commented on by those in Category 4 and Category 5, who had the highest levels and most varied patterns of participation in leisure activities.

Findings of this sort repeatedly raise the question of how individuals come to perceive their leisure to be constrained. Shortages of money and time were identified as constraints by people whose financial situations and time commitments were so obviously very different that this inevitably raises questions about how people with such diverse lifestyles can believe themselves to be constrained by the same factors. It appears implicit in the policies of public-sector leisure providers that low-participation groups are most constrained in their leisure, yet the relationship between levels of participation and perceived levels of constraint is not necessarily negative.

The findings relating to financial and time constraints in this study suggest that a constraint to leisure participation may be perceived when participation is not greatly affected. The majority of those affected by financial constraint participated less than they wished, but only a small minority did not participate at all. In most cases, therefore, individuals experienced constraint *while continuing to participate in the activities to which they said the constraint applied*. In more extreme cases, constraints were reported by a number of interviewees who did not reduce their participation at all, despite identifying the constraint as a major influence on their leisure. Through exerting effort to overcome the constraint, these individuals appeared to feel they had been affected by it, despite their success in maintaining their desired level of participation. As a result, constraints are likely to be reported by participants in an activity, as well as by non-participants; constraints may even be reported more frequently by participants than by non-participants. Any act of participation potentially exposes individuals to constraints which reflect the characteristics of the activity. It is therefore to be expected that high levels of constraint may be reported by those who participate.

The extent of perceived constraint may also reflect individuals' aspirations for participation, and these relate to their current levels of participation. Thus, those who are engaged in a high level of activity, are also more likely to be 'recreation literate', to be aware of further activities in which they could engage, and thus to have frustrated desires in this respect. At the other extreme, as e.g. Jackson and Searle (1983) have indicated, the low levels of participation of some individuals are the product of lack of awareness of participation possibilities, and this very lack of awareness makes them less likely to formulate leisure aspirations. If such aspirations do not exist, they cannot be consciously frustrated, and thus constraints will not be perceived. Perceived recreation constraint would thus appear to be substantially the result of frustrated aspirations: people's *feeling* of being constrained does not stem from not doing certain activities, but from not doing *activities which they want to do*. For this reason, too, those who participate most may report high levels of constraint.

A diverse range of factors contribute to the development of leisure patterns and restrict participation. Constraints form only a part of these: the range also includes a complex web of perceptual and attitudinal influences, and family, household and other lifestyle factors. It has become evident that these various factors and influences affect individuals multiply, and interact with each other - and that as most individuals are constrained by several different factors, there is no certainty that the removal of a specific form of constraint will be significant enough to prompt participation to occur.

It seems important in the formulation of policy and practice to recognize the enormity, and complexity, of the task of removing constraints, and the paucity of the tools available with which this can be attempted. Once again, as implied above, it would appear theoretically most effective to increase participation levels by making apparently harsh decisions to reduce the emphasis given to providing for groups whose overall situation is so unfavourable that they are unlikely to respond to such strategies. This is obviously undesirable from a social welfare point of view. The alternative is to link leisure policy initiatives to those in other areas of social policy which can contribute to significant improvement in the lifestyles of these people.

5   References

Boothby, J., M.F. Tungatt, and A.R. Townsend (1981) Ceasing participation in sports activity: Reported reasons and their implications **Journal of Leisure Research** 12, pp. 20-33

Crawford, D.W. and G. Godbey (1987) Reconceptualising barriers to family leisure **Leisure Sciences** 9, 119-128

Goodale, T.L. and P.A.Witt Recreation non-participation and barriers to leisure in **Understanding Leisure: Mapping the Past, Charting the Future** E.L. Jackson and T.L. Burton (eds), 1989, pp. 421-449

Henderson, K.A., D. Stalnaker, and G. Taylor (1987) Personality traits and leisure barriers among women. Paper presented to the Fifth Canadian Congress on Leisure Research, Dalhousie University, Nova Scotia, May 1987

Jackson, E. L. (1990) Variations in the desire to begin a leisure activity: evidence of antecedent constraints? **Journal of Leisure Research**, 22.

Jackson, G.A.M. (1991) Recreation Constraint in an Urban Context Unpublished Ph.D. thesis, Staffordshire Polytechnic.

Jackson, G.A.M. and G. Oulds (1985) **A Social Area Analysis of Stoke-on-Trent** Occasional Papers in Geography, no. 4, North Staffordshire Polytechnic

Rodgers, H.B. (1977) **Rationalising Sports Policies**, Council of Europe, Strasbourg

LIFESTYLES AND SPORTS PARTICIPATION

H.A. McINNES[1]
Sports Council, London, England

Abstract
This paper sets out to examine individuals' patterns of leisure behaviour in order to identify and define sporting lifestyles. It is based on an empirical study of 460 individuals in Nottingham, England. Detailed records of activity patterns were collected using time-space diaries, supplemented by structured and semistructured questionnaire interviews to provide profile information about the individual. Association analysis was used to describe aggregate patterns of behaviour, whilst biographical analysis shifted the emphasis to the particular behaviour of individuals. Lifestyles were found to be diverse and complicated, however lifestyle groups could be identified. Gender influences were confirmed as important social profile indicators of behaviour, although differences relating to leisure pursuits complicated the situation. At the individual level, biographical analysis highlighted differences in the degree of commitment to sport even for those to whom sport was significant in describing their lifestyles. Thus, lifestyles may be described and ascribed to sport, yet there is no single sporting lifestyle.
Keywords: Lifestyles, Sports Participation, Time-Space Diaries, Biographies.

1 Introduction

Leisure and sporting lifestyles of individuals are poorly understood. Research to date has concentrated on specific activities or the use of facilities. It has been almost wholly descriptive in nature. This paper examines individuals' patterns of leisure behaviour in order to identify and define sporting lifestyles in terms of activity packages.

The analysis is based on a databank of 'time-space' diaries collected for the primary purpose of offering an insight into 'Leisure and the Home', a project commissioned by the Joint Economic and Social Research Council/Sports Council Panel on Leisure and Recreation Research. This paper draws upon one important

1 The research project on which this paper is based was funded by the Joint ESRC/Sports Council Panel on Leisure and Recreation Research, whose support is gratefully acknowledged.

aspect of the data; namely the information it gives us about the type and range of activities that people take part in.

Conventional surveys impose pre-conceived definitions of leisure upon respondents, with self-evident limitations. In this case leisure was defined by the respondents themselves. However defined, it is a fundamental component of our lifestyles. The term 'lifestyle' may be taken as the 'aggregate pattern of day-to-day activities which make up an individual's way of life' (McInnes, 1988). More accurately, and more problematic, lifestyle might subsume people's attitudes, beliefs, experiences and motivations (Tokarski and Uttitz, 1984).

A lifestyle approach to leisure studies focuses on the individual rather than social aggregates, and is concerned with the total package of activities which makes up an individual's normal routine. Thus, leisure behaviour can be seen in the wider context of life in general, rather than be examined in isolation as is more usual in leisure research.

2 Methodology

Customary aggregate analysis of participation data by social group divisions, such as age, sex and social class, does not adequately clarify or identify lifestyle variations. A 'lifestyle' approach facilitates the classification of people according to like patterns of leisure behaviour.

Identification of lifestyles in this manner requires some form of classification technique. One of the most widely used methods is cluster analysis (Everitt, 1974). Such techniques are used to sub-divide a population into constituent groups, so that individuals most similar in terms of defined characteristics are grouped together.

This type of analysis has rarely been applied in leisure research in Britain to date (exceptions include Glyptis, 1981; McInnes, 1989), yet it is potentially a powerful way of exploring the totality of people's behaviour.

A divisive clustering technique, namely association analysis, was used to disaggregate the whole sample into groups revealing similar behavioural patterns. Thus the clustering technique was used to see whether people did or did not take part in given activities.

Association analysis was complemented by biographical analysis to shift the emphasis from the aggregate characteristics of the whole sample to the particular behaviour of individuals. Adapted from the principles of time-geography, this was used to illustrate contrasting types of lifestyles (Glyptis, McInnes and Patmore, 1987).

3 Lifestyle Groups

A full discussion of the various analyses to identify lifestyle groups is beyond the scope of this discussion (McInnes, 1989). However, a brief explanation of their general progression is pertinent.

The first analysis provided a general examination of the whole sample of 460 individuals, and considered all the activities recorded within the three-day period of the time-space diaries. Activities that were almost universal, such as sleeping, eating and washing were all excluded. Equally, to satisfy the statistical conditions of the technique, all those activities with a particularly low frequency of events (ie less than 30) were also excluded. However, it must be acknowledged that for those individuals concerned, these minority activities may be of central importance to their lifestyles, eg gambling and playing musical instruments.

This initial investigation generated some 100 significantly different cluster groups. The resultant pattern indicates considerable diversity and complexity in individuals' lifestyles. The main criterion for cluster formation was indoor cleaning, and subsequent divisions were also based on domestic chore activities.

Follow-up analyses of the whole sample using varying activity ranges confirmed these findings, thus highlighting two important results. Firstly, the diversity and complexity of lifestyles, and secondly, to confirm the established strength of gender as a social profile predictor of behaviour.

Thus, lifestyle variations were apparent; although initially there was little evidence of **leisure lifestyle** variations.

The first instance of such variation emerged from an analysis undertaken with the exclusion of activities that were most obviously related to profile characteristics, such as paid employment or child care. One cluster group, defined according to participation in gardening, was the first group to be formed in terms of a shared leisure interest. Although primarily composed of men, this group came from a diversity of social backgrounds, thus suggesting that it may be possible to consider lifestyle groups based on people's leisure behaviour.

4   Lifestyles of Sports Participants

The next stage in the analysis was to focus on samples of individuals who were known to have a shared leisure interest (from the diary records) and study their patterns of behaviour in more detail both at the aggregate level and at the level of the individual.

One particular group to be considered was the sports participants. The original activity classification divided sport into four categories: individual sports, team sports, racquet sports and water sports. For the purposes of the cluster analysis, it was more appropriate to consider the four types together. This was firstly to see whether sports players in general displayed particular lifestyle patterns and, secondly, because the sample sizes for each of the four types were too small to be considered separately. Sixty-four individuals were divided into some sixty cluster groups. From this it would appear that sports players were a very disparate group of people, each revealing distinctly different lifestyles.

At the aggregate level, the cluster analysis produced a series of divisions based on leisure activities. This suggests that sports participants, although generally pursuing very individual lifestyles, also displayed particularly leisure-oriented patterns of behaviour.

The largest cluster group was described on the basis of a mixture of leisure and chore, namely individual sports and washing up. The group was five strong and, although predominantly young, was split between the sexes, further confirming the possibility of identifying leisure lifestyles.

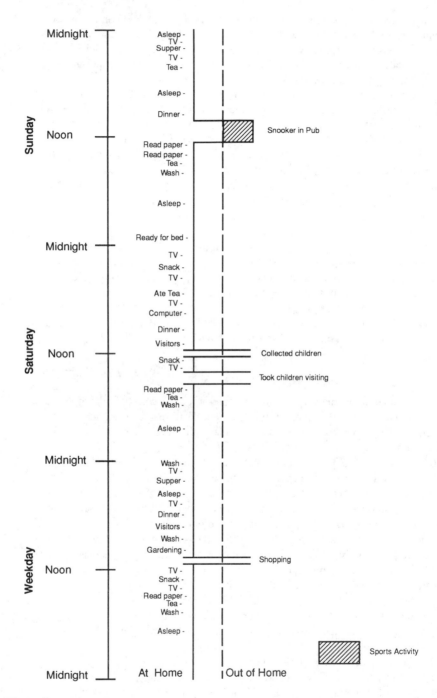

Figure 1:   *Person A*

Aggregate findings often obscure the differences between individuals within the same group, and biographical analysis can be used to illustrate the lifestyles of individual sports participants. These can be depicted in diagrammatic fashion to show activity patterns in time and space (Glyptis, McInnes and Patmore, 1987; Glyptis, 1989).

The biography of Person A, an unemployed married man aged between 30 and 44 years, is depicted in Figure 1. The shape of the diagram reveals a lifestyle spent almost entirely at home; some 94 per cent of his time was spent indoors over the three day period.

Much of his time was spent at leisure, the lack of paid employment being compensated for by leisure pursuits rather than work or chore. His leisure time was primarily spent at home, and much of it was in front of the television. Some ten events were recorded over the three days.

Sport was not a pivotal pursuit in his lifestyle, as he only recorded one such event, namely a game of snooker in the local pub. Furthermore, it only accounted for 8 per cent of his leisure time.

Thus, Person A, without the routine imposed by a job, spent much of his time at home, and a considerable proportion on leisure activities such as watching television and reading newspapers. Participation in sport may have been a defining attribute, yet it was seemingly of minor importance in his overall lifestyle.

This can be contrasted with the biographies of two other individuals in this group. Person B, a young schoolboy, displayed a more active lifestyle in terms of his activities and his movements away from home (Figure 4). Like Person A, almost half of his time was spent on leisure pursuits, and he recorded almost as many incidents of watching television. However, almost one third of his time was away from home, and some sixty per cent of this was sport. He recorded five sporting events, primarily football training, so clearly sport was far more important in Person B's lifestyle than in that of Person A.

Perhaps this would have been expected as it has been established elsewhere that school children, particularly boys, are generally more active in sports participation than other groups.

However, such conventional reasoning was less applicable in the case of Person C (Figure 2), a married woman without children aged between 25 and 29 years, and working in a skilled manual job. The shape of the biography reveals a lifestyle which took her away from home on a number of occasions and for lengthy periods of time.

Like the other two individuals much of her time was spent on leisure pursuits and, like the schoolboy, these primarily took place out of the home. Including preparation for sport, she recorded eight separate events, representing two-thirds of all her leisure time. The activities she recorded were skating and training (presumably for skating competitions), and allied to the preparation and sharpening of her skates at home, it is clear that skating was a pivotal influence in her lifestyle.

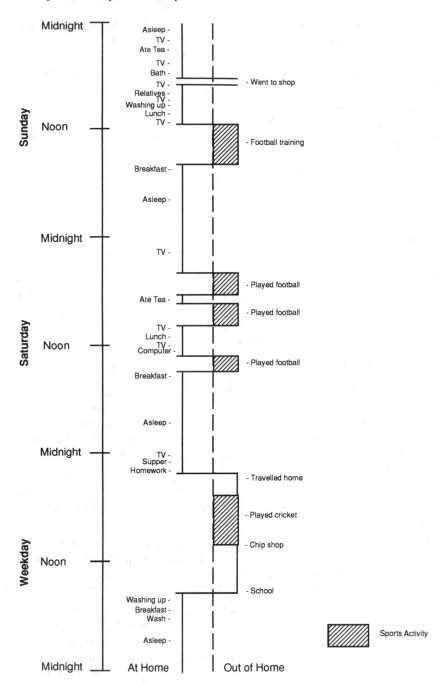

Figure 2   *Person B*

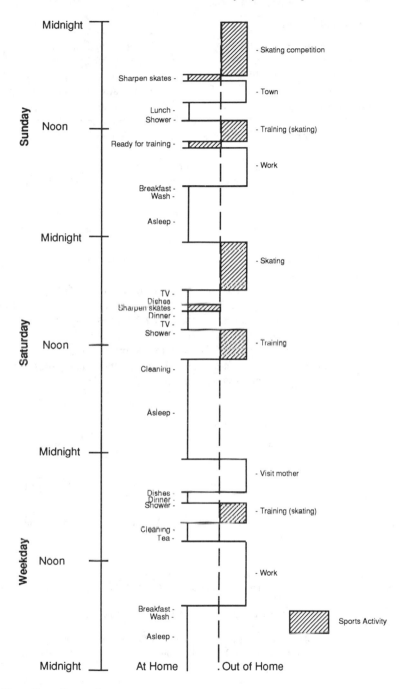

Figure 3   *Person C*

5   A Sporting Lifestyle?

This paper then, sets out to examine the application of cluster analysis and biographical analysis to participation data, to see whether or not lifestyle groups, and in particular sporting lifestyles, could be identified on the basis of activity packages.

The overall trend was one of diversity and complexity, indicating that people lead very different and complicated lifestyles. However, lifestyle groups (or clusters) could be identified. Initially such groups were described according to gender-related factors, confirming the importance of gender as a social profile predictor of behaviour.

The situation was complicated however by other differences relating to the influence of leisure pursuits. To a certain extent, leisure lifestyles could be identified and defined across social profile divisions.

Closer inspection of the lifestyles revealed differences between individuals as highlighted by the biographical analysis. The three individuals selected have, purely for illustrative purposes, all revealed a sporting lifestyle but to a markedly varying degree, in terms of the amount and frequency of participation, and the significance of sport within their leisure time.

Thus it may be concluded that there is no single sporting lifestyle to which sports participants adhere. Further investigation of people's activity patterns at this level of detail should be complemented by an understanding of the attitudes and satisfactions associated with participation. Such extra information would enhance our understanding of the individual, which would serve either to produce distinct lifestyle models with a practical and theoretical purpose, or finally to dispel lifestyle notions as a result of people's inherent diversity and individuality.

6   References

Everitt, B. (1974) **Cluster Analysis**. Social Science Research Council Review, Heinemann, London.

Glyptis, S.A. (1981) Leisure Lifestyles. **Regional Studies**, 15, 5, 311-326.

Glyptis, S.A. (1989) **Leisure and Unemployment**. Open University Press, Milton Keynes.

Glyptis, S.A. McInnes, H.A. and Patmore, J.A. (1987) **Leisure and the Home**. Sports Council/Economic and Social Research Council, London.

McInnes, H.A. and Glyptis, S.A. (1986) The use of leisure time, in **Sport, Culture, Society: International, Historical and Sociological Perspectives** (eds J A Mangan and R B Small), Proceedings of the VIII Commonwealth and International Conference on Sport, Physical Education, Dance, Recreation and Health.

McInnes, H.A. (1985) The Identification of Leisure Lifestyles: the Role of Cluster Analysis. Unpublished Conference Paper. Free Time, Culture and Society. World Leisure and Recreation Association - First World Congress. Alberta, Canada.

McInnes, H.A. (1989) Lifestyles and Leisure Participation. Unpublished PhD Thesis. Loughborough University of Technology.

Tokarski, W and Uttitz, P. (1984) Leisure lifestyles: some more differentiations from the sociological point of view, in **Le Temps Libre et Le Loisir**. Proceedings of Congress of WLRA, Paris.

MOVING TOWARDS EXCELLENCE

DAVID PICKUP
Sports Council, London, England

Abstract
This paper sets out the way in which the Sports Council has been developing a strategy for performance and excellence in sport, taking into account some of the contextual social changes that have been influencing its thinking. It argues that the growing emphasis on the individual perfomer is a logical conclusion of the way that sport has developed in Britain over the last two decades. In the seventies the emphasis was on facility development and in the eighties efforts were concentrated on increasing the number of people taking part in sport. The paper explains that the Sports Council's strategy for performance and excellence is underpinned by two basic assumptions: first, that more effort needs to go into the identification of talented youngsters and, second, that more attention needs to be given to the establishment of a comprehensive and coherent support structure for individual performers. The concept of a partnership approach to sports development is outlined, focusing on the improvement and extra provision of national facilities; the need to increase the accessibility of crucial back-up services such as sports science and sports medicine; and the stimulation of coaching development along properly professional lines.

1

Some months ago the *Independent on Sunday* ran a feature on junior tennis in the UK. The centrepiece of the article concerned the meeting of two young men in the final of last year's national under 18 championships. On one side of the net was Nick Adams, a star product of the Lawn Tennis Association's School of Excellence at Bisham Abbey, one of the Sports Council's National Centres. Adams, I seem to recall, was clad in the latest gear, and armed with a battery of rackets - a muscular, athletic, ebullient young man prepared to perfection - physically and mentally - by the land's finest coaches. His opponent was one Jonathan Haycock, a pupil from Dulwich College. Haycock - evocatively nicknamed 'The Rake' - caused something of a stir as he entered the arena. A slender, rather raffish figure, he was wearing a battered old raincoat over his tennis clothes and carrying but a single racket - it might even have been a wooden one.

To the uninformed observer it looked like no contest. Bristling with aggression and power, Adams would surely blow the dilettante off the court. It didn't, of course, work out that way. Haycock produced a fine performance of daring and finesse to emerge as clear winner.

A salutary lesson for the sports professionals? In some ways, yes. In others, no. The natural genius demonstrated by Haycock is not something that can be legislated for. It can't be guaranteed through careful planning; rarely can it be harnessed with any degree of consistency. We can't set out to engineer talent of that kind, nor in my view should we endeavour to do so. To adopt a wholly mechanistic approach to high performance leads one rapidly into areas of ethical dubiety. It would also tend towards the filtering out of idiosyncratic artistry - Pele, John McEnroe, Ian Botham spring quickly to mind - to the impoverishment of us all. To have imposed a strongly regimented approach on this kind of talent would have probably extinguished the spark that maketh the man.

But is this a reason for the coaches, the teachers, the medics and the administrators to pack up their kit bags and seek a new vocation? Of course not. Lawn tennis in the UK is a classic example of a sport which has, over the years, produced many young Haycocks. Very few of them, however - and no men at all - have gone on to achieve prominence on the international circuit. Something more than natural flair is required. It is an important part of our job at the Sports Council to help provide the sporting infrastructure - physical, social, economic and attitudinal - which will encourage performers, up to and certainly including the elite level, to fulfil their potential.

And, in one sense, we have not been doing too badly. British sport is still probably unique in its pluralism. Over the years we have managed to produce many international champions in a tremendous variety of sports. But impressive though the results may have been, they have come about with little sense of our having consciously directed our national resources to that end. Indeed, sometimes one has had the impression of talented performers achieving success in spite of the system rather than because of it.

2

This situation cannot, of course, be divorced from our history and tradition. It is not all that long ago that the whole concept of athletic performance and excellence, as currently understood, would, in Britain, have been looked upon with some distaste. And given the adverse consequences that can result from today's obsession with winning at all costs, the Corinthian approach should not too quickly be dismissed. That traditional view can be clearly seen in the following quotation:

> The gentleman athlete will not be seen training or practising for his event before the day of competition. To do so would be to attempt to gain an unfair advantage over his fellow.

This passage, taken from a Coaching Manual of 1870, demonstrates the revolution in attitude that has taken place in the world of elite sport.

In the middle of the 19th century there was very little preparation of athletes in the modern sense. Whilst coaches did exist they were often little more than bag carriers or ball retrievers for their masters. Nowadays the profile of the coach is more often than not as high as the athlete's.

Even with the advent of sport governing bodies in the later part of the 19th century, little consideration was given to the development of competition structures or coaching. Governing bodies saw it as their task to administer and control that which already existed. It was not until after the Stockholm Olympics, when the British Olympic Association reviewed the performance of the British team, that the first decision to employ coaches on a national basis was taken. The press in the latter part of 1912 was full of recrimination for the so-called 'failure' of the British athletes. Some things seemingly never change!

Even with these developments there was, in the period before the Second World War, nothing that could be described as a coaching profession in Britain. 'Coaches' were still very much untrained and related, not to high levels of performance, but to the improvement of the recreative players of a leisured class. Even in soccer the only coaches that existed were either managers or masseurs.

The seeds of coaching and a structured approach towards excellence were sown with the advent of the government backed National Fitness Campaign of 1939. The Campaign planned the establishment of three National Coaches for athletics and although war intervened, the coaching agenda had been firmly set. After the war the Amateur Athletic Association agreed the adoption of an AAA Coaching Scheme, many other governing bodies followed suit and the 1950s marked a rapid growth of coaching schemes.

The 'Chariots of Fire' era was slowly coming to a close and Britain through the '50s and '60s began to produce coaching schemes and technical materials which were well regarded in the western world. It was not, however, until the USSR entered the international sporting arena that Britain realized how much further it still had to go. The USSR and its satellites were the first to start to systematically train its athletes and to apply themselves methodically to sports performance.

The example set by the USSR spurred Britain into the realization that coaching was only one element in the complex chemistry of sports performance. Excellence of facilities, selective competition, the application of sports medicine and sports science all began to come to the fore. It became increasingly evident that all these elements had to exist in a dynamic balance if sporting excellence was to be achieved.

At the same time, the position of the coach and the importance of support services in the pursuit of excellence, was slowly filtering through to sports administrators. In 1965, the British Association of National Coaches was formed with the aim of bringing together on a yearly basis professional National Coaches of all sports. Theories of coaching developed and it was felt that there was a need for a coach-education programme revolving round central core elements, independent of specific sports.

It was around this theory that the National Coaching Foundation was created in 1983. Under its Director, Sue Campbell, the NCF has since become recognized as one of the world's major sources of core knowledge in coaching. The creation of the NCF brought into clear focus the lack of core elements in the education of many coaches. Areas such as psychology, child development and mobility had indeed been covered in many coach education programmes, but rarely in great depth, and programmes had often been sport-related rather than performer-related.

The NCF has made great strides but other aspects of our performance-related policies have tended to be neglected, mainly through a grave lack of resources but also because in key areas like sports medicine there has not been a consensus among experts and administrators as to how best to move forward.

There has, however, in the past two years been a clear recognition in British sport that it was time to combine all our resources and our thinking in order to build a coherent and constructive structure aimed at promoting excellence. And this recognition occurred at the same time that the Sports Council was beginning to be concerned about the need to define more precisely its aims in promoting performance and excellence.

To this end, the Council in spring 1989 established a widely-based consultative group specifically to help us identify the key elements of a policy framework within which talented and committed sportspersons would be most likely to realize their ambition.

3

I want to give you a feel for the way in which the Sports Council has been developing its strategy on performance and excellence, taking into account some of the contextual social changes that are influencing our interim conclusions. In doing so, I am lifting the veil on a number of ideas that have not yet formally been endorsed by the Sports Council. The conclusions I shall be describing are therefore more of the nature of preliminary sketches rather than the completed canvas; but I hope that they will serve to give an idea of the way in which our thinking is developing.

First, though, I think it is necessary for us to paint in some important background factors:

(a) Increasingly we are becoming a leisured society. When the Sports Council's Strategy Document was first published in 1983, it was established for example that almost all working people had 3 weeks or more paid holiday a year, that personal incomes had doubled in real terms over 20 years and that the number of private cars had quadrupled over the same period.

(b) In Great Britain approximately 21 million adults take part in sport or active recreation on a regular basis.

(c) Some £4.5 billion is spent annually on sport and recreation, which thus works out at over £200 per participant. Amongst providers, local authorities are known to spend almost £800 million annually on capital and revenue programmes. The Sports Council's own expenditure this year will exceed £52 million.

(d)   There are more people employed in the sport and recreation industry than work in such areas as chemicals and man-made fibres; agriculture, forestry and fishing; electricity and water; motor vehicles and parts; coal, oil and natural gas.

Sport, then, is big business. It helps bring material wealth to the nation. It helps to improve the quality of life and reduces boredom. Nor should it be forgotten that playing sport improves people's physical and mental well being, thereby helping to reduce public health costs and lost working days and remedial health measures.

The Sports Council is currently testing the hypothesis that sport is good for your health. Together with the Health Education Authority we are financing the first ever England-wide survey of the levels of fitness in the population. Sponsored by Allied Dunbar the survey measures, in particular, the causal relationship between the pursuit of an active lifestyle and the general health of an individual. Never before in this country has a study of this kind, or of this magnitude, been undertaken. I am sure we will all learn a great deal from this research.

The conviction that sport is both an intrinsic good and also economically profitable has underpinned the way that sport in the UK has developed over the last twenty years.

In the seventies, the emphasis was on the development of facilities - a prerequisite for the growth of participation. The construction of a wide range of facilities at community, district, county, regional and national level provided the foundation for increasing involvement. Investment by newly-established Leisure and Recreation Departments at local government level resulted in the first major explosion in facility development this century. In the eighties, with the Sports Council in the vanguard of the movement, efforts were concentrated on increasing the number of people taking part in sport. Marketing strategies, campaigns, outreach work and the establishment of special development projects all contributed to the drive to attract non-participants into sport - often for the first time since school.

Mass participation will, of course, remain a major plank in the Sports Council's policy. But I also strongly believe that the Council has a clear duty to help sportsmen and women realize their potential. We should not shy away from the determination to provide elite services for elite performers. There is of course a continuum here. The elite performer provides a role model for the more ordinary participant. One only has to look at what the achievements of Bjorn Borg and Boris Becker have done for tennis in Sweden and Germany.

Britain has often demonstrated a reluctance to focus on the individual but we need to recognize that the production of champions is the most effective way of showing others with ability what they too might be able to achieve. It is also the surest way of igniting public enthusiasm for just getting involved. In this sense, we must regard the time, energy and resources committed to the accomplished performer as an investment in the participation stakes as well.

Any strategy for performance and excellence must therefore direct itself towards two fundamental objectives; first, to put more effort into the identification of, and maintenance of information about, talented youngsters and, second, to give more attention to the establishment of a comprehensive and coherent support structure for individual performers.

There are unfortunately no hard and fast rules to help us determine where, when or why talented performers will emerge. Some youngsters, of course, are actively encouraged from an early age. Others are inspired by watching the stars; Nick Faldo had never held a golf club until, at the age of 14, he saw Jack Nicklaus winning the Masters on TV. Within a few months, he was shooting sub-80 rounds on a full size course. Some have been driven on by hunger, by the desire to escape from poverty, discrimination or the ghetto. In their very different fields, Lee Trevino and Mike Tyson come to mind as representatives of this genre.

But whatever background the performer comes from, it is clear that his or her talent is prey to a whole range of potentially destructive factors which together may conspire to prevent that talent from flourishing. Amongst these I count the lack of leadership, absence of suitable, accessible facilities, inadequate financial resources and the non-availability of quality coaching.

4

The Sports Council has a current research project studying the Training of Young Athletes, a project which is being carried out by a team from the Institute of Child Health and which is now in its third year. One part of the study explores the reasons why children retire from or change their involvement in sport. Of a sample of 69 young athletes, the majority of whom had participated at national and international level, 10% cited their social life as the primary reason for retiring from, or changing their involvement in sport. There will, I guess, always be 'distractions' which divert young people away from competitive sport and over which no-one can, or should, claim to exercise any control.

Other frequently cited reasons, however, are rather more illuminating. 'Disinterest' accounted for 12%, 'problems with coach' for 9%, 'injury' for 10%, 'disappointing results' for 10%, 'pressure of the sport' for 6% and 'illness' for 6%. One might speculate that with better support, encouragement and coaching a significant proportion of these youngsters might have been helped to overcome their difficulties and disillusionment. Other interesting results from the research indicate that there are inequalities in access to intensive participation in sport, with children from the lower socio-economic groups being significantly under-represented across each of the four sports examined (tennis, swimming, gymnastics and soccer), a problem sometimes compounded by the distance that young athletes are required to travel to training facilities. Part of the move towards excellence will require us to take more conscious heed of these results and to seek to counter them as part of the process of identifying and nurturing young talent.

One should perhaps pause at this stage to point out one major problem that lies across our path. In the past the UK has benefitted from an educational system that has, however inadequately, been broadly supportive of the concept of providing youngsters with the best opportunities to develop their sporting performance. In England and Wales, however, the public education system is now experiencing major turbulence. Changes over the last few years have included:

(a)   the introduction of new conditions of service for teachers which means that fewer non PE specialists are able to give their time to extra-curricular sport;

(b)   the devolution of budgetary control to school governors and head teachers through the Local Management of schools, which could operate to the disadvantage of sport in that there might be a growing reluctance to allow school facilities to be used by the wider community;

(c)   the introduction of a National Curriculum and system for pupil profiling. The National Curriculum will provide the framework within which children will be introduced to physical education and thence to sport and is therefore of vital interest, as this will determine the grounding for future sporting champions.

The Sports Council is concerned to help the physical education profession play a leading role in the formulation of policy for the teaching of PE in schools, a task which will be undertaken by a subject-specific working party set up by the Secretary of State for Education and Science. However, we have to be realistic and recognize that progress is likely to be limited. We also have to recognize the limitations of the most often argued alternative, namely that responsibility for getting young people involved in sport, and for encouraging and supporting them once they are there, is increasingly going to reside with parents and with clubs.

I am sure that there are many people attending this conference who will be able to offer an opinion to my British colleagues on whether or not these changes will lead to a diminution in the foundation for our sporting talent or, as some have suggested, to a greater focusing of expertise and facilities within certain schools.

This is one area of policy which must not be neglected. It is the foundation on which everything else in sport is erected. I do not pretend to have the answers. Some were provided in the recent report of the School Sports Forum, but the Government has so far proved unreceptive to those ideas insofar as they involve extra resources.

I have a feeling that the way ahead will entail introducing some form of sport leadership auxiliaries into the schools, perhaps with a responsibility for promoting games in a number of adjacent schools within a community. This may not be an easy concept for the fully professional teachers to accept, but it may require some innovation of this nature to ensure that the nation does not produce a generation of youngsters deprived of the opportunity to take part in sport and to identify their talents to themselves and to others best placed to nurture and develop it.

Certainly we see local authorities generally as having an important role in terms of performance and excellence, quite apart from their educational responsibilities.

Local authorities have traditionally tended to focus on the 'sport for all' end of the sporting spectrum, ensuring that sport and recreation opportunities are available for the casual player. They do, however, value the civic prestige and public enthusiasm which emerges when a local boy or girl makes good. Several, have, therefore, developed policies which provide a hierarchy of skill development through subsidized use of facilities and assisted coaching and squad systems.

We will certainly need to develop this approach, not least by fostering closer, more creative linkages between the local authorities and the Governing Bodies of sport who have a crucial co-ordinating role to play at local and regional levels. The Sports Council acknowledges that it needs to assist the Governing Bodies in discharging these responsibilities perhaps through creating more specifically-funded liaison and development staff. There are already examples of such posts being established, partly with private sector financial support, and in connection with different sports. In the London area, for instance, the Hockey Association has secured financial support from Pizza Express for the funding for a Hockey Development Officer post. London also boasts a thriving Community Cricket Association which exists without funding from any other cricket or statutory body and enjoys considerable private sector support. In Yorkshire, exciting initiatives have taken place in connection with the development of Rugby League, also with commercial sponsorship.

5

I now want to look at the means by which support can be offered to those performers identified as possessing the stuff of champions. The four areas on which I shall concentrate are facilities, sports science, sports medicine and coaching.

Despite the facilities explosion of the seventies that I mentioned earlier, Britain still lacks a range of facilities suitable for national and international competition and competitors.

There are eleven National Centres which make a considerable contribution to the nation's sporting excellence. In England, Lilleshall (Soccer, Cricket, Gymnastics, Table Tennis, Hockey, Archery), Bisham Abbey (Lawn Tennis, Hockey, Weightlifting), Crystal Palace (Swimming, Diving, Athletics, Martial Arts), Holme Pierrepont (Rowing, Canoeing and other water sports) and Plas y Brenin (Mountain and Outdoor activities) represent our strongest and most visible commitment to the promotion of performance and excellence. The competitive tendering arrangements which are being phased in for the management of each of the centres are providing us with a renewed determination to ensure that the facilities and back-up services provided support their objectives in the most effective way possible. They are all dedicated to fostering excellence in sport and recreation.

Bisham Abbey and Lilleshall host the tennis and football academies. Five members of the England Soccer Team's current under 21 squad spent two formative years at the FA School at Lilleshall. At Bisham Abbey the 13 teenage boys will soon be joined by girls. The schools are examples of the integrated approach towards excellence which is the cornerstone of our future strategy. At Bisham the pupils attend local schools and have daily fitness and skills training sessions on the three most commonly used international surfaces, and in conditions which can be adjusted for light, heat and humidity. They have two sessions a week with a sports psychologist, either as individuals or in a group. Their physiology is constantly checked and their diet adjusted to ensure adequate nutrition. Visiting tutors from other sports stimulate new perspectives on their training.

The British Olympic Association is now actively developing an exciting initiative making use of the Centres. This summer they will be holding combined training camps at our National Centres. Players, coaches, officials and team managers of sports with similar interests will combine to explore issues of common interest and share intelligence about the international scene and particularly, I suspect, about the conditions in Barcelona.

The National Centres offer a unique environment for a whole range of Governing Bodies. Amongst our most notable customers in recent times have been our national rugby, cricket and soccer squads - and it would be nice to think that the unprecedented standards of fitness achieved by the England XV which so nearly brought them a grand slam last season, the unexpected challenge to the West Indies by Graham Gooch's men in the winter, and the media-silencing exploits of Gascoigne, Lineker and company in Italy, can be attributed in part to the support and back-up offered to them at Lilleshall and Bisham.

But apart from these Centres, the UK is still gravely deficient in many sports in terms of modern facility provision for both training and competition. The Sports Council is endeavouring to address these deficiencies with the working up of a National Strategy for Facilities Provision, the aim of which is to assist each sport with the provision of a facility of the standard necessary for staging international competition or for national training purposes. The basic criteria will be that any national facility proposals are part of a comprehensive development plan for each sport under review. We would have to think long and hard about investing significant amounts in a high quality mega-pound training facility for a sport that offered only limited potential for increasing participation. Front runners in terms of their claim upon Sports Council resources are, however, a National Hockey Centre, a National Ice Skating Training Centre, a National Velodrome and a National Sailing Centre.

The Sports Council fully acknowledges its responsibility for helping the relevant Governing Bodies to provide these high-level facilities. Now that England has acquired superb athletics stadia and a second Olympic-standard swimming pool at Birmingham and Sheffield we shall be able to begin the task of redirecting resources to these ends.

But training provision for the elite level performers may not be enough. We are now looking closely at a proposal that has been put to us that in formulating a strategy for performance and excellence, the Sports Council has a unique opportunity to create new types of centres of national significance, based on the concept of development. The designation of and investment in selected institutions of higher education as National Centres for Sports Development would give the institutions the status they need to increase their contribution to British sport and to attract other investment, and allow them to develop a more strategic approach to their established activities in sports development training, sports coaching education, sports training provision and sports science support.

The concept of Centres for sports education and development, based on existing centres of excellence, would add a human resource dimension to the Sports Council's strategy for performance and excellence.

The record and tradition in the UK of education as a major patron, catalyst and provider of sports facilities and services is exemplified in its most integrated form in the institutions of higher education. These institutions have contributed not only the context and support for many performers to reach levels of excellence, but have also provided the initial and further training for generations of teachers, coaches, researchers and sports administrators. Sports governing bodies, local authority recreation departments and individual sports clubs and groups have all benefitted from the support of various institutions of higher education, and the students of these institutions have gained professional knowledge, experience and insight from these links.

Over the last three years, the National Coaching Foundation has recognized and capitalized on the expertise and services available at selected institutions, in setting up the National Coaching Centre network. The result has been to add to the 'critical mass' of sports development opportunities at some of these institutions, by providing a focus for sports coaching education, and by attracting a number of well qualified and enthusiastic young people as development officers. This had added to and strengthened the already well established services which some institutions had been providing for their communities and regions. The development of a range of services had been in response to local, regional and national needs, and was achieved by individuals and groups with the capacity for recognizing the potential for co-operation and the need to work across the institutional boundaries which have for so long limited the development of British sport.

An extension of this type of cluster of services and facilities, to cover strategic approaches to sports development and other training, and to develop and monitor good practice, might be a logical progression to what has already been achieved, and is a possibility that we are examining closely.

This leads me fairly naturally into the subject of sports science.

It is a matter for conjecture whether sports science has been the chicken or the egg in the theory of causation, but its rapid growth over the last 10 or 15 years is incontrovertible. Sports scientists nowadays fall into four main categories - psychologists, physiologists, biomechanics and match or performance analysts. Their expertise finds four main means of expression - consultancy, information, education and applied research or problem solving.

We already have an excellent structure on the ground. The British Association of Sports Science and the National Coaching Foundation have together developed a nationwide network of accredited individuals and laboratories.

These two bodies now co-ordinate the Council's sports science grant scheme for Governing Bodies of sport. These include support to such projects as the design and monitoring of the training programmes of the Rugby Football Union's national squad, the implementation of psychological techniques to boxing with a view to maximizing the potential of national squads, and the biomechanical analysis of diving involving the use of high speed film. Regular workshops are also held for sports scientists and coaches.

The Sports Council manages the National Doping Control and Education programme. On the control side independent sampling officers are trained and appointed by us and they then conduct random tests both at events and out of competition. A range of information materials have been developed to advise competitors and other interested bodies on allowable and banned substances. Circulation of these materials exceeds 20,000 per year.

The Sports Council also commissions its own research in support of excellence in sport. For example the University of Sheffield Medical Care Research Unit, under Professor Brian Williams, has now started the National Study of the Epidemiology of Sports Injuries. And I have already mentioned the Training of Young Athletes Project (TOYA) being carried out by a team from the Institute of Child Health, is now in its third year and publication of its initial findings is imminent.

The problem to date has been one of underfunding; governing bodies have found themselves limited in their purchasing power and consequently restricted to the use of sports scientists largely as consultants. The Sports Aid Foundation and commercial sponsors can help lucky individual performers with their training and competition expenses, but there is little enthusiasm from the business world to underpin the costs of support services. The Sports Council's sports science programme however is a priority area for increased funding and we intend, in collaboration with the British Olympic Association, to develop the linking of individual scientists with specific sports.

Sports medics have been less enthusiastic about accrediting themselves in the manner of the sports scientists, and this has led to severe difficulties in establishing a nationwide data-base of suitably qualified doctors to whom sportsmen and women might be able to refer themselves in different parts of the country. The other significant problem that bedevils this area is the lack of specialized knowledge amongst doctors about soft tissue injuries and about the suitability of different means of treatment and rehabilitation for performers involved in different sports. Now there are signs that a new co-operative approach is being adopted and a clearer strategy is emerging in the field of sports medicine. A seminar of key personnel earlier this year identified a number of key issues for concerted action. These include:-

(a) the need for a standardized approach to qualification training, with the main thrust being directed at post-graduate level.

(b) the establishment of a network of accredited sports medicine clinics throughout the country, with specific information provided on the standard of facilities and the services available.

(c) the establishment of a national sports medicine institute responsible for the co-ordinated accreditation and education of the different bodies involved in the field.

If we can begin to take more seriously the need for proper medical back-up for elite performers at both team and individual level, and in training and competition situations, then perhaps we can start to make inroads into the 25% of Britain's medal winning potential which it has been estimated we lose at each major athletics competition through illness or injury.

This brings me back to the subject of coaching itself. I have referred already to the increasing professionalization of sport and sportspeople, and to the many pressures which are nowadays brought to bear upon them. These contextual changes are not without their implications for coaches - in fact, the reverse is true. Whilst once upon a time a coach, professional or otherwise, might have been expected to do little more than to 'get their player in shape', we have now moved into an era when the coach to a top performer or team has become as much of a personal manager as an overseer of physical fitness. He or she will require a range of skills - from performance development (and by this I mean the ability to arrange access to the necessary facilities, to manage a competition preparation programme, and to understand their charge's psychological, biomechanical and nutritional requirements), to medical management, to what has been termed 'lifestyle counselling'.

Although the value of good coaching is therefore widely appreciated, the view of the Sports Council working group on performance and excellence is that this value has been reduced in Britain 'because of the lack of any generally accepted policy for the identification, training, employment and deployment of coaches.... Without good coaching , concluded the group, 'every other piece of the performance and excellence jigsaw will be worthless since it is the coach who can identify the talent, nourish it and help it grow'.

The Sports Council has accordingly set up a Coaching Review Group to consider the way forward for coaching in the United Kingdom. Although the Review Group has yet to publish its final report, I would expect its conclusions to centre on the need for the status and the power-base of coaches to be raised and on the need to delineate clearly between what one might call 'performance coaches' and coach educators. At the performance and excellence end of the spectrum, our concern must be to help the coach to coach and not to spend his or her time, as some National Coaches might have done in the past, as some sort of inter-agency go-between.

Some of the key issues emerging from the Review Group will focus on:-

(a)   The identification of people to coach both at a voluntary and professional level.

(b)   The improvements necessary in the employment and deployment of coaches - again both voluntary and professional. In relation to professional coaches, these improvements should help to ensure they are paid at a professional rate to reflect their professional input.

(c)   The need for a more explicit and generally accepted code of ethics for coaches. An excellent start has been made by the British Institute of Sports Coaches in its published work in this area.

(d)   The benefits of a more integrated approach to coach provision at all levels of sport and, particularly, a matching up of skills of the coach to the right audience group - for example, the recognition of different groups, such as young people, who require a different approach by the responsible coach.

(e)   The need for greater co-ordination and co-operation among different organizations employing or deploying coaches, whether at local, regional or national level. In particular, we will look for a rationalisation of the work of the many organizations involved in training, employing and receiving the benefits of the work of coaches and improved integration with others in the field administrators, development officers and other office bearers.

(f)   The introduction of an accreditation system for coaches and the coach education systems of governing bodies to ensure that a measure of quality assurance can be introduced, both for the individuals concerned and for the coach education systems they operate.

(g) An improvement to coaching support services provided, including better pre- and in-service training; more and better data on which decisions can be made; more support through the emerging coaching network centres; apprenticeship services for coaches eager to progress to a higher level, more support for international contacts to be made and improved research, both of a speculative and applied nature. And of course improved support services in sports medicine and sports sciences .

Sport enters the 1990s with a good but far from complete stock of community facilities, an excellent tradition of development projects geared to promoting Sport for All and a relatively knowledgeable population aware of the opportunities to participate. However, many of the participants now appear to want to improve, to move onto the performance ladder and it is clear that this desire to improve at the chosen sport will continue. This will have a significant influence on the type and level of provision of facilities and the ways in which the sports development service is provided. Most significantly of all, in the 1990s there will be an increased focus on giving more opportunities to improve by providing more and better leadership and coaching - at all levels.

6

I started with an anecdote and I'll finish with one. For some people sport is an art, for others a science. Other still confer a religious-like status upon it - so it is perhaps appropriate that this story concerns the Pope.

Several years ago, you will recall, the Pontiff visited our shores as part (it seemed at the time) of a never-ending world tour. When the tour was being planned, Kenny Dalglish was despatched to the Vatican to persuade the Pope to go to Liverpool. One Great Man granted the other Great Man an audience, listened carefully to the arguments and mused for a moment or two. Finally, he stated, 'No, Mr Dalglish I cannot come to Liverpool. I don't want to spend two years in the reserves!'

I think an apocryphal story !! But, like the Pope, we all know that the planning and preparation that goes on in the famous Anfield Boot Room is the key to Liverpool's almost unchallenged domination of the Football League over the past 20 years. Their success has not been achieved by chance or by the fortuitous coming together at one point in time of a bunch of gifted footballers. At Liverpool, players are taught to play in the Liverpool way, to acknowledge that the team is the thing, that there is a corporate tradition to be maintained. It is a lesson that we would be foolish not to learn from.

The drive for excellence is the joint responsibility of a multi-agency partnership whose members include schools, local authorities, clubs, Governing Bodies of sport and private sector interests. The Sports Council is committed to working in concert with these agencies to identify and nurture talented performers; to improve and extend the provision of national facilities; to increase the accessibility of crucial back-up services such as sports science and sports medicine; and to stimulate the development of coaching along properly professional lines. We have already produced detailed guidelines for national sports bodies on development planning and are offering financial incentives to enable many of them to make greater use of the unique facilities offered at our National Centres.

By promoting a corporate approach to sports development, the Sports Council aims to encourage a shared understanding of the role that different interests can play in the effort to get our sportsmen and women on the winning path.

THE DISINTEGRATION OF SPORT

K. ROBERTS
University of Liverpool

1   Introduction

Sport is breaking up. Top sport, amateur club sport and mass participation are losing their former inter-dependence in terms of personnel, organization, finance and ideology. This means that sport's several layers have ceased to be mutually supporting. What strengthens one no longer necessarily benefits the others. This does not mean that sport must decline. All the layers may flourish in the future. It is simply that current trends are undermining the bonds and culture of an older, more integrated world of sport.

2   The classical model

Modern sport is a nineteenth century invention and Britain was the main birthplace. Of course, sport has a much longer history. All known societies have possessed games based on the still primary sport activities of running, throwing and swimming. However, during the nineteenth century the rules of older sports were redrafted, and new sports were invented with rules of play consistent with the rhythms and values of industrial life. Some writers regard the rise of modern sports as part of a broader civilizing process.

The main agents responsible for drafting the new rules of play, then governing and popularizing modern sports, were voluntary associations which were created by English gentlemen. Sport was not pioneered primarily as a commercial enterprise for profit. It was neither under the direct control of, nor did it receive much patronage from, the state in its early years. The new sports were played and governed principally by amateurs. They did it for the love of sport, or so they said. This ethic was enshrined in the modern Olympic movement whose founders (wrongly) believed that the ancient Greeks had similar ideals.

Ever since the late nineteenth century most competitive sport has been amateur club sport. Commerce has penetrated sport in all market economies, particularly in North America. Governments have also become more involved, especially in socialist societies. Nevertheless, sport has carried the ethos of amateur club organization into every country to which the games have spread. Everywhere most sport has been played and organized by amateurs as a leisure activity. Their achievements discredit the notion that only financial incentives will induce people to push themselves to their limits.

Historically, elite sport grew out of amateur club sport. The most skilled and successful players progressed to national and international arenas. Whenever top players could command pay for their performances there was invariably some tension with the amateur grassroots, but often more so with amateur governing bodies. Sometimes professional clubs and leagues declared independence, but even then amateur sport remained their main source of players. Elite performers set the standards at which amateurs aimed, and reached usually only in daydreams. The top players were better by definition, but they did not necessarily move in entirely different sporting worlds from amateur competitors. Most amateur clubs would have had former players who had 'made it', and at any time there would be hopefuls who were on the fringes of the big time. The rise of top sport, therefore, did not automatically undermine the 'backbone' position of the amateur club. These clubs had links with the sporting elite, and with casual players.

Much sport-play has always been unorganized. Informal games in parks and streets are older than, and did not disappear with the rise of modern sports. Rather, the new games were adopted in casual play. Streets and parks became the places where children and young people could develop the skills with which to become competent players for school teams and other clubs.

This meant that all the different layers of sport were mutually supporting. It could be argued that the larger the pool of casual players, the healthier would be the condition of club sport, and that the larger the pool of amateur club players, the stronger would elite sport become. Elite players and teams generated mass interest and inspired novices. Mass interest and experience of playing the games created a knowledgeable audience for elite sport. What was good for any level could normally be relied on to benefit the others. There was a sufficiently integrated sport system for politicians, businessfolk or whoever to be pro-sport, and for everyone to understand what this meant. Whichever branch or level was supported directly, the entire sport system could be appreciative. In this sense the sports world was a real community in which all participants, players and officials, whatever their levels, shared common purposes and interests.

3   Contradictions

A sign that things have changed and that the classical model no longer works in its traditional way is the difficulty that now confronts anyone trying to select or interpret indicators of sport's condition. It is unsurprising that recent trends in sport have differed from country to country. It is less expected, and certainly would not be predicted from the classical model, that there should often be contradictory evidence of trends within countries (see Kamphorst and Roberts, 1989).

How healthy a country's sport appears nowadays can depend on which indicators are inspected. In terms of international success a country's sport may be ascending, but today it is unwise to infer that there will be a parallel upward trend in mass participation. Growth in the proportion of people playing sport sometimes co-exists with a decline in club membership. The apparent health of sport can vary dramatically depending on the indicators inspected - spending on sport goods and services, numbers playing, Olympic medals, or club membership for instance. The underlying reason for the indicators often pointing in different directions is that the classical model is breaking up with sport's several layers becoming increasingly independent.

4   Top Sport

The principal cause of top sport's separation is media coverage, especially by television. Most spectators now watch sport 'on the box'. The world-wide viewing audience for one major soccer fixture can exceed an entire season's attendances at Football League matches. Sports such as snooker and indoor bowls have been able to command massive television audiences the vast majority of whom have never attended live events let alone played the sports.

Television coverage multiplies the earning power of top sport. The fees paid by television companies are only the beginning of this story. Advertisers will pay handsomely to link their names with well-publicised events and performers. Needless to say, it is only the elite performers and events, those covered regularly by television, that have this attraction which sets them apart from run of-the-mill games and players.

Top performers invariably seek maximum control over their earnings. They also have vested financial interests in controlling the timing and organization of events, and in making their own deals with the media and other sponsors. They may or may not wish to tamper with the actual rules of play to shape their sports to the needs of the media and advertisers. Traditional amateur governing bodies may remain in nominal control, but only by respecting the elite's wishes and interests. This frequently involves some imaginative rule-stretching, to allow top athletes to remain officially amateur for example. There is also inevitable tension at governing body level between the interests of club players and the demands of the elite. One solution is for top sport to break away with its own governing organizations, as has happened in golf and tennis.

A related development has been the escalation of standards of play in top sport to levels that are far beyond the reach of most amateurs. Of course, the bulk of amateur players have never been able to compete with the best on level terms. The recent development has been for the threshold for admission to elite competition to rise beyond even extraordinary expectations in amateur play. Initially becoming an aspirant top performer nowadays can require years of dedication and training in which the sport is effectively a full-time occupation. It may be necessary to have special training and coaching from a very young age, and a consequence can be that future top players and amateurs hardly ever compete together. They may undergo entirely different processes of sport socialization, and recruitment to the ranks of elite performers therefore becomes independent of amateur club sport. Above-average club athletes in Britain compete for places in Olympic teams, but usually with no hope of winning in such international contests or even of becoming regular high earners at televised Grand Prix events.

Governments have encouraged and subsidized both amateur and top sport, but for rather different reasons. Their interest in the latter is linked with national identity and pride, and international prestige. It used to be argued that the best way to improve a nation's top performers was to widen the pool of amateur talent. The more people initially brought into and retained in sport, the argument ran, the larger and more talented would be the pools from which to draw elite players. However, country after country and government after government have discovered that it is possible nowadays to develop national elite squads to match the world's best without a broad base of mass participation in amateur sport. This reinforces top sport's independence and separation. It no longer needs amateur roots. Money and players can be drawn directly into the elite, just as mass audiences for top events can be attracted without other teams, players and fixtures generating any significant spectator interest.

There are senses in which contemporary top sport has less in common with amateur clubs and players than with other branches of mass entertainment - films, television, music and publishing for example. Top sport's organizations and organizers need connection with, and skills common to, other branches of mass entertainment. The scheduling and presentation of top sport events has to be shaped more by the logic of the broader entertainment business than the traditions of specific games. Elite players share levels of income and lifestyles with other media stars. The top professionals in sport are no longer paid just ordinary wages, much the same amounts as players in amateur clubs earn in their own paid occupations. The elite's incomes set them in a class apart from other players and merge them into the broader ranks of top entertainers.

Of course, there are still events that bring top performers and other players together. The annual London Marathon attracts top athletes, club runners and fun runners. Needless to say, they are not really competing against each other, and the event has several layers of organization. It is partly top sport, partly a festival and tourist attraction, but also an event in club calendars and in the lifestyles of many unorganized athletes.

5   Sport for all

While top sport has been captured by the entertainment industry, mass participation has also been breaking away from sport federations, leagues and clubs. There are two main sources of this trend. Firstly, facilities have been built that enable unorganized members of the public to take noncompetitive exercise and to play competitive games such as squash and badminton without joining clubs. It used to be the case that young people were introduced to team sports at school, then, if they wished to play subsequently, it was necessary to join a club that had facilities of its own or rented space in someone else's premises. Today, however, the spread of genuinely public sports centres has multiplied opportunities for casual play. Casual sport is no longer confined to streets and parks. Rather, the casual player can command first-class facilities. Any group can organize a squash ladder, badminton contest or football match with six, five, four or three per side and book top class accommodation. There is simply no need to join a club that is affiliated to a sports federation. Sport has become another literally do-it-yourself activity.

The second source of this development has been the rise in standards of living and the spread of consumerism which have enabled and encouraged more people to purchase the clothing and equipment needed to ski, surf, run for fun, train with or without weights, and play court games. Proper sport equipment used to be the almost exclusive property of proper clubs. Nowadays most equipment is owned by private individuals.

Patterns of mass sport participation cannot be explained in terms of the rules of sports associations. The key to making sense of sport-for-all is to relate these activities to the participants' values and broader styles of life. In Britain in recent years casual sport participation has been absorbed into, and adopted by, sections of the population seeking generally health-promoting ways of life which regulate diets and alcohol consumption as well as daily or less frequent exercise (Roberts et al, 1990)

Unorganized players may or may not follow top sport. Their approach to exercise may be casual or serious. Some are highly committed and spend considerable sums on clothing and equipment. Owning and wearing the 'right' shoes and shirts, and using a branded racquet can allow everyday players to feel part of a sport world that includes international stars. Pop music fans derive similar sensations by adopting their stars' clothing and coiffure. Catering for mass sport participation has become big business. The sale of sports clothing and equipment are major elements in the present-day sports industry. Marketing exercise facilities can also be highly lucrative. The point is that all this is now possible without organized club sport winning even a slice of the action. Sport participation can rise while club membership declines. The commercial sports industry can be buoyant while sports clubs are in increasingly dire financial straits. Neither top sport nor the majority of everyday players any longer require the mediation and support of amateur associations.

6 Theoretical implications

Disintegration is not synonymous with decline. There may be a buoyant future for all levels of sport, but they are no longer so bound together and inter-dependent that trends in one necessarily pull or drag the others in its wake. Sport has become a less coherent entity, which means that the prospects for a coherent and specialized sport science are receding.

Every layer in present-day sport is best understood, in the first instance, as part of the broader, lateral social formation in which it is most firmly embedded. Club sport, therefore, and the trends therein, need to be examined and interpreted as one example of the broader category of voluntary leisure organizations. Casual sport participation needs to be set in the context of different groups of players' everyday lifestyles and distinctive value orientations. Top sport is best understood as part of the broader entertainment business. Each of these broader formations, in turn, can be related to the evolving macro-organization of contemporary society. The study of present-day sport diminishes its ability to understand its own subject matter by endeavouring to go independent. Trends in sport itself require that its analysis becomes more firmly integrated into the broader sciences of society.

7   References

Kamphorst, T.J. and Roberts, K. eds (1989), **Trends in Sport**, Giordano Bruno, Amersfoort, The Netherlands.

Roberts, K., Asturias, L., Campbell, R., Chadwick, C. and Brodie, D. A. (1990), Health and fitness consciousness and the lifestyles of adult sport participants, paper presented to conference on **The Future of Adult Life**, The Netherlands.

CENTRAL ISSUES IN CHILDREN'S PLAY

KATE STEPHENS
National Children's Play and Recreation Unit, London

1   Introduction

Extreme playfulness and humour are conspicuous in dolphins and may be found in whales also, although they are harder to observe. Despite its low status in puritanical value systems, play is a hallmark of intelligence and is indispensable for creativity and flexibility. Its marked development in Cetaceans makes it likely that they will frolic with their minds as much as with their bodies. (Taken from an American article on comparative behaviour in Cetaceans)

I start this presentation with two sizeable disadvantages: firstly, as you will have spotted - and as our Chairperson, Sue Glyptis has already explained - I am **not** Mike Nussbaum, who was expecting to make this presentation. Secondly, unlike my colleagues on the platform, I am going to address you on a subject on which **everyone** is an expert. However unlikely it may seem, all of us here today were once children, all of us have played - some of us still do!

Think back to your own childhood to how and where you played, to favourite games and treasured toys, to the rich landscape of childhood, where play was at the centre.

In this paper I will do some scene setting with a brief glance at how we respond to the word 'play', I will explore the way that provision for children's play is organized - or perhaps more appropriately in this century disorganized, then raise some questions about what it is we want for our children and finally, by looking at the work of the NCPRU, set some goals for the year 2000.

2   Scene Setting

First of all some facts and figures. Children under 15 make up 20% of the population. For the average 7 year old 37% of waking hours is spent at play in one form or another. By contrast less than a third of a child's year is spent in school - a statistic that sometimes surprises.

Contrary to general opinion children's play is not restricted to designated play areas. Children play anywhere and everywhere. They do it all day long, and it is their principal means of assimilating the world around them and of finding their own place within it.

Broadly speaking we have developed three sets of arenas for play:

(a)   the home;
(b)   the context where play is peripheral to some other activity, e.g., garden centres, hyperstores and the long string of waiting rooms of every ilk; and
(c)   the context that is play dedicated. And this last category in itself covers a wide range of settings.

Play happens in playgrounds, play centres, playschemes in schools, other buildings, open spaces, hospitals, residential settings, commercial settings, in shops, in theme parks, on adventure holidays, in private/domestic settings, in childcare settings (workplace facilities or otherwise). Play opportunities are provided by:

(a)   Local Authorities: at County, District and parish level and often across a staggering number of departments,
(b)   Voluntary Organizations: big and small from Save the Children to the 5 parents running the neighbourhood play scheme, and
(c)   of course increasingly by the Private Sector, yet funding is patchy, complex and thin on the ground and policy co-ordination often conspicuous by its absence.

At Central Government level alone there are numerous Ministries with a finger in the pie:

(a)   the Department of the Environment,
(b)   the Department of Health,
(c)   the Department of Education & Science,
(d)   the Home Office,
(e)   the Department of Trade & Industry,
(f)   the Department of Employment,
(g)   the Cabinet Office

and even the Ministry of Defence, where they are responsible for 1,200 playgrounds, and an enormous number of service family children.

Yet play, and the business of working with children - 'playwork', are not always recognized as central even to all the settings I have already mentioned. As a result, play people, if they want to follow a career, are not well paid, do not have access to training (whether they are paid or voluntary staff), have no qualification framework, are not recognized as 'professional' in their work and, compared with parallel professions such as youth work, teaching or social work, they have no status. Part of the reason for this is the extraordinarily low value we place on the word 'play'.

Let us pause on that for a moment and just think of the throwaway, derogatory manner in which we use 'play'. Here are a handful of phrases - Play nicely!, go away and play!, you're playing me up!, it's child's play! and play down that noise!

Yet play is serious -

(a)   if it's for adults (think how much we spend on leisure centres alone!),
(b)   if it's called education with measurable educational outputs,
(c)   if it's called therapy,
(d)   if it's a strategy in preventing riots and hooliganism, and if it diverts criminal tendencies.

Why then can play not be taken seriously in its own right as the cornerstone of our whole childhood experience? Why is it that we continue to apologize for its very existence by disguising it under other apparently 'worthier' titles? We call it 'childcare', 'supervised activity', 'day care', 'recreational activities', 'creche provision'. Maybe all that is meaningful for adults, but to children **it is all play**.

In the adult mind play is juxtaposed to work; the right to play is an added extra - a bonus, earned as a reward for earnest work-worthy endeavours. For the child, play and work are the same things - its chief characteristic is that it is fun. In short, adults find 'play' a very difficult word to handle. And if adults find play difficult to handle then bureaucracies (the epitome of adult-centred constructions) find it almost impossible. They are confused and bemused and they relegate it to the bottom of the pile. I've already spoken about Central Government, but let me just give you one example of conflicting and inconsistent attitudes to play within a single department.

In the report of 1985, entitled 'Better Schools', the Department of Education and Science (DES) clearly states that: 'the education of children is founded in play'. In October 1989 at the instigation of Mrs Angela Rumbold, the DES wrote to all local authorities re-enforcing the importance of play, by encouraging them to make schools' premises available for child care and children's activities out of school hours. And yet in March of this year, in response to the Unit's expression of concern that in the two years since its foundation the DES had never managed to attend any of its Management Committee meetings, an official in the Department wrote:

> In fact, looking at recent papers. . .there is very little which actually impacts on this Department. . . .Neither I, nor my predecessor see a major role for us in the work of this Committee. . . (Letter dated March 7th)

Now if the Department of Education and Science find it difficult to establish a coherent approach to play, how much more difficult is it for other departments whose work is less directly concerned with children?

At local government level the picture is, if anything, even more confused - 17 departments or sub-departments dealing with play provision: housing, leisure, education, social services, community relations, planning, engineers and in some local authorities even graves and cemeteries!

And while we adults are making such a pig's ear of our response to play needs, radical changes are happening in our children's lives.

A year ago, I completed a research study on patterns of play in one local authority in the South East. It was not a deprived area, either in income terms or in environmental terms. It had no high rise blocks and one-third of the total area was open space, so in principle children should have had plenty of play opportunities. But, what we found in fact was that children's lives were becoming more and more restricted. The increase in traffic limited the distance they can safely travel from home; poor housing design meant that there was little easily accessible play space; they weren't allowed to go to the park alone, and if they did, it was often only to find that all the play equipment had been removed because local authorities couldn't afford the cost of impact absorbing surfaces; there was virtually no provision of safe supervised activities for children; school-based after-school activity groups (chess club, netball, football, etc.) had almost disappeared following the teacher's strike of three years ago, and of course the current pressure on teachers in preparation for the advent of the National Curriculum; changing patterns in parents' lives meant that there was little shared play between adults and children during the working week; and finally, parents anxieties for their children's personal safety meant that even 9 and 10 year olds were not allowed out after school.

For most children the play environment meant the confines of their bedroom, and their play companions were the television and the computer. How long, I wonder, before we produce the totally plug-in child with only second-hand experiences to draw on and to signpost their way towards adulthood. As one child said to us: 'Even the dogs round here have more fun than we do!'

For much of their lives our children find themselves in situations that are simply not geared to their needs. Just imagine yourself as the average six year old, what does the world look like? Look at how we plan housing areas, what is it like to live in a flat on the 14th floor or to be hemmed in by traffic? Look as the size of things and everywhere evidence of your unwelcomeness from the 'Keep off the grass' sign. What is it like to spend Saturday mornings in that greatest of British leisure pursuits in the weekend shop either with your bottom squeezed into the shopping trolley or in the supermarket creche that advertizes itself as 'Room to park the car and the kids!' What messages are we giving to our children?

No, planning for children has to offer something more qualitative than merely car-parking for kids and it is vital that in planning for children's play environments we are clear about what we want. Firstly it should be a child-centred environment, not an adult one - a learning space and a caring place. It should provide easy access to a range of stimulating activities and experiences, water and paint, sand and clay, construction activities and destruction activities, imaginative play, co-ordinative play, physical play and access to the natural environment. It should be close to home, so that you can grow up with your neighbourhood pals. It should be a place where children participate in creating the environment and in being responsible for it. A place where children are encouraged to explore and experiment, and to participate in making decisions. A place where co-operation, sharing and learning to give and take have a central role. It should be a place where everyone feels accepted in their own right, and has equal access to all that is on offer. It will have large spaces for noisy big group games and smaller spaces for quiet times or for playing in two or threes or even on your own. It will have a rich seam of stimulating play materials, from assorted junk to sophisticated equipment, toys and games, books and puzzles - everything to respond to the ever-changing agenda of childhood enquiry. And most of all, it will have the one toy with most play value of all - it's one that no manufacturer has yet managed to put into production - the support and interaction of skilled and interested playful adults.

3   The National Children's Play and Recreation Unit and its Work

I have already said that children make up 20% of the population. If you are 5 now you will be 15 by the year 2000.   If you are 10 you will be 20 - and the rest of us will be getting on some. You will inherit not just the decade, not even the century, but the millennium. What we do now will influence the way our children shape that new millennium, and if our society is not child-friendly, if it is negligent of their needs, what kind of world will they create? This is where all of us here today have a central role to play. The National Children's Play and Recreation Unit is funded through the Department of the Environment to develop a national framework for children's play. Everything we are doing is designed to create a national picture that cuts through the confusion and brings together an **HOLISTIC** approach to children. Our work centres on 4 main areas:

Awareness where we are working in various contexts to emphasize the need to 'think child', - in the media, at conferences, through the local authority associations where we are setting up a range of demonstration projects, with individual authorities helping them in planning for children across departments, and with central government to make links for them where ministries are coming at common issues from different perspectives.

Legislation Here we are working to clarify the implications of major pieces of legislation for children and children's play, not just the Children Act, but the Education Reform Act (Local Management of Schools), the Local Government Act (Compulsory Competitive Tendering), the Broadcasting Bill, the Community Care & Health Service Bill as well as working on strategic reports such as Sport and the Inner City and the Wilding Report on the Arts. In fact we are pressing for a Working Group on Children's Issues (comparable to the Ministerial Group on Women's Issues which has received so much attention in the media recently), and with a Cabinet ranking minister to lead its work.

Training and Education where as part of its strategic role the Unit is working to produce a National Framework for Training Education and Qualification (which will provide a training structure for everyone from parents and volunteers to full-time career play staff). Key to this work is the development of a network of National Centres to act as a focus for training in play, not just for play staff but also for a range of parallel professions for whom play is an important part of their work.

Resources We are working both directly and indirectly to develop the resources for children's play. Directly, through the work of the National Play Information Centre, which is based at our offices in the Euston Road and which houses a unique collection of play literature and documentation, and associated with that through our publications on Good Practice, such as the 'Safety Guidelines on Playground Planning and Design', which we have been commissioned to write for the Department of the Environment, and our study on 'In-Service Training of Play Staff'; and indirectly by working with local authorities to encourage planning across departments to enact legislation that considers children not as an adjunct - a scaled down version of the adult population - but as a group of people in their own right. It is our belief that this approach together with a growing recognition of the value of play work will enable existing resources to be deployed in more effective ways and ultimately deliver a better quality of experience to children.

Now you may have spotted that these key areas of:

A -WARENESS
L -EGISLATION
T -RAINING and
E -DUCATION
R -ESOURCE

give us a useful mnemonic - ALTER - and that is exactly what we plan to do. But the Unit cannot do it alone. The Unit already has a clear commitment to working in partnership with the statutory, voluntary and commercial sectors, and we are working to broaden that constituency by, among other things, speaking at conferences such as this. I hope that over the next four years we will establish a strong and dynamic focus on children and their need for play. I hope that it will be as articulate as the Arts lobby, as vigorous as the Sports lobby and yet have an energy and commitment that is all its own; so that well before we get to the end of the century it will be evident that together we have substantially enriched the play experience of our young people, and substantially altered the agenda for children.

It was George Bernard Shaw who said:

We don't stop playing because we grow old; we grow old because we stop playing.

I hope we can all look forward to a long and very playful future.

SPORT AND LEISURE CHANGES AND CHALLENGES: ACTIVE LIFESTYLES - FROM SCHOOL TO COMMUNITY

ROBERT. M.E. LAVENTURE
Coventry Education Department

1   Introduction

This paper presents an overview of the work of teachers in the City of Coventry in addressing the post school participation of young people in sport and recreation.

In the 1980's, in its work to promote the philosophy of Sport for All, the Sports Council mounted a series of 13 demonstration, action research projects, working with a range of new partners and organizations to encourage greater co-operation in promoting mass participation at all levels and particularly amongst non participant groups.

Active Life Styles is one such demonstration project and a partnership between the Sports Council and the City of Coventry Education Committee. Its aim was to address the issues surrounding post school participation in sport and recreation in the 13-24 age range, and in particular to focus upon the role of physical education and teachers in selected secondary schools (11-18) using an action research style of work.

2   The starting point

The work of the project had its philosophical roots in

(a)   the need to re-examine the relevance of the concept of 'the gap' as identified by Wolfenden (1960);

(b)   the relevance of the concept of Sport for All to the aims and objectives of the physical education curriculum;

(c)   the beliefs of physical education teachers in Coventry as articulated in **Physical Education for Life**: (Coventry LEA, 1984) a policy document for the development of Physical Education, which amongst other things, identified the need to prepare school leavers for the transition from physical education and school based participation to community based forms of sport and recreation activity.

Our philosophy is summed up in the question:- What will young people take with them from school into society?

Answer:- The desire to remain active throughout life. More specifically - what will any young person do with their PE kit and sports equipment once they leave school? Does it go in the rubbish bin for good? Such a philosophy has been met certainly in Coventry by an increase in the community provision for young people, in the form of the growth of sports and leisure facilities, the growth of sports development officers attached to the governing bodies of sports with a brief to work with young people, and by the appointment of youth liaison officers within sports clubs and centres providing an identifiable point of contact in the community for students and teachers alike.

3   Methods of Working

The following methods of working were adopted by the project.

The use of two project staff, one a physical education teacher with a specific brief to work with teachers, and a leisure co-ordinator employed to work with the local sporting community, to assist teachers and others to develop new methods of working with the 13-24 age range and specifically the later years of secondary schooling.

The work was supported by joint funding from the Sports Council and the Coventry City Council which included resources for equipment, transport, facility hire and staff development including inservice training for teachers. Additionally the Sports Council is undertaking a long term monitoring and evaluation programme, jointly agreed by both partners.

Four secondary schools were chosen on the basis of their collectively representing a socio-economic cross section of the city as well as having physical education departments with stable staffing situations and an open mindedness and willingness to work in new ways.

The project adopted three long term strategies:

(a)   to examine curriculum developments in the form of a relevant curriculum in physical education in the 14-16 age range in relation to the adoption of an **Active Life Style** as a means of promoting life long participation in sporting and recreative activity;

(b)   to examine and develop the nature of school to community links to enable school leavers to continue such participation beyond compulsory schooling;

(c)   to act as a catalyst amongst the local sporting community in encouraging, promoting and developing opportunities for young people.

Individually, these three concepts are an increasing feature of work throughout the country, but it was the opportunity to work in all three phases under the one structure that has given the project a unique flavour if also a distinct advantage.

4   A Relevant Curriculum

In order to develop a more relevant curriculum (Coventry, 1985), the project enabled teachers to develop styles of work some of which are a feature of other presentations at this conference - those of health related fitness and health related activity.

However, in addition to teaching the knowledge, skills and understanding required to develop an awareness of the functions of the body during activity, the effects of exercise, planning exercise programmes has been developed in the context of young people acquiring the skills and confidences required for them to join aerobics classes and similar user groups in local centres and facilities, or to develop their own groups and opportunities.

Education for Active Leisure is another focus of curriculum development. As a city, Coventry is well resourced with sports centres both multi-purpose and sports specific. Our research confirmed that of Stevens (1985) in that knowledge of such centres amongst school leavers was poor.

But more importantly the barriers identified by young people themselves included a host of issues and perceptions as yet unconsidered.

How much will it cost?
What should I wear?
Will I feel silly?
Can I book in advance?
Am I good enough?
How do I find out?

Collectively these questions and others formed the basis of young people's reservations and hesitancy concerning sports participation and for many non-users, could be considered almost as a form of intimidation.

The concept of Education for Active Leisure took the form of planned visits to a variety of sports and leisure centres, hereby giving young people the opportunity to find out about facilities and programmes, meet staff and take part in activities in what is considered to be the adult leisure environment.

5   School to Community Links

The development of School to Community links (Laventure, 1987), between the physical education curriculum and the local sporting community, has enabled teachers to maximize the use of local resources, people, activities, facilities and expertise. These developments have been seen as part of a two way process - in and out of school; pupils in school have the opportunity to work with local sports coaches and club personnel who visit schools; similarly schools have the opportunity to make use of local sports facilities and activities that would not otherwise be available to pupils and teachers, both on and off the school site.

Such methods of working will raise questions of curriculum breadth and the supermarket approach to activity. However such strategies have been developed with the express purpose of introducing young people to activities and venues to which they may reasonably gain access in the future. By such processes we hope that these young people will become active participants in the future.

5.1 *Providing Information*

Underpinning much of this work was the critical need to provide a variety of forms of information for students, teachers and sports clubs. Our research told us that young people were ignorant of many opportunities. Consequently teachers devised a number of methods of 'finding out', providing opportunities for enquiry and information including maps of local facilities and school leavers' pocket books with discount vouchers for introductory activities. A data base for schools with up to date sports and recreation information was placed in school libraries, physical education departments and pastoral bases. Such information was also vital for teachers in addition to the value of such work to local clubs and centres.

The models illustrated so far are based upon preparing young people to move into adult organized activities. For many this is appropriate, but not always. A group of school leavers wanted to play cricket together, but for a number of reasons, including in this case racism, the local clubs structures were inappropriate. Consequently a style of work has been adopted that encourages school leavers to set up their own sports and activity groups that are not adult organized. This process can be very difficult for young people and we are all aware of the number of problems and issues that any such group faces in organizing their own activities.

But given appropriate help and support and access to the sorts of information that adults take for granted this group of young people has operated now for four years, runs two cricket teams and holds an annual presentation dinner. The model has been adopted for other sports such as basketball, volleyball, table tennis and soccer although we would recognize certain sports and activities where this would be inappropriate. It has also been successful in the formation of health related activity groups - jogging, weights, multigym, aerobics and jazz dance.

6   Issues arising - What have we learned?

From six years of action research development in Coventry, a number of significant issues have arisen, critical to the ongoing progress of the Active Life Styles Project.

6.1 *Progress through partnership*
It is clear that a significant amount of what has been achieved has depended upon the establishment of new forms of partnership between the education world (in the form of teachers and students) and the local sporting community. The interaction and co-operation between schools, local sports clubs, sports centres and the governing bodies forms part of a new agenda in the development of youth sports participation. School Sport Forum (1988)

6.2 *Local strategies and structures*
The successful partnerships which benefit young people, must recognize the uniqueness of local sporting structures, organizations and controlling bodies. Strategies for specific sport will also reflect particular strengths and weakness and be built upon opportunities identified according to need and resource.

6.3 *The local sporting network*
The sorts of information, knowledge and interaction required for this style of work makes considerable demands upon teachers and others. Teachers must feel that they have a role to play and are contributing to a local sports development network.

6.4 *The role of the teacher*

All of these developments described and much more have had a considerable impact upon the role of any teacher who adopts this style of work with obvious implications for inservice and initial teacher training.

7   Monitoring and Evaluation

Previous well documented research had pointed to the evidence of non participation in sport and recreation by school leavers. A more specific research base was felt desirable in terms of issues and trends relating to young people in Coventry. A survey of 1500 school leavers from the four original project schools Coventry LEA (1988) was undertaken, which examined amongst others, the following areas.

(a) Pupils' attitude to leisure and spare time.
(b) Pupils' knowledge of sports and leisure facilities, both in the school catchment area and the City.
(c) Pupils' reflections on their PE careers, and the programme of activities offered.
(d) Significant influences that might have affected their participation, including methods of introduction and parental involvement.
(e) Pupils' future intentions and aspirations with regard to their sporting interests.

In addition individual schools conducted their own surveys. Such a database with over half a million individual responses had been used in two ways:-

(a) As a diagnostic tool of research. The responses to the survey work indicated here, were disseminated to schools so that the information could be used to inform and affect school practice.
Two examples.
 (i) the method of off site visits to centres and providing information were developed as a response to student knowledge and awareness of opportunities in sports centres.
 (ii) the use of teachers to introduce pupils to local centres and activities was a result of the finding that to date, teachers had played little part in this process of introduction to sport and recreation.
(b) It has been used as a means of comparison with follow up surveys in longitudinal research to compare different cohorts of the school population, in addition to following up on previous pupils and their expressed intentions and aspirations. This research was carried out by the Sports Council research and evaluation team. (Sports Council, 1990)

8   Significant outcomes

As a result of the independent monitoring and evaluation of the Active Life Styles project, the following have been identified as significant outcomes of the project's work.

8.1 *Cross-curricular links*

Such work has enabled PE to greatly impact upon the whole curriculum. There has been the opportunity to develop cross curricular links with other aspects of leisure education in personal development programmes, health education and information technology and provide teachers with confidence in looking forward to the New National Curriculum.

8.2 *Health Related Fitness*

Research indicates that Health Related Fitness has had a significant impact upon casual and informal participation in health related activities by young people.

8.3 *Off site visits*

Through an ongoing monitoring process there is evidence that independent follow up visits to sports centres by young people have continued post school.

8.4 *Future Intentions*

73% of students are reported to be leaving school with intentions of continuing in sport and recreational activities. Two years on those aspirations have been translated into practice.

8.5 *Multi sport*

The nature of post school participation is very much one of involvement in many sports and activities at a variety of levels of ability. Evidence reports participation in 3, 4 or more different sports activities and single sports careers are very much in a minority.

8.6 *Long term partnerships*

Those partnerships developed between education and the local sporting community are continuing to be a significant feature of the local sporting scene. Many are now established as the long term *modus operandi* throughout the City of Coventry.

9   Ongoing Development

Like all action research projects, development is ongoing, but the following summarizes a number of issues that are still to be addressed in full.

(a) Can the local sporting community cope with the demands placed upon it by such work? Has it the resources to devote to such development?

(b) The multi-sport phenomenon and young peoples' ability to transfer from one activity to another needs further investigation. We need to examine more closely what sort of physical education curriculum can accommodate and assist this process.

(c) The assumption that transfer to post or out of school sports participation best occurs at the end of a school career. Such transfer is more successful when related to the nature of the activity, the type of provision available and the developmental needs of the participants.

(d) Youth participation both in schools and out of school must be perceived in the context of the sports development model proposed by Campbell (1990) which considers the concepts of foundation, participation, performance and excellence. The level of performance and motivation are critical features of sustained sports participation.

10 Conclusion

As an action research project, Active Life Styles will soon be drawing to its end. Some valuable lessons have been learned supported by a considerable research base of evidence. The project is now embarking upon a dissemination phase whereby such information and examples of practice will become available to a broader audience. In Coventry, there is an intention and will to continue such working amongst all secondary schools within the context of the National Curriculum in physical education which will begin in 1992, thus continuing to implement the philosophy of promoting an Active Life Style.

11 References

Campbell (1990) Sports Development. Unpublished paper given to Coventry Sports Development Group.

Coventry L.E.A. (1984) **Physical Education for Life**, Coventry L.E.A.

Coventry (1985) **Towards a relevant curriculum**. Conference Proceedings. Coventry L.E.A.

Davies, R. (1988) Information and an Active Life Style. **British Journal of Physical Education** Vol. 10 No. 4.

Laventure, R.M.E. (1987) Linking School to Community. **British Journal of Physical Education** Vol. 16 No. 4.

School Sport Forum (1988) **Sport and Young People: Partnership and Action** . The Sports Council London.

Sports Council (1990) **Active Life Styles**. Monitoring Report. The Sports Council Research Unit, Manchester.

Stevens, J.E.R. (1985) Developing post School participation in Sport and recreation. **British Journal of Physical Education**. Vol. 16 No. 4.

Wollfenden (1960) **Sport and the Community**. The report of the Wollfenden Committee. C.C.P.R. London.

Coventry L.E.A. (1986) School leavers' Life Styles and Sports participation. Unpublished survey. The Sports Council Research Unit. Manchester.

LEISURE, THE LOCAL STATE AND THE CHANGING ECONOMY IN BRITAIN

I. HENRY[1] AND P. BRAMHAM[2]
[1] *Department of of Physical Education and Sports Science, Loughborough University*
[2] *Faculty of Cultural and Educational Studies, Leeds Polytechnic*

1   Introduction

The aim of this paper is to identify the nature of the strategic options facing local government in the 1990s in terms of leisure policy. In the context of British politics in the 1980s local governments in the major metropolitan areas have been predominantly Labour controlled. Such local authorities have operated in tension with, sometimes in opposition to, and occasionally in partnership with, Conservative controlled central governments. This paper will define three types of policy strategy open to local government and the problems which such strategies pose for the political left in local government.

Perhaps the most powerful explanatory framework to emerge in the recent work in urban political economy follows the development of arguments derived from the 'regulation school' of political economy (Aglietta 1979, Boyer 1986, Lipietz 1987) which identifies the nature of regimes of capital accumulation and their associated methods of regulation, tracing shifts from 'Fordism' to 'Post-Fordism' or flexible accumulation. This theoretical project seeks to avoid both functionalist and structuralist weaknesses of earlier Marxist accounts of political economy (Jessop 1988) since the establishment of new forms of capital accumulation do not take place without the contingent efforts of political actors to establish an environment which will foster new methods of accumulation. The impact of changes in mode of accumulation and method of regulation on urban leisure politics will therefore be central to the concerns of this paper and to the choice of policies available to the local state.

The first section introduces the central arguments of the regulation school and its distinction between Fordist and Post-Fordist accumulation regimes and their distinctive consequences for leisure policy. The second section will deal with the failure of the economy in the 1970s, the breakdown of political consensus within and between parties, and the implications for leisure policy of the reemergence of ideology. The third section will focus on central-local relations in the 1980s, and in particular local socialist attempts (employing leisure policy) to resist the establishment of new hegemony by the New Right. Finally the paper outlines the consequences of attempts by central government to reshape local government in a post- Fordist image, and the new role of leisure policy implicit within such a scenario. In developing this line of argument the paper draws on work by Stoker (1989), Geddes (1989) and more specifically Gamble (1988) who have sought to identify the nature of political hegemony in Britain and its implications for both national and local state by reference to the role of Thatcherism in promoting a set of social and institutional relationships consistent with flexible accumulation or Post-Fordism.

2   Fordism, Social Democracy and Leisure Policy in Post-war Britain

Fordism is a currently popular, although fiercely contested, term used to describe the social democratic settlement achieved between capital and labour in the post-war period. The term sensitizes the reader to the central importance of the USA and its dominance of international finance and currency arrangements. It also characterizes a particular form of industrial organization, namely assembly-line techniques and thus a 'deskilled' work force. Economies of scale were achieved by standardisation of production and mass production. This was mirrored by mass consumption underwritten by increases in real wages and substantial national economic growth. Industrial labour, organized within unions, achieved real gains both in private standards of living but also in the 'social wage' sustained by public expenditure; the outcome witnessed a post-war settlement between labour and capital which can best be described as social democratic both in outlook and content. Although Taylorism and the deskilling thesis have been subject to intense intellectual and empirical scrutiny as regards its relevance to the UK, the role of the UK state in such Fordist economies was one of intervention to manage demand by Keynesian methods, the provision of an infra-structure to sustain production and improve productivity, and increasing collective consumption to ensure the compliance of both capital and labour in the system of Fordist production. The state's role in accommodating the interests of capital and labour was sustainable so long as economic growth provided the resources to undertake the role, and the legitimacy of the state was underpinned by the incorporation of the major interest groups into decision making on economic and social issues. The political discourse centred upon citizenship rights and the work of Marshall claimed that all citizens in advanced industrial societies had benefitted from the universal extention of legal, political and social rights which in their totality constituted the welfare state. The approach to leisure policy to date then had been what one might term 'traditional pluralism', that is that the market and voluntary sectors should predominantly provide for the public's needs except where externalities such as preservation of the environment, the 'cultural heritage', national sporting prestige, or of social stability might accrue. A 'reformist pluralism', bearing the hallmarks of a social democratic recognition of people's right to access to leisure opportunities for their own sake only began to emerge in the modernizing approach of the Wilson government of 1964-70 with its avowedly Fordist aims of developing industrial opportunities.

3   The Failure of Fordism, the Breakdown of Ideological Consensus and the Implications for Leisure

The problem for leisure of course was that at the very moment when it was being recognized as having a legitimate place in the scheme of social democracy, the mode of accumulation which had underpinned that hegemonic system was crumbling. Britain's economic performance had been deteriorating since the war and its ability to operate successfully in world markets was already severely compromised. A further cataclysmic set of events served to accelerate the exposure of the inadequacies of the Fordist regime of accumulation and the social democratic framework which supported it. The corporatism of the post war settlement became increasing fragile and appeared less relevant and serviceable to both capital and labour towards the end of the 1970s.

Fordism was underwritten in the post-war period by the US dollar, the value of which was tied to gold reserves. US military supremacy also provided a stable framework for world trade among the capitalist economies of the 'first' and 'third' worlds. However the US carried a considerable balance of trade deficit over an extended period, in part to finance its military supremacy with troops in Europe and Asia and defence hardware. This severely weakened the US economy. At the beginning of the 1970s it became clear that the financing of the US dollar's trade deficit by gold holdings was no longer viable and the US abandoned the policy. The value of the dollar which had been sustained at a falsely high position fell sharply, and American domestic demand was severely reduced. Given the size of the American domestic market there was an immediate negative impact on world trade. Currencies went onto the unprotected market and the value of sterling fell. In 1973-4 oil prices quadrupled accelerating the world recession, while Britain was also further affected by having to meet the costs of entry into the EEC. The cornerstone of social democratic economics, the Keynesian economic policy of demand management, no longer offered the opportunity to trade off inflation against unemployment. As the world recession deepened domestic demand management appeared powerless to alleviate either inflation or unemployment; both continued to grow alarmingly.

In such circumstances it is hardly surprising that the legitimacy of social democracy seemed bankrupt. The settlement between capital and organized labour seemed increasingly unfair to urban social movements and to those living in cities transformed by unemployment caused by shifting patterns of international trade. The welfare state was attacked by the Left for having failed to meet the needs of working class communities who generally received poorer quality education, poorer housing, were more likely to suffer ill health and were also less likely to benefit from public sector leisure investment. The state was increasingly drawn into dealing with policy issues which were generated by settlement of racial minorities in inner city areas, which historically constituted a reserve army of labour for unskilled and semiskilled work in both the public and private sectors of the UK economy. The women's movement was able to point to gender inequalities perpetuated within welfare services and black communities became more vociferous in reaction to the institutionalized racism inherent in the welfare system and elsewhere. However, the most successful attack came from the Right, which claimed that the economic ills of

Britain were largely the product of the overburdening of industry with high levels of taxation (Bacon and Eltis 1978), and that state subsidy produced inefficiency and reduced self reliance. The key features of social democracy, relatively full employment, a general increase in standard of living, and a broadening of social welfare programmes, were crumbling.

Throughout the nineteenth and twentieth centuries, the dominant political elite within the UK had managed to construct a substantial political consensus amongst the electorate behind existing political arrangements. Although industrial relations were often riven by industrial conflict and anomie over wage levels, industrial unrest never spilled over to undermine the existing political consensus. Stated briefly, the major political achievement of the dominant UK elite was to separate political and economic policy demands. Working class struggle and dissensus about economic affairs never were superimposed on political demands with the result that working class organizations and demands was accommodated within the existing and practically inevitable horizon of capitalism.

The two major means of mobilising consent in twentieth century parliamentary politics had been by popular vote and parliamentary leadership, or corporatist strategies of accommodation of interests within the machinery of government decision-making. In the 1970s, as Gamble (1988) points out, social democracy failed to realize either of these. The majorities gained by governments in the 1970s were thin, and the industrial strife which contributed to the demise of the Heath and Callaghan governments was considerable. Social democracy was faced with the problem of economic malaise spilling over to corrode the political legitimacy of the central state. Faced with disillusionment and disarray, politicians of all parties were starting to reassess Fordism in a changed international economy in the 1970s. Consensual politics was replaced by an authoritarian state strategy in which state imposed solutions to social, economic and political problems were developed. During this decade there was growing evidence of the racism embedded within state practices and within popular consciousness in civil society. One potent explanation for the crisis was to blame the black population for inner city decay, urban crime and high public welfare spending. The Labour government's imposition of spending limits in 1976, and the battles with public sector trade unions in the winter of discontent constituted elements of this authoritarian style. Particularly when the strategy was manifestly unsuccessful, the state's popularity inevitably weakened. The Right under the leadership of the new Tory Party leader, Margaret Thatcher, was able to appeal to an anti-collectivist, anti-statist, anti-social democratic disaffection when it came to develop an alternative project to social democracy (Gamble 1988).

4   Thatcherism as a Hegemonic Project, Post-Fordism, and the New Roles of Urban Leisure Policy in the 1990s

The fact that Fordism has been in crisis since the early 1970s does not of itself signify that developed economies will evolve a new Post-Fordist accumulation regime, and a new method of regulation to replace social democracy. Politico-economic systems develop their own trajectories influenced by the political, economic and ideological actors and historical alliances within those systems. Structuralist and postmodernist accounts provide powerful theoretical critiques of mainstream thinking in the social sciences but frequently fail to identify precisely the agents and social movements which are the carriers of these transformative cultural changes. Regulation theory represents an attempt to escape the notion that capitalism has a single inevitable logic of development. A simplistic theory of social change becomes impossible to sustain once nation states are conceptualized within a world economic system. Regulation theory also attempts to recast the traditional base-superstructure paradigm and acknowledges the centrality of human agency within social and political relations. Historical struggle and resistance over cultural forms within the state and civil society become more central in any further analysis.

Some writers, as Stoker (1989) points out, have explicitly rejected the notion that Britain has already moved into a Post-Fordist accumulation regime, suggesting that the continuities between the post 1970s and the dominantly Fordist period, are more significant than the contrasts. These writers prefer to refer to a Neo-Fordist accumulation regime. It is certainly the case that despite radical changes in the industrial structure of post-war Britain and of other industrialized nations, together with the loss of US economic hegemony, no new accumulation regime is as dominant as the Taylorist US post-war regime. The Japanese, West German and US economies therefore continue to strive for dominance (Lipietz 1987) and the development and restructuring of state socialist economies in Eastern Europe will play a crucial part.

Nevertheless despite the disputed nature of claims that Britain has moved into a Post-Fordist accumulation regime, there is good evidence (as Gamble, 1988 illustrates) to support the claim that Thatcherism constitutes a hegemonic project which has sought in the 1980s to establish elements of a new accumulation regime, in large part by establishing elements of a new method of regulation. Hegemony in Gramsci's terms relates to the struggle to provide moral and political leadership which usually resides in class dominance although his analysis acknowledges the fluidity of class alliances and the possibility of constructing active popular support outside the traditional lines of class. One of the sites on which historical alliances are fought relate to the division between the state and civil society. Gramsci's own work sensitizes the reader to the problematic of hegemony - the need for leadership to win the active popular support of civil society to provide the ideological bedrock for successful hegemonic leadership and political practice. Leisure has been one of the sites of ideological and economic activity on which the political leadership has lighted as a means of shifting the nature of accumulation and its legitimation.

A brief consideration of the main policy thrusts of the Conservative Governments since 1979 illustrates the nature of the attempts to dismantle Fordist structures and discredit their support amongst the electorate.. The government abandoned the corporatist practices of its predecessors, which had been a key feature of the political compromises underpinning Fordist regulation. The monetarist attacks on welfare spending sought to reduce spending on services such as health and education, and though public spending in revenue terms was not significantly reduced these attempts were seen as consistent with the aim of dismantling the apparatus of the welfare state. A major deliverer of welfare services, local government was also subject to intense pressure by central government.

By tackling one of the cornerstones of collectivism, the power of the trade unions, the government has sought to sweep away a major barrier to the restructuring of accumulation. Thus it has introduced legislation to require ballots for strike action, to limit numbers of pickets, to prevent secondary picketing, to require union leaders to subject themselves to regular elections, and to require authority from the membership via a ballot for the use of union funds for support of political parties. In addition the government successfully took on public sector unions, most notably the steel workers, the miners, and (less successfully) the teachers in major strikes which illustrated the strength of government in opposing worker organizations.

In abandoning Keynesian economic strategy, the Conservatives, employing monetarist tactics inherited from their Labour predecessors, accelerated the restructuring of British industry. Under Thatcherism there have been some heavy losers, most notably heavy engineering and chemical production, while other areas of capital have enjoyed growth throughout the recession, including banking and finance, food, oil, and the protected sectors of defence and agriculture. The substantial revenues from North Sea oil were consumed in funding high rates of unemployment and substantial tax cuts rather than long-term investment in collective consumption goods, as was the experience of other European oil producers. The dramatic loss of manufacturing industry was complemented by (though not compensated for) the increased growth of the service sector. In the early days of the Thatcher government, between 1981 and 1984, 700,000 new jobs were claimed to have been created in the service sector, of which 230,000 were in the banking, finance sector and related areas, and were predominantly located in the South of England.

The traditional class divisions of Fordist industrial organization do not disappear under a Post-Fordist regime but are reshaped and deepened as core workers in the new industries are recruited and retained with packages of inducements, both monetary and in terms of enhanced conditions and other perquisites, while those in the peripheral industries to which work is sub-contracted and for which job security is therefore low, are subject to insecurity and low wages. Often such jobs will involve part-time work. The need to cut guaranteed minimum wages rates, monitored by the Wages Councils, is a crucial stage in this overall strategy, as is the need to educate young workers into the realization that past practises would price them out of employment. The establishment of a Social Fund has not only had the impact of cutting public expenditure on the poor but also does the ideological work of making those on income support pay back money loaned from the state for the purchase of major household items. It also explains the reluctance of the present government to embrace the EC Social Charter and its concomitant rights of employment, pensions, health and welfare. Consequently, the low paid, the underemployed and the unemployed are those for whom the loss of welfare services is most keenly felt. They are unable to avail themselves of the new rights of consumer choice in welfare services - they do not live in those more salubrious areas where schools may have the resources (parental and financial) to opt out. They are unable to avail themselves of leisure services in contracted out leisure centres because of the price levels implied by the limits set on local poll tax levels by central government, they cannot afford the health insurance premiums required by private medical companies. Thus a two tier welfare system is implied in the Post-Fordist mode of accumulation with consumer choice for flexibly provided and managed welfare services (including leisure services) and safety net provision for those without the resources to benefit.

Gamble (1988) portrays the Government's industrial strategy in the following terms:

> Thatcherism has no industrial strategy except to promote the complete integration of Britain into the world economy. Companies must survive unaided if they are to have a future in the British industry. (Gamble 1988: p.195)

Manufacturing investment which has been lost has predominantly been that which required labour intensive production. These jobs have been lost to low wage economies. Automation of production which may save on costs also loses jobs, but may allow more flexibility in production. The technology of robotics and the speed and accuracy of market intelligence thus allows mass marketing to be superseded in these areas by the identification of market segments and production for market niches. Debates about postmodernity highlight the sensitivity that different consumer groups have to distinctive styles and the consumption of particular leisure experiences and leisure lifestyles. It is no irony that manufacturing centres of the North and the Midlands have been preserved as museums, suitable for the 'postmodernist tourist gaze'. The industrial past and its local cultures are reduced and reproduced as stylized and sanitized experiences for the visitor. Postcards, photographs, exhibits etc. provide tourist experiences and interpretations of history as museums sell the past, becoming more like shops and conversely shops become more like museums. Thus the manufacturing which remains is likely to be of a different type to that lost to the developing economies. The traditional industrial base is reworked as a leisure experience for those with substantial disposable incomes.

The evolving industrial structure of British industry is not however a self generating, it requires the agency of a political and economic personnel, and in multinational capital and the Conservative Government it has effective proponents. The Government has aided restructuring directly, consider for example the provision of infrastructure for the prosperous South East, while traditional industries were denied state support. Gurr et al (1987) point out that it has been political choices that have left some cities to decline and others to stagnate. There is nothing inevitable or natural in permitting market forces decide the fate and futures of UK cities. In addition it has aided indirectly in, for example, the case of the financial services sector which has been given a considerable boost by the Government's programme of privatization. The various privatization programmes have resulted in short term gains for some investors as well as wider share ownership blurring traditional class divisions and drawing larger numbers of the electorate into the world of enterprise and finance.

As the concept of hegemony implies, the Government's programme has however operated on more than simply the economic plane. Ideological change has been seen as more than a mere byproduct of economic change, in that the Government has sought to put values on the agenda in an overt way, opening up debates about values which had been seen as virtually beyond politics in the period of social democratic consensus. With the 'end of ideology' in the 1960s, it witnessed a resurgence in the 1970s with appeals to self reliance, new realism and the enterprise culture. It also fuelled a 'new racism' (Husband 1986) which sought to stress the natural differences between ethnic cultures, leaving a selective 'English' to dominate.

Few areas of social relations have been left untouched by this new discourse and leisure has proved to be no exception. Individualism within the family has been used in justification of the reduction of welfare provision and policies such as the reintroduction of those in institutional care into the community and the onus of individuals to make their own pension arrangements. The state is no longer the final arbiter and guarantor of income support in old age. The shift away from statutory state provision for instance in community care initiatives introduces a tension in that community care, because of traditional gender roles, means care by women, and yet flexible employment of women is seen as one of the major employment changes to aid capital.

Law and order and the strong state are also key ideas in the Government's ideological programme which have been used to justify the considerable strengthening of police powers, and the protection of police pay. The legitimation crisis of the state in the the 1970s and 1980s has most clearly found its expression in the importance of race and race relations on the political agenda. Race and the nation state provide an important dimension to the hegemonic struggle taking place. Anti-police riots in 1981 become recast as black riots in the mid 1980s (Solomos 1986) and there is growing racism and racist attacks within inner city areas. Positive discrimination to redress disadvantages experienced by racial minorities becomes unfashionable as a policy option and good race relations are seen to demand tighter controls on immigration and growing fears that multi-culturalism will dilute the English tradition and heritage. This appeal to nationalism which invoked such a strong positive reaction from the electorate following the Falklands conflict is used to justify the position taken by Mrs. Thatcher in for example the Brugges speech and her subsequent resistance to joining the European Monetary System.

However the conflicting ideological messages of Thatcherism are not solely to be communicated by the medium of political pronouncements but through, for example, the reshaping of the education system. The introduction of initiatives such as 'enterprise in the curriculum' designed to infuse entrepreneurial messages into higher education and the development of a core curriculum, with for example its attendant encouragement to study 'British history', and the denigration or marginalization of critical areas of social analysis (witness the restructuring of the SSRC, and attacks on Peace Studies). The significance of ideology in establishing a new hegemony has clearly not been lost on the Conservatives in the 1980s. It is worth noting that the most stringent attacks on Thatcherism have come from within the established church in civil society, particularly with its publication 'Faith in the Cities 1984'. Particular clerics have attacked the lack of collectivism and compassion within enterprise culture whereas for their part, the government appears irritated by the 'political' pronouncements of senior clergy and instead urges the church to provide society with religious and moral leadership.

Table 1 presents an idealized form of the Fordist - Post-Fordist regimes of accumulation and their associated forms of regulation. The first four headings relate to the 'industrial' dimensions of the distinctions drawn in the literature. The next two relate to the different cultures and concepts of citizenship, while the remaining headings contrast the nature of local- central relations, of local government and of leisure policy under the respective regimes.

As we have seen the ideological agenda of Thatcherism holds as central the need to break the 'chains of welfare dependency' and instil entrepreneurial spirit. Rights of citizenship are to be replaced by consumer rights since commercial organizations are seen as responding to dynamically changing needs more quickly, efficiently and ultimately effectively. Large scale bureaucratic provision whether in production

Table 1   *Ideal typical illustrations of Fordist and Post-Fordist regimes of accumulation and methods of regulation*

DIMENSION	FORDISM	POST-FORDISM
Manufacturing	Mass production, low innovation, economies of scale, deskilled labour	Flexible production, small batch processing, skilled labour information technology
Product Markets	Mass consumption of standard products; product orientation	Market niches; target marketing; customer care
Organizational Types	Mechanistic - fixed structure relating to predictably stable environment	Organizmic - flexible structure adapting to variable environmental conditions and markets
Hierarchy	'Tall' organization, vertical command, bureaucratic structure, salaried full time employment	'Flat' organization, self-contained and relatively autonomous work groups organized around particular problems, flexible part-time employment and consultancies
Management Type	Corporate management, centralized control, market concentration in organizations of increasing size	Emphasis on the deconcentration of corporate organization: divisional structures with autonomous roles; scaling down organizations through the sub-contracting of functions to satellite specialist firms
Politico- economic system	Corporatism - unions, business, government in policy discussion; Keynesian macro-economic planning	Strong state - exclusion of business and union interests from government to generate 'free economy'
Social Impacts	Task specialization and alienation of workforce compensated by rising real wages, and welfare provision	'Core' workforce of service professionals; 'peripheral' workforce of part-time, low paid, temporary, government scheme workers

(the nationalized industries) or in consumption (public sector health, education, housing, leisure services) are regarded as invariably inferior. The inevitable consequence of such a move towards private provision for such services is that those who cannot afford to take advantage of these more flexible forms of commercial provision will be reduced to receipt of a residual, low level, safety net, state provision. The divisive nature of Post-Fordist regimes is evident in the deepening divisions between core and peripheral workforces, between affluent regions such as the M4 corridor and regions in decline such as Tyneside, and within cities. Indeed Esser and Hirsch (1989) describe Post-Fordism as effectively reshaping West German cities reducing them to three principal types of area. The first of these is the internationally competitive urban area which predominantly takes on functions which are aimed at internationally oriented business people, visitors to meetings, conferences. This consists of conference facilities, museums, airport facilities, hotel accommodation, administrative complexes and cultural facilities. This area, where it exists in cities (it may be absent in some) is in direct national and international competition with other cities. The second type of area is the 'normal' residential area for the middle classes. The third area is that inhabited by the urban poor, the permanently underemployed, drug addicts, and other marginal groups.

The Post-Fordist city therefore requires a very different form of local government strategy and central-local relations from that implied by the social democratic structures of Fordism. Under Fordism there was a tendency to separate production concerns which were dealt with predominantly by central government through corporatist structures, and consumption issues which were largely consigned to local (though not necessarily pluralist) politics (Saunders 1984, Dunleavy 1984), or to quangos. This has given way to a much greater concern with controlling local spending levels, local service delivery structures, and aspects of local planning. Local government itself has been encouraged to scale down its activities, to divest itself of some responsibilities, and is much more tightly constrained. In this new environment local government professionals, particularly in the leisure sphere, are more likely to adopt a view of efficiency and effectiveness which draws form the ideology of the industrial professions (accountancy, marketing) than the liberal welfare profession.

The disintegration of social democracy has impacted upon central government policy on the leisure quangos. The Sports Council's role, far from promoting access to recreation as a right of citizenship, is reduced to a residual social policy role in the inner city and a health promotion role. The Arts Council is not to be seen as a politically disinterested body promoting critical evaluation of the nature of life in contemporary Britain, but is charged with weaning arts organizations onto commercial sponsorship. The Countryside Commission's position has been marginalized by the granting of quango status, reducing its opportunities to defend recreation or conservation interests from within Government (Blunden and Curry 1985, Coalter et al 1987). The dissolution of the Nature Conservancy Council is viewed by many as a direct attempt to dilute conservation policies which interfere with producer policies. Local government is no longer the arbiter of and provider for the 'community's every day needs'. It is central government that determines the Standard Assessment Spending for local authorities and it is central government that distributes the nationally determined business rate. The aims of leisure policy more generally have shifted from a dominant emphasis on achieving social benefits, to one which stresses an economic rationale for leisure policy.

However the emergence of Post-Fordist leisure policy structures is not to be seen in any way as a functional requirement of a changing regime of accumulation. Shifts in the nature of regulation are initiated and contested by economic, cultural and political actors. Significant differences emerge within and between local governments as to the appropriate direction of leisure policy and these can perhaps best be characterized under three main headings. Left Post-Fordist strategies, left Fordist strategies, and right or mainstream Post-Fordist strategies. We will consider each of these in turn.

4.1   Left Fordist Strategies of Resistance

One of the problems Labour local government has had in defending local services in the social democratic mould has been that these tended to reinforce, as well as to address, certain forms of inequality. These forms of inequality were features not simply of services delivered (since in many instances the disadvantaged were underrepresented among users of such services), but were also reproduced by the ways in which local government organizations operated, with hierarchically ordered structures, dominated by white, male, middle class professionals and incorporating taylorist control of an alienated workforce. Nevertheless, left Fordist strategies have sought to oppose the attack on welfare services and Keynesian planning by resorting to, or modifying, traditional Fordist approaches. In terms of economic development, for example, Geddes (1989) cites the West Midlands Enterprise Board as adopting a typically left Fordist strategy since it has sought to combat deindustrialization by substituting public sector capital for 'missing' private investment.

Table 2.   Post-Fordism and the role of the central State

DIMENSION	FORDISM	POST-FORDISM
Dominant Culture	Welfarism	Enterprise culture
Rights of the Individual	System of universal rights of citizenship	Dual system: consumer rights and (safety net) welfare provision
Central-Local Relations	Local determination / influence on local spending and taxation levels; local management and policy for major consumption services, central responsibility for economic planning	(a) Service Provision Central control of minimalist policy - local concern for locally flexible and appropriate means of implementation
		(b) Economic Development centrally devised policy implemented by local organs of the central state e.g UDCs, Enterprise Zones etc.
		(c) Taxation Levels largely decided centrally

Table 3   *Post-Fordism and Local Government leisure policy*

DIMENSION	FORDISM	POST-FORDISM
Local Government	Large scale bureaucratic corporate policy and management approach to social provision and accountability	Flexible forms of management and policy control: introduction of area management, decentralization: Enterprise Zones, Urban Development Corporations, CCT and LMS bring with them new management approaches and structures
Orientation of Local Government Professionals	Bureaucratic, and (liberal welfare) professionalism	entrepreneurial and 'industrial' professionalism (e.g. accountancy, engineering, etc.)
Leisure Policy Emphasis	Social democratic orientation - leisure opportunities are a right of citizenship - leisure investment may achieve externalities (reduce anti-social behaviour and increase health)	- Provide cultural infrastructure to attract investment from new industries; and generate tourism multiplier effect; - provide infrastructure for new cultural industries (in some authorities); - Provide safety net welfare service in inner city; - Minimize costs of achieving externalities. Leisure
Policy Rationale	Largely social with some economic benefits	Largely economic with some social benefits

In the leisure sphere however, perhaps the most obvious form of left Fordism is in the planned response of a number of Labour authorities to the requirement to put leisure services out to private tender. The strategy here is to construct tendering packages which are so large that it is unlikely that any commercial concern would have the resources to compete effectively to win the contract or meet its requirements. Where virtually the whole of a department's work is put out to a single contractor, the existing management is likely to retain this work. Although winning the contract will place on management the requirement to achieve a specific return on investment (Walsh 1988), management practices in respect of the workforce are unlikely to be significantly altered. Indeed, management is likely to have to both cut costs, and generate increased revenue in ways which are likely to damage the interests of both the workforce and the less affluent market segments served by leisure services. Thus the strategy of constructing large-scale contracts to stave off commercial interest, even where it is allowed by the Secretary of State who must approve such tenders documents, is likely to reinforce existing inequalities.

4.2   Left Post-Fordist Strategies and Leisure Policy

The rejection of the Morrisonian model of the local state as neither efficient nor democratic has led some members of the Left to adopt a more positive approach to the opportunities offered by Post-Fordist regulation and accumulation. The Greater

London Council's challenge to Thatcherism has been influential here in inspiring alternative agendas to that framed by central government. In particular the cultural industries strategy of the GLC has generated considerable interest on the left, in cities such as Sheffield and Manchester. Wolverhampton too has acknowledged the central role the local state can play, particularly in relation to youth policy and it has conducted an external audit of all its local authority services and has demanded that young people should have material democracy (control over resources) as well as political democracy and involvement in community affairs. It is interesting to note that such a demand grew out of the Thompson Report in 1982 which failed to raise any commitment from central government during the 1980s. On the contrary, training and social policies during the 1980s have encouraged a new realism and conformism amongst young people and its here that the cutting edge of Thatcher's hegemonic project can be felt at its sharpest. The collective consumption arrangements made as part of the post-war social democratic settlement are being consumed by the middle aged and the elderly but the latter do not intend such univeral and generous benefits will be made available for the next generation to inherit. To do so would run directly counter to the demand for flexibilization and fragmentation inherent in Post-Fordist regimes of capital accumulation.

Unlike many other Labour authorities concerned with regeneration, Sheffield's cultural policy has been developed with capital from the local state rather than from private-public partnership. An initial concern was with the creation of a cultural industries quarter. This centred on two complexes - the Leadmill opened in 1982 initially as a venue for rock bands and subsequently expanded into an arts and media training and exhibition centre; and the Audio-visual Enterprise Centre, linked with Red Tape municipal recording studios and rehearsal rooms, photographic gallery, civic cinema, and Sheffield Independent Film, an umbrella organization for local film and video producers. (Bianchini 1989b).

The thinking underpinning this approach to development is influenced by critical theory in the tradition of the Frankfurt School (particulary Adorno's aesthetics) and the analysis of the political economy of the culture industries undertaken by Garnham (1983) on behalf of the GLC. Because ownership in the cultural industries in terms of both production and distribution has been highly concentrated, the industries have been dominated by the production of mass products, and cultural diversity and critical art have been stifled. The aim of municipally provided training, production and trading opportunities in the cultural industries is therefore to foster opportunities for cultural minorities, particularly those disadvantaged by race, class or gender, without the market requirement of the immediate adoption of mass appeal. However, as Garnham argues, market survival should be an important goal for the groups supported, and the old Arts Council approach of continuing revenue subsidy should be abandoned. This strategy is Post-Fordist rather than Fordist in that it provides resources for disadvantaged groups without seeking to manage or control those resources directly through managerialist methods, and because it represents public investment not as a replacement for the private sector, but as a stimulus for new forms of market niching.

Traditional cultural forms are also being supported in Sheffield, centred around the Tudor Square with the development of the Crucible theatre, the restored Lyceum

Theatre, the Ruskin Art Gallery, with new hotel and gallery developments proposed (Bianchini 1989b). This, together with the staging of the World Student Games represent a rather more traditional form of post- Fordist cultural development.

A further element in left Post-Fordist thinking is the recapturing of city space through cultural development of unused city areas (Chambers and Curtis 1983). Following the experience gained in Western European cities, particularly in Italy with the staging of feminist torch-lit processions to 'reclaim' certain areas of the city, and the 'estate romana' promoted in Rome by the PCI administration, there has been a realization on the left that cultural animation and development can bring night life to underused city centres, rendering them potentially safer, particularly for women, to use at night. This approach is evident in Glasgow's campaign to redress its reputation as a city of macho violence, drunkenness and poverty. Glasgow Action was a public-private coalition which sought to update the city centre environment, to improve the image of the city, and to develop Glasgow's tourism potential (Bianchini 1989b). The first of these aims represents an element of left Post-Fordism, using the reconstruction of the city to challenge the spatial expression of oppressive structures.

A third aspect of left Post-Fordism is evident in the attempts of a number of Labour controlled authorities to introduce decentralization of service decision-making and delivery. Decentralization has been adopted by the left as a means of overcoming problems of insensitivity to local needs, and alienation of the work force in large scale bureaucratic local government organizations. The benefits of decentralization are said to be a more flexible response to local needs, greater opportunity for community involvement, and the generating of opportunities for the workforce for job enrichment, involvement in decision-making and reduced alienation from the public. Among the more publicized of decentralization schemes developed in respect of leisure include those of Hackney, Middlesborough and St. Helens. However though the thinking behind these approaches may have been influenced by a radical critique of the professions, the practice of design, implementation and control of decentralization has been dominated by professionals, the top tier of whom have not been decentralized. The 'dispersal' of the workforce may make the organization of labour more difficult but the dominance of decision-making by professionals remains (Hoggett 1987). In a sense then decentralization, despite the intentions of Labour politicians, may represent a managerialist tool, strengthening professional autonomy (Geddes 1989).

4.3 Post-Fordism, the Right, and Leisure Policy

The momentum of Post-Fordist strategies, in public sector leisure services as elsewhere, has of course received greatest support from the political right. Flexible units of production have been encouraged through the introduction of Compulsory Competitive Tendering, Urban Development Corporations, Local Management of Schools. These units of production break with the corporate management approaches of the early 1970s and mirror management styles introduced in the private sector (Quinn 1980, Peters and Waterman 1982). Thus in many instances even where local authorities win their own contracts to manage existing services, they will do so through new mechanisms such as management boards (analogous to boards of directors incorporating professionals and politicians) with autonomy to act within the parameters laid down by the contracts concerned.

Locally managed schools will have control over education facilities outside school hours, a valuable leisure resource in many communities. Urban Development Corporations are freed from the constraints of local democracy to plan (through meetings which may be held in camera) the future of the areas under their control. Development Corporation plans are likely to include significant leisure elements, particularly when such elements imply economic development. Thus London Docklands and the Merseyside Development Corporations have used waterside leisure developments to render housing attractive to an affluent market, and as an incentive for capital investment in profit-making facilities, as well as facilitating direct investment in profit generating leisure facilities such as the Docklands Arena. Consequently, new governing bodies are restructured and peopled with 'right minded' individuals essentially committed to new discourse about efficiency and accountability through consumer choice. The professional power bases of the social democratic past are gradually diluted and traditional discourses about public service, professionalism and autonomy, become recast into the discourse of 'new realism', profitability, income generation and rational and efficient allocation of resources. Myerscough (1988) illustrates this shift in discourse within the Arts - the aesthetic discourse is superceded by the business discourse.

Investment, in what Esser and Hirsch (1989) refer to as 'internationally competitive urban areas', is a function of the nature of industrial location decision criteria for the new service industries. Whereas traditional manufacturing industry had to locate itself close to sources of raw materials or skilled labour, the new service industries, it is assumed, are able to locate in cities which provide the cultural infrastructure which is likely to attract and retain geographically and socially mobile core workers, such as financial service and information technology personnel.

Allied to this strategy of facilitating the recruitment of key personnel to the new industries, is the development of an infrastructure for tourism, generating business opportunities for small and large-scale capital in for example, hotels and themed attractions. In Bradford for example the refurbishment of the city centre has incorporated the development of the National Museum of Film and Photography (with an estimated annual attendance of 3/4 million), the renovation of the St. George's Hall (a major concert venue), the modernization and redevelopment of the Alhambra Theatre, together with proposals to develop the West End area of the city. The West End proposals include a major private investment in a tourist facility, with discussions currently focusing on an electronic theme park or adventure facility.

The Bradford example is an interesting one since it is an authority which has not only been subject to changes in party control during the period of redevelopment, but also the Conservative group to assume power in 1988 is one dominated by a New Right leadership. The Conservative administration in fact introduced one of the most highly publicized programmes of radical cuts in jobs and spending in 1988, but has continued to support the programme as broadly developed under previous administrations controlled by both Labour and Conservative parties. There have been different nuances of policy. For example some members of the Labour Groups originally sought to use the West End development to celebrate the city's multicultural background, by incorporating an eastern bazaar into the new shopping element of this development. But the plans for restructuring of the city in other respects have been remarkably similar. In Liverpool also, following the disqualification of the majority of the Labour Group, its successor has cooperated with the Development Corporation in the redevelopment of the city's cultural facilities including the Albert Dock project, and the development of a tourism package based on the city's pop music heritage.

Though economic development does constitute the major new state interest in leisure, consumption or service provision issues are of significance in a Post-Fordist scenario. The dislocation implied in restructuring the accumulation regime means that some care must be taken to provide for those who lose out in the restructuring process. Provision for sport and recreation has traditionally been seen as a means of reinforcing social order. Even in the 1975 White Paper 'Sport and Recreation' which advocated the view of leisure as a 'right of citizenship', a dual rationale for provision was put forward since it was also argued that;

By reducing boredom and urban frustration, participation in active recreation contributes to the reduction of hooliganism and delinquency among young people .... The need to provide for people to make the best use of their leisure must be seen in this context. (Department of Environment 1975: p. 2)

Similar claims were repeated in the White Paper 'A Policy for the Inner Cities' (Department of Environment 1977). The continued funding of schemes such as Action Sport funded by the Sports Council and local authorities, and of schemes for the unemployed, during times of pressure on public sector service budgets reinforces the notion that this is an important function of leisure policy. This is all the more impressive since there is little evidence to support the assertion that participation in recreation influences other forms of behaviour (Bramham, Haywood and Henry 1982). Thus a two tier notion of leisure provision is fostered, with local authorities encouraged to either sell off facilities, or to run them in ways more akin to commercial operations, while at the same time making residual provision in areas of high social need.

5   Conclusion

The politics of leisure as we move in to the 1990s then, continue to reflect something of a fudged consensus. Central government appears to tolerate the cultural industries strategy of authorities such as Sheffield, but is unlikely to tolerate left Fordism, since this will generate increased costs in the public sector. However, were the cultural industries strategy to generate high profile, critical, collective cultural responses to the New Right, then central government opposition might become manifest. At present left Post-Fordism represents a highly localized and marginal response to the pressures placed on the local state.

Most authorities would seem to be following a right Post-Fordism line, but this places Labour controlled authorities in a difficult position. The attracting of high technology industry or financial and administrative services, through development of an attractive cultural infrastructure, is a zero sum game. More jobs are not created by the transfer of the administrative headquarters of a multi-national from one city to another, thus alleviating local problems may mean inflicting further difficulties on others. Where investment in the leisure industries is to generate local economic activity directly (rather than by attracting investment) then flexible accumulation through, for example, the tourist industry may well result in low paid, part-time, insecure jobs. Thus Labour authorities may be associated with the active reproduction of exploitation of a peripheral workforce. Finally the two tier system of provision implied by the abandonment of social democratic rights of citizenship in favour of consumer rights and residual welfare provision, means that Labour local authorities will be seen as presiding over the local dismantling of welfare services. The experiments of the 1980s of local resistance to central government initiatives through cultural politics has become increasingly difficult to sustain. Thus, as in the case of other recent attacks on local government by central government, Labour may well find it difficult to distance itself from the negative electoral connotations of right Fordism, further alienating itself from its traditional electoral consituency

6   REFERENCES

Aglietta, M.A. (1979) **Theory of Capitalist Regulation: the US Experience**. Verso 1979

Audit Commission. (1984) **The Impact on Local Authorities' Economy, Efficiency and Effectiveness of the Block Grant Distribution System**. HMSO

Bacon, R. and Eltis, W. (1978) **Britain's Economic Problem: Too Few Producers**. Macmillan, London.

Bianchini, F. (1989a) Cultural Problems and Urban Scoila Movements: the Response of the 'New Left' in Rome (1976-1985) and in London (1981-1986), in **Leisure and Urban Processes: Critical Studies of Leisure Policy in Western European Cities** (ed. P. Bramham et al.), Routledge, London.

Bianchini, F. (1989b) **Urban Renaissance? The Arts and the Urban Regeneration Process in 1980s Britain**. University of Liverpool, Centre for Urban Studies, Working Paper No. 7.

Blunden, J. and Curry, N. (1985) **The Changing Countryside**. London, Croom Helm.

Boyer, R. (1986) **La Theorie de la Regulation: un Analyse Critique**. Paris, Editions de la Decouverte.

Bramham, P., Haywood, L. and Henry, I. (1982) Recreation versus Vandalism: a Rationale for the Profession? **Leisure Management**, 2, 12.

Carr, M. and Weir, S. (1983) Sunrise City. **New Socialist**, 41, 7- 10.

Chambers, I. and Curtis, L. (1983) Italian Summers. **Marxism Today**. July.

Centre of Contemporary Cultural Studies. (1983) **The Empire Strikes Back**. Hutchinson.

Coalter, F. with Duffield, B. and Long, J. (1987) **The Rationale for Public Sector Investment in Leisure**. Sports Council.

Department of Environment. (1975) **Sport and Recreation**, HMSO, London

Department of Environment. (1977) **A Policy for the Inner Cities**. HMSO, London.

Dunleavy, P. (1984) The Limits to Local Government, in **Local Socialism?** (eds. M. Boddy and C. Fudge), London, Macmillan.

Erikson, R. and Syms, P. (1986) The Effects of Enterprize Zones on Property Prices. **Regional Studies**, 20, 1, 1-14.

Esser, J. and Hirsch, J. (1989) The Crisis of Fordism and the Dimensions of a 'postfordist' regional and Urban Structure. **International Journal of Urban and Regional Research**, 13, 417 - 437.

Gamble, A. (1988) **The Free Economy and the Strong State: the Politics of Thatcherism**. London, Macmillan.

Garnham, N. (1983) Concepts of Culture, Cultural Policy and the Cultural Industries, paper presented at the Cultural Industries and Cultural Policy in London Conference, London, Riverside Studios, December 12-13.

Geddes, M. (1989) The Capitalist State and the Local Economy: 'Restructuring' for Labour and Beyond. **Capital and Class**, 35, 85-120.

Greater London Enterprise Board. **Altered Images: Towards a Strategy for London's Cultural Industries**. GLEB, London (nd)

Glyptis, S. and Pack, C. (1989) **Developing Sport and Leisure: Good Practice in Urban Regeneration**. London, Department of Environment, HMSO.

Gurr, T., King, D., and Gyford, J. (1987) **The City and the State**. MacMillan.

Gyford, J. (1985) **The Politics of Local Socialism**. London, Allen and Unwin.

Hall, S. et al. (1978) **Policing the Crisis**. Hutchinson.

Husband, C. (1986) **Race in Britain Today**. Hutchinson.

Hoggett, P. (1987) Farewell to Mass Production? Decentralisation as an Emergent Private and Public Sector Paradigm, in **Decentralisation and Democracy: Localising Public Services**, (eds. P. Hoggett & R. Hambleton), Universty of Bristol, School of Advanced Urban Studies, Occasional Paper 28.

Jessop, B. (1988) Regulation Theory, Post-Fordism and the State. **Capital and Class**, 34, 147-168, Spring.

Klausner, D. (1986) Beyond Separate Spheres: Linking Production with Social Reproduction and Consumption. **Environment and Planning D: Society and Space**, 4, 29-40.

Lipietz, A. (1987) **Miracles and Mirages: the Crisis of Global Fordism**. London, Verso.

Mulgan, G. and Worpole, K. (1986) **Saturday Night or Sunday Morning? From Arts to Industry: New Forms of Cultural Policy**. London, Comedia.

Myerscough, J. (1988) **The Economic Importance of the Arts in Britain**. Policy Studies Institute.

Newton, K. & Karran, T. (1985) **The Politics of Local Government Expenditure**. London, Macmillan.

Quinn, J. (1980) **Strategies for Change: Logical Incrementalism**. Homewood, Illinois, Irwin.

Peters, T. and Waterman, R. (1982) **In Search of Excellence**. London, Harper Row.

Saunders, P. (1984) Rethinking Local Politics, in **Local Socialism?**, (eds. M. Boddy & C. Fudge), London, Macmillan.

Solomos,J. (1986) Political language and Violent Protest. **Youth and Policy**, 18.

Stoker, G. (1989) **The Politics of Local Government**. Macmillan.

Walsh, K. (1988) The Consequences of Competition, in **The Future of Leisure**, (eds. J. Benington & J. White), London, Longman.

Willis, P. (1988) **Youth Review**. Gower.

THE ROLE OF HISTORY IN THE CONCEPTUALIZATION OF LEISURE: A CASE STUDY OF THE MINERS OF EAST NORTHUMBERLAND, 1800 TO 1914

ALAN METCALFE
University of Windsor, Canada

Obviously a basic question that must be addressed pertains to the relevance of a history paper in the examination of the role of sport and leisure in contemporary society? This question becomes even more pertinent when one considers the basically ahistorical, structural functionalist approach of many leisure researchers[1]. Very simply, I argue that without an understanding of the historical antecedents of any set of events one's understanding of those events is, by definition, incomplete. It is the nature of the particular situation and the questions being asked that determine the degree to which historical analysis can be useful[2]. In a more general sense historical analysis pinpoints continuities and discontinuities. Additionally, historical studies can be used to illustrate things that are hidden in a cross sectional ahistorical approach.

Attitudes to and concepts of leisure are historically created, flowing out of the conditions of work and the nature of social relationships. Like other aspects of life, leisure was a contested domain. This paper will examine the development of and changes in the concept of leisure amongst the miners of East Northumberland, 1800 to 1914. The changing working conditions and changes in the mining industry will provide the foundation for an analysis of the changing concept of leisure. Leisure, itself, will be studied through the histories of 16 sporting activities. These histories provide evidence of traditional, residual and emergent practices which together constituted leisure at any given time. In particular attention will be focused on how the miners actively created their own views of leisure. At the same time there was never a single uncontested definition of leisure[3]. Leisure practices were a contested domain with influences from both within and outside the communities influencing the particular view of leisure. At any given time leisure practices reflected a

---

[1] This approach is typified in Smith, et al. (1973)
[2] Examples of the historical approach to leisure are Cunningham (1980), Clarke and Critcher (1985).
[3] Leisure has been studied by psychologists, economists, geographers, sociologists and historians. All these approaches are predicated on different sets of assumptions. The assumptions underlying this paper are that leisure cannot be divorced from the society of which it is a part. Therefore attempts to isolate leisure from the society provide incomplete pictures of leisure.

divergent set of attitudes towards leisure and its uses. It is the changing definitions of leisure that are the focus of this paper.

In the final analysis all definitions of leisure come down to the lowest common denominator, free time. While the association of leisure with time is patently obvious, it serves to obscure other elements that influence our view of leisure. The ways in which individuals and groups conceptualize leisure are not just contoured by the availability of free time but are structured by the physical, economic, social and intellectual environments. Thus, we must shift the focus from time *per se* to a broader consideration of the structural elements.

The coal miners of East Northumberland lived in 66 towns and villages contained within an area of approximately 20 by 7 miles[4]. During the nineteenth century the population grew from around 20,000 to 110,000. Throughout this period sport played a central role in their lives. This, of course, was predicated on the availability of free time. Control of time both at work and non work was one of the major preoccupations of the miners and their leaders during the nineteenth century. Thus, although I wish to shift the focus from time *per se*, it did form the foundation stone of work, leisure, and life; therefore we must consider it first.

Central to any understanding of time are two elements, the actual free time available and how individuals and groups conceptualize it[5]. Modern society defines time as a commodity to be controlled, thus the emphasis upon records, schedules, the work day and, of course, free time. It was not always such and certainly not amongst the miners of East Northumberland. In fact, during the first half of the century the miners, to some degree, controlled their own time. In the 1850s some hewers, the elite workers, determined the time they went into and came out of the pit. However, during the second half of the century the owners made efforts to exert control over the working day. This was resisted by the miners. The definition of the working day was the site of ongoing dispute between the Miners Union and the owners. While the move to standardize the work day, fortnight, and year met with some success one thing did not change, uncertainty. The work day and fortnight were of unpredictable length as they responded to fluctuating economic conditions. Thus time, and in particular free time, was always an uncertain commodity. This had consequences for the way in which the miners approached life. The future oriented philosophy of the middle classes had little meaning for people whose lives were predicated on uncertainty, basically they lived for the present. One consequence of the focus on control of time was the fact that throughout the century the miners always had considerable amounts of free time. However they clearly differentiated between two types of free time, that which was useful and wanted and that which was useless and unwanted. Idle time was unwanted and psychologically debilitating. Very simply this was time without money, when they were on strike or laid off or had unwanted holidays. These punctuated the year and were a reality of mining life. Very simply useful free time was that time in which they had money. It was the availability of money that was the foundation stone of useful free time and gave meaning to the miner's concept of leisure.

---

4   Data for this paper was gathered under SSHRC Grants in 1979 and 1987.
5   The classic starting point for the re-conceptualization of leisure was Thompson (1967)

Money lay at the heart of miners' sport[6]. In the very popular traditional sports rarely was the competition not for a money prize or stake. It was only with the advent of team sports that games were played for no money prize. One of the consequences of this was that unlike the advocates of muscular Christianity and amateurism few miners used sport to achieve ends other than victory. In fact, even in prestigious championship matches once a competitor realized he was beaten the contest ended. Thus, it was not the process but the product, victory, that was important. Competitive sport was a vehicle for testing an individual against another not for developing character or leadership qualities. The important question is how does this different focus influence the meaning attached to leisure?

In order to explore the meaning of leisure we have to delve into the activities that constituted the free time activities and the ideas that underlay these activities. Until the explosion of interest in football in the 1890s the mining sports were exclusively competitions that placed an individual or animal in competition with another individual or animal. Potshare bowling, quoits, rabbit coursing, dog racing, shooting, rowing, boxing, fives, and fishing constituted the miners' sports. Without exception these sports had been long associated with the miners and were deeply rooted in their culture. The second half of the century witnessed the gradual commercialization of these sports and the intrusion of sports from outside the community. In particular football, codified and organized by the middle classes, changed the focus of activities. Thus there was a gradual, subtle shift in focus to sports either organized or controlled from outside the community. At the same time up until 1914 these sports served as a means of testing individuals against individuals and village against village. In this instance sport served as a way of measuring oneself or one's colliery village against others. Thus, leisure and the meaning attached to it arose out of a sense of community and tradition. This was changed subtly during the later decades of the century as ideas that filtered in from the outside influenced the ways in which they thought about life, work, and leisure. Thus like many other areas of life leisure was a contested domain, a contest between traditional ways of life and new ideas[7].

In fact, there were other events lying outside the control of the miners that changed the way in which they participated in sport. First through the development of the railway network and newspapers the miners were increasingly brought in contact with ideas and sports from outside their communities. Increasingly with the advent of football the miners competed against teams from outside the mining districts. However, the impact of these team games must not be over emphasized as the failure of cricket to find a real foothold attests. The power of traditional social relationships was strong. One of the most important changes was the introduction of compulsory education. No longer did the young males go straight down the mines. They received educational experiences from men and women who were not of the coalfield. Instead of being introduced to the traditional sports of the miners they soon become ardent supporters of football. Basically what I am arguing in this segment is that throughout the nineteenth century the miners were gradually exposed

---

6   The centrality of money to mining sport cannot be over emphasized especially in the traditional mining sports. It was only in cricket and football, games with a heavy middle class presence, that money was not at stake in the contests.

7   One of the most provocative discussions on structure and agency is Callinicos (1989)

to sports and ideas from outside the area. Thus the way in which they conceptualized life, its possibilities, and leisure were subtly changed. New sports and new ideas filtered into the communities.

Having a more direct and visible impact upon life within the district were the changes wrought by the increase in population. This placed severe pressure on land and resulted in legislative actions being taken to force the miners from their traditional playgrounds on Newcastle Moor, Newbiggin Moor, the beaches, and on the highways. In 1870 there were no enclosed facilities for sport. Between then and 1914 the authorities through legislative action attempted with some success to force the miners from these traditional locations into sporting grounds where admission could be charged. By 1914 the district boasted over 170 enclosed sporting grounds. The miners' sport associated with public space had been forced within the confines of enclosed grounds to which access was limited. Thus the activities themselves were changed and also what leisure could be was changed.

What I have been arguing in the foregoing is that while time is the foundation stone of leisure the way in which it is used and the meanings attached to it are created within the context of the society of which it is a part. The way in which the miners viewed leisure was contoured by their own life experiences. Thus in the earlier years the meaning was derived from within the traditional activities of the miners, the material conditions within which they lived, and the values they lived by. However, within the confines of this relatively small area there were distinctively different views of leisure represented in the activities themselves and the meanings attached to these activities. These were related to occupation, gender, and age. It is obvious that the activities of the miners were different from those of Lord Hastings, Sir Matthew White Ridley and other landowners. However, within the context of mining society sport and perhaps leisure were the exclusive preserve of males and thus sport reflected predominantly male characteristics - strength, endurance, and to the modern mind, brutality. Until the last two decades of the century age was no barrier. As soon as a child was old enough to work he went down the pit and was also introduced to the sports of his father. This changed with the advent of universal education and thus the beginning of change for their concept of leisure. Additionally leisure knew no age boundaries. Miners participated actively in sport throughout their lives. In fact, many of the great potshare bowling champions were champions into their 50s. Even as late as 1912 65 year old men competed for a stake of £100 on the River Blyth[8]. The idea of sport as the exclusive domain of the young had not yet taken hold. Thus what sport was and the meaning attached to it were different.

Very simply what I have tried to argue is that simplistic definitions of leisure based on time obscure the reality of many leisures. In fact, leisure was simply an integral part of life. What it meant shifted as the conditions in society changed. The concept of leisure is socially constructed within the reality of lived experience. What the history of leisure in the twentieth century has demonstrated has been on the one hand an attempt to impose the values of the dominant culture upon all segments of society and on the other the impact of rampant commercialization. To some degree

---

[8]   The history of one of these racers, Lewis Lewis, provides a fascinating insight into attitudes to sport. Lewis Lewis first raced for a stake in 1867. He was still racing for large stakes in 1912; a racing career of 45 years!

leisure and commercialization become synonomous. Thus, within sport the advocates of amateurism have since the beginning fought a battle against the reality of sport. Any view of leisure that fails to take into consideration the material conditions of the society of which it is a part is doomed to failure. Perhaps the consequences of the dominant approach to leisure can be best illustrated in the failure of the British to come to grips with an important leisure time pursuit - soccer hooliganism. Until people accept that it is related to the material conditions of society and is rooted in society itself all the well meaning efforts to eliminate it are doomed to failure. Basically the majority of people focus on the symptoms and not the causes.

Basically all I have attempted to do through this brief analysis based on an historical case study is to broaden our perspective on leisure. It is a plea for decision makers in leisure to broaden the base from which they draw their ideas about what leisure is and its meaning. A plea to allow people to become involved in constructing their own leisure rather than 'experts' determining what is 'best' for them. The attempts of the nineteenth century middle classes to impose 'rational recreation' and amateurism on the working class ultimately failed. What is to say that modern day leisure practitioners who believe that they know the answers will achieve any greater degree of success. It is when people are involved in their own lives that initiatives with any chance of long term success are undertaken.

References

Callinicos, A. (1989) **Making History**. London: Polity Press.

Clarke J. and Critcher, C. (1985) **The Devil Makes Work. Leisure in Capitalist Britain**. Chicago: University of Illinois Press.

Cunningham, H. (1980) **Leisure in the Industrial Revolution, c1780-c1880**. London: Croom Helm Ltd.

Smith, M., Parker, S. and Smith, C. S. (eds). (1973) **Leisure and Society in Britain**. London: Allen Lane.

Thompson, E.P. (1967) **Time, Work-Discipline and Industrial Capitalism, Past and Present**, 38.

INDEX

This index has been compiled using the keywords assigned to each chapter. The numbers are the page numbers of the first page of the paper referred to.